TAXATION,

REVENUE, EXPENDITURE,

POWER, STATISTICS,

AND

DEBT

OF THE

WHOLE BRITISH EMPIRE;

THEIR

ORIGIN, PROGRESS, AND PRESENT STATE.

WITH AN ESTIMATE OF THE

CAPITAL AND RESOURCES OF THE EMPIRE,

AND

A Practical Plan

FOR APPLYING THEM TO

THE LIQUIDATION OF THE NATIONAL DEBT.

THE WHOLE FOUNDED ON, AND ILLUSTRATED BY,

OFFICIAL TABLES, AND AUTHENTIC DOCUMENTS.

BY PABLO PEBRER,

MEMBER OF SEVERAL SCIENTIFIC AND LITERARY SOCIETIES.

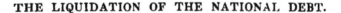

". . . . Non ego paucis
Offendar maculis, quas aut incuria fudit,
Aut humana parum cavit natura. . . . ." HOR.

LONDON:
BALDWIN AND CRADOCK, PATERNOSTER ROW.

1833.

DEDICATION.

TO HER MOST GRACIOUS MAJESTY THE QUEEN OF SPAIN.

When all the Provinces, Towns, and even the most humble Villages of Spain, raise their unanimous and grateful voices to proclaim the great, wise, and beneficent measures of your Majesty, in promoting public instruction, encouraging the meritorious, consoling the unfortunate, and advancing the national wealth and prosperity:—when they proclaim the admirable act of opening the scientific institutions and universities, by which ignorance, that monster that annihilates the most powerful nations, will be made to disappear:—when thousands of wretched Spanish families who were wandering in foreign lands oppressed with misery and poverty, and lamenting in silence their hard fate, are restored to their country and friends; and civil rancour and discord, the cancers that corrode and destroy mighty empires, give place to peace and contentment:—at a time, in short, when all the economical societies of the kingdom are addressing and congratulating your Majesty on the sound and politic arrangements you have made, by the establishment of a separate minister and establishment, to give energy and encouragement to agriculture, commerce, industry, and all the sources of public wealth:—it may not appear strange that an individual, belonging to a nation on which such bounties have been bestowed, should, although absent, join to the general voice, his own hearty thanks to the beautiful Benefactress of a country which gave him birth.

But another not less powerful motive leads him to Dedicate to your Majesty these, his humble exertions. In detailing the Revenue, Statistics, and Power of the greatest of modern nations, it has been shewn that the true foundations of the unparalleled grandeur and wealth of the British Empire, were the financial measures towards establishing a solid basis of public faith and credit, adopted by a Queen who bore the very name of your Majesty's August Daughter, who is destined to reign over the Spanish Dominions under your Majesty's maternal influence.

Spanish credit has already experienced the good effects of your Majesty's policy; and may Divine Providence grant to your Majesty length of days to pursue the glorious career so happily commenced; to continue the financial and economical measures for the amelioration of a gallant nation, worthy of being raised to that pitch of grandeur, opulence, and prosperity reached by the British Empire, over which "the solar orb never sets"—once the proud but just motto of the Spanish Monarchs.

A. L. R. P. DE V. M.

PABLO PEBRER.

London, April, 1833.

PREFACE.

In contemplating the mighty structure of the British Empire, while the reflecting mind is astonished at the solidity of its constituent parts, it is no less surprised at the many and striking evils which are visible at the very foundations of that wonderful fabric, and which seem to pervade its whole frame. The greatest contradictions, the most unaccountable economical paradoxes, the most perplexing anomalies, are met with at every step of the inquiry. There is found an immense excess of capital, the very source of production, causing distress instead of prosperity amongst its owners! an extraordinary excess of labour, the very cause of wealth, producing poverty, ruin, and misery amongst the labourers, themselves a great and powerful empire, where knowledge, invention, and art have multiplied in a boundless manner the means for the enjoyment of life, and for the satisfaction of all its wants, comforts, and luxuries; but where the very perfections of these springs of human and social happiness occasion misfortune, distress, and perpetual agitation, amongst the members of that great empire itself! There must, therefore, be some hidden defect in that mighty structure, something wrong in the combination of that wonderful system, or some misdirection of the immense resources of that greatest of empires.

The exertions of the patriotism, talent, and intelligence,

so abundant in this country, have been unremittingly directed to the discovery and cure of that deep-seated and all-pervading evil; but unfortunately, the opinions of the many eminent men, who have attempted to point out the cause of such transcendant calamity, are so various, so partial, and so contradictory, that the most important of all national questions, on the solution and right understanding of which the welfare of millions depends, is left involved in doubt, confusion, and uncertainty.

However, after carefully comparing these opinions, and examining the foundations on which they rest; after bestowing the most serious reflection on the subject in all its bearings; and considering, with mature attention, the various parts of the wonderful system, on which the financial concerns of this mighty empire are conducted; the author of this work is forced to the conclusion, "*that the main source of the deplorable evils which afflict this empire, is, the enormous pressure of the national debt on the vital parts of that system, and its baneful effects on the sources of production.*" All other causes are deemed merely accessary and partial. These may be clearly demonstrated by national writers, and even utterly removed; but while the *chief cause* remains behind, all their labours will be vain and fruitless, like palliatives applied to a cancerous or consumptive disease.

Firmly impressed with this conviction, the author has conceived the plan (perhaps too boldly) of attacking and annihilating the evil at its very source, *by the payment of the debt itself.* Most economical writers, deterred perhaps by the magnitude of the undertaking, and the apparent impossibility and doubtful result of the operation, and dreading the intolerable shafts of ridicule, have entirely neglected this great financial problem; and the few, who have laudably attempted to discuss it, have executed their task in the most awkward and imperfect manner. Rather opposing, than consulting, the interests of those powerful parties, on whose cordial co-operation the success of the measure itself depended; resorting to partial expedients, instead of recommending general measures, and confining their inquiries to *portions*, instead of taking into consideration the *whole* economical system of the empire, and the reciprocal action of its parts one upon another, and contemplating the measure as one that could not be effected without the joint concurrence of all the branches of that system,—these writers have, in fact, with the best intentions, adopted the worst and most inadequate means to attain their end; and have proposed measures calculated rather to defeat, than to accomplish, the great national object they had in contemplation.

The mode in which this important inquiry is conducted in this work, is entirely the reverse. It sets out on the principle, that no financial measure of this magnitude should be proposed or attempted, without taking into consideration the whole system of national economy in all its branches and ramifications; without duly estimating the sources of production, consulting the various and conflicting interests of all portions and classes of the empire, and calculating the effects of such a measure upon all those branches, sources, and interests, along with its general results, and the great and important benefits it will eventually bestow upon the whole extent of the British dominions.

Pursuing this plan, it was indispensable, in order to trace the evil to its most remote source, to discover the very origin of the excessive *pressure* to which it is attributed; and—1. to ascertain the origin, progress, and present state of taxation and expenditure in all their branches, and the progressive and actual amount of the national income; to notice the objects to which it has been directed, the perversions and abuses of it, and particularly the large portion applied to the payment of the interest of the debt, which those perversions have rendered necessary. 2. To consider the origin, follow the course, and state the actual amount of this debt; to examine the measures and schemes by which it has been created; and, in connection with these, the engines which have so strenuously contributed to raise such a portentous mass of treasure, have been deemed worthy to be described, and their abuses denounced. 3. The amount of the national debt, thus created, being so enormous, it became necessary to estimate the extent and amount of capital in all parts of the empire; to calculate the annual produce and determine the assets and means actually available to the grand operation of its liquidation, without impairing the capital itself, or injuring the sources of production; and preserving at the same time unhurt, the main springs which supply the means for the unavoidable expenditure. 4. Having arrived thus far, it became important to ascertain the effects produced by the pressure of the interest of the debt upon the springs and great agents of production, and its blighting influence upon all classes of society; and finally, to sugges the only remedy for this overwhelming evil, by pointin out the mode in which the means of the empire may b effectively applied to the liquidation of the debt itself; b demonstrating the practicability of the plan, explainin the general and particular advantages which would infallibly result from the measure, and answering the objections that might be urged against it.

In treating a question, where the rights of property are so complicated, the interests of all ranks so various and opposite, the opinions of national writers so contradictory, and the collateral economical questions so many and so important—the task of steering successfully through such a mass of jarring interests, and such a chaos of conflicting opinions, was extremely arduous. Indeed, the uncommon dryness of the subject, the difficulty of unravelling the accounts, the monotony of reciting almost the same measures to raise revenue and debt—in fine, the novelty and vastness of a design, assuming to develope the economical system of the whole empire, explain its practical effects throughout its whole extent, shew the foundations upon which the power, resources, and prosperity of the British empire rest, and solve the greatest of all national problems; all these presented, to the mind of the author, obstacles and difficulties of such magnitude, as to produce extreme diffidence in regard to the result of the enterprize, and almost to deter him from the attempt.

But convinced that any development of the productive powers, any increase of the wealth of the British Empire, will influence and augment those of all other nations; and animated by the pleasing and flattering idea of the beneficial results which such a measure would produce, in alleviating the distresses, miseries, and burdens of a mighty nation, and in diffusing happiness throughout the world at large (of which that nation has become the very centre)—he was emboldened to undertake a task, perhaps exceeding his abilities, but to which his attention has been long directed; and to which he has been at length impelled, by the cheering prospects opened by the great measure of Reform.

Intent solely on the grand object of the universal happiness of mankind, not a line has been written with reference to personal reputation, not an idea has been expressed through flattery or fear, nor has an intention existed of offending any individual or corporation. The constant endeavour has been, to collect and offer authentic facts, to state them fairly, reason upon them correctly, and deduce from them necessary consequences. The feelings which naturally arose when describing extortion, tyranny, injustice, and the oppression of nations by their rulers, or when contemplating the immense waste of human blood and treasure for objects generally unconnected with, and often contrary to, the true national interests,—have been openly, freely, and candidly expressed.

To remove the dryness of the subject, and render it if possible agreeable to all classes of readers, the tiresome accounts and details of figures have been relieved by and interwoven with a relation of the most remarkable historical events, and greatest revolutions of the world; pointing out their fundamental causes, and the fiscal measures which brought them into immediate action; and distinguishing the personages who figured most conspicuously in them, by their characteristic features: and, in a few instances, the satirical and ridiculous have been attempted.

Unfettered by party spirit, and regardless of forms of government, equal impartiality has been shown to republicans and royalists, whigs and tories, serviles and liberals. The tyrannical proceedings of Charles I., and the infamous excesses of the republican *saints*, have been alike condemned: and while some of the financial measures of Pitt, and of the ministers who have succeeded him during this peaceful period, have been willingly admired, others, which have inflicted the most positive and unmerited evils on the nation, have been unsparingly denounced. Never losing sight of the grand object, praise or blame has been bestowed upon men and measures according to their real merits, without regard to party principles or political systems; on the conviction, that sound reason is not limited to any particular sect, nor public wisdom and national virtue confined to any particular sphere.

Sensible of the little weight attached to foreign authorities, in matters of national interest and internal economy, great care has been taken to select native authors, and great exertions employed in consulting national authorities: a considerable number of historical works have been perused; the best writers on the National Debt, Taxation, Public Revenue and Expenditure (among whom Sir J. Sinclair ranks pre-eminent) have been examined and compared; parliamentary records and official accounts, have been checked and collated; and it may be safely asserted that few facts are stated, which do not rest upon the most approved domestic authority, and the most authentic documents [a].

In estimating the capital of the whole empire, the principle of moderate valuation has been strictly adhered to; national records, the best statistical writers, and the

[a] Should any discrepancies be found in the Official Tables, they must be attributed to the mystified, confused, and complicated manner in which the public accounts are kept: they have been selected and compiled with considerable labour and research, from hundreds of folio volumes; and the author takes this opportunity of thanking the gentlemen of the British Museum for their great trouble, and for their kindness in occasionally allowing him the use of a private room.

most eminent economists, have been the guides: and in stating the produce annually raised and property yearly created, by the combination of capital with all the animate and inanimate powers of the empire, the same means have been employed to attain moderation and accuracy; but in a matter of this nature, an approximative estimate is all that can be reasonably expected. In the construction and arrangement of the numerous statistical and financial Tables, every exertion has been used to obtain symmetry of construction and comprehensiveness of detail, combined with clearness, copiousness, and a strict adherence to official data; so as to render them intelligible at a glance, and at the same time convey important information, collected from many costly works and numerous documents, not easily accessible to the public [a].

Before establishing the basis upon which the liquidation of the Debt can be effected, the urgent and absolute necessity of resorting to such a measure, and the utter insufficiency and uselessness of any partial operations, have been abundantly demonstrated; and the inevitable consequence of the ever-increasing pressure of the Interest of the Debt; upon the three primary sources of production in a mercantile and manufacturing empire, and the comparative decrease of the demand for her produce and manufactures, have been clearly and unanswerably shewn.

In the arrangement of the Plan for the Payment of

[a] In the few Tables taken from Colquhoun, the correction of the numerous and unaccountable errors with which, notwithstanding the reputation of the author, they abounded, has been more tedious and troublesome than the construction of new ones. In one of the Tables of Queen Anne's reign, for instance, there was an error of above *nine millions* in an amount of sixty-two.

the Debt, the universal interests of all the integral parts of the Empire have not for a moment been lost sight of. The interests of the West India Planter, the Merchant and the Shipowner, have been combined with the benefits that will result to the British consumer, the Landowner, and the Manufacturer: Canadian commerce and agriculture, with the benefits to the Negro Population and West India Proprietor; the increase of East Indian commerce, the improvement of the defective agriculture of those remote regions, and the advance towards civilization of that abject race of men, have been combined with the augmentation of British shipping and the greater demand for English manufactures.

In the selection of the taxes to be repealed, care has been taken to point out only those which greatly press upon the productive sources, and the repeal of which would be most advantageous to the branches of the revenue, and most likely to facilitate the operation in question. Due regard has also been paid to the contrary opinions entertained on this subject by a powerful party of national financiers; but their high respectability has not been thought a sufficient reason for deviating from the straight-forward course.

With respect to the great and daily agitated questions connected with this plan, such as the Currency question, the opposite views of colonial policy, free trade, &c., &c., the greatest deference has been shewn to the opinions expressed in the periodical publications—those crucibles of reasoning and knowledge, those admirable engines of power and civilization, which are the pride of England, and which have so largely contributed to advance her greatness and prosperity. Preserving, however, the strictest impartiality and independence, the opinions of contending parties have been alternately followed, according as they seemed more conducive to the grand object in view—the welfare and happiness of the empire.

The national writers who have attempted this great question, having treated it (as before observed) in a superficial and imperfect manner; the works on this important subject being exceedingly few, and the only one connected with it, which shews the wealth, power, and resources of the empire, being composed rather, as the author says, "to tranquillize the minds of the people and prepare them for greater taxation and increase of debt," rather than with a view to diminish their burdens, and alleviate its pressure; the author, though fully aware of the narrow limits of individual capacity, and diffident of his own mental powers, thought that it would greatly facilitate the discussion of this urgent and momentous inquiry, to unite and condense in the smallest compass, all the essential materials dispersed in hundreds of expensive and unmanageable volumes and musty records; to notice the leading points in all the great questions connected with it; to present an uninterrupted chain of historical, economical, and official facts and data; and to demonstrate the effects of the system, and the results that might be expected from the adoption of the measure proposed. He thought that it would further the great object to place before the British legislature, at one view, the whole statistical and financial economy of the British Empire in all its ramifications; to furnish the British reformed parliament with all the essential elements of discussion and elucidation, in order that their wisdom may more easily decide a question deeply affecting the actual prosperity, the permanent stability, and the vital existence of this mighty empire.

The great disadvantage, under which the author

labours, of writing in a language not his own, and expressing his thoughts in a form and idiom different from the order in which they arise in his mind, is offered as an apology for the numerous defects and irregularities which may be discovered in the course of this production: to which may be added, the difficulty of comprising in the narrowest compass such a variety of complicated objects—historical, statistical, moral, political, and economical, and of reconciling such diversity of opinion regarding the vast and intricate financial system of this country. When the extreme difficulty of arriving at accuracy in the comparatively trifling accounts of a household or mercantile establishment is considered, allowances will readily be made for the errors of figures and calculations which must unavoidably occur in analyzing all the financial concerns of an empire. Besides which, the shortness of the time employed in the production, in order to present it to the public on the first meeting of the Reformed Parliament; *and the determined resolution of the author to consult no individual whatever in its conception, arrangement, and composition*, have no doubt contributed to increase those errors, defects, and omissions. The reader must expect, therefore, to find facts, *data*, and conclusions, rather than elaborate composition, refined expressions, or brilliancy of style. It will be satisfactory to know, that the words used in many instances, do not convey an idea different from the one meant: the general bearing and connexion of the subject must be considered, rather than the perfect fitness or propriety of certain words and forms of expression.

It will be highly gratifying, should the imperfect work now submitted to the public, be the means of exciting some more able, steady, and profound writer, to devote his powers to this comprehensive and important subject. Should it, however, prove acceptable in its present state, the author himself will undertake to give it that due and ample extension and revision, which a work upon a subject of such magnitude justly deserves.

If his suggestions attract the attention of the Legislature, and of the reflecting men of this country; if they lead to the adoption of any measure for alleviating the burdens of the British people; and tend to improve the moral and social condition, increase the power, and promote the comforts and happiness of the millions who inhabit the British empire,—the great object of the author will be accomplished, his ardent wishes will be fulfilled, and he will find ample compensation for all his labours, in the delightful consciousness of having contributed to the happiness of mankind.

London, April, 1833.

CONTENTS.

b

PART III.

ESTIMATE OF THE CAPITAL, POWER, AND RESOURCES OF THE BRITISH EMPIRE IN ALL PARTS OF THE WORLD.

PART IV.

EFFECTS OF THE TAXATION REQUIRED TO PAY THE INTEREST OF THE NATIONAL DEBT; AND A PRACTICAL PLAN FOR ITS LIQUIDATION.

ERRATA.

Page 45, line 6—*for* "his troops," *read* "him."
—— 45, — 7—*for* "their," *read* "his."
—— 64, — 26—*dele* "important."
—— 78, Note b—*for* "six," *read* "five."
—— 314, line 9—*for* "two," *read* "twenty."
—— 314, — 14—*for* "5,330,000," *read* "23,730,000."
—— 314, — 15—*for* "25,670,000," *read* "7,270,000."
—— 470, last line of the Table—*for* "49," *read* "40," making the total "89,577,206," instead of "98,577,206."

PART I.

ORIGIN, PROGRESS, AND PRESENT STATE

OF

TAXATION,

REVENUE, AND EXPENDITURE.

inhabitants of the northern regions paid to their chiefs and princes grain and cattle, as a mark of respect and honour. Such was the case in England, when divided into so many parts, and governed by such numerous chieftains. This period of English history, involved (like that of other European nations,) in obscurity, does not furnish any authentic data: but it is most probable that these barbarous chiefs, besides the grain and cattle they were entitled to, appropriated to themselves a large share of the booty arising from their uninterrupted petty wars.

The Romans, more expert tyrants than the little chiefs whom they conquered, introduced a regular system of taxation, of which the "Tributa et Vectigalia" were the two constituent parts. The latter, (comprising tillage, pasturage, and the conveyance of goods,) not yielding enough for the rapacity of these oppressors, they had recourse to the "Tributa", the capitation tax, an impost on goods sold by auction, or in the public market, and a duty on imports and exports: high duties were also levied on legacies, houses, slaves, hearths, and different animals; human bodies, even, could not be interred, without paying a heavy duty [a]. The financial ministers of these barbarous robbers, (not unlike Pitt in more enlightened times,) profusely rewarded those unfeeling monsters to their own race, who could point out a new article for taxation. The revenue was increased so much by these measures, that the cruel

Tacitus says in another place: "Reges ex utilitate, Duces ex virtute sumunt: nec regibus infinita aut libera potestas; et duces exemplo potius quam imperio; si prompti, si conspicui, si ante aciem agunt admiratione, præsunt."

[a] Henry, Hist. Great Brit. Vol. I. p. 238. Whittaker, Hist. of Manchester. Vol. I. p. 212.

Roman proconsuls not only covered the expenditure of the country, but even sent considerable sums to the capital of the world [a].

Six hundred and twenty years elapsed between the departure of these fierce conquerors and the arrival of new ones. In this long interval of warfare and bloodshed, we see the rise, progress, and downfal of the Heptarchy. The country being divided into seven kingdoms, and the greatest part of the land distributed amongst such barbarous chiefs, the regularity of the contributions disappeared, and the cultivators of the land paid personal service to their chiefs, instead of money. This was a considerable source of revenue in war time, but we discover another no less productive, arising from the commutation of all punishments for crimes and atrocities, for a pecuniary fine.

The Danes threatened and infested the country so much, that a temporary land tax became necessary to purchase their forbearance. King Ethelred therefore, (anno 991), created the "Danegeld" [b], which produced

[a] The Roman proconsuls acted in the same manner in the other conquered countries. They extorted from that part of the Spanish peninsula called Galicia, and Lusitania, 2000 pounds of gold (or 645,834*l.*) a year. Cæsar got from Gaul "quadringentia," (or 322,916*l.*) a year. (Arbuthnot):—his triumph was embellished with 2,822 massive crowns of gold, which, when melted, amounted to 22,414 pounds weight of gold!—the greater part of these treasures were from conquered Spain and Gaul. The emperors were not less rapacious than the proconsuls and generals. In Spain, the Tarraconenses were forced to present Claudius with a crown of gold of 700 pounds weight; and the Gauls with another of 900 pounds weight.

[b] Danegeld, or Hidagium, Mort. Hist. Eng. The tribute paid to the Danes, in 1002, was 24,000*l.*, in 1007, 36,000*l.*, the last was in 1018, when Canute exacted the sum of 72,000*l.* from the kingdom in general, and 11,000*l.* from the city of London—a proof of

10,000*l.*, equal to 360,000*l.* of our present money. This tax, (which was afterwards increased,) although originally imposed for a specific object, was made permanent until 1051, when Edward the Confessor entirely repealed it [a].

The reader must be fully aware of the difficulty of ascertaining the amount of the revenue and expenditure of England, at a period of such confusion: however, many economists and historians, who have taken the trouble to calculate it, assert, that it was between two and two and a half millions of the present money; but we cannot pledge ourselves for their accuracy.

NORMAN CONQUEST.

The bastard, William the Conqueror, ascended the throne on the 14th of October, 1066; and with him, a new financial and political era commenced in England. The revenue of this king may be classed under four principal heads;—royal demesnes, voluntary gifts, legal taxes, and tyrannical exactions: the subdivision of these branches formed a catalogue of oppressions [b]; and the odious Danegeld, varying from one shilling to six on each hide of land, was extorted with the greatest

its importance at that time. All these sums were raised to induce the Danes to leave England. (Sinclair.)

[a] Webb, "Account of the Danegeld." This tax, at the rate of a shilling for each hide of land, produced 12,180 Saxon pounds, or 360,000*l.* sterling. A hide is calculated by some at "as much as one plough can work in a year"; by others, a "quantity necessary to maintain a family." Mort. Hist. Eng.

[b] William began and finished a survey, not only of the royal demesnes, but of all landed property in the kingdom: six years were employed in this undertaking, the result of which was the "Dom-boc," or final sentence, better known as the "Doomsday Book."

rigour[a]. At this period, the royal demesnes furnished the principal part of the revenues of the English sovereigns; and it was only in the emergency of a war, that extraordinary aid was required.

Vitalis[b], who was born nine years after the Conquest, calculates William's annual income at 400,000*l.*; but Hume, with great sagacity, observes, that a pound of silver of that time, containing three times the weight it does at present, would make it amount to 1,200,000*l.*; which, moreover, would purchase ten times more of the necessaries of life, than in our times: consequently his revenue would have been equal to ten millions of our money,—a sum rather large for those times. Henry[c] computes the Conqueror's revenue to have been equal to 5,808,975*l.*; Littleton, to 5,369,925*l.*; and Voltaire, to 5,000,000*l.* But these estimates are rather high.

WILLIAM RUFUS.

The rapacious atrocities of this king procured him the appropriate name of "Red Lion." He increased the "Danegeld" by charging four shillings on every hide of land[d]; plundered his elder brother of the Duchy of Normandy; and loaded the wretched Britons with double taxes to enable him to conquer not only Aquitaine, but all France. Most fortunately, when out hunting, an arrow pierced his heart, while meditating foreign conquests at the expense of his already miserable and overtaxed subjects.

HENRY I.

The third son of the Conqueror, taking advantage of

[a] Matthew of Paris calls it, "gravissima pecuniarum exactio."

[b] "Ipsi vero Regi mille et sexaginta libræ sterlinenses, &c. &c."

[c] Hist. Great Brit. Vol. III. p. 28.

[d] Matthew Paris, Hist. Ang. p. 42.

his brother's being engaged in the Crusade, mounted the throne with a questionable title; but promising his subjects a "charter, liberty, and relief from taxation," he was established on it. However, like some of our modern monarchs, he soon forgot his pledges, scorned the engagements contracted with his people, and even disregarded the charter, under which he took possession of the regalia, and of the treasure at Westminster.

On marrying his daughter Matilda to the Emperor of Germany, he levied three shillings on every hide of land [a]. This tax, which was exceedingly oppressive to the people, has been calculated at 800,000*l.* of our currency. But on his undertaking a continental expedition, a tax was levied upon monasteries, without exempting a single church. No less than 200 priests attired in their surplices, and bearing their crosses, met the king on the London road, and on their bare knees supplicated for a mitigation of this impost; but their humble prayers were of no avail [b]. If such was Henry's conduct towards the sacred churchmen, we cannot wonder at his arbitrary proceedings towards his lay subjects.

An essential alteration took place in the revenue during this reign: the rents of the royal demesnes, which, before, were chiefly paid in kind, were ordered to be paid in specie [c]. We must remember, that at that time, an ox was worth one shilling; and a sheep four pence, or about a shilling of our present money.

STEPHEN.

This prince—bold as his grandfather William the Conqueror—not only expelled Matilda, the true re-

[a] Brady, Vol. II. p. 270. [b] Mortimer, Vol. I. p. 212.
[c] Maddox's Exchequer, p. 186. Carte, Hist. Eng. Vol. I. p. 518.

presentative of the royal line, but introduced numbers of barbarians to support him in his usurpation: to pay these, he alloyed the coin—sold the offices, honours, and dignities of the church—and even alienated the estates of the crown. Agriculture was abandoned, the towns deserted, and famine desolated the land [a]; and as Stephen had recourse to all kinds of extortions to supply his rude and needy supporters, the complicated misery, distress, and devastation which ensued, compelled the English to abandon their native land. The abhorred Danegeld, which the king had sworn to abolish, when he assumed the crown, was continued with the utmost severity.

Stephen was the last of the Norman line. During this dynasty, the revenue, aided by extortion, met the expenditure: public credit, a weapon unknown at that time, could not forward the cruel or ambitious views of those monarchs. (Table I. Part I.)

SECTION II.

SAXON OR PLANTAGENET LINE.

HENRY II.

The first tax on personal property, amounting to two pence in the pound, was established by the first king of the Saxon line, (the Danegeld being discontinued.) But unfortunately, the Sultan of Egypt having conquered Jerusalem [b], this tax was immediately raised

[a] Lytt. Vol. I. p. 328. Stevens, p. 21.

[b] 35 Hen. II. Hoveden, p. 366. This is the first instance of a *tenth* being exacted: it was called "Saladin Tithe." Carte, Vol. I. p. 719. The "scutage" was attempted in the second year of this reign.

to one "tenth part" of all personal property: thus, the English were compelled to pay the large sum of 70,000*l.* in consequence of that event; and the Jews themselves were forced to contribute 60,000*l.*, for the religious and Christian object of retaking Jerusalem. The sums altogether collected are said to have amounted to two millions of the present money [a].

RICHARD I.

The folly of this king, and the treachery, cowardice, and avarice of Austria [b], in detaining the brave "Cœur de Lion" on his return from the Holy Land, and then requiring 100,000 marks [c] (or 300,000*l.*) for his ransom—quite empoverished the English people. The Danegeld was changed to the less odious name of "Hydage" [d] at the rate of five shillings per hyde; and the first impost was laid upon public amusements and tournaments.

JOHN.

His successor—is better known by his connexion with Magna Charta, than by his mis-deeds and his cruelty to the Jews—from whom he exacted 60,000 marks. One of them, a resident of Bristol, being rated at 10,000 marks, resisted the payment of so large a sum; but John ordered a tooth to be pulled out every day till the

[a] The amount of treasure left by Henry, was 900,000*l.*, according to Matthew Paris.

[b] "—Oh! Austria . . thou slave, thou wretch, thou coward,
Thou little valiant, great in villany,
Thou ever strong upon the strongest side!"
SHAKSP. JOHN, ACT. II.

[c] MS. of Chester says 160,000 marks.

[d] Stevens, p. 40. Hoveden affirms, that in two years, 1,100,000 marks, or 753,332*l.*, had been collected for public services.

payment was completed; on the eighth day, the Jew's fortitude failed him, and he paid the money [a]. By such financial means did this *mild* king provide for the public expenditure.

HENRY III.

This king's reign was long [b]; but his power was respected neither at home, nor abroad. Commerce, however, flourished, as the revenue of the customs [c] reached 60,000*l.* a year [d].

EDWARD I.

The English Justinian has been very properly distinguished for the important articles he added to Magna Charta, and for abolishing the practice of taxing the inhabitants of cities and boroughs without the consent of their representatives in parliament. "The famous statute, entitled 'Tallagio non concedendo,' was," says a clever writer, "exacted by the English people from the most able, warlike, and ambitious of their princes; who was thus bereaved of the power which his predecessors had assumed, of imposing tributary taxes."

The duties of tonnage and poundage, and the first charter granted to alien merchants, (in which for the first time a tariff [e] of duties appeared,) had their ori-

[a] Matthew Paris. Tovey, Anglia Judaica, p. 70.

[b] The historical events of this country, and of the rest of the world, are so intimately connected with the history of Taxation and Revenue, that it has been deemed indispensable to subjoin a Chronological Table of the Wars and Treaties of all Nations, which will be found at the end of this Part.

[c] Noy, Rights of the Crown.

[d] Matthew Paris, p. 647. "He pawned the jewels of the crown, and even the shrine of Edward the Confessor." (Noy.)

[e] They were called "nova custuma". Gilb. Excheq. p. 275.

gin in this reign. Edward has been admired by many as a great hero and statesman; but plundering the clergy in spite of the Pope's bull [a], confiscating the property of the Jews to increase the revenue, exiling 15,000 Israelites, and hanging 250 of these persecuted people in one day [b], are certainly no great proofs of Edward's heroism, nor of his economical and statesman-like proficiency.

EDWARD II.

This king attempted to recover the prerogative which his father had abandoned, but he possessed neither the valour nor the talents of his predecessor. He endeavoured to raise supplies by imposing duties on merchants and by customs, but it was contrary to the principle of the laws of England to levy new duties or add to old ones without the authority of parliament or a "consensus mercatorum." Imposts laid on by royal authority were called "maltolets" or evil duties [c].

England was desirous of conquering Scotland. Large imposts were consequently levied to defray the expenses of the war: and the loss of the battle of Bannockburn, (the Marathon of Scotland,) on the 23d of June 1314, did not damp the British courage; for in 1316, the parliament passed an act levying new impositions, by which every city, town, and village in the kingdom was compelled to furnish a number of armed men to reduce that country:—and to achieve that much desired conquest, even one fifteenth of all moveables of the laity

[a] Edward declared, (alluding to the Church,) that those who refused to support the civil government were not entitled to receive any advantage from it. Carte, Vol. II. p. 265. Sinclair.

[b] Tovey, Anglia Judaica, p. 232. Stevens, p. 48.

[c] Noy's Rights of the Crown, p. 77. Gilb. Excheq. p. 272.

was granted [a]. This was the only conquest of sufficient importance to the British nation to justify the imposition of taxes. However it was not effected: these abundant supplies were of no avail.

EDWARD III.

The glory of Cressy, Sluys, and Poictiers, was approaching, but was attended with a great expense without any return to England. The parliament was unbounded in its prodigality;—the most exorbitant taxes were levied for these expeditions;—the greatest variety of imposts, grants of all denominations, "tenths [b], fifteenths," subsidies in kind, (as on wool, &c.,) called "the ninth sheaf, the ninth lamb," &c., were exacted. The first parliamentary grant of money took place in 1371, when the sum of 50,000*l.* was voted to carry on the war against France [c]. The customs produced 12,000 marks annually [d]; every parish in England was assessed 1*l.* 3*s.* 4*d.*, which was afterwards raised to 5*l.* 18*s.*; the first poll-tax, of fourpence upon every individual above the age of fourteen, was levied [e]; in short every species of extortion was practised. But the people became sick of glory, and began to revolt against these continual extortions. However his brave son, Edward the Black Prince, requiring supplies to reinstate on his throne Pedro the Cruel, (the legitimate sovereign of Spain,) the king, to supply his wants, ap-

[a] Gilb. Excheq. In the second year of this reign, a commission was granted to farm waste lands "si absque injuriâ alterius fieri potest."

[b] Rot. Par. Edw. III. Vol. II. p. 232. [c] Stevens, p. 109.

[d] Noy, Rights of the Crown, p. 86. The Commons complained that the manner in which the tax upon wines, &c., was imposed, was a violation of their privileges. Gilb. Excheq. p. 217.

[e] Rot. Par. 47 Edw. III. Vol. II. p. 317.

plied to the conquered countries for the ransom of their respective sovereigns. That of the king of France amounted to 3,000,000 crowns of gold, (equal to 1,500,000*l.*,) one half of which was paid [a]: that of the king of Scotland to 100,000 marks [b], the greater part of which was also paid. Edward also received 50,000*l.* for the marriage portion of his daughter [c], and Ireland yielded 30,000*l.* after paying the expenses of its government. Yet all these sums, added to the ordinary revenue of England, being insufficient to relieve Edward from his distress, he pledged the royal crown (which remained eight years unredeemed) and the most valuable jewels of the queen [d].

Notwithstanding this monarch plundered France, and exhausted England by taxation, at the end of his career he not only lost all his conquests (Calais excepted), but his own patrimony was reduced to Bayonne and Bourdeaux; and this conqueror of kings was forced to accept whatever humiliating terms his enemies thought proper to dictate [e]. A mighty lesson to all nations, not blindly to squander their financial resources for the empty glory of foreign conquests, or the ambitious folly of their chiefs.

RICHARD II.

Succeeded his grandfather Edward. The revenue could not prosper during a minority where all was faction and disorder. The first subsidy granted by parliament amounted to 160,000*l.*, the largest sum ever before voted by the legislature [f]. It was levied by a poll and

[a] Hume, Vol. II. p. 469. [b] Mortimer, Vol. II. p. 605.

[c] Stevens, p. 124. [d] Hume, Vol. II. p. 482.

[e] The revenue of the Crown in the twenty years of Edward's reign, amounted to 154,139*l.* 17*s.* 5*d.* per annum.

[f] Rot. Par. Rich. II. No. 15. Vol. III. p. 90.

income tax, and the rich contrived to throw the burden upon the poor, by raising the money by means of an assessment of one shilling on every person above fifteen years of age. The English always hating this sort of capitation tax, an insurrection was the result, headed by Tyler and Straw; who, though not the best leaders, fought bravely, but were beaten. The young king showed himself to the people, made great promises, and gave hopes of reducing their burdens. He was perhaps the only sovereign (Queens Mary and Anne excepted) who returned part of the supplies granted him; but his sudden death put an end to the improvement of the revenue as well as to his line[a]. The tax on real and personal property commenced during this dynasty. No knowledge of finance existed; but the Pope's sanction for the imposition of taxes was no longer considered necessary, an evident proof that the doctrine of Wickliffe (the great father of the Reformation[b]) began to

[a] Hume, Vol. II.

[b] This great man, the precursor of John Huss, Jerome of Prague, and Luther, was born in the village which bears his name, about 1324. He began by attacking the Mendicant orders, who like locusts infested the best parts of Europe and England, and under pretext of devotion and virtue, devoured the fruits of the earth, and the labours of the people. In 1360, he published his famous "Objections to the Friars". But Edward III. quarrelling with Pope Urban V., in consequence of a demand of a thousand marks as an acknowledgement of the feudal dominion of the Popedom over England and Ireland, the Monks (those soldiers of the Pope) defended their leader by publishing several tracts, maintaining the Pope's rights, and calling upon Wycliffe to answer them. He published a work, defending the right of the King and his Parliament "to refuse the infamous tribute demanded by the Papal court,—the right to subject all ecclesiastics to the secular jurisdiction in all civil cases,—and even the right to alienate the property of the Church." At the accession of Richard to the throne, the Parliament, vexed by the continual Papal extortions, resumed the subject; and the fol-

produce the most salutary effects: we shall see their development in the subsequent reigns.

We now enter upon a dreadful period of eighty-six years of civil war, anarchy, bloodshed and crime. The revenue could not be benefited during these unsettled times; but the contest between the houses of York and Lancaster produced a good effect, as regarded the national rights, and the imposition of taxes. The charter was not violated, and no taxes were imposed without the consent of parliament; both parties respecting this basis of national liberty. (Table II. Part I.)

lowing question was submitted to Wycliffe,—"Whether a kingdom might not in case of necessity prevent its treasures from being conveyed to foreign countries, although it should be demanded by the Pope himself".

Wycliffe, the better to destroy the Pope's power, completed that most extraordinary task, the "Version of the Bible." The Old Testament has not yet been printed; but it is time that such an important publication should appear. "Copies of those translations were multiplied", says Lingard, "by the aid of transcribers, and recommended by this poor priest to the perusal of his hearers: in their hands they became an engine of wonderful power, and the seeds were sown of that religious revolution, which took place in little more than a century." Wycliffe, however, continued his march; he had the courage to attack the still strong bulwark of modern Rome,—transubstantiation. The servant of the servants of God fulminated bull after bull against John, ordering him to be imprisoned and tortured; but the good sense of the British people refused to execute the cruel mandates of Gregory II. (See "Life and Opinions of Wycliffe", by Vaughan, and "Life of Wiclif", by Le Bas.) The object of this digression has been, to show that, 130 years before Luther, an Englishman had set forth the three great fundamental principles of the Reformation,—to remark the spirit of the British people in defending such a champion, and the honourable resolution of the English parliament, in resisting all sorts of encroachments on its resources, and all foreign interference in the finances of the country.

SECTION III.

LINE OF LANCASTER.

HENRY IV.

HENRY IV., son of John of Gaunt, Duke of Lancaster[a], the patron of Wycliffe and Chaucer, (the one the father of English prose, as the other was of English poetry,) ascended the throne; and filled it better than many who were not usurpers. The customs became more productive. A tax on places and pensions was imposed by "Parliamentum Indoctum", or a parliament into which "no individual conversant with the law was admitted."[b] The expenses of the king's household were augmented from 10,000*l.* to 16,000*l.* But the most remarkable financial feature of this reign was the income or real property tax, which was granted with

[a] When Wycliffe was accused of heresy, and summoned to appear before the Convocation (1377), where the Bishop of London was performing the part of the Inquisitor Torrequemada, Percy, Marshal of England, out of tenderness for the respectable old man, and having but little regard for a court which owed all its authority to foreign power, bid him sit down; telling him "that he had many things to answer for, and therefore had need of a soft seat to rest him upon during so tedious an attendance." The Bishop of London, hearing that, answered, "he should not sit there," adding, "that if he could have guessed that the Earl Marshal would have played the master there, he would not have suffered him to come into the court." Gaunt, Duke of Lancaster, replied, "that the Earl Marshal's motion was but reasonable; and that as for him, who was grown so proud and arrogant, he would bring down the pride not only of him, but of all the prelacy of England." The bishop's hypocritical answer did not satisfy the duke, who said softly to one sitting by him, that "rather than take what the bishop had said, he would pluck him by the hair of his head out of the Church."

[b] Noy's Rights of the Crown, p. 4. Gilb. Ex. p. 240.

the express understanding, that "it should not become a precedent, lest it should be handed down to posterity as an impost of monstrous birth": and all documents relating to it were to be burned[a]. The clergy having refused to contribute their part of the subsidy, the "Indoctum Parliamentum" in 141[illegible] proposed that the church property and income, which amounted to 485,000 marks, should be divided among 15 earls, 1500 knights, 6000 squires and 100 hospitals[b].

HENRY V.

It is difficult to ascertain the amount of the revenue of England, during this monarch's reign: his great enterprises, however, are well known: consequently his expenses must have been adequately large. Hume, to excite our admiration of Henry, makes the supplies much less than were actually granted[c]; but Sinclair (perhaps the best authority on the subject) calculates Henry's income at 160,000 pounds of silver, or 500,000*l.* of the present money. The above-mentioned plan of the "Unlearned Parliament" was renewed in the second year of this reign: the Commons proposed to seize all property of the church and appropriate it to the use of the crown[d].

HENRY VI.

At the age of only nine months was proclaimed king of France and England. He lived long enough to find himself without a home, or even a subject. The parliament was sparing in granting subsidies; but taxes

[a] Hist. Ang. p. 369. Bacon's Discourses, Part II. c. 13.

[b] Hume, Vol. III. p. 81.

[c] Hume says that all the extraordinary supplies granted to Henry during his reign amounted to 203,000*l.*—Vol. III. p. 120. According to Rymer's Fœdera, the total income was 76,643*l.* 1*s.* 8*d.*

[d] Hume, and Par. Hist. Vol. II. p. 136.

were imposed under the name of benevolences, or "populi liberalitas"[a], accompanied by a threat, that should they not be complied with, they would be taken by force. Subsidies, however, were granted to the king in the tenth, fourteenth, and twenty-seventh years of his reign; and in the last was introduced for the first time, the principle of the gradation, which has been adopted in modern taxation[b]. Individuals enjoying an income of

from	1*l.*	to	20*l.* paid	6*d.* in the pound.
	20*l.*		200*l.*	1*s.*
above 200*l.*				2*s.*

How far the principles of commerce were understood at this period may be judged of, by the persecutions experienced by the foreign merchants, and the poll tax to which they were subject, from which the natives were exempt: even aliens who accidentally landed, and resided in England "six weeks", paid a tax of twenty shillings[c]. No wonder that the customs declined, and that the revenue fell off to 64,946*l.* 16*s.* 4*d.*: this fact is preserved in one of the parliamentary rolls, and shows that the same causes produce, in all times, the same effects[d].

Henry released his prisoner the Duke of Orleans, on the payment of 54,000 nobles, or 36,000*l.*[e]; and James of Scotland, (though not a prisoner,) was compelled to pay 40,000*l.*; notwithstanding which, the debts of this extravagant sovereign amounted to the enormous sum of 372,000*l.*; a part of which the parliament paid, by levying taxes on the British people, as we have seen done in more modern times[f]. (Table III. Part I.)

[a] Stevens, p. 157. Cotton, p. 177.
[b] Rot. Par. 28 Henry VI.
[c] Idem.
[d] Idem, Vol. IV. p. 33.
[e] Hume, Vol. III. p. 178.
[f] Idem, Vol. III. p. 215.

SECTION IV.

LINE OF YORK.

EDWARD IV.

Edward IV., the first prince of the house of York, and the handsomest man of his time, increased his revenue, by confiscating the estates of the nobility and gentry who supported his rival, Lancaster. The poverty of the treasury when he ascended the throne was extraordinary; and the grants of parliament being scanty, and insufficient to cover the expenditure, he had recourse to the "benevolence" of the clergy, and submitting his wants to the people, succeeded in obtaining considerable sums [a].

The expenses of the French expedition were defrayed by Louis XI., who gave 75,000 crowns, and an annuity of 50,000 [b]: the nation, however, considered this a most disgraceful transaction. Edward, by questioning the titles of those estates thought to be defective [c]—by fining the temporalities and bishoprics—and by engaging in commercial pursuits, acquired large sums; notwithstanding which, the exchequer was constantly exhausted, and the sums granted for the expenses of the household were always deficient, on account of the great

[a] Par. Hist. Ed. IV. Vol. VII. An old widow, who was personally applied to by Edward, was so much pleased with his appearance, and the graceful manner in which he made the request, that she immediately answered, "By my troth! for thy lovely countenance thou shalt have twenty pounds." The sum was so considerable, that the king, in token of his satisfaction, gave the old lady a kiss; which unexpected mark of royal condescension so pleased her, that she added 20*l.* more to her former donation.

[b] Hume. Stevens, p. 163.

[c] Carte, Vol. II. p. 796.

hospitality which the custom of the age rendered unavoidable. Parliament voted 11,000*l.* towards defraying these expenses; but the whole revenue applied to these purposes is estimated at 100,000*l.* [a]

EDWARD V. AND RICHARD III.

In these short reigns we do not discover any financial feature of importance, except the repeal *for ever* of the "benevolence"; but we find a superabundance of crime, treachery, and deceit; as well as the murder of Richard's two young and innocent nephews. (Table IV. Part I.)

SECTION V.

HOUSE OF TUDOR, TO THE END OF THE REIGN OF MARY.

HENRY VII.

The most avaricious of kings, and the first of the Tudor dynasty, (by the union of the houses of York and Lancaster effected by his marriage,) put a stop to the bloody civil wars, and commenced a regular system of exactions; all the penal statutes, all obsolete practices and customs, however ancient or cruel, were revived and enforced to extort money [b]. The only good act performed by Richard III.—the repeal *for ever* of the "benevolence," was rescinded by Henry, under the pretext, that the acts of an usurper were null [c]: thus the city of London [d] was compelled to pay a "bene-

[a] Rot. Par. 22 Ed. IV. No. 2. Vol. VI. p. 796.

[b] Bacon says, "they converted law and justice into wormwood and rapine."

[c] Hist. Hen. VII. p. 58.

[d] Act 2 Henry VII. Chap. 10. One of the new taxes was called "Morton's purge", from its being originally contrived by Bishop Morton.

volence" of above nine thousand pounds. (9688*l.* 17*s.* 4*d.*)

If the demands of Henry on the parliament were excessive, that assembly was no less prodigal of the public money. He obtained from them above thirty-one thousand pounds, for the marriage of his daughter to the King of Scotland [a]; which unjust grant was directed to be levied on the feudal lords and their vassals. He received from Charles VIII. of France 745,000 crowns, or 186,450*l.* [b]; and an annuity of 25,000 crowns, in consideration of his claim on Brittany. He received also 200,000 ducats from Ferdinand of Spain with his daughter Catherine, who was married first to Arthur, and afterwards to his brother, the cruel Henry.

Yet all these sources of revenue did not satisfy the avarice of this king. The Spaniards had discovered the new world; and the Portuguese, the passage to the East Indies; which opened new channels to commerce, industry, and enterprise. Henry let out ships, and lent money, at the highest interest, to merchants and adventurers [c]: but such usurious and unfair proceedings, joined to his uninterrupted exactions, produced disgust and discontent, which ended in revolt. Yorkshire and Durham were the first to rise in open rebellion; and Cornwall followed: 16,000 armed people came up from this last county to attack the capital, but were defeated near Blackheath, and 2000 of their number were either killed, or afterwards hanged [d].

However, the grants of parliament and the king's ex-

[a] Rot. Par. Henry VII. Vol. VI. p. 447.

[b] Par. Hist. Vol. II. p. 747.

[c] Noy's Rights of the Crown, p. 176.

[d] Par. Hist. Vol. II. p. 452. Bacon, Hist. Hen. VII.

tortions, combined with the small expenditure, produced a large surplus in the revenue, which accumulated from year to year; for Henry (like Ferdinand VI. of Spain) glutted his avarice in amassing treasure, which, like manure, could only benefit his subjects when spread. The amount of this treasure has been variously computed: Fabian Phillips calculates it at four millions sterling [a]; the most moderate estimate makes it three millions.

HENRY VIII.

The prodigality and extravagance of this king, exceeded even the avarice of his father. As soon as he had dissipated all the immense sums left to him, he had recourse to the most tyrannical means to extort money. The parliament voted him supplies of all denominations; but in 1523, when Wolsey demanded 800,000*l.*, they expressed their astonishment at such an exorbitant sum, and only granted one half [b]:—Henry became furious, and sending for Montague the lawyer and leader of the house, told him in plain terms, "if the supply does not pass, I shall have your head to morrow." [c] With such polite, mild, and constitutional measures, no grant could be refused, nor any tax resisted, even in the "land of freedom."

In the fourth year of this tyrant's reign the abhorred poll-tax was voted [d], by which a duke paid 10 marks, an earl 4*l.*, a baron 2*l.*, and a knight 1*l.* 10*s.* In 1523, a loan for the monarch, rated at 5*s.* in the pound on the clergy, and 2*s.* on laymen [e], was demanded; and as soon as it was collected, a decree was published

[a] Restauranda, p. 24.
[b] Par. Hist. Vol. III. p. 35.
[c] Anecdote related by Sinclair.
[d] Lords' Journal, Vol. I. p. 25.
[e] Hume, Vol. IV.

"cancelling all debts which the king had incurred since his accession to the throne:"[a] but, by a sort of retributive justice, Wolsey's favourites were the chief sufferers by this shameful violation of public faith.

But Henry's expenses exceeded all the ordinary resources; he had recourse therefore to extraordinary ones. Being declared the head of the church, he appointed Cromwell his vicar-general, to reform the hideous vices of the monks. The report made by the minister was as just in its strictures on the morals of the monks, as it was favourable for the revenue. The character of those unproductive and infamous hypocrites was shewn in all its abominable colours; the nation contemplated it with disgust, and saw, without expressing any mark of discontent[b], the suppression by one act only, of 376 monasteries and convents, whose land, personal property, and effects, produced at the lowest estimate the annual income of 132,000*l.*[c] But this was only a part of Henry's plan: two years afterwards, the larger monasteries, 605 abbeys, 90 colleges, and 110 hospitals for the relief of the poor[d], were also abolished. The suppression of the last was the only one injurious to the public.

Henry did not even respect the secular clergy, but took seventy manors from the Archbishop of York[e], and rated the other dioceses in the same proportion. The monasteries and convents of Ireland, as well as those belonging to the Knights of St. John of Jerusalem, were also suppressed[f]. To complete this wise and bold

[a] 35 Henry VIII. chap. 12.

[b] Burn's Eccles. Law, voce Monasteries.

[c] Stevens, p. 212; and Hume.

[d] 31 Henry VIII. cap. 13.

[e] Stevens, p. 193. Hume, Vol. IV.

[f] 37 Henry VIII. cap. 16.

scheme, the king ordered the parliament to pass an act, granting to him "the revenue of the two universities, and of all chantries, free chapels, and hospitals in the kingdom"[a]; and although the obstacles were considerable, he employed effective means to surmount them. He ordered those who returned to their convents, to be hung in the habits of their order. Never were the vices and crimes of a monarch more beneficial to the interests of the nation. Henry achieved with ease, at the commencement of the sixteenth century, what the National Assembly could not perform in the eighteenth, and what the Cortes of Spain intended in the nineteenth: no wonder that the English nation is two centuries further advanced than the French, and more than three centuries beyond the Spaniards.

However all these immense sums[b] did not cover the extravagant expenditure of this remorseless murderer of his beautiful wives. The value of the suppressed religious houses has been computed at five millions, but we think this estimate much too moderate: certain it is, that the most important moral and political effects resulted from their suppression. The origin of poor rates must be traced to these strong measures; but the baneful effects of this tax, so oppressive to the present generation, must be imputed to the abuses committed in its administration, and not to the principle or source from which it emanated.

All means were devised to supply Henry's whims and prodigality. A general survey was made of the state

[a] 37 Henry VIII. cap. 4.

[b] The revenues of the religious houses suppressed amounting on a moderate calculation to 272,000*l.*, their value at the present time would be six millions. (See Sinclair.) See also "A Summary of all the religious Houses at the time of their dissolution," p. 63.

of the kingdom, the number of the inhabitants, their age, profession, wealth, and income; but unfortunately this document has been lost, and the only point in it which has reached the present times, is the information that the annual income of the whole kingdom was estimated at four millions [a]. We must not omit to mention, that if the war with France gratified Henry's vanity by conquering Boulogne, it was expensive to England, as it cost the nation 1,340,000*l.*

EDWARD VI.

Succeeded his father Henry. The minority of this monarch was accompanied by the usual consequences of all minorities—the rapacity and misgovernment of ministers at home, and disgrace and disrespect abroad. France refused to pay 2,000,000 crowns, the arrears of her tribute [b]. Seymour, Edward's maternal uncle, who ruled the nation under the name of Protector, sold Boulogne for 400,000 crowns [c], (or 133,333*l.* 6*s.* 8*d.*); while his ministers and favourites divided among themselves the property of the church and the spoils of the Friars. To defray the expenses of the wars with France and Scotland, the Protector obtained from the parliament several subsidies, besides the tonnage and poundage. A most curious poll-tax of 1½*d.*, 2*d.*, and 3*d.*, on sheep (for one year) took place during this administration [d]. The impost of 8*d.* on each pound of cloth was no less ridiculous; indeed these taxes were all too unpopular to be well collected [e].

[a] Par. Hist. Vol. III. p. 26; and Sinclair.

[b] Henry II., the French king, answered, "that he would not be tributary to any body." 2 Edw. VI. cap. 36. Stevens, p. 225.

[c] Carte, Vol. III. p. 246.

[d] 3 Edw. VI. cap. 36.

[e] Stevens, p. 225.

A remarkable financial measure of this reign, was the suppression of a monopoly granted to foreign merchants, called the "Corporation Steel Yards." The abolition of these obnoxious privileges, by placing all merchants on an equal footing, produced the most advantageous results to the revenue [a]: the customs experienced a considerable increase.

However, these, and all other expedients and resources, did not supply the deficiencies of the treasury, and the profligacy of the administration. Money was therefore borrowed from the rich and mercantile towns of Flanders [b]. The city of Antwerp lent the Protector a large sum, at 14*l.* per cent. interest, to carry on the government: a national debt of 240,000*l.* was the result. The average revenue of this reign has been estimated at 400,000*l.* (Table V. Part I.)

MARY.

It has been said that it was most happy for England that Mary reigned only five years. However, the parliament was, at first, as humble as it was prodigal towards this queen. The tonnage and poundage duties were granted to her for life, by "your poore and obedient subjects of Commons": three subsidies, and five-fifteenths were also voted [c]. Her revenues, during all her reign, in Hume's opinion, exceeded three millions [d]: others have estimated them at 4,500,000*l.*, which is more probable, as the revenue may be supposed to have been greatly benefited during Mary's reign by the Union of Scotland, which terminated the depredations of the Scots, on account of which, the counties of Northum-

[a] Hume, Vol. IV. p. 348. [b] Sinclair.

[c] 1 Mary, cap. 18.

[d] Stevens. Hume, Vol. IV. p. 433. Rossi, "Successi d'Inghilterra."

berland, Cumberland, and Westmoreland, and the towns of Berwick and Newcastle, had hitherto been exempted from the payment of subsidies.

But Mary's bigotry, her persecution of the Protestants, (the *Liberals* of the age,) and her infatuated attachment to a husband who loathed her, roused the spirit of the legislature, which refused her a subsidy on the ground "that it was in vain to bestow treasures on a monarch whose revenues were wasted"[a]. In fact the crown revenues suffered considerably in Mary's reign.

She was determined to take more care of her soul than her kingdom; and as ready to aid her consort Philip in his foreign enterprises, as to follow his infernal persecuting policy[b]. For this purpose, she had recourse to forced loans, embargoes, and extortions of all sorts:—240,000*l.* were raised by these unjust means. She also fitted out an armament to assist Philip, and to victual it, plundered the counties of Suffolk and Norfolk,—seizing the corn and grain, without making any compensation.

The revenues of Ireland afforded but slender relief to Mary's exchequer. To have mixed up the history of the origin and progress of the revenues of this part of the United Kingdom with the preceding details, would have engendered confusion, without any advantage. The revenues of that country originated like those of England, (already described,) and were at first paid in kind. Ware[c] asserts, that 1450 oxen, 3650 cows,

[a] Parl. Hist. Mary.

[b] She said, "Albeit you may object again, I set more store by the salvation of my soul, than by ten kingdoms." A Bill was passed restoring to the Church first fruits and tenths; new convents were founded, &c.

[c] Hist. of Ireland, Vol. X. p. 413.

4800 pigs, 100 horses, &c., &c., were annually contributed to the palace of Kincora; but we suspect the number is exaggerated. Henry II. made grants of land to his followers, "subject to such imposts as were necessary for the maintenance of the government." John created a Court of Exchequer to decide about the collection and management of the contributions. Henry III. oppressed his Irish subjects with extortions, as all his predecessors had done: in 1226, all cathedral and ecclesiastical revenues were demanded by this king. Edward I. obtained all the clergy revenues, under pretext of conquering the Holy Land. In Edward the Second's time, after Bruce's invasion, "the only mode by which the English could maintain themselves", says Sinclair, "was by forcibly extorting money and provisions from the wretched inhabitants." Davies affirms, that in the same reign "the revenue of Ireland was far short, and yet no supply of treasure was sent out of England." Edward III. obtained from the Pope all the English revenues in Ireland for two years: Leland [a] says, "the laity were duly obedient, but the clergy absolutely refused." A remarkable financial measure, by which a tax was imposed upon absentees, was effected by the government of Richard II. During the reigns of Henry IV. and V., the disorder of Ireland was such, that in 1433 the revenue only amounted to 2,339*l.* 18*s.* 6*d.* [b], while the expenditure was 2,348*l.* 16*s.* 11*d.* Under Edward IV., we see money raised by the imposition of duties upon all merchandise sold in Ireland, excepting "hides and the

[a] Vol. I. p. 282.

[b] Leland, Vol. I. p. 284. Rymer's Fœdera, Vol. X. p. 113; and Rose, Vol. II. p. 433.

[illegible] of freemen of Dublin and Drogheda*. A [illegible] was granted in Henry [illegible] of a shilling in the pound on all merchandise imported and exported. It is from this reign that we may date the revival of English power in Ireland; which, since the time of the [illegible] war, had declined into a miserable and precarious state of weakness.

However we do not find that the revenue made any considerable progress: it seldom exceeded 5,000l. per annum. The dissolution of the monasteries, and the result of the laws against absentees, in the reign of Henry VIII., produced some addition to the Irish income; but it did not increase during the reign of his daughter Mary. Indeed, Ireland seldom contributed any large income, but on the contrary, became a burden to England.

CONCLUSION.

But we must conclude this long period exceeding [illegible] centuries, during which we unfortunately discover the most complete ignorance of commercial and financial principles, accompanied by a long and uninterrupted series of extortions to raise money, but without any regular system of taxation. The irregular, unprofitable, and anti-national objects upon which the sums raised were expended, has been sufficiently indicated.

It appears that the tax on personal property (at 2*d.* in the pound) commenced, and the first tenth (called Saladin tithe) was exacted, in the reign of the first king of the Saxon line:—the first charter was granted

* Leland, Vol. II. p. 617.

to merchants, the first duty of tonnage and poundage, and the first tariff on goods, were imposed by Edward I., who also compelled the church to contribute to the revenues of the state;—the first poll-tax (at 4*d.* a-head) was granted to Edward III., and the first grant in money (of 50,000*l.*) voted by parliament to achieve the victories of Poictiers, &c.;—the income tax, or tax on real and personal property, was established during the Saxon dynasty, and was granted to Henry IV. on the express condition, that it should be concealed from posterity "as an impost of monstrous birth;"—subsidies were a tax on income, and have continued almost without interruption;—the doctrines of Wickliffe (whose bold spirit first burst the trammels of superstition) spread to such an extent, that not only was the church considered liable to share the expenses of the state, but the "indoctum" parliament thought a distribution of its property among the people and hospitals would be expedient;—the house of commons[a] renewed the proposal to seize all the church property in Henry the Sixth's reign, and the principle of gradation in the imposition of taxes was introduced about the same time;—immense treasures were accumulated by the extortion and parsimony

[a] In the dispute between Edward III. and Urban regarding the payment of 1000 marks, the Lords Spiritual and Temporal and the Commons were unanimous in stating, that "neither King John nor any other sovereign had power to subject the realm of England without the consent of Parliament—that their consent was not obtained—and that, passing over other difficulties, the whole transaction, on the part of the king, was a violation of the oath which he had taken on receiving the crown." It was farther determined by the temporal nobility and the popular representatives that, "should the pontiff issue his threatened process against the monarch of England as his vassal, the strength of the nation should be instantly called to the king's aid."—Vaughan, Life of Wycliffe. Vol. I.

of Henry VII.;—his son, Henry VIII., largely increased the revenue by confiscating the property of the church: the origin of poor rates may be traced to this measure; —finally, the crown revenues were diminished by the injudicious restitutions and mismanagement of Mary. The revenues of Ireland had the same origin as those of Great Britain, and were at first paid in kind;—its income was always small, and inadequate to cover the expenditure;—Richard II. was compelled to impose a tax upon absentees, the same causes operating in the earliest times, as in the present.

But with Elizabeth a new era, more favourable to the finances of Great Britain, commences.

PART I.

PROGRESS OF TAXATION, REVENUE, AND EXPENDITURE.

SECOND PERIOD.

FROM THE ACCESSION OF ELIZABETH TO THE REVOLUTION IN 1688.

Progress of Taxation and Public Revenue.—Financial measures of Elizabeth.—Their effects on Public Credit and on the Revenue.—Resources of Elizabeth, applied to forward the first great European Revolution.—Immediate cause of its explosion.—Financial causes of the important part which the Commons began to play, and which occasioned the consolidation of British liberties.—The first Lottery established in the reign of James I., and where the produce was sent.—Title of Baronet originated in the same reign.—Conditions upon which that dignity was conferred.—Revenue derived from it, and from houses licensed to play at cards.—Bill of Rights purchased from Charles I., and for what amount.—His enterprises, and illegal financial measures; and the effects they produced.—When, and by whom, the Land-Tax, Customs, Excise, and Post Office were systematically constituted regular branches of revenue.—When the first Stamp Act was established,—and what financial measures caused the entire abolition of feudal rights, and the introduction of a uniform system of taxation and representation.—Revenue of Ireland,—continued small.—When the Excise was first introduced into that country.—Liberality of the Irish parliament towards Charles II.—Measures adopted by James II. in consequence of not being able to collect a grant accorded to him by the Irish parliament.—Objects to which the whole amount of the Public Revenue of Great Britain and Ireland, and of the illegal exactions, were applied in this period.

Coincident with the discovery of the New World, burst forth the first great revolution in Europe. To the downfal of the Roman empire succeeded the irruption of the northern barbarians, and to this, a much greater evil, the overwhelming tyranny, crimes, and profligacy, of the Roman pontiffs. The mighty monarch and the abject vassal were equally slaves to the crafty dictates of the church. But a coarse, though bold and talented Augustinian Friar[a], had the undaunted

[a] The mine that was to explode against superstition and the profligate abuses of the Church, already strongly loaded, only required a steady and expert hand to apply the match; and Martin Luther,

courage to resist their infamous oppressions and unjust fiscal measures, to set the papal power at defiance, and the son of a Saxon miner, was the person ordained to perform this critical task. This extraordinary man was born in 1483, in the small town of Eisleben. Actuated by the fears of that superstition and ignorance he was destined to destroy,—struck at the death of a friend killed by his side by lightning, he abandoned the study of the law for that of divinity, and the lawyer's brief, for the friar's cowl. He soon became a Doctor (1512), upholding and defending all the subtleties and absurdities of the faculty with far greater power than the prejudiced and ignorant contemporary doctors of his university. But Luther visited Rome, and saw that court, where irreligion, deception, and profligacy, have always kept perpetual and undisturbed possession of the throne: his religious fervour and mystic enthusiasm cooled at the sight of the corruption, the crimes, and the infamy of the high ministers of the *Divine Church*. Rome, at all times subsisting by plunder, or the ignorance of nations, wanted money; and her great pontiff, finding his exchequer exhausted, adopted the same measures, the same deceptions, and infamous means to fill it, that all his predecessors had done. Nay, Leo, educated in a great mercantile place in those times, and a more clever financier than his predecessors, followed the sound principle of levying a smaller tax upon larger numbers, in order to obtain the greatest amount of revenue. Never, in fact, were indulgences so cheap—fourpence could get a soul out of the flames. But the collectors of the Papal revenue did not second their master's fiscal intentions: they were more attached to their rights of sale, and to their sordid and large profits, than intent on the relief of the treasury, or of the sufferers in purgatory. The Augustins were in possession of the right of selling that most precious merchandise —'Indulgence', in the province where Luther resided; but the Dominicans were unjustly appointed in their stead. The auctioneers began to quarrel; and Luther, who, but for an awkward fiscal blunder of the administration, would have been the best of all Papal collectors, turned furious, not only against his rivals the Dominicans, but, with his characteristic determination and boldness, menaced even the annihilation of the treasury and of the Pope himself. He directly (1517) affixed on the door of the University of Wittemburg, the famous ninety-five propositions, attacking the whole foundation and frame of the doctrine of Indulgences. Such was the motive for the first step towards that grand revolutionary

raise the standard of civil and religious liberty. The Spaniards, the most powerful, the most free people of

movement, which separated and set free one half of Europe from the shameful tyranny of modern Rome.

But in this very year, Luther, pursuing his plan with indefatigable exertions, translated the Penitential Psalms, and began to distribute and sell the Scriptures to the people; thus attacking the other basis on which the Church of Rome rests—ignorance. Leo, astonished at such boldness, and indignant at the stoppage of the supplies to the treasury, excommunicated Luther (1520): but that blunt Saxon, surrounded by immense crowds as coarse as himself, in the market-place of Wittemburg, took the excommunicating Bull in his hands, and shewing it to the people, flung it along with a whole collection of Papal decrees and decisions into the fire. A new and more formal excommunication being fulminated against him in the following year, he appealed to the General Council of the Universal Church. But Charles V., whose Spanish ambassador at Rome had most strenuously entreated him to promote and protect a German friar who gave so much trouble to the Pope, wishing to see Luther, and become acquainted with the opinions of such a courageous man, invited him to the Diet of Worms, offering him an ample 'safe conduct'. The friends of the Reformer, remembering the 'safe conduct' of Sigismund, insisted, in the most positive manner, on his declining the Imperial invitation: to all their entreaties, however, the bold Luther only replied, "I shall go, were I to meet with as many devils in the Diet as there are tiles on the roofs of the houses in the town." All the Emperor Charles's mighty allurements and all his natural and persuasive eloquence, could not prevail on Luther to desert his opinions. The bishops advised the emperor to act like the religious Sigismund,—break his promise, and burn Luther, as the other did Huss and Jerome of Prague: but Charles was more honourable, more enlightened, more humane: he only permitted an edict of outlawry against the Reformer. Never has a similar measure produced more important effects upon the state of religion, and particularly upon the German language and literature. Luther, compelled to remain concealed, translated the New Testament into his native idiom; and thus the dialect of his native district superseded the common language, and has become ever since the general literary language of Germany. In the same year in which he published the translation of the

that age, whose policy it was to direct that glorious movement by putting themselves at its head, were mis-

Psalms (1525) he married the Lady Boren, *a nun*, by whom his descendants are yet existing. But while the Catholic Charles V. was keeping the Pope in prison, his measures against the Reformers in Germany were not the less severe. The princes of Germany were compelled to league themselves at Smalcald in defence of their opinions. The Reformers delivered at the Diet of Spires that famous protest, which gave them the name of Protestants; and while Luther was directing all their movements from his retreat at Cologne, he was concocting with the dialectic Melanchthon the confession of Augsburg. By this act was formed and consolidated the Protestantism, which he saw spread, before his death, over Germany, Denmark, Sweden, England, France, and Spain. The Lutheran churches of Seville, Avila, Valladolid, &c., offered the first martyrs to the Protestant religion; and Lutheranism was spreading so fast, that the Spanish government became alarmed lest all Spain should become Protestant. (See "History of the Reformation in Spain," a very valuable work; also "Llorente's History of the Inquisition"; and Puigblanch's ditto.)

Such were the wonderful effects of that astonishing combination of intellectual and moral qualities, which constituted the character of this man. As Melanchthon says, "Pomeranus is a grammarian, and explains the force of words: I am an analogian, and point out trains of connexion and argument: Jonas is an orator, and discourses copiously and ornately; but Luther is all in all, and a miracle among men. Whatever he utters, whatever he writes, penetrates the minds of men, and in some wonderful manner leaves, as it were, a sting in their hearts."—"It is indeed true," says Bossuet, "that there was a force of generous vehemence in his discourses,—he possessed a lively and impetuous eloquence, by which people were drawn along and charmed, and an extraordinary boldness when he found himself supported and applauded, together with an air of authority, which made his disciples tremble in his presence, so that they dared not to contradict him, either in great matter or small." Such is the character of this extraordinary man, drawn by both friends and enemies. To shew how powerfully he contributed towards the first great European revolution, which exploded on account of a mistaken and badly contrived Papal measure of finance, was the motive which led to this digression.

led by their great military despot Charles V., the destroyer of Castilian privileges[a]. He was at first inclined to adopt the true policy, but wavered, hesitated, and at last mistook his own and the interests of the world. The gloomy Philip inherited with the honour of leader of European politics, the bad policy, the errors, and the mighty power of his father; he employed all his means, and directed all his vast financial resources, against the sacred principles of that revolution, and of European liberty.

An Englishwoman, however, with a nobler mind, and superior good sense, placed herself in front of the opposite party, and gave a far better direction to her energies and financial resources, by employing them to aid all those who fought for the grand contested principle—liberty of conscience.

ELIZABETH.

Elizabeth, on ascending the throne, began her financial measures by paying the debts of her father, her sister, and her brother, Edward, the whole amount of which has been computed at 4,000,000*l.*; but Hume thinks (very justly) there must be some mistake in this estimate. At the same time, she adopted the measures best calculated to establish national credit, by restoring

[a] The towns and communities of Spain rose against the encroachments and violations of their liberties by Charles V. This gave occasion to the war called "Communidades". Padilla and Bravo were the generals of the "Communeros", and fought most bravely at the famous battle of Villalar; but were defeated by the regular troops of Charles. The next day they were hanged; and with them expired Castilian liberty. From these leaders, and from this cause, the party who have latterly experienced the same fate in Spain, assumed the name of "Communeros".

the debased coin of the realm to a proper standard, and strictly upholding the basis of public faith[a].

The parliament was liberal; as no less than thirty-eight fifteenths and nineteen subsidies were voted, and the tonnage and poundage were granted for her life[b]. The clergy also contributed eighteen more subsidies, valued at 20,000*l.* each; and the total grants during her life amounted to 280,000*l.*[c]: but the total amount of her permanent income, including her hereditary revenues, and the Duchy of Lancaster, exceeded 350,000*l.*[d].

The progress in the discovery of the New World, promoted commerce and adventurous maritime speculation; thus the customs became one of the most productive sources of the revenue[e]. But unfortunately for that branch, and for the commercial interests, the crown held the monopolies of "salt, oil, starch, aniseed, and vinegar." "Is not bread in the number?" exclaimed Hackwell, a patriotic member of parliament[f]. She abused most shamefully the baneful prerogative; no mercantile article could escape her mortiferous grasp. A single patent, granted to four of her base and profligate courtiers, utterly ruined 800 industrious fami-

[a] See Camden's Eliz.; Folkes on Coinage, p. 58; and Harris on Coins, Part II. p. 9.

[b] Par. Hist. Vol. IV. p. 73. Statute Book.

[c] Commons' Journal, Vol. I. p. 395. Thus stated by Cotton and Salisbury.

[d] Stevens, p. 247. Par. Hist. Vol. IV. p. 80.

[e] See Forbes, Vol. I. p. 133. Philipps says they produced 50,000*l.*; Naunton, that in ten years the receipts were doubled.

[f] "For I assure you if affairs go on at this rate, we shall have bread reduced to a monopoly." D'Ewes, p. 648. Par. Hist. Vol. IV. p. 402.

lies[a]! In vain the people complained, in vain the parliament remonstrated: Elizabeth, as haughty as her cruel father, and infatuated with her prerogative, like the fanatic James, replied, "that it was the chief flower in her garden, and the principal and head point in her crown and diadem."[b]

From such extortionate sources were the revenues derived, which supplied the great expenditure of the state and of her numerous enterprises. She assisted the Dutch against Spain, lending them 800,000*l.*, but receiving as security their most valuable fortress; aided the French Protestants[c], lending to their king, Henry, 450,000*l.*, but at fourteen per cent. interest; expended (between 1589 and 1593) 1,200,000*l.* in the war with Spain, and against the "invincible Armada"[d]; and carried on a most cruel and horrible war in Ireland, during eight years, at an expense of above three millions[e]. So extraordinary an expenditure required an augmentation of the circulating medium; accordingly we find the amount of silver coined during Elizabeth's reign to be 5,513,717*l.*, and that of gold 795,138*l.*[f]. The consolidation of the laws previously enacted for the relief of the poor, was another great economical measure of this reign[g].

But let not the reader conclude that Elizabeth's con-

[a] D'Ewes. Camden's Hist. Eliz.

[b] See her speech on the occasion, Par. Hist. Vol. IV. Camden's Eliz.

[c] Camden's Eliz. Par. Hist. Vol. IV.

[d] Par. Hist. Vol. IV. p. 364.

[e] Cecil has estimated the amount of the expenditure in ten years at 3,400,000*l.*

[f] Harris on coins; and Folkes.

[g] A bill for relieving the poor out of church livings was lost by twenty-nine votes. D'Ewes.

duct was exempt from the mal-practices and extortions of her predecessors. She imprisoned her beloved subjects, as former kings had done, when they refused to lend her money; laid embargoes, like Mary, on all sorts of merchandize; and (a greater hypocrite than her half-blood sister) obtained, by cunning, more reasonable prices; she extorted 100,000*l.* from the Catholics for licenses to say mass[a]; and plundered Ireland, by means of a debased coin, against the advice of her able minister Burleigh. This virgin queen, like the notorious Catherine of Russia, squandered prodigious sums on her numerous and successive favourites[b], but, worse than that empress, butchered them afterwards. Her gifts to Dudley, Leicester, and Essex, were as boundless as they were scandalous; the presents to the latter were immense; but the expenses of her household and her dresses were carried to such extravagance, that no less than 3000 suits of different colours and shapes were found at her death, with which she used to adorn her ugly person.

This profligate expenditure left an unpaid debt of 400,000*l.*[c]; but notwithstanding all her errors, we must remember (as has been already stated) that the basis of public credit was laid by Elizabeth, who may also be called the founder of our immense Indian empire. All the branches of the revenue, especially the customs, increased. The consolidation of the acts and measures of Henry VIII., relative to church and monastic property,

[a] Strype's Annals of the Reformation.

[b] Naunton in his Fragmenta Regal. gives an account of Elizabeth's favourites, twenty-two in number: the presents made to Essex were calculated at 300,000*l.* "The queen," it was said, "pays bountifully while she rewards sparingly."

[c] Restauranda, Part IV. Vol. V. p. 147.

combined with the progressive diminution of the royal demesnes, gave rise to the importance of the commons, to the liberties of the people, and laid the foundation of the present power, prosperity, and glory of the whole British empire[a]. (Table V. Part I.)

JAMES I.

The son of Queen Mary of Scotland, uniting the two crowns, was the first sovereign styled King of Great Britain. This monarch's revenue arose from the same sources as that of his predecessors; demesnes[b], which yielded 80,000*l.* per annum, and a royal and feudal prerogative, in virtue of which goods were forcibly sold at whatever price the officers of the crown chose, whereby this branch was made to furnish 200,000*l.* per annum[c]. The parliament was likewise liberal enough with regard to grants and subsidies. They granted to James, besides the tonnage and poundage, nine subsidies and ten fifteenths[d]; calculating the former at 70,000*l.*, and the latter at 36,000*l.*[e], they altogether amounted to about 1,000,000*l.*; to which, when we add twenty ecclesiastical subsidies, the whole would exceed an average of 60,000*l.* per annum[f]. Notwithstanding

[a] Harrington says, "that though the perpetual love-tricks, which passed between Elizabeth and her people, converted her reign into a kind of romance, the House of Commons, even then, began to raise that head, which soon became so high and formidable to their princes, that they looked pale upon those assemblies." See also Nickolls' "Calvinism and Arminianism compared."

[b] Noy's Rights of the Crown, p. 8.

[c] Com. Jour. Vol. I. p. 864.

[d] Idem, Vol. I. p. 264. Macauley's Hist. Vol. I. p. 251.

[e] "Brief declaration of the present state of His Majesty's Revenue, ann. 1651."

[f] Sinclair.

which, Salisbury, in his speech to the parliament, lamented its want of liberality, observing that "in 600 years previous, in only three instances the supplies were refused by the Commons." But these Commons were justly irritated with the bad conduct and expedients of James, who (on the subject of forced loans) declared, "that no man should be forced to lend money, nor give reason why he would not." [a]

The first lottery took place in this reign [b], and the greater part of its proceeds was sent to give impulse to the American colonies. In 1620, a number of houses were licensed in London to play at cards, and yielded a revenue to the state, long before such a source was thought of by our neighbours the French. But the "monopolies," another important source of James's revenue, destroyed commerce and paralysed rising industry. "All the trade of England," says Hume, "was in the hands of a few rapacious engrossers, and all prospect of future improvement was sacrificed for a little temporary advantage to the sovereign." [c] The commons came forward, and by an act, condemned "all monopolies as contrary to law, and the known liberties of the people;" [d] but this pedantic king had recourse to other contrivances to supply his whims, and those of his equally pedantic courtiers [e]. He sold the dignities of baron, earl, and viscount, to any body who chose to become a purchaser: the price of one of these titles was from 10,000*l.* to 20,000*l.* [f]. The title of baronet also originated at this time: no less than ninety-three of these

[a] Com. Jour.

[b] Mortimer, Vol. II. p. 512.

[c] Hume, Vol. V. p. 103.

[d] Par. Hist. Vol. V. p. 228.

[e] Noy, Rights of the Crown. See the excellent treatise, "Cottoni Posthuma."

[f] Franklyn, Annals, p. 33.

dignities were created, which at the rate of 1095*l.* each, (the fixed price,) produced to the revenue 98,550*l.*[a]; they were bound besides to maintain thirty-four soldiers for three years, at 8*d.* a-day each. The fines produced still larger sums; Benet paid 20,000*l.*, Suffolk 30,000*l.*, Middlesex 50,000*l.*, and the great Bacon was sentenced to pay 40,000*l.*[b] Under such a system, the star-chamber formed the best mint.

But the most productive branch, and that which gave occasion to radically establish the rights of the British nation, was the customs. James considered that, like some of his predecessors, he could raise supplies from the customs on his own authority; but the parliament, more enlightened, and less intimidated than some previous ones, thought, and with justice, otherwise. The commons passed an act against these arbitrary imposts, but the lords, seldom in favour of the liberties of the people, most shamefully refused their assent to this important bill[c].

We may judge how rapidly commerce was increasing, by the account of imports and exports. The receipts of customs amounted to 190,000*l.* at the end of this reign, (see Table VI. Part I.); and the total revenue may be computed at the annual sum of 600,000*l.*[d]. Let us see how James expended a great portion of these sums. He paid considerable attention to the naval establishment, devoting to it 50,000*l.* a-year; he

[a] Hume, Vol. VI. p. 23. See also "Brief Declaration," &c.

[b] Macauley, Vol. I. p. 230. Par. Hist. Vol. V.

[c] Lords' Journal, Vol. VI. Hume, Vol. VI. p. 61. The best publications on this important question are, in support of the prerogative, "The Question concerning Imposition fully stated," by Davis; in defence of the national rights,—"The Liberty of the Subject Maintained against the power of Imposition," by Hackwell.

[d] Sinclair, Vol. I.

paid off 400,000*l.* of debt contracted by Elizabeth; kept three courts in a most luxurious and profuse style[a]; and gave 93,278*l.* to the Palatine with his daughter. His large presents to his infamous Scotch and English courtiers, the profligate Carr, Earl of Somerset, Rich, Earl of Holland, and Villiers, Duke of Buckingham, are well known. In the first fourteen years of his reign, no less than 424,464*l.* in money only, was lavished on those perverse favourites[b]; still larger sums were expended in the romantic expedition of his son Charles to Spain, and in the unsuccessful conquest of Bohemia, to gratify the ambition of the Palatine. (Table X. Part I.)

CHARLES I.

Was one of the greatest, but (happily for England) most unsuccessful of tyrants. He inherited, along with the crown, the despotism and the absurd notions of "prerogative" of his father. He began his reign by wasting the English blood and treasures in wars against Austria, France, and Spain; contending with the two latter powers at the same time. (See Chronological Tables.) But all these enterprises turned out as unfortunate as they were impolitic[c]. Charles, after having excited the Huguenots to an open rebellion, basely abandoned them to their executioner Louis[d]. Before, however, he had quite concluded his wars with these nations, he began to turn his arms against a portion of his own peaceful sub-

[a] Macaulay's Hist. Vol. I. p. 22. "Brief Declaration", &c.

[b] "Brief Declaration", &c. [c] Hume, Vol. VI.

[d] Vassor, Histoire de Louis XIII. "Les Reformés de France ne furent point compris (dans le traité): une si grande infidelité après des paroles donneés et souvent reitereés, sera une fletrissure éternelle à la mémoire de Charles."

jects; who, detesting the ceremonies and hierarchy of the Episcopal Church, preferred the simple but stern doctrines of Calvin. Charles, like a blind fanatic, twice put himself at the head of a powerful army and fleet, destined to massacre his Scotch subjects: while twenty-four palaces completely furnished, afforded his troops the unknown luxury of resting on their march to enforce his arbitrary and despotic views [a].

But all this required immense expenditure. The sources of Charles's revenue were the same as those of his father's: it will therefore be unnecessary to repeat them. The parliamentary and clerical subsidies, twenty in number, granted to Charles, were considerable: they exceeded 600,000*l.*[b] The customs yielded 500,000*l.* a year; the royal demesnes not only produced a large income, but even afforded Charles the means of borrowing 300,000*l.* on their security. The total sums raised during Charles's reign, including all these items, amounted to 21,495,000*l.* [c], averaging 895,819*l.* per annum [d]; a revenue amply sufficient to defray the ordinary expenses of the kingdom.

But this income was inadequate to cover the expenses of Charles's unjust and extraordinary enterprises; he had recourse, therefore, to all sorts of extortions.—200,000*l.* were raised by means of the illegal, and already abolished expedient of "a forced loan"; and those who refused to lend on these arbitrary terms were imprisoned, or had soldiers quartered in their houses [e]. But the city of London having openly refused to supply the sum demanded, could not so easily be imprisoned or punished! Places

[a] Hume, Vol. VII. p. 341.

[b] See the famous "Remonstrance", 1640. Rush. Vol. I. p. 190.

[c] Hume, Vol. VII. p. 34.

[d] Commons' Jour. Vol. VIII. p. 150.

[e] Stevens, p. 247.

and offices were invented with the sole view of charging heavy duties upon them. Merchants, traders, and vintners, were compelled to pay illegal duties on the goods and wine retailed by them[a]. An ancient duty for furnishing the soldiery with coat and conduct-money which had long been abolished, was revived[b]. 100,000*l.* were extorted by means of fines on people who were compelled to receive the order of knighthood. The Star Chamber also inflicted its terrible pecuniary fines. Fowles was mulcted 5000*l.*[c], for merely dissuading a friend from compounding with the commissioners of knighthood;—30,000*l.* were exacted from those who had trespassed on an obsolete law against converting arable land into pasture. Encroachments on the king's forests were punished in the same manner; and those who resisted these illegal extortions were forcibly enlisted as soldiers and sailors[d].

An act was passed by the second parliament, granting to Charles 250,000*l.*, on the express condition that he should give his assent to the Bill of Rights; and among other clauses contained in this act, the most important was one, "that no gift, loan, benevolence, tax, or such like charge, be exacted without the consent of the Commons' House of Parliament"[e]: in spite of which, Charles, forgetting his sacred engagements and blinded by despotism, imposed, without any consent of parliament, the famous tax, called "ship money." 800,000*l.* was the produce of this odious tax, enforced by Charles during four years with an unparalleled and tyrannical

[a] Macaulay, Vol. II. p. 218. [b] Stevens, p. 250.
[c] Macaulay, Vol. II. p. 218. Naunton, Frag. Regal.
[d] Hume, Vol. VI. p. 230.
[e] Par. Hist. Vol. VIII. p. 256. 17 Char. I. cap. 41. Rush. Vol. II. p. 103.

perseverance, which ultimately cost him his head. But Pym [a], Selden, St. John, and above all, the brave Hampden, resolutely and steadily withstood the storm of royal persecution. The fourth parliament rejected with dignity the insidious overtures made by Charles to countenance his arbitrary imposition of the "ship money." But the Long Parliament was at hand. Its first important decision declared, that the "ship money" was illegal and arbitrary, and for ever abolished, and that the sentence against Hampden was contrary to law: the judges who condemned that patriot were impeached, and the officers collecting the impost declared highly culpable [b]. But such strong resolutions were of no avail against the king. That military despot, far from stopping in his illegal course, sent money to Germany, to raise and bring over 1000 horse, to aid in oppressing his subjects. He ordered a number of horse, foot, and carriages, to be furnished by every county and town, against the Scotch: until at last he unfurled the bloody standard of civil war, and commenced butchering his British subjects [c].

[a] Pym (as Lord Nugent observes in his excellent Memorials of Hampden) said, "when the citadel of public liberty was menaced, he defended it as one who thought, in such a battle, all arms lawful." (Macaulay, Vol. II. Hume, Vol. VI.) Selden, the Author of the "Analectum Anglo-Britanicum," or the form of the British government before the Normans; the "Titles of Honour"; the "De Diis Syriis", an elaborate oriental investigation; the "Mare Clausum", or defence of the rights of the British to the surrounding seas; in answer to the "Mare Liberum" of Grotius; and above all, of the "History of Tithes", in which he refutes the doctrine of their divine origin,—was one of the ablest debaters, as well as one of the most learned and patriotic writers of the time.

[b] 16 Char. I. cap. 14.

[c] In the first engagement, the deformed Prince Rupert killed a party of soldiers belonging to the Commons.

Such proceedings exhausted the patience of the nation, as it exhausts the patience of every impartial man to hear statistical writers assert, "that historians are all of opinion, that Charles was a man almost without blemish"[a]; when Hume himself, the partial and able defender of the House of Stuart, who with uncommon abilities has excused and defended Charles's conduct, is obliged to declare, "that his disasters ought to be ascribed neither to the rigours of destiny, nor to the malignity of his enemies, but to his own precipitancy and indiscretion."[b]

But the reader is no doubt utterly tired and disgusted with the uninterrupted recital of the crimes, extortions, cruelties, tyranny, and injustice, perpetrated by the rulers of the British people. It was not, however, from choice, but with the greatest reluctance, and entirely in opposition to his own feelings and inclinations, that the author entered upon such unpleasant topics; but the taxes imposed during these transactions were so intimately connected with the facts themselves, that it would have been impossible to describe the origin and progress of the one, without referring to the other. (Table X. Part I.)

COMMONWEALTH.

The Long Parliament could not keep a numerous army with the ordinary resources; they therefore resorted to all sorts of contributions: but the national opinion was in their favour—the cause they defended was that of the people. Large sums were raised by voluntary contributions. The plate of almost every inhabitant of London was brought in to be coined;—

[a] Moreau, "Chronological Tables." [b] Hume, Vol. VI. p. 472.

no article, however mean, no ornament, however valuable, was spared;—the very thimbles and bodkins of the women were not withheld;—every one was anxious to maintain the cause of the "Godly" against the King and the "Malignants."[a] Never was the cause of liberty better seconded; every person retrenched a meal a week towards its defence[b]: this whimsical tax existed during six years, in which time it produced 608,400*l.*

A new and more comprehensive financial system began now to be acted upon. In lieu of subsidies, a most productive land-tax was levied; which was for the first time regularly established. Pym formed a new plan for the excise[c]: thus this branch was systematically introduced, but with the express condition that "at the end of the war it should cease." In the mean time, not only wine, liquors, &c., but even salt, meat, and bread, were subject to excise[d]. The customs also considerably increased, and became very productive, in spite of the civil war[e]. A tax of four shillings a chaldron was laid on coals. In short, these two branches of revenue—the Customs and the Excise,—became so important, that, in 1657, Cromwell refused to let them on lease at 1,100,000*l.* per annum[f].

The Long Parliament also established the post office, which yielded 10,000*l.* annually, besides saving considerable expense. The republicans exacted with rigour the dues payable by the holders of Charles's feudal possessions[g]. The crown lands of the principality of Wales were cheaply sold at the rate of ten years' purchase; and the numerous palaces, with their furniture

[a] Hume, Vol. VI. p. 532. [b] Stevens, p. 290.
[c] Walker's Hist. Vol. VIII. Part II. p. 193.
[d] Black. Vol. I. p. 318. [e] Walker's Hist. Part II. p. 193.
[f] Ibid. p. 260. Black. Vol. I. p. 318. [g] Ibid.

and effects, were disposed of at low prices. The church was also compelled to contribute: not only the lands of the bishops, but even the glebe lands, were disposed of at ten and twelve years' purchase [a]; and the tithes sequestrated for the public service [b]. They likewise had recourse to compulsory loans, which were extorted from "hearty malignants:" [c] and if we may believe Walker, "On the colour of Malignancy," about one-half of their personal as well as their landed property was sequestrated. Thus the republicans forced the enemies of the new system to contribute towards its support [d]. But when military despotism was established, these oppressive exactions increased: soldiers were quartered in the houses, the kingdom being divided into twelve military districts; and a tax, under the name of "decimation," was imposed and cruelly exacted [e].

The permanent income of England, during the Protectorate, was 1,517,274*l.* 17*s.* 6*d.*;—that of Scotland, 143,652*l.*;—that of Ireland, 207,790*l.*; making a total of 1,868,719*l.*: and the sums raised during the republican period, from all legal sources of revenue, and all exactions and extortions, amounted altogether to 83,331,198*l.*—or about 4,300,000*l.* a year. Nothing can convey a better idea of these infamous exactions, extortions, confiscations, and robberies, than Table VII. at the end of this Part.

But how was this immense sum expended? The very men who so heroically opposed the tyrant, and defended the rights of the nation—when they in turn became sovereigns, entirely forgot their oaths, and openly betrayed their constituents. They voted 4*l.*

[a] Walker's Hist. Part II. p. 260.

[b] Hume, Vol. VII. p. 99.

[c] Walker.

[d] Ibid.

[e] Ibid. Vol. IV. p. 27.

a week to each member of parliament, and distributed 300,000*l.* among themselves; the *Godly* gave 679,800*l.* to the *Saints*: public frauds were openly permitted; and parliament bestowed 1000*l.* a week on itself, while the soldiers were destitute and starving, their arrears amounting to 331,000*l.*[a] Is it to be wondered at, then, that Cromwell, with a few soldiers, ignominiously expelled from the House those traitorous miscreants, who betrayed the cause they pretended to defend. "For shame, get you gone," said Cromwell, "give place to honest men, the Lord has done with you."

But if, during the Republic, we find extortions to execrate and abuses to condemn, we are equally compelled to acknowledge that the taxes were better and more efficiently applied to their sacred object—the true national interest,—than under monarchical government. For under Cromwell, (the great man of his age—that wonderful man—the only military despot who has ever been useful to his country,) impartial justice was strictly administered [b]—a new financial system was introduced—the navigation laws were enacted—learning was protected—the foundation of commerce and industry laid—and England elevated to the highest influence and glory. The Dutch were compelled to surrender their republican and naval superiority to the British Commonwealth[c]. Proud Spain was punished—France humi-

[a] Walker, Vol. IV. Part II. p. 109.

[b] "Dissimulation", as Lord Nugent very justly says, "was the weapon used by many bad men, with whom Cromwell had to deal; and Cromwell took it up and vanquished them." (Memorials of Hampden.) Lingard says, "his two objects were civil and religious freedom."

[c] One of the articles of the peace of 1654 was, "that the ships of the Dutch, as well ships of war as others, should lower their

liated—Portugal frightened. The important possessions of Dunkirk and Jamaica were added to the new republic—Ireland was reduced, and Scotland subdued. A strong army at home, and numerous and invincible fleets abroad, caused the British name to be respected by all nations, in a manner unknown before, or perhaps since [a]. (Table VII. Part I.) But the nation, oppressed and tired of military despotism, and without that strong hand that kept the most discordant elements together, was ripe for a change: it only required an impulse, which was not long wanting. Monk, (a traitor to the party which had raised him to his eminent military rank, after granting him the life he had forfeited [b],)

flag, and strike their topsail, on meeting any of the ships of the English Commonwealth at sea."

[a] See Dryden's "Heroic Stanzas on the death of Oliver Cromwell."

[b] Cromwell died 3d Sept. 1658; Charles landed 25th May, 1660. —"George Monk", says Aubrey, "was a strong, lusty, well-set fellow, and in his youth happened to slay a man, which was the occasion of his flying into the Low Countries, where he turned to be a soldier." Such was the commencement of the first Duke of Albemarle! He was born in 1608, at Petheridge, in Devonshire, served in the army under Charles against the Scotch, and for his bold conduct, and service rendered to that king at the time of the Revolution, was made a lieutenant-colonel. But at the battle of Nantwich, in 1644, where the king's army under Byron, was defeated by that of the Commons under Fairfax, Monk was made prisoner and sent to the Tower, where he composed his "Observations on Military and Political Affairs." He there became acquainted with Clarges, the daughter of a blacksmith in the Strand, who was his laundress, and whom he married after having kept her as his mistress, and whose husband, Radford, (as was known at the time,) was still living when Monk gave her his hand. The above quoted Author asserts, "that her mother was one of the fine women's barbers, and that her father's was the corner shop, the first turning on the right as you come out of the Strand into Drury-lane." However, many entertained an opinion, that to his high

found ample time, during nearly two years that elapsed since the Protector's death, to carry on his treasonable manoeuvres. The fugitive Charles was recalled, and landed at Dover, hardly believing the evidence of his own senses, that his once hated family was restored to the throne.

CHARLES II.

New financial arrangements took place on the accession of this king. The rights of parliament were much better understood and defined. But the enthusiasm of the moment, produced by the change, caused a general

and respectable connexion, Monk was indebted for all his fortunes. By accepting a command against the Irish, who were considered in a state of rebellion, he was liberated from prison; and after fighting against the Irish, went to do the same thing against the Scotch. Cromwell, who was particularly partial to him, not only gave him a command in the war for the conquest of Scotland, but when he was compelled to return to England to stop the progress of the king's arms, left Monk in that country at the head of the republican army. He took Stirling and Dundee, entered Aberdeen, and remained in Scotland, ruling it with the heavy hand of a tyrant, until the death of Cromwell in 1658; after which he came to England, leading his principal force to oppose Richard, the son of his patron. It has been affirmed that he intrigued with the French ambassador to usurp the Protectorate; but his wife, Clarges, and her brother, powerfully contributed to incline him to restore the king. Monk was too reserved and prudent to disclose his intentions so early to such people, but he soon openly declared himself for Charles, whom he went to receive at Dover on the 25th of May, and by whom he was honoured with the order of the garter, and soon afterwards created Duke of Albemarle. In 1665, he was appointed naval commander, and in conjunction with Prince Rupert, completely defeated the fleets of the Dutch admirals, Ruyter the Younger, and Van Tromp, in the Downs, 24th July, 1666. In this sanguinary battle, which lasted two days, twenty Dutch vessels were burned and sunk, and 4000 men killed and wounded. Such was the career of Monk, who ended it in 1670, at the age of sixty-two.

display of loyalty, and the economy of the parliament degenerated into prodigality. It granted to Charles 1,200,000*l.* as the fixed revenue of his crown: the total "miscellaneous" amounted to 4,168,926*l.*, and the total supplies[a] voted to the king during his reign, amounted to 13,414,858*l.*—a sum hitherto unparalleled. The different sources of these grants are shown in Table VIII. Part I. Commerce increased,—as the imports and exports amounted to six millions, according to Munn and the inspector Davenant. The customs, consequently, became one of the most productive branches of the revenue, yielding 400,000*l.* a year: the excise was calculated at 300,000*l.*[b]: the stamp duty was for the first time introduced[c]: the taxes on personal property produced 69,786*l.* 10*s.* a month[d]. Such were the ordinary resources; but Charles had extraordinary ones. Clarendon sold Dunkirk in the king's name, which brought 400,000*l.* to the Exchequer; but he was afterwards impeached on that account. The plunder in the first Dutch war produced 340,000*l.*[e]; and Charles received 30,000*l.*, in consideration of signing the second peace. 100,000*l.* were raised by illegal and arbitrary extortion; and 1,200,000*l.*, by the most infamous breach of faith towards his creditors, when the Treasurer Clifford shut the Exchequer, and instead of paying the principal sums which had been advanced on its security, issued only the legal interests of six per cent.[f] The King of Portugal, dismembering his dominions, gave Charles Tangiers and Bombay, (the con-

[a] Commons' Journal, Vol. VIII. p. 498.

[b] 12 Car. II. cap. 4.

[c] 22 Car. II. cap. 3.

[d] 15 Car. II. cap. 9. An assessment of 70,000*l.* a month was imposed in 1660.

[e] D'Estrades.

[f] Com. Jour. Vol. X. p. 109.

quest of the brave discoverers,) and bestowed half a million of money with the pretty Catherine; of which Hume thinks only 250,000*l.* were paid. The King of France, Louis XIV., considered him both his tool and pensioner, and regularly paid him an annual pension, which amounted to 950,000*l.*; while Charles was betraying Holland, Austria, and Spain. All the sums received by Charles during his reign, amounted, in the opinion of some writers [a], to 53,824,492*l.*; while according to the more moderate estimate of others, they only formed a total of 43,983,390*l.* [b] (Table VIII. Part I.)

Let us see how this immense treasure was expended by the king. His debts, contracted previous to the restoration, were paid by parliament [c]; and he was the first sovereign in England who kept a standing army in time of peace, which cost 212,000*l.* per annum; while the navy absorbed 300,000*l.*, and the ordnance 40,000*l.* (in 1675). But the profusion of Charles—the rapacity of his favourites—the extravagance of his numerous mistresses—and the expenses of his harems, disgraced even royalty, and dissipated the greatest part of these sums. No less than five of his bastards were created dukes, namely, Richmond, St. Albans, Grafton, Cleveland, and Monmouth. Such profligate expenditure brought the king to such extreme poverty, that it was publicly advertised, "that whoever discovered a mode of supplying his necessities, should be rewarded with the office of Treasurer."

The amount of gold and silver coined during this reign was very considerable,—being nearly eight millions (7,899,435*l.* 15*s.* 1½*d.*). (Table IX. Part I.)

The feudal rights and exactions of "wardship mar-

[a] Carte, Vol. VI. [b] See "A Letter to Carte."
[c] 12 Car. II. cap. 21 et 29.

riage" were abolished, and two very remarkable financial measures took place; by one of which, the clergy were placed on the same footing with the laity, both in regard to taxation, and the right of choosing representatives in parliament; the other, no less important, provided, "that for the future, the grants of parliament must specify the purpose to which each sum voted is to be applied." (Table X. Part I.)

JAMES II.

A bigot, fanatically attached to the absurd doctrine of the prerogative, succeeded his brother Charles. His plan was to get money "by all means," in order to destroy both the established religion, and the English liberties. The crown had such power, and the parliament was so prodigal, that two millions per annum were granted to James for life [a]; the greatest revenue ever before enjoyed by any English monarch. Only one temporary grant of 400,000*l.* was made, to suppress the rebellion of his nephew Monmouth, ***whom he ordered to be beheaded.*** In short we find no branch of James's government in which arbitrary principles were not exercised. "Any attempt," says one of his speeches to the parliament, "to secure your frequent meetings by granting moderate supplies, would be resented;"—"I plainly tell you," said the despot, "that such expedients would be very improper to employ with me; and that the best way to engage me to meet you often is to use me well." [b] Was not the ignominious expulsion of such a tyrant both just and natural? (Table X. Part I.)

The revenue of Ireland during this period (of 130

[a] See "An Account laid before Parliament", Com. Jour. Vol. X. p. 37. Hume, Vol. VIII. p. 221. Mortimer, Vol. VIII. p. 658.

[b] "Collection of Kings' Speeches", p. 177.

years) continued insignificant, and always inadequate to the expenditure. At the beginning of this epoch it was reduced to 6000*l.*; and the immense sums which Ireland cost England in Elizabeth's time [a], have been already noticed. It was to make good this insufficiency, that baronets were created in James the First's reign [b]. At the restoration, Ireland participated in the temporary enthusiasm of England. The Irish parliament granted Charles the hereditary revenues, the excise, the tonnage and poundage, and a tax of two shillings on fire-hearths. A voluntary contribution was also raised to be paid in three years, by way of subsidy to the king; and another subsidy was granted to be raised on lands and all chattels. The first mention of the excise is made in this reign [c]. James II. was not so fortunate: the Irish parliament granted him 20,000*l.* to be raised on lands; and he imposed a tax upon all chattels equal to the same amount; but not being able to collect it, issued a base and false coin to indemnify himself,—a curious, and indeed unusual mode of compensation. (Table X. Part I.)

RECAPITULATION.

In this period, we have seen—that Elizabeth's ministers began to establish the basis of public faith, by restoring the standard of the coin, and by paying off the debt; and that they devoted part of the financial resources to consolidate the great European revolution produced by the Reformation:—that the Commons

[a] See "Collection of Papers of Thurlow."
[b] Hume; and Leland, Hist. Ireland, Vol. IV. p. 483.
[c] Leland, Vol. II. p. 512.

began to play an important part in financial measures, in consequence of the diminution of the royal demesnes, and the consolidation of the preceding acts relating to church property. The poor laws were also consolidated. The lottery had its origin in James's time; and its first produce was sent to forward the agriculture of the now powerful republic of the United States.

We have seen that the Bill of Rights, in which was the clause "that no gift, benevolence, &c. be exacted without the Commons' consent," was purchased from Charles I. That a regular financial system was created —that the land tax, the customs, the excise, and the post office, were systematically established, and that commerce, industry, and naval superiority were founded, during the republic. The first stamp act was introduced by Charles II.; in whose reign feudal rights were entirely annihilated:—the clergy were placed on the same footing with the laity, in respect both to taxation and representation; and the grants voted by parliament specified the purposes to which each sum should be applied. In fine, James II., having resorted to arbitrary principles to supply the deficiencies of his revenue, was expelled.—Such are the leading features of this period. But an extraordinary financial epoch commenced with William III.

PART I.

PROGRESS OF TAXATION, REVENUE, AND EXPENDITURE.

THIRD PERIOD.

FROM THE BEGINNING OF THE REIGN OF WILLIAM III. TO THE PEACE OF PARIS, 20TH NOV. 1815.

Progress of Taxation and Revenue.—Malt-tax introduced.—Taxes on hawkers and pedlars, marriages, bachelors, &c.—The republican system of taxation followed and improved.—Sound principles of commerce introduced.—When bounties were first granted, and upon what produce.—Amount reached by the Land-Tax in Queen Anne's reign.—Repeal of the duties on the raw materials of manufactures.—Effects of the aristocratical power in parliament on taxation.—Pitt's universal taxation.—Progress and extent of taxation and public revenue in Ireland.—Its amount exceeding eight millions.—The same of Scotland.—Influence of modern discoveries on taxation and expenditure.—Astonishing progress made by the customs, land-tax, post office, stamps, and excise, and highest point reached by these branches.—To what objects their produce was applied.—Total net produce of all taxes from the accession of George III. to the peace of Paris in 1815, amounting to 1,386 millions, chiefly expended in opposing the principles of the second great European revolution, brought on by the miscalculating policy of the sovereigns and aristocracy.—Good and bad financial measures of their ministers during this period.

WILLIAM III. AND MARY.

The two cousins, after defeating Mary's father at the Boyne, ascended the throne. A mere aristocratical revolution was effected; but the constitution, (that grand political compact,) after centuries of the most bloody contest, was consolidated. Population increased, consumption augmented, importation, commerce, and navigation continually advanced in England; and Europe began to change its aspect. The customs and excise each produced above a million a year; and the land tax more than a million and a half. However, deficiencies were on the increase, and William had recourse to all sorts of new taxes. The malt tax, the hackney-coach tax, and the tax on hawkers and pedlars, were first introduced: marriages, births, and bachelors were taxed, —a gentleman paid 6*s*., a duke 12*l*.; yet all this was insufficient. William imported the borrowing system; he borrowed above thirteen millions; thus the total revenue (loans included) of this twelve years' reign was above seventy-two millions. (Table XI. Part I.)

The income of England, the year preceding that in which the king broke his collar bone, reached 3,896,205*l*. (Table XII. Part I.): while at his accession, it was only about two millions. But 30,477,382*l*. were expended in the wars against France and Ireland. (Table XIII. Part I.); the interest of the Debt absorbed 13,691,498*l*.; and the Civil List 8,800,506*l*. (Table XIV. Part I.)

Nevertheless, a new era commenced in this reign; mercantile, industrious, and economical principles began to be developed. A duty was imposed on the exportation of woollen manufactures, which was repealed, because (as the act recites) "the wealth and prosperity of the kingdom depend on the improvement of its woollen manufactures, and the profitable trade carried on by the exportation thereof."[a] Taxes were imposed on the exportation of corn, bread, meal, and biscuit: afterwards, opinion passed to the opposite extreme, and a bounty was granted upon the exportation of these very articles.

Two great economical engines originated in this reign, the Bank—and Paper Credit—that immense power, which can accomplish, as the greatest of British poets beautifully expresses it, the hardest things;—

> "Can pocket states, can fetch and carry kings:
> A single leaf shall waft an army o'er,
> Or ship off senates to some distant shore."

We shall soon see its wonderful effects.

[a] 12 Will. III. cap. 20.

ANNE,

The second daughter of James II., succeeded her sister Mary; and a novel and extraordinary financial system began to be acted upon, which bears the strongest resemblance to that of Pitt, in the enormous sums extracted from the people by taxation, and borrowed on its credit, in the opposite views of the Whigs and Tories, and in the objects to which the produce of those prodigious burdens was applied. It is true, the kings of England at this time could not oppress their *living* subjects, either by cruel extortions, or illegal impositions; but they possessed far greater power,—they could legally enslave, ruin, and oppress posterity. This Anne did. Her administration, by accumulating new taxes upon articles of consumption, increased the excise to nearly two millions a year; and by keeping the land-tax at four shillings in the pound, rendered it as productive as it is at the present day. Thus, the aggregate revenue during the reign of Anne (twelve years) amounted to above sixty-two millions and a half (Table XV. Part I.); making her ordinary annual income 5,691,803*l.* (Table XVI. Part I.) But she burdened future generations with nearly sixty millions more: thus upwards of one hundred and twenty-two millions was the prodigious sum received by this queen. (Table XVII. Part I.)

But how was this immense treasure employed? The Whigs were active, restless, and anxious for war. Under pretext of humbling despotism in Europe, and defending popular rights, they applied large sums to purposes contrary to sound policy, and for objects unconnected with the true British interest. To place on the throne of Spain a wretched despot in preference to a Frenchman, or to uphold the ignorance, superstition, and tyranny of either of the two worthless competitors, did not justify the waste of British blood, and the burdening of posterity with many millions of debt [a]. (Table XV. Part I.) The wars during this reign cost above forty-three millions. (Table XVIII. Part I.)

But if the aristocratical party in parliament was so prodigal of the public money, for purposes quite foreign to British interests; the great political "desideratum," on which the elevation of the British empire depended, "the Union of Scotland"—was accomplished by Queen Anne's administration. However, this unfortunate mother of eighteen children, had not one to inherit her crown.

GEORGE I.

The great-grandson of James I. by Elizabeth, rose, from elector of the small circle of Hanover, to the first European throne. He was perhaps the only monarch not ungrateful to his people; and one of the few, who did not forget their engagements. He respected the British constitution, which was enough for that admirable work to produce its glorious effects. He was a true friend to his people, and his ministers were not less true patriots. No wonder then, that almost uninterrupted peace was preserved, and the taxes, expenses, and national debt reduced. The total sums which passed into the Exchequer during his reign, amounted to 79,832,160*l.* (Table XIX. Part I.); out of which forty-one millions were applied to the payment of the principal and interest of the debt contracted by his predecessors. (Table XX. Part I.) The total annual expense of the nation was only 2,583,000*l.* (Table XXI. Part I.); and

[a] War was declared by England in May, 1702. Peace was signed at Utrecht, 13th April, 1713. (See Chronological Tables.)

the total extraordinary expense of the army, navy, and ordnance, during seventeen years, was no more than 6,048,267*l.* (Table XXII. Part I.) The public revenue, on an average of the four years preceding the king's death, was 6,762,463*l.* (Table XXIII. Part I.)

But in this reign economical principles advanced a step farther. George and his ministers bestowed an open protection on manufactures: they passed an act repealing "all duties on exportation of goods, the produce of British manufacture"[a]; and another, entirely abolishing "the duties on importation of raw material, as all sorts of drugs, &c." Such were the beneficial results of the peaceful policy of this reign.

GEORGE II.,

His violent, rough, and ill-tempered son, preferred perpetual warfare to the happiness of his people. Carteret[b] betrayed his duty to obtain an increase of taxation. The oppression of the people, and the augmentation of the national debt, were the infallible results. We find that the customs did not prosper during this period—from 1729 to 1759—as in the former year their produce was 1,872,342*l.*, and in the latter 1,911,072*l.*, showing an insignificant increase of 38,730*l.* in thirty years: but there were twelve intermediate years, in which they produced only somewhat above a million; while we observe that the excise reached near four millions. (Table XXIV. Part I.) The total public income in the year 1759 amounted to 8,523,540*l.*

[a] Com. Jour.

[b] See "Selection from the Papers of the Earl of Marchmont, in possession of the Right Hon. G. Rose, illustrative of the events from 1685 to 1750." Carteret's party was at last defeated by the Pelhams.

The aggregate revenue of the thirty-three years during which this reign lasted, was 217,217,301*l.* (Table XXV. Part I.); but fifty-nine millions of debt were incurred; consequently the whole receipts amounted to upwards of 276 millions. (Table XXVI. Part I.)

How were these immense sums disposed of?—The civil list and king's expenses absorbed twenty-seven millions. George declared war against Spain on the most frivolous pretext [a]. A trifling sum (about 100,000*l.*) was the bone of contention, yet this war cost forty-six millions [b]. (Table XXVII. Part I.) The object of the second, called "the seven years' war," [c] was, if possible, more ridiculous. For an object so impolitic as the placing a German damsel on the remote throne of Austria, the barbarous Muscovites were, by George's policy, brought to figure in European concerns, and British blood and treasure flowed in torrents; while the discontented at home, secretly encouraged by France, were emboldened to break into open rebellion, and a hundred and eleven millions of money were squandered. (Table XXVIII. Part I.)

But what advantages were derived from sacrifices of such magnitude? The honour of supporting Austria, which a few years afterwards made war against England (See Chronological Tables); and the acquisition of the important colonies of Grenada, Tobago, St. Vincent, and Canada, on payment of three millions to the French proprietors and planters for the rights of the soil [d].

George's administration misunderstood the true in-

[a] Begun 1739, and concluded at Aix-la-Chapelle in 1748.

[b] "Present State of the Nation", 1748.

[c] Commenced in 1755, terminated at Paris, 1763.

[d] Chalmers, "Political Annals of British Colonies", Vol. I. p. 63.

terest of the nation. But the above mentioned misfortunes must not be exclusively attributed to the king; for ever since the accession of William III., the kings of England are not to be considered entirely responsible for the oppressions practised, or the blood and treasure squandered. The power of the ministry had exactly replaced the tyranny and despotism formerly exercised by the kings over the parliament. The legislature, chosen by the combined influence of the aristocracy and the administration, was constantly as subservient to the dictates of the ministry, as it had been to Henry VIII. A striking instance in confirmation of this, occurred in this reign. A most obnoxious tax upon salt, being considered injurious to our fisheries (the foundation of the naval power) was repealed in 1730; but Walpole, the very minister who introduced the repeal, having reduced the land tax to one shilling to please the aristocracy, moved without shame for its revival [a].

George's ministry not only sustained an expensive war on account of the colonies, but devoted sums, amounting in the whole to 1,697,424*l.* to forward their prosperity. (Table XXVI. Part I.) The sum of 152,037*l.* was much better employed in purchasing the feudal rights and obnoxious privileges exercised by the Scotch barons. In fine, the peace establishment being only 2,766,000*l.*, (Table XXIX. Part I.) the expenses of George's reign would have been only eighty-eight millions instead of 276, had not his administrations pursued a policy contrary to the national, as well as to the financial interests of the British empire [b].

[a] Commons' Jour. Sinclair.

[b] See "History of National Taxes"; and "History of Public Revenue", printed in 1759.

GEORGE III.

The greatest financial era, not only of England, but of all the civilized nations of the world, begins in the reign of George III. All the objects which we have till now thought great, appear in miniature when compared with those of the present period. We shall see thousands converted into millions—divisions into armies—squadrons into fleets[a]: we shall see the ablest economists disappointed in their theories—the most sagacious statesmen deceived in their views—the greatest calculators foiled in their demonstrations: finally, we shall see the British nation supporting burdens so enormous, as had not before been even imagined. The rule, however, that has been adopted, of stating facts, and leaving the reader to draw conclusions, will not be departed from. At the same time it is to be regretted, that the "mystification" displayed in the accounts for ministerial purposes, combined with the confusion and complication of those of Ireland and Scotland, renders it impossible to present such a clear and perfect view of this mighty period as could be wished: nevertheless, an attempt will be made to treat the subject in such a manner as to attain a great and useful end, and render it intelligible even to those least initiated in these abstruse matters.

It appeared as if, with George III., interminable war came to ravage and destroy the world. Pitt's father was

[a] All the British troops during the seven years' war, and at the commencement of this reign, amounted to 70,000 men of all descriptions. The military establishment in 1814, exclusive of all foreign troops in English pay, was 721,897 men; or about three times the forces of Augustus, who maintained only about 242,000 men for the empire of the world. (Arbuthnot. Gibbon.)

compelled to tender his resignation[a]. In 1762, war was declared against Spain, on the pretext of "family

[a] William Pitt's father, who was born in London in 1708, changed a military for a political life, and the regiment of the Blues for the representation of Old Sarum (1735). His vehement, powerful, and convincing eloquence, soon raised him to the highest importance, and gave the last blow to the Walpole administration. He was chosen for the first time in 1746 to the office of Vice-Treasurer for Ireland, and in 1746 was appointed to the premiership of the State. But George III. and his ministry brought new principles into the Cabinet, contrary to the views and opinions of Pitt, which compelled him to retire. The State was embarrassed with the Rockingham ministry, and the foolish American stamp act was passed. But the nation wanted a wiser and better pilot to steer the vessel of the State: Pitt was called to direct it, and raised to the Upper House with the title of Lord Chatham. He directly employed all his efforts to settle the differences with America; but his wise measures being opposed and thwarted by his own colleagues, he was again compelled to resign (1768). This great statesman, while he promoted the glory of his country abroad, bestowed the most strenuous exertions at home,—defending the British Constitution from the erroneous conduct of the House of Commons, which endeavoured to establish the most dangerous principle of expulsion, by the repeated rejection of Wilkes, who had been legally returned a member to that house. Chatham opposed also, with the greatest energy and eloquence, the infamous "general warrants", which, without mentioning any person by name, were directed against all who came, or were imagined to come, under the most general description. No wonder that the patriotic Pynsent left him his estates in Somersetshire, imitating the generosity of the Duchess of Marlborough, who, as far back as 1744, had left him a legacy of 10,000*l.*, mentioning it in her will, "as a reward for the noble disinterestedness with which he had maintained the authority of the laws, and prevented the ruin of his country." But it was the great question of America which called forth the dying energies of the great Chatham, and which crowned his glorious life. He made his appearance in 1778 for the last time in the House of Lords, leaning on the arm of his son Pitt, his majestic figure wrapped in flannels, and his face pale as death; and, after delivering his sentiments with the strongest emotion against the most infa-

compact"; and in 1765, the American stamp act gave rise to the most unjust, unnatural, and impolitic bloodshed: and as it was impossible to maintain these measures with the ordinary revenue, the ministers and their friends devoted the utmost ingenuity to discover new taxes, and adopted the deepest contrivances to impose new burdens. But the people were already tired of a war, which, as Pitt truly said when reproaching the ministers, "was a fruitless waste of blood and treasure, without even a reasonable object." But "that apostate, that traitor to the party that made him known to the world"[a]—upbraided and attacked the ministry, only to obtain place, and to increase ten-fold the taxation he had before declaimed against. He came into office by opposing American and continental war; but as soon as he got power, embroiled the country more than ever. The unparalleled wars against France were undertaken; and the expenses increased in proportion to those gigantic contests: all means, therefore, were devised and put in execution to augment taxation, and oppress the people. The inventors of the most destructive and whimsical impositions, were rewarded with greater profusion than the victorious naval officers. "Every thing that could be seen, and every thing that could be touched," locomotion, and *even light* "was *taxed.*"

It would not be difficult to relate the various plans

tuated measures, fell insensible in the arms of the Duke of Cumberland and Lord Temple, and expired—as if he could not support the sight of that unjust and parricidal war, which led to the dismemberment of the British empire.

[a] Such was the language of the member of the opposition (Grey), who attacked Pitt when he deserted. (Life of Pitt.) See also "History of Taxes", by Cunningham, as relating to the taxes till this period.

and contrivances by which Pitt, and his fanatic scholars, augmented all branches of the revenue, during this period; they were as numerous as they were extraordinary. But such a narration, far from conveying a distinct knowledge, would only confuse the reader. The sums are so vast, that simple assertions would appear paradoxical or erroneous, did not authentic documents exhibit to demonstration the increase, progress, and wonderfully high point of elevation reached by the principal branches of the public income. The reader will observe that, in 1798, the produce of the assessed taxes was trebled: that on the 3d of April of the same year, Pitt proposed his plan of redeeming the land tax; and on the 3d of December, 1799, carried the motion of the income tax. It will be seen by inspecting Table XXX., Part I., that the customs, at the accession of George III., produced 1,960,000*l.*; in 1804, above seven millions; three years afterwards, exceeded nine millions and a half; and at the conclusion of the war (1815) reached their highest point, 10,960,775*l.* The land tax, in 1790, produced 3,600,000*l.*; in 1804, yielded 5,300,000*l.*; three years later, 6,900,000*l.*; and at the end of the war reached 7,543,865*l.* The stamps, which in 1760 produced 263,207*l.*, in 1804 rendered 3,170,000*l.*; in the three following years, 4,132,000*l.*; and at the conclusion of the war, 5,601,791*l.* The post office experienced even a greater proportionate increase, the returns being, in 1760, 83,493*l.*; and, in 1815, 1,541,000*l.* Lastly, the excise, which produced 3,837,000*l.* at George's accession, yielded, in 1804, 17,900,000*l.*; three years later, above 23,000,000*l.*; and in the last year of the war, 26,537,633*l.*!!—while the property tax reached nearly 12,000,000*l.* The net public revenue, in the first year of George's reign, amounted to 8,800,000*l.*; in 1793, reached 17,600,000*l.*; in 1808, 61,500,000*l.*; and at the end of the war 76,833,494*l.*! The total aggregate net amount produced by all branches of the revenue, from the accession of George III. to the close of the war in 1815, was 1,386,268,446*l.*!!! (Table XXXI., Part I.)

Such was the prodigious sum raised during this extraordinary period—a sum three times greater than all the stock of gold and silver existing in the world in 1809, the epoch of the greatest known abundance of those metals[a]. Such an enormous amount of treasure was never before imagined: such amazing increase of taxation never before recorded in history.

Had these immense sums been sufficient to meet the expenses incurred by Pitt, and the ministers who ruled the nation during this period, posterity would be merely astonished that there was a people capable of supporting such prodigious burdens, and suffering such enormous exactions. But it was far otherwise: they fell infinitely short of the expenditure. It was not enough for Pitt and his successors to torture and oppress their *own* generation; they wrested from Parliament the dangerous power of drawing bills upon posterity, like a prodigal son drawing upon his father's banker. They contracted debts, and added loans to loans at the lowest interest[b]; adding, (as we shall shew in the proper place,) the unparalleled sum of 531 millions to the immense amount already noticed; the whole constituting a grand total of 1,917,367,587*l.*!! Truly, North, Pitt, and Castlereagh, were wonderful men: George III., that good

[a] Calculated by Jacob at 380 millions, by Humboldt at 325 millions, and by Storch at 220 millions.

[b] See the Tables to the Second Part.

man, but inflexible king, certainly possessed extraordinary ministries.

Let us see for what purposes these vast treasures were expended. However incredible it may appear, the facts prove that such immense sums were chiefly expended for three grand objects—to enforce unjust laws in our colonies—first to keep down, and afterwards to replace on the throne, the Bourbon dynasty—and to support the various branches of the royal family. Immense sums were wasted in the American contest, besides three millions and a half granted to the "Loyalists"; and from the beginning of George's reign to three years after the peace, in virtue of which we finally lost these colonies, "we see," says Sinclair, "98,565,762*l.* exclusively applied to the military service, without a single brilliant military exploit, the defence of Gibraltar excepted."[a] But greater events are approaching.

The grand principle of the first European revolution was ratified at Passau: liberty of conscience and the free exercise of the Protestant religion were solemnly established at Augsburg.—(See Chronological Tables.) But civil and religious liberty (so intimately connected) though publicly recognized, were not yet consolidated. Elizabeth and Cromwell did all in their power towards that great object: but Europe was divided—one portion supporting ignorance and slavery, the other contending for knowledge and freedom. This cruel and unparalleled contest was protracted nearly two centuries: the sword of despotism, and the flames of the Inquisition, raged in all their fury and horrors over the finest countries of Europe, until the first was blunted by the constancy of the champions of freedom, and the last quenched with the blood of the martyrs of religious

[a] Sinclair, Vol. III.

liberty. The Church, although repeatedly defeated, never despaired; but, rallying all its energies, and being seconded by the besotted aristocracy, formed a most powerful alliance with its once inveterate enemy, the throne: thus the church, the throne, and the aristocracy, became united and natural allies in the common cause of upholding oppression, ignorance, and absolutism. Meanwhile the Press (that formidable engine of knowledge—that salutary corrector of abuses—that bulwark of popular rights) continued, in spite of a cruel and uninterrupted persecution, to heap the most terrible ridicule upon the Church; to expose the frivolity of the aristocracy; and to point out the vices of courts, and the excessive abuses of royal power.

At length a revolution in the New World came, to precipitate the explosion of the already tremendously loaded mine. A new, poor, and persecuted people, had the boldness to assert, in the woods of America, the imprescriptible rights of man, against the wealth and power of one of the greatest European nations. The aristocracy, (deluded and charmed by the philosophical doctrines of the time,) and even monarchs themselves, misunderstanding their own interest, gave them their powerful aid [a]. The volunteers, who left Europe to aid

[a] "Such is the strange infatuation of the human mind, that those who governed a monarchy armed it for the support of two republics against a king, and sustained, by the most painful exertions, the cause of a people in a state of insurrection! The whole youth were excited by the higher orders to regard the American patriots as the first of the human race; and our aristocratic youth, the future supports of the monarchy, rushed to the shores of America, to imbibe the principles of equality, hatred to the privileged ranks, and horror at despotism, whether ministerial or sacerdotal. Though still young, and carried away by the spirit of the time, this whirlwind of error did not entirely blind my eyes to the consequences it

in that glorious enterprise, were ashamed, on their return, of the expensive, corrupt, and rotten system of the old governments. Lafayette appeared[a]—and a

must produce. I shall never forget the astonishment with which I heard all the court, at the theatre of Versailles, applaud with enthusiasm Brutus, the celebrated republican play of Voltaire, and especially the two lines,

'Je suis fils de Brutus, et je porte en mon cœur,
La liberté gravée, et les rois en horreur.'

When the higher classes in the monarchy are seized with such fanaticism as to applaud the most extravagant republican maxims, *a revolution cannot be far distant, and should not be unforeseen;* but since that time, the most ardent enemies of liberty, the most zealous defenders of the ancient order of things, have completely forgotten what a large share they themselves had in pushing the people to that rapid descent, where it soon became impossible to arrest their progress." (Segur.) "The general illusion spread even to royal heads. Frederick the Great and Catherine of Russia did not, it is true, openly adopt the counsels of our modern Platos, but they applauded and consulted them. Joseph II., without asking their advice, advanced even more rapidly than they had recommended. He imprudently carried into practice what with them was only matter of speculation." (Idem.)

[a] For their distinguished services in America, the decoration of the order of Cincinnatus was conferred on Lafayette and Segur by the republican government. "This decoration", says Segur, "consisted of an eagle of gold suspended by a blue ribbon edged with white; on the one side Cincinnatus was represented quitting his cottage to assume the office of Dictator, on the other he was to be seen laying aside his buckler and sword and resuming his plough." "Such a decoration, so republican in its import, displayed with pride in the capital of a great monarchy, afforded ample subject for meditation. It was evident how profound was the impression produced by the first sight of that emblem of freedom; but Lafayette and I were too proud of displaying it on our breasts, to attend to any thing but the admiring crowds which it drew around our persons. In their eyes, that decoration appeared as a new order of chivalry; and confounding democratic passion with aristocratic distinctions, they gave it, both in the city and at the court, the name of the 'order of Cincinnatus'. This expression gave rise to a lu-

second grand revolution burst forth, like a furious volcano, in the centre of Europe: her mighty powers were all astounded at the explosion: the mere attempt to reform abuses and limit absolute power, was considered by all monarchs as a political blasphemy: the just proposal to equalize burdens was resented by the aristocracy as the greatest insult; and the Church became frantic at the bare idea of losing her tithes. Never did the great powers of the earth so heartily join in defending their common cause—their vital interest: never were their combined efforts greater. Their resistance, indeed, was immense, but the force which overcame it was superior.

The National Convention, that wonderful government, whose power can only be conceived by the obstacles which it overcame, and whose measures can only be judged of by the astonishing results they have produced—not only cut off the head of the representative of the most ancient dynasty in Europe, (using it to block up the way to all retreat and render retraction impossible,) stopped civil war, and defeated the European armies, but boldly declared war, even against England. It is true that the machinations of the Congress of Pilnitz, dexterously promoted by the secret intrigues of Pitt, and his unfriendly and even insulting acts towards France, accelerated the terrible declaration of that irritable,

dicrous mistake on the part of an officer of high rank, who had served with distinction in the American war, but whose education had not been so sedulously attended to as his manners. 'You are really', said he to me, 'well provided with saints, for you have three—Saint Louis, Saint Lazare, and *Saint* Cincinnatus: but as for the latter saint, may the devil take me if I can discover where our good friends in America have contrived to disinter him.' This officer had himself received this decoration for his gallant conduct in the transatlantic contest."

bold, and resolute assembly; but the grand question at issue was, *the sovereignty of nations—the rights of the people—and their freedom to choose or limit their own form of government.*

Pitt, however, adopting a policy quite opposite to that of the great Elizabeth's minister *in the first European revolution,* grasped with avidity the "declaration of war," as a plea to oppose the second: it was, besides, an excellent opportunity to consolidate himself at the head of the European aristocracy. He pleaded the necessity of defence, in order the better to blind the people, and as he expressed himself, "to crush the hideous Hydra of the revolution in its birth." The taxation of the British nation formed the ponderous stone to crush that phantom. All expedients were employed towards that main object. The first alliance was formed[a] with Austria, Prussia, and the savage Muscovites; and the partition of Poland among those three powers, was consequently overlooked by England. A second coalition was formed, of which British gold was the prime mover. The ferocious Turks, and the barbarous Russians, naturally enemies, were made friends, and compelled to fight by the side of the British. The torpid Austrians were paid, on condition "*that they would not make peace.*"[b] The most savage hordes of the North were hired in this second crusade. The courts of Germany, Naples, Portugal, Spain, and even the Barbary States, were bought, and combined to fight

[a] The first coalition was formed in 1792, when the King of Prussia issued his manifesto and commenced the aggression against France: in February 1795, England entered into the alliance with Russia; and the partition of Poland took place in November of the same year.

[b] See Treaty with Austria.

against a nation which was resolved to abolish a frivolous and oppressive aristocracy, and choose its own form of government. *Two hundred and ninety-seven millions of money*, exclusive of the charges of the peace establishment, were expended in the first revolutionary war; or above three times the amount of the total expenses incurred during the nineteen years of the Commonwealth. Thus British capital and labour were unproductively squandered by this deluded minister, and the most subservient and corrupt of parliaments. Whether the intended object was attained is not so easily determined; but it may be safely asserted that no regard was paid to that salutary maxim of a great orator of antiquity, that national economy is the best source of revenue [a].

But if frugality did not preside in the first war, profusion certainly reigned in the second. If Pitt has met with defenders to excuse him in the first contest, he could not find panegyrists in the second: the aggression was entirely on his side. Pitt, with all his penetration, did not perceive that the Corsican monster, devouring the mother that gave him birth (the revolution), was creating a new aristocracy by the amalgamation of the modern and ancient nobility; was meditating family alliances with the most ultra-aristocratic house in Europe; and even contemplating the recal of the Pope. He rashly declared war in 1803, and after immense expenses incurred during two years, formed (in 1805) the third grand coalition, composed of Russia, Austria, Sweden, and Naples.—(See the Chronological Tables.) Every body is aware what enormous sums were expended to overcome the immense difficulties of bringing

[a] "Optimum est in privatis famulis, et in Reipublicæ vectigalibus, parsimonia." (Cicero, De Repub.)

together such heterogeneous materials: but Buonaparté was at the head of the soldiers of the republic, and in three months the whole of these immense sums were lost, and the coalition itself entirely annihilated [a].

But fortunately for Pitt and his successors, "steam", a new and wonderful power, made its appearance. The discoveries of Hargraves, Arkwright, and Watt, in applying the capabilities of this powerful engine to the operations of manufactures, combined with a more extensive commerce, produced the most surprising results. Here lies the secret,—from this inexhaustible mine flowed the unexpected supplies. But although Fate did not allow Pitt to witness their wonderful effects, his spirit and policy did not die with him, but descended to his successors. Percival and Castlereagh continued and redoubled their efforts and their oppressions. Three successive and even more powerful coalitions were formed: all the principal European powers were brought into action: armies increased to such numbers as had not before been imagined; and the expenses augmented in proportion to these gigantic enterprises. But two of these coalitions, after immense sums expended, were completely defeated: the fifth was concluded in March 1813. By this wonderful and unprecedented combination, all the barbarians of the north were paid, brought out from their remote haunts, and marched into the most civilized part of Europe. England had a million of fighting men in her own pay [b]; and nearly 114 millions of money were expended in this year only (1814), or three millions more than the cost of the

[a] At the battle of Austerlitz in December 1805.

[b] Such is the number according to the official statements.

"seven years' war."[a] The military, naval, and ordnance expenses absorbed the immense sums shown in Table XXXII. Part I. The grand result of all this was, that Napoleon was sent to Elba, and Louis was reinstated on his throne.

But neither the incorrigible Bourbon administration of the latter, nor the restless ambition of the former, were of long duration. Buonaparte again appeared in France, and a new coalition was required: the sixth and last, combining all Europe, again marched towards France, England leading the van[b]. What power could resist such a tremendous shock? Napoleon was crushed, and Louis made his second triumphant entry into Paris, surrounded by Calmucks, Baskiers, Cossacks, and all sorts of savages, mixed with the free Britons. Undoubtedly, the king of England had the glory of replacing the abhorred family on the throne of France, but at a cost of above *one thousand millions sterling!* Did this immense waste of blood and treasure correspond with the true interests of England and France? Or has the civilized world reaped from it any beneficial result? (See Table XXXIII. Part I.)

Having endeavoured to present a sketch of the finan-

[a] This impolitic war of George II. against Austria, Russia, and Sweden, cost 111,271,996*l.*, exclusive of the peace establishment.

[b] But her army and ordnance alone cost, in this year only, six millions more than during all the wars in the reign of Queen Anne.

Total in 1815	Army	£33,795,556
	Ordnance	4,480,729
		£38,276,285
Ditto in Anne's reign		£32,975,331

(See the Tables.)

cial effects of these wars, let us now proceed to notice the third chief branch of expenditure, the support of the splendour of the crown. The expense of the royal family had always been considered enormous. In 1780, Burke brought in a bill "for the better regulation of his majesty's civil establishment"; and Dunning moved, "that it is necessary to declare, 1st. that the influence of the crown has increased, is increasing, and ought to be diminished; 2dly. that it is competent for parliament to examine and correct the abuses and the expenditure of the civil list, as well as every other branch of the public revenue, whenever it shall appear expedient to do so."[a] This resolution was carried by a majority of 113: however, a saving of only 32,000*l.* (which was reduced to 16,000*l.* in the next year) was effected. Such was the grand result of Burke's eloquence on this subject, which created such a great sensation at the time. The fact is, that between 1786 and 1802, above sixteen millions were appropriated to the civil list only; of which more than eight millions were applied to the personal expenses of the royal family[b]; and the whole amount devoted to this branch, from George's accession to the end of this period (1815), exceeded *fifty-eight millions!*[c]

[a] Com. Jour. Vol. X. 1780.

[b] The actual sum paid to the branches of the royal family in the year 1802, was 348,000*l.* (Colq. p. 207.) The above calculation is made at the rate of only 250,000*l.* per annum.

[c] A Parliamentary Paper has been printed, shewing what the Crown has gained or lost during the reigns of George III. and IV. by surrendering the hereditary revenues enjoyed by George II. From 26th Oct. 1760 to 26th June 1830, the total revenues alienated have produced 94,871,427*l.*: whereas the annuity paid to the Crown under the head of Civil List, including the occasional grants of parliament for the discharge of arrears due at nine different periods,

Nations, in a feverish excess of loyalty, have addressed their prayers to the Almighty to increase the number of the royal scions; but unfortunately for the British exchequer, the royal family has been too numerous. The amount paid in the shape of annuities to the several members of the royal family (fifteen in number), from 1760 to 1815, was 12,600,000*l.*; while the whole sum granted for the encouragement of useful discoveries during forty-seven years, was only 77,463*l.* (Colq.) Nearly a million was given to Wellington for his services in six years of war; while in twenty-one years, only 68,300*l.* was advanced to that great institution, the Board of Agriculture, one of the foundations of the power and prosperity of the nation. 1,361,707*l.* was granted for ecclesiastical purposes, and only 4,600*l.* to the institution for the destitute, and to that for the prevention of contagious fevers. Six millions were paid to the Bank, between 1801 and 1812, for mere services and jobbing, (exclusive of the interest on Exchequer bills); while only 141,198*l.* was granted for the encouragement of commerce.

These are a few of the features of our financial policy at home: while abroad, nearly five millions sterling were applied to rebuild the fortifications which the Emperor Joseph had demolished. A line of fortresses was constructed under the superintendence of Wellington, with a view to curb the ambition of France, and secure the peace of Europe, to be again demolished some years afterwards, with the express consent of the British government (1832). Considerable sums were expended, and great pains taken, to unite and place within this

and the whole extra payments, amounted to a grand total of 65,823,428*l.* Deducting this sum from the hereditary revenue, leaves the public a gainer of 29,000,000*l.*

line of fortresses, two distinct and separate nations, differing in language, character, habits, interests, and religion. But while British policy was thus trying to unite the most discordant elements, to construct (as it were) a triangle with four angles, her agents were persecuting and thwarting that strong, numerous, and enlightened party, whose object was to unite, under one sceptre, the whole Spanish peninsula, the natural ally of England, the natural enemy of France, and the true grand barrier to French ambition: but, "sic parvâ sapientiâ regitur mundus."[a]

[a] Whoever has read the "Strategie" of the Archduke Charles, and the "Guerres de la Revolution" of Jomini, will be convinced of the importance of this line of fortresses, and of their absolute necessity as a basis of operations either for defence or aggression. But for Great Britain to amalgamate such opposite nations in order to oppose a barrier to French irruption, while at the same time she discouraged the attempt to raise, for the same end, a much stronger barrier, by the union (so easy to be effected) of two nations of the same character, habits, interests, language, and religion, was to throw away the second opportunity that has occurred of consulting her true interest, and is a proof that the same extraordinary absurdities are committed age after age by the most enlightened nations. The Spanish peninsula, divided in itself, intersected by a frontier of 300 miles towards Portugal, offering two other long lines of frontier on the sides of Galicia and Andalusia, and ruled by different sovereigns, actuated by contrary policy,—is useless to itself, powerless as opposed to France, and utterly null in the great European system of a balance of power. Every motive for national enmity between two people is to be discovered in France and the Spanish peninsula: proximity of frontiers, non-intercourse of commerce, in consequence of similarity of productions, the frivolity of one people, and the serious character of the other, the undying spirit of irruption in France, from Charlemagne to the conqueror of Trocadero, and her ever-working policy, to render the peninsula powerless, and reduce it to a barren Africa. On the contrary, all the essential materials to form a true and natural alliance, are to be found in England and the Peninsula: distance of frontier, necessity for commerce, resulting from the mutual wants of the nations,

Thus the reader may form an adequate idea upon what objects the wisdom of parliament and the policy of Pitt (continued by Castlereagh), expended nearly two thousand millions of money. But in taking a financial view of the subject, it is impossible to refrain from asking—what has England gained by opposing the European revolution with such immense sacrifice of blood and treasure? Would not a policy opposite to that of Pitt, have been more beneficial to the British empire? The offer understood to have been made by the French government, to exchange their East India establishments for a part of our West India islands, would have placed England in a situation to extend her power in that part of the world at a very trifling expense: whilst the confusion of parties in France—the fanaticism of the clergy—the infatuation

the superabundance of natural productions in the one, and their scarcity or absence in the other, the want of industry and manufactures in the one country, and the superior industry, and imperious necessity of extending the consumption of manufactures in the other; the thinness of population, and the vast uncultivated tracts of land in the Peninsula, and the excess of people, and exhausted state of the soil in England; in fine, the common antipathy of both nations towards France;—all these are more than sufficient grounds for abandoning that limited, short-sighted, and absurd policy of strengthening one part of the Peninsula against the other, and perpetuating its disunion; preferring to exercise an imperfect influence over a fraction of it, when the whole might be effectively influenced, and directed towards the true interest of both countries. Surely the grand European object of curbing Gallic ambition and irruption, might be effected with far more stability by this means, than by aiming at it on the side of Belgium. The battle of Baylem neutralized all the grand victories of Marengo, Austerlitz, and Jena: the surrender of Dupont's army, produced more effects in rousing depressed, humiliated, and conquered Europe, than all the advantages obtained by the coalitions and victories of the continental powers. Not Portugal alone, but the united Peninsula, is the grand basis of British and Spanish power, and the true fulcrum of European liberties against the unceasing ambition of France.

of the nobility—the unsettled state of all the aristocratical powers of the continent—the extra-continental or insular position of England—and the superiority of the British navy,—all combined to give her the most decided advantages; and, had she maintained a strong armed neutrality, would undoubtedly have thrown the commerce of all the world into her hands, without her being excluded from that of almost all the Continent, as was the case in consequence of her interference.

But Pitt and his admirers thought otherwise. They thought, like some modern writers on political economy, that taxation was a practical source of riches to the country [a]—that its imposition was a blessing to manufacturers, agriculturists, and merchants. It is unnecessary to discuss these opinions here: however, (with all deference be it observed,) it is a principle in political economy that capital is better managed and rendered more productive by individuals than by governments, even when the latter employ it in objects useful and beneficial to the community. It has been observed by Vauban, that "l'argent le mieux employé est celui que le roi laisse entre les mains de ses sujets." [b] Had only one half of the amount spent been left in the possession of the industrious and persevering Britons; had the thousand millions sterling [c], which was employed in the payment of so many millions of destructive labourers,

[a] Chambers. Canard. Spence. Colquhoun. Gray. This last author calls public debt "service capital".

[b] "Nul sentiment dans l'homme retienne son intelligence, ni l'éveille autant que l'interêt personel,—il donne de l'esprit aux plus simples." (Say.)

[c] The total money raised in Great Britain by loans and taxes, during the twenty-three years that elapsed between the beginning of 1793, and 1816, was about 1,564,000,000*l.*, of which 1,100,000,000*l.*! were expended in the charges of the war, according to the calculations of Lowe and Hamilton.

remained in the hands of active British producers, the result would have been infinitely superior. The argument that the nation has increased in wealth, proves nothing: how much richer would it be, had a contrary system prevailed? Above two millions were granted in this period for public works, and 141,000*l.* for the encouragement of commerce and navigation. If, in the opinion of this able party, these comparatively small sums produced the most astonishing and beneficial effects, what would have been the result *had five hundred times the amount been appropriated to the same objects?*

But leaving all these questions to British statesmen, and confining ourselves to facts, let us observe, that from the accession of William III. to 1815, above *one thousand one hundred millions* were chiefly expended in depressing the house of Bourbon; while, during the same period, *an equal sum* was appropriated to raise it to the splendour, and strengthen it in the possession of the throne! When one seriously considers, that all this has been done by the most free, the most enlightened, and the most calculating nation of the world—when one reflects on the inconsistency, the ignorance, and the folly of mankind, one is certainly not inclined to be proud of the genius, nor to admire the boasted excellence of the human race.

The public revenue of Ireland, although small at the beginning of this period, constantly and progressively increased: it even exhibited a greater relative increase than that of Great Britain. When Schomberg landed in that country in 1689, its income amounted to the insignificant sum of 8,884*l.*; five years afterwards, it rose to 430,000*l.*; five years later, to 710,000*l.*; and, at the end of the century, it was 766,000*l.* (Table

XXXIV. Part I.)—the amount continued nearly stationary at this, until the accession of George III. (Table XXXV. Part I.) when all its branches received more regularity: its gross annual produce, on an average of the first ten years of his reign, was 892,287*l.*—of the following ten years, 1,335,100*l.*—and at the beginning of the French revolution, it reached 2,161,983*l.*—(Table XXXVI. Part I.)

The great political event, so much praised by one party, and so much blamed by the other, took place in 1802. The union with Ireland was undoubtedly beneficial both to Ireland itself, and to its revenue, as in 1803 it increased to above 4,830,000*l.*—(Table XXXVII. Part I.) Commerce and industry have progressed in that island ever since this epoch. The several branches of the revenue received great improvements and a better organization, its heads being the same as those of England, as customs, land tax, excise, &c. &c. The results were favourable, as in four years after the Union, the revenue increased nearly two millions, when the gross income amounted to above 5,816,000*l.* The public income kept pace with the tranquillity of the country and the increase of its population, and in 1709 added another million to its amount. Agriculture was visibly advancing: the demand for its produce during the war was very considerable. The constant supplies required by the army in Portugal, gave a great impulse to this branch of industry, and had the most salutary effects on the income, which, in 1812, reached 6,698,537*l.* But if agriculture was improving, commerce and manufactures (particularly that of linen) were not less on the advance. The demand for this last article increased considerably in the Spanish peninsula, as well as in the vast dominions of Spanish America.

Exports and imports increased, and consumption augmented in Ireland. The effects were perceived in the customs and excise, and the grand result was, that in 1813, the revenue reached 7,326,000*l.*; and these causes continuing their beneficial influence, the revenue of Ireland, at the end of this period when the French boundaries were fixed, reached the extraordinary amount of 8,335,966*l.*—(Table XXXVII. Part I.) Such was the high point reached by the ordinary revenue of Ireland[a]; but if we include the loans contracted, the whole will amount to 9,217,000*l.* in 1803; to more than 12,800,000*l.* in 1812; and to above 19,700,000*l.* at the end of the war. (Table XXXVIII. Part I.)

The reader is aware, that in the general history and account of the Revenue and Expenditure of Great Britain, the revenue of Scotland, as well as that of Ireland, has been included; but as it may perhaps be gratifying to know what has been its progress, it may be mentioned, that, at the commencement of the present century (1804), the total gross produce of the revenue of Scotland was 2,734,429*l.*; in 1807 was above 3,800,000*l.*; in 1812, 4,600,000*l.*; and at the end of this period reached the considerable amount of 5,368,487*l.* (Table XXXIX. Part I.)

RECAPITULATION.

But let us conclude this extraordinary period of British taxation, revenue, and expenditure; in which we

[a] The numerous Tables relating to Ireland, formed by Moreau from official documents, are elaborate and complete in all the details of the revenue, commerce, manufactures, &c. of that country; and are earnestly recommended to all who take an interest in those matters.

have seen, that the system of taxation introduced by the Republic, was continued and improved by William III., who was placed on the throne by an aristocratical revolution; that he introduced the malt tax, and the taxes on hackney coaches, hawkers and pedlars, marriages, births and bachelors; that from the imposition of taxes upon bread, corn, &c., he went to the opposite extreme, and granted bounties upon the same articles; that, coming from the first commercial country, he introduced the borrowing system, the Bank, and the funding system, as well as more sound commercial principles, which began to be developed in his reign; that the basis of industry and manufactures began to be much better understood, as the duties on the exportation of woollen manufactures were entirely repealed.

We have seen—that Queen Anne's time bore a great resemblance to that of Pitt, both in the system of borrowing money, and increasing taxation. The excise reached two millions, and the land tax, by assessing it at four shillings, produced as much as it does at present. The objects to which the produce of these exactions was applied, were not the most beneficial to the British interest; but the great "desideratum" the union with Scotland, effected in this reign, was an ample compensation for many disadvantages.

We have seen—that George I., a true father to his people, maintained peace, reduced the expenditure, paid part of the debt contracted by his predecessors, and instead of burdening his people with new taxes, gave open protection to the manufacturer, by abolishing the duties upon the exportation of British goods, and repealing the taxes upon raw materials.

That his successor, preferring war to the happiness of his people, increased the taxes and burdens; notwithstanding which, the customs remained stationary, while the excise reached nearly four millions, and the whole public income was eight millions; that in order to gratify the aristocracy, the land tax was reduced to one shilling, while the duty upon salt, which had been repealed with a view of forwarding our fisheries and navigation, was revived; and that 157 millions were expended in the war of Spain, and in that for supporting Maria Theresa.

Lastly, we have seen—that the greatest financial epoch of the world commenced with George III.; that Pitt came into power, by opposing the ministry, the American and continental wars, and the heavy taxation of the people; but soon forgot his engagements,—doubled and trebled their burdens—renewed the income and property tax—and imposed duties upon *every thing that could be seen or felt*; that the customs, from a million and a half, increased to 11,000,000*l.*, at the end of this period; the land tax, from 3,600,000*l.* to 7,500,000*l.*; and the excise from 3,800,000*l.* to 26,500,000*l.*; that the useful discoveries in directing steam to manufacturing operations, had the greatest influence on commerce and manufactures—increasing the extent of the one, and the productions of the other; whereby consumption was augmented, and the revenue progressively and uninterruptedly increased from 8,800,000*l.* to nearly 77,000,000*l.*!—while its total net aggregate amount, from the accession of George III. to the end of this period, exceeded the prodigious sum (never before imagined) of 1,386 millions! to which were added, 531 millions of debt!—lastly, that this stupendous sum was chiefly expended—in enforcing unjust laws in the American colonies; in upholding the dethroned house of Bourbon; in fostering the aristocracy; and in opposing the principles of the second great European revolution.

Let us now proceed to a more happy period—a period of peace.

[illegible]

[illegible] OF TAXATION, [illegible]

[illegible]

[illegible] PRESENT TIME.

[illegible] —Their influence on the reve- [illegible] several obnoxious [illegible] property taxes [illegible] revenue of Great [illegible] assessed taxes [illegible] Russia and Hol- [illegible] —Their [illegible] sums were ap- [illegible] taxation, [illegible] building pa- [illegible] Windsor Castle.— [illegible] means adopted [illegible] ministry.— [illegible] revenue and [illegible]

THE war ceased its horrors; and that "[illegible]-minded" man, born to enslave and degrade the human race, was chained to the rock of St. Helena. A new era arose in economical policy, and a new financial system became necessary. The peace establishment of 1792 was discussed and adopted, "subject, however, to those qualifications rendered necessary by the new state of things."

The amount (27 millions) of the supplies for this year (1816) was certainly considerable, although wonderfully reduced when compared with that of preceding ones; an arrangement was entered into between the Government and the Bank of England, by which the latter aided in raising the necessary sum [a].

Reduction being now the order of the day, the na-

[a] See "State of the Nation", p. 17; and Com. Jour.

tional burdens were diminished: 18 millions of taxes were repealed within the year; while above 39 millions were struck off the expenses of the army and navy, by the discharge, since 1814, of 300,000 soldiers and sailors; 99,000 men being considered amply sufficient for the peace establishment [a]. Thus, notwithstanding the terrible effects of the sudden and violent transition from one extreme to another, the British nation began to breathe, and to enjoy the beneficial effects of peace.

It is satisfactory to observe, that the principle of a diminution of taxes being, in this year, once established, the government have uniformly adhered to it; and that, although slowly, the reductions have progressed. But the contraction of general commerce and trade, and the deficiency of the harvest by one-third, caused them to adopt two excellent measures in the following year (1817), viz.:—the appropriation of a million and a half for the employment of the poor, and the abolition of sinecures amounting to 100,000*l.* [b] The funding operations effected in 1818, although closely connected with revenue and taxation, are described in a separate Part.

Upon the opening of parliament in 1819, the Prince Regent, in his speech, congratulated the country upon the novel circumstances of "the withdrawal of the army from France, the great reduction of the naval and military establishments, and the progressive improvement of the revenue, and of all resources." For once

[a] Of these, 25,000 men (or more than one fourth of the whole number) were required to keep the peace in Ireland. They were distributed throughout the country, in no less than 400 barracks. Unfortunately, almost as large a force is necessary in the present time.

[b] Com. Journ.; and Report of Financial Committee.

the King's speech spoke truth: the revenue for this year amounted to 54 millions, being an excess of two millions and a half over that of 1818, which was estimated by the Finance Committee at 51½ millions, and the expenditure at 50 millions—thus leaving a surplus of one million and a half; while in 1819 the surplus was three millions. Ten millions, however, being due the same year, five millions to the Bank, and five millions for the payment of Exchequer Bills, the Committee passed the important resolution, "that the finances of the country would not be established upon a basis solid and permanent, until the income of the year should exceed the expenditure by at least five millions."[a] The ministry, acting upon this resolution, imposed three millions of new taxes, the selection of which was formed upon the most approved principles of political economy. Twelve millions were taken from the sinking fund,—a deposit hitherto considered sacred,—and applied to the loans and the Exchequer bills. The great measure of establishing the ancient security against an excess of paper money by a return to payment in gold, (the discussion of which is reserved for another place,) was effected in this year.

The national revenue increased, notwithstanding the abolition of the war taxes. Its principal heads, the customs and excise, were very productive: in 1820, the former reached 14,700,000*l.*, and the latter nearly 28,000,000*l.* (Table XLI. Part I.) The settlement of the civil list, upon the plan of 1816, was effected this year; and no less than twelve millions were taken from the sinking fund, by that very party who had so much vaunted its extraordinary efficacy, and so earnestly insisted upon its inviolability[b]. But in 1821, the finan-

[a] See the Report. [b] Com. Jour.

cial prospects of the kingdom bore a more favourable aspect. The excise reached the enormous sum of 31,200,000*l.*; the stamps above 7,000,000*l.*; and the land tax 8,182,000*l.*, as appears by Table XLI. The King had promised in his speech to direct the efforts of his ministers to farther reductions: they redeemed that pledge; and consequently, a reduction of nearly two millions was made in the supplies, compared with their amount in the preceding year[a]. The lottery was abolished about this time.

It would be tedious to pass in minute review the financial measures connected with taxation, and the progress of the public revenue in the succeeding years: to relate how the property tax ceased—how that most obnoxious and abhorred tax upon income was repealed, and how a new source of revenue was added to the others by the "Corn Act" passed in 1828, which furnished a considerable item of increase to the income. It will be sufficient to state, that while all the branches of income have been on the increase, the exertions both of the opposition and of the government have been constantly directed to the reduction of the expenditure.—Thus, in 1829, the ministers congratulated the House on the increasing prosperity of the country as evinced in the improvement of the "excise and customs"—the two chief branches of revenue; in consequence of which, its produce had exceeded the estimate by upwards of two millions; while the expenditure was no less than 767,000*l.* under it.—(See the Chancellor of the Exchequer's Budget of this year.) In 1830, the Chancellor of the Exchequer announced a reduction of 1,300,000*l.*, and signified his intention of totally remit-

[a] See "State of the Nation."

ting the excise duties on beer, cider, and leather—a relief which he calculated would amount to nearly five millions.

The civil list of William IV. was soon brought forward by the ministers; but it was not so easily settled as that of his predecessor, George IV. The mighty aristocratical party, which for more than a century had almost uninterruptedly ruled the destinies of the nation, was too confident of its power to carry this measure. Wellington being at its head, it thought itself irresistible, and unconquerable; but the enemies of this chief were not idle. The motion for a select committee was carried by a majority of twenty-nine; and the proud conqueror of the French was worsted and completely defeated, by so small a number of Englishmen. Thus a motion, having for its object the saving of a few thousand pounds, occasioned, in England, perhaps the greatest of her revolutions—the introduction of the Reform Bill.

But a far more violent struggle was going on in France:—almost at the same time, blood was running in torrents in Paris, to bring about another democratic revolution.

The grand European revolution had almost failed in the objects for which it was intended. Napoleon, its traitorous and ungrateful offspring, usurping all its advantages, becoming possessed of all the immense means which that wonderful phenomenon had produced, and placing himself at the head of the invincible arms of the republic, turned all those immense means against the revolution itself. He brought together the men of the old and the new order of things (so opposite to each other), filled the Tuileries with the ancient and the modern aristocracy, converted France into a barrack of soldiers, a bagnio of slaves, a country of spies, and all Europe into a bloody field of battle—into a region of plunder, slaughter, and devastation. The name of *liberty* became a bye-word, and an object of ridicule; the rights of men were scoffed at, and trampled upon; and the idea of a limited monarchy was punished with death, by this most insolent, but most powerful, of all military tyrants. Sovereigns and their subjects, were equally confounded in the desolating ruin—in the universal military oppression. Nations were already tired out; and eagerly expected the first favourable opportunity to throw off the yoke. It came at last:—monarchs uttered the sacred name of "liberty", and held forth the consoling, the intoxicating idea, of "constitutional monarchy": nations rose *en masse*, and the greatest of tyrants was suddenly crushed. It was not the frosts of Moscow, nor the gold of England, which precipitated the fall of Napoleon; but the long-provoked desertion of the people—the unanimous and mighty will of nations.

But scarcely was the victory obtained, when the monarchs (yet celebrating with their people the jointly-acquired triumph,) forfeited their specious promises of "constitutions", and "limited charters."[a] A hypocrital woman, Krudner, suggested the idea of the "Holy Alliance" (in 1815); and the very sovereigns, who had just been liberated by the blood and exertions of their subjects, and who gave the most solemn pledges to repay the obligation, united in a "Holy Alliance"; whose ostensible object was, "to govern them in justice

[a] See the proclamations of the King of Prussia, and the Princes of Germany.

and equity, taking the divine precepts of the Christian religion as the rule of their conduct"[a]; but its real object was, to keep them in greater slavery and subjection, and, far from conceding the often promised "liberal institutions", to destroy those which they had granted.

At length, forbearance was exhausted. "The Charter", was the cry of the people of Paris, when attacking the hired Swiss at the king's palace: the "Charter", was the tremendous cry, when they flocked to the barricades. All Europe was convulsed; and all nations, from the Pillars of Hercules to Warsaw, commenced the reclamation of their just rights. The "sovereignty of the people" a second time reared its head in Europe: the empty shadows "legitimacy" and the "Holy Alliance" were compelled to give way; and monarchs themselves were the original and the principal cause of this new democratic revolution,—this "third great European revolution."[b]

[a] See the letter of George IV. in answer to the invitation of the Allies to become a member, declining the honour, as being incompatible with the liberty of the people.

[b] Although the revolution of Paris excited a general insurrectionary movement throughout all Europe, still it would not have been worthy to be numbered among the great European revolutions undertaken for the happiness and true liberty of mankind, had it not been coupled and contemporary with, the great measure of British reform. For it is absurd to expect that rational liberty and freedom, can be established among a people who, by their topographical and political situation, are compelled to be a nation of soldiers, and whose character is so volatile, that their attention is far more absorbed by theatrical exhibitions and idle pageants, than by the endeavour to obtain for themselves sound, peaceful, and well regulated constitutional liberties. This is abundantly proved by the events subsequent to the revolution, and by the facts exposed in

The people, proud of their conquest, and in the full exercise of their sovereignty, chose a "Citizen King", and placed him on a "popular throne, surrounded by republican institutions"; these were his own words when he accepted their conditions, and swore to the new constitutional compact. If he destroy the conditions of the contract, all his rights are at an end—they have no other foundation. But the king of the French has acted in open contradiction to those stipulations: he is perhaps convinced, that civil and well-understood liberty never has been, nor ever will be, established, in a vast barrack of soldiers like France: he has paralysed the revolution, but its movement is

the "Histoire des choses et des hommes de Juillet", by Sarrans; in "England and France, or a Cure for Ministerial Gallomania"; and in the "Calendrier de la liberté de la presse, et de l'ordre publique en France, depuis la Revolution de Juillet 1830." The perpetual tumults, the violations of essential rights, and the infringement of the principal articles of the Charter so recently sworn to, and so ostentatiously proclaimed, suggested to these authors and to the judicious editor of the last Quarterly Review, the following striking parallels, which are well worth attention. Charles was expelled for four chief heads of offence:—1. For attempting to control the press. *There have been more state prosecutions of the press, more printing-houses destroyed, more publications arbitrarily suppressed, in two years of Philippe's reign, than in the whole reign of Charles.* 2. Charles was expelled for attempting to remodel, by the authority of one branch of the legislature, the composition and numbers of another. *Philippe—one branch of the legislature,—took upon himself, on his own single authority, to remodel the composition and numbers of another.* 3. Charles was expelled for having "mitraillé" his subjects in the streets of Paris in July 1830. *Philippe "mitraillèd" a greater number of his fellow-citizens in June* 1832. 4. Charles was expelled for having on 27th July, while the revolution was flagrant, proclaimed martial law in the capital. *Philippe, in June* 1832, *after the tumults had been suppressed, proclaimed martial law in the capital, and maintained it till the indignant tribunals declared its illegality.*

not annihilated. The two principles, the "sovereignty of the people"—and "absolute monarchy", are afresh struggling, and contending for victory: the contest is open in France, and secret, though intense, throughout all Europe. If the first gain the ascendancy, will they again trust to the promises of monarchs?

But will this revolution be conducted by the peaceful, determined, united, but a thousand times stronger means, by which the British people directed theirs? "We will pay no more taxes until the bill is passed": no bloodshed—no "barricades."; this simple resolution was the weapon used by the British people—the great engine furnished by the representative system, and by enlightened modern civilization. But they proceeded further: convinced that all revolutions of the world are secured or lost through money, they acted upon this principle, the more effectually to secure their object. "There is no return of gold to the Bank," (says Palmer, the governor, before the Committee,) "there is no return down to this day of any part of this issue," (between the resignation of Earl Grey and his restoration) "and the Bank, during that run, paid out 1,600,000*l.*!!![a] Consequently, had the Reform Bill been delayed, had the powerful aristocratic party gained their point—the most powerful government of the earth would have found itself utterly destitute, the greatest mercantile nation in the world would have been paralysed in its operations, and the most wealthy establishment on record would certainly have failed[b]. These

[a] See evidence of Mr. Palmer before the Committee on the Bank Charter.

[b] On 9th May, 1832, Earl Grey and the Lord Chancellor, on presenting petitions in favour of Reform, took occasion to inform the House, that they, together with their colleagues, had tendered

facts sufficiently explain why all Wellington's exertions to form an anti-reform ministry were ineffectual.

Such was the salutary, the grand practical lesson, given to all nations by the sound sense of the British people,—*to conduct their revolutions peaceably, in order to succeed.* Should the Reform Bill cause one half of the changes which the reformers expect, and the anti-reformers dread—should the financial measures which can be effected in consequence of this event be carried into effect, the greatest results will be felt throughout the mercantile world, and the greatest influence directed towards universal civilization. And if (as we have noticed) English policy, and English means and measures, acted so prominent a part in the *First* and *Second* grand European revolutions, this coincident British reform will undoubtedly most powerfully influence, retard, or consolidate, the *Third.*

their resignations as ministers, in consequence of having been left in a minority on the division on the Reform Bill on May 7th.

On 11th May, a petition was presented from the Common Council of London to the House of Commons, praying the House to withhold the supplies till the Reform Bill was passed into a law. Viscount Ebrington then moved an address to his Majesty, expressing the regret of the House at the retirement of the ministry, and praying him to call to his councils such persons only as would carry into effect the Reform Bill unimpaired in all its essential provisions. After a long debate, the motion was carried on a division of 288 against 208.

On 17th May, the Duke of Wellington, on presenting a petition to the House of Lords against Reform, stated to the House that the negotiation for the purpose of forming a new ministry under his auspices, which had been in agitation for some days, had failed, and that Earl Grey was again in communication with the King. This was confirmed by that nobleman, who added, that his retention of office must depend on the conviction of being able to carry the Reform Bill unimpaired in all its principles. (See the Note on the Savings' Banks in the Third Part.)

The reformers having triumphed, the reforming ministry remained in office, and the Chancellor of the Exchequer immediately presented his budget (Feb. 1831). It must be confessed, that although his financial plan was not the most sound, nor the most conformable to the principles of the science of taxation, still his intentions to relieve the public burdens were most honourable and praiseworthy. He announced the intention to abolish 210 places; and proposed to reduce the duties on tobacco, newspapers and advertisements, and to repeal those on coals, candles, printed cottons, glass, and on a number of miscellaneous small ones, which, while they caused great inconvenience to the people, produced only 2000*l.* to the government. He estimated the amount of the relief to be afforded to the people, at 4,080,000*l.*; but to supply part of the deficiency occasioned by the remission, he proposed an equalization of the duties on wine, an alteration of those on timber, an imposition of a penny per pound on imported cotton, *a tax upon passengers by steam boats*, and a *duty on the transfer of stock or funded property* [a]. From these items, and from the increased consumption occasioned by lowering the proposed duties, he expected to derive the sum of 2,740,000*l.*: thus, he asserted, "the income of the year would exceed the expenditure by 4,500,000*l.*" The proposed tax on funded property was too anti-economical to be persisted in; it was utterly abandoned, as well as the alteration in the timber duties, and the tax on steam-boat passengers. Our financial condition in this year may be compared with what it was at the beginning of this period (1816), by inspecting Table XLI. of this Part: this shows the produce of customs, ex-

[a] Ward, J. Smith, and Goulburn strenuously, and with great propriety, opposed this measure.

cise, stamps, post office, &c. &c.; and gives a complete idea of the progress, alteration, highest point reached, and present state (1832) of the principal heads of revenue. It must be remarked, that although it appears by Table XLI., that the gross amount produced by the excise in 1822, was 31,800,000*l.*, and in 1831, only 22,352,000*l.*, we must not conclude on that account, that consumption has decreased, or that this source of income has made no progress, as the duties remitted on various articles must be taken into consideration. By Tables XLII. and XLIII., the progress, or decrease, and alterations on all the heads, may be examined and compared up to the present year.

The revenue of Ireland has kept pace with that of Great Britain. In 1818, it was under five millions (Table XLIV. Part I.); but in 1822, exceeded that sum by 250,000*l.* Table XLV. shows the past and present state of the customs, excise, post office, &c.

It should be particularly observed, that in this epoch, property was very lightly taxed, and that the most productive branch of the public revenue was that which arose from taxes on articles of consumption. Also, that in six years (from 1822 to 1828), there was a surplus of nearly nineteen millions, while an extraordinary diminution was simultaneously effected in taxation; nay more, if we may place implicit reliance upon the Finance Committee of 1828, "a reduction in the rate of taxation equivalent to a revenue of twenty-seven millions a-year had been effected, when compared with the year 1816."[a] But the most remarkable circumstance is, "that a greater progressive increase was effected on those articles precisely, upon which the duties have been reduced": a most salutary lesson for those theoretical

[a] See the Report.

ministers who are entrusted with the reins of the state, but whose ideas are diametrically opposed to practical facts.

The aggregate produce of all the branches of the revenue, and its progress and present state, are shewn by Table XLI. Part I. The excise, in some years, produced more than all the revenue of France![a] The customs, in the last year, yielded more than the united revenues of Russia and Holland! The stamps, only a million less than all the public income of Prussia! And the land and assessed taxes, a sum equal to the income of Spain!

The general result is, that the grand total of all the revenue of Great Britain and Ireland, during this period of peace, amounted to 933,084,153*l.* (Table XLVI. Part I.) But in what manner, and upon what objects, have such enormous sums been expended? The laudable efforts both of the administration and of the opposition to reduce the estimates of the navy, army, and ordnance, have already been noticed (and with the greatest satisfaction): however, the expenditure of the navy has varied in the following ratio: in 1817, 9,500,000*l.*—in 1823, 4,900,000*l.* (the lowest) and in 1832, 5,689,858*l.*

[a] The public income of France was,

	Francs.		Francs.
In 1819......	808,312,572	In 1826......	976,948,919
1820......	875,352,252	1827......	915,729,742
1821......	882,321,289	1828......	872,746,938
1822......	949,134,984	1829......	1021,714,602
1823......	1092,094,282	1830......	1177,000,000
1824......	951,994,200	1831......	1122,197,435
1825......	946,948,411		

For Russia, see "Storch on Political Economy"; and for Holland, "Bydragen tot dehnishouding van Staat in he het Koningryk der Nederlander", by Count Van Hogendorp. Also "Richesse de Hollande."

(Tables XLIII. and XLVII.)—the total amounting to 99,178,184*l.*: that of the army was, in 1817, 13,000,000*l.* in 1831, 6,900,000*l.* (the lowest), and in 1832, 7,216,293*l.* —the whole amounting to 134,867,875*l.*: the total amount of the ordnance (which shows a proportionate variation) is 25,673,243*l.*:—the aggregate of these three heads of expenditure amounts to 259,719,202*l.* But the efforts of the Opposition to reduce the several items of the miscellaneous, have not been so successful. The praiseworthy and persevering exertions of Brougham, Hume, Graham, &c., to lessen the useless expenses incurred in building, demolishing, and rebuilding palaces, have been of no avail. Equally unavailing was that important motion of Taylor, to inquire into "the misapplication of the public money, and violation of the privileges of the House, in directing the large sum of 250,000*l.*, belonging to the British claimants on the French Government, to be expended in the absurd and useless alteration of Buckingham Palace." The sums expended in repairing and furnishing Windsor Castle, exceed any thing witnessed in modern times: they amount, up to the present day, to 1,092,000*l.*! and after all, this *palace*, as it is called, appears no better than a pigeon-house to any one who has seen the magnificent palaces on the Continent. Unbounded sums also were applied to build numerous churches and chapels, during the reign of one of the least bigoted kings that ever swayed the British sceptre: and this expenditure is still going on profusely, although, according to the 12th Report of the Commissioners, 168 churches and chapels are already completed, 19 are now in progress, and plans have been approved for building 8 more; and the Commissioners have proposed to make further grants, in aid of building 11 churches and chapels more in different places. Up to 24th July 1832, the considerable sum of 1,440,000*l.*! in Exchequer bills, had been issued for these purposes. Thus the total "miscellaneous" amount to 40,467,838*l.*

We now proceed to notice the civil list. In January 1820, the equally vain and handsome George IV. ascended the throne. This King was as loose in his own morals, as he was rigid towards those of his wife; and if this Queen's innocence was not superior to that of Queen Boleyn, the intentions of her husband were certainly not inferior in malignity to those of Henry: but the times were quite different. This domestic quarrel, however, coupled with the most vain and pompous of coronations, occasioned a perilous national conflict, an abridgement of constitutional liberties (the "Six Acts" as they are called being passed for that purpose) and an immense increase of expenditure. The moderate expenses of the coronation of his present Majesty, form a striking contrast to the vast sums squandered on a similar occasion by his proud predecessor: the present sensible and excellent King preferring the good of his people to all foolish pageant and fantastical show. The expenses of the coronation of the King and Queen, only amounted to the inconsiderable sum of 43,159*l.* 11*s.* 6*d.*[a]

	£	*s.*	*d.*
[a] In the several departments of their Majesties' household	22,234	10	3
By the office of arms, for the King's heralds and poursuivants	1,478	3	9
In the office of works, for fitting up the Abbey, &c.	12,085	14	5
In the Mint, for coronation medals	4,326	4	6
The amount expended for fireworks and for keeping open the public theatres on the night of the coronation	3,034	18	7
Total	£43,159	11	6

The civil list, during this period, reached the enormous sum of 16,630,253*l.*; and the amount of the pensions and allowances for the support of the branches of the Royal Family is no less than 6,284,572*l.* (Table XLVIII. Part I.). All the remainder of the immense aggregate noticed above, has been swallowed up by the Debt—that millstone, which, as Hume in his time said, "must be destroyed, or it will destroy the nation."

Table L. exhibits, at one view, the amount of the public revenue in each reign, from William the Conqueror to the present time; and Table LI., shewing the variation in the fineness and weight of gold and silver coins, during the same period, furnishes the means of calculating the amount of that revenue, according to the present value of money.

But to come to a general conclusion—we have seen, that the public revenue of Great Britain and Ireland, from the most humble beginnings of contributions in fish and cattle, gradually rose until it reached a point hardly imaginable: that the first grant in money, amounting to 50,000*l.*, was voted by Parliament for the expedition of Poictiers; while for those which ended at Waterloo, above 700 millions were granted!—we have seen a nation, struggling in all periods against extortions, obtain the right of self-taxation, and control even its representatives in the exercise of that power: we have seen, that the income and real property tax was granted in the time of Henry IV.; and producing at first but a small sum, has reached an enormous amount in our days:—that the system of taxation organized by the republic under the heads of customs, excise, post-office, land tax, &c.:—producing comparatively small sums during the preceding periods, has become, in our days, so productive, that each of these heads has equalled, and even exceeded, the whole public revenue of some great modern empires!!—that all these immense sums, to raise which, the application of modern discoveries to manufactures, the extension of commerce, and the use made of public credit, so largely contributed, were sufficient to provide for the immense expenditure required, for the support of the crown—for the prodigious expenses of the last wars—and for the payment of the interest of the National Debt:—lastly, we have seen, that although all these vast sums are absorbed, this is far from being the *whole* result of an unparalleled expenditure; its most terrible effects—its most oppressive consequences, are still left behind, in the shape of the *National Debt!* —the rise, progress, and present state of which, are examined in the next Part.

TABLES TO PART I.

A CHRONOLOGICAL TABLE of the more IMPORTANT TREATIES between the principal civilized Nations; with notices of the WARS and other Events with which they are connected; from the beginning of the Fourteenth Century to 1833.

1326. War between England and France, on the subject of a fortress in Guienne, which Edward II. claimed as his of right.

1327. Peace between Robert Bruce and Edward III. The independence of Scotland acknowledged.

1336. Edward III. renews his pretensions to the crown of France, and enters into a league with the revolted Flemings.

1356. The German Constitution, known by the name of the *Golden Bull*, sanctioned; and the mode of electing the Emperor determined.

1360. May 8. Peace concluded with France, at Bretigny near Chartres, whereby England retained Gascony and Guienne, acquired Saintonge, Agenois, Perigord, Limosin, Bigorre, Angoumois, and Rovergne, and renounced her pretensions to Maine, Anjou, Touraine, and Normandy; England was also to receive 3,000,000 crowns, and to release King John, who had been long prisoner in London.

1370. War recommenced between France and England.

1381. Peace ratified between Venice and Genoa.

1385. The French united with the Scotch against England, upon which Richard II. invaded Scotland, and burnt Edinburgh.

1390. The Sultan Bajazet ratified a treaty with the Greek Emperor, John Paleologus.

1412. Henry IV. of England leagued with the Duke of Orleans, Regent of France, in order to oppose the Duke of Burgundy.

1415. August. Henry V. of England commences war against France.

1420. May 21. *Treaty of Troyes* between England, France, and Burgundy, whereby it was stipulated that Henry V. should marry Catherine, daughter of Charles VI., be appointed Regent of France, and after the death of Charles should inherit the crown.

1423. Treaty between England and Burgundy.

1435. September 22. *Treaty of Arras* between France and Burgundy. Several towns annexed to the duchy of Burgundy.

1439. The *Pragmatic Sanction* settled in France, regulating the election of bishops, and moderating the power of the pope.

1453. The first alliance entered into between the French and Swiss.

1464. A league, designated "*For the public good,*" formed between the Dukes of Burgundy, Brittany, and Bourbon, and others, against Louis XI. of France.

1465. *Treaty of Conflans*, between Louis XI. and the chiefs of the above league. Normandy ceded to the Duke of Berri.

1468. Louis XI., having placed himself in the power of the Duke of Burgundy, was forced to sign a treaty at Peronne, confirming those of Arras and Conflans, with some other stipulations.

1474. Peace concluded between Edward IV. of England and Louis XI. of France.

1475. The *peace of Pacquigni.*

1475. Charles the Bold, of Burgundy, concluded a treaty with the French king, but speedily afterwards leagued against him with Edward IV. of England, and the Duke of Brittany. Louis XI., on the other hand, entered into a treaty with the Switzers, and succeeded ultimately in becoming an ally of England, which unexpected change determined the Duke of Burgundy to conclude a truce at Vervius for nine years.

1476. Charles of Burgundy commenced war against the Switzers, in which he eventually lost his life.

1482. The *treaty of Arras*, between Maximilian of Austria, the husband of Mary of Burgundy, and Louis XI. of France, whereby Margaret, daughter of the former, was espoused to the dauphin, son of the latter, with Artois and Burgundy as a dowry.

1482. Peace concluded at Edinburgh between England and Scotland.

1494. War commenced by France for the possession of Naples, bequeathed to the king by Charles du Maine, which was opposed by the Pope, the Emperor, the King of Spain, the Venetians, and the Duke of Milan—France being ultimately forced to abandon her claim.

1497. Treaty between England and Scotland, by which Perkin Warbeck was compelled to quit the latter kingdom.

1501. Treaty between Louis XII. of France and Ferdinand of Spain, for the division of the kingdom of Naples; this partition, however, gave rise to a war between those powers, and eventually Naples remained in possession of Spain.

1508. December 10. The *league of Cambray* against the Republic of Venice, comprising the Pope, the Emperor, and the Kings of France and Spain. Venice forced to cede to Spain her possessions in the kingdom of Naples.

1510. *Holy league* against Louis XII. of France.

1514. France obliged to sue for peace, which was obtained from the Pope, by promising to abolish the Pragmatic Sanction; from the King of Spain, by uniting his grandson, the Duke of Ferrara, to Renée, daughter of the King of France; and from England, by Louis XII. espousing Mary, sister of Henry VIII.

1515. On the accession of Francis I., a war was commenced by France for the recovery of the Milanese.

1516. August 16. The *treaty of Noyon.*

1521. *Edict of Worms,* proscribing Luther and his adherents.

1521. First war between France and Charles V.; France endeavouring to reinstate Henry d'Albert in the kingdom of Navarre.

1521. The emperor Charles V. prevailed upon Henry VIII. to declare war against France.

1522. War commenced between France and Scotland, and also between France and England.

1525. A treaty concluded between France and England.

1526. Francis I., to release himself from captivity, signed a treaty with Charles V., surrendering Burgundy, Artois, Flanders, &c., and renouncing all pretensions to Italy.

1527. Second war between France and Charles V. The Pope taken prisoner at Rome.

1527. A treaty of mutual obligation entered into between France and England; and in the same year a fresh treaty, for the purpose of carrying war into Italy to restore the Pope to liberty.

1529. August 5. The *peace of Cambray.*

December. The *league of Smalcald* in Franconia, entered into between the Elector of Brandenburg and other princes of Germany, in defence of Protestantism.

1532. June 23. A new treaty of alliance ratified between the kings of England and France.

1532. August 2. The *treaty of Nuremburg* ratified.

1536. Third war between France and Charles V. for possession of Milan.

1538. June 18. *Treaty of Nice* between Francis I. and Charles V.

1541. Fourth war between Francis I. and Charles V.

1542. Henry VIII. of England attacked Scotland, in order to force an alliance between the young Queen Mary and his son Prince

Edward, which was terminated by a peace the following year. This attempt was as unsuccessfully renewed in 1547, after the accession of Edward VI.

1544. League between England and the Emperor Charles V. against France; shortly after which, peace was concluded with France, and signed at Cressy in Valois.

1548. May 15. The *Interim* granted by the Emperor Charles V. to the Protestants of Germany.

1549. Peace ratified between France and England. Boulogne restored to France.

1551. October 5. *Treaty of Friedwald*, between France and the Protestant princes of Germany.

1552. January 15. *Treaty of Chambord*, confirming the league between France and the Protestant princes of Germany.

August 12. *Treaty of Passau*, ratified between Charles V. and the Protestant princes of Germany. Freedom of religion established.

1554. *Treaty of Naumburg*, between Augustus Elector of Saxony, and the deposed elector John Frederic—the electorate to descend to John Frederic and his heirs, in default of heirs male of Augustus.

1555. *Peace of Religion*, concluded at Augsburg,—a confirmation of the treaty of Passau, establishing the free exercise of the Protestant religion.

1556. England entered into an alliance with Spain against France.

1558. February. The French took Calais, which had been in possession of the English since 1347.

1559. *Peace of Chateau Cambresis*, between France, Spain, and Piedmont. France ceded Savoy, Corsica, and nearly 200 forts in Italy and the Low Countries.

1560. Peace ratified between England, France, and Scotland.

1561. *Treaty of Wilna*, between the Northern Powers.

1562. The French Protestants having had recourse to arms, Elizabeth sent over succours to their assistance.

1563. War between Sweden and Denmark.

1564. April 29. Peace ratified between France and England.

1570. *Peace of St. Germain*.

December 13. *Peace of Stettin*, between Sweden and Denmark.

1571. Spain, Venice, and the Pope, combine against the Turks, who were endeavouring to subdue Cyprus.

1572. Peace concluded between England and France.

1576. The United States of the Netherlands send deputies to the Hague, who declare Philip II. divested of his principality, and appoint William, Prince of Orange, for their governor or stadtholder.

November 8. *Pacification of Ghent*, by which foreign troops were expelled from the Netherlands and the Inquisition abolished.

The *League* begins in France.

1579. January 22. The *union of Utrecht*, formed by Holland, Utrecht, Zealand, Friesland, and Guelderland, by which the republic of Holland was constituted. Overyssel joined in 1580, and Groningen in 1594.

1595. War declared by France against Spain.

May 18. *Peace of Teusin*, between Russia and Sweden, which powers had been at war, with an interval of seven years' truce, from 1572.

1598. May 2. Peace ratified at Vervins between France and Spain; Spain restores her conquests of Calais, Amiens, &c.

1603. A treaty between James I. of England and Henry IV. of France, in order to support the States General against the Spanish branch of the house of Austria.

1604. August 18. Peace between England and Spain ratified.

1609. April 4. The truce of twelve years between the Spaniards and Dutch.

1610. *Treaty of Halle*, between the Protestant princes of the empire.

League of Würzbourg, between the Catholic princes of the empire.

1613. *Peace of Siöröd*, concluding a war of two years between Sweden and Denmark.

1619. Peace between France and Spain; marriage of Louis XIII. with Anne of Austria, infanta of Spain.

September 5. The Elector Palatine, Frederic V., son-in-law of James I., accepted the crown of Bohemia offered to him by the Protestant states. This was the beginning of the Thirty Years' War.

1620. July 3. *Peace of Ulm*, by which Frederic V. lost Bohemia.

1622. Conquest of the Palatinate, by the Emperor Ferdinand II.

1625. *Danish period* of the Thirty Years' War, when Christian IV. became the head of the Protestant party. Treaty between Denmark, England, and Holland.

1626. League of the Swedes, Dutch, and the Protestant princes of Germany, against the Emperor.

1627. War commenced by England against France, in favour of the distressed French Protestants.

1629. War commenced by the King of France against the Emperor, the King of Spain, and the Duke of Savoy, in favour of the claims of the Duke of Nevers to the territory of Mantua.

April 14. Peace ratified with France.

May 22. *Peace of Lubeck*, between the Emperor and King of Denmark.

1630. France joined the Protestant princes of Germany, Gustavus Adolphus of Sweden, and Holland, against the house of Austria, in Germany and Spain.

England also acceded to the above alliance, with a view of procuring the restoration of the Elector Palatine.

June 24. *Swedish period* of the Thirty Years' War, when Gustavus Adolphus made a descent on the Isle of Rügen.

October 13. *Peace of Ratisbon*, between France and the Emperor; terminating the war for the Mantuan succession.

November 27. Peace proclaimed between England and Spain.

1631. January 13. Subsidizing alliance of France with Sweden.

April. *Alliance of Leipsig*, between the Elector of Saxony and the Protestant princes.

Treaty of Chierasco, by which the Duke of Nevers finally takes possession of his Mantuan territories.

1633. March. *Treaty of Heilbron* between Sweden and the Northern Protestant States of Germany, after the death of Gustavus Adolphus.

1635. February 28. Alliance between France and Holland.

May 19. War declared by France against Spain. France entered actively into the Thirty Years' War, forming *the French period.*

May 30. *Peace of Prague* between the Emperor and the Elector of Saxony.

1640. Civil wars in England commenced; the Scotch army take Newcastle.

1641. The Duke of Braganza, having been declared King of Portugal, entered into an alliance with France, in their contest against Spain.

1648. January 30. *Peace of Munster* between Spain and the Dutch. Independence of Holland fully recognized.

1648. October 24. The *peace of Westphalia* signed at Munster and at Osnaburg, between France, the Emperor, and Sweden; Spain continuing the war against France. By this peace the principle of a balance of power in Europe was first recognized: Alsace given to France, and part of Pomerania and some other districts to Sweden; the Elector Palatine restored to the Lower Palatine; the civil and political rights of the German States established; and the independence of the Swiss Confederation recognized by Germany.

1651. October. War commenced between the English Commonwealth and the Dutch.

1654. April 5. Peace ratified between the Dutch and the Commonwealth of England.

1655. November 3. Articles of peace signed between England and France.

1656. February 15. Spain declared war against England.

November 10. *Treaty of Liebau*, which annulled the feudal subjection of the duchy of Prussia to the crown of Sweden.

1657. March 23. Treaty of alliance between England and France against Spain.

May 27. Alliance of Vienna between Poland, Denmark, and the Emperor, against Sweden.

1659. May 21. *Treaty of the Hague* between England, France, and Holland, to maintain the equilibrium of the North.

November 7. Peace concluded between France and Spain, by the *treaty of the Pyrenees*; Spain yielding Roussillon, Artois, and her rights to Alsace; and France ceding her conquests in Catalonia, Italy, &c., and engaging not to assist Portugal.

1660. May 3. The *peace of Oliva* ratified between Sweden, Poland, Prussia, and the Emperor. Esthonia and Livonia given up to Sweden.

September. A proclamation issued at London for the cessation of hostilities with Spain.

May 27. *Peace of Copenhagen* between Sweden and Denmark.

1661. June 23. Treaty of Alliance between England and Portugal.

1663. France entered into a defensive alliance with Holland and Switzerland.

1664. November. The second war commenced between England and Holland.

War between the Turks and the Emperor of Germany; after the Turks had been defeated the *truce of Temeswar* was concluded, on September 7, for twenty years; the Emperor ceding Great Waradein and Neuhäusel.

1666. January 26. France declared war against England; the Danes also entered into a league with the Dutch against England.

October. War declared by England against Denmark.

1667. July 25. *Peace of Breda* concluded between England, France, Holland, and Denmark.

1668. January 28. A treaty of alliance ratified between the States General and England, against France, for the protection of the Spanish Netherlands; Sweden afterwards joining the league, it was known as the *Triple Alliance.*

February 13. *Peace of Lisbon* concluded between Spain and Portugal through the mediation of England. Independence of Portugal acknowledged by Spain.

May 2. *Peace of Aix-la-Chapelle* between France and Spain signed. France yields Franche Comté, but retains her conquests in the Netherlands.

1669. May 7. *Treaty of the Hague* between Holland and Portugal: the Dutch allowed to retain their conquests in India.

1672. Treaty between France and England (12th February), and Sweden (14th April) against Holland.

August 30. An alliance entered into between the Emperor, Spain, and Holland, against France.

1673. June 16. *Peace of Vossem* between the Elector of Brandenburg and France. The former engaging not to assist the Dutch.

France declared war against Spain.

1674. February 19. *Peace of Westminster* between England and Holland.

June. The Empire declared war against France.

1678. January 10. Treaty concluded between England and Holland, by which Holland detached Charles II. from the interests of France.

August 11. *Peace of Nimeguen* concluded between France and Holland. Spain accedes to the peace 17th September, giving up Franche Compté, &c.; the Emperor on the 5th Feb. following; and Sweden on March 29.

1679. June 29. *Peace of St. Germain en Laye* concluded between France, Sweden, and the Elector of Brandenburg.

September 2. *Peace of Fontainebleau* between France and Denmark.

1683. March 31. *Alliance of Warsaw,* between Austria and

Poland, against Turkey, in pursuance of which John Sobieski assisted in raising the siege of Vienna, on Sept. 12.

1684. August 15. Truce of Ratisbon concluded by France with Spain and the empire, terminating the war of the previous year.

1686. *League of Augsburg* entered into by Holland and other European powers, for the purpose of causing the treaties of Munster and Nimeguen to be fulfilled on the part of France.

1688. France commences hostilities against the confederated States, and ravages the Palatinate.

1689. May 7. War declared by England against France.

May 12. The *Grand Alliance* signed at Vienna between England, the Emperor, and the States General; to which Spain and the Duke of Savoy afterwards acceded.

1696. August 29. The Duke of Savoy quitted the coalition, and entered into a treaty with France.

1697. September 20. *Peace of Ryswick,* between France, England, Spain, and Holland; signed by Germany 30th October.

1698. October 11. *First treaty of Partition* signed between France, England, and Holland, for the purpose of regulating the succession of the territories of the King of Spain. Joseph Ferdinand, electoral prince of Bavaria, declared presumptive heir.

1699. January 26. *Peace of Carlowitz,* between Turkey and Germany, Poland, Russia, and Venice.

1700. March 13. *Second treaty of Partition* between France, England, and Holland, declaring the archduke Charles presumptive heir of the Spanish monarchy, Joseph Ferdinand having died in 1699.

October 2. Charles II., last male branch of the house of Austria reigning in Spain, bequeaths the kingdom to Philip of Anjou.

November 1. Charles II. of Spain died, and the claim of Philip of Anjou was recognized by the court of France.

1701. September 7. England and Holland conclude a formal alliance at the Hague, to resist the claim of Philip of Anjou, to which almost all the European states successively accede.

November 16. King James II. dying, his son was proclaimed King of England by France, upon which William III. commanded the return of his ambassadors from France, and ordered the departure of the French ambassador from London.

1702. May 4. War declared against France and Spain, by England, the Empire, and Holland.

1703. The *Methuen Treaty* between England and Portugal, principally for the regulation of commerce.

1706. September 24. *Peace of Alt Ranstadt*, between Charles XII. of Sweden and Augustus of Poland.

1711. July 2. *Peace of Falczi* concluded between Russia and Turkey, the Russians giving up Azoph and all their possessions on the Black Sea to the Turks; in the following year the war was renewed, and terminated by the *peace of Constantinople*, on April 16, 1712.

1713. April 11. *Peace of Utrecht*, signed by the ministers of Great Britain and France, as well as of all the other allies, except the ministers of the empire. The most important stipulations of this treaty were the security of the Protestant succession in England, the disuniting the French and Spanish crowns, the destruction of Dunkirk, the enlargement of the British colonies and plantations in America, and a full satisfaction for the claims of the allies.

April 17. The Emperor Charles VI. published the *Pragmatic Sanction*, whereby, in default of male issue, his daughters should succeed in preference to the sons of his brother Joseph I.

July 13. The *treaty of Utrecht* signed by Spain.

1714. March 6. *Peace of Radstadt* between France and the Emperor.

September 7. *Peace of Baden*, between France and the Emperor. Landau ceded to France.

1715. November 15. The *Barrier Treaty* signed at Antwerp, by the British, the Imperial, and Dutch ministers. Low Countries ceded to the Emperor.

1717. January 4. *Triple Alliance of the Hague* between France, England, and Holland, to oppose the designs of Cardinal Alberoni, the Spanish minister.

1718. July 21. *Peace of Passarowitz* between the Emperor, Venice, and Turkey.

August 2. The treaty of alliance between Great Britain, France, and the Emperor, signed at London. This alliance, on the accession of the states of Holland, obtained the name of the *Quadruple Alliance*, and was for the purpose of guaranteeing the succession of the reigning families in Great Britain and France, and settling the partition of the Spanish monarchy.

November 18. The Duke of Savoy joined the Quadruple Alliance, signing the treaty by his envoys at Whitehall.

1718. December 16. War declared by England against Spain.

December 22. War declared against Spain by France, under the administration of the regent, Duke of Orleans.

1719. November 20. *Peace of Stockholm* between the King of Great Britain and the Queen of Sweden, by which the former acquired the duchies of Bremen and Verden as Elector and Duke of Brunswick.

1720. January 26. The King of Spain accepts and signs the *Quadruple Alliance.*

1721. August 30. *Peace of Nystett,* in Finland, between Sweden and Russia, whereby Livonia and Ingria were ceded to Russia.

1724. March 23. *Treaty of Stockholm* between Russia and Sweden, in favour of the Duke of Holstein Gottorp.

1725. April 30. The *Vienna treaty,* signed between the Emperor of Germany and the King of Spain, by which they confirmed to each other such parts of the Spanish dominions as they were respectively possessed of, and by a private treaty the Emperor engaged to employ a force to procure the restoration of Gibraltar to Spain, and to use means for placing the Pretender on the throne of Great Britain. Spain guaranteed the Pragmatic Sanction.

September 3. The *Hanover treaty,* concluded between the Kings of England, France, and Prussia, as an act of self-defence against the provisions of the Vienna treaty.

1726. War between England and Spain commenced.

August 6. Treaty of alliance between Russia and the Emperor.

1727. May 31. Preliminary articles for a general pacification, signed at Paris by the ministers of Great Britain, the Emperor, the King of France, and the States-General. Ostend Company suspended.

October 21. *Treaty of Nipchoo* (Nerchinsk) between Russia and China, by which the boundaries of the two empires were settled, a Russian resident at Pekin allowed, and 200 merchants allowed to trade to China once in three years. Not ratified until June 14, 1728, in consequence of the death of Catherine.

1728. June 14. A congress commenced its sittings at Soissons.

1729. November 9. The *peace of Seville,* between the courts of Great Britain, France, and Spain; and a defensive alliance entered into: to this treaty the states of Holland afterwards acceded, November 21.

1731. March 16. *The treaty of alliance of Vienna,* between the Emperor, Great Britain, and Holland, by which the Pragmatic

Sanction was guaranteed, and the disputes as to the Spanish Succession terminated; Spain acceded to the treaty on the 22d of July.

1732. October 7. Peace between Sweden and Poland.

1733. October 10. War declared by the King of France against the Emperor, on account of the latter combining with the Russians to drive Stanislaus, father-in-law of the French King, from the throne of Poland, to which he had been elected on the death of Augustus II.

1735. October 3. Preliminaries of peace signed at Vienna, between France and the Emperor. Spain acceded April 15, 1736.

1736. April 23. War commenced between Russia and Turkey.

1737. May 4. War declared against the Turks by the Emperor.

1738. November 18. *The definitive peace of Vienna*, between the Emperor and the King of France, the latter power agreeing to guarantee the Pragmatic Sanction. Lorraine ceded to France.

1739. September 18. *Peace of Belgrade* between the Emperor and the Turks, the Emperor giving up Belgrade and Servia; this was speedily followed by a peace between Russia and Turkey, Russia surrendering Azoph and all her conquests on the Black Sea.

October 23. War declared by England against Spain.

1740. August. A subsidy treaty concluded between Great Britain and Hesse.

October 20. Charles VI., Emperor of Germany died, and was succeeded by his eldest daughter, Maria Theresa, by virtue of the Pragmatic Sanction, which being opposed by the Kings of Spain and Poland, who supported the right of the Elector of Bavaria, founded on the will of Ferdinand I., gave rise to a war, in which most of the powers of Europe were engaged.

1741. Alliance between Great Britain, Russia, and Poland, with the Queen of Hungary, (the Empress Maria Theresa,) for the purpose of supporting the interests of the house of Austria; France, Spain, and Sardinia, uniting about the same time in the interest of the Elector of Bavaria.

1742. June 28. *Peace of Berlin*, between the King of Poland and the Queen of Hungary. Silesia given up to Prussia.

November 18. A treaty for mutual defence and guarantee signed at Whitehall, between Great Britain and Prussia.

1743. June 24. A defensive treaty concluded between Great Britain and Russia for fifteen years.

August 7. *Peace of Abo*, between Russia and Sweden.

1744. March 14. War declared formally by Louis XV. against

Great Britain, France having been previously engaged merely as ally of the Elector of Bavaria.

1744. April 27. War declared between the Queen of Hungary and King of France.

1745. April 23. *Peace of Fuessen*, between the Queen of Hungary and Elector of Bavaria.

December 25. *Peace of Dresden*, between Saxony, Prussia, and the Queen of Hungary, confirming the treaties of Berlin and Breslau.

1748. April 30. Preliminary articles for the *peace of Aix-la-Chapelle* signed by the ministers of Great Britain, France, and Holland, to which the Queen of Hungary, the King of Sardinia, and the Duke of Modena, shortly after acceded, and Spain and Genoa before the end of June; in September and October the definitive treaty was concluded and signed by the respective powers. By this peace the treaties of Westphalia in 1648, of Nimeguen in 1678 and 1679, of Ryswick in 1697; of Utrecht in 1713, of Baden in 1714, and of the Triple Alliance in 1717, of the Quadruple Alliance in 1718, and of Vienna in 1738, were renewed and confirmed.

1750. October 5. Treaty between England and Spain, by which England renounced the *Assiento contract* for the supply of slaves, included in the peace of Utrecht, in 1713.

1755. June 8. Commencement of war by the English, by the attack on two French frigates in America.

1756. January 16. Treaty of alliance between Prussia and England. Hanover put under the safeguard of the King of Prussia.

May 1. Alliance between Austria and France, concluded at Versailles.

June 9. War formally declared by France against England.

August 17. Saxony invaded by Prussia. Beginning of the Seven Years' War.

September 30. War between Austria and Prussia.

1757. July 17. War between Great Britain and Austria.

August 24. Hostilities commenced between Sweden and Prussia.

September 10. *Convention of Closterseven.*

October 22. Treaty of peace concluded between the province of Pennsylvania, and the Delaware and the Shawanee Indians.

1761. August 15. *The Family Compact* between the different branches of the House of Bourbon, signed at Paris.

1762. January 23. War declared by England against Spain, in consequence of the Family Compact.

May 1. The Spanish and French invade Portugal, and an army sent from England to assist the Portuguese.

— 5. *Peace of Petersburg*, between Russia and Prussia. Russia restored all her conquests to Prussia.

— 22. *Peace of Hamburg*, between Sweden and Prussia.

— 23. War declared by Portugal against Spain.

November 3. Preliminaries of peace signed at Fontainebleau, between France and England.

1763. February 10. *Peace of Paris* concluded between France, Spain, Portugal, and Great Britain. Cession of Canada by France, and of Florida by Spain.

— 15. *Peace of Hubertsberg*, between Prussia, Austria, and Saxony. End of the Seven Years' War.

1765. March 22. American Stamp Act.

1768. February 24. *Treaty of Warsaw*, between Russia and Poland.

October. War between Russia and Turkey.

1771. January 22. A treaty concluded between Great Britain and Spain, confirming the possession of the Falkland Islands to the former.

1772. February 17. Secret convention for the partition of Poland by Russia and Prussia.

August 5. *Treaty of Petersburg* for the same object, between Austria, Russia, and Prussia.

1773. December 21. The disturbances in America began with the destruction of the tea on board three sloops at Boston.

1774. July 21. *Peace of Kutchuk kainarji*, between Russia and Turkey. Crimea declared independent, Azoph ceded to Russia, and freedom of commerce and navigation of the Black Sea granted.

December 5. Congress opened at Philadelphia.

1775. April 19. Hostilities commenced at Lexington, North America, between Great Britain and the Colonists.

May 20. The American provinces sign articles of union and alliance.

1776. July 4. American declaration of independence.

1778. February 6. A treaty ratified with the states of America, by France, who acknowledged their independence.

March 13. War between England and France.

1779. May 13. *Peace of Teschen* ratified between Austria, Saxony, and Prussia.

1779. July 13. Spain joins the war against England.

1780. December 20. War declared by Great Britain against Holland.

July 9 and August 1. First conventions for the armed neutrality, between Russia, Denmark, and Sweden. December 24, the States-General acceded.

1781. May 8. King of Prussia accedes to the armed neutrality.

October 9. The Emperor of Germany joins the armed neutrality.

1782. November 30. The independence of America acknowledged by England, and preliminaries of peace signed at Paris between the British and American Commissioners.

1783. January 20. Preliminary articles of peace signed at Versailles, between Great Britain, Spain, and France.

Crimea passes under the dominion of Russia.

September 2. Preliminaries of peace between Great Britain and Holland, signed at Paris.

— 3. *Definitive treaty of peace* between Great Britain and America, signed at Paris; when the latter power was admitted to be a sovereign and independent State. On the same day, the definitive treaty was signed at Versailles between Great Britain, France, and Spain.

1784. June 20. *Definitive treaty of peace* between Great Britain and Holland signed at Paris.

1785. July 23. Germanic confederation between Saxony, Brandenburg, and Hanover.

November 8. The *treaty of Fontainebleau*, between the Emperor and Holland.

1787. August 18. The Turks declare war against Russia.

1788. February 10. The Emperor of Germany joined Russia against Turkey.

September 25. The King of France convened the States-General to assemble in January, 1789.

1790. September 27. The preliminary treaty ratified with Spain, relative to Nootka Sound; and the definitive treaty signed on the 28th of October following.

1791. July 20. *Convention of Pilnitz*, between the Emperor Leopold and the King of Prussia.

1792. April 20. The French National Assembly declared war against the Emperor of Germany.

June 26. The *first coalition* against France took place, and the King of Prussia issued his manifesto.

1792. September 16. War declared against Sardinia by the French National Assembly.

1793. February 1. France declared war against Great Britain and Holland.

— 9. The Duke of Tuscany acknowledged the French republic.

May 25. Spain engaged to assist Great Britain.

September 3. The King of Naples declared war against the French republic.

Great Britain concluded treaties, July 14, with Prussia; Aug. 30, with Austria; and Sept. 26, with Portugal.

1795. February 15. The first pacification between the National Assembly of France and the Vendeans, concluded.

— 18. A defensive alliance entered into with Russia, by Great Britain.

April 5. *Peace of Basle*, between the King of Prussia and the French republic.

May 16. Treaty of alliance signed at Paris, between France and the United Provinces, against England. Dutch Flanders ceded to France.

July 22. Peace ratified at Basle between France and Spain. Spanish St. Domingo ceded to France.

November 25. *The partition of Poland* took place between Russia, Austria, and Prussia.

1796. May 15. *Treaty of Paris*, between the French republic and the King of Sardinia, the latter ceding Savoy, Nice, the territory of Tende, and Beuil, and granting a free passage for troops through his states.

August 5. The *treaty of Berlin* ratified between Prussia and France, whereby the neutrality of Germany was guaranteed.

— 19. An *alliance* offensive and defensive concluded at *St. Ildefonso*, between France and Spain.

October 6. War declared by Spain against Great Britain.

1797. February 19. *Treaty of Tolentino*, between the French republic and the Pope.

April 18. Preliminaries of the *peace of Leoben* signed between Austria and France.

October 17. *Treaty of Campo Formio*, between France and Austria, the latter power yielding the Low Countries and the Ionian Islands to France; and Milan, Mantua, and Modena, to the Cisalpine republic.

December 9. *Congress of Radstadt* commenced its labours to treat concerning a general peace with the Germanic powers.

1798. Switzerland invaded by the French.

September 12. War declared against France by the Porte, and an alliance, offensive and defensive, entered into between the latter power, Russia, and Great Britain.

October 3. Naples and Sardinia commence hostilities against France.

December 29. A treaty of alliance and subsidies, agreed upon between Great Britain and Russia, against France.

1799. June 22. The *second coalition* against France, by Great Britain, the Emperors of Germany and Russia, part of the German empire, the Kings of Naples and Portugal, Turkey, and the Barbary States. Conference of Radstadt broken up.

1800. June 20. A treaty of subsidies ratified at Vienna, between Austria and England, stipulating that the war should be vigorously prosecuted against France, and that neither of the contracting powers should enter into a separate peace.

September 30. A treaty of amity and commerce ratified, between France and the United States of America. Stipulated in the treaty that the flag should protect the cargo.

December 16. A *treaty of armed neutrality ratified*, between Russia, Denmark, and Sweden, at Petersburg, in order to cause their flags to be respected by the belligerent powers. The principle, that neutral flags protect neutral bottoms, being contrary to the maritime system of England, the British Cabinet remonstrated, when the Emperor Paul caused an embargo to be laid on all English vessels in his ports, detaining their crews, whom he marched up the country. Prussia afterwards acceded to this treaty.

1801. January 14. A proclamation issued by Great Britain, authorizing reprisals, and laying an embargo on all Russian, Swedish, and Danish vessels.

February 9. *Peace of Luneville*, between the French republic and the Emperor of Germany, confirming the cessions made by the treaty of Campo Formio, stipulating that the Rhine, to the Dutch territories, should form the boundary of France, and recognizing the independence of the Batavian, Helvetic, Ligurian, and Cisalpine republics.

March 3. War declared by Spain against Portugal.

— 21. A treaty signed at Madrid between France and Spain, whereby the estates of Parma were yielded to France, who in return ceded Tuscany to the Infanta Prince of Parma, with the title of King of Etruria.

— 28. A treaty of peace between France and the King of

Naples, signed at Florence, by which France acquired the isles of Elba, Piombino, and Presides.

1801. June 17. A treaty concluded between Great Britain and Russia at Petersburg.

July 15. The *Concordat* between Buonaparte and Pius VII., signed at Paris.

August 8. A treaty of peace concluded between Spain and Portugal.

September 29. A treaty of peace signed at Madrid, between France and Portugal.

October 1. Preliminary articles of peace between France and England, signed at London by Lord Hawkesbury and M. Otto.

— 8. A treaty of peace ratified at Paris between the Emperor of Russia and the French government.

1802. March 25. *Peace of Amiens* between Great Britain, France, Spain, and Holland.

June 25. Definitive treaty between France and the Ottoman Porte.

September 11. Piedmont united to France.

1803. March 14. Hostilities renewed between Great Britain and France.

May 18. War declared by Great Britain against France.

June 17. Great Britain declared war against the republic of Batavia.

August 1. A treaty ratified between Great Britain and Sweden.

1804. December 12. Spain declared war against Great Britain.

1805. January 24. War declared against Spain by Great Britain.

April 8. The *treaty of Petersburg* entered into for a third coalition against France, England and Russia being the contracting parties.

August 9. The Emperor of Austria acceded to the treaty of Petersburg.

— 31. An alliance offensive and defensive, entered into at Beekaskog, between Great Britain and Sweden.

September 8. *Third coalition* against France, the parties being Great Britain, Russia, Austria, Sweden, and Naples.

— 21. A treaty of neutrality signed between France and Naples.

December 26. *Peace of Presburg* between France and Austria, by which the ancient states of Venice were ceded to Italy; the principality of Eichstett, part of the bishopric of Passau, the city of Augsburg, the Tyrol, all the possessions of Austria in Suabia, in Brisgau, and Ortenau, were transferred to the Elector of Bavaria and the Duke of Wirtemberg, who, as well as the Duke of Baden, were then created kings by Napoleon: the independence of the Helvetic republic was also stipulated.

1806. April 7. War between Great Britain and Prussia.

July 12. The Germanic *confederation of the Rhine* formed under the auspices of Napoleon.

— 20. *Peace of Paris* between France and Russia, which Alexander subsequently refused to ratify.

August 1. The treaty of the 12th of July notified to the Diet at Ratisbon, when the German princes seceded from the Germanic empire, and placed themselves under the protection of Napoleon.

October 6. The *fourth coalition* formed against France, by Great Britain, Russia, Prussia, and Saxony.

November 21. The *Berlin decree*, issued by Buonaparte after the battle of Jena, declaring the British islands in a state of blockade, and interdicting the whole world from any communication with them.

— 28. War declared against France by Russia.

December 11. A treaty of peace and alliance signed at Cosen, between Napoleon and the Elector of Saxony, who then assumed the title of king.

— 17. War declared against Russia by Turkey.

— 31. A treaty of commerce entered into between Great Britain and the United States of America, which the latter state afterwards refused to ratify.

1807. July 2. The President of the United States ordered all British ships to evacuate the ports of America, in consequence of the capture of the Chesapeake by an English ship of war.

— 7. *Peace of Tilsit* concluded between France and Russia, when Napoleon restored to the Prussian monarch one half of his territories, and Russia recognized the Confederation of the Rhine, and the elevation of Napoleon's three brothers, Joseph, Louis, and Jerome, to the thrones of Naples, Holland, and Westphalia; this treaty was ratified on the 19th.

August 16. A Danish declaration published against Great Britain.

October 8. The Prince Regent of Portugal ordered all his ports to be shut against the British, which order was speedily revoked, and on the French approaching Lisbon, he embarked on Nov. 27, for the Brazils.

1807. Oct. 31. A treaty of alliance entered into between France and Denmark.

November 1. Russia declared war against England.

— 10. A treaty ratified at Paris between France and Holland, whereby Flushing was ceded to the French.

December 17. *Milan decree* issued by Napoleon; England declared in a state of blockade.

1808. February 8. Treaty of peace between Great Britain and Sweden.

— 18. A declaration issued by Austria, breaking off all connexion with England.

— 29. Denmark declared war against Sweden.

March 30. A treaty of alliance and subsidy entered into between England and Sicily, whereby the latter was to be garrisoned by 10,000 British troops, and to receive an annual subsidy of 300,000*l*.

May 1. The Regent of Portugal declared war against France.

— 5. *Treaty of Bayonne*, whereby Charles IV. ceded all his titles to Spain and its dependencies to Napoleon, expressly resigning to him the right of transmitting the crown to whomsoever he should think fitting.

On the festival of St. Ferdinand, insurrections broke out in several parts of Spain, at Cadiz in particular.

June 6. War commenced between the Spanish insurgents and France.

— 16. Insurrection of the Portuguese at Oporto, which spread so rapidly as to occasion the evacuation of the northern provinces by the French troops.

— 25. A Spanish proclamation of peace with England, and Sweden, her ally, published at Oviedo.

August 30. The *convention of Cintra* signed, the French agreeing to evacuate Portugal.

November 5. The *convention of Berlin* entered into, whereby Napoleon remitted to Prussia the sum due on the war-debt, and withdrew his troops from many of the fortresses in order to reinforce his armies in Spain.

1809. January 5. Peace ratified between Great Britain and the Ottoman Porte.

— 14. A treaty of alliance ratified between England and the Spanish insurgents.

1809. April 6. War declared against the French by the Austrians.

— 9. The *fifth coalition* against France by Great Britain and Austria.

May 3. Russia declared war against Austria.

July 25. Armistice between Sweden and Norway.

September 17. A treaty of peace signed between Russia and Sweden.

October 14. *Peace of Vienna*, between France and Austria; Austria ceding to France the Tyrol, Dalmatia, and other territories, which were shortly afterwards declared to be united to France under the title of the Illyrian provinces, and engaging to adhere to the prohibitory system adopted towards England by France and Russia.

1810. January 6. *Peace of Paris*, between France and Sweden, whereby Swedish Pomerania and the island of Rugen were given up to the Swedes, who agreed to adopt the French prohibitory system against Great Britain.

February 19. Treaties of alliance and commerce signed between Great Britain and the Brazils.

April 13. Sweden interdicts all commerce with England.

— 19. The South American provinces of Caraccas, &c., form a federative government, under the title of the Federation of Venezuela.

May 1. All French and English vessels prohibited from entering the ports of the United States.

— 29. The Dey of Algiers declared war against France.

July 9. Holland incorporated with France on the abdication of Louis Buonaparte.

November 19. Sweden declared war against Great Britain.

1812. March 13. Treaty of alliance signed at Paris between France and Austria.

— 24. Treaty of alliance, signed at St. Petersburg, between Bernadotte, Prince Royal of Sweden, and the Emperor Alexander; the former agreeing to join in the campaign against France, in return for which Sweden was to receive Norway.

April 1. The Berlin decree revoked as far as respected America.

May 28. Preliminaries of peace ratified at Bucharest between Russia and Turkey, it being stipulated that the Pruth should form the limits of those empires.

June 18. The United States of America declare war against Great Britain.

1812. June 22. Napoleon having assembled an immense army in Western Prussia declared war against Russia.

July 6. A treaty of peace between Great Britain and Sweden ratified at Orebo.

— 20. Treaty signed between the Emperor Alexander and the Regency of Cadiz, in the name of Ferdinand the Seventh of Spain.

August 1. Treaty of peace and union ratified at St. Petersburg between Great Britain and Russia, renewing their ancient relations of friendship and commerce.

1813. January 25. *Concordat at Fontainebleau*, between Napoleon and Pius VII.

March 1. The *sixth coalition* entered into between Russia and Prussia against France, the treaty being ratified at Kalisch.

— 3. The *treaty of Stockholm* entered into between England and Sweden.

April 1. France declared war against Prussia.

June 14. A treaty of alliance concluded between Great Britain, Russia, and Prussia.

July 8. The *convention of Peterswalden* took place between Great Britain and Russia.

— 10. A reciprocal treaty of alliance and guarantee entered into between France and Denmark, ratified at Copenhagen.

September 3. War declared by Denmark against Sweden.

— 9. A triple *treaty of alliance* ratified at *Toplitz* between Russia, Austria, and Prussia.

October 3. A preliminary treaty of alliance signed at *Toplitz* between Austria and Great Britain.

December 8. *Treaty of Valençay*, between Napoleon and Ferdinand the Seventh of Spain, whereby the latter was put in full possession of that kingdom, on agreeing to maintain its integrity.

1814. January 14. *Treaty of Kiel*, between Great Britain, Sweden, and Denmark. Norway ceded to Sweden.

February 5. The Cortes of Spain renounce the treaty ratified at Valençay.

Congress of Chatillon between the four great powers allied against France, at which Caulaincourt attended on the part of France; the Congress broke up on the 19th of March.

March 1. *Treaty of Chaumont* between Great Britain, Austria, Russia, and Prussia.

April 11. The *treaty of Paris* ratified on the part of Napoleon and the Allies, by which Napoleon renounced his sovereignty over

France, &c., stipulating that the island of Elba should be his domain and residence for life, with a suitable provision for himself and Maria Louisa, who was to have vested in her the duchies of Parma and Placentia, the same to descend to her son.

1814. April 23. A convention signed at Paris between the Count d'Artois on the one part, and the Allied Powers on the other, stipulating that all hostilities should cease by land and sea; that the confederated armies should evacuate the French territory, leaving its boundaries the same as they were on the 1st of January, 1792.

May 30. *Peace of Paris* ratified between France and the Allied Powers, in a supplemental article of which Louis XVIII. stipulated that he would exert his endeavours with the continental powers to ensure the abolition of the slave trade, in conjunction with Great Britain.

July 20. A treaty of peace signed between France and Spain at Paris, confirming the stipulations of previous treaties which had existed on the 1st of January, 1792.

— 26. Norway and Sweden commence hostilities. Norway opposing her separation from Denmark, but eventually submitting in the following August.

August 13. Convention between Great Britain and the Sovereign Prince of the Low Countries respecting the Dutch colonies.

September 28. A convention ratified at Vienna, whereby Saxony was placed under the control of Prussia.

December 24. *Peace of Ghent* between Great Britain and the United States of America.

1815. March 13. The eight powers, who had ratified the treaty of Paris, issued a manifesto after the escape of Napoleon from Elba, declaring him a common enemy to the repose of the world.

— 23. *Treaty of Vienna* between Great Britain, Austria, Russia, and Prussia, confirming the principles on which they had acted by the treaty of Chaumont, March 1, 1814.

— 28. War commenced by Murat against Austria.

May 18. Peace ratified between Saxony and Prussia.

— 20. A convention signed at Zurich between the Swiss Diet and the plenipotentiaries of Great Britain, Austria, Russia, and Prussia.

A convention entered into near Capua between the Austrian commander and the English envoy and Joachim Murat, by which the latter surrendered his kingdom to King Ferdinand.

— 31. *Treaty of Vienna* between the King of the Low Countries on the one part, and Great Britain, Russia, Austria, and Prussia, on the other, agreeing to the enlargement of the Dutch territories, and vesting the sovereignty in the House of Orange.

1815. June 4. *Treaty of Vienna.* Denmark cedes Swedish Pomerania and Rugen to Prussia, in exchange for Lauenburg.

— 8. Federative constitution of Germany signed at Vienna.

— 15. Hostilities began by Napoleon's entry into Belgium.

July 3. The convention of St. Cloud entered into between Marshal Davoust on the one part, and Wellington and Blucher on the other, by which Paris was surrendered to the Allies, who enter it on the 6th.

August 2. A convention signed at Paris between Great Britain, Austria, Russia, and Prussia, styling Napoleon the prisoner of those powers, and confiding his safeguard particularly to the British government.

September 14. A convention entered into at Vienna, whereby the duchies of Parma, &c., were secured to the Empress Maria Louisa, and on her demise to her son, by Napoleon.

— 26. The treaty denominated of the *Holy Alliance* ratified at Paris by the Emperors of Austria and Russia, and the King of Prussia.

November 5. A treaty ratified at Paris between Great Britain and Russia respecting the Ionian Islands, which were declared to form a united state under the sole protection of the former power.

— 20. *Peace of Paris* between France on the one part, and Great Britain, Austria, Russia, and Prussia, on the other, establishing the boundaries of France, and stipulating for the garrisoning of several of the fortresses in France by foreign troops for three years.

— 20. The *treaty of Paris* executed between Great Britain, Russia, Austria, and Prussia, confirming the treaties of Chaumont as well as those of Vienna.

1816. March 13. A treaty entered into between France and the Swiss Cantons, whereby 12,000 Swiss troops were admitted into the French service.

1817. June 10. *Treaty of Paris* between Great Britain, France, Spain, Russia, and Prussia, in order to fulfil the articles of the Congress of Vienna.

August 28. A treaty concluded at Paris between France and Portugal relative to the surrendering up of French Guiana.

1818. April 25. A convention signed at Paris between France on the one part, and the allied powers on the other, releasing

France from all debts referred to in the treaties from the 30th of May, 1814, to the 20th of November, 1815.

1818. April 25. A convention ratified at Paris between England and France, whereby the latter power undertook to liquidate all further demands on the part of British subjects.

May 4. A treaty ratified between Great Britain and the Netherlands for abolishing the slave-trade.

October 9. A convention entered into by the great powers of Europe, assembled at Aix-la-Chapelle, on the one part, and the Duke de Richelieu on the other, whereby it was stipulated that the army of occupation should quit the French territory on the 30th of November ensuing; it was also agreed that the remaining sum due from France to the Allies was 265,000,000 francs.

1819. August 1. *Congress of Carlsbad.*

1820. October 20. *Congress of Troppau.*

— 24. Treaty between Spain and America: Florida ceded to the United States.

1821. May 6. The *congress of Laybach,* which had been for some time attended by the sovereigns of Austria, Russia, and Prussia, finally broke up, having issued two circulars stating it to be their resolution to occupy Naples with Austrian troops, and proscribe popular insurrection.

1822. January 1. Greeks declare their independence.

March 19. The independence of Columbia, Mexico, and Peru, recognized by the United States of America.

August 25. *Congress of Verona.*

1823. April 7. The French invaded Spain, alleging the necessity of protecting Ferdinand against the Liberal party.

October 30. British Consuls appointed to the South American states.

1824. February 4. A convention between Great Britain and Austria laid upon the table of the House of Commons, by which the former agreed to accept 2,500,000*l.* as a final compensation for their claims upon the latter power, amounting to 30,000,000*l.*

June 16. Commercial treaty between Great Britain and Denmark.

1825. January 9. The British government determined to acknowledge the independence of Mexico, Columbia, and Buenos Ayres, by sending out Commissioners charged with full powers to conclude treaties of commerce between them and this country, founded on that recognition.

1825. February 2. Treaty of commerce signed at Buenos Ayres between Great Britain and the united province of Rio de la Plata.

— 28. Convention between Great Britain and Russia; frontier of north-west coast of America settled.

April 17. France recognizes the independence of St. Domingo.

— 18. Treaty of amity between Great Britain and Columbia.

September 20. Commercial treaty between Great Britain and the Hanse towns.

October 18. Treaty between Great Britain and Brazil for abolition of Slave trade.

1826. January 26. Treaty of navigation between Great Britain and France.

May 19. Treaty of navigation between Great Britain and Sweden.

September 4. *Treaty of Akermann.*

— 28. Russia declares war against Persia.

November 13. Convention concluded between England and the United States, concerning indemnities to American subjects injured by the war.

1828. February 22. *Peace of Turkmauchay* between Russia and Persia. Erivan and Nakhitchwan ceded to Russia.

April 26. Russia declares war against Turkey.

June 26. Convention between Great Britain and Spain for satisfying claims of British merchants.

August 6. Convention between Viceroy of Egypt and Sir E. Codrington for the evacuation of the Morea.

— 29. Treaty of peace between Brazil and Buenos Ayres, at Rio Janeiro.

October 28. Peace between Naples and Tripoli.

1829. July 6. *Treaty of London* between Russia, France, and Great Britain, for the settlement of the affairs of Greece.

September 14. Peace between Russia and Turkey.

1830. May 7. Treaty between Turkey and the United States. American vessels allowed to pass to and from the Black Sea.

July 5. Algiers taken by the French.

1830. Nov. 29. The Polish revolution commenced at Warsaw. The Polish army immediately declares itself in favour of the people, and on the 4th of December the Grand Duke Constantine abandons the neighbourhood of Warsaw.

Dec. 26. M. Van de Weyer announces to the Congress, that the Allied Powers had recognised the independence of Belgium.

1831. Jan. 25. The Diet at Warsaw declare the throne of Poland vacant.

Feb. 20. The battle of Grochow, near Praga, a suburb of Warsaw, took place between the Poles and Russians. After an obstinate contest, continuing the whole of that day, and great part of the next, the Poles remained masters of the field of battle. The Russians shortly after retreated, having been foiled in their attempt to take Warsaw, by this battle, in which they are stated to have lost 7000 men, and the Poles 2000.

24. The Congress of Deputies at Brussels elect M. Surlet de Chokier Regent of the Belgic States.

March 1. The ministerial measure for Parliamentary reform introduced to the House of Commons by Lord John Russell.

31. The Poles, under General Skrzynecki, attacked the Russians at Wawz, and after fighting the whole of this and part of the following day, all the positions of the Russian army were carried by storm, and themselves compelled to retreat, with a loss, as stated, of 12,000 men in killed and wounded, 2000 prisoners, several pieces of cannon, and much baggage. The loss of the Poles was represented as comparatively trifling.

April 3. The Polish insurrection spreading into Wilna and Volhynia, the Emperor of Russia issues a decree, confiscating the estates of those nobles who shall join therein, persons of inferior ranks to be sent to the Siberian battalions. The children in both cases to be taken as military cantonists.

7. Revolution at Brazil. The Emperor Don Pedro abdicates in favour of his son, Don Pedro II., a child of five years of age, and embarks with the rest of his family on board of a British ship of war. The representatives of the nation immediately met and appointed a regency to act in the name of the young Emperor.

10. The Poles gain another victory over the Russians at Siedlez, taking several cannon and between 3000 and 4000 prisoners.

May 8. General Chrzanowski, with a division of Poles, succeeds in forcing his way through the Russian positions into Lithuania, in order to support the insurrection there in the place of General Dwernicki, who had been forced to surrender to the Austrians.

26. Battle of Ostrolenka, between the Poles and Russians, with great loss on both sides. The Poles remained masters of the field of battle, but shortly after retreated unmolested to Praga, their object having been to forward succours to Volhynia, which was effected.

27. The Belgic Congress decide, by a large majority, on enter-

taining the proposition for electing Prince Leopold to the throne of Belgium.

1831. May 28. Frederick King of Denmark issues a proclamation, bestowing a new constitution on his kingdom and the duchies of Sleswick and Holstein, including a provision for a system of representative local councils.

June 4. Prince Leopold elected King of Belgium by the Congress at Brussels. On the 6th, M. Surlet de Chokier, Regent of Belgium, addresses a letter to the Prince announcing the fact.

26. Prince Leopold addresses a letter to the Belgic deputation, which had been sent to him at London, announcing his acceptance of the crown.

July 21. Leopold I., the new King of Belgium, makes his entrance into Brussels, after a most triumphant progress through his dominions, from Ostend, where he landed from England. On the 22d his inauguration took place, and, in the presence of the Congress, he took the oaths to preserve and defend the Belgic constitution.

August 3. The King of the Netherlands resumes war against Belgium, and obtains several advantages over the Belgic troops. King Leopold applies for protection to the five Powers under whose auspices the settlement of the differences between the two states was proceeding. France immediately despatches 50,000 men to his assistance; upon which, on the 13th, the King of the Netherlands agrees to withdraw his troops, and consents to another armistice.

Sept. 7. After two days' hard fighting, Warsaw capitulated, and was taken possession of by the Russians. Great part of the Polish army retired towards Plock and Modlin.

Oct. 20. In the Belgian Chamber of Representatives, the Secretary for Foreign Affairs submitted the protocol agreed upon by the plenipotentiaries of the Five Powers, respecting the terms of the division of Belgium and Holland, which is declared to be final, and to be enforced by the whole of the subscribing powers.

Nov. 3. The Belgian Congress, after several days' debate, adopt the articles of separation from Holland proposed to them by the Conference, by a majority of 35 to 8.

December 4. In consequence of the epidemic disease prevailing in Sunderland, Government issued an order that all vessels bound from that place, to London, should be stopped at the Nore to perform quarantine.

— 6. President Jackson's message to both houses of Congress in the United States, detailing the present state of American affairs, and congratulating his fellow-citizens on the prospect of a speedy extinction of the public debt.

1831. Dec. 6. A suit to nullify the will of the late Duc de Bourbon, was entered this day in the Court of First Instance, at Paris, by the Princes de Rohan, heirs at law of the deceased; it being alleged that the will, which went to benefit the family of the King of the French, had been procured by improper means, and that the Duc de Bourbon had not come fairly to his death. After a trial of great length, the court subsequently decided in favour of the will.

— 12. The new ministerial measure of Parliamentary Reform was introduced to the House of Commons by Lord John Russell.

— 27. The Bill for the abolition of the hereditary peerage in France passed the Upper Chamber by a majority of 36.

1832. February 23. A French expedition landed at Ancona, and took possession of the citadel. The Pope called it an "invasion," and protested against it several times.

— 26. Ukase issued by the Emperor Nicholas, decreeing that the kingdom of Poland shall henceforth form an integral part of the Russian empire.

May 4. The Russian ratifications of the treaty respecting the affairs of Holland and Belgium, were exchanged at the Foreign Office.

— 7. Ministers defeated in the House of Lords by a majority of 35, on the motion of Lord Lyndhurst for postponing the disfranchisement clauses in the Reform Bill.

June 28. The Diet at Frankfort issued their manifesto of measures adopted by the German Confederacy, for the maintenance of order and tranquillity within their respective dominions. The publication of this manifesto occasioned great agitation throughout the German States, as it was mainly directed against the liberty of the press.

— 30. The Court of Cassation decide that the ordinance declaring Paris in a state of siege, and subject to military law, was illegal; and consequently annul the sentences pronounced by courts-martial on the prisoners who had been convicted by them of rioting and rebellion at the funeral of General Lamarque.

July 8. The expedition of Don Pedro landed on the Portuguese coast near Oporto, and took possession of that city without opposition.

October 10. A new French ministry formed under the direction of Marshal Soult, President of the Council.

1832. Oct. 25. Queen of Spain appointed Regent during the King's indisposition, and a complete change made in the ministry.

November 4. The combined English and French fleet sailed from Spithead, under the command of Sir Pulteney Malcolm and l'Amiral Villeneuve.

— 6. A deputation, headed by Sir John Key, the Lord Mayor, waited upon Lords Grey, Althorp, and Russell, and presented their Lordships with gold cups, the produce of a penny subscription, to which 300,000 persons had contributed. A similar cup was presented to the Lord Chancellor, on the 3rd of December.

—. An embargo was laid on all Dutch vessels within the British ports.

— 13. The Belgian Chambers opened by the King in person. His Majesty announced the recognition of Belgium, as an independent state, by the leading powers of Europe; and likewise his recent marriage with one of the daughters of the King of the French. He also alluded to the situation of their affairs with regard to Holland, of which, however, he declared his confidence of obtaining a satisfactory settlement.

Dec. 24. The citadel of Antwerp having been battered and bombarded by the French, till it was no longer tenable, General Chassé surrendered it to the French commander. Baron Chassé and the garrison were held as prisoners of war till the surrender of Lillo and Liefkenshoek, two other Belgian fortresses on the Scheldt, in the possession of the Dutch. The King of Holland having refused to allow of the surrender of these forts, the garrison were marched into France, and the French army proceeded immediately to evacuate Belgium.

TABLE I.

Estimated Revenues of the Norman Line.

William the Conqueror, at the commencement of his reign		14 Oct. 1066	£400,000
William Rufus	Idem	9 Sept. 1087	350,000
Henry I.	Idem	2 Aug. 1100	300,000
Stephen	Idem	1 Dec. 1135	250,000

TABLE II.

Estimated Revenues of the Saxon or Plantagenet Line.

Henry II., at the commencement of his reign		25 Oct. 1154	£200,000
Richard I.	Idem	6 July 1189	150,000
John	Idem	6 April 1199	100,000
Henry III.	Idem	19 Oct. 1216	80,000
Edward I.	Idem	16 Nov. 1272	150,000
Edward II.	Idem	7 July 1307	100,000
Edward III.	Idem	27 Jan. 1327	154,139
Richard II.	Idem	21 Jan. 1377	130,000

TABLE III.

Estimated Revenues of the Line of Lancaster.

Henry IV., at the commencement of his reign		29 Sept. 1399	£100,000
Henry V.	Idem	20 Mar. 1413	76,643
Henry VI.	Idem	31 Aug. 1422	64,976

TABLE IV.

Estimated Revenues of the Line of York.

Edward IV., at the commencement of his reign		4 Mar. 1460	£100,000
Edward V.	Idem	9 April 1483	100,000
Richard III.	Idem	22 June 1483	100,000

TABLE V.

Estimated Revenues of the House of Tudor.

At the commencement of the reign of

Henry VII.	22 Aug. 1485	£400,000
Henry VIII.	22 April 1509	800,000
Edward VI.	28 Jan. 1547	400,000
Mary	6 July 1553	450,000
Elizabeth	17 Nov. 1558	500,000

TABLE VI.

General Statement of the real total value of Imports into, and Exports from, England, between 1612 and December 1613.—(From Misselden.)

EXPORTS TO ALL PARTS OF THE WORLD.

	£	s.	d.
1613	2,090,640	11	8
The customs on those goods	86,794	16	2
The import paid outwards on woollen goods, lead, tin, &c.	10,000	0	0
The merchants' gains, freight, &c.	300,000	0	0
Grand total	2,487,435	7	10
Imported during that time in silk, gold and silver stuffs, Spanish wines, linen, &c. &c.	2,141,151	10	0
Balance gained in this year	346,283	17	10

REVENUE OF THE CUSTOMS IN THE YEAR 1613.

		£	s.	d.	£	s.	d.
London	Outwards	61,322	16	7	109,472	18	4
	Inwards	48,150	1	9			
In all the outports, the revenue of the Customs,							
	Outwards	25,471	19	7	38,502	9	4
	Inwards	13,030	9	9			
Total for England					147,975	7	8

TABLE VII.

ABSTRACT of the MONEY raised in ENGLAND during the COMMONWEALTH; from November 3, 1640, to November 5, 1659.

	£
Six subsidies at 50,000*l.* each	300,000
Poll money and assessments, to disband the Scotch and English armies	800,000
Voluntary contributions for the support of the "good cause" against malignants	300,000
Voluntary contributions for the relief of the Irish Protestants	180,000
Land tax on various assessments for the maintenance of the army	32,172,321
Excise for sixteen years at 500,000*l.* per annum	8,000,000
Tonnage and poundage for nineteen years, at 400,000*l.* a-year	7,600,000
Duty on coals	850,000
Duty on currants	51,000
Postage of letters	301,000
Weekly meal for six years	608,400
Court of wards and other feudal prerogatives	1,400,000
Wine licenses	312,200
Vintners' delinquency	4,000
Offices sequestered for the public service	850,000
Sequestrations of the lands of bishops, deans, and inferior clergy for four years	3,528,632
Tenths of all the clergy and other exactions from the church	1,600,320
Sale of church lands	10,035,663
Fee farm rents for twelve years	2,963,467
Other rents belonging to the crown and the principality of Wales	376,000
Sale of the crown lands and principality (120,000*l.* per annum)	1,200,000
Sale of forests, lands, and houses, &c., belonging to the king	656,000
Sequestrations of the estates and compositions with private individuals in England	4,564,986
Composition with delinquents in Ireland	1,000,000
Carried forward	£79,653,989

	£
Brought forward.........	79,653,989
Sale of the estates of the delinquents in Ireland	2,245,000
Sale of Irish lands	1,322,500
Ransom of captives..	102,000
New river water	8,000
Total..	83,331,489

INCOME OF SCOTLAND DURING THE COMMONWEALTH.

	£	s.	d.
The whole annual income of Scotland, arising from ten different sources, is..............................	143,652	11	11

INCOME OF IRELAND.

The whole annual income of Ireland, arising from five different sources, is..............................	207,790	0	0

INCOME OF ENGLAND.

The whole annual income of England, arising from forty-five different sources, is	1,517,274	17	1

TABLE VIII.

General View of the Money received by Charles II. during the whole course of his reign.

MISCELLANEOUS RESOURCES.

	£
1. Queen's portion	250,000
2. Sale of royal domains....................................	500,000
3. Price of Dunkirk	400,000
4. Pensions from France	950,000
5. Plunder	640,000
6. Shutting up the exchequer	1,328,526
7. Extortions	100,000
Total miscellaneous resources	4,168,526

2. PARLIAMENTARY GRANTS.

Parliamentary grants for public services	13,414,863
	17,583,389

	£
Brought forward.........	17,583,389

3. THE PERMANENT REVENUE.

Permanent revenue, or the income of the Crown at 1,000,000*l.* a year	26,400,000
Total.........	£43,983,389

Sources of the Revenue of Charles II.

PARLIAMENTARY GRANTS.

(For the debts of the republic and disbanding the army.)

		£
1661.	1. Three months' assessment at 70,000*l.* per month	210,000
	2. The first poll-tax	252,167
	3. Two months' assessment at 70,000*l.* per month	140,000
	4. Six months' assessment at 70,000*l.* each ...	420,000
		1,022,167

2. TEMPORARY GRANTS.

1660.	1. For the speedy supply to his Majesty	70,000
	2. Ditto for the expenses of the coronation	70,000
	3. Forfeited estates of traitors [a]..................	75,000
1662.	4. Grant for paying the king's debts	1,260,000
	5. To be distributed among the loyal cavaliers	60,000
1663.	6. Four entire subsidies from temporality and clergy	282,000
1664.	7. First aid for the Dutch war	2,477,502
1665.	8. Second aid for ditto	1,250,000
1666.	9. Third aid for ditto	1,256,345
	10. Second poll-tax for ditto	500,000
1668.	11. Grant for fitting out a fleet	310,000
1670.	12. Personal tax on bankers, and for the king's debts	800,000
	Carried forward.........	9,433,014

[a] It appears from Commons' Journal, Vol. VIII. p. 498, that the clear annual value of these estates amounted only to 5000*l.*; they were not probably worth more than fifteen years' purchase.

		£
	Brought forward.........	9,433,014
1673.	13. Grants during the Dutch war, voted in order to procure the repeal of the declaration of indulgence	1,238,750
1677.	14. Grant for building 30 ships of war	584,978
	15. Third poll-tax for preparations against France	150,000
	16. Grant for disbanding the army	414,000
	17. Grant for ditto	241,464

3. PERMANENT GRANTS.

1670.	1. Additional tax on wine for eight years	456,000
	2. Additional Excise for nine years, about	300,000
	3. Stamp duty for twelve years	266,666
		13,084,872
	Arrears of Excise, voluntary presents from Parliament to the King and the Duke of York, and money in the hands of receivers at the Restoration,—supposed	400,000
		£13,484,872

TABLE IX.

The author of "Britannia Languens", in order to shew that the commerce of England had been for some years in a declining state, (according to perpetual lament,) made an account of all gold and silver coined in seventy-six years, from 1st October 1599, to November 1676.

				£	s.	d.
1st Period, 19 years,		from Oct. 1599 to March	1619............	4,779,314	13	0
2d do.	do.	to March	1638............	6,900,042	11	1
3d do.	do.	to do.	1657............	7,733,997	16	0
4th do.	do.	to Nov.	1675............	2,238,997	16	0
Total coined in England in 76 years......				£21,652,352	16	1

TABLE X.

			£
Estimated PUBLIC REVENUE at the commencement of the reign of		Elizabeth, 17th Nov. 1558.....	500,000
Do.	do.	James I... 24th March 1603...	600,000
Do.	do.	Charles I. 27th March 1625...	895,819
		Commonwealth, 1648	1,517,247
Do.	do.	Charles II. 30th Jan. 1649	1,800,000
Do.	do.	James II. 6th Feb. 1685	2,001,885

TABLE XI.

AGGREGATE RECEIPTS of KING WILLIAM'S REIGN.

	£	s.	d.
Customs	13,296,833	14	6
Excise	13,649,328	0	5¼
Land-tax	19,174,059	8	3½
Polls	2,557,641	7	7¼
Tax on marriages, births, &c.	275,517	18	1
Various articles (including permanent loans)...	9,745,300	10	9
Temporary loans unpaid	13,348,680	5	10¼
Total.........	72,047,361	5	6¼

TABLE XII.

INCOME of ENGLAND, ANNO 1701.—(The year preceding the monarch's death.)

	£
Customs	1,539,100
Excise	986,004
Post Office, &c.	130,399
Land-tax, at 2*s*. in the pound............................	989,965
Various small taxes	249,737
	3,895,205
Income at the Revolution	2,001,855
Total additional revenue at the death of William	£1,893,350

TABLE XIII.

EXPENSE of the WAR against FRANCE and IRELAND.

	£
Extra expenses of the navy	9,622,141
Extra expenses of the army	14,566,051
Extra expenses of the ordnance	2,408,535
	26,596,727
Expenses of the reduction of Ireland	3,851,655
Total	£30,448,382

TABLE XIV.

AGGREGATE EXPENDITURE of KING WILLIAM'S REIGN.

	£
The naval expenses	19,822,141
The military expenses, exclusive of Ireland	18,165,051
The ordnance department	3,008,535
The expenses of the Revolution, paid to the United Provinces for the expenses of the charges of the king's expedition to England	600,000
The expenses of the war in Ireland	3,851,655
The expenses incurred on recoining the money of the realm	3,170,840
Miscellaneous expenses	272,845
Principal and interest of public debts	13,691,458
Balance of accounts ending Lady-day 1702	624,477
Expenses of the civil list, as above stated	8,880,506
Total	£72,087,508

TABLE XV.

AGGREGATE RECEIPTS of QUEEN ANNE, during twelve years and three quarters.

	£
The Customs, which had greatly increased with other small branches, produced in this reign to the exchequer	24,113,811
The Excise, which had also been augmented in consequence of a variety of new duties, comprehending soap, candles, starch, leather, paper, printed linen, &c.	20,859,311
The land-tax during this reign was rendered very productive, from its being generally kept up at 4*s.* in the pound: it produced	12,285,909
The Post Office, Stamps, and smaller branches of the revenue, produced a total of	5,261,346
	62,520,377
The amount of the loans on temporary as well as perpetual taxes, borrowed to carry on the wars during this reign	59,853,154
Total	£122,373,531

TABLE XVI.

Total revenue, 5,691,803*l.*

THE PEACE ESTABLISHMENT.

	£
The civil list	700,000
The navy	765,700
The army	425,905
The ordnance	58,000
Miscellaneous services	16,000
Aggregate total	£1,965,605

TABLE XVII.

AGGREGATE EXPENDITURE of QUEEN ANNE'S REIGN, during twelve years and three quarters.

	£
The civil list	7,604,848
The expenses of the navy	23,484,574
The expenses of the army	32,975,331
The expenses of the ordnance	2,100,676
The transport service	796,220
The repairing and building of churches	482,508
The equivalent paid to Scotland on equalizing the taxes at the Union	398,085
Recompense for tolls abolished at the Union	7,641
Expenses incurred in the coinage	81,934
Expense of the government in the West Indies	37,100
Money lent to Sweden	20,095
Miscellaneous services	200,000
Temporary loans repaid	31,661,176
Interest of the permanent national debt	22,523,351
Total expenses	£122,373,539

TABLE XVIII.

COST of the WARS of QUEEN ANNE.

	£
Extra expenses of the navy	13,913,323
Extra expenses of the army	27,014,691
Extra expenses of the ordnance	1,404,676
Extra expenses of the transport service	796,220
Sufferers at Nevis and St. Christopher's	141,093
Total	£43,270,003

TABLE XIX.

AGGREGATE RECEIPTS of GEORGE I. during twelve years and a half.

	£
The Customs	21,632,985
The Excise	30,421,451
The Stamps	1,675,609
The Land-tax	18,470,022
Incidents	4,800,000
	77,000,067
Loans	2,832,093
Total during the whole reign	£79,832,160

TABLE XX.

AGGREGATE EXPENSES of GEORGE I. during twelve years and a half.

	£
The Civil List	10,632,514
The Navy	12,923,851
The Army	13,842,467
The Ordnance	1,064,449
Miscellaneous Services	150,000
Total	£38,613,281
Interest of the Public Debt, Loans, and Land-tax deficiences	41,218,879
	£79,832,160

TABLE XXI.

PEACE ESTABLISHMENT.

	£
The Civil List	850,000
The Navy	740,000
The Army	900,000
The Ordnance	73,000
Miscellaneous Services	20,000
Total	£2,583,000

TABLE XXII.

TOTAL EXTRAORDINARY EXPENSES during this reign.

	£
The Navy	3,303,851
The Army	2,592,467
The Ordnance	151,949
Total	£6,048,267

TABLE XXIII.

PUBLIC REVENUE at the time of GEORGE the FIRST's death, June 1727; a Four Years' Average.

	£	£
The Customs	1,530,361	
Excise (deducting 6*d*. per bushel on Malt)	1,927,354	
Stamps	132,665	
Duty on Houses and Windows	131,011	
Hackney Coaches and Chairs	9,523	
Hawkers and Pedlars	8,055	
Sixpence in the pound for places and pensions	31,504	
First fruits and tenths	16,473	
Post Office	75,545	
Salt Duties	185,505	
Small branches belonging to the Civil List	55,892	
Taxes known then under the name of the General Fund	58,755	
		4,162,643
Land-tax at 4*s*. in the pound	2,000,000	
Malt-tax at 6*d*. per bushel	750,000	
	2,750,000	
Deduct deficiencies in 1726	150,000	
		2,600,000
Total		£6,762,643

TABLE XXIV.

PUBLIC REVENUE in the year preceding the death of GEORGE II.

	£	£
Customs		1,985,376
Excise (including annual Malt)		3,887,349
Stamps		263,207
Incidents		650,000
		6,785,932
Land-taxes 4*s*., given for	2,000,000	
Deduct deficiencies as per account, 1760	262,392	
		1,737,608
Total		£8,523,540

TABLE XXV.

AGGREGATE RECEIPTS of GEORGE II.; reigned thirty-three years and four months.

	£
Customs	49,838,854
Excise (including annual Malt)	93,747,167
Stamps	4,377,957
Land-tax	49,453,323
Miscellaneous taxes	19,800,000
	217,217,301
Loans during this reign	59,132,472
Total	£276,349,773

TABLE XXVI.

AGGREGATE EXPENDITURE of GEORGE II.; reigned thirty-three years and four months.

	£
Civil List	27,280,000
Navy	71,424,171
Army	73,911,521
Ordnance	6,706,674
Other military expenses	28,869
Ecclesiastical expenses	152,240
Westminster bridge	216,500
London bridge	45,000
Military roads	24,000
Making harbours	43,360
Public rewards	22,000
Public monument to Captain Cornwall	3,000
Heritable jurisdiction in Scotland	152,037
Debts due to the Scotch forfeited estates	72,410
Charges on the Mint, 7000*l.* per annum for thirty-three years	231,000
Extra expenses of the Mint	31,364
Horned cattle	208,123
Foundling Hospital	182,277
Earthquake at Lisbon	100,000
African forts and settlements	420,000
American expenses	1,697,424
Miscellaneous expenses	25,496
Money paid pursuant to addresses	25,000
	183,002,466
Interest of public debts and payment of principal	93,347,184
Total	£276,349,650

TABLE XXVII.

EXPENSES of the FIRST WAR, of eight Years.

	£
Eight years' Land-tax at 4s. in the pound	16,000,000
Eight years' Malt	6,000,000
Taken out of the sinking fund	7,800,000
	29,800,000
Deduct eight years' expense in the time of peace	14,720,000
	15,080,000
Add the public debt contracted	31,333,689
Total expense of the war, 1739	£46,413,689

TABLE XXVIII.

EXPENSES of the SECOND WAR, called the SEVEN YEARS' WAR.

	£
The sums voted by parliament for the support of this war commenced in the year 1754, and continued until the year 1767, before the expenses were finally ascertained and wound up	150,442,820
Deduct the peace establishment, at 2,797,916l. for fourteen years	39,170,824
Net sum applicable to the war	£111,271,996

TABLE XXIX.

PEACE ESTABLISHMENT.

	£
The Civil List	836,000
The Navy	900,000
The Army	900,000
The Ordnance	80,000
Miscellaneous expenses	50,000
Total	£2,766,000

TABLE XXX.

Official Accounts of the Net Revenue of Great Britain.

Customs, Excise, Stamps, Land and Assessed Taxes, and Post-Office—showing the Progress of Revenue. (Moreau.)

	Years: W for years of War, P for years of Peace.		Customs.	Excise.	Stamps.	Land and Assessed Taxes.	Post Office.
Ending 25th March.	War	1760	1,969,933	3,847,349	263,207	We have carefully examined a great number of Official Documents laid before Parliament on the Revenue of Land and Assessed Taxes of Great Britain, but we have not been able to find any materials to exhibit the Net produce paid into the Exchequer prior to 1790. (Moreau.)	83,493
	W	61	1,888,151	4,612,220	280,751		86,689
	W	62	1,858,417	4,592,523	265,614		77,795
	W	63	2,249,663	4,480,147	278,914		97,833
	P	64	2,169,472	4,808,610	278,269		116,182
	P	65	2,271,231	4,732,307	281,914		157,571
	P	66	2,448,280	4,921,421	285,266		161,943
	P	67	2,355,830	4,800,650	In all the Official Documents we have examined we have not found any materials distinguishing the Net Revenue of Stamps, from 1767 to 1789.		161,944
	P	68	2,445,016	5,013,534			165,783
	P	69	2,639,086	4,731,309			164,760
	P	70	2,546,143	4,613,217			156,062
	P	71	2,642,129	4,507,766			155,543
	P	72	2,525,596	4,659,157			165,503
	P	73	2,439,017	4,782,446			167,176
	P	74	2,567,769	4,570,835			164,077
	P	75	2,481,031	5,031,006			173,188
	W	76	2,480,402	4,866,813			167,482
	W	77	2,229,105	5,079,106			157,575
	W	78	2,162,681	5,074,102			137,994
	W	79	2,502,273	5,287,047			139,248
	W	80	2,723,920	5,749,060			136,409
	W	81	2,791,428	5,828,022			154,157
	W	82	2,861,563	5,758,657			137,325
	W	83	2,848,320	5,515,009			152,858
	W	84	3,326,639	5,534,237			197,655
	P	85	4,592,091	5,462,385			265,679
	P	86	4,076,911	5,530,643			287,509
	P	87	3,673,807	6,071,952			283,005
	P	88	3,780,770	6,503,655			294,792
	P	89	3,686,994	6,861,067			319,297
	P	90	3,357,001	7,255,263	1,214,969	3,622,542	320,000
	P	91	3,764,483	8,082,391	1,293,432	2,776,810	342,000
	P	92	3,925,386	8,524,523	1,385,495	3,013,839	339,000
	P	93	3,988,591	8,780,020	1,420,546	2,865,509	382,484
	W	94	3,947,372	8,333,918	1,361,753	2,918,249	379,000
	W	95	3,521,236	8,778,933	1,411,074	2,900,767	431,000
	W	96	2,535,184	9,591,673	1,671,133	2,800,931	419,000
	W	97	3,612,725	9,588,468	1,771,976	3,090,682	491,000
Ending 5th January.	W	98	4,055,608	10,470,610	2,093,716	3,310,847	586,000
	W	99	5,570,675	11,212,725	2,433,789	3,903,154	669,000
	W	1800	7,498,614	12,121,523	2,642,497	4,325,172	713,000
	W	01	6,763,297	10,832,749	2,645,375	4,302,821	716,000
	W	02	5,871,200	11,260,110	2,876,986	4,187,541	827,000
	P	03	6,058,626	14,644,159	3,025,323	4,783,047	932,000
	W	04	7,179,620	17,975,373	3,177,604	5,309,699	835,000
	W	05	8,357,871	20,604,143	3,354,322	5,309,130	924,000
	W	06	9,084,458	22,281,539	3,918,964	5,545,887	1,057,000
	W	07	9,733,813	23,184,067	4,132,516	5,815,989	1,101,000
	W	08	9,207,735	23,808,226	4,274,555	6,384,750	1,082,000
	W	09	8,797,823	24,650,712	4,536,311	6,909,788	1,076,000
	W	10	10,259,806	22,390,397	5,124,739	7,863,231	1,168,000
	W	11	10,819,151	24,767,772	5,336,455	7,177,897	1,253,000
	W	12	9,436,321	24,900,054	5,090,478	6,868,230	1,274,000
	W	13	10,029,747	22,472,113	5,078,837	6,985,544	1,322,000
	W	14	10,291,327	24,113,252	5,344,486	7,433,496	1,403,000
	W	15	10,960,773	25,264,076	5,601,791	7,543,865	1,462,000
	W	16	10,526,764	26,537,633	5,869,376	7,299,241	1,541,000

TABLE XXXI.

Public Revenue and its Progress, from the commencement of the Reign of George III. to the General Peace of Paris, November 20th, 1815, when the Boundaries of France were established:—Comprising the Land and Malt Taxes, the Customs, Excise, Stamps, Assessed Taxes, and Miscellaneous Duties: the "Net" sums which passed into the Exchequer.

Period	Year	£.
	1761	8,800,000
	62	8,950,000
	63	9,100,000
Period of Peace.	64	9,250,000
	65	9,300,000
	66	9,350,000
	67	9,200,000
	68	9,250,000
	69	9,350,000
	70	9,510,000
	71	9,650,000
	72	9,850,000
	73	10,066,661
	74	10,285,673
American and French War.	75	10,138,061
	76	10,265,405
	77	10,604,013
	78	10,732,405
	79	11,192,141
	80	12,255,214
	81	12,434,936
	82	12,593,297
	83	11,962,718
	84	12,905,519
Peace.	85	14,871,520
	86	15,196,112
	87	15,360,857
	88	15,572,971
	89	15,565,642
Peace.	1790	15,986,068
	91	16,631,000
	92	19,382,435
	93	17,674,395
French Revolutionary W.	94	17,440,809
	95	17,374,890
	96	18,243,876
	97	18,668,925
	98	20,518,780
	99	23,607,945
	1800	29,604,008
	01	28,085,829
Peace.	02	28,221,183
	03	38,401,738
War with France.	04	49,335,978
	05	49,652,471
	06	53,698,124
	07	58,902,291
	08	61,524,118
	09	63,042,746
	10	66,029,349
	11	64,427,371
	12	63,327,432
	13	63,211,422
	14	70,926,215
	15	72,131,214
	16	76,834,494
	Total	£1,386,468,445

TABLE XXXII.

Showing the MILITARY, ORDNANCE and NAVAL EXPENSES in each Year, from the Accession of George III. to the Peace of Paris in 1815.

MILITARY SERVICES.

		£.			£.			£.
War.	1761	8,344,030	War.	1780	6,589,080	War.	1799	11,840,000
	62	7,657,205		81	7,723,912		1800	11,941,767
	63	4,593,805		82	7,645,237	Peace.	01	12,117,839
Peace.	64	2,267,867		83	5,577,474		02	11,211,795
	65	1,784,856	Peace.	84	3,153,191		03	11,786,619
	66	1,910,413		85	1,689,169		04	19,108,859
	67	1,[illegible]37,314		86	1,594,115		05	18,581,127
	68	1,472,484		87	1,831,069		06	18,507,518
	69	1,497,921		88	1,979,020		07	19,875,946
	70	1,547,931		89	1,917,062		08	19,439,189
	71	1,810,319		90	1,609,574		09	21,144,770
	72	1,551,428		91	2,062,548		10	20,337,080
	73	1,516,402		92	1,819,460		11	21,287,004
	74	1,549,720	War.	93	3,993,715		12	25,174,756
War.	75	1,597,051		94	6,641,060		13	33,089,334
	76	3,500,366		95	11,610,008		14	33,797,556
	77	3,797,632		96	14,911,899		15	23,172,136
	78	4,333,666		97	15,488,083		16	13,047,582
	79	6,013,082		98	12,852,844		Total	£514,432,059

ORDNANCE EXPENSES.

	£.		£.		£.
1760 to 1788	17,079,011	1797	1,643,056	1808	3,713,071
		98	1,303,580	09	5,311,675
		99	1,500,000	10	3,819,466
89	459,444	1800	1,695,956	11	4,352,628
90	455,872	01	1,639,055	12	4,620,147
91	594,678	02	1,952,274	13	4,464,273
92	422,001	03	1,125,921	14	4,480,729
93	783,776	04	3,737,091	15	2,963,891
94	1,345,008	05	4,436,994	16	2,661,711
95	2,321,010	06	4,328,144		
96	1,954,665	07	3,321,216	Total	£82,526,345

NAVAL CHARGES.

		£.			£.			£.
War.	1761	5,072,602	War.	1780	6,777,362	War.	1799	13,642,000
	62	5,688,012		81	8,603,884		1800	13,619,079
Peace.	63	1,975,661		82	7,095,228	P.	01	15,857,017
	64	2,953,200		83	6,197,832		02	13,833,573
	65	2,886,876	Peace.	84	3,086,269	War.	03	10,211,278
	66	2,680,683		85	2,054,507		04	12,350,606
	67	1,400,409		86	2,381,526		05	15,035,630
	68	1,238,883		87	2,286,000		06	15,864,341
	69	1,828,057		88	2,236,000		07	17,400,337
	70	1,580,467		89	2,328,570		08	18,317,547
	71	2,967,409		90	2,483,636		09	19,578,467
	72	1,813,164		91	4,008,405		10	19,829,434
	73	1,833,573		92	1,485,482		11	20,935,894
	74	2,052,917	War.	93	3,971,975		12	20,442,149
	75	1,599,493		94	5,525,331		13	21,212,011
War.	76	3,092,967		95	6,315,523		14	21,961,566
	77	4,053,666		96	11,883,693		15	16,373,870
	78	4,779,151		97	13,033,673		16	9,519,325
	79	4,106,374		98	13,449,388			
							Total	£453,864,992

To face page 154.]

In each Y to the House of Commons. (Moreau.)

Years ending 5th Jan.	ON A Interest on the Permanent Debt.	Charges of Managem	ubsidies, Loans, mittances, and Advances to other Countries.	Issues from appointed Funds for Local Purposes, including the Remittances to Ireland.	Miscellaneous Services at Home and Abroad.	Charges of Collection of the Revenue.	Exchequer Bills diminished.	Total Amount of Expenditure, including the Sinking Fund.
	£.		£.	£.	£	£.	£.	£.
1794	8,921,835		,196,200	200,000	1,125,512	1,122,271	..	22,754,366
95	9,296,247		ly 4,000	..	517,654	1,150,346	1,737,000	29,305,477
96	9,871,896		810,500	..	861,468	1,167,014	..	39,751,091
97	10,856,632		99,500	..	1,245,454	1,174,525	562,400	40,761,683
98	12,923,263		..	1,454,069	1,470,239	1,554,720	..	50,739,857
99	12.251.184	206,528	190,012	2,000,000	827,600	1,614,990	..	51,241,798
1800	15,689,143	212,227	225,000	3,000,000	1,177,958	1,639,770	..	59,296,061
01	15,888,263	238,294	,613,178	2,000,000	1,255,589	1,828,124	..	61,617,988
02	17,139,720	236,773	200,114	2,500,000	2,305,427	2,025,469	5,492,000	73,072,468
03	18,144,873	263,105	..	2,000,000	3,494,320	1,982,079	4,132,100	62,373,480
04	17,728,945	247,538	..	2,117,444	2,800,500	1,955,368	..	54,912,890
05	18,925,797	267,787	..	3,738,292	1,882,075	2,135,177	..	67,619,475
06	19,598,306	271,912	..	3,211,062	2,845,728	2,257,186	..	76,056,796
07	20,410,716	292,127	..	1,768,000	2,766,698	2,375,825	..	75,154,548
08	20,701,252	297,758	..	3,681,250	1,227,383	2,699,048	..	78,369,689
09	20,771,872	210,549	,400,000	2,569,167	2,920,490	2,816,569	..	84,797,080
10	20,996,653	292,775	,050,000	2,921,528	1,459,434	2,886,201	929,100	88,792,551
11	21,555,401	217,826	,060,102	5,294,417	2,270,868	2,934,876	877,700	94,360,728
12	22,100,845	228,350	,977,747	4,482,293	1,962,636	3,096,582	..	99,004,241
13	23,890,912	233,706	,315,838	2,868,500	5,652,231	3,273,243	..	107,644,085
14	24,055,666	238,828	,294,416	4,700,417	4,010,350	3,504,988	..	122,235,660
15	26,292,496	242,264	,024,624	8,723,982	2,384,592	3,573,261	..	129,742,399
16	27,176,930	259,970	,035,248	7,277,082	3,871,178	3,663,663	16,499,800	130,305,958
	419,669,894		,528,470	66,482,443	49,855,874	51,421,425	30,230,100	1,699,910,239

mmencement of 1703.

1700	1701	1702
£.	£.	£.
56,620	697,955	581,886

e Reign of George II.

BLE XXXVI.

Years	uce.	Net Produce.	Average Ten Years. Gross.	Net.
From 1730 t	16	7,471,948	892,071	747,194
From 1749 t	18	7,495,073	971,041	949,507
From 1750 t	79	9,505,111	1,335,097	950,511
	97	15,753,597	2,161,939	1,575,359

TABLE XXXVII.

An Account of the Ordinary Revenue of Ireland since the Union, including only, and showing the progress of, the Customs, Excise, and Taxes, Stamps, Postage, Poundage and Pells, Fees, and Casualties. (Moreau.)

Years.	Gross Receipts.	Net produce applicable to the National objects and for Payments into the Exchequer.	Charges of Management.
	£.	£.	£.
1802	3,738,755	3,056,610	383,529
03	4,830,352	4,036,592	411,045
04	4,401,449	3,662,069	440,661
05	5,291,979	4,476,852	449,094
06	5,329,869	4,611,331	461,468
07	5,816,777	5,125,918	455,653
08	6,708,944	5,896,818	528,663
09	6,823,848	5,921,670	646,692
10	6,551,552	5,551,729	788,318
11	6,233,622	4,851,644	877,507
12	6,698,537	5,488,887	898,073
13	7,326,921	6,239,590	895,085
14	7,478,932	6,454,932	897,591
15	8,118,777	6,944,756	969,435
16	8,335,985	7,128,607	1,039,623

TABLE XXXVIII.

Ordinary and Extraordinary Resources of Ireland since the Union: Loans included.

Years ending 5th Jan.	Gross Receipts within the Year.	Net produce applicable to the National objects and to Payments into the Exchequer.	Payments into the Exchequer.	Charges of Management.
	£.	£.	£.	£.
1802	8,189,660	7,505,497	6,838,597	308,529
03	9,217,516	8,422,705	7,697,789	411,155
04	6,922,207	6,181,375	5,305,572	440,716
05	10,870,630	10,050,116	8,841,069	449,175
06	10,609,754	9,889,361	8,620,054	451,545
07	10,656,947	9,963,159	8,656,221	455,752
08	10,064,475	9,250,132	7,746,934	528,771
09	12,468,179	11,564,289	10,192,019	646,790
10	11,090,333	10,089,817	8,795,830	788,318
11	12,181,643	10,790,259	9,559,708	877,681
12	12,884,814	11,633,172	10,309,862	898,264
13	13,907,203	12,816,610	11,469,314	895,121
14	15,395,146	14,368,146	12,968,470	897,653
15	16,235,989	15,058,695	13,635,899	969,560
16	19,757,157	18,546,928	17,168,432	1,039,731

TABLE XXXIX.

An Abstract of the General Official Account presented to the House of Commons 26th May, 1815, showing the Gross and Net Produce of the Ordinary Revenues of Scotland during the War, from 1803 to 1815,—the Years ending 5th January,—Customs, Excise, Land and Assessed Taxes, Post-Office, War, Property, and Income Taxes included.

Years.	Total Gross Produce.	Total Net Produce.	War Taxes.
	£.	£.	£.
1804	2,784,429	2,246,027	193,449
05	2,759,278	2,271,972	536,961
06	3,227,005	2,692,624	728,907
07	3,805,108	3,182,677	8[illegible]8,591
08	4,385,442	3,558,783	1,114,724
09	4,201,810	3,544,100	1,011,517
10	4,439,157	3,632,831	1,157,004
11	4,882,206	4,188,814	1,614,254
12	4,699,752	4,031,347	1,513,707
13	4,988,965	4,296,796	1,634,198
14	5,294,577	4,419,751	1,869,806
15	5,368,487	4,463,013	1,796,964

TABLE XL.

ESTIMATED PUBLIC REVENUE.

	£.
The Year preceding the Death of William III.	3,895,205
Average of Queen Anne's Reign	5,691,803
At the Death of George I.	6,762,643
The Year preceding the Death of George II.	8,523,540
At the Accession of George III.	8,800,000
In the Year 1788	15,572,971
——— 1800	29,604,008
——— 1810	66,029,349
——— 1815	72,131,214

TABLE XLI.

GENERAL OFFICIAL ACCOUNTS of the ORDINARY and EXTRAORDINARY RESOURCES constituting the Public Income of Great Britain and Ireland: distinguishing the Amount of the Gross Receipts, Rate of Collection, Signature and Date of the Accounts: Showing its progress in the Five principal Heads of Revenue,—Customs, Excise, Stamps, Land and Assessed Taxes, and Post-Office, from 5th January, 1817, to

Years.	Customs.	Rate of Collection.	Excise.	Rate of Collection.	Stamps.	Rate of Collection.	Land and Assessed Taxes.	Rate of Collection.	Post-Office.	Rate of Collection.	Name, Signature, and Date of the Account.
	£.	£. s. d.	£.	£. s. d.	£.	£. s. d.	£.	£. s. d.	£.	£. s. d.	
1817	10,714,762	10 15 6	21,239,509	4 3 1	6,255,956	2 10 6	7,347,473	4 0 6	2,002,566	23 8 3	S. R. Lushington, 25 Mar. 1817
18	15,866,673	10 1 2	24,713,720	5 17 1	7,270,723	3 0 9	8,354,761	4 7 3	2,093,028	30 14 0	S. R. Lushington, 25 Mar. 1818
19	15,946,776	10 12 9	28,316,919	4 17 7	7,330,637	3 1 3	8,290,174	4 10 6	2,139,263	31 10 9	S. R. Lushington, 25 Mar. 1819
20	14,734,562	10 19 6	27,955,810	4 19 4	7,113,266	3 9 2	8,172,851	4 15 1	2,129,821	26 18 2	S. R. Lushington, 1 May 1820
21	14,100,521	10 9 10	31,298,733	4 10 6	7,027,837	3 3 0	8,182,819	4 13 3	2,068,061	28 9 2	S. R. Lushington, 24 Mar. 1821
22	14,789,705	10 0 1	31,812,985	4 9 4	7,078,790	3 3 10	8,042,304	4 17 3	2,044,802	30 3 6	S. R. Lushington, 22 Mar. 1822
23	14,364,710	10 15 2	31,190,948	4 7 3	7,106,745	2 18 0	7,538,826	5 1 11	2,128,926	23 4 2	J. C. Herries, 11 Mar. 1823
24	15,504,869	10 2 3	29,308,986	4 11 3	7,216,373	2 15 0	6,595,820	5 12 9	2,154,294	26 8 4	J. C. Herries, 11 Mar. 1824
25	15,491,158	9 8 9	30,779,302	4 5 8	7,672,411	2 16 7	5,228,197	5 15 8	2,255,239	26 12 6	J. C. Herries, 10 Mar. 1825
26	20,367,652	7 7 9	26,089,408	4 16 0	7,881,150	2 6 11	5,183,012	5 11 10	2,367,567	25 11 10	J. C. Herries, 20 Mar. 1826
27	20,582,924	7 9 4	22,541,969	5 13 7	7,101,503	2 12 5	5,030,028	5 14 9	2,392,272	28 8 11	J. C. Herries, 24 Mar. 1827
28	21,009,052	7 1 10	22,224,443	5 11 3	7,275,552	2 12 8	5,092,078	5 16 6	2,278,412	30 8 11	G. R. Dawson, 6 Mar. 1828
29	20,608,710	7 1 1	24,802,507	4 17 6	7,605,107	2 19 3	5,169,874	5 8 7	2,287,961	29 0 2	G. R. Dawson, 23 Mar. 1829
30	20,571,837	6 13 9	23,052,186	5 6 4	7,586,318	2 10 11	5,212,569	5 10 3	2,265,482	29 16 2	G. R. Dawson, 6 Mar. 1830
31	21,084,524	6 2 10	22,354,887	5 8 5	7,555,065	2 10 4	5,301,279	5 6 4	2,301,432	30 3 4	T. Spring Rice, 24 Mar. 1831
32											
33											
34											
35											
36											
37											
38											
39											
40											

TABLE XLIV.

General Official Accounts of Ordinary and Extraordinary Resources constituting the Public Income of Ireland, independent of Loans; distinguishing the Amount of Gross Receipts, Net Produce, Payments into the Exchequer, Total Discharge applicable to National Objects, the Signatures and Dates of the Accounts; the Years ending 5th January, from 1817 to

PROGRESS OF REVENUE.

Years.	Gross Receipts.	Net Produce applicable to National Objects, and to Payments into the Exchequer.	Payments into the Exchequer.	Signature and Date of the Account.
	£.	£.	£.	
1817	6,524,916	6,300,766	4,941,465	G. Cavendish, 25 March, 1817
18	5,672,518	4,931,323	4,438,161	S. R. Lushington, 25 March, 1818
19	5,775,730	5,076,289	4,632,091	S. R. Lushington, 25 March, 1819
20	5,474,783	4,691,680	4,304,497	S. R. Lushington, 1 May, 1820
21	4,918,116	4,066,275	3,652,108	S. R. Lushington, 24 March, 1821
22	6,171,314	5,255,682	4,843,798	S. R. Lushington, 23 March, 1822
23	5,131,152	5,134,884	3,690,973	J. C. Herries, 24 March, 1823
24	4,592,335	4,586,268	3,199,128	J. C. Herries, 11 March, 1824
25	4,910,029	4,927,849	3,690,090	J. C. Herries, 10 March, 1825
26	5,007,260	4,981,250	3,624,799	J. C. Herries, 20 March, 1826
57	4,649,306	4,789,446	3,622,593	J. C. Herries, 24 March, 1827
28	4,676,160	4,797,959	3,682,341	G. R. Dawson, 6 March, 1828
29	4,755,156	4,839,312	3,749,401	G. R. Dawson, 20 March, 1829
30	4,568,617	4,660,983	3,654,609	G. R. Dawson, 3 March. 1830
31	4,313,609	4,409,632	3,530,751	T. Spring Rce, 24 March, 1831
32				
33				
34				
35				
36				
37				
38				
39				
40				

I.

E—18

of the

RE
Civil D
Prevent

nd Land
nary rev

Perman
l Paym
l Paym
Excheq
nt . .

Privy
nces to
Highnes
Lieutena
es and c
artment
nd Ordn
n the C
Civil L

Justice i
Crimina
Conv
Convi
Other

nd Retir

ingencie

Effec
Nc
Effec

Effec
Nc
Effec

Effec
Nc
Effec

or prom
s Reve
rks
out of
Public
Charg
e and
laims,
eous Se
s of Pa
st . .

Termi
Corre

, Trea

O aym
e of

	1
	Net receipts.
	£.
Bal	. .
Cust	98,32
Exci	61,65
Sta	55,97
Tax	06,39
Post Dut	84,66
C ar	76,63
	. .
Ded	. .
Tot	. .
Oth	. .
	. .
Pa	
Cha Div	. .
F e si I	. .
Issu si	
Civ	67,00
Pen	49,94
Con	55,61
Mis	80,42
Arm	09,37
Na	02,33
Ord	69,15
Mis	95,66
Ded N Is	
Adv	. .
Tot to	. .
Sur	. .
	. .

R. I

TABLE XLVI.

General Official Accounts of Ordinary and Extraordinary Resources constituting the Public Income of Great Britain and Ireland, independent of Loans; distinguishing the Amount of Gross Receipts, Charges of Management, Net Produce, Payments into the Exchequer, Total Discharge applicable to National Objects, and the Signatures and Dates of the Account. The Years ending 5th January, from 1817 to

PROGRESS OF REVENUE.

Years.	Gross Receipts within the Year.	Charges of Management.	Net Produce applicable to National Objects, and to Payments into the Exchequer.	Payments into the Exchequer.	Signature and Date of the Account.
	£.	£.	£.	£.	
1817	81,901,801	4,755,327	72,880,186	68,605,355	S. R. Lushington, 25 March, 1817
18	61,736,344	4,351,836	55,836,888	52,240,887	S. R. Lushington, 25 March, 1818
19	74,610,318	4,403,756	68,348,714	65,093,375	S. R. Lushington, 25 March, 1819
20	61,872,588	4,249,236	56,040,108	53,388,248	S. R. Lushington, 1 May, 1820
21	63,828,420	4,136,641	57,304,650	54,534,262	S. R. Lushington, 24 March, 1821
22	64,784,460	4,161,833	58,108,855	55,334,192	S. R. Lushington, 23 March, 1822
23	63,801,494	4,160,270	63,104,999	54,414,650	J. C. Herries, 24 March, 1823
24	67,476,515	4,105,182	66,236,776	57,672,999	J. C. Herries, 11 March, 1824
25	69,310,912	3,967,641	67,516,785	59,362,403	J. C. Herries, 10 March, 1825
26	68,111,052	3,898,377	65,324,376	57,273,869	J. C. Herries, 20 March, 1826
27	63,408,347	4,030,337	62,472,259	54,894,989	J. C. Herries, 24 March, 1827
28	63,768,671	3,966,456	62,306,214	54,932,518	G. R. Dawson, 6 March, 1828
29	64,662,799	3,890,151	62,710,108	55,187,142	G. R. Dawson, 23 March, 1829
30	59,723,483	3,797,038	58,008,437	50,786,682	G. R. Dawson, 6 March, 1830
31	59,308,872	3,713,944	56,884,798	50,056,616	T. Spring Rice, 24 March, 1831
32					
33					
34					
35					
36					
37					
38					
39					
40					

TABLE XLVII.

EXPENDITURE of GREAT BRITAIN and IRELAND, under the several Heads of Interest of Debt, Civil List, Navy, Army, &c., in each Year, from 1817 to 1822.

Years.	National Debt. Reduction, Interest, and Charges of Management.	Interest on Exchequer Bills.	Loans and Remittances.	Civil List.	Courts of Justice, Allowances to the Royal Family, Miscellaneous, &c.	Civil Government of Scotland.	Payments in anticipation, Bounties, &c.	Navy.	Ordnance.	Army.	Miscellaneous Services.	To be deducted.	TOTAL.
	£.	£.	£	£.	£.	£.	£.	£.	£.	£.	£.	£.	£.
1817	45,004,889	2,196,177	4,312,287	1,028,000	696,739	128,514	358,582	9,516,325	2,661,711	13,047,582	3,909,161	2,714,146	80,185,828 *
18	44,108,233	1,815,926	75,857	1,191,168	1,112,494	130,646	451,403	6,473,062	1,435,401	9,614,864	2,466,483	165,039	68,710,502 *
19	44,648,738	2,200,414	60,284	1,236,167	1,139,912	129,627	483,471	6,521,714	1,407,807	8,517,044	2,620,891	144,636	68,821,437 †
20	46,467,999	779,922	53,101	1,181,056	1,357,610	129,988	389,167	6,395,552	1,538,209	9,450,650	1,855,948	150,376	69,448,899 ‡
21	47,070,927	1,849,219	50,357	1,062,011	1,072,202	132,080	438,339	6,387,799	1,401,585	8,926,423	2,616,700	156,906	70,850,741 ‡
22	47,130,171	2,219,602	48,464	1,054,877	1,203,946	133,077	476,873	5,943,879	1,337,923	8,932,779	3,870,042	163,739	72,198,017
				6,763,279				41,238,331	9,782,636	58,489,342	17,339,225		430 215,424

The Form of the Accounts was altered in 1823. (See Tab. XLIII). * Signed C. Arbuthnot, 21 March, 1817. † S. R. Lushington, 25 March. ‡ C. Arbuthnot, 2 March.

TABLE XLVIII.

ALLOWANCES to the ROYAL FAMILY, PENSIONS, &c., in each Year, from 1817 to

	£.
1817 . . .	427,009
18 . . .	447,637
19 . . .	457,678
20 . . .	472,233
21 . . .	327,066
22 . . .	439,299
23 . . .	378,432
24 . . .	377,776
25 . . .	371,644
26 . . .	366,028
27 . . .	364,268
28 . . .	365,908
29 . . .	370,867
30 . . .	378,691
31 . . .	370,018
32 . . .	370,018
33 . . .	
34 . . .	
35 . . .	
36 . . .	
37 . . .	
38 . . .	
39 . . .	
40 . . .	

TABLE L.

Public Revenue of England, from the Conquest to the present Time.

	Anno.	£.
William the Conqueror	1066	400,000
William Rufus	1087	350,000
Henry I.	1100	300,000
Stephen	1135	250,000
Henry II.	1154	200,000
Richard I.	1189	150,000
John	1199	100,000
Henry III.	1216	80,000
Edward I.	1272	150,000
Edward II.	1307	100,000
Edward III.	1327	154,139
Richard II.	1377	130,000
Henry IV.	1399	100,000
Henry V.	1413	76,643
Henry VI.	1422	64,976
Edward IV.	1460	100,000
Edward V.	1483	100,800
Richard III.	1483	100,000
Henry VII.	1485	400,000
Henry VIII.	1509	800,000
Edward VI.	1547	400,000
Mary	1553	450,000
Elizabeth	1558	500,000
James I.	1602	600,000
Charles I.	1625	895,819
Commonwealth	1648	1,517,247
Charles II.	1648	1,800,000
James II.	1685	2,001,855
William III. and Mary	1688	3,895,225
Anne (1706)	1704	5,691,803
George I.	1714	6,762,643
George II.	1727	8,522,540
George III. (1783)	1760	15,372,971
Ditto	1800	36,728,000
Ditto	1815	71,153,142
George IV. average 1820 to	1826	58,000,000
Ditto ditto 1826 to	1830	60,000,000
William IV. average of last three years	1840	46,620,165

TABLE LI.

An Account of the quantity of *fine* Silver coined in Twenty Shillings or a Pound sterling; the quantity of standard Silver of eleven oz. two dwts. fine, and eighteen dwts. alloy, contained in twenty shillings or a pound sterling in the different reigns from Edward I. to William IV. A similar account with respect to Gold: an account of the proportional value of *fine* Gold to fine Silver, according to the number of grains contained in Coins, calculated in graine and one thousand parts of Troy weight. (Taken from Essays on Money, Exchanges, and Political Economy, by H. James.)

A. D.	Anno Regni.	Number of grains of fine Silver in twenty Shillings or a Pound sterling, as coined by Mint Indentures.	Number of grains of standard Silver of eleven oz. two dwts. fine in twenty Shillings, or a Pound sterling, as coined by the Mint Indentures.	Number of grains of fine Gold in twenty Shillings, or a Pound sterling, as coined by the Mint Indentures.	Number of grains of standard Gold, twenty-two carats fine in twenty Shillings, or a pound sterling, as coined by the Mint Indentures.	Proportionate value of fine Gold to fine Silver, according to the quantity of each metal contained in the coins.
		Grains.	Grains.	Grains.	Grains.	Gold to Silver.
1066	Conquest	4,995,000	5,400,000	——	——	——
1280	8 Edw. I.	4,995,000	5,400,000	——	——	——
1344	18 Edw. III.	4,933,333	5,333,000	407,990	445,080	1 to 12,901
1349	23 ——	4,440,000	4,800,000	383,705	418,580	1 — 11,571
1356	30 ——	3,996,000	4,320,000	358,125	390,682	1 — 11,158
1401	3 Hen. IV.	3,996,000	4,320,000	358,125	390,682	1 — 11,158
1421	9 Hen. V.	3,330,000	4,320,000	322,312	351,613	1 — 10,331
1464	4 Edw. IV.	2,664,000	3,600,000	257,850	281,291	1 — 10,331
1465	5 ——	2,664,000	2,880,000	238,750	260,454	1 — 11,158
1470	49 Hen. VI.	2,664,000	2,880,000	238,750	260,454	1 — 11,158
1482	22 Edw. IV.	2,664,000	2,880,000	238,750	260,454	1 — 11,158
1509	1 Hen. VIII.	2,664,000	2,880,000	238,750	260,454	1 — 11,158
1527	18 ——	2,368,000	2,880,000	210,149	229,253	1 — 11,208
1543	34 ——	2,000,000	2,560,000	191,666	209,090	1 — 10,434
1545	36 ——	1,200,000	2,162,162	176,000	192,000	1 — 6,818
1546	37 ——	800,000	1,297,297	160,000	174,545	1 — 5,000
1547	1 Edw. VI.	800,000	864,864	160,000	174,545	1 — 5,000
1549	3 ——	800,000	864,864	155,294	169,412	1 — 5,000
1551*	5 ——	400,000	864,864	——	169,412	1 — 5,150
——	——	1,760,000	——	——	——	——
1552	6 ——	1,768,000	1,902,702	160,000	169,412	1 — 11,000
1553	1 Mary.	1,760,000	1,911,351	160,000	174,545	1 — 11,050
1560	2 Elizabeth.	1,766,000	1,902,702	159,166	174,545	1 — 11,057
1600	43 ——	1,718,000	1,920,064	160,000	171,940	1 — 10,904
1604	2 James I.	1,718,000	1,858,064	157,612	154,838	1 — 12,109
1626	2 Charles I.	1,718,709	1,858,064	141,935	148,487	1 — 13,346
1666	18 Chas. II.	1,718,709	1,858,064	128,780	129,438	1 — 14,485
1717	3 Geo. I.	1,718,709	1,858,064	113,001	123,274	1 — 15,209
1816†	56 Geo. III.	1,614,545	1,745,454	113,001	123,274	1 — 14,287

* The coinage of debased Silver money in the fifth year of Edward VI. of three oz. three dwts. fine, ought more properly to be considered as tokens. The sum of £120,000 only was coined.

† The Government having taken the coinage of Silver into their own hands, there is at present no fixed price paid to the public by the Mint for standard Silver; and supposing the Government to continue the present Mint regulations, and to keep Gold at 77*s.* 10½*d.* an oz., as the price of Silver varies, the relative value of Gold to Silver will vary in the same proportion.

PART II.

ORIGIN, PROGRESS, AND PRESENT STATE OF THE NATIONAL DEBT AND FUNDING SYSTEM.

FIRST PERIOD.

FROM THE EARLIEST TIMES TO THE ACCESSION OF GEORGE III.

Origin of the National Debt.—Measures adopted by the kings of England to borrow money in the earliest times.—Attempt of the kings and governments to defraud their creditors.—Resolution of the British people in insisting on being repaid the money lent.—Second method of borrowing.—Funding system introduced by William III.—carried into execution in all its essential branches in the same reign.—Original amount of the present national debt, and its total increase during the same reign.—Its progress, the measures adopted to increase it, and its total amount in the succeeding reign.—When exchequer bills first made their appearance, and when the sinking fund was first established.—How the present Consols originated, and the original amount of that stock.—State of the public debt in the time of George I. and the amount redeemed.—Its progress in the reign of George II., and amount at the death of that monarch.—Objects to which the sums borrowed in this period were applied.

THE difficulties in which individuals are involved by their real wants, but oftener by their unruly passions, are the source of their debts. The debts of nations have not a different origin. When the ordinary resources of a country were insufficient to carry into effect the private views, or impolitic wars, of the despots who ruled, or the ministers who directed it, they simply resorted to the expedient of borrowing: but when the sums lent were inadequate to the increased expenditure, they had recourse to all sorts of schemes, deceptions, and contrivances, the better to delude the lenders, and allure their avarice. Such is the origin of the funding system.

The kings of England, like those of all other nations, have contracted debts from the most remote antiquity. As early as the 12th century Richard I. pawned the revenues of the crown, "for the payment of monies borrowed to defray the expenses of the fanatical conquest of the Holy Land." Henry III. pawned the crown jewels, the regal ornaments, and the robes of state [a]. Edward I. borrowed money to pay the debts of his father, in order to get his soul "out of purgatory"; as the record states, "ad exonerationem animæ Henrici patris nostri." Richard II. was deposed for extorting 1,100,000*l.* sterling under pretext of borrowing, which was never repaid: this was one of the chief causes of the horrible civil wars of York and Lancaster [b]. In 1346, Edward III. ordered a sum of money to be lent to him. Henry IV. obliged the rich men of the kingdom to lend him money upon the growing taxes. (See Macpherson's History of Commerce.) But Henry VIII. escaped the punishment he so justly merited for defrauding his creditors. He compelled the parliament to pass two acts offering him "all the money he had received in loans"; thus "discharging him of all obligations he had come under, and all suits that might arise thereupon." [c] Elizabeth found the people quite indifferent as to any form of religion, but far otherwise in money matters: they insisted on the payment of the sums advanced to her predecessors; a demand she was wise enough to comply with. The political chameleon, Burleigh, counselled her to lay the foundation of public credit; and never did that versatile statesman give her better advice, during the 40 years he administered the affairs of the state [d]. The republic contracted a large debt; and

[a] Stevens, History of Taxes.—"He was so poor, that it was more charitable to give him money than to a beggar."

[b] Bacon, Hist. Hen. VII. p. 46. The parliament particularly insisted on the payment of 372,000*l.*, or 1,100,000*l.* of our currency.

[c] Par. Hist. Henry VIII. p. 6.

[d] Nares' Life of Cecil, Lord Burleigh. In the review of this

at Cromwell's death it amounted to 2,474,290*l*. (Table I. Part II.) Charles, by shutting the Exchequer, (in 1672,) defrauded the creditors of the state of the sum of 2,800,000*l*.; but an arrangement took place, by which the sum of 664,226*l*. was left, at an interest of 19,927*l*. 18*s*. 9*d*½. This was the origin of the present national debt, and its whole amount before the Revolution.

In former times, loans were generally contracted for short periods: it was, moreover, an established principle or practice, that the funds assigned for the repayment should be sufficient to pay the principal and interest, and that, within a determinate number of years. In those times, the sums borrowed were measured by the amount of existing revenue; in fact they were mere anticipations of its proceeds for a fixed number of years. Whether that mode of borrowing was beneficial or injurious, compared with the present, the reader can best judge.

The system of our times is quite the reverse. *Modern* ministers are fully satisfied if they provide for the payment of the interest, without even contemplating the discharge of the principal; or if they *do* think about

work, the Edinburgh Editor has justly described this extraordinary man. "He paid", he says, "great attention to the interests of the state, and great attention to the interest of his own family also. He never deserted his friends till it was very inconvenient to stand by them. He was an excellent Protestant when it was not very advantageous to be a Papist. He recommended a tolerant policy to his mistress as strongly as he could recommend it without hazarding her favour. Never put to the rack any person from whom it did not seem probable that very useful information might be derived; and was so moderate in his desires, that he left *only* 300 distinct landed estates; though he might, as his honest servant assures us, have left much more, if he would have taken money out of the treasury for his own use, as many treasurers have done."

it, it is in conformity to the maxim of Linguet and Terney, "to cancel the capital by a general bankruptcy, *is in order to bring a state home.*"[a] The new system, not

[a] The maxim of Terney and Linguet, "that a bankruptcy is required in every century, and that the king risks nothing in borrowing, since he has the liberty to cancel the older debt whenever it suits his purpose," was practically adopted in France some centuries before that singular Abbé was born. That nation has, from the most remote periods, adopted the principle. Brisson, in his excellent history, enumerates only five French national bankruptcies: but in the financial history of that country may be found a great many more; and one act, that has never before nor since been perpetrated by that or any other nation, namely, the decree noticed by the Author of "Observations sur les Ministres de la France depuis 1660 à 1791," by which it was declared (in 1808) that "those who do not present their titles for liquidation within a certain period, shall forfeit their claims": this ordinance was not promulgated, but concealed, and after the term had expired, "le publique apprit son existence" (13 Jan. 1810). Such was the unprecedented, barefaced, and infamous proceeding by which the creditors of the state were robbed and mocked at the same time. But though France has committed more bankruptcies than any other nation, there is no doubt that she will commit yet more. The Monarchy, the Directory, the Republic, the Empire, all agreed to, and deemed essential, the financial tenet of Terney. The English have contracted and increased their debt in time of war; but, on the contrary, French financial talent has prodigiously increased theirs in time of peace. Napoleon, waging war throughout all Europe, added only 240,000l. sterling annually to the debt. When the Bourbons returned, the annual interest was scarcely two millions and a half sterling. They gave the extraordinary sum of forty millions sterling to the "Emigrés"; and in 1821, the French debt had increased to 3468 millions of francs! In 1829 it was largely augmented, and at the present moment, if we can rely upon the last statement, the debt amounts to the prodigious sum of 5135 millions of francs!!! There is good reason to fear, that the Citizen King's government will soon commence like the Legislative Assembly (27th April 1792), by issuing 300 millions monthly; continue, like the Convention (7th May 1792), issuing 800 and 1200 millions; and conclude, like the Directory (1797), by wiping out

imagined by the ancients, originated in the republics of Venice and Genoa—was considerably improved by the Dutch republicans—and, being imported by William III., has been carried by the English to the highest perfection.

With William III. a new era in the borrowing system commenced in England. James and Tyrconel had revolutionized Ireland. The obstinate Sarsfield continued the contest, after the runaway bigot was gone, and the battle of the Boyne won. William applied to individuals and public bodies, for money to defray the large expenses of that most cruel civil war: but the sums thus raised were soon expended. The Parliament also was liberal, but its grants were insufficient. William had recourse, therefore, to better expedients, and new contrivances, to supply the deficiency. The Long Annuities were created in 1692: 881,493*l.* were raised upon annuities of ninety-nine years, bearing interest at 10 per cent. until 1700, and at 7 per cent. after that year, with benefit of survivorship for the lives of the nominees of those who contributed[a]. The Short Annuities began in the following year (1693). A million was borrowed by this expedient; every subscriber receiving 14 per cent. for sixteen years, besides a beneficial "lottery ticket."[b] But the wants of the treasury went on increasing. The unfortunate and persecuted Patterson made his appearance, and contrived the scheme of the "Bank," of which Houblon was the first governor, and Smith, Ward, Tench, Huband, Patterson, and others were the first directors. (See charter of the Bank.)

two-thirds of the debt. However, the French five per cents are at 105. How forgetful—how ignorant—how incorrigible is the human race!

[a] 4 and 5 William and Mary, cap. 7.

[b] 6 William and Mary, cap. 7.

They lent William 1,200,000*l.*, *at* 8 *per cent. interest.* It appears, that they knew how to take advantage of the public distress; thus setting an example to their successors in the Bank direction.

The New East India Company was quarrelling with the Old one; and both were threatened with the loss of their monopoly. The New Company, to secure its privileges, came forward and offered two millions at 8 per cent.; with the proviso, that the principal should be repaid before the expiration of their charter in 1711: thereby hoping to perpetuate their monopoly. However, as the government never contemplated the repayment of the principal sums lent, either by the Company, or the Bank, we may safely consider these loans as perpetual annuities.

But William began to forget, that he had no other right to the crown, than what the free election of the nation gave him. He began to forget the "Bill of Rights," by which he was bound by the unanimous coalition of Whigs and Tories. He wished to continue the standing army; but this could not be effected without incurring the resentment of the Whigs, thus making enemies of those who placed him on the throne [a]. He also wished to preserve the illusory balance of power in Europe, and indulge his private revenge against the arch-infamous tyrant Louis XIV.; but this could not be done without money, which could not be obtained without fresh contrivances. To aid his master, the Chancellor Montague invented the scheme of issuing bills; thus "Exchequer Bills" first made their appearance (1696); and their issue has been continued at in-

[a] The Whigs, the Duke of Marlborough, Godolphin, and even the Princess Anne, were suspected of conspiring to dethrone William.

tervals ever since. New Lotteries were planned: the most exorbitant premiums were given for money: the natural consequence was, that the debt was considerably increased by these miscalculated operations. Public credit became so low, that out of the five millions granted to carry on the war, only two and a half, in Davenant's opinion, ever reached the Exchequer.

One of the constituent parts of the funding system is the reduction of interest from the higher to the lower denomination. This expedient, which has played so conspicuous a part in our days, was originally resorted to in 1699, when the higher interests were reduced to five per cent.[a]; as if it was the destiny of King William's reign to create, improve, and complete all the essential parts of the Funding System. From the 5th Nov. 1688 to 1702, 44,100,795*l.* were borrowed, and 34,034,518*l.* repaid, according to Grellier's History of the National Debt; thus leaving a national debt, at the end of this reign, of 16,394,702*l.* (Table II. Part II.)

ANNE.

When the grand-daughter of Hyde ascended the throne, the annual interest of the debt was 1,310,942*l.*; but the Whigs, who before were against the war, became all at once the greatest warriors and alliance-makers[b]. The efforts of the Tory party (whose chief leader, Rochester, was the queen's own cousin) were of no avail: the Whig faction ruled this woman by means of her confidante, Marlborough's wife; war was therefore declared, at the same time, against France and Spain.

[a] Par. Hist. Vol. X. Cunningham's History of Taxes.

[b] They formed the second grand alliance with Portugal and other powers. (See "Collection of Treaties"; and Chronological Tables.)

Soon after the commencement of the war, the most disadvantageous schemes to raise money were brought into the market. Annuities for ninety-nine years were granted at fifteen years' purchase[a]; annuities for lives followed; one life was rated at nine years' purchase; two lives at eleven years'; three at twelve years'[b]. No wonder that by such operations the Whigs ruined the national credit: in 1710, the "Tallies" and "Deficiencies" were sold in the public market, at forty per cent. discount. The Bank, taking advantage of this state of affairs, lent 400,000*l.* to the government without interest, on condition of being allowed to increase their capital, and of having their monopoly prolonged without any farther advance[c]. The East India Company followed their example; and, this time, were more generous, as they lent 1,200,000*l.* without interest; also on condition of having their monopoly continued.

However, the extensive and impolitic wars absorbing all these sums, Tontines, Lotteries, &c., were resorted to. Gambling was the last, but the most powerful resource of the government. The nation was infected with that irresistible passion, and as Pope has admirably described it,

> "Statesman and patriot ply alike the Stocks,
> Peeress and butler share alike the box,
> And judges job, and bishops bite the town,
> And mighty dukes pack cards for half-a-crown."

[a] Com. Jour. Vol. IX. p. 240. History of our National Debts, Part II. p. 45.

[b] Anne, sec. 2. cap. 3. Price, "On Civil Liberty and Debt of the Kingdom", calculates, that to borrow for two lives at twelve years' purchase, and for three lives at ten years'—is to give ten per cent. in the first case, and nine per cent. in the second. See also Swift's History of Anne.

[c] 7 Anne, sec. 2. cap. 3.

The South Sea Company was established about 1711, to carry on, in appearance, commerce in the South Sea, and on the west coast of Africa; but the *real* object was, to extricate that spendthrift government from its financial embarrassments. Every idle and preposterous wish of the projectors was complied with: the perpetual annuities were created, and no less than 800,000*l.* per annum allowed to the company for mere management (1711), besides six per cent. interest for the capital advanced. Thus the Company's capital reached the enormous sum of ten millions: the arrears of interest were converted into stock, in lieu of dividends, and the stock was made transferable, "for the public benefit", as it was hypocritically said; and all this, under the special direction of the Treasury itself. The malversations were so considerable, that the Commons made a remonstrance to her majesty, "that 35,302,107*l.* were not accounted for": the amount is certainly greatly exaggerated[a]. But it must be agreed, that if these operations were ruinous to the nation, they were most beneficial to the gamblers, "who," as Hutchinson says, "in a short time, increased so much in wealth, as to outtop all the ancient gentry, and vie with the first of the nobility in the kingdom."[b] In this manner, stock jobbing and gambling were encouraged, and the national debt was increased from sixteen millions to fifty-four millions, by the very party which, in latter times, so strenuously opposed this nefarious system[c]. (Table II. Part II.)

[a] See "Harley's (Lord Oxford) Tracts on Loans and Public Credit." They are exceedingly clever.

[b] Treatise on National Debt.

[c] According to another account, the amount of the debt at Queen Anne's death was 52,145,363*l.*, and the annual interest, 3,351,358*l.*

GEORGE I.

As soon as this peaceful monarch*, whose favourite maxim was "to be friends with all the world, and to fear no man," ascended the throne, the important measure of reducing the interest from six per cent to five, was adopted; and in 1716, followed the still more important measure of establishing the first sinking fund, "to discharge the principal and interest of such national debts as were incurred before December 1716; to be discharged therewith, or out of the same, and for no other use, intent, or purpose whatsoever." The interest on further sums was reduced from six per cent to five, effecting a large annual saving of [illegible]l. 15s. 7d. But the cunning Blount, who possessed all the qualities of a [illegible] schemer, proposed to the ministry in the name of the South Sea Company, "to buy up all the debts of the different companies, and that the South Sea Association should become the sole creditor of the state." Stanhope accepted the proposal, and a bill was passed to carry it into effect. The delusion commenced: the scheme exceeded the most sanguine hopes of the projectors: the nation was possessed with the spirit of gambling, avarice, and fraud: the stock fetched ten times its value: the nobility, the principal members of both houses, and some of the ministers themselves, were deeply concerned in these fraudulent and infamous

* He was peaceful in spite of the Whigs themselves, who impeached Bolingbroke, Ormond, and Oxford, for having made peace. Ormond, on taking leave of Oxford, when he escaped to France, said, "Farewell Oxford without a head." To which the other replied, "Farewell Duke without a duchy." When Walpole impeached Bolingbroke, Coningsby rose and said, "the chairman has impeached the scholar, and I impeach the master; I impeach Robert, Earl of Oxford and Mortimer, for high treason."

transactions. At length the bubble burst: the imagined gains disappeared like smoke: the people cried aloud with despair. Every body knows the ultimate result of this nefarious scheme—encouraged by a ministry whose only aim was to get money, "whatever be the means;" but perhaps it is not known to all, that the immense capital of the company, amounting to 33,802,203*l.* 5*s.* 6*d.*, was divided into two portions, one half remaining as their trading fund, the other half, to be invested in joint stock, with interest at five per cent. till June 1727, then to be reduced to four per cent. This arrangement gave name to the Old South Sea Annuities. Only about two millions and a half were borrowed during this peaceful reign: however, at its close, the principal of the national debt amounted to 52,092,235*l.* [a]; while the amount of the annual interest was reduced one million; an evident proof of the benefit the funding operations effected, and of the good effects of a peaceful policy. (Table II. Part II.)

GEORGE II.

The long reign of this monarch was composed of intervals of peace and war. Of course the national debt followed these fluctuations in its increase and decrease. The king in one of his first speeches assured the house, "that the glory and reputation of the nation were at the highest pitch, and he was never better able to vindicate the honour of the crown, and defend its just privileges and possessions [b]." Peace was preserved for

[a] According to another account, published by Cohen in 1822, it amounted to 53,331,155*l.* 17*s.* 5½*d.*, and the interest to 2,181,602*l.* 16*s.* 4½*d.*

[b] Com. Jour.

twelve years: and in this period the debt was reduced 5,137,612*l.*, and the annual interest no more than 253,526*l.* (Table II. Part II.) Public credit ascended to the highest point. In 1737, the three per cents. reached 107; when the ministry, taking advantage of that favourable circumstance, introduced a bill to convert four per cents. into three per cent. annuities; but the Jacobites or Tories, who had assumed the name of the "country party," acting against it in the Commons, the bill was lost, and the good intentions of the ministers frustrated.

But the king, anxious to reduce the debt by preserving peace with Spain, wrote to the monarch of that country, "that he would do the utmost in his power to restore Gibraltar to him." However, the Tory party had far greater propensity for war, than the king had for peace: they introduced a clamorous sailor at the bar of the House of Commons, who affirmed, with the coarsest gestures, that the Spaniards had mutilated him, and that he looked up "to his God for pardon, and to his country for revenge." This was considered a sufficient pretext to declare war[a]. The public credit was impaired, and the reduction of the debt discontinued; while, to increase the evil, Robinson and Thomson, two of the managers of a charitable corporation for lending money to the poor, &c., absconded with 500,000*l.* belonging to the institution. Persons of the highest

[a] Thomson, the poor Scotchman, but superior poet, was hired by his aristocratical friends to compose his "Britannia" for a similar purpose, in 1726; namely, to rouse the nation to revenge against the Spaniards; "who (as an English writer says) were not the aggressors, but justly defended themselves and their coasts against the continual encroachments, the uninterrupted smuggling, and the insatiable cupidity of the English." The "Britannia" was published in 1727.

rank and quality countenanced these thieves, and were implicated in this abominable robbery.

The British glory was tarnished before Carthagena[a]; and the extent of the disasters by land and sea exceeded even the corrupt means employed to raise money for those fruitless expeditions. But Walpole weathered the rising storm, not by his mean and miserable eloquence, but by the irresistible power supplied to him by the operations of the funding and borrowing system. He established the corrupt system of bribing the members of both houses with money, pensions, and places; who consequently voted him as many millions as he asked for, as they themselves had no small share of the plunder. The war, therefore, was continued, in spite of Wyndham's cutting invectives, and severe attacks on the low origin and avarice of the minister[b]. Walpole only redoubled his efforts. The discontented Whigs, who, betraying their party, had reinforced the Tories, were bought with pensions and places, and became

[a] The armament against Carthagena was one of the greatest that England had fitted out; it consisted of twenty-nine ships of the line, besides an equal number of frigates, with 15,000 seamen, and as many land forces: never was a fleet more completely equipped. But the commanders, Wentworth and Vernon, after quarrelling and being defeated, at last agreed in one mortifying measure, to re-embark their troops, and withdraw them as quickly as possible from that scene of slaughter and contagion.—(Goldsmith.)

[b] One of the leading men of the "country party" in George the Second's time alleged, "that septennial parliaments were an encroachment on the rights of the people, and that there was no method to overturn a wicked ministry, but by frequent changes of parliament." Attacking, and alluding to, Walpole, he said, "let us suppose a man of no great family and of but mean fortune, without any sense of honour, advanced to be chief minister of the state: suppose this man raised to great wealth, the plunder of the nation, with a parliament chiefly composed of members whose seats are purchased, and whose votes are venal, &c."

eager for a new exploit [a]. The Duchess of Tuscany aspired to the crown of Augsburg. (Chronological Tables.) The ministry of England declared themselves her champions; and paid the Hungarian hordes, the Poles, and the savage Muscovites, to join in the bloody tournament. These great coalitions and enterprises could not be prosecuted without immense expenditure, and a proportionate increase of debt: consequently we find, that "shortly after the peace of Aix-la-Chapelle, (31st Dec. 1749) the national debt amounted to 76,138,858*l.* 10*s.* 11½*d.*" (Grellier and Cohen.)

But with the blessings of peace, came also a revival of the financial operations. Barnard and the minister Pelham combined, and renewed the proposal, ineffectually made before, for a reduction of the rate of interest. This time they completely succeeded: upwards of fifty-seven millions and a half (57,703,475*l.* 6*s.* 4*d.*) of four per cent. stock, were converted into three per cents. As this operation has been so well imitated in 1822 and 24, it is useless to describe it: suffice it to say that, by these and similar funding contrivances, the debt was reduced, in seven years, 3,721,472*l.* In 1752, an act was passed for the consolidation of several stocks, amounting to 9,137,812*l.* 5*s.* 1*d.*; which sum forms the original capital of the three per cent. Consolidated Annuities.

We come now to the third epoch of the national debt in this reign. The English commenced the war of 1755, by roughly attacking two French frigates. (Chronological Tables.) The king contracted to advance 100,000*l.* annually to the Czarina, to engage her to ravage Germany with 50,000 ferocious Russians: but

[a] Sandys was appointed a lord of the treasury; Carteret, secretary of state; Pulteney, afterwards Earl of Bath, privy counsellor.

that extraordinary woman did not need this inducement to do what entered into her own deep designs. The great Frederick better understood his interest: he promised George the preservation of his "idolized" Hanover. Immediately, the most inveterate enemies—France, Austria, Russia, and Sweden, formed a coalition against the two kings. The war became universal. The expenditure increased amazingly, and the debt followed its steps. In 1759, a loan of 6,600,000*l.* [a], the largest yet known, was contracted at 85½, at an interest of three per cent.; by which an addition of above seven millions and a half was made to the debt; and eight millions were borrowed in the following year, by which 8,200,000*l.* stock were created. But to obtain such large sums, great deceptions were practised—the most enticing allurements were held out. The bad, the ruinous practice, commenced in Queen Anne's reign, of adding an artificial to the real capital, was renewed: but the immense expenses incurred, and the large sums required to be sent to Hanover and Prussia, could not be provided for, even by such stratagems. The aggregate of all these operations almost doubled the debt, which swelled to nearly 146 millions. (Table II. Part II.) Such were the results of this war.

But the objects will appear on a larger scale in the next period.

[a] 32 Geo. II. c. 12.

PART II.

PROGRESS AND PRESENT STATE OF THE NATIONAL DEBT AND FUNDING SYSTEM.

SECOND PERIOD.

FROM THE ACCESSION OF GEORGE III. TO THE PEACE OF PARIS IN [illegible].

Reduction of the National Debt at the commencement of this period.—Bad measures which occasioned the loss of the American colonies and the increase of the national debt.—Alarm and distress caused by the transition from the American war to peace.—Amount of the debt at that time.—Pitt's able measures in annexing the sinking fund to [illegible].—Rise in value and prosperous state of the funds at that time.—Pitt [illegible] his liberal principles, and abandons the system of peace for that of war.—Its consequences.—Extraordinary means employed by him to borrow money.—Fall and low ebb of public credit.—Grand measure of the restriction of cash payments adopted; its effects.—Increase of the national debt in the eleven years of the first French war, and amount at its close.—Powerful aid afforded by the Bank and Stock Exchange.—Origin, progress, and present state of these establishments.—By whom the plan of the Bank was formed, and how the scheme was [illegible].—Its original and present capital.—Its [illegible].—Public and private securities and bullion held by this establishment.—Profits and dividends distributed to the proprietors from its commencement to the present time.—Influence of its operations on the value of all property whatever, and upon all the commercial transactions of the world.—Bad effects, to the public interest, of the restraining clause, in preventing the formation of chartered banking companies.—Total annual expenses and losses of the establishment.—Average annual amount of losses incurred by forgeries, including those of Fauntleroy.—Report of the Secret Committee on the affairs of the Bank.—Influence of this establishment on the origin of the Stock Exchange.—How this association was originally formed, and became a powerful engine in creating the national debt.—Its greatest epoch.—Its constitution, rules, and ceremonies on the admission of members.—Their number.—Services rendered to the Government and the Bank.—Laws enacted against the operations of this establishment.—Their effects.—When the Government began to bestow upon the Stock Exchange marks of public consideration.—Attacks it has suffered from public writers, which have occasioned a general opinion of its insignificance.—Its real and great power.—Its influence over the financial operations of all governments, and amount of the sums raised for them.—Its services to the American republics, and sums raised for their [illegible].—Distinguished individuals who have belonged to the association.—Its exertions [illegible] the government and increasing the debt, at the end of this period.

[illegible] measures of Pitt, and increase of the national debt in the second French war.—Unprecedented extent to which this war was carried.—Measures

of Percival, Vansittart, and Castlereagh.—Enormous sums raised and expended in their enterprises, particularly in 1813.—Vansittart's plan.—Effect of the operations of creating and redeeming immense sums annually.—Increase of the national debt at the peace of Paris, its total amount, and the terms and conditions of the loans contracted.—Objects to which these immense sums were applied.

THE reduction of the National Debt commenced at this epoch. During the twelve years of peace which preceded the late wars, all the advantageous parts of the funding system were in full play, and scarcely a year passed without some funding operation. A large portion of the 4 per cents and navy bonds was paid off, in 1766, by an arrangement with the East India Company: the remainder of the 4 per cents. created in 1763, was paid off in 1768: and the 3½ per cents. created in 1756, were redeemed in 1770. A more judicious operation took place in 1772, by means of which one million and a half of several stocks was reduced; and by a similar arrangement in 1775, another million was saved. These combined operations produced a beneficial reduction in the capital of the debt of 10,739,793*l.* and of only 364,000*l.* in the annual interest. Such were the financial results of the funding system in 1775. (Table II. Part II).

But the wishes of those who considered the war as a great boon—" a means ", as they expressed it, " of freeing the country of a number of turbulent and vicious characters, the pest of society,"[a] were soon accomplished.

At the time when barbarous Russia granted freedom of commerce and navigation to the people she had just conquered, free and commercial England caused an insurrection in her American colonies, by shutting the

[a] Ramsay, " Essay on the Constitution of England," p. 70.

port of Boston, restricting their commerce, depriving them of their currency[a], and imposing illegal and oppressive duties in specie, while she deprived them of the means of obtaining it[b]. "Place us", they exclaimed, "as we were at the close of the late war, and our former harmony will be restored: we will endeavour to live without trade, and recur for subsistence to the fertility of our soil: we will defray our civil list, and we promise to give 100,000*l.* per annum, for a hundred years, in aid of the sinking fund to pay the national debt. England calls us her children; let us, by our behaviour, give her reason to pride herself on the relationship."[c]

But folly, instead of justice, reigned in the British councils. The parricidal war commenced. The cruel minister employed the Indians to destroy their brethren in a manner revolting to humanity: while to the atrocities of savages, and the cruelties of civil war, were added the misfortunes of foreign interference. France dragged in Spain, as she always did in wars opposed to her true interest. Thus, a contest which began with a dispute about some tea-boxes[d], became the most horribly destructive, as well as expensive war, England had ever waged.

[a] In 1764, an act was passed imposing duties payable *in specie* on all articles imported from France and the West India Islands.

[b] Another act followed, restricting the currency of paper money. And to these succeeded the famous Stamp Act, called "the Folly of England, and the Ruin of America"; but, "Oh! miseras hominum mentes, oh! pectora cæca," it ultimately became the cause of happiness to the latter country, and even beneficial to England.

[c] See "Petition of the Commissioners of America"; and "State Papers." Also Franklin's "Miscellanies," and Jefferson's "Correspondence."

[d] The disturbances commenced at Boston, by throwing overboard some boxes of tea from three sloops in the harbour.

The ministry refused the contribution offered towards the extinction of the debt: they preferred resorting to funding measures to increase it. The funding operations, so wisely effected in time of peace, were now reversed. Five millions of 4 per cents. were created in 1770: six millions were added in the next year; and seven millions more of 3 per cents. in the year following. In 1780, the 4 per cents. were increased twelve millions more; and in the succeeding year, the 3 per cents. were augmented by a sum of 18,986,300*l.* At last, the war was closed by a loan of twelve millions, made in 1783. With such rapid strides did the debt increase in this war, that, after taking into consideration the unfavourable terms on which the loans were contracted, the artificial capital added to the real, and the long annuities granted as inducements to the lenders—we shall not be surprised to find, at the close of the American war (1783), 102,541,819*l.* added to the capital of the debt, and 3,843,084*l.* to the annual interest. (Table II. Part II.)

The party which so confidently maintained, that "every addition to the national debt was a real augmentation in the amount of gold and silver all over the country"[a], was not yet convinced of its error. The people, however, began seriously to reflect, that facts contradicted those agreeable theories; for gold certainly did not flow in such abundance over the land: they chose Pitt, therefore, as the champion to assert their rights. This man was selected to introduce a Reform Bill (similar to the one just passed)—to terminate the war—and to reduce the national debt[b]. We shall see how he fulfilled those sacred engagements.

The termination of that unfortunate war produced

[a] Mortimer's Elements of Finance. Hope's "Letter on Credit."
[b] See Pitt's Life.

effects similar to those we have witnessed at the close of the late war. The sanguine expectations of the ablest economists of that age were entirely disappointed. But it was no more than the cessation of an artificial stimulus —the sudden transition from a violent to a quiet state: nevertheless, men's imaginations were seized with a panic, and the funds fell to 54. However, Pitt was at the helm of affairs, and Price was at his elbow. The doctor, who, as far back as 1772, had been struck with the idea of the first sinking fund, (before mentioned,) now conceived that, by the addition of compound interest, a new and grand scheme might be formed. He proposed to Pitt the prompt reduction of the national debt, " by a sum annually set apart to be exclusively appropriated to the purchase of stock at the market prices; the interest of the debt redeemed to be added to the original sums, to multiply the operations of the fund". Pitt, more sagacious than the preceding ministers, who had rejected this plan, readily adopted the proposal. He proved to the House by figures, " that a surplus of 900,000*l.* would remain, after satisfying all branches of expenditure:"[a] he proposed farther, " to raise the sum to a million, by new taxes."

Such was the sinking fund established in 1786. Its effects were magical. The inclination of the people to see the debt extinguished was transformed, by an Act of Parliament, into something approaching a positive payment: never was delusion more complete; never did deception produce more wonderful results:[b] as if it were the destiny of the human race to be led by deceit.

But Pitt was not satisfied with one fund; he created, in the same year, another, called the " Consolidated

[a] Com. Jour. 1786. [b] The funds rose to 76; or 26 per cent.

Fund," composed of the aggregate duties on "houses, windows, hackney-coaches, male and female servants, hawkers and pedlars, &c. &c." An Act was passed by which all annuities payable to the public creditors, were made redeemable; giving, however, to the holders till the 1st of June to dissent. This was the principal basis of Pitt's great financial system: nevertheless, the debt only experienced the very insignificant reduction of little more than four millions and a half (4,751,260*l.*) in the long space of ten years' peace.

However, Pitt, the very man who had concluded the most liberal treaty of commerce with France, (a treaty which would astonish even our present supporters of *free trade*[a],) who, opposing the opinions of the 'anti-free-trade' people, declared, "that his mind revolted from the opinion of those who thought France the unalterable enemy of England,—that the position was monstrous and impossible, and that it was a libel against the constitution of political societies"[b]: this very man soon changed his opinion; stopped the corn already shipped for France, when her inhabitants, particularly the people of Paris, were starving; and adopted several not less abominable measures: thus forcing the Convention to declare the war of 1793, while the odium of aggression was thrown upon that Assembly.

The funds had risen before that declaration to 96; but this was rather owing to the prosperous state of our industry and agriculture, than to the sinking fund. Although the revolutionary contest was the most extraordinary that ever happened, the progress of the debt

[a] Debrett's Par. Register, Vol. XXI. anno 1787. See the Treaty in Buchanan, Appendix.

[b] Nichols' "Recollections of George III." "Biographical Sketch of Fox", by Man.

contracted to oppose it, was by no means inferior in magnitude and importance. Loans succeeded loans; and England being at the head of the European powers, they all thought themselves entitled to borrow money in the English market. The firm of Boyd, Binfield and Co., being employed by the slothful Austrians to raise two loans of 6,220,000*l.*, that house, as well as its employers, was ruined. The republicans were everywhere victorious, and the cause of nations was triumphant. Our expenses could not be provided for, and the staunchest aristocrats began to despair. Government, greatly embarrassed, determined (in 1796) to have recourse to violent measures "to compel all persons of a certain income to lend one-fourth"; when the gamblers came forward, and subscribed eighteen millions in a few hours. This proceeding, though in reality infamous and Jewish, was nevertheless pompously embellished with the name of "the Loyalty Loan." [a]

At length the modern Huns were expelled from Italy (Chronological Tables). Whole armies surrendered their arms, and could only be again raised by the magical power of the gold of England. Pitt applied to the Bank of England for assistance; but his extravagant demands were resisted with honourable firmness: he redoubled his efforts, pressed, coaxed, insisted; but the directors distrusted his promises [b]. They plainly told him, "you have deceived us several times"; and at last absolutely refused his proposals. But the mighty Pitt was not deterred. It was out of his power to

[a] Government, besides paying a bonus for the 18 millions, funded 20,124,843*l.* at 5 per cent.; mortgaging the revenue of the nation for 1,006,243*l.* interest, exclusive of the charges for management.

[b] "Historical Sketch of the Bank of England."

compel the directors to give "what they had not"; but he made them declare "that their coffers were replete with gold, and that a favourable balance of 3,826,899*l*. was at their disposal": and notes being prepared before-hand, the Restriction Act was passed, forbidding the Bank "to issue or pay in gold." This Act has been severely censured; but it must be allowed that, taking all the circumstances into consideration, such a bold, grand, and wise financial measure had never before been adopted. According to the Act, the restriction was only till the 24th of June following; but this temporary stopment, continued from year to year, was prolonged to a rather long period of twenty-four years (1797 to 1821).

But what effects had this measure on the progress of the debt, and the funding system? The Bank directors, disengaged from cash payments, were enabled to give unlimited support and assistance to the extravagant financial schemes and funding operations of the minister; and the latter were immediately commenced on a more extensive scale. The two other propelling powers of the system—the Stock Exchange and the delusive Sinking Fund,—joined hand in hand with the Bank, and all its several parts combined were in full play. The Bank increased its circulation immensely; and Exchequer Bills, hitherto issued in moderate sums, were thrown upon the market by eleven and twelve millions at a time. The Bank gave the signal to the Stock Exchange: that centre of gamblers sent forth its thousand agents in as many divergent directions: these enticed the public with promises of the greatest advantages, allured their avarice by hopes of exorbitant gains, excited all interests, and made it appear that nothing could be more beneficial than the war: while servile writers seconded their efforts, and confirmed the delusion. Never could the words of Lucan be better applied :—

> "Hinc usura vorax, avidumque in tempore fœnus,
> Hinc concussa fides, et multis utile bellum."

A complete view is given in Table III. Part II. of all the loans contracted from 1793 to 1819, with the terms on which the bargains were made, and all the particulars of the transactions. It will there be seen, that twenty millions were subscribed in 1800, by which 32,185,000*l.* of consols, and three per cent. reduced were created : the enormous sum of forty-nine millions was raised in the next year, to which must be added eleven millions of Exchequer Bills funded, making a total of above sixty millions! and thirty-three millions more were created in the year following. Is it to be wondered at then, that the debt was increased in the prodigious sum of 327 millions![a] in the short space of eleven years: or that the whole amount of the national debt exceeded 561 millions!!! (Table IV. Part II.)

It has already been remarked, that the Bank and the Stock Exchange were the principal instruments employed in raising this enormous sum. A sketch of their history, and of the steps by which they have risen to their present commanding position, is necessary to

[a] Sinclair and Colquhoun say, that the increase in this war, was 327,469,665*l.*; and the total debt at the conclusion of the war in 1801, 561,203,234*l.* Cohen states the increase during the war at 367,626,912*l.* According to the official account of Higham, the debt was

In 1793	£244,440,306
Increase in 1802	284,438,000
Total	£528,878,306

confirm and illustrate many of the statements contained in this work; while, at the same time, it may serve to relieve the monotony of these dry details.

SKETCH OF THE HISTORY OF THE BANK.

Five years after the Revolution (in 1694), an enterprising Scotchman came forward to relieve the treasury from its embarrassments. He proposed to raise 1,200,000*l.* (Table V. Part II.) an immense sum for that time; but his scheme was adopted, and he carried it into effect. The subscribers were to receive 100,000*l.* a year; they had also the faculty of issuing bank notes convertible into gold, and were formed into a corporate body, under the name of "The Governor and Company of the Bank of England;" the charter to expire in 1705, but "on payment, by the public to the Bank, of all demands in this act expressed."[a] Little did the talented and clever founder think, while forming a mercantile company whose power has never been paralleled before nor since, that he should perish in the wild woods of Darien, abandoned and cruelly persecuted by the very king and government whom he had extricated from their difficulties, and upon whom he had bestowed such immense power. The unfortunate Patterson might justly complain of men's ingratitude, and exclaim "*Oh nescia mens fati, sortisque futuri.*"[b]

[a] This charter is dated 27th of July, 1694.

[b] This talented man was not only persecuted by his contemporaries, his partners, and his king, but has been so unfortunate, that even in the present time, we daily hear the most bitter invectives against one of those singular beings who had the greatest share in the civilization and prosperity of his country; as if genius were answerable for the abuses of the perfect works of its inven-

But the association was progressing. Its chief object was to supply money to the government. To effect this, a public subscription of a million took place three years after the charter was granted; and a fresh one, to the same amount, was effected twenty-four months after. The capital of the Bank was increasing, in proportion as the wants of the government were augmenting: in 1709, it reached 4,400,000*l.* (Table V. Part II.)

tion; or, as if it were just to attribute to the original projector, the clumsiness of the subsequent management. We cannot let this opportunity pass without rendering homage to an individual, who, although poor, proceeding from a miserable place, without friends, and without resources, contrived not only an "American, African, and Indian trading company," which filled the country with admiration at the time, but whose mind conceived, and whose determination brought forward, the great designs of the banks of Scotland and England; without the imperfections which, by an act of parliament, have been inflicted on the first, and without the defects which at present deform the last. Patterson must have been a man of no ordinary stamp, not only to have raised in those times the large subscriptions required for the Banks of England and Scotland, but to have made the Scotchmen pay, with public joy and rejoicings, 400,000*l* towards the colony of Darien. The obstacles which were encountered in that unfortunate expedition, were either not imagined by him, or if they were, his adventurous spirit despised the danger. King William had no right to act with such vindictive feeling against this poor and unfortunate Scotchman, abandoned on that dreadful and mortiferous coast. "I have," said this king, "been ill served in Scotland, but I hope some remedies may be found to prevent the inconveniences which may arise from this act," (the Act of Incorporation.) Immediate instructions were sent to colonial governors not to give any assistance to the Scotch colonists; while foreign courts were answered, that "the British cabinet had no knowledge of such Scotch colony." Thus humanity and policy were abandoned for revenge and ingratitude: the colonists were left to be starved and murdered, and nobody knows the spot where the principal victim was sacrificed, or where rest the mortal remains of Patterson.

The profits of the subscribers having excited cupidity, some competitors thought themselves entitled to form a similar association. The "Mine Adventure Company" stepped forward to claim a fair and just participation; but it was quite disappointed: its competitor was already more powerful than the government, towards which it exercised the power of a proud and rich man towards his needy creditor.

The charter had judiciously provided, that the Bank "should make no purchase of lands or revenues belonging to the crown," nor "advance any sums to their majesties"; but no restriction whatsoever was enacted in regard to the number of members in any other company. But to suppress the "Mining Company," the directors artfully contrived to obtain from the government a declaration, "that it should not be lawful for any body politic erected or to be erected, other than the governor and company of the Bank of England, or for other persons whatsoever, united, or to be united in covenant or partnership, *exceeding the number of six persons*, in the part of Great Britain called England, to borrow, owe, or take up any sums of money on their bills or notes payable on demand, for any less time than six months from the borrowing thereof." The "Mine Company" was annihilated by this act; while the most extraordinary privilege ever known—"an exclusive privilege of creating money for their own private benefit"—a monopoly to coin paper money for their own advantage, was granted to a corporation of dealers.

However, the directors of that time did not fully comprehend their immense power: perhaps, they had not yet recovered from the panic which seized them when they stopped payment in 1696. Government had several times assisted them; but notwithstanding this, they issued no notes under twenty pounds previous to 1756. But if they were timid on this point, they were quite conscious that the continuation of their monopoly depended more on their own pleasure, than on the government. Thus, their charter was renewed from time to time, during a period of exactly a century and a year (1732 to 1833)[a]; and they obtained acts and privileges in behalf of the corporation, "whose mere titles alone extend to about 200 pages," according to the declaration of the Bank Secretary[b]. But it must be observed that, as the debt of the government was increased, so the capital of the company was augmented: thus, in 1742, it reached the enormous amount of 8,900,000*l.*, increased to 11,642,000*l.* in 1782, and in 1816, amounted to 14,953,000*l.*—this being the actual sum lent to the government. (Table V. Part II.)

The British ministers, virtually invested with the dangerous power of raising money, widened their operations, as has been already noticed, in consequence of the perpetual wars and alternate alliances. The national debt was amazingly increased by these operations, managed between the government and the Bank; and the profits of the latter, in consequence of the part it acted in those measures, were augmented in a corresponding ratio. In proof of this it may be mentioned, that the distribution of profits made to the proprietors since 1790, amounts to 51,546,666*l.* (Table VI. and

[a] 1694......Charter granted. 1697...... do. extended. 1708...... do. do. 1713...... do. do. 1742......Charter extended. 1764...... do. do. 1781...... do. do. 1800...... do. do.
It expires this year.

[b] Secret Committee on the Bank Charter, Appendix 6.

VII. Part II.), a sum almost ten times greater than the average produce of all the mines of the world during the last nine years and a half[a]. And while such a profitable distribution has taken place, the average of losses, during the same interval, is only 31,696*l.* a year; and the average loss by forgeries, during the last ten years, is 40,204*l.* a year. (Tables VIII. and IX. Part II.).

It appears impossible to conceive a more advantageous commercial association, or a company in which the profits should be so certain and enormous, and the losses so casual and insignificant. It has therefore been publicly maintained, that the profits of the Bank have been excessive. But the fact is certainly quite the contrary. For, considering the boundless sources of those profits—the power of the company over the government, over the currency, over the public and private property and the commercial credit of a country like this, and over all the mercantile movements and transactions of the world—it would really appear, not only that the profits have not been excessive, but that the directors have not been clever enough to take all the advantages of such resources which they might have done.

The power of the Bank was great before 1797; but when the government, by one magic Act, restricted that corporation from paying in cash, and at the same time exempted it from the universal liability to bankruptcy, its power became without limits. Before that time, the power of the Bank over the government was disputed, or only partially avowed; but since this Act, it

[a] Jacob calculates the total produce of the mines of America, during the twenty years ending in 1829, at 80,736,760*l.*, or 4,036,838*l.* a year; and of all the mines of the world, at 5,500,000*l.* a year. (Historical Inquiry.)

has been openly acknowledged, and no man in his senses has dared to call it in question.

The profits, therefore, derived from the transactions with the government and the circulation of paper, have been proportioned to the magnitude of the transactions themselves. Some idea of this may be formed, from the fact, that the amount of the loans contracted between 1793 and 1815, exceeds 618 millions! and more especially from the operation carried on with Vansittart (now Lord Bexley) in 1816, when he exalted and praised the extreme generosity of the Bank in lending the government three millions at three per cent. interest, "while at the same time they had a disposable balance lying in the hands of the Bank, amounting to the enormous sum of 10,807,660*l.*, for which the Bank paid no interest whatever!!!" Notwithstanding this, in consideration of such *extreme* liberality, the Chancellor advised the Crown to permit the Bank to add these three millions to its pre-existing capital. This dishonourable arrangement took place in April, and on the 23d of the same month was announced to parliament. The three millions thus raised were then offered to the public, as a clever public writer has observed, at 215½, and rose in a few days to 223: in this manner the Bank proprietors realized no less than 6,600,000*l.*!! Such an enormous profit, in the very year when the greatest distress prevailed, and 2730 commissions of bankruptcy were issued, was neither creditable to the minister, nor generous on the part of the Bank direction.

The functions of the Bank, according to the evidence of the governor before the committee, are, "to furnish the paper money with which the public act around them, and to be a place of safe deposit for the public money, or for the money of individuals who prefer a public body like the Bank to private banks." They act also as a bank to the government, managing the public debt by keeping a register and the accounts of the fundholders; paying the dividends, and taking upon themselves the risk of forgeries. And lastly, they act as a bank of discounts for the accommodation of the commercial and manufacturing districts [a].

The profits derived from all these sources are consequently very large. Those arising from the circulation of bank notes are considerable.

Before the Restriction Act, the amount of the circula-

[a] The Bank of England acts as a private bank also: they ought to allow interest on the deposits as the banks of Scotland do. The facilities granted by the Bank to their customers ever since 1825, according to the statement of the chief cashier before the committee, were as follows:—

1. The Bank receives dividends by power of attorney for all persons having drawing accounts at the Bank.

2. Dividend warrants are received at the warrant office for ditto.

3. Exchequer bills and other securities are received for ditto; the bills exchanged, the interest received, and the amount carried to their respective accounts.

4. Cheques may be drawn for 5*l.* and upwards, instead of 10*l.* as heretofore.

5. Cash boxes taken in, contents unknown, for such persons as keep accounts at the Bank.

6. Bank notes are paid at the counter, instead of drawing tickets for them on the pay clerks as heretofore.

7. Cheques on city bankers paid in by three o'clock may be drawn for between four and five; and those paid in before four will be received and passed to account the same evening.

8. Cheques paid in before four are sent out at nine o'clock the following morning, received and passed to account, and may be drawn for as soon as received.

9. Dividend warrants taken in at the drawing office until five in the afternoon, instead of until three as heretofore.

10. Credits paid into account are received without the Bank

tion was about ten millions; two years afterwards, it increased to thirteen millions; in 1803, to sixteen millions; and subsequently to twenty-nine millions and a half! (Tables X. and XIV. Part II.) The annual amount of the profits from this source has been stated at 178,875*l.* (Table XI. Part II.) The Bank has the power, by increasing or decreasing the circulation, of raising or depressing the price of the funds, as well as the value of all property. Nothing is more evident than that the enlargement of issues, one, two, or three millions, in a few months, would raise the price of the public funds ten or fifteen per cent.; and that, by the contraction of them again, the price would be proportionably depressed. This operation has been actually performed, and may be repeated. The circulation is contracted by selling exchequer bills and refusing discounts: it is extended by opposite operations, and by issuing fresh bank notes. Consequently, the prices of the public securities, as well as all the exchanges in general, are subordinate to and dependent on the Bank directors, or the leading man amongst them.

The profits arising from the mercantile discounts have not been so proportionably large as those resulting from circulation, nor so considerable in their influence over all the objects of commerce. Table XII. Part II. shows that the accommodations afforded to commerce have been comparatively limited, except in one year.

book (the pass-book), and are afterwards entered therein without the party claiming them.

11. Bills of exchange accepted payable at the Bank are paid with or without advice, heretofore with advice only.

12. Notes of country bankers, payable in London, are sent out the same day for payment.

13. Cheques are given out in books and not in sheets as heretofore.

These facilities amounted, in 1795, to two millions and a half; in 1803, to ten millions; in 1810, reached the high point of twenty millions; and from that point declined to 919,000*l.* in 1830; and were only 600,000*l.* more than that sum in the following year. Table XIII. shews the amount of accommodation given to bankers, which is comparatively trifling. By reflecting that the discounts have been decreasing, while commerce has been considerably increasing; by considering the narrowness of the discounts in the late years, compared with the expansion of commerce; the most important conclusions could be drawn; but such observations cannot be introduced with propriety here. A more complete idea of all the profits of this colossal establishment may be formed from the amount of public and private securities held at different periods. These were, in 1778, above thirteen millions; in 1789, above twenty millions; at the declaration of war against France in 1803, thirty-one millions; after the peace of Paris, forty-eight millions; and are at present, thirty-three millions. (Table XIV. Part II.)

It has already been observed, that the power of the Bank extends over all the commercial movements and transactions of the world. Nobody will deny, that the abundance or scarcity of the precious metals is the ultimate regulator of the value of all things, as well as of all commercial operations. Besides the above mentioned deposits, the greatest part of the produce of the American mines arriving in this country passes through the Bank. Thus an enormous deposit of precious metals is formed, and eventually becomes at the disposal of the Bank directors: they may, at their pleasure, open or shut the flood-gates of this immense reservoir. There is an extraordinary person, who, in less than five weeks, will draw from it and spread over the world 885,000*l.*! (Table XV. Part II.)—a sum equal to the fourth part of the annual produce of all the American mines. Rothschild—that wonderful man, whose individual financial operations are unprecedented, and whose power is unknown even to himself, entirely confirms this assertion, when in his straight-forward evidence he says, that "not only all the gold and silver of the world will tend to come here, but that all the mercantile transactions of the globe are balanced in this emporium."[a]

Thus it evidently appears, that the power of this establishment extends, not only over the government and over all the mercantile transactions of the globe, but even to all the foundations of society itself. Whether this colossal power should be contained in the hands of twenty-four private individuals, is the most important of all questions; a question affecting the interests of the whole world; but a question out of the pale of this enquiry. Indeed, it would be presumptuous for an individual to attempt the decision of such a point, when one of the most enlightened committees, after having put 5978 questions to, and elicited an equal number of answers from, twenty-four practical and clever men, solemnly declared, that "*it was not justified in giving a decided opinion.*" But it is hoped, that the subjoined tables and statements, and the Report of the committee, purposely inserted to afford the public the grounds and materials for discussing and deciding this grand question, will be read with interest[b]. However, it may be

[a] "Question,—If there be no importation of corn, and no foreign loans, the exchanges always being in favour of this country, must it not inevitably follow, that all the gold and silver in the world will tend to come here? Answer,—It will tend to come here." (Evidence before the Committee on the Bank Charter.)

[b] The Secret Committee appointed to inquire into the expediency

observed that, from the most remote period, the patriotic economists of this country have strongly declaimed

of renewing the charter of the Bank of England, and into the system upon which banks of issue in England and Wales are conducted; and to whom the petition of certain Joint Stock Banking Companies in England was referred; and who were empowered to report the minutes of evidence taken before them; have agreed upon the following Report:—

Your Committee have applied themselves to the inquiry which the House has committed to them, by calling for all the accounts which appeared to them necessary for the purpose of elucidating the affairs of the Bank of England, and have examined evidence for the purpose of ascertaining the principles on which it regulates the issue of its notes, and conducts its general transactions. They feel bound to state, that the directors of the Bank of England have afforded to them every facility in their power, and have most readily and candidly answered every question which has been put to them, and produced every account which has been called for. The Committee have also examined such witnesses as appeared to them, from their practical knowledge and experience, most likely to afford information on the important subjects under their consideration, who have all been ready to give the Committee the most ample information.

The principal points to which they have directed their attention, are—

First. Whether the paper circulation of the metropolis should be confined, as at present, to the issues of one bank, and that a commercial company; or, whether a competition of different banks of issue, each consisting of an unlimited number of partners, should be permitted.

Secondly. If it should be deemed expedient that the paper circulation of the metropolis should be confined, as at present, to the issues of one bank, how far the whole of the exclusive privileges possessed by the Bank of England are necessary to effect this object.

Thirdly. What checks can be provided to secure for the public a proper management of banks of issue, and especially whether it would be expedient and safe to compel them periodically to publish their accounts.

With respect to the circulation of paper in the country, the Com-

[illegible]

[illegible]

In all these, and in some matters [illegible] more or less information will be found in the minutes of evidence; [illegible]

In their opinion no public inconvenience will arise from this publication. The only parts of the evidence which they have thought it necessary to suppress, are those which relate merely to the private interests of individuals.

The House will perceive that the Committee have presented, as part of the evidence which they have taken, the actual amount of bullion at different times in the coffers of the Bank of England. This information has never been given to the public. It is, however, very essential to a complete knowledge of the subject; and if it had been suppressed by the Committee, many parts of the evidence would have been unintelligible, and a false impression would have been produced in the minds of the public, that the Bank were not as well provided with bullion as is desirable, which might have a very injurious effect. The House will, however, observe, that the Bank is amply provided with bullion at the present time; and it does not therefore appear to the Committee, that this information being now given to the public can be productive of any injurious consequences.

The Committee, however, by no means wish it to be understood, from their having felt themselves called upon to include this evidence in their report, that they have formed any opinion as to the propriety of periodically publishing the affairs of this or of any other bank of issue. There appears to be a difference between the

writer 125 years ago, "is of that extent, that I know not well where to begin my account of it: *this voracious animal* (!!!) spreads its malignity even to the land, and the natural productions of the country."[a] And the same opinion may be traced, maintained, and alternately expressed in equal or more becoming terms, by a long catalogue of national writers from that time down to the superior and convincing publication of Sir H. Parnell[b]; an evident proof of the reasonable and uninterrupted national feeling, as well as of the overwhelming power of the Bank.

But all the charges brought against the conduct of the Bank, and all the recriminations and invectives against their proceedings and profits, are here readily passed over; because in justice they, like any other

publication of the affairs of the Bank when an inquiry is instituted for the purpose of deciding whether the Bank charter shall be renewed or not, and a periodical publication during the course of its ordinary transactions.

Of the ample means of the Bank of England to meet all its engagements, and of the high credit which it has always possessed, and continues to deserve, no man who reads the evidence taken before this Committee can for a moment doubt, for it appears that, in addition to the surplus left in the hands of the Bank itself, amounting to 2,880,000*l.*, the capital on which interest is paid to the proprietors, and for which the state is debtor to the Bank, amounts to 14,533,000*l.*, making no less a sum than 17,433,000*l.* over and above all its liabilities.

11th August, 1832.

[a] "Reasons against the continuance of the Bank." London, 1707.

[b] "Plain Statement of the Power of the Bank of England, and the use made of it, with a refutation of, and reply to, the Historical Sketch of the Bank"; by Sir H. Parnell. The most interesting publication on this important question is the excellent "Analysis of the Currency Question, and origin and growth of Joint Stock Banking", by Joplin.

corporation or merchant, are entitled to act according to their opinion, and in conformity to their own interest: farther, if the public, and particularly the government, require a banker, they certainly could not find one richer, more solid, or better in all respects, than the Bank of England. But it does appear utterly impossible to conceive, that so eminent and wealthy a corporation *will strive to preserve any longer that infamous clause, which prevents the introduction of the unrivalled banking system of Scotland into this country*[a]: a clause seriously affecting the interests of all individuals, the progess, the solidity, the public and private wealth of the British empire. Indeed, after reflecting on the baneful effects resulting from the restraining clause, and considering that in a mercantile country like England, it has been steadily maintained for upwards of a century, while in one portion of Great

[a] The Bank of Scotland was established by an Act of William III. passed in 1695, conferring an exclusive privilege of banking; and the first issue of notes of twenty shillings was in 1704. The present banking system was not introduced until the monopoly of the Bank of Scotland was abolished in 1715. The English government supposed that the Bank had assisted the Pretender, and on that ground the monopoly was abolished, and rivals were created. Never has a measure been more favourable to the country. If it be asked, in what consists the superiority of the Scotch banking system? the reply is, that it mainly consists in four advantages. 1st, Greater security of capital; the failure of a bank with a paid-up capital being almost impossible. 2dly, In the interest received on the capital itself, which is paid from the very day on which it is deposited. 3dly, "Cash accounts", in virtue of which not only the commercial and manufacturing, but the agricultural, the industrious, and even the poorer classes receive aid and accommodation. 4thly, That by this system the precious metals are rendered comparatively unnecessary, the bankers and the nation becoming almost independent of them; whilst all the capital existing in the country is gaining interest and continually augmenting.

Britain, the most perfect system of banking imaginable has been carried on, during the same long period, with the greatest success,—one is really at a loss whether to be more astonished at the stupidity and weakness of the human race, or at the perseverance and cunning of a mercantile corporation.

But coming to the real effects produced by the exercise of the above-mentioned power: one of the cleverest writers on the subject (Mushet) states, "that in no less than seven instances has the Bank abused its power, and caused, or greatly contributed to cause, immense injury to the public interests, since 1780."[a] In fact, the Bank, possessing the means of increasing or decreasing the circulation *ad libitum*, and this having a direct action on the funds, on credit, and on commercial transactions, as is demonstrated by the comparison of Tables XIV. and X., no wonder, that to the imprudent exercise of this power, have been attributed the confusion, the embarrassments, and the agricultural and commercial distress, of the years 1783, 1797, 1816, 1818, and 1825[b]. After perusing, in the history of the rise and progress of the National Debt, the accounts of the financial and funding operations which took place, the reader will be able to form a decided opinion upon the merits of the

[a] "What has the Currency to do with the present Discounts?" by Lambert; "A Letter on the Currency", by Mushet, an interesting tract, and full of merit. Also, "Currency Question free from Mystery", a most excellent production, by P. Scrope; and, "On Paper and Banking", by Sir H. Parnell. Also, "Report of Select Committee on Promissory Notes in Scotland and Ireland", 1826.—&c.

[b] See the above-named authors, and especially Sir H. Parnell. The author of the "Historical Sketch" has excused the distress of 1797, on account of the importunate demands of Pitt; and that of 1825, on the ground of a *mistake* of the Bank directors. But "risum teneatis, amici?"

question, as to the influence of the Bank over these periods of distress. But in regard to the last named convulsion (1825), although newly arrived in England on a mission from a foreign government, and having his thoughts chiefly engrossed by his duties, and although not very conversant with the economical affairs of this country, whilst all the writers of the time assigned it to other causes, as overtrading, loans, mining speculations, &c. &c., the author of this work was perhaps the only one who openly attributed it to the operations of the Bank[a]; nor is the truth of his assertion in any

[a] "Five Questions on the Actual Mercantile Distress," by P. Pebrer. London, 1826.

In discussing one of these five questions, viz. "How did the present mercantile distress come on?" not only did I attribute it to the Bank, but by a curious coincidence, used almost the same words as Mr. Rothschild has since done in his evidence before the Committee on the Bank Charter, (1832). In answer to "Question 4846," "How did the distress of 1825 come on?" he says, "when the Bank found that a great deal of gold was going away, the Bank drew in, and would not discount; there was an immense deal of speculation; the Bank then began to refuse to discount the corn bills, the Vienna bills, and other bills," &c. &c. The words in the above mentioned pamphlet, page 13, are, "*At the time when speculation and facilities were immense, and the great mercantile machine was at its most rapid rotation; at the time when the January accounts became due, that is, at the period when more money and circulation are required, then it was, that the Bank curtailed their discounts, and restricted their accommodation; this was the fatal moment:* the alarm spread, nor was the liberality with which the Bank afterwards acted, sufficient to restore confidence, and stop the panic, and the effects of this sudden measure: 'other bankers may fail,' was re-echoed from every mouth; and soon the convulsion became general. The public became alarmed—the runs began, and instantly increased, discrimination was not thought of—there was no time for reasoning. Every one hastened to withdraw his funds from his bankers: while the latter experience the effects of their want of confidence, and their determination to restrict their discounts; soon finding themselves

manner shaken by the statement made by some of the directors (in the secret committee) to justify their conduct on that occasion.

obliged to make great sacrifice in order to stand their ground: some, however, are unable to stem the torrent: a number of country bankers suspend their payments. The alarm spread throughout the country even with more rapidity than it had done in the city; and in direct ratio to the lesser knowledge of the state affairs, and the greater dread experienced by a multitude of small capitalists and labourers. The exaggerated declamations of the public papers, the malignant and gloomy pictures drawn by some of them, added to the cries and lamentations of a multitude of weavers thrown out of bread, who are partly cast into that deplorable state by natural prejudices, and the mistaken interest of some individuals belonging to a class of manufactures, 'who will soon supplant French silks,' completed the picture of confusion, alarm, distrust, and discredit, generally felt among all classes. Such in our opinion is the simple history of the late mercantile distress, as well as of its progress and immediate origin. We indeed agree, that the mercantile machine suffered in its rotation, its accelerated movement was obstructed, some misfortune was in reality felt; but the real extent of this misfortune, of this distress, is what is misunderstood by the public at large. In so many speeches, pamphlets, and public papers, as have been written on the subject, the exaggerations have been palpable and great. At one time, the manufactures and commerce of this country have been represented as being at the lowest ebb, and even the government in a state of penury; whilst at another, the imprudence of the merchant in his hazardous speculations, and his want of foresight in over-trading, are the favourite topics of the day."

The prediction in regard to the increase of the silk manufacture, on account of which such loud complaint was made at the time, has been tolerably fulfilled; as well as the assertion that such exaggerated and clamorous distress would not ruin the country, and that all the other branches of national prosperity, being unimpaired, would continue their uninterrupted progress. But I cannot omit mentioning in this place, another subject deeply affecting the British commercial interests (also touched upon in the same pamphlet), viz. the grand question of Spanish American Independence, and its relative effects on the commerce of this country. Mr.

But by consulting the Bank statements themselves, the reader will come to more clear and correct con-

Canning (wishing to know my opinion more fully upon this subject) was quite astonished, and I dare say did not form the highest opinion of my sagacity, when I told him in the most plain language, that it was the greatest absurdity to expect tranquillity or any thing like order from those immense countries, in which the mixed and naturally inimical population was so thinly scattered, that in several provinces there were only two inhabitants to a square mile; all the social elements of those regions presenting a heterogeneous and anomalous mass of contrarieties: that every district and petty village was to be considered an "Independent State," or *Republic*, as it was called, every soldier an officer, every officer a general, and every general as struggling to be President of the *Republic*. "Such being the *true* state of Spanish America, in which it is likely to continue *at least* for the remainder of the present century, your Excellency," I added, "will draw the inference in regard to the prospects and prosperity of our commerce in those countries." I am sorry to say, these predictions have been hitherto verified: unfortunately for that quarter of the world, and for the interests of the other three, it continues, and will continue, in the same anarchical, unproductive, and disjointed state. That eminent, good, and patriotic statesman, was not correctly informed of the physical, moral, political, and economical state of Spanish America. Never has a more erroneous policy been pursued, both in regard to the true interests of those countries themselves, and to the manufacturing and commercial interests of Great Britain, than was adopted in promoting the insurrection of those states, in the great question of recognizing their independence, and in the manner in which the whole affair was conducted. Mercantile England experiences its results. But the ministry was not enlightened nor firm enough, to resist the clamours of that senseless herd among the commercial class, whose avarice made them imagine those countries to be "the land of promise," and that—

"—— There the molten silver
Runs out like cream on cakes of gold;
—— And rubies
Do grow like strawberries."

However, the manner in which some European governments so earnestly and powerfully urge the Spanish cabinet to recognise the

clusions on the subject, than any reasoning can lead him to: he will see the relative increase or decrease of bank

independence of those vast regions, is not less absurd and inconsiderate. For should Spain be so destitute of common sense as to acknowledge their independence on the terms they require, they *would not be any nearer to a state of tranquillity, nor would their intestine disorders and anarchy cease.* The elements of discord are inherent in a mixed population, dispersed over an immense surface, struggling for command, and addicted to gambling, idleness, and many other vices. No doubt the true interest of Spain would be promoted by recognizing the independence of those countries, but it must be on condition of receiving a just compensation for the immense labour and capital invested by her subjects in the civilization and cultivation of those wild regions, where no vestiges of civil life existed till they were introduced by the Spaniards, and where every town and house is the result of Spanish capital and labour, as appears by the name and date affixed on every building by the authorities. It would be the height of folly in Spain, to give up her right and title to her former possessions for nothing, or indeed without having a suitable indemnity solemnly guaranteed by the European powers, who are deeply interested in the tranquillization of those countries. This basis once admitted, the Spanish government *ought not to delay for an hour the full and ample recognition* of the independence of all those numerous American republics and governments: such a measure becomes the more urgent, as not only those countries and Spain, but the mercantile and manufacturing interests of Europe, are injuriously affected by the unsettled and anarchical condition of one of the most important parts of the world. It is especially the interest of England, with such an immense capital embarked in those countries, to put a stop to such a state of things; but it is to be feared this will never be effected, without the direct intervention of her power and capital, combined with the rights of Spain. A powerful and well organized military and mercantile association, with a large subscribed capital, in which not only the Spanish and English, but all the trading interests of Europe, were freely permitted to take a part, is perhaps the sole expedient for accomplishing the grand object of putting down anarchy, and establishing peace and regular government in South America: a result which would be equally important and beneficial to the country itself, and to the parties that effected it.

notes, deposits, and circulation, in the periods of distress; he may even foretel the coming evil, by remarking the preparatory issues of the preceding year, &c. &c. This brings us to notice the historical fact, that the over issue of these notes, at one time, was bringing the Bank of England to a manufactory of valueless paper. This establishment, which before 1740 had not two millions of notes in circulation, and which had increased its circulation in 1792 to about eleven millions, in 1810 had above 21,000,000*l.* in circulation!—but the value of its notes, compared with gold, became depreciated 13 per cent.: in 1812, its circulation was increased to 23,360,220*l.*—but its notes were depreciated 20 per cent.: lastly, in 1814, it was carried to 28,308,290*l.*—but its notes were depreciated 25 per cent. (Table X. and XIV. Part II.)

Had the war been protracted, had the Bank continued the enlargement of its circulation, and the abuse of its issues, there can be no doubt that Bank of England notes would have become like the Austrian or French

Twenty thousand European soldiers with *an enlightened European prince at their head,* would certainly meet with little or no resistance in Mexico, which is the principal part of Spanish America. An armed mercantile association, such as is here proposed, might be easily formed, in which the profits of the members, the interests of the presiding prince and his dynasty, and the advantages of all the countries concerned, should be equally secured: it is merely necessary for the British government to lend its countenance to the scheme, and the requisite capital could be subscribed, and the details arranged, with great facility. An ardent desire to see a termination of the wretchedness and anarchy of eighteen millions of human beings, at present oppressed, ruined, and spoiled, by a thousand inhuman, despotic, petty military tyrants, and to promote human happiness and civilisation all over the world, have perhaps carried the author beyond his subject; the magnitude and importance of the objects aimed at must be his apology.

assignats. But, fortunately for it, the war ceased—cash payments were re-established—and the credit of this establishment revived. The following facts and statements fully establish these truths.

Table XVI. Part II. shows the amount of gold coined and possessed, in each year since the peace of Paris, amounting, in the whole, to above 83 millions: besides the silver melted and coined, a specimen of the amount of which is given in Table XVII. Table XVIII. showing the highest and lowest amount of bullion and coin possessed by the Bank, in each year since 1815, is very important, as the public was never correctly informed on this point previous to this "Report". Table XIX. exhibits the total amount of gold and silver held in the several years since the peace; which, in 1815, was 2,179,000*l.*—in 1821, was about 8,000,000*l.*—in 1825, reached 11,000,000*l.*—and in 1831, was above 10,330,000*l.* Table XX. shows that the dividends paid in the present year amounted to 1,164,235: and Table XXI. that the net annual profits, on an average of four years, (including the present,) were 1,214,444*l.*; the profits of the present year reaching 1,689,176*l.* according to Table XXII.: while Table XXIII. shows the annual expenses to be only 339,000*l.*; and by Table IX. it appears, that the loss by forgeries in the last year, was no more than 1,891*l.* Table XIV. shows the amount of all securities and bullion held by the Bank from 1778, when it was about 13,000,000*l.* to 7th August, 1832, when it reached the prodigious sum of 33,130,000*l.*!!! the "rest" of 2,880,000*l.* not included. Tables XXIV. and XXV. show the present state of the affairs of the Bank: it appears by them, and according to the declaration of the committee, that it possesses 17,190,760*l.* over and above all its liabilities.

Such is the immense wealth of this establishment: such are the rise, progress, and actual state of this stupendous engine of the National Debt: and such have been some of the uses which the directors have made of their unrivalled power [a].

But, as a well-informed writer said above a century ago,—" since the Bank directors have obtained, that no society or corporation shall issue out bills of credit as a Bank, they have become the Stock Jobbers' Masters ". It remains, therefore, to show the origin and progress of that other engine of the National Debt—the Stock Exchange; which, though subordinate to the Bank, has powerfully contributed to increase the debt.

[a] The wealth and importance of this Corporation have become so immense, that it may not be uninteresting to know the names of the first Directors, which are here given from a copy of the Charter.

Sir John Houblon, Knight.—*Governor*.
Michael Godfrey, Esq.—*Deputy Governor*.

Directors.

Sir John Huband, Bart.
Sir James Houblon, Knt.
Sir William Gore, Knt.
Sir William Scawen, Knt.
Sir Henry Furnese, Knt.
Sir Thomas Abney, Knt.
Sir William Hedges, Knt.
Brook Bridges, Esq.
James Bateman, Esq.
George Boddington, Esq.
Edward Clerke, Esq.
James Denew, Esq.
Thomas Goddard, Esq.
Abraham Houblon, Esq.
Gilbert Heathcote, Esq.
Theodore Janssen, Esq.
John Lordell, Esq.
Samuel Lethieullier, Esq.
William Paterson, Esq.
Robert Raworth, Esq.
John Smith, of Beaufort Buildings, Esq.
Obadiah Sedgwick, Esq.
Nathaniel Tench, Esq.
John Ward, Esq.

SKETCH OF THE HISTORY OF THE STOCK EXCHANGE.

The Israelites, abhorred, detested, and persecuted by all other nations of the world, found at last a peaceful retreat and protection in Spain, which they enjoyed for above 1400 years. Their natural activity, their shrewdness, and their prudence, caused many of them to become the directors and managers of the revenues, and the advisers of the financial concerns, both of the Spanish and Moorish kings: thus the Jews acquired possession of the greater part of the commerce, and of all the money transactions of that rich peninsula. But after the conquest of Granada, and the union of the Spanish kingdoms, the universal tide of human persecution against the Jews reached even that country: and being partial to the conquered Moors, whom they aided and abetted in their revolts against their conquerors, the best pretext was afforded for their persecution and plunder. The superstition, the abuse of religion, the dereliction of the precepts and doctrine of the Gospel as taught by their Master, by a prejudiced clergy, joined to the bigotry of the kings and the ignorance of the Spanish ministers, led to the cruel and impolitic measure of their expulsion: and Spain was thus deprived of her capital and her monied men, who spread their skill over all the world. But by a natural feeling, the Spanish Jews, proud of their origin, flocked in greater numbers to those nations which were under Spanish sway, than to any other[a]: and by that anti-economical persecution

[a] The Spanish Jews were considered the nobility and aristocracy of the Jewish nation; and preserve this proud distinction, at Rome, Leghorn, Constantinople, and in Asia and Africa, to the present day.

in Spain, the Low Countries and Holland obtained the greatest commercial benefits. The commercial towns of the last increased in importance: her markets were in full activity; and Amsterdam became the centre of all money transactions, by the addition of so many practical, rich, and skilful individuals. Many of these, attentive to profit, and following the customs of their ancestors towards the Moorish and Spanish kings, accompanied the army of King William when he came to this country.

The decided propensity of that monarch for war, and the sums required to defray its expenses, involved him in great difficulties; and, consequently, money transactions were multiplied. One of the principal of these was the large loan, in virtue of which the Bank of England was established. But this establishment, which had obtained the exclusive privilege of dealing "in all jewels, plate, bullion, or other goods, chattels, or merchandise whatsoever, which shall be pawned into this corporation", could not exercise this lucrative prerogative without the aid of the intelligent men, who had for ages carried on that business. Thus the Bank became crowded with busy Jews—the most active and necessary agents of the corporation. The charter, moreover, contained a proviso, "that the capital stock and yearly fund of 100,000*l.* shall be assignable, assigned, transferable and transferred, and that there shall be constantly kept in the public office of the said Governor and Company of the Bank of England, a register, or book or books, where all assignments and transfers shall be entered" (see the original charter): but it was impossible either to effect this, or to enhance the price of that stock, without the active interference and capital of the most practised men of the age in operations of that sort. The jobbing system, therefore, with all its cunning tricks, and all the machinery of the Stock Exchange, commenced under the roof of the Bank itself.

In the succeeding reign, foreign war was continued on a larger scale; and the national debt following, in its increase, the destructive course of those wars, stock jobbing equally advanced: the nation became infected with it. Every battle, every defeat or victory, furnished the Stock Exchange people with the grounds for their operations, and gave rise to new combinations, and to new and more refined improvements. The great and wealthy Jew Medina, was to be seen accompanying the great English hero Marlborough in his campaigns; alluring his avarice, and bribing his partiality, with a pension of 6000*l.* a year. This great monied man of the time, was to be seen getting thousands on the Stock Exchange, by sending quicker advices of the battles of Ramilies, Oudenarde, Malplaquet, and Blenheim; just as has been effected in our time, by early intelligence of those of Talavera, Salamanca, Victoria, and Waterloo.

However the Stock Exchange people becoming too numerous, and encumbering too much the Bank offices, were compelled, about this time, (1700,) to choose a larger place for their meetings, and the exercise of their avocations. 'Change Alley became their famous place of resort: "The centre of jobbing," exclaims a writer of that time, "is the kingdom of 'Change Alley." The enormous profits made by the association, the malpractices of the greater part of its members, and the insolence of the richer ones, excited the just alarm of a steady and reflecting nation, unaccustomed to such manœuvres; and public and patriotic writers began to attack their increasing power. "The villany of stock jobbing is called a mystery, or machine of trade," says one of these: "this destructive Hydra, this new corporation of hell," exclaims another: while one of them gives the most skilful military directions, in order to besiege, and bring to surrender, "that infamous place, 'Change Alley,'—" to storm it, and put to death all the inhabitants, without giving quarter to any." Another writer declares in the most serious manner, that "the general cry against stock jobbing has been so long, and it has been so justly complained of as a public nuisance, that these people are hardened in crime: all their art is a mere system of cheat and delusion; their characters are as dirty as their employments, and the best thing that can be said of them is, that there happen to be *two* honest men amongst them":—"their employment becomes a crime: this sort of men are more dangerous than all national enemies abroad, an evil more formidable than pestilence, and more fatal to the public than an invasion of Spaniards":—"Exchange Alley, in fact, is as dangerous to the public safety, as a magazine of gunpowder to a populous city."[a]

Such were the attacks against the corporation of the Stock Exchange, and such was the general opinion entertained of it above a century ago: an opinion which has continued, and unfortunately has not entirely subsided at the present day. However, all those invectives, insults, and cruel attacks, did not obstruct the progress of the establishment: on the contrary, it became more powerful, and increased in proportion as the government was more extravagant and careless of the public

[a] "Anatomy of Exchange Alley," 1719.

money. It became, in fact, an indispensable engine of the government itself: but the latter was compelled, by the public opinion against the detested operations of the Stock Exchange, and in order to keep up appearances, to pass several acts against the very operations and the very gambling, it was so deeply though secretly fomenting. But those numerous acts had precisely the same effect that is justly attributed by Gibbon to the laws against usury enacted by the Twelve Tables, and by the government and clergy of the eastern and western empires. The mutual sense of benefit, and hope of profit, which triumphed over the laws of the republic and the empire, equally resisted the decrees of the church, and even overcame the prejudices of mankind. Such has been exactly the result of the acts of the British legislature against the gambling of the Stock Exchange. Avarice, idleness, and the hope of becoming rich in a short time without exertion, eluded and evaded all the laws of British wisdom, and sometimes disregarded even the common law of the land. Indeed the frequenters of the Stock Exchange increased in number. Sweeting's Alley was their next resort: Garraway's Coffee House was selected as a more convenient and comfortable place for the members; and any man might transact business there, by paying the moderate contribution of sixpence for entrance.

This powerful engine remained in this humble state, till the immense operations of the government and the Bank in 1802, required a proportionably greater support. Forty-nine millions (as has been before stated) were borrowed in that extraordinary year. It was already high time that the submissive but powerful supporters of operations of such magnitude and importance, should leave that obscure place, and get rid of such clumsy and wretched arrangements. Accordingly, in this very year, the leading men came forward, entered into a subscription, and erected the present building of the Stock Exchange: appointed trustees and managers, and a select committee of thirty; and formed a regular corporation and monopoly. They declared, "that the Committee for general purposes shall admit such persons (whether proprietors or not) as they shall think proper, to attend or frequent the Stock Exchange, for transacting therein the business of a stock broker or jobber, &c., at the price which, for the time being, shall have been fixed by the trustees and managers for such admission." (Deed of settlement, sec. 37). And, following the charter of the Bank in all its bearings, they appointed officers, &c.: using the word chairman instead of governor: deputy chairman instead of deputy governor: and, instead of direction, committee for general purposes, of whom "seven are to be a quorum, and to have *the sole management, regulation, and direction* of the concerns of the undertaking, except the treasurership thereof, and the management and direction of the buildings." (Deed of settlement, sec. 9). "The chairman shall have a casting vote" (sec. 11): and "the secretary shall hold his office during the pleasure of the committee." It is true, the chairman and deputy chairman do not take the oath after their election, that the governor and deputy governor of the Bank do, in virtue of which they "do promise and swear, that they will do the utmost in their power, and *by all lawful ways and means* endeavour, to support and maintain the body politic and fellowship of the government and company of the Bank of England (Stock Exchange!) and the liberties and privileges thereof, and that in the execution of the said office, they will faithfully and honestly demean themselves, according to the best of their skill and understanding, so help them God" (see the original charter of the Bank); but this corporation is invested with the power of enacting "Rules, Orders, and Bye-Laws", more imperative, strong, and exclusive, than those of the Bank itself.

The regulations state, that "every member of the Stock Exchange shall attend the committee for general purposes when called upon."—"The committee have the right to expel any of their members who may have been guilty of dishonourable or disgraceful conduct."—"The committee is endowed with the power of dispensing with the rules and regulations of the corporation itself." "A foreigner, not naturalized, or not having the letter of denization, is inadmissible, unless he shall have been a *constant resident in this country during the five years immediately preceding his application for admission,* and unless he be recommended by *five* members of the Stock Exchange, who are required also *to join in the usual pecuniary engagement.*"—"*Any person who shall be admitted, and shall afterwards engage in other than Stock Exchange business, or business connected therewith, shall cease to be a member.*" But the founders of the Stock Exchange, with a more profound knowledge of the human heart than the Bank directors, and convinced how strongly exterior objects act upon the senses of the multitude, gave, to the admission of new members to their corporation, that solemnity which might impress upon their minds the high duties they are called upon to perform. The candidate, accompanied by three members if an Englishman, and by five if, unfortunately, he be a foreigner, "shall appear in the presence of the chairman of the committee, who shall put to him the following questions, the answers to which shall be entered on the minutes."

1. Is this your signature? (showing him his letter of application.)

2. Have you read the resolution on the back of this letter?

3. Are you a natural born subject?

4. Are you of age?

5. Are you engaged in partnership?

6. Are you, or is your wife, (if he has any,) engaged in business?

7. Are you a clerk in any public or private establishment?

The chairman, in addition to any other questions that may appear to be necessary, shall, to each of the recommenders, put the following[a], &c. &c. (Regulations, p. 10.)

[a] One of these is:—"Have you accepted, or are you hereafter to accept, either directly or indirectly, from the party or his friends, an indemnity for the sum in which you are bound?"

Another of the regulations is:—"Members who recommend any person for admission, *must attend, with the person recommended*, at one o'clock of the day on which the ballot for him is to take place; and they are expected to have *a personal knowledge of the party and his circumstances*, so that each of them shall be enabled to give a satisfactory account of the same, when called upon by the committee. And this regulation shall be inserted at the foot of the letter of admission."

The letter of recommendation runs thus:—"We recommend Mr. —— as a fit and proper person to be admitted a Member of the Stock Exchange; and in case he shall be *publicly declared to be a defaulter, either in the Stock Exchange or Foreign Stock Market, within two years from the date of his admission*, we each of us hereby engage to pay to his creditors, upon application, the sum of three hundred pounds, to be applied in discharge of the said defaulter's debts."

One

The ceremonial performed at the installation of a chevalier of the Order of the Garter, or even of the Golden Fleece, is certainly not more impressive, nor the act of the *accolade* itself so awful, as the admission of a member to the Stock Exchange.

But however laughable and ridiculous all this may appear to unreflecting minds, it is by this means, by "the deed of settlement," and by its "regulations and bye-laws," that the Stock Exchange has become a more politic, exclusive, and corporate body, than the Bank of England, without incurring the expense of a charter, or the odium of possessing one. Its power, consequently, received a greater impulse; and in spite of public opinion, and the disgraceful conduct of some of its members, the government began to treat that body with some little consideration: they even ventured to mention the Stock Exchange in the House of Commons with a certain degree of respect: the commissioner for the reduction of the national debt was sent into the house of the Stock Exchange; and the Bank, the moment they received an order to enter into any financial operation with the government, sent a message to that corporation, giving the full particulars of it.

How much this body politic, after it received its organization, aided the operations of the Bank combined with those of the government, is shewn by the immense debt annually created from 1802 till the peace of Paris. The facts speak for themselves. The activity, the exertions, the contrivances, the allurements, displayed by its 700 members towards all classes of society, to induce them to part with their money, can

One of the regulations states:—"That no application, which has for its object *the annulling of any bargain*, in the Stock Exchange, shall be attended to by the Committee."

may be judged of by the magnitude of the operations, and the success which attended them. They evidently prevailed in falsifying that elegant verse of Juvenal. "— quando major avaritiæ patuit sinus!" for in these epochs that passion was still more largely excited.

The power of the corporation at the peace, therefore, was very considerable: but the operations of the government and the Bank having comparatively ceased since that period, the power of that body might naturally be expected to have decreased also. This however was not the case. An immense and boundless field was opened to the establishment by the new system of *rentes* and borrowing adopted by the continental powers. Members of the Stock Exchange who had never before travelled further than from their lodgings to Sweeting's Alley or the new 'House,' ran, with perfect ease, the extraordinary distances from London to Paris, and from Petersburgh to Madrid. The French *rentes*, and Russian, Prussian, Austrian, Spanish, Portuguese, and Poyais bonds, were as easily sold in London, as consols or omnium before the peace. Their security, stability, and the certain payment of the dividends, were most positively assured and guaranteed, by the most clever and influential members. John Bull was led to believe, that M'Gregor's faith was as good as the Bank of England, and that Great Britain was nothing compared to the unbounded and productive territory of the "kingdom of mosquitos."* It is not surprising that, with such assurances, the most cautious of the John Bull tribe preferred the large annual interest of the Cacique, to the small one which the British funds yield. Thus the enormous sum of 72,694,571*l.*

* The [illegible] sold as high as 75: they may now be bought for 1[illegible]

was borrowed by foreign powers, in the incredibly short period of seven years (1822 to 1829), through the agency and influence of this powerful body!! (Table XXXI. Part II.)

All sorts of people, and even the most grave and respectable members of the corporation, regardless of the dignity of their establishment, began to deal in those securities, in the open air of the Royal Exchange. It was impossible that such extraordinary events, such a new field of Stock Exchange operations, could be foreseen, even by the comprehensive minds of the founders of the modern House: consequently, the deed of settlement did not provide for them. But the most reflecting members soon came forward, and, to remedy this defect, and put a stop to such transcendant evils, conceived the just idea of monopolizing all the profits. They contrived a plan-for creating a Foreign Stock Exchange, but entirely dependent on, and subservient to, their own. A subscription was raised for this salutary purpose, in a few hours; and a building erected communicating with the "house." Regulations, bye-laws, and a committee followed, but all subservient to the great committee for general purposes; and by these wise and temperate measures, not only its own stray members, but the new votaries and their unforeseen but profitable business, were brought under the judicious control, and lucrative monopoly, of the old establishment.

By these simple and unobtrusive measures has the power of this corporation reached its present height. Its members have not only become the exclusive masters of the British market, but have acquired the immense power of directly controlling and regulating the funds and money markets of all Europe. No financial operation whatever can be safely undertaken in any of those markets, without consulting and obtaining the approbation of the "Committee of the Stock Exchange." The agents of the Bank of England have surpassed their principals: they really possess far greater power than their masters. A mere decision of a committee composed of individuals unknown beyond their own immediate circle, is more powerful, and will produce more effects in regard to any loan or financial measure, than all the laws of the sovereigns of Europe put together. Facts have, in several instances, demonstrated the truth of this assertion; and woe to the plans of Russian, Prussian, Austrian, or French ministers, unless they take proper measures to combine with the influential men of the English Stock Exchange. The unaccountable awkwardness of the Spanish ministers in neglecting this necessary precaution, has rendered the credit of Spain the lowest in the world: her funds are twenty-eight per cent. lower than those of the Pope himself! Those who are at present confidently asserting, that Don Miguel will be confirmed on the throne of Portugal by the produce of a loan raised here, or in any market in Europe, are but little acquainted with the construction, machinery, and influence of the London Stock Exchange. They ought to remember, that the loan of Don Pedro was, in the first instance, rejected; and that the emperor might be still under the refreshing shades of the orange trees of the Azores, had not another party, either forming a part of the committee, or enjoying its special favour, brought forward and contracted that very loan (or a similar one) which had been so solemnly disapproved.

But the power of the Stock Exchange is not limited to Europe: the New World has experienced its wonderful effects. The boundless Pampas, the colossal Cimborazo, and the deepest caverns of Guanaxuato, have equally felt the effects of its magical power: the armies of Bolivar, San Martin, and O'Higgins, were clothed, armed, and accoutred by its exertions; and to it the Spanish Americans are indebted both for their independence and their perpetual anarchy. It is unquestionably true that, without its interference, without its unremitting toils and efforts, England never would have sent, to those remote and wild regions, upwards of twenty-three millions and a half sterling, exclusive of the large sums sent on account of the mining companies. (Table XXXI.) The value of the American mining shares now, compared with what it was when the bubble began to burst, and the considerable sum paid and sent to Spanish America on account of these ruinous undertakings, are exhibited in Table XXXII. The schemes of 1824 would never have been carried to such an extent without the power of this establishment. This, therefore, must be considered as the grand epoch of the corporation: the number of its members reached a thousand, and each became in himself a small centre of operations and activity; at the east-end and the west-end—in the counting house of the merchant and the drawing-room of the peer—in the lobby of the House of Commons and the vestry-room of the church,—the shares of the establishment were bartered with equal eagerness; they superseded the most profitable national undertakings of Great Britain, and many of them were elevated to five times the amount of the original subscriptions. The spirited writer, who, exaggerating the crimes and the power of the people of Change Alley, and attacking them in the most unbecoming manner, said, above a century ago, "that the new corporation of hell could levy troops—set company against company—and alderman against alderman,"—certainly could not contemplate that a day would arrive, when these people would be so powerful, as not only to "set alderman against alderman," but to draw up armies against armies —and this, at the distance of thousands of miles from England; increasing, at the same time, the value of their own property five hundred per cent. by these very operations!

But the coarse style, and bitter invectives, so repeatedly employed against an association, necessary to the Bank, indispensable to the *system*, and encouraged by the government itself, must be strongly disapproved by every impartial and sensible man. These declamations, when uttered by disappointed gamblers, who ought to be aware of the infallible certainty of losing their property, and of the disastrous consequences of that abominable passion, lose their strength, from the very source whence they originate; and produce no other effect on the public than would result from the clamours raised by a set of unsuccessful gamblers, against their infamous and proscribed house of resort [a]. But when such invectives are delivered by the most respectable, well intentioned, and high class of public writers, they only produce an erroneous impression, without in any manner remedying the unavoidable evil of Stock Exchange gambling. It has been represented as an insignificant association, without power, and undeserving any serious consideration; as a body containing many members of the most despicable and contemptible character; but however true the latter part of the accusation may be, these pages abundantly prove the opinion of its insignificance and unimportance to be entirely unfounded: it has been clearly shewn, that this corporation actually possesses a

[a] It has been shewn and is capable of demonstration, that the disadvantages attending an operator in the Funds out of doors, and not being a member of the House, are considerably greater than the chances against a gambler at *Rouge et Noir*, or even at *Roulette*.

power equal to, or greater than, any in the state; and that its influence in creating the national debt has been immense. The association has besides given rise to several opulent and independent families, and even to some illustrious and noble houses, as Lord Eardley, and Lady Say and Sele, the grandchildren of the famous Israelite Gideon, Lord Dudley, &c. The name of Ricardo is well known to the financial world; and those of Bailey and Gompertz are equally celebrated in the sciences of astronomy and calculation.

However, the importance of the Stock Exchange has somewhat declined, since the failure of its gigantic operations on the other side of the Atlantic; and since the immense losses sustained by the public on that occasion, it has been less attended; the number of its members being reduced, at one time, as low as 400: at present their number is about 600[a]. It is worthy of remark, that during all these vicissitudes, the Israelite nation has maintained its original ascendancy in this branch; and that very few (comparatively speaking) of that calumniated people, have dishonoured their engagements.

But the Stock Exchange still preserves its immense power without any essential diminution, and its engrossing monopoly without the least encroachment. The

[a] It would have been gratifying to the author, and perhaps not uninteresting to the public, to have ascertained with exactness the number of the members, as well as many other important and well combined regulations and particulars, of this corporation. But his most active inquiries have been utterly fruitless: the members being exceedingly cautious; and the fittest person, who has had the honour of being in the service of the corporation for no less than twenty-one years, not daring to disclose any particulars or give any information whatever, without consulting the powerful committee for general purposes, and obtaining its express consent.

[illegible] infinitely [illegible] those of the Bank [illegible] of all the [illegible] monopoly, [illegible] expenses [illegible] advantages.

But [illegible] the Bank [illegible] preserving the restraining [illegible] banking com-panies [illegible] has in-[illegible] of all reflecting men, [illegible] allowing its members, most of whom [illegible] themselves brokers, to de-[illegible] from the [illegible] practice of the commercial world, by refusing to give the *principal* the means of verifying the terms on which his broker has made a con-tract for him. In mercantile transactions, every prin-cipal has the ready means of assuring himself of the price at which his broker has bought or sold any goods; it being the sacred and bounden duty of the opposite party's broker to give him a true and faithful answer as to the price, the terms of the bargain, &c. This essen-tial right of the employer, the foundation of reciprocal confidence, the mutual security of the contracting par-ties against fraud, is entirely frustrated and annulled by the practice of the Stock Exchange. In that establish-ment, when a principal, anxious to ascertain what has been the real conduct of his broker, (of whose fidelity he has perhaps well founded doubts,) addresses himself to the member whose name is mentioned in the contract, he is answered in the most uncivil and ungentlemanly manner—" Sir, you do not belong to the house—I have nothing to do with you." This unfair and unjust mode of proceeding, which has thrown, and continues to throw, the greatest dishonour upon this powerful cor-poration, ought not to be suffered: the sooner it is discontinued, the better for the welfare and credit of the establishment; or it may induce the belief, that this association, not satisfied with its immense power over all the financial operations of the world, wishes to surpass all other monopolies, in taking unfair advantage of the public against the generally received customs and laws of commerce among all nations.

But resuming the narrative of the history of the Debt, let us examine the effects of the active exertions of the component engines of the *system* in raising the amount of the national debt, during the brightest historical period of its increase.

The peace of Amiens came to relieve both humanity and the finances of the country. But Buonaparte and Pitt, those two monsters born for the extermination of their own race[a], soon deprived us of this blessing: it lasted only twelve months, nine days, and five hours. Pitt recommenced hostilities 14th March, 1803: the war was carried on on a larger scale, and with greatly increased slaughter and destruction: and of course the national debt kept pace with this increasing velocity. Loan succeeded loan in each year, to cover the accruing deficiencies. Nineteen millions were instantly created, in 1803; twenty-six millions more in the next year: the extraordinary sum of thirty-nine millions was created

[a] It may perhaps sound harsh to some readers to hear such strong epithets applied to Napoleon and Pitt; but they ought to reflect that, from the time that the first was infatuated with the desire of being an emperor, to the time when he was imprisoned in St. Helena, *above five millions of human beings were massacred—murdered—destroyed*, through the blind ambition of one, and the infamous policy of the other. The tears shed in eleven years on account of those wars would form a considerable river. Dupin calculates only two millions of Frenchmen: but in the Spanish peninsula alone, 450,000 French troops, and 800,000 Spaniards, were killed!

in 1805; and thirty-three millions more in the succeeding year*. (Table III. Part I.)

But all these immense sums did not pay the expenses of the coalition. The armies of the Republic, eager for victory, were ready to shew of what they were capable. But the greatest military man perhaps ever born, unfortunately directed his courage and abilities to satisfy his inordinate ambition. 220,000 men started at the same instant from the remote points of Europe: the grandest combined movements of immense corps d'armée, were performed with the rapidity and exactness of a military parade. The grand army, destined to conquer England, found itself, as if by enchantment, in the centre of Germany; opposing its front to the enemy on one side, while the army of Bernadotte faced them on the other. By unparalleled marches, they advanced to the distant Moravia; halting at Austerlitz to destroy the Austrian armies, and threaten the annihilation of the

* In 1803	£9,600,000	3 per cents.
	9,600,000	ditto reduced.
	£19,200,000	
1804	11,890,000	3 per cents.
	14,500,000	ditto reduced.
	£26,390,000	
1805	33,750,000	Consols.
	4,950,000	3 per cent. reduced.
	360,000	5 ditto ditto.
	£39,060,000	
1806	20,000,000	Consols.
	13,200,000	3 per cent. reduced.
	£33,200,000	

ancient House of Hapsburgh; and driving the Muscovites, with the Czar at their head, back to their remote haunts, prescribing the roads and marches they were to take.

Thus the coalition was defeated; and the spirit of Pitt sunk in affliction, despair, and disappointment. But he had formed a sect of fanatics, who affirmed "that the artificial capital created by the loans, was transformed into a fixed and solid one; and that it was as advantageous to the public, as if so much real additional treasure were added to the kingdom."[a] The system of parliamentary corruption, improved by Walpole, was consolidated by Pitt. The efforts of the Opposition to prevent the extravagant increase of the debt, were laughed at and easily overcome by a parliament composed of his creatures, and bought to vote as he commanded.

Percival, Vansittart, and Castlereagh, the successors and excellent disciples of Pitt, had only to pursue the system of their master: but they did more; and, like all sectarians, carried it to extremes. They borrowed, in 1809, above 17 millions and a half; in the years 1810 and 1811, they added above 31 millions, and in 1812 and in 1813, the enormous sum of 114 millions, to the debt: and lastly, in the two following years, 98 millions more were created by these statesmen[b]:

[a] "Reflections on the National Debt."

[b]

In 1809		£8,760,000	4 per cents.
		8,760,000	3 ditto reduced.
		£17,520,000	
1810	12,000,000	15,600,000	3 per cents.
		1,245,000	Consols.
1811	12,000,000	12,000,000	3 per cent. reduced.
		2,400,000	Consols.
		£31,245,000	

1812

how else, indeed, could they have paid such swarms of northern barbarians?

Those who have so often boasted, "that for gold, fertilized by gallant British blood, this country has reaped incorruptible honour," cannot reasonably be dissatisfied with the measures adopted by these ministers to effect this result.

But let us proceed to notice the great financial plan of Vansittart. It was composed of ten resolutions, all of which received the sanction of parliament: the second of these declared, "that 238,355,143*l.*, (a sum exceeding, by 118,893*l.*, the whole unfunded debt of 1786,) were already redeemed; that such sum ought to be cancelled; and that ministers could make use of a part of the Sinking Fund, *without infringing or contradicting the views upon which it was established by Pitt.*" They made use, therefore, of this fund, and, like unprincipled merchants, abused the credit of the British nation: for, not contented with adding immensely to the *funded* debt, they increased the *unfunded* by prodigious issues of Exchequer Bills; so

1812 ...	22,500,000 ...	27,126,000 ...	3 per cent. reduced
	12,000,000 ...	12,000,000 ...	Consols.
	27,000,000 ...	23,100,000 ...	3 per cent. reduced.
1813	....	12,600,000 ...	Consols.
	22,000,000 ...	24,500,000 ...	3 per cent. reduced.
		14,940,000 ...	Consols.
		£114,266,000	
1814 ...	24,000,000 ...	5,640,000 ...	Consols.
		7,200,000 ...	5 per cents.
		19,200,000 ...	3 per cent. reduced.
1815 ...	36,000,000 ...	46,800,000 ...	ditto.
		3,600,000 ...	4 per cents.
		15,840,000 ...	Consols.
		£98,280,000	

that, in 1815, their amount exceeded 67 millions and a half—a sum larger than the whole national debt in the middle of George the Second's reign.

These immense transactions enable us to conceive the enormous losses sustained, the extent of the operations of the funding system, and the rapid progress of the debt. But the official Tables annexed, which the reader is particularly entreated to examine, give a more correct and complete idea of these extraordinary operations: they afford incontestible evidence that in 1807 thirty-five millions of debt were created, and fifteen redeemed—in 1813, fifty millions were created, and twenty-four redeemed—finally, that in 1814, one hundred and six millions were raised, and twenty-seven redeemed!! (Table IV. Part II.) The result of this grand process of creating and redeeming was, that during the second mis-called revolutionary war, in the short space of eleven years, the debt was increased 335,983,164*l.*; as, after the peace of Paris, its total amount was 864,822,441*l.*!!! (Tables II. and IV. Part II.)—a sum four times greater than all the stock of coined money existing in the world, according to Storch's calculations [a].

The party who style the funding system "the master-piece of human policy," have here the most ample field to indulge their reveries: let it merely be observed, that the national debt, like a snowball, insignificant at first, has increased in size during its course, till it has become an awful and tremendous *avalanche!*

However, in the next peaceful period, its violent and overwhelming course is arrested.

[a] Storch's "Economie Politique" calculates it at £221,000,000
Humboldt at 325,000,000
Jacob at 380,000,000

PART II.

PROGRESS AND PRESENT STATE OF THE NATIONAL DEBT AND FUNDING SYSTEM.

THIRD PERIOD.

FROM THE PEACE OF PARIS TO THE PRESENT TIME.

Financial measures adopted by the Administrations in this period towards the reduction of the National Debt.—Rise in the value of the Funds and in public credit.—Reduction of the interest on Exchequer Bills from 5½ to 3½ per cent.—Conversion of the 3 per cents. into 3½ per cent. Stock.—Cash payments resumed.—Opposite opinions of the two powerful parties as to the results of this great measure.—Conversion of the 5 per cents. into 4, and of the 4 per cents. into 3½.—Late prospective operation for the reduction of the Debt.—Origin, progress, and end of the Sinking Fund.—Violation of the Acts to regulate its application.—Its delusive nature, and the effects produced by it on the public mind and national credit.—The absurd manner in which the Funding System has been conducted, and the original cause of those measures.—Final results of the Fund in regard to the reduction of the Public Debt.—Opinion of the Finance Committee on this subject.—Trifling and almost incredible amount of the reduction of the National Debt in this long period of peace.—Its present actual amount.

THE artificial stimulus ceased with the war. The effects produced by the sudden transition to peace, although similar, were much greater than those which took place at the peace of 1783, and after the first war of the revolution. A reduction of forty-four millions per annum in the expenditure, in consequence of the peace, could not fail to be severely felt by all the productive classes: but we ought not to conclude from this, as one party contended, that the national debt was "a bounteous inundation, which carried riches and fertility along with it," or "that it was additional and substantial property produced by the funding system, combined with taxation": in the opinion of an opposite party, the debt, instead of "riches and fertility," carried with it "distress and terror." Let us, therefore, examine the various stages of its increase and decrease during this peaceful period.

The Chancellor of the Exchequer combining with the Bank, (that powerful engine on the enlargements or contractions of which, as has been observed, public credit mainly depends,) very soon increased the value of the public securities nearly 20 per cent. (Table XXXIII. Part II.) The funds, which in 1816 were at 62, rose at the commencement of 1817 to 79. This favourable circumstance was not overlooked: the interest on exchequer bills was reduced, in this year, from 5½ to 3¼ per cent.; and, while only three millions were added to the debt, above twenty-three millions were cancelled in the same year. (Table IV. Part II.) This was the first operation of the funding system after the peace. But the Bank continued its enlarging operations, and the public securities followed the rising movements. The interest of a portion of the public funds was transferred from a lower, to a higher denomination: the 3 per cent. stock was converted into 3½ per cent.; thereby effecting a reduction of the debt, by inducing the holders of the former stock to buy into the latter at a higher price. Thus the small sum of 3,000*l.* was created, while more than nineteen millions of the national debt were reduced in this year (1818).

The great measure for re-establishing a security against the excessive issue of paper money, the act for the resumption of cash payments, passed in the following year[a]. The ministry, with the most honourable

[a] In a pamphlet published by the late Mr. Huskisson it is stated, "that as far back as 1797, it had been foreseen, that should this

firmness, held a middle course between the two powerful contending parties; and although the beneficial results of that great national measure have been practically experienced, its supporters and opponents have not, and never will, come to an understanding. Circumstances not unlike those which happened in Pelham's time, occurred on this occasion, but with greater advantages.

The grand measure of reducing the five per cents. into fours, was next proposed. Never had the Bank possessed such an amount of coin and bullion at one time. They had above thirteen millions in their coffers, (Table XVIII. Part II.); and they further increased the circulation, by throwing a large amount of paper into the market, by lowering the rate of interest from 5 to 4 per cent., and by the produce of the arrangement with government respecting the half-pay and pension annuities. Thus, by the union of the ministerial and banking powers, the enormous sum of 140,250,828*l.* of 5 per cents., was easily converted into 147,263,328*l.* of 4 per cents. It is true, the capital was increased; but an annual saving of 1,222,000*l.* was effected in the interest. Such was the advantageous operation of 1822, stigmatized by a powerful party, " as a fraud committed on the public creditors." [a]

temporary expedient be attempted to be converted into a system for an indefinite number of years, every creditor, public and private, to whom the law had secured the payment of a pound of gold for every 46*l.* 17*s.* 6*d.*, would be obliged to accept about ten and a half ounces, or 17*s.* in the pound, in satisfaction of his demand: and that it is impossible to conceive, that parliament would not be alive to such enduring injustice, and ultimate public calamity, and provide for the termination of the restriction."

[a] " An Account of the Manœuvres between the Bank and the Government."

The continuation of the same favourable causes produced similar effects in 1824. Four per cents., to the amount of 76,806,882*l.*, were changed into an equal amount of stock bearing an interest of three and a half per cent. This operation, besides effecting an annual saving of 381,034*l.*, had the particular advantage of making no addition to the capital of the debt. Nobody would believe, had not some of the directors solemnly declared it to be so, that this operation was effected by the issue of Bank notes! It is not surprising that the convulsion, the distress, and the horrors, of the panic of 1825, resulted from those artificial measures.

However, the funding system continued its operations; and in 1827, 8,500,000*l.* of debt were created, while 2,866,528*l.* were redeemed. (Table IV. Part II.) But in 1828, the "sinking fund," one of the three co-operative powers of that system, was destroyed. This engine of delusion was condemned by the finance committee of this year; as well as the system of borrowing upon its principle. This powerful piece of the funding machinery is so important that it is necessary to give a sketch of its origin, progress, and end.

It has already been mentioned, that as far back as 1717, a sinking fund was established "for the redemption of the national debt incurred before 1716, and for none other use, intent, or purpose whatever." Notwithstanding which, this arrangement was violated, and the public faith built upon it most shamefully insulted, twelve years afterwards, by charging this fund with the payment of the interest of the loan; and to this breach of faith, succeeded another, of even a more destructive character, by which the very design of its foundation was frustrated. The supplies for the year 1733 were

[illegible]

... raised by loans on perpetual or terminable annuities, a sum equal to one per cent. on the stock created by such loans, should be issued out of the produce of the consolidated fund quarterly, to be placed to the account of the commissioners." These measures accelerated the progress of the sinking fund, while the future loans carried in themselves the principle of self-extinction.

By this means the original sinking fund had increased in 1802 to 2,551,157l. 1s. 9d.; which sum was then added to 3,275,143l. 2s. 3d.—the amount of the new. Thus a new sinking fund made its appearance, the whole amount of which was to be exclusively

* Budget of 1791.

applied to the redemption of the debt; providing also, that "the fund should accumulate until the existing redeemable annuities should be paid off." In this manner, the former limitation of this fund, established on the great principle of compound interest, was done away with.

Vansittart, considering the amount of this sinking fund insufficient, proposed, that even "on exchequer bills, and other floating unfunded property, a sinking fund of one per cent. should be annually voted." It has been already stated, in the history of the revenue, how this minister dealt with the sinking fund, and how he repealed the act of 1802, as far as it directed, "that the produce of the sinking fund should accumulate at compound interest for the extinction of the debt;" contending at the same time, that "the public faith was strictly preserved": and while he disposed of the sinking fund in this manner, he created another, by enacting "that whenever the sum borrowed in any year should exceed the sum to be paid off, a sinking fund should be provided for the excess of the loan, equal to one and a half per cent. of its interest."

The ministers who succeeded Vansittart were even less considerate towards the sinking fund. They took twelve millions from it in 1819, without the least compunction; and in the following year, under the pretext that its amount was seventeen millions, twelve millions more were appropriated to purposes quite foreign to its original institution. In 1820, similar operations were repeated[a]; the still larger sum of thirteen millions being taken from it. In this manner, these pitiless ministers boldly went on bleeding that robust body; until at last, the finance committee of 1828 completely exhausted it,

[a] Com. Jour.

and condemned both it, and the system of borrowing upon its principle. The Chancellor of the Exchequer, adopting this sentence of condemnation, signed its death warrant on the 11th July, when it was enacted, that for the future "the amount of the sinking fund, be the actual surplus of the revenue over the expenditure."[a] Thus breathed its last that wonderful being, the hope of the past generation, and of Pitt's votaries; that wonderful engine, whose lever, resting on the public imagination, was moved by the powerful and natural wish of the nation to see that enormous burden, the debt, extinguished.

Those who so much admire the unbroken faith of the financial engagements of the British parliament, should not overlook in their enthusiastic encomiums the above statement of historical facts. Had the operation of the sinking fund been always confined to the legitimate and proposed ends of its institution, there would be no question of its great and beneficial results, in ultimately redeeming the debt: but the deception of the sinking fund consisted, not in its original and essential constitution, but in the extension of its operation when no *surplus*, but on the contrary a large *deficiency* of income existed: when, for the purpose of maintaining that public delusion of redeeming the national debt, it was necessary to increase the debt itself in a larger amount than the sum redeemed.

But although one of the three elements of the funding system was lost, the action of that system was not on that account discontinued. A prospective operation was contrived in May, 1830, to transfer into Three-and-a-half per cents. the Fours created on the reduction of the Fives in 1822 (above mentioned). One of the

[a] Act 10 Geo. IV. c. 27.—Came into operation, 5th July 1829.

conditions of this transaction was, "that the new Stock should not be subject to redemption at any time before the 5th January, 1849": and an option was offered to the holders to receive 70*l.* of new Fives, or 100*l.* of 3½ per cents. for every 100*l.* of 4 per cent. annuities. This operation is called *prospective*, because the advantage of the plan is, that when the stipulated term shall have expired, as much relief may be obtained by the nation from every payment of 70*l.* employed in cancelling 5 per cents., as by the payment of 100*l.* when applied to the discharge of 3½ per cents.; both being redeemable at par. The ministers departed, in this instance, from the almost general rule observed in the Funding System; notwithstanding which, the measure produced a beneficial annual saving of 700,000*l.*

The author has entered into the details of these operations, not only to show the progress of the plans and mode in which the Funding System acted, (more especially after the peace,) but from the great pleasure he feels when he sees the attempt made to reduce the National Debt, and consequently to alleviate its pressure upon the British people. Nevertheless, he is bound in justice to declare, that the operations of that System were conducted, on the whole, in a manner equally awkward and absurd. Large issues of money were yearly made to the Commissioners, who, acting in accordance with the principles of the System, added and redeemed annually. In 1829, 4,900,000*l.* were created, and 6,000,000*l.* reduced: 154 millions were created in 1830, and 168 millions reduced; but what was the result? (Table IV.) The Committee of 1828 itself shall tell us:—"in a few years (says the Fourth Report) which preceded the virtual abandonment of the system, one hundred and twenty millions had been added to the capital of the

National Debt, while the purchases of the Commissioners had fallen so far short of that sum, that the unredeemed capital of the Unfunded Debt was greater at the commencement of 1823 than it had been in 1818, by the large sum of 25 millions"! Such was the *wisdom* displayed in the management of this system.

What then has been the actual reduction in the long period of peace? The Finance Committee—that combination of knowledge, patriotism, and talent—declares, "that the total reduction effected from 1816 to 1828 in the National Debt, was *three millions and a half!!!!* Is it possible to believe our senses? In fourteen years of peace, with an immense increase of resources, with an augmentation of industry, prosperity, manufactures, and commerce, with the talents of the ministers, the power of the Bank, the manœuvres of the Stock Exchange, and the means of the Sinking Fund,—is it possible, that with all these amazing and combined forces, only a paltry reduction of three millions and a half could be effected in the National Debt? The total of this Debt, on the 5th January, 1832, amounted to 782,667,234*l.*[a] (Tables IV. and XXXIV. Part II.)

[a] Besides this amount, which constitutes the Funded and Unfunded Debt, there are the terminable annuities. The amount of these, for lives and terms of years, is about 3,297,375*l.* per annum. Estimating these annuities at their market value, the capital which they represent may be stated at £56,055,375
To which adding 782,667,234

Total amount of Debt £838,722,609

CONCLUSION.

Thus we have seen, that the National Debt of England originated in the real or fictitious wants of her rulers. We have remarked that some of her proud kings pledged their crowns, their royal robes, and even the jewels of their wives, to borrow money, while others shamefully defrauded their creditors; but it appears that the British people, more than any other, constantly insisted on being repaid the cash they advanced to their sovereigns. We have noticed the practice of contracting loans for short periods, assigning funds to redeem the principal and interest; and that practice changed, by the adoption of new principles. We have seen that a system, till then quite unknown, was introduced by William III.; and that the funding system was brought into action in all its essential branches, in the very reign in which it originated. It has been shewn, that the National Debt, amounting at the Revolution to only 664,000*l.*, was increased to above 146,000,000*l.*! by two aristocratical factions—by the sums expended for the preservation of Hanover—and by the expenditure in several foreign wars; and that men in power not only imposed on the nation such an enormous burden, but contrived to raise money by drawing upon posterity, and establishing the first regular system of corruption, avarice, fraud, malversation, and gambling.

The reign of George III., however, commenced with better auspices: ten millions of the Debt were reduced; the Sinking Fund of Price was adopted; and above four millions and a half more were redeemed, in the interval of peace and by Pitt's measures. One of these, that bold and wise project, the Restriction Act, gave the greatest power to the propelling engines of the Funding System, namely, the Bank—the Sinking Fund—and the Stock Exchange, which acted in union, and consequently with a force proportionably increased. We have traced the origin and progress of this System, and have seen its immense power, and the use made of it to increase the Debt. We have seen Pitt, pursuing his policy of foreign interference, widen the range of that System; and his successors carry it to the greatest extreme, by issuing enormous sums in Exchequer bills, and by creating 100 millions and redeeming 27 millions in one year. The general effect of all these combined powers and operations, even exceeded the expectations of the most enthusiastic founders of the System: but the grand general result was, the creation of a National Debt of 864 millions!!!

Lastly, we find that the ministers, combining with the Bank, began by reducing the interest on Exchequer bills from 5¼ to 3¼ per cent.: to that operation succeeded the conversions of 3 per cent. Stock into 3½ per cent.—of 5 per cent. into 4—and lastly, of 4 into 3½. The restoration of cash payments also took place in this period. We have seen the Sinking Fund often and shamefully infringed upon, until at last it has been entirely annihilated. The absurd manner in which the operations of this fund have been conducted, has been demonstrated by the fact of there being 25 millions more Debt in 1823 than in 1818, although 120 millions were issued to the Commissioners for its redemption. In short we find ourselves, at the end of this period, with almost the same amount of Debt as at its commencement.

It appears then, that this enormous debt has been chiefly raised by means of the Bank and the Stock Exchange, aided by the delusion of the sinking fund; and that it has been principally expended in wars, most of them undertaken against the true interests of a maritime, manufacturing, and commercial nation like England—a nation whose happy topographical situation renders her entirely independent of continental broils and quarrels. Its amount has been immensely increased in time of war; while the reductions effected in time of peace have been exceedingly limited. In the first period of peace, of twelve years' duration, ten millions were reduced; in the second, which lasted ten years, only four millions and a half; and in the last and longest, exceeding fifteen years, the amount of the reduction has been so trifling, that it seems almost incredible. When we consider the very inconsiderable reduction effected during so protracted an interval of peace, with all our immense resources, and increasing revenue, the most alarming considerations naturally arise for the time to come. The legislature, the economists, and the reflecting men, so numerous in England, have, in this subject, an unbounded field for the most serious meditation. But leaving them to speculate on the probability of future reduction, let us proceed to examine the effects of this debt, and its annual interest, upon the sources of production, upon the wealth and capital, and upon the happiness and prosperity of the people. And first, let us endeavour to ascertain what are the Means and Capital of the British empire.

TABLES TO PART II.

TABLE I.

State of the Debts of the Commonwealth.

	£.	s.	d.
To the Navy, 1658	541,465	14	7
To the Army in England, 1659	223,747	8	5¼
To ditto in Scotland	93,827	13	0¾
To ditto . . Citadel of Leith	1,800	0	0
To ditto in Ireland	299,225	5	4
To ditto ditto	71,903	12	0
To the Forces in Jamaica, abating for the provisions . .	110,228	11	3¾
To several persons for provisions in Flanders	13,153	6	1
To ditto for monies charged by Acts of Parliament	268,047	19	6
To ditto charged upon the Exchequer . .	124,184	15	6
The whole Debt at present is . .	£1,747,584	5	9¾
Besides which there is a growing Debt incurred for the Navy	393,882	8	0
And for the Issues exceeding the Income	332,823	6	4
The whole Debt of the Public at present and before the year's end is, and will be (1659)	£2,474,290	0	1¾

TABLE II.

Showing the Comparative Increase and Decrease of the National Debt, from its commencement, arising from the arrangement made by Charles II. with his Creditors, to the present time.

	Principal.	Interest.
National Debt at the Revolution . . .	664,263	39,855
Increase during the Reign of King William .	15,730,439	1,271,087
Debt at the Accession of Queen Anne . .	16,394,702	1,310,942
Increase during the Reign of Queen Anne .	37,750,661	2,040,416
Debt at the Accession of George I. . .	54,145,363	3,351,358
Decrease during the Reign of George I. . .	2,053,128	1,133,807
Debt at the Accession of George II. . .	52,092,235	2,217,551
Decrease during the Peace	5,137,612	253,526
Debt at the commencement of the Spanish War 1739	46,954,623	1,964,025
Increase during the war	31,338,689	1,096,979
Debt at the end of the Spanish War 1748 .	78,293,312	3,061,004
Decrease during the Peace	3,721,472	664,287
Debt at the commencement of the War 1755	74,571,840	2,396,717
Increase during the War	72,111,004	2,444,104
Debt at the conclusion of the Peace 1762 .	146,682,844	4,840,821
Decrease during the Peace	10,739,793	364,000
Debt at the commencement of the American War 1776	135,943,051	4,476,821
Increase during the War	102,541,819	3,843,084
Debt at the conclusion of the American War 1783	238,484,870	8,319,905
Decrease during the Peace	4,751,261	143,569
Debt at the commencement of the French Revolutionary War	233,733,609	8,176,336
Increase during the War	295,105,668	12,252,152
Debt at the Peace of Amiens—1st Feb. 1801 .	528,839,277	20,428,488
Increase during the second War . . .	335,983,164	20,796,796
Debt at the Peace of Paris—1st Feb. 1816 .	864,822,441	41,225,257
Decrease since the Peace	82,155,207	12,883,841
Debt on 5th Jan. 1832	782,667,234	28,341,416

TABLES TO THE BANK.

TABLE V.

An Account of the Variations which have taken place in the Amount of the Capital of the Bank, at different periods, from the date of the first Charter to the present time.

Year		£.	s.	d.
1694	Original Subscription	1,200,000	0	0
1697	New Subscription	1,001,171	10	0
		2,201,171	10	0
1707	Subscription returned	1,001,171	10	0
		1,200,000	0	0
1709	New Subscription	1,001,171	10	0
		2,201,171	10	0
1709	New Subscription	2,201,171	10	0
		4,402,343	0	0
1709	A call of	656,204	1	9
		5,058,547	1	9
1710	A call of	501,448	12	11
		5,559,995	14	8
1722	New Subscription	3,400,000	0	0
		8,959,995	14	8
1742	A call of	840,004	5	4
		9,800,000	0	0
1746	A call of	980,000	0	0
		10,780,000	0	0
1782	A call of	862,400	0	0
		11,642,400	0	0
1816	Addition to the Stock of the several Proprietors of 25 per cent.	2,910,600	0	0
		£ 14,553,000	0	0

WILLIAM SMEE, Chief Accountant.

Bank of England, 3 June, 1832.

To face page

A View [illegible] her in Cash or by funding of Exchequer Bills; the amount of Cash a[illegible] the Stock from the Annuities; the Rates per £100 Cash at whi[illegible]nding of Exchequer Bills and Annuities, distinguishing the amoun[illegible] Funds by the Commissioners of the Sinking Fund in Great

ΓS.

ıding the Austrian and Portuguese Loans, ɜ Amount of the Funded Debt contracted, and also the Total Amount of Unredeemed th their Value, calculated at Eighteen Years' chase.

Navy and Ordnance Debt, &c. included prior to 1822 in the Unfunded Debt Accounts.	Total Unfunded Debt.	Total Unfunded and Unredeemed Debt.
£.	£.	Col. 6. £.
. . . .	8,759,500	248,453,400
1,608,208	10,010,177	249,210,896
1,918,320	10,161,889	247,859,554
2,216,651	11,637,020	247,828,335
2,382,002	12,642,485	247,274,950
1,929,338	13,076,902	246,121,867
2,301,280	12,488,649	244,026,514
2,837,491	14,825,860	244,440,306
5,747,824	18,501,116	252,535,834
7,863,637	19,036,475	266,913,712
12,024,615	26,913,307	328,774,613
4,921,897	19,300,989	374,624,763
7,006,722	21,233,906	402,759,742
6,539,282	21,736,158	436,672,492
6,624,119	28,328,219	451,695,766
9,537,999	37,318,037	484,465,201
9,774,498	31,795,788	528,839,277
3,505,408	20,997,352	543,229,138
4,719,650	25,384,173	553,644,815
5,193,578	31,213,231	577,016,549
7,016,100	34,227,792	607,757,724
6,775,278	33,982,378	627,936,665
6,159,371	38,471,501	640,204,574
5,486,688	45,725,888	650,013,362
6,931,760	46,701,148	661,490,239
6,681,263	45,072,851	669,374,787
5,969,250	49,159,953	684,743,401
6,958,273	54,680,617	716,090,575
9,232,383	59,264,952	799,288,487
7,154,995	68,882,979	821,740,215
4,571,678	48,510,501	864,822,441
2,127,372	52,082,287	848,282,479
5,358,349	66,772,364	843,514,767
5,939,608	53,095,008	844,962,322
[illegible]123	48,408,323	843,388,805
[illegible]	40,860,481	842,425,792
[illegible]	32,671,731	827,984,489
[illegible]	[illegible]	[illegible]

TABLE VI.

A STATEMENT of the ANNUAL DISTRIBUTIONS to the Proprietors of Bank Stock in the shape of Dividend, or otherwise, and the Amount per Cent. of such Distributions upon the Capital of the Bank, at the same time they were made, in each year, from 1790.

Years.	Capital.	Annual amount of Dividend.	Rate per Cent. per annum.	Bonuses.	Rate per Cents.	
1790	11,642,400	814,968	7			
1791	ditto	ditto	do.			
1792	ditto	ditto	do.			
1793	ditto	ditto	do.			
1794	ditto	ditto	do.			
1795	ditto	ditto	do.			
1796	ditto	ditto	do.			
1797	ditto	ditto	do.			
1798	ditto	ditto	do.			
1799	ditto	ditto	do.	1,164,240	In 5 per Cents. per Cent. on ca-	1797, being £10. pital of Bank Stock.
1800	ditto	ditto	do.			
1801	ditto	ditto	do.	582,120	In 5 per Cents. N Cent. on Capital	avy, being £5 per of Bank Stock.
1802	ditto	ditto	do.	291,060	In 5 per Cents. N per Cent. on cap	avy, being £2. 10s. ital of Bank Stock.
1803	ditto	ditto	do.			
1804	ditto	ditto	do.	582,120	£5. per cent. in	money.
1805	ditto	1,397,088	5 April 10 Oct.	£ [illegible] £ [illegible] } 12		
1806	ditto	ditto	5 April 10 Oct.	£ [illegible] £ [illegible] } 12		
1807	ditto	1,164,240	10			
1808	ditto	ditto	do.			
1809	ditto	ditto	do.			
1810	ditto	ditto	do.			
1811	ditto	ditto	do.			
1812	ditto	ditto	do.			
1843	ditto	ditto	do.			
1814	ditto	ditto	do.			
1815	ditto	ditto	do.			
1816	ditto	582,120 (half year)	do.			
	14,553,000 (5 Apr.—10 Oct.)	727,650 (half year)	do.	2,910,600	£25 per Cent. inc	rease of Capital.
1817	ditto	1,455,300	do.			
1818	ditto	ditto	do.			
1819	ditto	ditto	do.			
1820	ditto	ditto	do.			
1821	ditto	ditto	do.			
1822	ditto	ditto	do.			
1823	ditto	1,164,240	8			
1824	ditto	ditto	do.			
1825	ditto	ditto	do.			
1826	ditto	ditto	do.			
1827	ditto	ditto	do.			
1828	ditto	ditto	do.			
1829	ditto	ditto	do.			
1830	ditto	ditto	do.			
1831	ditto	ditto	do.			
		46,016,526		5,530,140	Total	51,546,666

WILLIAM SMEE, CHIEF ACCOUNTANT.

Bank of England, 13 June, 1832.

TABLE VII.

An ACCOUNT of all DISTRIBUTIONS made by the Bank of England amongst the Proprietors of Bank Stock, whether by Money Payments, Transfers of £5 per cent. Annuities, or otherwise, under the heads of Bonus, Increase of Dividend, and Increase of Capital, betwixt the 25th February, 1797, and 31st March, 1832, in addition to the Ordinary Dividend of £7 per cent. on the Capital Stock of that Corporation existing in 1797, including therein the whole Dividend paid since June 1816, on their increased Capital; stating the period when such Distributions were made, and the Aggregate Amount of the whole.

	£.			£.	£.
In June 1799,	10	per Ct. Bonus in	5 per Cents. 1797	on 11,642,400 is	1,164,240
— May 1801,	5	ditto	Navy 5 per Cents. . . .	ditto	582,120
— Nov. 1802,	2½	ditto	ditto	ditto	291,060
— Oct. 1804,	5	ditto	Cash	ditto	582,120
— Oct. 1805,	5	ditto	ditto	ditto	582,120
— Oct. 1806,	5	ditto	ditto	ditto	582,120
From April 1807 to Oct. 1822, both inclusive		Increase of Dividend, at the rate of £3 per Ct. per Ann. on £11,642,400, is 16 Years			5,588,352
From April 1823 to Oct. 1831, both inclusive		Increase of Dividend at the rate of £1 per Ct. per Ann. on £11,642,400, is 16 Years			1,047,816
In June 1816		Increase of Capital at 25 per Cent. is			2,910,600
From Oct. 1816 to Oct. 1822, both inclusive		Dividend at the rate of 10 per cent. per Annum on £2,910,600 increased Capital, is 6½ Years			1,891,890
From April 1823 to Oct. 1831. both inclusive		Dividend at the rate of 8 per Cent. per Annum on £2,910,600 increased Capital, is 9 Years			2,095,632
		Aggregate Amount of the whole . . .			£17,318,070

Annual Dividend payable on Bank Stock in 1797, on a Capital of £11,642,400 at the rate of 7 per Cent. per Annum	814,968
Annual Dividend payable since June 1816 on a Capital of £14,553,000 to October 1822 inclusive, at the rate of 10 per Cent. per Annum	1,455,300
Annual Dividend payable from April 1823, to 31 March 1832, both inclusive, on a Capital of £14,553,000 at the rate of 8 per Cent. .	1,164,240

WILLIAM SMEE, CHIEF ACCOUNTANT.

Bank of England, 27 June, 1832.

TABLE VIII.

An Account of the Annual Average of Loss by Bad Debts on the Discounts of the Bank of England, from the year 1795 to 1831, both inclusive.

£31,696

WILLIAM SMEE, Chief Accountant.

Bank of England, 13 June, 1832.

An Account of the Average Amount of Loss to the Bank of England from Forgeries in the Public Funds, during the last Ten Years.

The Average Amount in each Year is £40,204

WILLIAM SMEE, Chief Accountant.

TABLE IX.

An Account of the Average Loss per Annum incurred by the Bank from Forgeries in the Public Funds, during the last Ten Years, and the actual Loss in each Year.

		£.
In the Year	1822	12,676
Ditto	1823	Nil.
Ditto	1824	360,214
Ditto	1825	972
Ditto	1826	10,996
Ditto	1827	1,612
Ditto	1828	1,110
Ditto	1829	700
Ditto	1830	11,869
Ditto	1831	1,891
	10)	402,040
		40,204 Average Loss per Ann.

WILLIAM SMEE, Chief Accountant.

An Account of Forgeries of Bank Notes, discovered to be forged by presentation for Payment, or otherwise.

Years.	£1	£2	£5	£10	£20	£25	Total number of Notes.	Total nominal Value.
1828	725	34	358	66	4	..	1,187	£ 3,343
1829	613	30	432	40	3	..	1,118	3,293
1830	273	23	281	37	..	1	615	2,119
1831	193	28	134	12	2	..	369	1,079

TABLE X.

An Account of the Average Amount of Bank Notes in Circulation in each Quarter of the Year, from 1792 to the present time; distinguishing Notes under £5.

Averages in the Quarters ending	31 March.	30 June.	30 September.	31 December.
1792 Bank Notes of £5. and upwards	[illegible]	11,759,100	11,367,160	11,202,840
1793 ditto	[illegible]	12,257,430	11,023,190	11,066,460
1794 ditto	[illegible]	[illegible]	10,422,900	10,964,990
1795 ditto	[illegible]	[illegible]	11,[illegible]25,840	11,596,520
1796 ditto	[illegible]	[illegible]	9,696,410	9,609,340
1797 ditto including under £5.	[illegible]	[illegible]	11,003,070	11,386,460
1798 ditto ditto . . .	[illegible]	[illegible]	12,152,010	12,253,220
1799 ditto ditto . . .	[illegible]	[illegible]	13,364,660	13,776,160
1800 ditto ditto . . .	[illegible]	14,955,370	15,129,250	15,491,750
1801 ditto ditto . . .	16,443,710	[illegible]	[illegible]	15,680,310
1802 ditto ditto . . .	[illegible]	16,757,410	16,955,800	17,397,760
1803 ditto ditto . . .	[illegible]	16,233,690	16,780,380	17,266,510
1804 ditto ditto . . .	[illegible]	[illegible]	17,133,570	17,248,690
Bank Notes of £5. and upwards	17,618,460	12,449,050	12,063,970	12,063,360
Ditto under £5. . . .		4,481,100	4,424,430	4,431,620
1805 . .	[illegible]	16,930,150	16,488,400	16,494,980
Bank Notes of £5. and upwards	12,425,470	12,715,090	12,410,430	12,422,260
Ditto under £5. . . .	4,427,970	4,304,910	4,263,230	4,190,430
1806 . .	16,853,440	17,020,000	16,673,660	16,612,690
Bank Notes of £5. and upwards	12,427,290	12,731,850	12,744,520	12,257,470
Ditto under £5. . . .	4,230,180	4,059,370	4,230,140	4,142,710
1807 . .	16,657,470	16,791,220	16,974,660	16,400,180
Bank Notes of £5. and upwards	12,524,810	13,189,270	13,060,650	13,259,780
Ditto under £5. . . .	4,121,050	3,995,490	4,113,970	4,163,380
1808 . .	16,645,860	17,184,760	17,174,620	17,423,160
Bank Notes of £5. and upwards	13,504,510	13,978,370	14,144,960	14,464,730
Ditto under £5. . . .	4,335,880	4,555,880	5,195,830	5,477,730
1809 . .	17,840,390	18,534,250	19,340,790	19,942,460
Bank Notes of £5. and upwards	14,544,420	15,177,400	17,075,640	16,873,760
Ditto under £5. . . .	5,898,320	6,168,700	7,094,330	7,333,130
1810 . .	20,442,740	21,346,100	24,170,270	24,206,890
Bank Notes of £5. and upwards	16,096,080	16,274,680	15,717,320	15,413,310
Ditto under £5. . . .	7,237,350	7,334,550	7,562,240	7,495,180
1811 . .	23,333,430	23,609,230	23,279,560	22,908,490

Average Amount of Bank Notes in Circulation, &c.—*Continued.*

Averages in the Quarters ending	31 March.	30 June.	30 September.	31 December.
Bank Notes of £5. and upwards	15,816,350	15,458,660	15,833,770	15,647,350
Ditto under £5. . .	7,505,670	7,465,560	7,626,500	7,672,170
1812 . .	23,322,020	22,924,220	23,460,270	23,319,520
Bank Notes of £5. and upwards	16,144,920	16,138,590	15,899,210	16,092,590
Ditto under £5. . .	7,788,220	7,807,600	8,057,120	8,165,940
1813 . .	23,933,140	23,946,190	23,956,330	24,258,530
Bank Notes of £5. and upwards	16,803,390	17,237,670	19,067,920	18,502,690
Ditto under £5. . .	8,354,320	8,626,600	9,571,950	9,465,910
1814 . .	25,157,710	25,864,270	28,639,850	27,968,600
Bank Notes of £5. and upwards	18,075,430	17,936,610	17,714,910	16,912,840
Ditto under £5. . .	9,222,860	9,076,830	9,456,520	9,161,730
1815 . .	27,298,290	27,103,440	27,171,430	26,074,570
Bank Notes of £5. and upwards	17,484,520	17,311,280	18,063,320	17,472,630
Ditto under £5. . .	9,088,760	9,051,960	9,170,380	8,656,410
1816 . .	26,573,280	26,363,240	27,233,700	26,129,040
Bank Notes of £5. and upwards	18,900,600	19,645,180	21,517,920	21,167,300
Ditto under £5. . .	8,237,690	7,896,020	7,986,160	7,748,640
1817 . .	27,138,290	27,541,200	29,504,080	28,915,940
Bank Notes of £5. and upwards	20,957,420	20,113,410	19,356,050	18,523,430
Ditto under £5. . .	7.458,310	7,379,930	7,537,460	7,481,810
1818 . .	28,415,730	27,493,340	26,893,510	26,005,240
Bank Notes of £5. and upwards	18,363,220	18,165,090	18,182,030	16,950,240
Ditto under £5. . .	7,431,220	7,226,880	17,301,930	6,960,560
1819 . .	25,794,440	25,391,970	25,483,960	23,910,800
Bank Notes of £5. and upwards	17,375,740	17,099,080	17,707,470	16,708,650
Ditto under £5. . .	6,758,110	6,662,920	6,757,020	6,569,380
1820 . .	24,133,850	23,762,000	24,464,490	23,278,030
Bank Notes of £5. and upwards	17,635,790	17,489,950	18,030,900	16,558,730
Ditto under £5. . .	6,521,270	5,398,330	2,718,460	1,957,190
1821 . .	24,157,060	22,888,280	20,749,360	18,515,920
Bank Notes of £5. and upwards	17,136,470	16,256,140	17,503,640	16,402,170
Ditto under £5. . .	1,450,330	1,063,170	875,800	763,770
1822 . .	18,586,800	17,319,310	18,379,440	17,165,94[illegible]

Average Amount of Bank Notes in Circulation, &c.—*Continued.*

Averages in the Quarters ending	31 March.	30 June.	30 September.	31 December.
Bank Notes of £5. and upwards	17,447,550	17,375,760	18,709,020	18,603,210
Ditto under £5.	689,560	617,510	557,010	518,480
1823	18,137,110	17,993,270	19,266,030	19,121,690
Bank Notes of £5. and upwards	19,174,890	19,442,730	20,177,820	19,913,040
Ditto under £5.	490,310	464,060	446,590	431,930
1824	19,665,200	19,906,790	20,624,410	20,344,970
Bank Notes of £5. and upwards	20,665,600	19,429,990	19,378,290	19,245,430
Ditto under £5.	418,870	407,780	398,070	503,410
1825	21,084,470	19,837,770	19,776,360	19,748,840
Bank Notes of £5. and upwards	23,135,690	21,563,030	20,517,790	19,055,600
Ditto under £5.	1,343,980	1,489,940	1,215,850	895,670
1826	24,479,670	23,052,970	21,733,640	19,951,270
Bank Notes of £5. and upwards	20,583,570	21,054,260	21,916,750	20,314,060
Ditto under £5.	686,670	558,420	487,770	448,320
1827	21,270,240	21,612,680	22,404,520	20,762,380
Bank Notes of £5. and upwards	21,118,540	20,256,960	21,166,790	20,041,510
Ditto under £5.	419,980	399,510	384,250	371,820
1828	21,538,520	20,656,470	21,551,040	20,413,330
Bank Notes of £5. and upwards	19,971,690	19,222,300	19,425,030	18,575,980
Ditto under £5.	358,860	344,750	335,010	326,170
1829	20,330,550	19,567,050	19,760,040	18,902,150
Bank Notes of £5. and upwards	19,663,950	20,694,890	21,041,660	19,301,630
Ditto under £5.	321,330	317,010	313,720	310,220
1830	19,985,280	21,011,900	21,355,580	19,611,850
Bank Notes of £5. and upwards	19,268,840	18,339,130	18,446,600	15,980,990
Ditto under £5.	307,270	304,850	302,760	301,070
1831	19,576,110	18,643,980	18,749,360	16,282,060
Bank Notes of £5. and upwards	17,900,950	17,579,920		
Ditto under £5.	299,280	297,110		
1832	18,200,230	17,877,030		

NOTE.—The Books not having been preserved which contained the particulars for ascertaining the distinct Amounts of Bank Notes in circulation of £5. and upwards and those under £5. from March 1797 (when the latter were first issued) to 17th April 1805, the Bank is unable to furnish the separate Average Amounts previous to June 1805.

Bank of England, 10th August, 1832. WILLIAM SMEE, CHIEF ACCOUNTANT.

TABLE XI.

An Estimated Account of Profit derived by the Bank from Circulation of Promissory Notes, and from Government Business.

Circulation . . . £ 20,000,000				
Government Deposits . 4,000,000	. . . .			£ 24,000,000
	Of which 2-3rds are estimated to be invested in Securities and 1-3rd in Bullion.			

Securities £16,000,000, viz.

9,000,000	Exchequer Bills . . at	$2\frac{1}{4}$	per cent.	£202,500	
800,000	Stock	3	"	24,000	
1,000,000	Advances for Circulation on Discount .	3	"	30,000	
500,000	Country Discounts .	$3\frac{1}{2}$	"	17,500	
4,700,000	. . . .	$4\frac{1}{8}$	"	193,875	
					467,875
16,000,000					

Deduct:

Expense of Circulation	£106,000		
Expense of Government Deposits	10,000		
Stamp Duty on Circulation	70,000		
One per cent. on Capital (held by Government at 3 per cent.)	147,000		
		333,000	
			134,875

THE PUBLIC DEBT.

Amount received from Government for Management of the Public Debt, for the Year ending 5th April, 1832, including Life Annuities .	£251,000		
Management of Life Annuities, proposed to be transferred	3,000		
		248,000	

Deduct:

Expenses for Management of the National Debt .	£164,000		
Average of Forgeries per Annum during the last ten Years	40,000		
		204,000	
			44,000
		Estimated Profit . . .	£178,875

WILLIAM SMEE, Chief Accountant.

TABLE XII.

An Account of the Annual average Amount of Commercial Paper under Discount at the Bank, in London, in each Year, from the Year 1795.

Years	£.	Years	£.	Years	£.	Years	£.
1795	2,946,500	1805	11,366,500	1815	14,947,100	1825	4,941,500
1796	3,505,000	1806	12,380,100	1816	11,416,400	1826	4,908,300
1797	5,350,000	1807	13,484,600	1817	3,960,600	1827	1,240,400
1798	4,490,600	1808	12,950,100	1818	4,325,200	1828	1,167,400
1799	5,403,900	1809	15,475,700	1819	6,515,000	1829	2,250,700
1800	6,401,900	1810	20,070,600	1820	3,883,600	1830	919,900
1801	7,905,100	1811	14,355,400	1821	2,676,700	1831	1,533,600
1802	7,523,300	1812	14,291,600	1822	3,366,700		
1803	10,747,600	1813	12,330,200	1823	3,123,800		
1804	9,982,400	1814	13,285,800	1824	2,369,800		

An Account of the average Amount of Bills and Notes under Discount, in each of the Quarters of the Years 1815 to 1831.

Years.	First Quarter, ending 31st March.	Second Quarter, ending 30th June.	Third Quarter, ending 30th Sept.	Fourth Quarter, ending 31st Dec.
	£.	£.	£.	£.
1815	13,611,500	13,846,500	16,613,200	15,717,300
1816	14,315,900	13,380,400	10,569,400	7,399,800
1817	5,823,500	4,148,300	3,329,300	2,541,200
1818	2,976,900	2,847,800	4,610,400	6,865,700
1819	8,363,700	6,632,300	6,021,600	5,042,200
1820	4,810,700	3,605,500	3,987,600	3,130,700
1821	3,238,300	2,715,100	2,294,100	2,459,300
1822	3,137,000	3,216,500	3,388,700	3,724,600
1823	4,107,200	3,252,200	2,801,400	2,334,200
1824	2,226,800	2,553,500	2,449,800	2,248,900
1825	2,466,800	3,973,700	5,486,000	7,839,500
1826	9,586,700	5,037,400	2,950,500	2,164,800
1827	2,198,600	1,226,400	1,107,500	1,239,800
1828	1,298,400	1,165,600	1,170,800	2,157,200
1829	3,952,900	3,283,700	2,611,800	2,152,700
1830	1,860,500	1,414,600	1,275,000	1,930,700
1831	2,549,200	3,240,200	3,422,500	3,771,500

WILLIAM SMEE, Chief Accountant.

TABLE XIII.

An Account of the average Amount of Bills under Discount for Bankers, during the Year 1831.

In 1831 . . . . £844,077

N. B.—No separate Account of Discount for Bankers was kept prior to 1831.

WILLIAM SMEE, Chief Accountant.

BRANCH BANKS.

An Account of the average Amount of Bills under Discount at the Branch Banks, during the Years 1828, 1829, 1830, and 1831.

In 1828	£281,000
1829	750,000
1830	700,000
1831	1,718,000

WILLIAM SMEE, Chief Accountant.

TABLE XIV.

An Account of the Amount of the Notes of the Bank of England in Circulation, distinguishing those under Five Pounds; of the Amount of all Deposits; and of the Amount of all Securities held by the Bank, on the 28th February and 31st August in each Year, from the Year 1778 to 7th August, 1832, (so far as the same can be ascertained).

February 28, 1778.		February 28, 1778. Securities:		
Circulation	7,440,330	Public	7,898,292	11,220,520
Deposits	4,662,150	Private	3,322,228	
		Bullion		2,010,690
	£ 12,102,480	Rest £1,128,730		£ 13,231,210

August 31, 1778.		August 31, 1778. Securities:		
Circulation	6,758,070	Public	6,540,433	9,627,970
Deposits	4,715,580	Private	3,087,537	
		Bullion		3,128,420
	£ 11,473,650	Rest £1,282,740		£ 12,756,390

February 28, 1779.		February 28, 1779. Securities:		
Circulation	9,012,610	Public	8,862,242	10,935,910
Deposits	4,358,160	Private	2,073,668	
		Bullion		3,711,150
	£ 13,370,770	Rest £1,276,290		£ 14,647,060

August 31, 1779.		August 31, 1779. Securities:		
Circulation	7,276,540	Public	7,493,649	9,849,840
Deposits	5,201,040	Private	2,356,191	
		Bullion		3,983,300
	£ 12,477,580	Rest £1,355,560		£ 13,833,140

February 29, 1780.		February 29, 1780. Securities:		
Circulation	8,410,790	Public	9,145,659	10,901,030
Deposits	4,723,890	Private	1,755,371	
		Bullion		3,581,060
	£ 13,134,680	Rest £1,347,460		£ 14,482,090

August 31, 1780.		August 31, 1780. Securities:		
Circulation	6,341,600	Public	6,740,514	10,345,540
Deposits	6,655,800	Private	3,605,026	
		Bullion		4,179,370
	£ 12,997,400	Rest £1,527,510		£ 14,524,910

February 28, 1781.		February 28, 1781. Securities:		
Circulation	7,092,450	Public	8,640,073	11,186,140
Deposits	5,796,830	Private	2,546,067	
		Bullion		3,279,940
	£ 12,889,280	Rest £1,576,800		£ 14,466,080

Notes in Circulation, Deposits, and Securities.—*Continued.*

August 31, 1781.

August 31, 1781.		August 31, 1781. Securities:		
Circulation	6,309,430	Public	6,609,457	11,110,510
Deposits	5,921,630	Private	4,501,053	
		Bullion		2,862,590
	£ 12,231,060	Rest £1,742,040		£ 13,973,100

February 28, 1782.		February 28, 1782. Securities:		
Circulation	8,028,880	Public	10,346,055	13,794,070
Deposits	6,130,300	Private	3,448,015	
		Bullion		2,157,860
	£ 14,159,180	Rest £1,792,750		£15,951,930

August 31, 1782.		August 31, 1782. Securities:		
Circulation	6,759,310	Public	8,987,573	13,483,790
Deposits	6,759,450	Private	4,496,217	
		Bullion		1,956,550
	£ 13,518,760	Rest £1,921,580		£ 15,440,340

February 28, 1783.		February 28, 1783. Securities:		
Circulation	7,675,090	Public	10,016,349	12,795,780
Deposits	4,465,000	Private	2,779,431	
		Bullion		1,321,190
	£ 12,140,090	Rest £1,976,880		£ 14,116,970

August 30, 1783.		August 30, 1783. Securities:		
Circulation	6,307,270	Public	9,566,037	13,841,800
Deposits	6,105,650	Private	4,275,763	
		Bullion		590,080
	£ 12,412,920	Rest £2,018,960		£ 14,431,880

February 28, 1784.		February 28, 1784. Securities:		
Circulation	6,202,760	Public	7,789,291	11,619,220
Deposits	3,903,920	Private	3,829,929	
		Bullion		655,840
	£ 10,106,680	Rest £2,168,380		£ 12,275,060

August 31, 1784.		August 31, 1784. Securities:		
Circulation	5,592,510	Public	8,435,777	12,524,380
Deposits	6,267,130	Private	4,088,603	
		Bullion		1,539,830
	£ 11,859,640	Rest £2,204,570		£ 14,064,210

February 28, 1785.		February 28, 1785. Securities:		
Circulation	5,923,090	Public	7,198,564	12,172,490
Deposits	6,669,160	Private	4,973,926	
		Bullion		2,740,820
	£ 12,592,250	Rest £2,321,060		£ 14,913,310

Notes in Circulation, Deposits, and Securities.—*Continued.*

August 31, 1785.

Circulation	6,570,650
Deposits	6,252,030
	£ 12,822,680

August 31, 1785.

Securities:

Public	6,725,891	9,944,570
Private	3,218,679	
Bullion		5,487,040
Rest £2,608,930		£ 15,431,610

February 28, 1786.

Circulation	7,581,960
Deposits	6,151,660
	£ 13,733,620

February 28, 1786.

Securities:

Public	6,836,459	10,353,240
Private	3,516,781	
Bullion		5,979,090
Rest £2,598,710		£ 16,332,330

August 31, 1786.

Circulation	8,184,330
Deposits	5,867,240
	£ 14,051,570

August 31, 1786.

Securities:

Public	7,988,241	10,378,780
Private	2,390,539	
Bullion		6,311,050
Rest £2,638,260		£ 16,689,830

February 28, 1787.

Circulation	8,329,840
Deposits	5,902,080
	£ 14,231,920

February 28, 1787.

Securities:

Public	7,642,587	11,359,050
Private	3,716,463	
Bullion		5,626,690
Rest £2,753,820		£ 16,985,740

August 31, 1787.

Circulation	9,685,720
Deposits	5,631,540
	£ 15,317,260

August 31, 1787.

Securities:

Public	8,066,303	11,853,660
Private	3,787,357	
Bullion		6,293,000
Rest £2,829,400		£ 18,146,660

February 29, 1788.

Circulation	9,561,120
Deposits	5,177,050
	£ 14,738,170

February 29, 1788.

Securities:

Public	7,833,857	11,864,510
Private	4,030,653	
Bullion		5,743,440
Rest £2,869,780		£ 17,607,950

August 30, 1788.

Circulation	10,002,880
Deposits	5,528,640
	£ 15,531,520

August 30, 1788.

Securities:

Public	8,840,068	11,570,320
Private	2,730,252	
Bullion		6,899,160
Rest £2,937,960		£ 18,469,480

February 28, 1789.

Circulation	9,807,210
Deposits	5,537,370
	£ 15,344,580

February 28, 1789.

Securities:

Public	8,249,582	10,960,690
Private	2,711,108	
Bullion		7,228,730
Rest £ 2,844,840		£18,189,420

Notes in Circulation, Deposits, and Securities.—*Continued.*

August 31, 1789.

Circulation	11,121,800
Deposits	6,402,450
	£ 17,524,250

August 31, 1789.

Securities:		
Public	9,661,859	11,697,760
Private	2,035,961	
Bullion		8,645,860
Rest £2,819,370		£ 20,343,620

February 28, 1790.

Circulation	10,040,540
Deposits	6,223,270
	£ 16,263,810

February 28, 1790.

Securities:		
Public	8,347,387	10,332,120
Private	1,984,733	
Bullion		8,633,000
Rest £2,700,310		£ 18,965,120

August 31, 1790.

Circulation	11,433,340
Deposits	6,199,200
	£ 17,632,540

August 31, 1790.

Securities:		
Public	10,047,257	12,003,520
Private	1,956,263	
Bullion		8,386,330
Rest £2,757,310		£ 20,389,850

February 28, 1791.

Circulation	11,439,200
Deposits	6,364,550
	£ 17,803,750

February 28, 1791.

Securities:		
Public	10,380,358	12,602,640
Private	2,222,282	
Bullion		7,869,410
Rest £2,668,300		£ 20,472,050

August 31, 1791.

Circulation	11,672,320
Deposits	6,437,730
	£ 18,110,050

August 31, 1791.

Securities:		
Public	10,921,300	12,819,940
Private	1,898,640	
Bullion		8,055,510
Rest £2,765,400		£ 20,875,450

February 29, 1792.

Circulation	11,307,380
Deposits	5,523,370
	£ 16,830,750

February 29, 1792.

Securities:		
Public	9,938,799	13,068,560
Private	3,129,761	
Bullion		6,468,060
Rest £2,705,870		£ 19,536,620

August 31, 1792.

Circulation	11,006,300
Deposits	5,526,480
	£ 16,532,780

August 31, 1792.

Securities:		
Public	10,715,041	13,905,910
Private	3,190,869	
Bullion		5,357,380
Rest £2,730,510		£ 19,263,290

February 28, 1793.

Circulation	11,888,910
Deposits	5,346,450
	£ 17,235,360

February 28, 1793.

Securities:		
Public	9,549,209	16,005,250
Private	6,456,041	
Bullion		4,010,680
Rest £2,780,570		£ 20,015,930

Notes in Circulation, Deposits, and Securities.—*Continued.*

August 31, 1793.

Circulation	10,865,050	Securities: Public	10,381,838	14,809,680
Deposits	6,442,810	Private	4,427,842	
		Bullion		5,322,010
	£ 17,307,860	Rest £2,823,830	£	20,131,690

February 28, 1794.

Circulation	10,744,020	Securities: Public	9,950,756	14,524,550
Deposits	7,891,810	Private	4,573,794	
		Bullion		6,987,110
	£ 18,635,830	Rest £2,875,830	£	21,511,660

August 30, 1794.

Circulation	10,286,780	Securities: Public	1,863,048	12,446,460
Deposits	5,935,710	Private	3,583,412	
		Bullion		6,770,110
	£ 16,222,490	Rest £2,994,080	£	19,216,570

February 28, 1795.

Circulation	14,017,510	Securities: Public	13,164,172	16,811,340
Deposits	5,973,020	Private	3,647,168	
		Bullion		6,127,720
	£ 19,990,530	Rest £2,948,530	£	22,939,060

August 31, 1795.

Circulation	10,862,200	Securities: Public	13,250,904	16,989,920
Deposits	8,154,980	Private	3,739,016	
		Bullion		5,136,350
	£ 19,017,180	Rest £3,109,090	£	22,126,270

February 29, 1796.

Circulation	10,729,520	Securities: Public	12,951,812	17,139,840
Deposits	5,702,360	Private	4,188,028	
		Bullion		2,539,630
	£ 16,431,880	Rest £3,247,590	£	19,679,470

August 31, 1796.

Circulation	9,246,790	Securities: Public	10,875,347	17,025,470
Deposits	6,656,320	Private	6,150,123	
		Bullion		2,122,950
	£ 15,902,110	Rest £3,245,310	£	19,148,420

February 28, 1797.

Circulation	9,674,780	Securities: Public	11,714,431	16,837,750
Deposits	4,891,530	Private	5,123,319	
		Bullion		1,086,170
	£ 14,566,310	Rest £3,357,610	£	17,923,920

S 2

Notes in Circulation, Deposits, and Securities.—*Continued.*

August 31, 1797.

Circulation:		
Bank Notes of £5 and Post Bills	10,246,535	..11,114,120
Bank Notes under £5	867,585	
Deposits		7,765,350
		£ 18,879,470

Securities:		
Public	8,765,224	18,261,170
Private	9,465,946	
Bullion		4,089,620
Rest £3,471,320		£ 22,350,790

February 28, 1798.

Circulation:		
Bank Notes of £5 and upwards, and Post Bills	11,647,610	13,095,830
Bank Notes under £5 . .	1,448,220	
Deposits		6,148,900
		£ 19,244,730

Securities:		
Public	11,241,333	16,799,500
Private	5,558,167	
Bullion		5,828,940
Rest £3,383,710		£ 22,628,440

August 31, 1798.

Circulation:		
Bank Notes of £5 and upwards, and Post Bills	10,649,550	12,180,610
Bank Notes under £5 . .	1,531,060	
Deposits		8,300,720
		£ 20,481,330

Securities:		
Public	10,930,038	17,349,640
Private	6,419,602	
Bullion		6,546,100
Rest £3,414,410		£ 23,895,740

February 28, 1799.

Circulation:		
Bank Notes of £5 and upwards, and Post Bills	11,494,150	12,959,800
Bank Notes under £5 . .	1,465,650	
Deposits		8,131,820
		£ 21,091,620

Securities:		
Public	11,510,677	17,039,030
Private	5,528,353	
Bullion		7,563,900
Rest £3,511,310		£ 24,602,930

August 31, 1799.

Circulation:		
Bank Notes of £5 and upwards, and Post Bills	12,047,790	13,389,490
Bank Notes under £5 . .	1,341,700	
Deposits		7,642,240
		£ 21,031,730

Securities:		
Public	9,452,955	16,930,440
Private	7,477,485	
Bullion		7,000,780
Rest £2,899,490		£ 23,931,220

February 28, 1800.

Circulation:		
Bank Notes of £5 and upwards, and Post Bills	15,372,930	16,844,470
Bank Notes under £5 . .	1,471,540	
Deposits		7,062,680
		£ 23,907,150

Securities:		
Public	13,975,663	21,424,050
Private	7,448,387	
Bullion		6,144,250
Rest £3,661,150		£ 27,568,300

August 31, 1800.

Circulation:		
Bank Notes of £5 and upwards, and Post Bills	13,448,540	15,047,180
Bank Notes under £5 . .	1,598,640	
Deposits		8,335,060
		£ 23,382,340

Securities.		
Public	13,586,590	22,138,420
Private	8,551,830	
Bullion		5,150,450
Rest £3,906,630		£ 27,288,870

Notes in Circulation, Deposits, and Securities.—*Continued.*

February 28, 1801.

Circulation:		
Bank Notes of £5 and upwards, and Post Bills	13,578,520	16,213,280
Bank Notes under £5	2,634,760	
Deposits		10,745,840
	£	26,959,120

February 28, 1801.

Securities:		
Public	15,958,011	26,424,730
Private	10,466,719	
Bullion		4,640,120
Rest £4,105,730	£	31,064,850

August 31, 1801.

Circulation:		
Bank Notes of £5 and upwards, and Post Bills	12,143,460	14,556,110
Bank Notes under £5	2,412,650	
Deposits		8,133,830
	£	22,689,940

August 31, 1801.

Securities:		
Public	11,926,873	22,209,570
Private	10,282,697	
Bullion		4,335,260
Rest £3,854,890	£	26,544,830

February 28, 1802.

Circulation:		
Bank Notes of £5 and upwards, and Post Bills	12,574,460	15,186,880
Bank Notes under £5	2,612,020	
Deposits		6,858,210
	£	22,045,090

February 28, 1802.

Securities:		
Public	14,199,094	21,959,820
Private	7,760,726	
Bullion		4,152,950
Rest £4,067,680	£	26,112,770

August 31, 1802.

Circulation:		
Bank Notes of £5 and upwards, and Post Bills	13,848,470	17,097,630
Bank Notes under £5	3,249,160	
Deposits		9,739,140
	£	26,836,770

August 31, 1802.

Securities:		
Public	13,528,599	27,113,360
Private	13,584,761	
Bullion		3,891,780
Rest £4,168,370	£	31,005,140

February 28, 1803.

Circulation:		
Bank Notes of £5 and upwards, and Post Bills	12,350,970	15,319,930
Bank Notes under £5	2,968,960	
Deposits		8,050,240
	£	23,370,170

February 28, 1803.

Securities:		
Public	9,417,887	23,914,900
Private	14,497,013	
Bullion		3,776,750
Rest £4,321,480	£	27,691,650

August 31, 1803.

Circulation:		
Bank Notes of £5 and upwards, and Post Bills	12,217,390	15,983,330
Bank Notes under £5	3,765,940	
Deposits		9,817,240
	£	25,800,570

August 31, 1803.

Securities:		
Public	13,336,179	26,918,840
Private	13,582,661	
Bullion		3,592,500
Rest £4,710,770	£	30,511,340

February 29, 1804.

Circulation:		
Bank Notes of £5 and upwards, and Post Bills	12,546,560	17,077,830
Bank Notes under £5	4,531,270	
Deposits		8,676,830
	£	25,754,660

February 29, 1804.

Securities:		
Public	14,684,686	26,998,970
Private	12,314,281	
Bullion		3,372,140
Rest £4,616,450	£	30,371,110

Notes in Circulation, Deposits, and Securities.—*Continued.*

August 31, 1804.

Circulation:		
Bank Notes of £5 and upwards, and Post Bills	12,466,790	17,153,890
Bank Notes under £5	4,687,100	
Deposits		9,715,530
		£ 26,869,420

August 31, 1804.

Securities:		
Public	14,993,395	25,826,680
Private	10,833,285	
Bullion		5,879,190
Rest £4,836,450		£ 31,705,870

February 28, 1805.

Circulation:		
Bank Notes of £5 and upwards, and Post Bills	13,011,010	17,871,170
Bank Notes under £5	4,860,160	
Deposits		12,083,620
		£ 29,954,790

February 28, 1805.

Securities:		
Public	16,889,501	28,661,390
Private	11,771,889	
Bullion		5,883,800
Rest £4,599,400		£ 34,545,190

August 31, 1805.

Circulation:		
Bank Notes of £5 and upwards, and Post Bills	11,862,740	16,388,400
Bank Notes under £5	4,525,660	
Deposits		14,048,080
		£ 30,436,480

August 31, 1805.

Securities:		
Public	11,413,266	27,772,850
Private	16,359,584	
Bullion		7,624,500
Rest £4,960,870		£ 35,397,350

February 28, 1806.

Circulation:		
Bank Notes of £5 and upwards, and Post Bills	13,271,520	17,730,120
Bank Notes under £5	4,458,600	
Deposits		9,980,790
		£ 27,710,910

February 28, 1806.

Securities:		
Public	14,813,599	26,591,070
Private	11,777,471	
Bullion		5,987,190
Rest £4,867,350		£ 32,578,260

August 31, 1806.

Circulation:		
Bank Notes of £5 and upwards, and Post Bills	16,757,930	21,027,470
Bank Notes under £5	4,269,540	
Deposits		9,636,330
		£ 30,663,800

August 31, 1806.

Securities:		
Public	14,167,772	29,473,100
Private	15,305,328	
Bullion		6,215,020
Rest £5,024,320		£ 35,688,120

February 28, 1807.

Circulation:		
Bank Notes of £5 and upwards, and Post Bills	12,840,790	16,950,680
Bank Notes under £5	4,019,890	
Deposits		11,829,320
		£ 28,780,000

February 28, 1807.

Securities:		
Public	13,452,871	27,408,460
Private	13,955,589	
Bullion		6,142,840
Rest £4,771,300		£ 33,551,300

August 31, 1807.

Circulation:		
Bank Notes of £5 and upwards, and Post Bills	15,432,990	19,678,360
Bank Notes under £5	4,245,370	
Deposits		11,789,200
		£ 31,467,560

August 31, 1807.

Securities:		
Public	13,410,055	29,936,950
Private	10,526,895	
Bullion		6,484,350
Rest £4,953,740		£ 36,421,300

Notes in Circulation, Deposits, and Securities.—*Continued.*

February 29, 1808.

Circulation:		
Bank Notes of £5 and upwards, and Post Bills	14,093,690	18,189,860
Bank Notes under £5	4,095,170	
Deposits		11,961,960
	£	30,150,820

Securities:		
Public	14,149,501	27,384,080
Private	13,234,579	
Bullion		7,855,470
Rest £5,088,730	£	35,239,550

August 31, 1808.

Circulation:		
Bank Notes of £5 and upwards, and Post Bills	12,993,020	17,111,290
Bank Notes under £5	4,118,270	
Deposits		13,012,510
	£	30,123,800

Securities:		
Public	14,956,394	29,244,090
Private	14,287,696	
Bullion		6,015,940
Rest £5,136,230	£	35,260,030

February 28, 1809.

Circulation:		
Bank Notes of £5 and upwards, and Post Bills	14,241,360	18,542,860
Bank Notes under £5	4,301,500	
Deposits		9,982,950
	£	28,525,810

Securities:		
Public	14,743,425	29,118,200
Private	14,374,775	
Bullion		4,488,700
Rest £5,081,090	£	33,606,900

August 31, 1809.

Circulation:		
Bank Notes of £5 and upwards, and Post Bills	14,393,110	19,574,180
Bank Notes under £5	5,181,070	
Deposits		12,257,180
	£	31,831,360

Securities:		
Public	15,307,673	33,435,270
Private	18,127,597	
Bullion		3,652,480
Rest £5,256,390	£	37,087,750

February 28, 1810.

Circulation:		
Bank Notes of £5 and upwards, and Post Bills	15,159,180	21,019,600
Bank Notes under £5	5,860,420	
Deposits		12,457,310
	£	33,476,910

Securities:		
Public	14,322,634	35,378,580
Private	21,055,946	
Bullion		3,501,410
Rest £5,403,080	£	38,879,990

August 31, 1810.

Circulation:		
Bank Notes of £5 and upwards, and Post Bills	17,570,780	24,793,990
Bank Notes under £5	7,223,210	
Deposits		13,617,520
	£	38,411,510

Securities:		
Public	17,198,677	40,973,770
Private	23,775,093	
Bullion		3,191,850
Rest £5,754,110	£	44,165,620

February 28, 1811.

Circulation:		
Bank Notes of £5 and upwards, and Post Bills	16,246,130	23,360,220
Bank Notes under £5	7,114,090	
Deposits		11,445,650
	£	34,805,870

Securities:		
Public	17,201,800	37,122,350
Private	19,920,550	
Bullion		3,350,940
Rest £5,667,420	£	40,473,290

Notes in Circulation, Deposits, and Securities.—*Continued.*

August 31, 1811.

Circulation:			Securities:		
Bank Notes of £5 and upwards, and Post Bills	15,692,490	23,286,850	Public	21,884,248	37,083,280
Bank Notes under £5	7,594,360		Private	15,199,032	
Deposits		11,075,660	Bullion		3,243,300
		£ 34,362,510	Rest £5,964,070		£ 40,326,580

February 29, 1812.

Circulation:			Securities:		
Bank Notes of £5 and upwards, and Post Bills	15,951,290	23,408,320	Public	22,127,253	38,026,290
Bank Notes under £5	7,457,030		Private	15,899,037	
Deposits		11,595,200	Bullion		2,983,190
		£.35,903,520	Rest £6,005,960		£ 41,009,480

August 31, 1812.

Circulation:			Securities:		
Bank Notes of £5 and upwards, and Post Bills	15,385,470	23,026,880	Public	21,165,190	38,176,120
Bank Notes under £5	7,641,410		Private	17,010,930	
Deposits		11,848,910	Bullion		3,099,270
		£ 34,875,790	Rest £6,399,270		£ 41,275,390

February 27, 1813.

Circulation:			Securities:		
Bank Notes of £5 and upwards, and Post Bills	15,497,320	23,210,930	Public	25,036,626	37,930,950
Bank Notes under £5	7,713,610		Private	12,894,324	
Deposits		11,268,180	Bullion		2,884,500
		£ 34,479,110	Rest £6,336,340		£ 40,815,450

August 31, 1813.

Circulation:			Securities:		
Bank Notes of £5 and upwards, and Post Bills	16,790,980	24,828,120	Public	25,591,336	40,106,080
Bank Notes under £5	8,037,140		Private	14,514,744	
Deposits		11,159,730	Bullion		2,712,270
		£ 35,987,850	Rest £6,830,500		£ 42,818,350

February 28, 1814.

Circulation:			Securities:		
Bank Notes of £5 and upwards, and Post Bills	16,455,540	24,801,080	Public	23,630,317	41,989,910
Bank Notes under £5	8,345,540		Private	18,359,593	
Deposits		12,455,460	Bullion		2,204,430
		£ 37,256,540	Rest £6,937,800		£ 44,194,340

August 31, 1814.

Circulation:			Securities:		
Bank Notes of £5 and upwards, and Post Bills	18,703,210	28,368,290	Public	34,982,485	48,345,960
Bank Notes under £5	9,665,080		Private	13,363,475	
Deposits		14,849,940	Bullion		2,097,680
		£ 43,218,230	Rest £7,225,410		£ 50,443,640

Notes in Circulation, Deposits, and Securities.—*Continued.*

February 28, 1815.

Circulation:		
Bank Notes of £5 and upwards, and Post Bills	18,226,400	27,261,650
Bank Notes under £5	9,035,250	
Deposits		11,702,250
		£ 38,963,900

Securities:		
Public	27,502,804	44,558,500
Private	17,045,696	
Bullion		2,036,910
Rest £7,631,510		£ 46,595,410

August 31, 1815.

Circulation:		
Bank Notes of £5 and upwards, and Post Bills	17,766,140	27,248,670
Bank Notes under £5	9,482,530	
Deposits		12,696,000
		£ 39,944,670

Securities:		
Public	24,194,086	44,854,180
Private	20,660,094	
Bullion		3,409,040
Rest £8,318,550		£ 48,263,220

February 29, 1816.

Circulation:		
Bank Notes of £5 and upwards, and Post Bills	18,012,220	27,013,620
Bank Notes under £5	9,001,400	
Deposits		12,388,890
		£ 39,402,510

Securities:		
Public	19,425,780	43,401,310
Private	23,975,530	
Bullion		4,640,880
Rest £8,639,680		£ 48,042,190

August 31, 1816.

Circulation:		
Bank Notes of £5 and upwards, and Post Bills	17,661,510	26,758,720
Bank Notes under £5	9,097,210	
Deposits		11,856,380
		£ 38,615,100

Securities:		
Public	26,097,431	37,279,540
Private	11,182,109	
Bullion		7,562,780
Rest £6,227,220		£ 44,842,320

February 28, 1817.

Circulation:		
Bank Notes of £5 and upwards, and Post Bills	19,261,630	27,397,900
Bank Notes under £5	8,136,270	
Deposits		10,825,610
		£ 38,223,510

Securities:		
Public	25,538,808	34,278,630
Private	8,739,822	
Bullion		9,680,970
Rest £5,736,090		£ 43,959,600

August 30, 1817.

Circulation:		
Bank Notes of £5 and upwards, and Post Bills	21,550,630	29,543,780
Bank Notes under £5	7,993,150	
Deposits		9,084,590
		£ 38,628,370

Securities:		
Public	27,098,238	32,605,630
Private	5,507,392	
Bullion		11,668,260
Rest £5,645,520		£ 44,273,890

February 28, 1818.

Circulation:		
Bank Notes of £5 and upwards, and Post Bills	20,370,290	27,770,970
Bank Notes under £5	7,400,680	
Deposits		7,997,550
		£ 35,768,520

Securities:		
Public	26,913,360	30,905,330
Private	3,991,970	
Bullion		10,055,460
Rest £5,192,270		£ 40,960,790

August 31, 1818.

Circulation:		
Bank Notes of £5 and upwards, and Post Bills	18,676,220	26,202,150
Bank Notes under £5	7,525,930	
Deposits		7,927,730
		£ 34,129,880

Securities:		
Public	27,257,012	32,370,760
Private	5,113,748	
Bullion		6,363,160
Rest £4,604,040		£ 38,733,[illegible]

Notes in Circulation, Deposits, and Securities.—*Continued.*

February 27, 1819.

Circulation:		
Bank Notes of £5 and upwards, and Post Bills	[illegible]	[illegible]
Bank Notes under £5	7,[illegible]	
Deposits		6,4[illegible]
		£ [illegible]

Securities:		
Public	[illegible]	31,455,000
Private	[illegible]	
Bullion		4,184,620
Rest £4,[illegible],550		£ 35,639,620

August 31, 1819.

Circulation:		
Bank Notes of £5 and upwards, and Post Bills	[illegible]	25,252,[illegible]
Bank Notes under £5	7,255,2[illegible]	
Deposits		6,304,[illegible]
		£ 31,556,850

Securities:		
Public	25,[illegible]9,148	31,740,550
Private	6,32[illegible],402	
Bullion		3,595,360
Rest £3,779,060		£ 35,335,910

February 29, 1820.

Circulation:		
Bank Notes of £5 and upwards, and Post Bills	[illegible]	23,484,[illegible]
Bank Notes under £5	6,659,1[illegible]	
Deposits		4,093,[illegible]
		£ 27,577,6[illegible]

Securities:		
Public	21,715,168	26,187,490
Private	4,472,322	
Bullion		4,911,050
Rest £3,520,880		£ 31,098,540

August 31, 1820.

Circulation:		
Bank Notes of £5 and upwards, and Post Bills	17,[illegible]	24,[illegible]40
Bank Notes under £5	6,[illegible]	
Deposits		4,42[illegible]
		£ 28,720,250

Securities:		
Public	19,173,997	23,846,120
Private	4,672,123	
Bullion		8,211,080
Rest £3,336,950		£ 32,057,200

February 28, 1821.

Circulation:		
Bank Notes of £5 and upwards, and Post Bills	17,447,360	23,884,920
Bank Notes under £5	6,437,560	
Deposits		5,622,890
		£ 29,507,810

Securities:		
Public	16,010,990	20,796,270
Private	4,785,280	
Bullion		11,869,900
Rest £3,158,360		£ 32,666,170

August 31, 1821.

Circulation:		
Bank Notes of £5 and upwards, and Post Bills	17,747,070	20,295,300
Bank Notes under £5	2,548,230	
Deposits		5,818,450
		£ 26,113,750

Securities:		
Public	15,752,953	18,475,540
Private	2,722,587	
Bullion		11,233,590
Rest £3,595,380		£ 29,709,130

February 28, 1822.

Circulation:		
Bank Notes of £5 and upwards, and Post Bills	17,290,500	18,665,350
Bank Notes under £5	1,374,850	
Deposits		4,689,940
		£ 23,355,290

Securities:		
Public	12,478,133	15,973,080
Private	3,494,947	
Bullion		11,057,150
Rest £3,674,940		£ 27,030,230

August 31, 1822.

Circulation:		
Bank Notes of £5 and upwards, and Post Bills	16,609,460	17,464,790
Bank Notes under £5	855,330	
Deposits		6,399,440
		£ 23,864,230

Securities:		
Public	13,668,359	17,290,510
Private	3,622,151	
Bullion		10,097,960
Rest £3,524,240		£ 27,388,470

Notes in Circulation, Deposits, and Securities.—*Continued.*

February 28, 1823.		
Circulation:		
Bank Notes of £5 and upwards, and Post Bills	17,710,740	18,392,240
Bank Notes under £5 . .	681,500	
Deposits		7,181,100
		£ 25,573,340

February 28, 1823.		
Securities:		
Public	13,658,829	18,319,730
Private	4,660,901	
Bullion		10,384,230
Rest £3,130,620		£ 28,703,960

August 30, 1823.		
Circulation:		
Bank Notes of £5 and upwards, and Post Bills	18,682,760	19,231,240
Bank Notes under £5 . .	548,480	
Deposits		7,827,350
		£ 27,058,590

August 31, 1823.		
Securities:		
Public	11,842,677	17,467,370
Private	5,624,693	
Bullion		12,658,240
Rest £3,067,020		£ 30,125,610

February 28, 1824.		
Circulation:		
Bank Notes of £5 and upwards, and Post Bills	19,250,860	19,736,990
Bank Notes under £5 . .	486,130	
Deposits		10,097,850
		£ 29,834,840

February 28, 1824.		
Securities:		
Public	14,341,127	18,872,000
Private	4,430,873	
Bullion		13,810,060
Rest £2,847,220		£ 32,682,060

August 31, 1824.		
Circulation:		
Bank Notes of £5 and upwards, and Post Bills	19,688,980	20,132,120
Bank Notes under £5 . .	443,140	
Deposits		9,679,810
		£ 29,811,930

August 31, 1824.		
Securities:		
Public	14,649,187	20,904,530
Private	6,255,343	
Bullion		11,787,430
Rest £2,880,030		£ 32,691,960

February 28, 1825.		
Circulation:		
Bank Notes of £5 and upwards, and Post Bills	20,337,030	20,753,760
Bank Notes under £5 . .	416,730	
Deposits		10,168,780
		£ 30,922,520

February 28, 1825.		
Securities:		
Public	19,447,588	24,951,330
Private	5,503,742	
Bullion		8,779,100
Rest £2,807,890		£ 33,730,430

August 31, 1825.		
Circulation:		
Bank Notes of £5 and upwards, and Post Bills	19,002,500	19,398,840
Bank Notes under £5 . .	396,340	
Deposits		6,410,560
		£ 25,809,400

August 31, 1825.		
Securities:		
Public	17,414,566	25,106,030
Private	7,691,464	
Bullion		3,634,320
Rest £2,930,950		£ 28,740,350

February 28, 1826.		
Circulation:		
Bank Notes of £5 and upwards, and Post Bills	24,092,660	25,467,910
Bank Notes under £5 . .	1,375,250	
Deposits		6,935,940
		£ 32,403,850

February 28, 1826.		
Securities:		
Public	20,573,258	32,918,580
Private	12,345,322	
Bullion		2,459,510
Rest £2,974,240		£ 35,378,090

August 31, 1826.		
Circulation:		
Bank Notes of £5 and upwards, and Post Bills	20,402,300	21,563,560
Bank Notes under £5 . .	1,161,260	
Deposits		7,199,860
		£ 28,763,420

August 31, 1826.		
Securities:		
Public	17,713,881	25,083,630
Private	7,639,749	
Bullion		6,754,230
Rest £3,074,440		£ 31,837,860

Notes in Circulation, Deposits, and Securities.—*Continued.*

February 28, 1827.

Circulation:		
Bank Notes of £5 and upwards, and Post Bills	21,229,220	21,890,610
Bank Notes under £5	661,390	
Deposits		8,801,660
		£ 30,692,270

Securities:		
Public	18,685,015	23,529,530
Private	4,844,515	
Bullion		10,159,020
Rest £2,996,280		£ 33,688,550

August 31, 1827.

Circulation:		
Bank Notes of £5 and upwards, and Post Bills	22,267,400	22,747,600
Bank Notes under £5	480,200	
Deposits		8,052,090
		£ 30,799,690

Securities:		
Public	19,809,595	23,199,320
Private	3,389,725	
Bullion		10,463,770
Rest £2,863,400		£ 33,663,090

February 29, 1828.

Circulation:		
Bank Notes of £5 and upwards, and Post Bills	21,564,450	21,980,710
Bank Notes under £5	416,260	
Deposits		9,198,140
		£ 31,178,850

Securities:		
Public	19,818,777	23,581,270
Private	3,762,493	
Bullion		10,347,290
Rest £2,749,710		£ 33,928,560

August 30, 1828.

Circulation:		
Bank Notes of £5 and upwards, and Post Bills	20,975,170	21,357,510
Bank Notes under £5	382,340	
Deposits		10,201,280
		£ 31,558,790

Securities:		
Public	20,682,776	23,905,530
Private	3,222,754	
Bullion		10,498,880
Rest £2,845,620		£ 34,404,410

February 29, 1829.

Circulation:		
Bank Notes of £5 and upwards, and Post Bills	19,514,020	19,870,850
Bank Notes under £5	356,830	
Deposits		9,553,960
		£ 29,424,810

Securities:		
Public	19,736,665	25,384,750
Private	5,648,085	
Bullion		6,835,020
Rest £2,794,960		£ 32,219,770

August 31, 1829.

Circulation:		
Bank Notes of £5 and upwards, and Post Bills	19,213,530	19,547,380
Bank Notes under £5	333,850	
Deposits		9,035,070
		£ 28,582,450

Securities:		
Public	20,072,440	24,661,810
Private	4,589,370	
Bullion		6,795,530
Rest £2,874,890		£ 31,457,340

February 27, 1830.

Circulation:		
Bank Notes of £5 and upwards, and Post Bills	19,730,240	20,050,730
Bank Notes under £5	320,490	
Deposits		10,763,150
		£ 30,813,880

Securities:		
Public	20,038,890	24,204,390
Private	4,165,500	
Bullion		9,171,000
Rest £2,561,510		£ 33,375,390

August 30, 1830.

Circulation:		
Bank Notes of £5 and upwards, and Post Bills	21,151,390	21,464,700
Bank Notes under £5	313,310	
Deposits		11,620,840
		£ 33,085,540

Securities:		
Public	20,911,616	24,565,690
Private	3,654,074	
Bullion		11,150,480
Rest £2,630,630		£ 35,716,170

Notes in Circulation, Deposits, and Securities.—*Continued.*

February 28, 1831.

Circulation:		
Bank Notes of £5 and upwards, and Post Bills	19,293,270	19,600,140
Bank Notes under £5 . .	306,870	
Deposits		11,213,530
	£	30,813,670

Securities:		
Public	19,927,572	25,208,980
Private	5,281,408	
Bullion		8,217,050
Rest £2,612,360	£	33,426,030

August 31, 1831.

Circulation:		
Bank Notes of £5 and upwards, and Post Bills	18,236,240	18,538,630
Bank Notes under £5 . .	302,390	
Deposits		9,069,310
	£	27,607,940

Securities:		
Public	18,056,552	23,905,030
Private	5,848,478	
Bullion		6,439,760
Rest £2,736,850	£	30,344,790

February 29, 1832.

Circulation:		
Bank Notes of £5 and upwards, and Post Bills	17,752,610	18,051,710
Bank Notes under £5 . .	299,100	
Deposits		8,937,170
	£	26,988,80

Securities:		
Public	18,497,448	24,333,490
Private	5,836,042	
Bullion		5,293,150
Rest £2,637,760	£	29,626,640

August 7, 1832.

Circulation:		
Bank Notes of £5 and upwards, and Post Bills	18,523,880	18,819,000
Bank Notes under £5 . .	295,120	
Deposits		11,431,000
	£	30,250,000

Securities:		
Public	20,828,000	25,976,000
Private	5,148,000	
Bullion		7,154,000
Rest £2,880,000	£	33,130,000

In addition to the above Rest, the estimated value of the Bank Premises is £1,000,000.

NOTE.—The Account dated 7th August, 1832, is merely an Estimate; the real Statement cannot be rendered until the 31st August, 1832.

WILLIAM SMEE, CHIEF ACCOUNTANT.

Bank of England, August 10, 1832.

TABLE XV.

Balance of Gold Coin delivered to the Public between 1st July and 1st November, 1824.

Delivered to the Public	£675,000
Ditto to N. M. Rothschild, Esq.. from the 21st July to the 28th August, 1824, both Days inclusive	885,000
	£1,560,000

T. RIPPON, Chief Cashier.

Bank of England, 9th June. 1832.

Supplied by N. M. Rothschild, in 1825, £500,000 in Gold.

TABLE XVI.

An Account of the average Amount of Coined Gold in the possession of the Bank, for the Years ending the 28th February, 1815, to 1832.

		£.
For the Year ending	1815	1,631,000
	1816	1,468,000
	1817	1,366,000
	1818	3,311,000
	1819	4,805,000
	1820	2,957,000
	1821	3,162,000
	1822	4,805,000
	1823	7,509,000
	1824	7,575,000
	1825	6,405,000
	1826	2,682,000
	1827	3,769,000
	1828	7,987,000
	1829	7,230,000
	1830	5,047,000
	1831	6,761,000
	1832	4,772,000
		83,242,000

T. RIPPON, Chief Cashier.

TABLE XVII.

An Account of the Amount of Silver Coin Melted; also, the Loss sustained thereby, in 1831.

	£.	s.	d.
Amount of Silver Coin melted in Bars	565,000	0	0
Ditto melted and recoined	35,000	0	0
Amount of Silver Coin melted	600,000	0	0
Loss on Sixpenny Pieces	4,601	1	3
Ditto on other denominations	62,982	19	2
Loss sustained	£67,584	0	5

TABLE XVIII.

An Account of the Amount of Coin and Bullion, distinguishing Coin from Bullion, in the possession of the Bank, from 28th February, 1815, to the present time, stating the Highest and Lowest Amount in each Year, with the date of each; together with the Amount of the Securities held by the Bank, and its Liabilities at each of the same periods.

In the Year ending	Coin.	Bullion.	Highest and Lowest Amount of Coin and Bullion in each Year, ending February. Highest.	Lowest.	Securities.	Liabilities
	£.	£.	£.	£.	£.	£.
			Coin . . . 1,733,000 Bullion . . 428,000	Coin . . . 1,719,000 Bullion . . 290,000		
Feb. 28, 1815	1,726,000	310,000	Nov. 5, 1814, 2,161,000	Feb. 25, 1815, 2,009,000	46,395,000	38,963,000
			Coin . . . 1,348,000 Bullion . . 3,018,000	Coin . . . 1,749,000 Bullion . . 335,000		
Feb. 29, 1816	1,565,000	3,075,000	Feb. 17, 1816, 4,366,000	Mar. 4, 1815, 2,084,000	48,042,000	39,402,000
			Coin . . . 2,027,000 Bullion . . 7,963,000	Coin . . . 1,557,000 Bullion . . 3,121,000		
Feb. 28, 1817	1,939,000	7,748,000	Feb. 11, 1817, 9,990,000	Mar. 2, 1816, 4,678,000	43,950,000	38,328,000
			Coin . . . 3,437,000 Bullion . . 8,477,000	Coin . . . 1,932,000 Bullion . . 7,742,000		
Feb. 28, 1818	7,111,000	2,944,000	Oct. 11, 1817, 11,914,000	Mar. 1, 1817, 9,674,000	40,960,000	35,768,000
			Coin . . . 7,155,000 Bullion . . 2,923,000	Coin . . . 3,216,000 Bullion . . 1,038,000		
Feb. 27, 1819	3,396,000	850,000	Mar. 7, 1818, 10,078,000	Feb. 27, 1819, 4,254,000	35,680,000	31,546,000
			Coin . . . 3,152,000 Bullion . . 1,755,000	Coin . . . 3,072,000 Bullion . . 498,000		
Feb. 29, 1820	2,163,000	1,746,000	Feb. 26, 1820, 4,907,000	Sept. 4, 1819, 3,570,000	31,098,000	27,577,000
			Coin . . . 3,847,000 Bullion . . 7,792,000	Coin . . . 3,164,000 Bullion . . 1,800,000		
Feb. 28, 1821	4,189,000	7,680,000	Feb. 24, 1821, 11,639,000	Mar. 1, 1820, 4,964,000	33,066,000	29,567,000
			Coin . . . 5,695,000 Bullion . . 7,634,000	Coin . . . 6,631,000 Bullion . . 4,327,000		
Feb. 28, 1822	7,250,000	3,797,000	May 5, 1821, 13,329,000	Feb. 2, 1822, 10,958,000	27,090,000	28,355,000
			Coin . . . 7,705,000 Bullion . . 3,381,000	Coin . . . 7,994,000 Bullion . . 1,861,000		
Feb. 28, 1823	3,670,000	1,718,000	Mar. 16, 1822, 11,086,000	Nov. 2, 1822, 9,855,000	28,703,000	25,578,000

In the Year ending	Coin.	Bullion.	Highest and Lowest Amount of Coin and Bullion in each Year, ending February. Highest.	Lowest.	Securities.	Liabilities
	£.	£.	£.	£.	£.	£.
			Coin . . . 8,206,000 Bullion . . 5,936,000	Coin . . . 8,657,000 Bullion . . 1,715,000		
Feb. 28, 1824	7,717,000	6,092,000	Dec. 26, 1823, 14,142,000	Mar. 1, 1823, 10,372,000	32,682,000	29,894,000
			Coin . . . 7,832,000 Bullion . . 6,113,000	Coin . . . 7,285,000 Bullion . . 1,572,000		
Feb. 28, 1825	7,190,000	1,388,000	Mar. 20, 1824, 13,945,000	Feb. 28, 1825, 8,857,000	33,720,000	30,898,000
			Coin . . . 7,245,000 Bullion . . 1,368,000	Coin . . . 426,000 Bullion . . 601,000		
Feb. 28, 1826	1,043,000	1,415,000	Mar. 5, 1825, 8,613,000	Dec. 24, 1825, 1,027,000	35,278,000	32,408,000
			Coin . . . 7,547,000 Bullion . . 2,460,000	Coin . . . 920,000 Bullion . . 2,428,000		
Feb. 28, 1827	7,626,000	2,582,000	Feb. 24, 1827, 10,007,000	Mar. 4, 1826, 3,348,000	32,682,000	30,692,000
			Coin . . . 9,114,000 Bullion . . 1,563,000	Coin . . . 8,805,000 Bullion . . 1,391,000		
Feb. 28, 1828	8,942,000	1,404,000	June 16, 1827, 10,677,000	Jan. 26, 1828, 10,196,000	33,928,000	31,178,000
			Coin . . . 8,734,000 Bullion . . 1,746,000	Coin . . . 6,097,000 Bullion . . 730,000		
Feb. 28, 1829	6,100,000	725,000	Aug. 23, 1828, 10,480,000	Feb. 1, 1829, 6,827,000	32,219,000	29,494,000
			Coin . . . 7,086,000 Bullion . . 2,075,000	Coin . . . 5,311,000 Bullion . . 793,000		
Feb. 27, 1830	7,095,000	2,073,000	Feb. 27, 1830, 9,161,000	April 18, 1829, 6,104,000	33,575,000	30,314,000
			Coin . . . 8,891,000 Bullion . . 2,904,000	Coin . . . 6,088,000 Bullion . . 2,123,000		
Feb. 28, 1831	6,151,000	2,065,000	June 26, 1830, 11,795,000	Feb. 19, 1831, 8,211,000	33,426,000	30,318,000
			Coin . . . 6,179,000 Bullion . . 2,031,000	Coin . . . 4,267,000 Bullion . . 821,000		
Feb. 29, 1832	4,585,000	737,000	Mar. 5, 1831, 8,210,000	Feb. 6, 1832, 5,088,000	29,626,000	26,960,000

TABLE XIX.

An Account of the average Amounts of Gold and Silver Bullion held by the Bank, in the Years ending February 28, 1815 to 1828, inclusive, distinguishing Gold from Silver.

	Gold.	Silver.	Total.
Years ending	£.	£.	£.
February 28, 1815	1,938,265	240,882	2,179,147
1816	2,828,707	570,407	3,399,114
1817	6,643,100	861,184	7,504,284
1818	10,147,115	962,266	11,109,381
1819	6,066,603	655,044	6,721,647
1820	3,663,561	305,967	3,969,528
1821	6,291,446	1,882,973	8,174,419
1822	9,162,298	2,468,792	11,631,090
1823	8,135,629	2,119,069	10,254,698
1824	10,805,780	1,801,183	12,606,963
1825	10,213,247	1,645,348	11,858,595
1826	3,719,824	601,878	4,321,702
1827	5,880,811	727,165	6,607,976
1828	9,505,630	695,623	10,201,253

WILLIAM SMEE, Chief Accountant.

Bank of England, 29 May, 1832.

An Account of the average Amonnts of Gold and Silver Bullion held by the Bank, in the Years ending February 28, 1829, 1830, 1831, and 1832, distinguishing Gold from Silver.

		£.
In the Year ending February 28, 1829	Gold	8,749,920
	Silver	1,013,210
		9,763,130
In the Year ending February 28, 1830	Gold	5,736,186
	Silver	1,519,586
		7,255,772
In the Year ending February 28, 1831	Gold	8,235,162
	Silver	2,095,199
		10,330,361
In the Year ending February 29, 1832	Gold	5,853,334
	Silver	551,924
		6,405,258

TABLE XX.

An Account of the Amounts of the Dividends paid to the Proprietors of Bank Stock, in the Years ending February 28, 1829, 1830, 1831, 1832.

	£.
In the Year ending February 28, 1829	1,164,234
In the Year ending February 28, 1830	1,164,234
In the Year ending February 28, 1831	1,164,235
In the Year ending February 28, 1832	1,164,235

WILLIAM SMEE, Chief Accountant.

TABLE XXI.

An Account of the Amounts of the Net Annual Profits of the Bank of England, in the Years ending February 28, 1829, 1830, 1831, and 1832, out of which Interest has been paid on the Capital Stock.

In the Year ending	£.	In the Year ending	£.
February 28, 1829 . .	1,209,482	February 28, 1831 . .	1,215,085
February 28, 1830 . .	930,786	February 29, 1832 . .	1,189,627

WILLIAM SMEE, Chief Accountant.

TABLE XXII.

An Account of the Profits of the Bank of England, in the Year ending February 29, 1832, stating the Description of the Securities held by the Bank, and the Sources from which the said Profits have accrued.

	£.
Interest on Commercial Bills	130,695
Interest on Exchequer Bills	204,109
Annuity for Forty-five Years, (the Dead-weight Account)	451,415
Interest on Capital received from Government	446,502
Allowance received for management of the Public Debt	251,896
Interest on Loans on Mortgages	60,684
Interest on Stock in the Public Funds	15,075
Interest on Private Loans	56,941
Profit on Bullion, Commission, Rent, Receipts on Discounted Bills unpaid, Management of the Business of the Banks of Ireland, of Scotland, and Sundry Items	71,859
	1,689,176

WILLIAM SMEE, Chief Accountant.

TABLE XXIII.

An Account of the total Amount of Salaries, Morning Money, Gratuities, &c., paid to Servants of the Bank in London, and at the Bank of England Branches, and of the number of persons to whom the said Amount was paid.

For the Year ending February 29, 1832:	£.	s.	d.
820 Clerks and Porters			
38 Printers and Engravers	211,903	10	10
82 Clerks and Porters at the Branches			
940 . . Average £225 each.			
Amount of Pensions paid in the same period:			
193 Pensioners, average £161 each	31,243	18	11

WILLIAM SMEE, Chief Accountant.

An Account of the total Expenses of the Bank of England, in the Years ending the 28th February, 1829, 1830, 1831, and 1832, exclusive of the Amount paid for Stamp Duty and Losses sustained by the Bank from Forgeries upon Stock, Transfers, and Dividends.

In the Year ending	£.	In the Year ending	£.
February 28, 1829 . .	331,700	February 28, 1831 . .	336,300
February 28, 1830 . .	337,300	February 29, 1832 . .	339,400

WILLIAM SMEE, Chief Accountant.

TABLE XXIV.

Debtor and Creditor Account of the Bank, on 29th February, 1832.

Dr.

		£.
To Bank Notes outstanding		18,051,710
To Public Deposits, *viz.*		
Drawing Accounts	2,034,790	
Balance of Audit Roll	550,550	
Life Annuities unpaid	85,030	3,198,730
Annuities for terms of Years unpaid	38,360	
Exchequer Bills deposited	490,000	
To Private Deposits, *viz.*		
Drawing Accounts	5,683,870	5,738,430
Various other Debts	54,560	
To the Bank of England for Capital		14,553,000
To Balance of Surplus in favour of the Bank of England		2,637,760
		£ 44,179,630

Cr.

		£.
By Advances on Government Securities, *viz.*		
Exchequer Bills on the growing Produce of the Consolidated Fund in the quarter ending 5th April 1832	3,428,340	
Ditto 5th July 1832	697,000	4,134,940
Exchequer Bills on supplies 1825	7,600	
Ditto for £10,500,000 for 1825	2,000	
By the advances to the Trustees appointed by the Act 3 Geo. IV. c. 51, towards the purchase of an Annuity of £585,740 for 44 Years from 5th April 1823		10,897,880
By other Credits, *viz.*		
Exchequer Bills purchased	2,700,000	
Stock purchased	764,600	
City Bonds	500,000	
Bills and Notes discounted	2,951,970	9,166,860
Loans on Mortgages	1,452,100	
London Dock Company	227,500	
Advances on Security and Various articles	570,690	
By Cash and Bullion		5,293,150
By the permanent Debt due from Government		14,686,800
		£ 44,179,630
Rest or Surplus brought down		2,637,760
Bank Capital due to Proprietors		14,553,000
		£ 17,190,760

TABLE XXV.

Bank of England, 29th February, 1832.

Dr.	£.	*Cr.*		£.
To Annual Expenses, Forgeries, Losses, and sundry Items	428,674	Profit and Loss		2,612,368
Stamp Duty on Circulation	70,875	By Interest on Loans and Commercial Bills		248,321
Divided to Proprietors	1,164,235	Government Securities held by the Bank		670,598
	1,663,784	Interest on Capital received from Government		446,502
Rest . .	2,637,760	Allowances received for the Management of the Public Debt		251,896
	£ 4,301,544	Profit on Bullion, Rent and sundry Items		71,859
Rest, 29th February 1832	2,637,760			£ 4,301,544
Rest, 28th February 1831	2,612,368	Rest, 29th February 1832		2,637,760
Increase . .	25,392	Capital with Government	14,686,800	14,553,000
		Less so much included in the Rest . . .	133,800	
				£ 17,190,760

TABLE XXVI.

An ACCOUNT of the Amount of DEPOSITS held by the BANK on 26th February, 26th May, 26th August, and 26th November, in each Year, from 1814 to the present time, distinguishing Public and Private Deposits.

	26 February.	26 May.	26 August.	26 November.
1815	£.	£.	£.	£.
Public Deposits .	10,543,600	11,558,700	11,779,100	10,972,400
Private ditto . .	1,626,100	1,805,700	1,091,600	1,569,000
£	12,169,700	13,364,400	12,870,700	12,541,400
1816				
Public Deposits .	11,064,800	10,205,700	9,898,800	9,001,500
Private ditto . .	986,400	1,197,100	1,215,100	1,833,000
£	12,051,200	11,402,800	11,113,900	10,834,500
1817				
Public Deposits .	8,739,700	9,493,900	7,046,600	6,000,600
Private ditto . .	1,781,200	1,832,300	1,906,600	1,568,600
£	10,520,900	11,326,200	8,953,200	7,569,200
1818				
Public Deposits .	5,755,300	6,578,600	5,188,600	5,914,600
Private ditto . .	1,642,900	2,038,900	1,653,100	2,283,300
£	7,398,200	8,617,500	6,841,700	8,197,900
1819				
Public Deposits .	4,592,300	3,731,700	3,953,000	2,819,600
Private ditto . .	1,523,500	1,997,300	1,879,200	1,632,500
£	6,115,800	5,729,000	5,832,200	4,452,100
1820				
Public Deposits .	3,014,900	2,984,300	3,456,600	3,070,300
Private ditto . .	1,156,500	1,361,100	1,438,100	1,722,000
£	4,171,400	4,345,400	4,894,700	4,792,300
1821				
Public Deposits .	3,553,400	3,094,300	4,417,300	3,464,900
Private ditto . .	1,642,800	1,962,500	1,909,300	2,248,500
£	5,196,200	5,056,800	6,326,600	5,713,400
1822				
Public Deposits .	3,075,000	2,978,900	4,258,200	3,271,000
Private ditto . .	1,735,200	1,987,400	2,715,500	2,736,100
£	4,810,200	4,966,300	6,973,700	6,007,100
1823				
Public Deposits .	5,171,900	4,432,200	4,086,300	5,434,500
Private ditto . .	2,509,600	3,657,500	3,091,000	3,937,100
£	7,681,500	8,089,700	7,177,300	9,371,600

Account of the Amount of Deposits.—continued.

		26 February.	26 May.	26 August.	26 November.
1824		£.	£.	£.	£.
Public Deposits .	.	7,330,100	7,508,900	[illegible]	[illegible]
Private ditto .	.	2,323,100	[illegible]	[illegible]	[illegible]
	£	9,653,200	9,994,700	[illegible]	[illegible]
1825					
Public Deposits .	.	5,797,900	[illegible]	[illegible]	[illegible]
Private ditto .	.	3,346,400	[illegible]	[illegible]	[illegible]
	£	9,144,300	[illegible]	[illegible]	[illegible]
1826					
Public deposits .	.	3,489,900	3,643,900	[illegible]	[illegible]
Private ditto .	.	3,614,700	[illegible]	[illegible]	[illegible]
	£	7,104,600	[illegible]	[illegible]	[illegible]
1827					
Public Deposits .	.	3,459,800	[illegible]	[illegible]	[illegible]
Private ditto .	.	5,588,700	[illegible]	[illegible]	[illegible]
	£	9,048,500	[illegible]	[illegible]	[illegible]
1828					
Public Deposits .	.	3,278,000	[illegible]	[illegible]	[illegible]
Private ditto .	.	5,684,200	[illegible]	[illegible]	[illegible]
	£	8,962,200	[illegible]	[illegible]	[illegible]
1829					
Public Deposits .	.	3,433,600	[illegible]	[illegible]	[illegible]
Private ditto .	.	5,726,300	[illegible]	[illegible]	[illegible]
	£	9,159,900	[illegible]	[illegible]	[illegible]
1830					
Public Deposits .	.	3,592,700	[illegible]	[illegible]	[illegible]
Private ditto .	.	6,647,400	[illegible]	[illegible]	[illegible]
	£	10,240,100	11,664,500	[illegible]	[illegible]
1831					
Public Deposits .	.	4,195,800	[illegible]	[illegible]	[illegible]
Private ditto .	.	6,847,600	6,591,300	[illegible]	[illegible]
	£	11,043,600	[illegible]	[illegible]	[illegible]
1832					
Public Deposits .	.	3,137,900	[illegible]		
Private ditto .	.	5,422,600	5,764,100		
	£	8,560,500	[illegible]		

Bank of England, 3d July, 1832.

WILLIAM SMEE, [illegible]

TABLE XXVII.

An ACCOUNT of the Total Amount of all EXCHEQUER BILLS held by the BANK of ENGLAND, on the 1st June in each Year, from 1816 to 1832, inclusive.

	£.		£.
On the 1st June, 1816 ..	23,372,600	On the 1st June, 1825 ..	12,913,000
Ditto 1817 ..	24,000,500	Ditto 1826 ..	11,606,787
Ditto 1818 ..	26,342,400	Ditto 1827 ..	10,099,743
Ditto 1819 ..	21,669,900	Ditto 1828 ..	9,217,530
Ditto 1820 ..	18,711,900	Ditto 1829 ..	7,762,935
Ditto 1821 ..	14,461,900	Ditto 1830 ..	8,918,726
Ditto 1822 ..	12,169,200	Ditto 1831 ..	5,121,700
Ditto 1823 ..	12,127,800	Ditto 1832 ..	6,650,453
Ditto 1824 ..	11,593,800		

WILLIAM SMEE, CHIEF ACCOUNTANT.

An Account of the average Amount of EXCHEQUER BILLS, including DEFICIENCY BILLS, held by the BANK of ENGLAND, in the Years 1828, 1829, 1830, and 1831.

In the Year 1828	£9,367,630
Ditto 1829	8,664,020
Ditto 1830	8,783,730
Ditto 1831	6,733,260

WILLIAM SMEE, CHIEF ACCOUNTANT.

TABLE XXVIII.

BRANCH BANKS.

An ACCOUNT of the Number of COUNTRY BANKERS who have been supplied with, or are now receiving BANK NOTES and COIN, and who act only with BANK of ENGLAND PAPER, but who do not take fixed Amounts for Circulation.

13 Country Bankers.

WILLIAM SMEE, CHIEF ACCOUNTANT.

BRANCH BANKS.

An ACCOUNT of the Number of COUNTRY BANKERS who issue their own NOTES, and who have been supplied with, or are now receiving COIN, as occasion may require.

126 Country Bankers.

WILLIAM SMEE, CHIEF ACCOUNTANT.

TABLE XXIX.

An ACCOUNT of the PLACES at which the BOARDS were established for ADVANCES on GOODS by the BANK of ENGLAND, and the Amounts of such ADVANCES, in the Year 1826.

Manchester . . .	115,490	Huddersfield . . .	30,300
Glasgow	81,700	Birmingham . . .	19,600
Sheffield	59,500	Dundee	16,500
Liverpool	41,450	Norwich	2,400

WILLIAM SMEE, CHIEF ACCOUNTANT.

Bank of England, June 9, 1832.

[To face page 279.

TABLE XXX.

STATEMENT B, showing the GROSS RECEIPT of STAMP DUTY on BILLS of EXCHANGE and PROMISSORY NOTES; distinguishing the Proportion on the reissuable Notes of Country Bankers; the Number of Licenses granted to Country Bankers; Commissions of Bankruptcy issued against the same; the Amount of Commercial Bills discounted by the Bank of England, and Amount of Public and Private Deposits held thereby; and Annual Average Circulation of Bank of England Notes in each of the 25 years 1807—1831; being Appendixes Nos. 24, 32, 50, 73, 81, 99, 98, 101, to the Report of the Committee on the Bank of England Charter; to which is here appended the Amount of Bullion in Dollars coined at all the Legal Mints of Mexico, and the proportion thereof exported in each of the 23 years 1807—1829.

⁎ In 1808 the duty on the £1 reissuable Notes of Country Bankers was raised from 3d. to 4d., and in 1815 from 4d. to 5d.; and a proportionate advance on the rate of duty on all other stamps took place in those years. In 1825 the circulation of small notes was suppressed in all England and Wales: the contrast in the amount of commercial bills discounted in 1810 and 1830, as well as the increase of private deposits since 1825, deserve notice, and merit serious consideration.

Years.	Gross Receipt of Stamp Duty on Bills of Exchange.	Proportion on Reissuable Notes.	Number of Licences granted to Country Bankers.	Commissions of Bankruptcy issued against ditto.	Commercial Bills Discounted.	DEPOSITS. Public.	DEPOSITS. Private.	Annual average Circulation of Bank of England Notes.	Coinage in Dollars of all the Legal Mints of Mexico.	Proportion of Dollars Exported.
	£.	£.			£.	£.	£.	£.		
1807		52,442		1	13,484,600	12,647,551	1,582,720	16,705,903	22,014,700	19,297,710
8		108,031		5	12,950,100	11,761,448	1,940,630	17,128,649	21,886,501	11,883,044
9		152,205	702	4	15,475,700	11,093,648	1,492,190	18,927,833	26,172,982	21,793,500
1810	738,793	99,633	782	20	20,070,600	11,950,047	1,428,720	23,541,523	19,662,221	11,636,872
11	679,839	101,941	779	4	14,355,400	10,191,854	1,567,920	23,282,071	14,295,947	7,233,553
12	691,044	119,562	825	17	14,291,600	10,390,130	1,578,950	23,237,318	9,411,331	4,034,655
13	719,897	130,830	922	8	12,330,200	10,393,404	1,771,310	24,023,569	10,540,783	11,283,596
14	713,838	103,314	940	27	13,285,800	12,158,227	2,374,910	26,927,650	11,230,648	9,276,872
15	841,459	88,900	916	25	14,947,100	11,737,436	1,690,490	26,887,010	8,419,288	8,226,609
16	754,301	83,213	831	37	11,416,400	10,807,660	1,333,120	26,574,840	10,538,491	8,423,534
17	735,940	139,632	752	3	3,960,600	8,699,133	1,672,800	28,274,880	9,937,981	7,659,890
18	845,750	148,314	765	8	4,325,200	7,066,887	1,640,210	27,221,200	12,899,917	4,264,450
19	738,974	62,329	787	13	6,515,000	4,538,373	1,790,860	25,145,310	13,301,590	6,002,737
1820	697,406	53,657	769	4	3,883,600	3,713,442	1,325,060	23,920,080	11,586,656	10,104,645
1	691,335	66,961	781	10	2,676,700	3,990,157	1,326,020	21,577,670	8,067,560	10,683,020
2	668,057	62,182	776	9	3,366,700	4,107,853	1,373,370	17,862,890	11,066,950	9,338,357
3	681,881	65,035	779	9	3,123,800	5,526,635	2,321,980	18,629,540	9,458,536	3,391,924
4	723,920	93,277	788	10	2,369,800	7,222,187	2,369,910	20,135,300	9,680,583	6,503,648
5	790,876	114,916	797	37	4,941,500	5,347,314	2,607,900	20,105,030	9,193,686	2,714,354

3	[illegible]	[illegible]	17,710,740	[illegible]	7,191,100	[illegible]	[illegible]	[illegible]	[illegible]	[illegible]	[illegible]	759,748
4	60,115,864	55,918,734	19,250,860	486,130	10,097,850	29,834,810	14,341,127	4,580,873	13,810,060	32,682,060	2,847,220	4,065,075
5	58,363,801	54,980,128	20,337,030	416,730	10,168,780	30,922,540	19,447,588	5,503,742	8,779,100	33,730,430	2,807,890	4,580,919
6	55,902,334	57,049,195	24,092,660	1,375,250	6,935,940	28,403,850	20,573,258	12,345,322	2,459,510	35,878,090	2,974,240	5,896,461
7	55,756,401	56,859,224	21,229,220	661,390	8,801,660	30,692,270	18,685,015	4,814,515	10,159,090	33,688,550	2,996,280	2,512,637
8	57,297,235	53,573,714	21,564,450	416,260	9,198,140	31,178,850	19,818,777	3,762,493	10,347,290	33,928,560	2,749,710	1,277,784
9	55,934,966	53,637,675	19,514,020	256,830	9,653,960	29,424,810	19,736,665	5,648,085	6,835,020	32,919,770	2,794,960	2,271,158
1830	54,932,287	51,430,877	19,730,240	220,490	10,763,160	30,813,880	20,038,890	4,165,500	9,171,000	33,375,390	2,561,810	No return
1	51,012,609	51,195,723	19,298,270	306,870	11,213,530	30,813,670	19,927,570	5,281,408	8,217,050	33,496,030	2,612,035	Ditto
2			17,758,610	299,100	8,937,170	26,988,880	18,497,448	5,836,042	5,293,150	29,696,640	2,637,760	Ditto
	—(1)—	—(2)—	—(3)—	—(4)—	—(5)—	—(6)—	—(7)—	—(8)—	—(9)—	—(10)—	—(11)—	—(12)—

TABLE XXXI.

A LIST of the FOREIGN LOANS contracted in ENGLAND; with the Names of the Contractors, the Year in which the Contracts were made, and the Prices at which they were issued. Extracted from the Memorandums of Messrs. Wettenhall, Publishers of "The Course of Exchange," &c.

	£.	Per cent.			Per cent.
Austrian* ..	2,500,000	5	N. M. Rothschild	1823	82
Belgian* ...	2,000,000	—	Ditto	1832	75
Brazilian ...	3,200,000	—	T. Wilson and Co.	1824	75
Ditto*	2,000,000	—	N. M. Rothschild	1825	85
Ditto*	800,000	—	Rothschild and Wilson ..	1829	—
Buenos Ayres	1,000,000	6	Baring, Brothers	1824	85
Chili	1,000,000	—	Hullett, Brothers	1822	70
Columbian..	2,000,000	—	Herring, Graham and Co. .	1822	84
Ditto	4,750,000	—	B. A. Goldschmidt and Co.	1824	88½
Danish*....	5,500,000	3	T. Wilson and Co.	1825	75
Greek......	800,000	5	Loughan and Co.	1824	59
Ditto	2,000,000	—	Ricardo	1825	56½
Guatemala..	1,428,571	6	J. and A. Powles	1825	73
Guadalajara.	600,000	5	W. Ellward, Jun.	1825	60
Mexican....	3,200,000	—	B. A. Goldschmidt and Co.	1824	58
Ditto	3,200,000	6	Barclay, Herring and Co. .	1825	89¾
Neapolitan*.	2,500,000	5	N. M. Rothschild.....	1824	92½
Prussian*...	5,000,000	—	Ditto	1818	72
Ditto*	3,500,000	—	Ditto	1822	84
Portuguese .	1,500,000	—	B. A. Goldschmidt and Co.	1823	87
Peruvian ...	450,000	6	Frys and Chapman	1822	88
Ditto	750,000	—	Ditto	1824	82
Ditto	616,000	—	Ditto	1825	78
Russian* ...	3,500,000	5	N. M. Rothschild	1822	82
Spanish	1,500,000	—	A. F. Haldimand	1821	56
Ditto	1,500,000	—	J. Campbell and Co. ...	1823	30½
Total	56,694,571				

* Those marked thus continue to pay the Dividends.

MIEVILLE and DE LA CHAUMETTE, ANGEL COURT.

N. B. In this List have been omitted Sixteen Millions sterling of Spanish Loans, which, although ostensibly contracted by the French houses of Lafitte and Ardouin, were, in reality, sold in the English Market.

TABLE XXXII.

Comparative Statement of the Money raised for the Mines of America, and the Money actually paid; showing the Companies existing on 1st February, 1825, and on 2d February, 1833; the number of Shares, Money paid, actual Value of each Share, and total Amount paid at each of the above periods. (From the Public List of Shares, published at the Stock Exchange, on 1st February 1825, and 2d February 1833).

Names of the Companies.	February 1, 1825.					February 2, 1833.				
	Number of Shares.	Amount of each Share.	Money paid.	Price per Share.	Total Amount paid.	Number of Shares.	Amount of each Share.	Money paid.	Price per Share.	Total Amount paid.
		£.	£.	£.	£.		£.	£.	£.	£.
Anglo Mexican .	10,000	100	10	117¼	100,000	10,000	100	100	12	1,000,000
Ditto Subscription	...	..	..	..	....	...	..	..	25	250,000
Bolanos . . .	2,000	400	..	450pm.	....	2,000	150	150	160	300,000
Brasilian . . .	6,000	100	5	26	30,000	6,000	20	5	10s.	30,000
Ditto Imperial .	10,000	..	..	..	....	10,000	35	20	..	200,000
Ditto St. John del Rey . . .	5,000	..	..	..	....	5,000	20	10	3	50,000
Ditto Cocaes . .	14,000	..	..	..	....	14,000	20	5	..	70,000
Bolivar . . .	10,000	..	..	..	....	10,000	50	20	..	200,000
Columbian . .	8,500	100	5	39	42,500	8,500	55	49½	..	398,000
General Mining .	20,000	50	..	12	....	20,000	20	11	..	220,000
Mexican . . .	6,155	..	..	..	....	6,155	100	46	4	283,130
Pénoles	1,020	..	..	..	....	1,020	12	12	..	12,240
Potosi las Paz .	10,000	..	..	..	....	10,000	15	5	..	50,000
Ditto consolidated	...	..	..	..	....	...	..	10	..	100,000
Real del Monte .	11,500	400	70	..	805,000	11,500	400	..	23	805,000
Talpuxahua . .	1,000	400	20	250pm.	20,000	1,000	400	330	..	330 000
United Mexican .	30,000	40	20	130pm	600,000	30,000	40	40	9	1,200 000
Ditto Subscription	...	..	..	..	....	...	..	2	2	60,000
Ditto New Scrip	...	..	..	..	....	...	..	5	14	150,000
*Castello and Spirito Santo** .	10,000	100	5	..	50,000	10,000	100	5	..	50,000
Chilian . . .	10,000	100	5	..	50,000	10,000	100	5	..	50,000
Chilian Peruvian	10,000	100	5	..	50,000	10,000	100	5	..	50,000
Famatina . . .	1,000	250	12½	..	12,500	1,000	250	12½	..	12,500
Haytian . . .	10,000	100	5	..	50,000	10,000	100	5	..	50,000
Pasco Peruvian .	10,000	100	10	..	100,000	10,000	100	10	..	100,000
Rio de la Plata .	10,000	100	5	..	50,000	10,000	100	5	..	50,000
Anglo Chilian .	15,000	100	5	14 pm.	75,000	15,000	100	5	..	75,000
					2,035,000				Total £	6,215,870

* Those marked in italics have disappeared from the Market.

TABLE XXXIII.

An Account of the Price of £3 per cent. Consols, and the Premium or Discount on Exchequer Bills, from 1797 to 1832, on the 28th February and 31st August, in each Year, to the present time, (7th August, 1832).

Date.	Consols.	Exchequer Bills.
1797 Feb. 28	52⅜ 51⅞	3/ dis.
Aug. 31	52⅝ ¾ ½ ⅝	nil.
1798 Feb. 28	49½ ¾ ⅝ ⅞	nil.
Aug. 31	50 49⅞ 50	⅝ per cent. dis.
1799 Feb. 28	53⅜ ⅝ 54	nil.
Aug. 31	65⅜ 65 66⅞ ⅝	7/ pm.
1800 Feb. 28	6[illegible] ¾ ½	nil.
Aug. 30	65[illegible]	nil.
1801 Feb. 28	55[illegible] 6	nil.
Aug. 31	60⅝ ⅛	nil.
1802 Feb. 27	69½ 9¼ ⅜	nil.
Aug. 31	68 67⅝ ¼	3/ pm. 4/ pm.
1803 Feb. 28	71¼ ⅝ 71¼	nil.
Aug. 31	54¼ ½ ¼ ⅝	nil.
1804 Feb. 28	55⅝ ½ ¼ ⅝	nil.
Aug. 31	57½ 7⅛	nil.
1805 Feb. 28	58⅞ ¼ 8⅛	par 1/ dis.
Aug. 31	58½ ⅝ ¼	2/ pm. 1/ dis. 1/ pm
1806 Feb. 28	60½ ⅛	2/ pm. 4/ pm.
Aug. 30	63⅛ 2¾	1/ pm. 1/ dis. par
1807 Feb. 27	62⅝ ⅝	2/ dis. par
Aug. 31	62⅝ ½ ⅝	1/ dis. 1/ pm.
1808 Feb. 27	63¼ ¼	2/ dis. 1/ pm.
Aug. 31	65¼ ½ ⅝	6/ 3/ 2/ pm.
1809 Feb. 28	67⅝ ¾	9/ 12/ pm.
Aug. 31	68⅛	8/ 15/ pm.
1810 Feb. 27	67¾ ⅝ ¾	3/ 6/ pm.
Aug. 31	68⅝ ⅛ ¼	3d. p. d. par 4/ pm.
		3½d. 1/ dis. 3/ pm.
1811 Feb. 28	65⅝ ½ ¾ ⅝	9/ 11/ pm.
Aug. 31	64¼ ⅛ ¼	3d. p. d. par 4/ pm.
		3½d. 4/ 5/ pm.
1812 Feb. 28	62⅛ 1⅞ 2	3d. p. d. 5/ pm.
		3½d. 6/ 5/ pm.
Aug. 31	59⅝	3½d. 1/ dis. par
		3½d. 4/ 5/ pm.
1813 Feb. 27	58⅝ ½ ⅝	3½d. 4/ 6/ pm.
Aug. 31	56⅞ 76½ 7	1/ 4/ pm.
1814 Feb. 28	70½ ⅝ ⅝	2/ 5/ pm.
Aug. 31	65⅝ ⅝ ⅛ ¼	2/ 5/ pm.
1815 Feb. 28	64⅛ 3⅞	1/ dis. 2/ pm.
Aug. 31	56⅛ ⅝ ¼	2/ 3/ dis.
		3/ 5/ dis.
1816 Feb. 28	61¾ ⅛	2/ dis. 3/ pm.
Aug. 31	61½ ⅝ ¾	3½d. p. d. 2/ 3/ pm.
		3½d. 3/ 5/ pm.
1817 Feb. 28	67⅝ ¼ ¼ ⅛ ⅝	3d. 13/ 16/ pm.
		3½d. 10/ 16/ pm.
		2½ 5/ pm.
Aug. 30	79⅝ 8⅞ 9⅛ 9	{ 2½d. 32/ 34/ 31/ 26/ pm. . . .
		3d. 30/ pm.
		3½d. 29/ 27/ pm.
1818 Feb. 28	79¼ ⅝	2d. 16/ 18/ pm.
		2½d. 20/ 18/ pm.
Aug. 31	74¼ 3⅞ 4	2d. 20/ 19/ pm.
		2½d. 19/ 18/ pm.
1819 Feb. 27	73¾ 4⅛ 3	{ 2d. 1/ pm. 10/ 6/ 8/ dis.
Aug. 31	71⅛ ⅝	par 1/ dis.
1820 Feb. 28	68¼ ⅛ ⅝	1/ 2/ pm.
Aug. 31	67⅝ ¾ ¼	4/ 5/ pm.
1821 Feb. 28	73¼ 2⅞	5/ 3/ 4/ 3/ pm.
Aug. 31	76⅛ 6	3/ 5/ 2/ 3/ pm.
1822 Feb. 28	78⅝ ⅝ ¾ ⅝	par 3/ dis.
Aug. 31	80⅝ ⅛ ⅝	3/ 4/ 2/ pm.
1823 Feb. 28	73⅛ 2¾ 3⅛	8/ 7/ pm.
Aug. 30	82¾ ⅞	35/ 36/ pm.
1824 Feb. 28	92½ ⅜	43/ 38/ pm.
Aug. 31	93⅞ ¾	2d. p. d. 41/ pm.
		1½d. 39/ pm.
		advertised 38/ pm.
1825 Feb. 28	93⅝ ⅞	2 / 1½ } 58/ 56/ 58/ pm.
Aug. 31	86½ 7⅝	5/ 7/ 3/ pm.
1826 Feb. 28	77⅛ 6⅞ 7⅛ ¼	2 dis. par
Aug. 31	79¼ 8¼ 98⅞	18/ 19/ pm.
1827 Feb. 28	82⅛ ⅞	34/ 35/ pm.
Aug. 31	86½ ⅝ ⅞	59/ 61/ pm.
1828 Feb. 28	83⅛ ½	55/ 57/ pm.
Aug. 31	87½ ⅝ ½	75/ 76/ pm.
1829 Feb. 28	86¾ ⅞	56/ 55/ pm.
Aug. 31	88½ ⅝ ⅞	66/ 64/ 66/ pm.
1830 Feb. 27	91½ ¼ ⅛	2d. / 1¾ / 1½ } 77/ 76/ pm.
Aug. 31	90¼ ⅛ ⅜ ¼	76/ 77/ pm.
1831 Feb. 28	77¾ ½	17/ 18/ pm.
Aug. 31	81⅝ ¾ ½ ⅝	10/ 11/ pm.
1832 Feb. 29	82⅝ ⅝ ⅝ ⅝	7/ 8/ pm.

WILLIAM SMEE, Chief Accountant.

Bank of England, August 11, 1832.

TABLE XXXIV.

An ACCOUNT of the STATE of the PUBLIC FUNDED and UNFUNDED DEBT of the United Kingdom, on the 5th January, 1832.

FUNDED DEBT.

GREAT BRITAIN.	£.	£.
Debt due to the South Sea Company at 3 per cent.	3,662,784	
Old South Sea Annuities	3,497,870	
New ditto ditto	2,460,830	
South Sea Annuities, 1751	523,100	
Debt due to the Bank of England	14,686,800	
Bank Annuities, created in 1726	876,050	
Consolidated Annuities	348,017,532	
Reduced Annuities	123,604,712	
Total at 3 per cent.	. . .	497,329,679
Annuities at 3½ per cent., anno 1818	12,553,755	
Reduced Annuities, ditto	63,386,707	
New 3½ per cent. Annuities	138,078,982	
Total at 3½ per cent.	. . .	214,019,445
4 per cent. Annuities, created 1826	. . .	10,804,595
New 5 per cent. Annuities	. . .	462,736
Great Britain	. . .	722,616,456
IRELAND.		
Irish Consolidated Annuities, at 3 per cent. . .	2,673,545	
Irish Reduced Annuities ditto . .	145,078	
Total at 3 per cent.	. . .	2,818,624
3½ per cent. Debentures and Stock	14,520,904	
Reduced 3½ per cent. Annuities	1,277,768	
New 3½ per cent. Annuities	11,672,700	
Total at 3½ per cent.	. . .	27,471,373
Debt due to the Bank of Ireland, at 4 per cent. .	. . .	1,615,384
New 5 per cent. Annuities	6,661	
Debt due to the Bank of Ireland, at 5 per cent.	1,015,384	
		1,022,045
Ireland	. . .	32,927,428
Total, United Kingdom . . .	. . . £	755,543,884

UNFUNDED DEBT.

The total Amount of Exchequer Bills outstanding on 5th January, 1832	£27,123,350
Grand Total, Funded and Unfunded Debt	£782,667,234

TABLE XXXV.

The following STATEMENT of the REDUCTION in the SECURITIES held by the Bank in February, 1819, occasioned by the preparation for the withdrawal of the £1 and £2 Notes, and general resumption of Cash Payments, will explain the cause of the diminution of the Surplus, as stated in the Consecutive Account from 1778 to 1832.

SECURITIES HELD BY THE BANK.

	£.
February 28, 1819	31,455,000
August 31, 1819	31,740,550
February 28, 1820	26,181,490
August 31, 1820	23,846,120
February 28, 1821	20,796,240
N. B. The Small Notes withdrawn this year.	
August 31, 1821	18,475,540
February 28, 1822	15,973,080
August 31, 1822	17,290,510
February 28, 1823	18,319,730
N. B. The Dividend reduced this year 8 per cent. per annum.	
August 31, 1823	17,467,370

SECURITIES HELD BY THE BANK.

	£.
February 28, 1824	18,872,000
August 31, 1824	20,904,530
February 28, 1825	24,951,330
August 31, 1825	25,106,030
February 28, 1826	32,918,580
N. B. Panic.	
August 31, 1826	25,083,630
February 28, 1827	23,520,530
August 31, 1827	23,199,320
February 28, 1828	23,581,270
August 31, 1828	23,905,530

From which period the Securities have sustained little or no fluctuation, and the Income has, from February 1825, more than covered the Dividends paid to the Proprietors.

The progressive reduction of Surplus as exhibited from 28th February, 1819, to 28th February, 1825, was £1,300,000.

The former period	£4,100,000
The latter	2,800,000
Difference	1,300,000

In February 1830, £250,000 was written on account of Losses from Fontleroy, and on 7th August, 1832, the estimated Surplus is stated at £2,880,000.

The payment of £1 and £2 Notes (seven millions) entailed upon the Bank the necessity for reducing their Securities to that extent.

The loss which the Bank sustained during that period was owing, in a great degree, to the Government having authorized the continuance of the circulation of the Country Small Notes till 1833, without any previous communication with the Bank after the provision of Bullion was made for withdrawal. The consequence of that measure was, to leave the Bank with upwards of fourteen millions of Bullion in January, 1824, and their Securities diminished to between seventeen and eighteen millions.—Evidence, &c.

TABLE XXXVI.

ABSTRACT RETURN of the Number of COMMISSIONS of BANKRUPTCY issued against Country Bankers, in each Year, since 1780.

Year	Number	Year	Number	Year	Number
1780	none	1797	2	1814	27
81	2	98	3	15	25
82	2	99	6	16	37
83	2	1800	5	17	3
84	3	01	3	18	3
85	1	02	2	19	13
86	none	03	5	20	4
87	none	04	2	21	10
88	3	05	9	22	9
89	1	06	5	23	9
90	1	07	1	24	10
91	1	08	5	25	37
92	1	09	4	26	43
93	22	10	20	27	8
94	2	11	4	28	3
95	5	12	17	29	3
96	3	13	8	30	14

TABLE XXXVII.

ACCOUNT of the estimated EXPENSES for managing the PUBLIC ACCOUNTS at the BANK of ENGLAND, in 1831.

Expenses of Public Drawing-Office, twenty-eight Clerks and Porters, Pensions, Rent, Stationer, &c. &c. . . . . } £10,000

WILLIAM SMEE, CHIEF ACCOUNTANT.

ACCOUNT of the EXPENSES for Conducting the Business of the FUNDED DEBT, for the Year 1831.

Number of Clerks 405, Emoluments and Gratuities, Pensions, Retired Clerks, Stationery, Pencutter, Printer, Solicitor's Bills, Coals, Candles and Oil, Rent, Nightly Superintendence, Refreshment for Soldiers £224, Clothes for Porters £372, Allowance to the Directors £4000, Taxes £2624, &c. &c.—Grand Total . . . } £164,143

WILLIAM SMEE, CHIEF ACCOUNTANT.

An ACCOUNT of the Number of POWERS of ATTORNEY, 1832.

Grand Total 2,594

WILLIAM SMEE, CHIEF ACCOUNTANT.

An ACCOUNT of EXPENSES attending the Circulation of PROMISSORY NOTES, POST BILLS, &c. &c.

Clerks 242, Printer and Engravers' Wages £3,163, Cost of Bank Note Paper £10,912, Refreshment for Soldiers £224, Clothes for Porters £372, Allowance to the Directors £2,000, Taxes £1,307, Solicitors' Bills, &c. Expenses attending the Circulation of 250,000 of Branch Bank of England Notes in 11 Banks £28,508.—Grand Total . } £106,093

WILLIAM SMEE, CHIEF ACCOUNTANT.

TABLE XXXVIII.

An ACCOUNT of the RATE of EXCHANGE on PARIS, on the first Post-day in every Month since the Year 1820, and Premium on Gold at Paris at the same time.

Date.	Exchange in London 3 Months' date. Fr. C.	Date.	At Paris. Premium on Gold. Fr. C.
1820		**1820**	
January.... 4	25 15	January....	These cannot be obtained.
February... 1	25 22½	February...	
March 3	25 32½	March	
April 4	25 50	April	
May 2	25 67	May........	
June 2	25 80	June	
July 4	25 82½	July	
August..... 1	25 82½	August	
September . 1	25 87½	September 25	7 50
October 3	25 92½	October 2	9 —
November.. 3	25 85	November . 2	7 —
December.. 1	25 85	December.. 1	8 50
1821		**1821**	
January.... 2	25 90	January.... 2	8 —
February... 2	25 85	February .. 2	9 —
March 2	25 87½	March 1	7 50
April 3	25 90	April 3	7 50
May 1	25 95	May 2	9 —
June....... 1	26 00	June 3	13 —
July 3	26 05	July 3	10 —
August 3	25 75	August 3	5 —
September . 4	25 85	September . 4	7 —
October 2	25 87½	October.... 3	8 50
November.. 2	25 80	November.. 6	5 50
December .. 4	25 82½	December .. 3	7 50
1822		**1822**	
January.... 1	25 80	January.... 3	5 50
February... 1	25 60	February .. 1	4 —
March 1	25 55	March 2	4 —
April 1	25 50	April 2	4 —
May 3	25 57½	May 2	3 —
June....... 4	25 55	June 1	1 —
July 2	25 62½	July 2	4 50
August 2	25 70	August 3	5 50
September . 3	25 77½	September . 3	4 —
October 1	25 80	October 1	5 —
November.. 1	25 72½	November.. 2	7 50
December.. 3	25 72½	December.. 3	5 —
1823		**1823**	
January.... 3	25 75	January.... 2	8 50
February... 4	25 80	February .. 1	4 —
March 4	25 95	March 1	4 75
April....... 2	25 92½	April 1	7 —
May 2	25 95	May 1	9 50
June....... 3	26 00	June 2	14 —
July 1	25 90	July 2	11 —
August 1	25 95	August 2	12 —
September . 2	25 95	September . 2	10 —
October 3	25 95	October 2	11 —
November.. 4	25 85	November.. 4	8 —
December .. 2	25 80	December.. 4	7 50
1824		**1824**	
January.... 2	25 72½	January.... 3	6 75
February... 3	25 70	February .. 2	5 50
March 4	25 70	March 4	5 —
April....... 2	25 75	April 2	3 —
May 4	25 57½	May 3	2 50
June....... 1	25 60	June 3	3 —
July 2	25 62½	July 3	3 —
August 3	25 40	August 3	2 50
September . 3	25 40	September . 3	2 —
October 1	25 50	October 2	2 —
November.. 2	25 40	November.. 2	2 —
December .. 3	25 35	December.. 4	1 —
1825		**1825**	
January.... 4	25 32½	January.... 4	1 —
February .. 1	25 25	February .. 3	1 —
March 4	25 22½	March 3	2 —
April 1	25 35	April 2	2 —
May 3	25 35	May 3	75–100
June....... 2	25 32½	June 4	2 —
July 1	25 35	July 4	3 50
August..... 2	25 25	August 4	1 50
September . 2	25 37½	September . 4	1 50
October.... 4	25 32½	October 3	1 50
November.. 1	25 42½	November.. 5	1 50
December .. 2	25 45	December.. 2	2 —
1826		**1826**	
January.... 3	25 52½	January.... 4	4 —
February .. 3	25 62½	February... 4	3 25
March 3	25 80	March 3	7 25
April....... 4	25 95	April 4	10 —
May........ 2	25 87½	May 3	9 —
June 2	25 92½	June....... 3	8 —
July 4	25 85	July 3	9 —
August 1	25 90	August 4	9 50
September . 1	25 90	September . 4	9 —
October 3	25 85	October 3	7 75
November.. 3	25 87½	November.. 3	6 —
December.. 1	25 75	December.. 4	4 —
1827		**1827**	
January.... 2	25 75	January.... 4	3 75
February .. 2	25 75	February... 4	4 —
March 2	25 65	March 3	4 —
April 3	25 75	April 4	5 —
May 1	25 70	May 3	5 —
June 1	25 70	June....... 1	5 —
July 3	25 67½	July 3	4 —
August..... 3	25 57½	August 3	2 75
September . 4	25 55	September . 6	2 75
October 2	25 52½	October 3	3 —
November.. 2	25 50	November.. 4	1 50
December .. 4	25 40	December .. 4	2 —
1828		**1828**	
January.... 1	25 50	January.... 4	1 75
February... 1	25 42½	February .. 4	1 75
March 4	25 45	March 3	2 —
April 1	25 52½	April 5	2 50
May 2	25 50½	May 4	2 50
June 3	25 52½	June....... 4	3 —
July 1	25 55	July 4	3 50
August 1	25 52½	August 4	4 —
September . 2	25 47½	September . 3	6 50
October 3	25 50	October 3	7 50
November.. 4	25 52½	November.. 5	8 —
December .. 1	25 55	December.. 5	4 —
1829		**1829**	
January.... 2	25 50	January.... 3	8 50
February .. 3	25 55	February... 4	6 50
March 3	25 65	March 4	6 50
April 3	25 70	April 4	8 25
May 1	25 72½	May 4	7 75
June 2	25 77½	June....... 3	13 —
July 3	25 85	July 4	13 —
August 4	25 82½	August 6	11 75
September . 1	25 82½	September . 3	9 50
October.... 2	25 90	October 2	14 —
November.. 3	25 95	November.. 2	16 25
December.. 1	26 —	December.. 2	15 50
1830		**1830**	
January.... 1	25 97½	January.... 4	18 —
February .. 2	25 87½	February .. 4	13 —
March 3	26 —	March 2	16 50
April 2	25 95	April 2	12 75
May 4	25 85	May 6	10 50
June 1	25 70	June....... 5	9 —
July 2	25 77½	July 6	10 —
August 3	25 67½	August 5	10 —
September . 3	25 65	September . 3	7 50
October 1	25 65	October 5	4 —
November.. 2	25 60	November.. 4	7 —
December.. 3	25 60	December.. 4	8 —
1831		**1831**	
January.... 4	25 45	January.... 4	8 —
February .. 1	25 37½	February .. 4	6 —
March 1	25 37½	March 4	12 50
April 1	25 47½	April 4	11 —
May 3	25 37½	May 2	4 —
June 3	25 40	June 5	6 —
July 1	25 37½	July 4	6 50
August 2	25 35	August 4	7 —
September . 2	25 37½	September . 5	4 —
October.... 4	25 40	October 5	3 —
November.. 1	25 42½	November.. 4	1 75
December.. 2	25 50	December.. 5	3 75

Date.	Exchange in London 3 Months' date. Fr. C.	Date.	At Paris. Premium on Gold. Fr. C.
1832		**1832**	
January.... 3	25 62½	January.... 4	7 —
February .. 3	25 60	February .. 3	5 —
March 2	25 75	March 2	10 —
April 3	25 85	April 4	12 50
May 1	25 90	May 4	13 50
June....... 1	25 97½	June 6	17 —

PART III.

STATISTICS OF THE WHOLE EMPIRE.

ESTIMATE OF THE CAPITAL, POWER, AND RESOURCES OF THE BRITISH EMPIRE IN ALL PARTS OF THE WORLD.

SECTION I.

INTRODUCTION. DATA, AUTHORITIES AND REASONING, ON WHICH THE ESTIMATES ARE FOUNDED.

"THE capital of the British empire is amply sufficient to liquidate the total national debt, without impairing either individual or national resources."

This assertion is bold, and new in its shape: it shall be endeavoured to demonstrate its truth. The same principles which govern the commercial concerns of individuals, are applicable to the great financial affairs of nations. It is evident that the first step to be taken, the directing principle, in liquidating the debts of an individual without impairing his resources, is, to obtain a true knowledge of his capital. In the case of individuals, this is readily ascertained; but the capital of nations is not so easily defined. The economists themselves differ on this important subject, and various have been the definitions of the "Capital of Nations"[a]: but a modern writer, after examining that given by the father of the science (Smith) concludes, that "the capital of a nation is that portion of produce and industry existing in it, which can be made available, either to the support of human existence, or to the facility of pro-

[a] Smith. Storch, Revenue National. Say, Economie Politique, Ganilh Systemes d' Economie Politique. Destutt. Tracy, Economie Politique; and M'Culloch.

duction."[a] It is no easy task to discover the amount of that produce in *any* nation; but when the attempt is made to ascertain the nature, the extent, and all the component parts, of the total property of the British empire, the enterprise becomes incomparably more difficult. Perfect accuracy, therefore, is not to be expected in such a comprehensive subject: to attain it would be difficult even for a government, impossible for an individual, and perhaps of no great importance after all to the grand object in view: a reasonable and just approximation is the true general regulator in a matter like this.

But before entering upon this inquiry, it may be observed, that while numberless authors in this country have devoted their exertions to economical subjects, the number of those who have directed their talent to national statistics, is exceedingly limited: the subject being as disagreeable and laborious as it is important, it is not surprising that the national economists have been rather deterred by its dryness, than allured by its utility. There are no doubt superabundant scattered materials; there exists an almost infinite number of folios of records, accounts, &c.; there are partial statistical statements; but there is no complete general work upon the subject. The best and more systematic of the kind is generally allowed to be that of Colquhoun. The sound judgement of the author, his ample means of information, and the patronage afforded him by government, were adequate elements for his great undertaking. The most useful plan appears to be, to extend and improve his Tables, which are almost universally referred to by national economists. This is the plan adopted; in the

[a] M'Culloch, "Rise and Progress of Political Economy."

execution of which, official documents, a chain of evidence, and a series of facts, have been the only guides.

In forming the calculations of the *present* amount of capital, productions, &c., &c., $33\frac{1}{3}$ per cent. has been added to each head, and collectively to the whole of the sums, as stated in the Tables of Colquhoun; except in those of the West Indies, which have been left as in 1811. Considerable alterations, which appeared necessary on account of the change of circumstances, (particularly in regard to India,) have also been made in some of the other Tables; but should any particular item be under or over-rated, it is allowed for, so as not to affect the general result; which will thus be pretty accurately obtained. The statesman, the economist, the landholder, the manufacturer, the ship-owner, &c., being better judges in their respective branches, will decide for themselves: they are only entreated to submit these Tables to the test of the official records, and of their own solid calculations and experience. To assist them in this important object, to the explanatory notes annexed to the Tables in this and the succeeding sections, are joined a few observations from Colquhoun, to show the comparative increase or decrease in both periods, in the various objects constituting the wealth, means, and capital of the British Empire. However, far from presuming to claim implicit credit for mere assertions, it has been thought necessary to prove—1st. That the estimates of Colquhoun are formed on a moderate scale. 2ndly. That the additions made to their amount rest upon solid grounds: in order that the reader may judge of their accuracy. If the truth of these propositions can be established, it will follow, that the subjoined Tables afford the true approximate data required to ascertain the actual amount of British capital.

That the basis upon which Colquhoun proceeds to establish his Tables is moderate, appears by the fact, as stated by himself, that "the public property, as barracks, arsenals, ships of war, fortifications, &c. have greatly augmented in value." "His estimate", he says, "is considerably short of their real worth": and he declares, that "the public property, which is estimated at what is presumed to exist at the present time, is not valued at above one fourth of the actual cost."[a] The national economists who have succeeded Colquhoun entertain a similar opinion; and, although some of them taunt him with having contrived those statements to serve ministerial purposes rather than the national interest, they in general allow them to have been calculated on a limited scale. Those who have examined them with considerably more attention than others, go so far as to assert, that the estimates are made 20 or 25 per cent. below the currency of the times; and that when the landed property ought to be calculated at from thirty to forty years purchase, he estimated it at only twenty-four[b]. But without entering into details as to how particular articles were calculated, it is enough for our purpose to know, that the general opinion on this point is, that these estimates were extremely moderate.

But upon what foundation does the addition of one third, made to these estimates, rest? Has the national property increased one third since 1811[c]? Pledged to conciseness, the author cannot go into this question to the extent he wishes; but sufficient facts will be stated to convince the reader of the soundness of the grounds upon which the calculations and additions are made.

[a] Colquhoun, p. 238. [b] Lowe's "Present State of England".

[c] The Tables of Colquhoun are dated 1812; consequently they must have been formed in 1811.

The most accurate principle to ascertain the increase of wealth and capital, in a nation regularly constituted and governed, is the progress of her population: for it is an axiom acknowledged by all the economists[a] of the productive system, "that the increase of population measures the increase of wealth; the augmentation of numbers causes the multiplication of employments; and these increase the amount of produce." And from such principles they farther conclude that, "in the progress of society, individual income increases even in a greater ratio than the population itself."[b] The axioms of this economical school would be of little weight, did not *facts* come in confirmation of them; but in Europe, we see, to a demonstration, wealth following the density of the population: particularly in France, where the wealth and capital have increased since 1814 in a far greater ratio than the population[c]. In the United States, the population has doubled, on an average, in thirty years; the wealth and capital have trebled[d]. In England, more

[a] Gray, "Happiness of States."

[b] Montesquieu has long ago said—"Partout où il se trouve une place où deux personnes peuvent vivre commodement, il se fait une menage."

[c] See Dupin, Forces Productives. Also Sec. XI. and the Tables at the end of this Part.

[d] Hinton's "History of the United States".—The United States of America, since their separation from the mother country, present an extraordinary and unexampled political phenomenon. This confederation of republics, each state of which has a different constitution and government, is at present inhabited by 13 millions (12,816,161, census of 1830) of active individuals, governing themselves without either king or military control, although dispersed over an immense territory of 2,257,347 square miles. Their annual imports amount to 74,472,527 dollars; and their exports, which chiefly consist of the produce of their domestic agriculture and manufactures, to the enormous sum of 72,358,670 dollars. Their

particularly, the population has doubled since George I.'s time; while the capital has been augmented in a greater ratio. The argument to be collected from the eternally agitated question of "high and low prices", far from being against, favours this position; as the same capital would command more goods, provisions, necessaries or luxuries of life *now* than in 1811: prices having considerably fallen since that time. (Tables I., II. and III.

civil list is extremely moderate: their revenue is nearly double their expenditure; and they are on the point of totally paying off their National Debt. When this is accomplished, a question will arise as to what is to be done with the revenue derived from duties on foreign imports, which cannot be absolutely repealed.

However blameable the conduct of the British ministry may have been during the war of Independence, every impartial man must candidly acknowledge, that to the admirable effects and enlightened principles and guarantees of the British Constitution, improved perhaps by several new ones introduced at the time of the separation, this extraordinary republic is indebted for its liberty, its prosperity, its civilization, and its extraordinary increase of population. The original guarantees are, the right of personal liberty, freedom of speech, and printing; right of calling for special amendments of the laws when defective, and seeking general amendments in the forms of the constitution, when not adapted to their end—the public good; right to know the details of whatever concerns the people, and of assembling together to discuss these details; power of resisting or correcting evil rulers by indictments, impeachment, or otherwise; right of having arms; right of sending representatives to consent to taxes and laws when needed; the direct responsibility of every man for his own acts, and impossibility of the instructions of a superior being admitted as a bar to that responsibility.

The new guarantees introduced by the Americans are, the degree of control possessed by the people over all the authorities, by means of frequent elections; rotation of office; prohibition of orders of nobility; substitution of a temporary president, with a narrow income and power; abolition of primogeniture, exclusive privilege, church, and tithes; admitting it to be a public duty to educate the whole community; and frequent reference of great affairs to the people in conversation.

in Sec. II.) The principle, or rather sophism, of the Malthusian school, namely, the pretended geometrical and arithmetical proportions between the increase of population and subsistence, and the poverty consequent upon them, (which, if true, might invalidate this doctrine,) is in too open contradiction to daily experience, authentic data, and sound reason, to deserve any attention[a]. That when society is decidedly progressing, when a nation is improving in agriculture, manufactures, commerce, and knowledge[b], when a larger population is maintained in the same space of territory in superior abundance and comfort, wealth and capital must have increased in the same proportion, is rather a self-evident truth, than a mere doubtful assertion.

Such having been the situation and progressive state of Great Britain since 1811, we are justly entitled to conclude, that the capital has augmented in at least an equal ratio to the population[c]. According to the official returns, the population has increased, between 1811 and 1831, $41\frac{9}{10}$ per cent. (Tables IV., V. and VI. Sec. II.): an equal proportion, therefore, ought

[a] Sadler, "Balance of Food and Numbers in Animated Nature."—Godwin's Answer to Malthus.

[b] That this is the case in Great Britain is proved by the great number of private Bills for national and local improvements, which have passed since 1811, and particularly from 1825 to the present time: and this, notwithstanding the wants of the country, and the necessary improvements, have been gradually, but to a great extent, supplied and effected. One hundred and fifty-eight of these Bills were passed in 1831-2; and in some years the number is much greater.

[c] "Capital has doubled (in England) in less than eighty, and perhaps more than sixty years; and it may fairly be presumed, that sixty years is about the shortest period in which the capital of an old and densely peopled country can be expected to be doubled".—M'Culloch.

to be added to the amount of the national capital; however, a proportion no less than 9 per cent. under this ratio has been adopted. The reader may judge, therefore, by examining and comparing the Tables just referred to, whether the calculations and assumptions are made on a moderate scale.

This will no doubt be readily admitted in regard to England and Scotland: but as the same relative progress of wealth and capital may not be so readily granted in respect to the poor sister country, an extract from the Report of the select committee appointed by the House of Commons "to take into consideration the state of the poorer classes in Ireland in 1830," is submitted for inspection. No better judges could have been found. It appears by this document, that "the capital has increased in greater ratio than the population; that agriculture, manufactures, roads, canals, public works, steam navigation, banking system, and commerce, have augmented beyond expectation." "The exports of all Ireland to Great Britain in Sir Charles Whitworth's Tables," says the report, "during the seven years from 1723 to 1729, amounted in value to 2,307,722*l.*: in 1829, the exports from the single port of Waterford reached 2,136,934*l.*; a sum less by only 170,000*l.* than the whole trade of Ireland in seven years, as before." Great as has been the progress of exports, the increase of the consumption of British manufactures has been still more rapid:—"the quantity of British manufactures consumed in Ireland since 1793, has quadrupled, whilst the quantity of Irish produce has more than trebled, in the same period: the foreign trade having continued on the increase, it is not to be doubted that the British imports have augmented in the same ratio." The tonnage on the Grand Canal and the

Barrow navigation, have been commensurate to the extension of general commerce. The effects of steam navigation between Great Britain and Ireland, have produced the greatest and most beneficial results. "In 1824, the first steamer was established between Dublin and Liverpool, by Williams: at present (1830) a capital of 671,000*l.* is engaged in the steam navigation across the channel; forty-two steam vessels being established, registering 8423 tons: when, in the previous time, from the time when a sailing vessel was prepared to start from Liverpool, to the time of her arrival in Dublin, a week might be calculated as a fair average of her passage [a]. The banking business, the savings' banks, the public works, &c., carried on in Ireland since 1822, have extended the cultivation, improved the habits of industry, &c. &c." [b]

[a] See also Note 1, to Table XVI.

[b] See Parliamentary Report, 1831.—500,000*l.* to be issued in Exchequer Bills towards the public works of Ireland.

The following statements officially made by S. Rice in the House of Commons, 12 Feb. 1833, are unanswerable proofs of the benefits conferred upon Ireland by the Union. It will be seen that commerce and manufactures have nearly doubled since that measure; and there is no doubt that all other branches of industry have experienced a similar increase.

Imports into Ireland.

1777	£2,716,000
83	3,040,000
93	4,164,000
1800	4,002,000
26	7,491,000

Consumption of Cotton Yarn.

1777	8,883,000 lbs.
83	5,400,000
93	276,000

1800

After noticing these facts, and considering the immense political and economical advantages which result to Ireland

1800	558,000
11	972,000
20	1,279,000
26	2,510,000

The consumption of cotton wool during the same interval, has augmented from 429,000 lbs. to 4,368,000 lbs.

Import of Sugar.

1777	212,000 cwt.
83	140,000
93	184,000
1832	342,000

Import of Tea.

1777	808,000
1830	3,887,955

Wool Imported.

1777	857,000 lbs.
83	841,000
93	1,860,000
1800	1,800,000
11	4,065,000
20	6,608,000
26	6,682,000

Exports of Linen from Ireland.

1777	20,000,000 yards
83	18,000,000
93	34,000,000
1800	36,000,000
10	40,000,000
20	48,000,000
26	51,000,000

Coals.

1777	330,000 tons
83	227,000
1800	364,000
30	940,000

Advanced

from her union with Great Britain, which are shown in the subjoined note, it is impossible to restrain feelings of indignation on seeing men, who are proud of being called Irishmen, agitate and distract their countrymen, and urge them to call for a separation from England. Irishmen should first consider, what power Ireland possesses to resist the united force of Great Britain; what bloodshed, loss of public and private property, and utter ruin would take place, before a separation could be obtained; and, should such *an unfortunate* and morally impossible event take place, what advantages, political or economical, Ireland would reap from it. The most mature consideration of these important questions, ought certainly to precede any proposal for a separation; and a stop ought to be put to the disgraceful system of lawless violence and agitation which prevails in that important part of the British dominions, and which retards the progress of its prosperity, and has the most baneful economical effects on both countries.

Advanced and paid to Charities, Literature and Manufactures during the twenty years which followed the Union	£1,465,000
Up to the present day	6,697,000

Being an excess of 5,232,000 above what it was about twenty years after the Union. The Imperial Parliament has paid out of the consolidated fund 6,432,000*l.* for the benefit of manufactures, roads, and harbours; of which only 2,500,000*l.* has been repaid: so that at present, there is a capital advanced to Ireland for these purposes, and not yet repaid, of 3,932,000*l.* For charities, and literary institutions, there have been granted, since the Union, 4,225,000*l.*; for agriculture and manufactures 1,340,000*l.*; for public works 3,120,000*l.*; making a total, granted since the Union, of 8,685,000*l.* Government advanced for the establishment of Cholera Hospitals, &c., to England 12,000*l.*, and to Ireland 164,000*l.*

Such are the unexceptionable authorities—such the additional grounds, besides those already noticed in regard to Great Britain, (equally applicable in Ireland,) on which rest the calculations in respect to the increased capital of Ireland since 1811. In the following Section, these calculations will be further confirmed by facts, and official documents.

SECTION II.

CAPITAL OF ENGLAND, WALES, SCOTLAND, AND IRELAND.

PRIVATE CAPITAL, viz.:—Lands and implements of husbandry.—Mines and minerals.—Canals.—Rail-roads.—Houses, furniture, plate, and jewellery.—Specie in circulation.—Machinery.—Manufactured goods and merchandize.—Shipping.—Fisheries.—Animate power.—Capital in Savings' Banks, &c. &c.

PUBLIC CAPITAL, viz.:—Arsenals, dock-yards, stores, ships of war, fortifications, barracks, public buildings, palaces.—Church property and capital, &c. &c.

PRODUCE AND PROPERTY ANNUALLY RAISED AND CREATED. Effect of the combination of capital with animate and inanimate power; namely, labour and machinery, in raising all sorts of natural productions, as well as manufactures.—Annual value of all animate and inanimate forces, and produce of agriculture, &c.—Capital and labour employed in all manufactures and occupations.—Annual value of the produce of inland and coasting trades, fisheries, shipping, and foreign commerce; of cotton, silk, linen, woollen, hardware, pottery, jewellery, plate, furniture, paper, and various miscellaneous manufactures.—Profits of bankers.—Foreign income, &c. &c.

THE official Table VII., at the end of this Section, drawn from data afforded by the Commissioners of the Revenue Inquiry, is an excellent document by which to form a correct idea of the amount, not only of personal, but of real property in England. The amount of all private property in England and Wales, under the heads above mentioned, and others specified in Table XVI., is estimated at 2,428,900,000*l.*; that of Scotland, under the same heads, at 369,400,000*l.*; and that of Ireland, at 738,500,000*l.*; forming a grand total for Great Britain and Ireland, of 3,575,700,000*l.* The value of the public property of England and Wales, may be stated at 42,000,000*l.*; that of Scotland, at 3,900,000*l.*, and that of Ireland, at 11,900,000*l.*; and taking the navy dock yards, military and naval stores, and ordnance, in common for all parts of the kingdom, forms a total, for all the public property of Great Britain and Ireland, of [illegible]; thus constituting, for the whole capital, public and private, a grand total of 3,579,500,000*l.* The explanatory notes annexed to Table XVI., state the data and official documents upon which the calculations are founded, and afford the reader the means of entering into details. Let us now examine how this enormous capital is distributed and employed; and what is the amount of produce and property annually raised, by its combination with animate and inanimate power.

AGRICULTURE.

The largest part of the capital of the British empire is concentrated, to the advantage of the United Kingdom, in this sceptred little isle; and the largest part of the British capital in Europe is absorbed by agriculture. Table XVI. shows, that the capital invested in land for the cultivation of wheat, grain, hops, grass, &c., amounts to the enormous sum of 1,600,000,000*l.*: the value of agricultural property, including machinery, tools, implements, &c., is estimated at no less than 59,900,000*l.*; and if to these be added another considerable item, the value of all animals connected with, and depending on, the exertions of husbandry, and which (as may be seen by the Table) amounts to 242,000,000*l.*, the aggregate result shows, that 1,901,900,000*l.*, or more than one half of the whole British capital in the United Kingdom, is employed and invested in agriculture!

These estimates, it should be observed, are considerably below those which, *some years ago*, elevated the British capital devoted to agriculture to two thousand millions, without taking into account the large item last mentioned. The opinions of the writers who formed those estimates are of such weight, that the reader is referred to them, while the result of all their reasonings and calculations is here noticed [a]. They consider, that fifty millions of acres of land are in cultivation; and that the value of the land, and capital employed by the landlord is equal to 30*l.* per acre, and the value added by the exertions of the tenant, to 10*l.* per acre: thus fifty millions of acres require the investment of a capital of two thousand millions. It is true, the number of cultivated acres (as may be seen by Note A. to Table XVI.) is not so great as those able writers supposed; but the cultivation having increased largely since they wrote, the calculation evidently tends to show the soundness and moderation of the estimates in the Table; as well as how unfounded is the general opinion which prevails on the continent, and among a large party here, that England is a manufacturing but not an agricultural country; it may also serve to expose the error of those Englishmen who, disregarding facts, consider the agriculture of their country as a subordinate and insignificant branch, compared either to her manufactures or commerce.

But what are the results of this large capital, when combined with British industry, labour, and machinery? The annual value of agricultural produce raised by this capital is proportionate to its magnitude. Fifty-one millions of quarters of all sorts of grain, wheat, barley, oats, rye, &c., are annually raised; the value of which

[a] "An Essay on the application of Capital to Land," by West. "On Agriculture and Rent." Quarterly Review, No. 71, 1826. "The Principles of Agriculture," by Bland.

cannot be estimated under 86,700,000*l.*[a] The average quantity of wheat annually imported into Great Britain from Europe (about which so much noise is made) may be taken at 900,000 quarters, which does not amount to two weeks' consumption: and if Ireland continue its progress in cultivation, even this may be rendered unnecessary[b]. The value of hay, straw, grass, vetches, field turnips, &c., to feed 1,900,000 horses, twelve millions of horned cattle, forty-eight millions of sheep, lambs, goats, &c., may be estimated at 113,000,000*l.*[c] The consumption of potatoes in the United Kingdom, independent of the quantity exported, is immense: this article forms the principal food of eight millions of inhabitants in Ireland: the total consumption in the United Kingdom, together with the exportation, cannot be valued at less than 19,000,000*l.* The produce of orchards, gardens, and nurseries, of all descriptions, certainly amounts to above 3,800,000*l.* The value of

[a] This calculation is formed in the following manner:—

Wheat, thirteen millions of quarters, valued at		63*s.*	£39,600,000
Oats, twenty-two	do.	21*s.*	23,100,000
All other sorts, sixteen	do.	30*s.*	24,000,000
			£86,700,000

The prices are taken on an average of the last three years.

[b] The total quantity of foreign grain, &c., admitted into consumption in Great Britain, in the year ending 28th Feb. 1830, was 1,315,937 quarters, of which 909,205 were of wheat; and the total quantity imported into Great Britain in 1829, was 2,562,051. In 1829, there were also imported from Ireland, 2,307,817 quarters of grain of all sorts. The largest amount of foreign grain, &c., imported into Great Britain was in 1818, when it reached 3,522,739 quarters.

[c] This is only the amount as stated in 1811; because although the quantity has increased, the price is now much less.

timber cut down, the produce of hops, kelp, seeds of all descriptions, &c. &c., to 2,600,000*l.* Cheese, butter, eggs, &c., labour included, to 6,000,000*l.* Manure and labour employed in the management and rearing of cattle, horses, pigs, &c., calculating eight per cent. of additional value, exclusive of the prime cost of feeding them, to 3,500,000*l.* Hemp and wool, all labour included, to 12,000,000*l.* Thus the total annual value of the direct produce of agriculture amounts to 246,600,000*l.*

Without entering into the details and grounds upon which these estimates are formed, the reader may be assured that considerable attention has been given to them, and he is entreated to bring them to the test of the actual expense of animal subsistence, and the daily cost of rearing and keeping cattle, horses, sheep, &c.; they will be found correct and no wise overrated; and, considering the exports of butter, eggs, cheese, &c., from Ireland [a], and the great and universal consumption of these articles; and examining the cost and produce of wool, hemp, timber cut, &c. &c., it will be found that in these branches the just mark has not been overstepped. (Table XV.)

MINES.

But the mineral riches of England are as great in proportion as her agricultural powers. The capital applied to mines produces considerable annual returns. Many are the mines to which English labour and capital are applied, such as gravel, sand, slate, granite, paving stones, &c., which in other countries are thought little of. The amount produced by the immense consumption of these articles in keeping and repairing the 30,000

[a] "Fifty tons of eggs, and ten of live and dead poultry, are shipped from Dublin in a single day."

miles of roads, and more than that number of pavements in the towns and villages, including the labour of gravel-raisers, slate, brick, limestone, chalk, and stone quarriers, &c. cannot be estimated at less than 1,900,000*l.* and the produce of salt, alum, &c., labour included, at 600,000*l.* But these sums, large as they are, almost disappear when compared with the produce and value of the tin, lead, copper, and above all, iron and coal mines. The quantity exported, and the value of the articles manufactured from the raw material of these mines, are stated in Note C. to Table XVI. The annual produce of the first three cannot be rated under 3,800,000*l.*

The IRON MINES may be called the gold mines of England, as their annual produce has exceeded the united produce of all the gold mines of Brazil and Spanish America, even in their best years. It was truly said by Locke, (alluding to the produce of the iron mines) that "he who first made use of iron may be truly styled the father of arts, and the author of plenty." The progress of the iron mines has been uninterrupted since 1796, when they produced 125,000 tons, till the present time, when their annual produce, as may be seen in the Note C., is 700,000; the amount is daily augmenting, and will continue so doing, in consequence of the increase in rail roads, &c. both in Great Britain and America. But 700,000 tons, at the low rate of eighty shillings per ton, would give 2,800,000*l.*; and the additional expenditure in manufacturing pig iron, may be estimated at 1,300,000*l.*; making the entire value of this manufacture 4,100,000*l.*

The COAL MINES formed at Newcastle, and in several other parts of Great Britain, extend many thousand square miles. (See Buckland.) The amount of coals annually raised has been estimated as high as twenty-eight millions of tons: but Mr. Taylor computes the total consumption and exportation at only 15,580,000, an estimate which every body must feel convinced is exceedingly underrated. The actual quantity of this important and indispensable article raised for consumption and exportation, may be fairly estimated at twenty-two millions of tons (of twenty cwt. each) which, at the low rate of ten shillings per ton, would produce the annual sum of 11,000,000*l.* Thus the mines and minerals of the United Kingdom yield an annual produce amounting in value to 21,400,000*l.*

INLAND AND COASTING TRADES.

These trades, which every body is aware are the most profitable of all to a nation, are highly promoted by such vast mineral productions. Easy and multiplied communications in the interior of a country, the avidity for gain, industry, and capital, are the principal foundations of interior commerce: and there is no country in the world where these elements are better and more extensively combined than in Great Britain.

The number of "Families of Shopkeepers" in Great Britain in 1831, is estimated by Marshall in his Statistics, at 350,000, or 2,100,000 individuals. But adding to that number all warehousemen and vendors; all publicans, whose number is very considerable; the people employed in purchasing and selling to the consumer, as well as in exporting all sorts of British and foreign goods, merchandise, luxuries, and commodities of all descriptions, and in exchanging and re-exchanging them amongst all the community,—the labour and profits of capital thus employed, cannot be estimated under 60*l.* a year for each family: this would give a sum of 21,000,000*l.*[a] But in the Sister Island, where the commerce and communications are not so rapid, it will be taking a low computation to consider only one eighth of the above number of families, as employed in the inland trade; thus producing for Great Britain and Ireland the sum of 23,625,000*l.*

The number of millers, butchers, and bakers, has been estimated by the same author, and for the same year, at 900,000 individuals, or 180,000 families. The profits of this class are considerably greater than those of the preceding; but assigning 80*l.* a year for the labour and profits of each family, would give 14,400,000*l.*; and allowing the eighth, as before, for Ireland, would produce 1,800,000*l.*; constituting a total for Great Britain and Ireland of 16,200,000*l.*

The intercourse on all rivers, canals, and rail-roads, is very considerable. The wonderful effects of the internal intercourse, and the transport of thousands of tons of goods, by means of rail-ways has been already stated: but the resolution of the great problem of travelling by steam carriages on the common turnpike roads, was reserved for the indefatigable exertions of Gurney. Others have imitated and even improved upon his beneficial discovery, and several steam carriages are at this moment in full play. The noble and praiseworthy conduct of this man, the difficulties he overcame, and the

[a] The annual profits (exceeding 600,000*l.*) arising from the immense property, chiefly belonging to this class, and to labourers, deposited in Savings' Banks must not be forgotten. The sums received in deposits since their first establishment in 1817, amounted to 20,760,228*l.* of which the depositors have received in principal and interest 5,648,838*l.*; in Nov. 1831, the amount was 14,311,647*l.*, shewing an increase of 114,998*l.* The number of savings' banks is above 371; and the number of separate accounts opened by depositors 429,400. (See Note Q to Table XVI.)

expenses he incurred, well deserve the thanks and admiration of the public; which will also notice as it deserves the base and perfidious proceedings of his adversaries, who carried their opposition to this useful undertaking to such a pitch, as to encumber the Gloucester road with heaps of loose stones to the depth of 18 inches, in order to impede and shatter the steam carriages: they succeeded in their malevolent object; but Gurney, far from prosecuting them by law, as he might have done, contented himself with observing, "that he felt only pity and contempt for those who could resort to such means to prevent a great national undertaking." And this it truly is:—a new era will commence in England: the benefits will be great and important, not only to commerce, but to agriculture. It has been stated that a million of horses are now employed in the transport of goods: the land required to rear and feed them would supply corn and animal food for eight millions of men. The extraordinary change that this discovery will cause not only in this country, but in the world at large, will be so great, that the conclusions of the Committee of the House of Commons on this important subject are here given: it is to be hoped they will lead to the repeal of those Acts of Parliament, extorted by the opponents of this grand discovery, with the view of preventing its success, and ruining its supporters. The conclusions are as follow:—" 1. That carriages can be propelled by steam on common roads, at an average rate of ten miles an hour." "2. That at this rate they have conveyed upwards of fourteen passengers." "3. That their weight, including engine, fuel, water, and attendants, may be under three tons." "4. That they can ascend and descend hills of considerable inclination with facility and safety." "5. That they are perfectly safe for passengers." "6. That they are not, (or need not be if properly constructed,) nuisances to the public." "7. That they will become a speedier and cheaper mode of conveyance than carriages drawn by horses." "8. That as they admit of greater breadth of tire than other carriages, and as the roads are not acted on so injuriously as by the feet of horses in common draught, such carriages will cause less wear of roads than carriages drawn by horses." "9. That rates of toll have been imposed on steam carriages which would prohibit their being used on several lines of roads, were such charges permitted to remain unaltered."

In the mean time, besides the horses at present working in the transport of goods, the number of labourers employed on canals, rivers, rail-roads, &c., cannot be less than 100,000 for the United Kingdom; whose wages, estimated at 40*l.* a year, would yield 4,000,000*l.* The labour and profits of capital invested, after deducting wear and tear, wages and charges, of all the barge proprietors, and owners of small craft employed on the rivers, canals, &c., in transporting merchandise, coals, &c., cannot be stated at less than 1,600,000*l.* The labour and profits of coach and cart proprietors engaged in the conveyance of goods, and of persons employed in repairing roads, canals, and rail-ways, collecting tolls, &c., &c., cannot be estimated under 3,000,000*l.* Several small items, which would considerably increase the estimate, are left out from a desire to make it rather lower than otherwise: nevertheless, it produces a result of 48,425,000*l.*

COASTING TRADE.

This trade, one of the most important to all nations, is particularly valuable to a maritime nation like England. An idea of its vast extent may be formed from the official declaration of P. Thompson in the House of Commons (1832), that no less than 9,800,000 tons are annually entered inwards and outwards!!! The profits of capital, and labour of the proprietors of this immense tonnage, after deducting the wear and tear of the vessels, the insurance, and several other charges, cannot be less than 2,500,000*l.* But the wages of about 35,000 men employed on board these vessels, and in the multifarious operations relating to this trade, cannot be estimated under 30*l.* a year: altogether producing a total for the coasting trade of 3,550,000*l.*

FISHERIES.

The British fisheries round the coasts are very productive, although not to the extent that several writers have calculated. The abundance, however, of herrings, cod, haddock, whitings, oysters, lobsters, soles, turbot, &c., &c., is equal to the superior quality of the articles. The produce of these fisheries, taking the export as well as the immense home consumption, after deducting the wear and tear, &c., may be estimated at 1,900,000*l.* By the last official account for the year ending 5th of April, 1830, the total quantity of herrings cured in Great Britain was 329,557 barrels, and the exported was 181,654 barrels; of which 89,680 went to Ireland, 67,672 to places out of Europe, chiefly the West Indies, and 24,302 to places in Europe. The river fisheries of Great Britain are equally excellent. They produce a variety of fish—perch, pike, eels, trout, &c., and perhaps the best salmon in Europe. Several thousand people are employed in them; and, making deductions for all fishing implements and charges, their produce cannot be estimated under 900,000*l.* The "fisheries far distant from the British coasts," as those of Greenland, the South Seas, &c., produced, in 1811, according to the official returns, after deducting all the expenses of out-fits, seamen's wages, insurance, &c., 600,000*l.* net. This estimate may be considered far under the mark at present, as the colonial fisheries are not included in it. Thus the total for the coasting, river, and sea fisheries, of Great Britain, would be 3,400,000*l.*

SHIPPING AND FOREIGN TRADE.

If the productions, the fisheries, the inland and coasting trade of a country, are any measure of its shipping and foreign commerce, it would certainly be difficult to calculate the property annually raised by the combination of industry, labour, and capital, in these considerable branches. But in order to come to an approximate estimate, let us take the value of the imports into Great Britain in the year ending 5th January, 1832, which are perhaps inferior to some preceding ones: these amounted to 48,161,600*l.*; and the real or declared value of the exports, was 36,652,600*l.*, making together 84,814,200*l.* (Table IX.) Charging only 12 per cent. for the profits of capital employed, and for the merchants' commissions for buying and selling, (which is 4 per cent. for both operations, exclusive of "del credere",) would produce the sum of 10,177,704*l.* The profits and labour of underwriters on the value of shipping, and of goods exported and imported, (calculating three-fourths as insured in England,) at the rate of 2½ per cent. upon the whole, would yield 2,120,355*l.* The amount of British shipping entered inwards, on an average of the years 1829-30-

31, has been officially stated at 2,930,000 tons; and that entered outwards, for the same period, at 2,243,000 tons. Calculating the ship-owners' freights upon this tonnage, and estimating the net profits upon the immense sum produced by them, the amount cannot be under 3,800,000*l.* The profits of ship and colonial brokers, factors, and agents, engaged in the sale of all the imports, exports, and shipping, may be stated at 1,600,000*l.* The wages of the clerks concerned in mercantile affairs, whose number probably exceeds 50,000, and of the labourers employed in shipping and landing merchandise, keeping and managing goods, &c., whose number exceeds 70,000, calculating both at 60*l.* a year, will give a sum of 7,200,000*l.* The wages of 210,000 sailors employed in vessels carrying on foreign commerce, estimating them at the rate of 30*l.* per year, amount to 6,300,000*l.* For the wages and profits on capital, of the ship-chandlers, block makers, sail and rope makers, and the various other artificers employed in fitting and equipping the mercantile marine, say 2,200,000*l.* For miscellaneous charges on account of the dock companies, harbour, pier, and port dues, and for the people concerned in these branches, and employed in keeping them in repair, &c., 1,000,000*l.* Thus the total amount for the foreign commerce and shipping is 34,398,059*l.* (Table XV.)

BANKERS, AND FOREIGN INCOME.

But without money, or the means of facilitating the exchange of commodities, foreign commerce could not exist. What the circulation of the blood is to the *human* body, the circulating medium is to the *mercan-*

tile one: as the former promotes all human functions, so in commerce the latter facilitates all operations. The bankers and chartered banks of the United Kingdom, are the agents and promoters of this circulation; and they must derive profits for their labour and capital so employed. An idea of these profits, as well as of the immensity of the transactions of these powerful agents, may be formed from the demi-official statement, that the amount of the accounts balanced every day in London by these bankers, is eight millions sterling!!![a] The profits annually arising from this source cannot be estimated under 4,500,000*l.* The income resulting from interest on foreign loans, money contracts, &c., and from property possessed by British subjects in all parts of the world, (particularly in the East Indies, whence the annual remittances on account of individuals have been calculated at two millions, but which are here reduced to 1,500,000*l.*,) constitute an annual item of 4,500,000*l.* The total income, therefore, from all these sources will amount to 9,000,000*l.*

[a] An idea may be formed of what the profits of this branch must be, by contemplating the many large establishments of this kind, particularly the colossal one of the Bank of England, whose circulation in August, 1832, was 30,250,000*l.*, and the public and private securities and bullion amounted, at the same date, to 33,130,000*l.*, besides 2,880,000*l.* of "rest"; making a grand total of 66,260,000*l.*! The deposits in the Banks of Ireland are very considerable; and those of Scotland exceed 24,000,000*l.*; making altogether a grand total of 105,000,000*l.* The private bankers are very numerous throughout the kingdom. In Scotland there are thirty-four banks (Table VIII). The number of licenses granted in 1831 was no less than 641. The profits of these establishments undoubtedly exceed the estimate.

MANUFACTURES.

But these large incomes and profits necessarily promote industry and employment, by that natural inclination ingrafted in the human heart, to employ the fruits of its toils and exertions in indulging in the comforts and luxuries of life. Manufactures are the means conducing to this end. This wonderful and productive branch, in which the English nation is so superior to all others, is so extensive, and the divisions, forms, and shapes of British manufactures are so numerous, various, and diversified, that a catalogue of their names would almost fill a volume. It is unnecessary here to enter into the details of their almost infinite ramifications: let us pass in review only the principal and staple manufactures of the United Kingdom, referring at the same time to the data stated in the Notes to Table XVI. The comparative value of each branch may be seen in Table XV.

The COTTON Manufacture, or to speak more correctly, the Cotton Machine-facture, ranks first. The entire value of this manufacture, in 1760, did not amount to 200,000*l.*; but since that time, by the aid of human skill and machinery, it has not only extended its produce over all Europe and America, but has undersold the Asiatics in their cheap and home markets; sending a larger quantity of its produce to the East Indies and China, than to the United States[a]. In

[a] The Cotton Manufactures exported to the United States, in 1829, were—

	Real Value.
By the yard	£1,346,023
Hosiery, &c.	155,334
Cotton twist, &c.	1,928
	£1,503,285

To

1824, Huskisson stated in the House of Commons, that the annual produce of this manufacture was 33,500,000*l.*; in 1827, it was stated to be 36,000,000*l.*; and at present cannot be estimated under 37,000,000*l.* Deducting six millions for the cost of the raw material, (though it certainly does not amount to that sum,) leaves 31,000,000*l.* More than 850,000 weavers, spinners, bleachers, &c., are employed in this manufacture, the amount of whose wages, at 24*l.* per year, exceeds two millions; and the wages of 111,000 engineers, masons, smiths, joiners, machine-makers, &c., at the rate of only 30*l.* a year, would produce 3,330,000*l.*; making together 5,330,000*l.*; which, deducted from 31,000,000*l.*, leaves 25,670,000*l.* for the profits of capital invested in looms, workshops, mills, machinery, &c. This capital was estimated, in the year above mentioned, at 65,000,000*l.*, and at present exceeds 75,000,000*l.* The number of men altogether employed is 1,200,000, as is more fully stated in Note E to Table XVI.

Such is the prodigious annual amount raised by this single manufacture: exceeding by one million the total gross revenue estimated to be raised in the whole of the stupendous and "celestial" empire of China. Such are the results of the combination of capital with the wonderful powers of machinery, perhaps equal to the work of 80 millions of men. Even the most cool and inattentive observer is astonished, when inspecting the

To the East Indies and China—

By the yard	£1,346,020
Hosiery and small wares	28,395
Cotton twist, &c.	131,383
	£1,505,798

Shewing an excess to the latter of 2,513*l.*: and, since that time, the exportation to those parts has greatly increased.

prodigious effects of this combination of human skill and ingenuity at Manchester, Glasgow, Paisley, &c.—effects which, more than all the theological and metaphysical arguments of traffickers in religion, demonstrate to the greatest unbeliever,

——" how wonderful is man,
A beam ethereal, sullied and absorpt,
Though sullied and dishonoured, still divine!"

And these admirable effects are not only witnessed in large towns, but in the most profound caverns, at the tops of the highest mountains, and in the most retired spots in the island [a]. See Note E, to Table XVI, where more ample particulars are stated [b].

At present, the amount of cotton goods exported, forms nearly one half of the whole exports of the king-

[a] There is a Cotton Manufactory at Llangollen.

[b] According to the following statement, made in 1827, by Mr. Kennedy, the total value of cotton goods annually manufactured in Great Britain was 36,000,000*l.*: viz.—

Raw material, 130 millions of lbs. at 1s. 4d.	£9,000,000
Wages of 133,000 engineers, machine-makers, &c......	4,000,000
Ditto ... 705,000 weavers, spinners, bleachers, &c.....	15,000,000
Profits of the manufacturers, wages for superintendence, sums to purchase materials of machinery, coals, &c.	8,000,000
	£36,000,000

The capital employed may be estimated as follows:

Capital employed in the purchase of raw material......	£9,000,000
Ditto .... in payment of wages	19,000,000
Ditto .... in spinning mills, power and hand-looms, workshops, warehouses, &c.	37,000,000
	£65,000,000

dom. (Table X.) The quantity of raw material consumed in this manufacture, and its prices, may be seen in Table XI. It may be observed that the prices have declined considerably; while machinery has improved in almost the same ratio. It is demonstrated by Table XII. that the cost of manufacture, in 1830, was considerably less than in 1811; the result, however, has been so favourable to all parties, that the same sum will buy treble the quantity of cotton goods now, that it would in 1811-12, and yet allow a reasonable profit to the sellers. Thus that general cheapness, so much desired by the economists, has been realized in this extraordinary manufacture. (See Section XI., Cotton Manufactures.)

From all these elements, an idea may be formed, as to whether the estimates in the Tables are just and moderate. The manufactures of Wool, Silk, &c., are on the same extensive scale, and have increased with the same rapid strides as that of Cotton.

The "Silk Manufacture" has made the most extraordinary progress since 1823. It will be almost impossible to explain its actual state, and give an approximate estimate of its value, without acquainting the reader with the contrary opinions and principles of the two great contending parties—the "Free Trade" and the "Anti-Free Trade" people. The latter, backed by the silk manufacturers, represent the silk trade to be in a most depressed, ruinous, and deplorable state; while the opposite party assert, that its prosperity, progress, and increase, have exceeded the most sanguine expectations. Let facts speak for themselves, and decide the question, without appealing to the human passions, or the contradictory interests of parties.

The importation of all silks, according to the statement presented to the Silk Committee by the anti-French-silk party, was, in 1824, 3,867,791 lbs., and in 1830, 4,206,444 lbs.; thus showing an extraordinary increase [a]. But it must not be inferred from this, that an equal increase of profits has accrued to the manufacturers, or an equal increase of prosperity to the weavers: for it must be borne in mind, that the amount produced by a manufacture may increase, and yet the profits of the manufacturers and the comforts of the operatives, may be stationary, or even decrease. The truth of this is illustrated by the silk manufacture; in which the profits and benefits to the weavers, cannot be calculated by the weight of silk manufactured, but by the number of yards of thread which have been woven: the reason is, that a common piece of stuff may require 100 strokes of the shuttle to every two inches, while a superior piece will require 200; and the weavers are always paid in this proportion. In confirmation of this, one of the witnesses before the committee shows, that 100 looms, in 1822, worked 5964 lbs., and were paid 4803*l.*; while in 1831, the same number of looms worked 7680 lbs., and were paid only 3490*l.*; or 2000 lbs. *more* of work, for 1600*l.* *less* of wages. The "Free Traders" ought to meet their adversaries on this ground, and endeavour to prove that such a

[a] Total importation of silk of all descriptions into Great Britain, from 1823 to 1831. (Bowring's Evidence.)

	lbs.		lbs.
1823	2,415,759	1828	4,524,680
1824	3,867,791	1829	2,892,201
1825	3,408,145	1830	4,206,449
1826	2,253,513	1831	3,550,172
1827	4,213,059		

state of things is not so detrimental to the silk manufacture as it may appear; while at the same time, the latter are not warranted in drawing such absurd and unconnected conclusions from these premises. It does not follow, as this party would persuade us, that the duty ought to be increased, and the introduction of French silks totally prohibited, thus establishing a complete monopoly, and compelling the public to buy a dear and bad article when they could buy a cheap and good one: nor are national antipathies to be excited, the distresses of 700,000 operatives exaggerated, and the precious time of the legislature wasted, for such objects, or for the private interests of individuals. The legislature cannot consider the prosperity or distress of one *isolated* branch of industry separately from another; it must consult and protect the interests of all the manufactures of the country together. The public is not to be overcharged with imposts for the private advantage of one class: one branch of industry is not to be fostered to the injury of many: smuggling is not to be encouraged by increasing the profits of the smugglers:—if, with a duty of 30 per cent., 300,000*l.* worth of French silks are annually smuggled, as is admitted by the anti-French silk party, to what extent would that disgraceful practice be carried on, were the duty increased to 60 or 80 per cent. as this party desires? By such smuggling the revenue has lost 90,000*l.* in one year: what would be the loss, should the legislature comply with the wishes of the petitioners? The least reflecting man will perceive, that such measures as these persons pray for, would neither cure the distress complained of, nor confer any substantial benefit on the community at large. The writer of these pages ventures to suggest to the silk manufacturers and weavers, a measure that he feels convinced would prove far more beneficial and efficient. Let that numerous body form a subscription amongst themselves (to which the public would no doubt heartily contribute) to establish a "School of Taste and Arts", upon the plan of that at present existing at Lyons. It is admitted on both sides, that the superiority of the French manufacturer chiefly consists in taste, invention, design, and the admirable combination of colours. The students in the School of Taste at Lyons, of whom there are 200, are instructed in all branches of the elegant arts, in sculpture, botany, in the selection and arrangement of flowers, drawing, and design. If such a school were established in England, the silk manufacturers would soon equal, or even surpass their rivals, in these particulars. The Italian, the fine, and the superior sorts of silk, would soon be woven in this country in even larger quantities than in France. And not to lose time, while the establishment was forming, English capital could easily bring over the best talent, and as many excellent draughtsmen as the British manufacturers required: with the artists indeed, the question would only be, who would pay them best; their services might certainly be secured for a very trifling sum. By this simple means, the distress of the silk manufacturers and weavers might be radically and effectually remedied, and their profits considerably augmented, without injuring either the public or the revenue; inflicting, at the same time, a just and deserved punishment on a blind and ignorant government, which, taking advantage of the liberality of the English in admitting the staple articles of France, wine and silk, on the most advantageous terms, excludes and prohibits almost all British produce: a government whose financial views are so limited that it compels 32 millions of people to pay a high price for, and limits the consumption of, the two necessary articles of sugar and coffee, to forward the paltry interests of a few cultivators of beet root, and of 78,000 planters, existing on two small and miserable islands, which, in the first war, will instantly fall into the hands of another nation: a government whose plans of economy are so ill-judged and absurd, that while it boasts of protecting agriculture, and promoting internal communication in France, by means of rail roads, almost excludes the coals, steel, and cheap iron of England; restricting the commerce of 57 millions of inhabitants of two of the first nations of the world, to the miserable amount of 2,000,000*l.* of imports, and only 486,000*l.* for all British and Irish exports [a].

But, let us see what is the present state of the British silk manufacture. In 1831, there were imported of all sorts of silk 3,550,172 lbs. (See page 317, note.) The consumption of articles of silk has increased amongst the British people since 1825, above 60 per cent.; and the value of the exports has augmented from 160,000*l.* to above 500,000*l.* [b]; the British silk exported to France itself, has increased from 119,570 frs.

[a] See the Tables of Commerce of both countries, in Sec. 11.

[b] An Account of the Official Value of British Manufactured Silks exported in each Year, from 1821 to 1830.

	Manufactured Silks only.			Silks mixed with other materials.			Total.		
	£	s.	d.	£	s.	d.	£	s.	d.
1821	104,124	10	7	32,717	8	6	136,841	19	1
22	102,707	3	3	38,467	14	3	141,174	17	6
23	104,934	19	2	35,525	0	3	140,459	19	5
24	95,038	9	5	64,632	8	1	159,670	17	6
25	57,499	8	9	93,387	11	0	150,886	19	9
26	53,155	19	3	93,775	10	10	106,931	10	1
27	78,665	15	10	94,927	8	8	173,593	4	6
28	81,636	6	6	97,417	13	5	179,053	19	11
29	141,688	0	6	80,312	0	5	221,998	1	3
30	348,761	10	8	79,087	14	11	427,849	5	5
31							500,000	0	0

in 1828, to 643,720 frs. in 1830[a]. The consumption of French manufactured silks in England, which is "rapidly decreasing" (according to the evidence of Dillon, one of the greatest and richest men in this branch,) has been officially stated at about 15 millions of francs[b]: the statement of the manufacturers and weavers of Lyons, in their petition to the French Chambers, which makes it 25,000,000 frs., is naturally exaggerated. The value of the annual produce of this manufacture has been stated at 8,000,000*l.*, which exceeds that of France: 700,000 workmen are employed, and 1,500,000 persons directly or indirectly concerned in it, according to the evidence before the committee.

Such is the magnitude of this manufacture, the depressed state of which is so loudly complained of: let not the British manufacturers despair; they will soon supplant the French in their own market, as the cotton manufacturers have done the Indians.

The WOOLLEN MANUFACTURE, to foster which such cruel and curious acts were passed, (as those enacted by

[a] Importation into France of Manufactured Silks.

Countries whence Imported.	1828.	1829.	1830.
	Francs.	Francs.	Francs.
England	119,570	385,770	643,720
Prussia	505,230	361,290	469,480
Other countries	65,560	53,290	25,740
	690,360	800,350	1,138,940

[b] Real amount of French silk exported to England from 1824 to 1830.

	Francs.		Francs.
1824	3,856,465	1828	17,311,810
1825	6,104,103	1829	10,483,777
1826	7,596,421	1830	15,204,388
1827	11,460,119		

Charles, directing all the dead to be buried in woollen shrouds,) was the first great manufacture introduced into England. In the seventeenth century, the wool then shorn in England, was estimated at two millions, and the value of all the articles produced was calculated at above eight millions, of which two were exported. The largest amount ever exported was in 1802, when it reached 7,321,012*l.*:—in 1830, it sunk to 5,558,709*l.*; but it must be remembered that prices were lower in this last year, therefore the *quantity* might still be greater than in 1802. The value of this manufacture was estimated by Stevenson, many years ago, at 18,000,000*l.*; but at present it cannot be less than 22,300,000*l.* Deducting six millions for the cost of the raw material at home, and in payments to Spain and Germany, (the annual importation from the last amounting to above twenty-two millions of pounds,) it follows, that the produce of the woollen manufacture is 16,250,000*l.* It gives employment to above half a million of men, women, and children; paying their wages, and furnishing the profits of an extraordinary large capital invested in works, mills, machinery, &c.

In the promotion of the Linen Manufacture, peculiar to Ireland, was shown to what an extraordinary height the selfish, blind, and erroneous policy could be carried, of fostering one manufacture by depressing another. William III. said, "I shall do all that in me lies to discourage the woollen manufacture in Ireland, and encourage that of linen in England." Fortunately these erroneous principles are abandoned, and this manufacture has become very productive and valuable in both countries. It was estimated, in 1811, at 10,000,000*l.* raw material deducted. But when we find, that in 1830, no less than 57,698,372 yards were exported—

when we consider the enormous consumption of this article at home—when we see that the average declared value of its export to foreign countries, (particularly to the United States, the West Indies, and Spain,) is nearly 2,000,000*l.*, and consider the number of flax-dressers, spinners, bleachers, weavers, calenderers, &c., altogether 300,000, employed in it, we cannot estimate the annual produce of this important manufacture under 11,000,000*l.*, the cost of the raw material deducted.

Eden, thirty years ago, estimated the "Leather" annually manufactured into various articles in Great Britain alone, at 12,000,000*l.* How much the general and daily use of all articles of leather must have increased, in consequence of the increase of population, is evident. The exports of articles of leather have also been much greater since that period, and extend not only to the British possessions in the East and West Indies, but even to all foreign nations. The import of hides has doubled, while that of skins has been, and still continues, enormous [a]. The value of this manufacture

[a] An Official Account of the Number of Lamb and Kid Skins which have been entered for Home Consumption, etc.

Years.	No. of Lamb Skins.	No. of Kid Skins.	Total Lamb and Kid.	Dos. of Gloves produced each year.	Dos. of Gloves imported.	Total consumption of Gloves, Dozens.
1820	932,817	286,443	1,219,260	182,889		182,889
1821	1,202,029	242,996	1,445,025	216,756		216,756
1822	1,908,661	408,525	2,317,174	347,562		347,562
1823	1,974,143	497,444	2,471,587	370,728		370,728
1824	2,201,295	631,995	2,833,290	424,980		424,980
1825	2,098,553	771,522	2,870,075	430,506		430,560
1826	1,743,778	575,533	2,319,311	347,886	41,330	389,216
1827	2,749,399	640,863	3,390,226	508,536	68,123	576,656
1828	2,917,476	904,639	3,822,115	573,300	100.222	673,559
1829	1,888,487	697,413	2,585,900		72,096	
1830	1,804,714	1,086,489	2,891,203		91,128	
1831					100,600	
1832						
1833						
1834						

has perhaps doubled, since Eden's estimate was formed. In fact the glove trade, which at that time was so small and of such moderate value, is at present considerable and extensive: the hands employed in it are very numerous, and the articles produced are in such universal use, that, like boots and shoes, they may be considered of prime necessity. Authentic data cannot be readily obtained, on which to estimate the annual produce raised by all the branches of the leather manufacture; but in adding 3,000,000*l.* to Eden's estimate, and making the annual amount of all the branches of this manufacture 15,000,000*l.*, it is certainly not overrated.

HARDWARE MANUFACTURES.

These productions are spread over all the world: the names of 'Birmingham', and 'Sheffield', are read at the tables of the highest monarchs, and in the hovels of the savages of Africa, visited by Clapperton and his servant Lander. The laborious and well informed Stevenson valued these manufactures, in 1815, at 17,000,000*l.* But it should be observed that since that time, the consumption has increased considerably, probably more than a third; and the exportation of hardware has augmented in proportion. The declared value of

NUMBER AND WEIGHT OF HIDES TANNED AND UNTANNED, IMPORTED IN THE FOLLOWING YEARS, WITH THE AMOUNT OF DUTY.

Untanned.			Tanned.		Duty.
Years.	No.	Cwts.	No.	lbs.	£
1825	540	303,850	6,595	53,131	46,948
1826	36	194,243	1,990	62,313	26,239
1827	98	152,434	1,506	103,808	28,539
1828	182	225,975	7,621	103,876	37,353
1829		286,416	8,199	91,515	39,767
1830		339,773			

the exports, in 1830, was 3,789,209*l.*; being an excess of 873,578*l.* over those of 1820. Moreover, the cost of the raw material in this manufacture is very small; while the value it acquires in passing through different hands, is immense. A few pounds of rough material, the cost of which is perhaps twenty shillings, may be raised to the value of 200*l.*; and as little or nothing is paid to the foreigner on account of the raw material, this manufacture becomes one of the most profitable to the nation. The greatest part of the price of the manufactured article, resolves itself into profits and wages to the members of the community, throughout the numberless branches employed in its preparation. Deducting, therefore, notwithstanding this peculiar circumstance, the cost of the raw material required for this manufacture, its annual produce cannot be estimated, at present, under 17,300,000*l.*; besides which, it maintains and gives employment to 370,000 men, in the working of copper, brass, pewter, steel, tin, and other metals.

The EARTHENWARE, CHINA, PORCELAIN, and GLASS MANUFACTURES, rank after the preceding, in regard to their general utility to the nation, and the small capital required to be paid to foreign countries on account of the raw material; for, with the exception of some barilla and pearl-ashes, almost all the materials are to be found in this country. The consumption of porcelain and all sorts of pottery, is so extensive and so rapid, that it can only be compared to the immense and equally quick consumption of glass,—green and blue, broad and plate, crown, flint, &c. &c. The number of people maintained by this manufacture is considerable. The annual produce of the glass manufacture, the cost of the raw material deducted, is 2,500,000*l.*; and the pottery and

[illegible]

[illegible] manufactures, [illegible] paper of all sorts, [illegible] book and printing [illegible] fine arts and engravings [illegible] cabinet-makers, [illegible] wiggin, and [illegible] manufactures, &c.; [illegible], in 1811, were estimated at [illegible], cannot at present be estimated at less than [illegible]. Any person interested in the matter, and wishing to go into the details of these manufactures, would easily find, that the increase in the consumption of the articles produced by them, since that period, is enormous; and although the prices are lower, the *quantity* fully warrants the above estimate.

It would be tedious to proceed in reviewing the endless number of manufactures carried on in this country, some of which are exceedingly valuable and important; "as salt, alum, soap, tobacco, beer, cider, spirits, gunpowder, candles, and a long catalogue of others." It will be sufficient to state the general result. We find, then, that the annual produce of various miscellaneous manufactures was estimated, in 1811, at 23,000,000*l.*; and after bestowing serious attention on the basis upon which these calculations were formed, comparing the increase of consumption with the population, the exports, and the cost of materials, and taking into consideration all the favourable and disadvantageous circumstances, it has been concluded, that the actual annual aggregate produce of these miscellaneous manufactures, including some new ones that have arisen since that period, cannot be estimated under 31,200,000*l.* for the United Kingdom. In order that the reader may judge of the correctness of this statement, and examine the grounds of the computation, a Table of these manufactures, accompanied with notes explaining the grounds upon which the estimates are formed, is here annexed (Table XIII.): and though some of the calculations may seem overrated, others certainly fall far short of the truth.

Thus all the branches of manufactures and machinefactures of the United Kingdom, by converting raw materials into all sorts of useful and ornamental articles promoting the comforts and luxuries of life, annually create new produce and property, to the amount of 148,050,000*l.* And by the prodigious and united exertions of labour and machinery[a], detailed in the foregoing pages, combined with the no less prodigious aggregate capital of 3,575,700,000*l.*! produce and property are annually raised and created in the United Kingdom, to the amount of 514,823,059*l.*!! (Table XV.)

[a] The stupendous machinery employed in several manufactories, is powerful enough to raise, in a few hours, and several yards from the ground, the largest Pyramid of Egypt; in the construction of which, according to Herodotus, 100,000 men were employed for twenty years; and the weight of which is calculated to be 10,401,000 tons!

TABLE I.

An ACCOUNT of the PRICES of different Articles of PROVISIONS supplied to the ROYAL HOSPITAL, Chelsea, from 1818.

The whole Ration contracted for at per head per diem, consisting of Bread, Cheese, Butter, Beef and Mutton, Salt and Oatmeal		Potatoes per cwt. of 120 lbs.	Beer per Barrel. Table Beer of the quality fixed by the Chancellor of the Exchequer.	Candles per dozen.	Coals per Chaldron
1818	10*d*	—	10/6	Contracted for at 4d. per doz. lbs. below the market price.	38/10 44/4
19	1/0 ⅜*d*	—	8/6		45/10 and 46/10
20	11⅜ ⅞*d*	—	8/6	7/11 per doz. lb	41/10 43/10 44/10
21	10⅝ ⅞*d*	—	8/6	7/5	38/10 43/4
22	8⅜ ¼*d*	—	8/6	6/8	38/10
23	6⅝ ¾*d*	—	7/10	6/	38/10
24	8⅝*d*	—	8/	5/8	39/2
25	8¼*d*	—	7/9	5/7	43/6
26	9⅜*d*	6/5	7/3	5/9	41/11
27	9*d*	5/5	6/10	6/	42/
28	8¼ ⅝*d*	5/	7/	5/10	37/5
29	9⅛ ¼*d*	4/4	Porter per Barrel	6/	33/9
30	7⅜ ¾*d*	3/10	39/	5/7	36/
31	8½ ⅛*d*	4/2	90/ per Butt	5/10	33/4
32	8⅝ ½*d*	2/10	85/ ditto	5/3	Not yet contd.

REMARKS.—From the year 1818 to 1824, referred to in the second column, the ration for each person, consisted of 1 lb. of Bread daily 18 oz. of Beef and Mutton per day, for five days in each week, ½ lb. Cheese and ⅛ lb. of Butter per day, and 2 oz. of Butter on two banyan days in each week; the Contractor also supplied with the rations 4 bushels of Oatmeal and 4 ditto of Salt per month, for Soup. From the Year 1825 to the present time, the ration has been as follows:—1 lb. of Bread per day, 13 oz. of Meat, ½ lb. of Cheese, 2 oz. of Butter, per week; the Contractor also supplied with the ration 4 bushels or 4 cwt. of Salt, and 4 bushels or 4 cwt. of Oatmeal, per month, for Soup. From the year 1825, the Pensioners are allowed Potatoes, but they do not form part of the ration contracted for. In 1826 the Commissioners made an experiment, with a view of ascertaining whether it would not be more advantageous to the Public to contract separately for each article composing the rations; but in comparing the prices contained in the tender for separate articles. it was found that the latter was the least expensive mode, and it was accordingly ordered to be continued.

RICHARD NEAVE, SECRETARY.

Royal Hospital, Chelsea, 19th June, 1832.

A RETURN [illegible]

YEARS.	[illegible]
January, [illegible]	[illegible]
July . . . ditto	[illegible]
January, [illegible]	[illegible]
July . . . ditto	[illegible]
January, [illegible]	[illegible]
July . . . ditto	[illegible]
January, [illegible]	[illegible]
July . . . ditto	[illegible]
January, [illegible]	[illegible]
July . . . ditto	[illegible]
January, [illegible]	[illegible]
July . . . ditto	[illegible]
January, [illegible]	[illegible]
July . . . ditto	[illegible]
January, [illegible]	[illegible]
July . . . ditto	[illegible]
January, [illegible]	[illegible]
July . . . ditto	[illegible]
January, [illegible]	[illegible]
July . . . ditto	[illegible]
January, [illegible]	[illegible]
July . . . ditto	[illegible]
January, [illegible]	[illegible]
July . . . ditto	[illegible]
January, [illegible]	[illegible]
July . . . ditto	[illegible]
January, [illegible]	[illegible]
June 18 ditto . .	[illegible]

Office for Board of Trade.

[illegible]

TABLE III.

An ACCOUNT of the PRICES of SUGAR, COFFEE, COTTON, HEMP, FLOUR, TALLOW, WHALE OIL, DEALS, TIMBER, and TO... in the Months of January and July in each Year, from 1819 to the present Time.

YEARS.	SUGAR, per cwt.		COFFEE, per cwt.		COTTON, per lb.		HEMP, per ton.	
	Fine Jamaica.	Fine Havannah	Fine Jamaica.	Java.	Bowed Georgia.	Bengal.	Riga Rhine.	Petersburgh Clean.
	s. s.	s. s.	s. s.	s. s.	s. d. s. d.	d. d.	l. l. s.	l. s. l. s.
January, 1819 ..	66 to 89	60 to 68	143 to 146	136s.	1 5 to 1 8	6¼ to 9	50l.	46l.
July ....ditto ..	77 „ 81	53 „ 56	113 „ 116	127 to 137	1 0 „ 1 1	6 „ 7½	47l.	42 0 to 43 0
January, 1820 ..	73 „ 80	52 „ 56	131 „ 138	none	1 1⅛ „ 1 2	6¼ „ 8	49l.	44l. 10s.
July ....ditto ..	79 „ 86	64 „ 72	125 „ 128	ditto	0 11⅜ „ 1 0	6⅛ „ 8½	none	41l. 10s.
January, 1821 ..	77 „ 81	45 „ 53	118 „ 121	ditto	0 9 „ 0 11	5½ „ 7½	48l.	39l.
July ....ditto ..	74 „ 78	38 „ 56	119 „ 124	ditto	0 9¼ „ 0 11	5½ „ 6¾	40l.	36 0 to 36 10
January, 1822 ..	75 „ 82	41 „ 46	104 „ 109	ditto	0 9 „ 0 10⅛	5½ „ 6¼	54l.	32l.
July ....ditto ..	69 „ 72	36 „ 37	140 „ 156	ditto	0 9⅜ „ 0 10⅜	5⅛ „ 6¼	41l.	37l.
January, 1823 ..	73 „ 78	48 „ 44	131 „ 134	100 to 120	0 7 „ 0 9	5 „ 5⅜	44l.	none
July ....ditto ..	66 „ 70	44 „ 45	125 „ 128	110 „ 115	0 7 „ 0 9	5⅛ „ 6¼	41l.	ditto
January, 1824 ..	70 „ 74	37 „ 44	106 „ 120	none	0 7⅛ „ 0 9½	5½ „ 6¼	42 to 44 10	37l. 10s.
July ....ditto ..	67 „ 71	33 „ 40	87 „ 104	ditto	0 7⅜ „ 0 9¼	5⅜ „ 6¼	38 „ 39	35 5 to 35 10
January, 1825 ..	60 „ 73	39 „ 40	98 „ 108	72 to 76	0 8⅜ „ 0 10½	5½ „ 6⅜	none	42l.
July ....ditto ..	70 „ 71	50 „ 54	88 „ 94	none	1 1 „ 1 2¼	7⅛ „ 9¼	ditto	42 0 to 42 10
January, 1826 ..	71 „ 75	40 „ 38	92 „ 100	ditto	6½ „ 0 9	5½ „ 6¼	ditto	41l.
July ....ditto ..	65 „ 69	39 „ 42	85 „ 89	ditto	0 6 „ 0 8	4⅜ „ 5½	ditto	37 0 to 38 0
January, 1827 .	70 „ 75	41 „ 46	95 „ 95	ditto	0 6¼ „ 0 7½	4⅜ „ 5½	ditto	41 10 „ 42 0
July ....ditto ..	73 „ 74	41 „ 47	80 „ 85	ditto	0 5¼ „ 0 6⅜	4½ „ 5½	41 to 43	37 0 „ 38 0
January, 1828 ..	71 „ 73	45 „ 49	78 „ 80	43 to 48	0 5¼ „ 0 6⅜	3⅞ „ 5	none	39l. 15s.
July ....ditto ..	67 „ 69	45 „ 49	68 „ 77	34 „ 40	0 5 „ 0 6¼	3⅜ „ 4⅞	ditto	38l. 10s.
January, 1829 ..	67 „ 70	47 „ 50	69 „ 76	none	0 5⅜ „ 0 7⅜	3⅜ „ 5	39 to 42	39l. 10s.
July ....ditto ..	67 „ 72	46 „ 50	73 „ 76	32 to 36	0 5½ „ 0 6¼	3¼ „ 4⅞	40l.	39 15 to 40 0
January, 1830 ..	64 „ 68	46 „ 48	63 „ 78	none	0 5⅜ „ 0 7⅜	3⅜ „ 4½	45 to 45 10	45l.
July ....ditto ..	56 „ 68	34 „ 45	66 „ 78	ditto	0 6⅜ „ 0 7½	4 „ 5	40 „ 44	42 0 to 43 0
January, 1831 ..	56 „ 61	27 „ 30	75 „ 78	29 to 34	0 6 „ 0 7½	4⅜ „ 5⅛	none	none
July ....ditto ..	57 „ 62	28 „ 35	70 „ 82	35 „ 41	0 5½ „ 0 7	4 „ 4⅞	41 to 42	38 10 to 40 0
January, 1832 ..	56 „ 58	32 „ 38	96 „ 100	55 „ 62	0 5 „ 0 7	4 „ 4⅜	39 „ 40	37l. 10s.
July 12. .ditto ..	54 „ 58	32 „ 37	94 „ 96	32 „ 62	0 6 „ 0 7½	4⅜ „ 5⅛	not quoted	35l.

YEARS.	TALLOW, per cwt.		WHALE OIL, per ton of 252 Gallons.		DEALS, Memel, Yellow, per Standard Hundred.	TIMBER, Memel, per Load.	TOBACCO, per lb.	
	Yellow Soap.	Petersburgh.	New Greenland, without Casks.	Spermaceti.			Virginia Fine Black.	Brazil Leaf.
	s. d. s. d.	s. d. s. d.	l. s. l. s.	l. l.	l. s. l. s.	l. s. d. l. s. d.	d. d.	
January, 1819 ..	78s.	74s.	36 0 to 37 0	98l.	22 0 to 23 0	6 15 0 to 6 17 6	12 to 13	none
July ....ditto ..	64 0 to 65 0	59 0 to 60 0	33 0 to 34 0	96l.	21l.	6 10 0 „ 6 12 6	9 „ 10	ditto
January, 1820 ..	55 0 „ 56 0	51 0 „ 52 0	31l.	66l.	18l.	6 0 0 „ 6 5 0	8½ „ 10	ditto
July ....ditto ..	57 0 „ 57 6	56s. 6d.	23 0 to 24 0	74l.	18 0 to 19 0	6 0 0 „ 6 17 6	8 „ 9	ditto
January, 1821 ..	51s. 6d.	47s.	25 0 „ 25 10	72l.	17 10 „ 18 0	6 0 0 „ 6 6 6	7½ „ 8½	ditto
July ....ditto ..	45s. 6d.	42s.	22l. 10s.	65l.	17 10 „ 18 0	5l. 5s.	6 „ 7	ditto
January, 1822 ..	44s.	39s.	19 0 to 20 0	53l.	17 10 „ 18 0	5 0 0 „ 5 5 0	7 „ 7½	ditto
July ....ditto ..	35s.	31 0 to 32 0	19l.	48l.	17 15 „ 18 0	5 2 6 „ 5 5 0	7 „ 7½	ditto
January, 1823 ..	37 0 to 37 6	35s.	27l.	47l.	18 10 „ 19 0	5 15 0 „ 5 17 0	7 „ 7½	ditto
July ....ditto ..	34s. 6d.	35s.	22 0 to 10 0	48l.	19 0 „ 19 10	5l. 10s.	5½ „ 6½	ditto
January, 1824 ..	31 0 to 32 0	34 0 to 34 6	18l.	42l.	20 0 „ 21 0	5 10 0 to 5 12 6	6 „ 7½	ditto
July ....ditto ..	32s. 6d.	34 3 „ 34 6	20l.	37 to 38	18 0 „ 18 10	5 2 6 „ 5 5 0	5 „ 6	ditto
January, 1825 ..	none	37s.	25l. 10s.	48 to 48	19 0 „ 19 10	5 15 0 „ 6 0 0	5½ „ 7	ditto
July ....ditto ..	ditto	35 0 to 35 6	24l.	44l.	18 0 „ 19 10	5l. 15s.	6½ „ 8	ditto
January, 1826 ..	ditto	35 0 „ 35 3	31l.	52l.	19 0 „ 20 0	5 10 0 to 5 15 0	8 „ 8½	ditto
July ....ditto ..	ditto	32s.	29l.	48l.	17 0 „ 17 10	4 15 0 „ 5 0 0	6½ „ 7	ditto
January, 1827 .	38s. 6d.	37s.	34s. to 35s.	66l.	17 0 „ 17 10	4 15 0 „ 5 7 6	6½ „ 7	ditto
July ....ditto ..	38s.	38s.	28l.	70l.	16 0 „ 17 0	4 5 0 „ 4 7 6	6½ „ 7	ditto
January, 1828 ..	37 9 to 38 0	37s. 6d.	28l.	82l.	16 0 „ 17 0	4 15 0 „ 5 0 0	5½ „ 6	ditto
July ....ditto ..	38s. 9d.	36 0 to 36 6	24 0 to 25 0	78l.	15 0 „ 16 10	4 12 6 „ 5 0 0	5 „ 5½	ditto
January, 1829 ..	38s. 9d.	38 6 „ 39 0	26 0 „ 27	80l.	16 0 „ 17 0	5 0 0 „ 5 10 0	5 „ 5½	ditto
July ....ditto ..	37 3 to 37 6	none	26l.	68l.	16 0 „ 17 10	4 17 6 „ 5 7 6	5 „ 5½	ditto
January, 1830 ..	34s.	35s. 3d.	29l.	73l.	16 0 „ 17 0	4 17 6 „ 5 2 6	4½ „ 5	ditto
July ....ditto ..	33 6 to 34 0	35s.	30 10 to 31 0	74l.	16 0 „ 17 0	4l. 10s.	4 „ 5	ditto
January, 1831 ..	45s. 9d.	45s. 9d.	37 0 „ 38 0	85 to 86	16 0 „ 17 0	4 15 0 to 5 2 6	5 „ 5½	ditto
July ....ditto ..	40s. 6d.	41s.	none	78l.	16 10 „ 18 0	5 0 0 „ 5 10 0	4½ „ 5	ditto
January, 1832 ..	49s. 6d.	46s. 6d.	34l.	74l.	18 10 „ 18 0	5 0 0 „ 5 10 0	4½ „ 5	ditto
July 12. .ditto ..	none	41s.	30l.	65 to 66	18 10 „ 18 10	5 0 0 „ 5 10 0	4½ „ 5	ditto

Mem.—The Records of the Board of Trade do not furnish the means of supplying the prices of English Flour.

of Trade, 18th June, 1832. THOMAS LACK.

TABLE IV.

SUMMARY of the POPULATION of GREAT BRITAIN and IRELAND.

JOHN RICKMAN.

	1801.	1811.	1821.	1831.	1840.
England	8,331,434	9,551,888	11,261,437	13,089,333	
Wales	541,546	611,788	717,438	805,236	
Scotland	1,599,068	1,805,688	2,093,456	2,365,807	
Army and Navy	470,500	640,500	319,300	277,017	
	10,942,548	12,609,864	14,391,631	16,537,393	
Ireland	. . .	4,500,000	6,802,093	7,734,365	
Grand Total . .	10,942,548	17,109,864	21,193,724	24,271,758	
		17,109,864		24,271,758	

Increase $41\frac{8}{10}$ per cent. from 1811 to 1831

TABLE V.

SUMMARY of the POPULATION of COUNTIES in 1821 and 1831, distinguishing the Sexes.

ENGLAND.

	1821.			1831.		
	Males.	Females.	Total.	Males.	Females.	Total.
Bedford	40,385	43,331	83,716	46,350	49,033	95,383
Berks	65,546	66,431	131,977	72,453	72,836	145,289
Bucks	64,867	69,201	134,068	71,734	74,795	146,529
Cambridge	60,301	61,608	121,909	72,031	71,924	143,955
Chester	132,952	137,146	270,098	164,152	170,258	334,410
Cornwall	124,817	132,630	257,447	146,949	155,491	302,440
Cumberland	75,600	80,524	156,124	81,971	87,710	169,681
Derby	105,873	107,460	213,333	117,740	119,430	237,170
Devon	208,229	230,811	439,040	235,630	258,538	494,168
Dorset	68,934	75,565	144,499	76,536	82,716	159,252
Durham	99,100	108,573	207,673	121,701	132,196	253,827
Essex	144,909	144,515	289,424	158,895	158,332	317,227
Gloucester	160,451	175,392	335,843	185,063	201,841	386,904
Hants	138,373	144,925	283,298	152,097	162,216	314,313
Hereford	51,552	51,691	103,243	55,715	55,261	110,976
Hertford	64,121	65,593	129,714	71,395	71,946	143,341
Huntingdon	24,020	24,751	48,771	26,365	26,784	53,149
Kent	209,833	216,183	426,016	234,572	244,583	479,155
Lancaster	512,476	540,383	1,052,859	650,389	686,465	1,336,854
Leicester	86,390	88,181	174,571	97,556	99,447	197,003
Lincoln	141,570	141,488	283,058	158,717	158,527	317,244
Middlesex	533,573	610,958	1,144,531	631,493	727,048	1,358,541
Monmouth	37,278	34,555	71,833	51,095	47,035	98,130
Norfolk	166,892	177,476	344,368	189,305	200,749	390,054
Northampton	79,575	82,908	162,483	87,889	91,387	179,276
Northumberland	95,354	103,611	198,965	106,157	116,755	222,912
Nottingham	91,491	95,382	186,873	110,443	114,877	225,320
Oxford	68,817	68,154	136,971	76,055	75,671	151,726
Rutland	9,223	9,264	18,487	9,721	9,664	19,385
Salop	102,056	104,097	206,153	110,788	111,715	222,503
Somerset	170,199	185,115	355,314	194,169	209,739	403,908
Stafford	171,668	169,372	341,040	206,895	203,588	410,483
Suffolk	132,410	138,132	270,542	145,761	150,543	296,304
Surrey	189,871	208,787	398,658	230,855	256,471	486,326
Sussex	116,705	116,314	233,019	135,386	137,002	272,328
Warwick	133,827	140,565	274,392	165,781	171,227	336,988

Summary of Population, &c.—*Continued.*

	1821. Males.	1821. Females.	1821. Total.	1831. Males.	1831. Females.	1831. Total.
Westmorland	25,513	25,846	51,359	27,594	27,447	55,041
Wilts	108,213	113,944	222,157	117,118	122,063	239,181
Worcester	90,259	94,165	184,424	103,367	107,989	211,356
York—East Riding	92,761	97,688	190,449	98,524	105,484	204,008
North Riding	90,153	93,228	183,381	93,232	97,641	190,873
West Riding	397,542	401,815	799,357	485,845	490,570	976,415
Total of England	5,483,679	5,777,758	11,261,437	6,375,394	6,713,944	13,089,338

WALES.

	1821. Males.	1821. Females.	1821. Total.	1831. Males.	1831. Females.	1831. Total.
Anglesey	21,784	23,279	45,063	23,475	24,850	48,325
Brecon	21,853	21,760	43,613	23,896	23,867	47,763
Cardigan	27,898	29,886	57,784	30,868	33,912	64,780
Carmarthen	43,577	46,662	90,239	48,648	52,007	100,655
Carnarvon	28,412	29,546	57,958	31,810	33,943	65,753
Denbigh	37,785	38,726	76,511	41,388	41,779	83,167
Flint	26,733	27,051	53,784	29,924	30,088	60,012
Glamorgan	50,427	51,310	101,737	63,284	63,328	126,612
Merioneth	16,479	17,903	34,382	17,334	18,275	35,609
Montgomery	29,743	30,156	59,899	33,043	33,437	66,485
Pembroke	34,530	39,479	74,009	37,947	43,477	81,424
Radnor	11,266	11,193	22,459	12,453	12,198	24,651
Total of Wales	350,487	366,951	717,438	394,075	411,161	805,236

SCOTLAND.

	1821. Males.	1821. Females.	1821. Total.	1831. Males.	1831. Females.	1831. Total.
Aberdeen	72,383	83,004	155,387	82,582	95,069	177,651
Argyll	47,775	49,541	97,316	50,059	51,366	101,425
Ayr	61,077	66,222	127,299	69,717	75,338	145,055
Banff	20,193	23,368	43,561	22,743	25,861	48,604
Berwick	15,976	17,409	33,385	16,239	17,809	34,048
Bute	6,474	7,323	13,797	6,495	7,656	14,151
Caithness	14,196	16,042	30,238	16,359	18,170	34,529
Clackmannan	6,356	6,907	13,263	7,095	7,634	14,729
Dumbarton	13,046	14,271	27,317	16,321	16,890	33,211
Dumfries	33,572	37,306	70,878	34,829	38,941	73,770
Edinburgh	87,759	103,755	191,514	99,911	119,681	219,592
Elgin	14,292	16,870	31,162	15,779	18,452	34,231
Fife	53,540	61,016	114,556	60,780	68,059	128,839
Forfar	52,071	61,359	113,430	65,093	74,513	139,606
Haddington	16,828	18,299	35,127	17,397	18,748	36,145
Inverness	42,304	47,853	90,157	44,510	50,287	94,797
Kincardine	13,540	15,578	29,118	15,016	16,415	31,431
Kinross	3,660	4,102	7,762	4,519	4,553	9,072
Kirkcudbright	18,506	20,397	38,903	18,969	21,621	40,590
Lanark	115,385	129,002	244,387	150,229	166,590	316,818
Linlithgow	10,703	11,982	22,685	10,995	12,296	23,291
Nairn	4,082	4,924	9,006	4,307	5,047	9,354
Orkney and Shetland	24,070	29,054	53,124	26,594	31,645	58,239
Peebles	4,973	5,073	10,046	5,342	5,236	10,578
Perth	66,033	73,017	139,050	68,565	74,329	142,894
Renfrew	51,178	60,997	112,175	61,154	72,289	133,443
Ross and Cromarty	32,324	36,504	68,828	34,927	39,893	74,820
Roxburgh	19,408	21,484	40,892	20,761	22,902	43,663
Selkirk	3,205	3,432	6,637	3,394	3,439	6,833
Stirling	31,718	33,658	65,376	35,283	37,338	72,621
Sutherland	11,088	12,752	23,840	12,090	13,428	25,518
Wigtown	15,837	17,403	33,240	17,078	19,180	36,258
Total of Scotland	983,552	1,109,904	2,093,456	1,115,132	1,250,675	2,365,807
Total of England	5,483,679	5,777,758	11,261,437	6,375,394	6,713,944	13,089,338
Wales	350,487	366,951	717,438	394,075	411,161	805,236
Scotland	983,552	1,109,904	2,093,456	1,115,132	1,250,675	2,365,807
Grand Total	6,817,718	7,254,613	14,072,331	7,884,601	8,375,780	16,260,381

[illegible]

[illegible]

[illegible] [illegible] the errors arising from imperfect returns have been corrected.

Middlesex, East Riding of York, Somerset, and Hertford, the total population, and average rate of increase, are,—

Population, 1831.	Increase per Cent.			
	1801—11.	1811—21.	1821—31.	1700—1831.
5,319,756	16¼	18⅛	15⅜	147

The highest rate of increase, since 1700, in these counties, has been in Surrey, where it has been 214 per cent.; and the lowest, in Hertfordshire, of 103 per cent. Middlesex, since that period, has increased 117 per cent., and the rate of increase has diminished one per cent. since 1821, having been 19 per cent. for the last ten years. Its present population is 1,358,541.

Of the remaining nineteen English counties or districts, being almost entirely agricultural, viz. Devon, Essex, North Riding of York, Bedford, Suffolk, Berks, Oxford, Westmoreland, Northumberland, Cambridge, Norfolk, Buckingham, Lincoln, Dorset, Wilts, Huntingdon, Northampton, Hereford, and Rutland, the total population, and average rate of increase, are,—

Population, 1831.	Increase per Cent.			
	1801—1811.	1811—1821.	1821—1831.	1700—1831.
3,727,920	9½	15¼	10⅜	84

In the last mentioned counties, the highest increase, since 1700, has been in Devonshire, of 99 per cent.; and the lowest in Hereford and Rutland, being respectively 36 and 17 per cent. Norfolk is at about the average, being 86 per cent. The slow increase of the population of these agricultural counties, which has not nearly doubled itself in a period of 130 years, is worthy of observation, because the received law of population, according to Mr. Malthus, is, that population, when unchecked, increases in a geometrical progression of such a nature as to double itself every twenty-five years.

North and South Wales stand together as follows:—

Population, 1831.	Increase per Cent.			
	1801—1811.	1811—1821.	1821—1831.	1700—1831.
805,236	13	17¼	12	117

The territorial extent of the ten manufacturing counties first named, according to parliamentary documents, together with the value of property therein, have been thus estimated:—

Counties.	Superficies in Statute Acres.	Rental, 1815.	Average Rate per Acre.	Value for Property Tax, 1815.		Parochial Assessments, 1829.	Land and Assessed Taxes, 1829.
				Schedule A.	Schedule B.		
		£	s. d.	£	£	£	£
Lancaster . . .	1,171,840	1,270,344	21 8	3,139,043	2,222,080	413,530	184,383
York, West Riding	(Returns made for the whole County.)						
Warwick . . .	577,280	645,130	22 4	1,269,757	669,370	122,304	96,633
Stafford . . .	734,720	756,635	20 7	1,200,325	516,721	171,578	76,451
Nottingham . .	535,680	534,992	20 0	751,626	314,591	106,707	59,543
Chester	673,280	676,864	20 1	1,114,928	969,309	144,102	65,254
Durham . . .	679,040	506,063	14 11	885,590	253,631	100,647	{with Northumbld.
Monmouth . .	318,720	203,676	12 9	298,981	102,571	32,090	41,030
Worcester . . .	466,560	516,203	22 1½	890,021	273,303	97,176	69,165
Salop	858,240	738,495	17 2½	1,093,702	279,983	89,656	65,467

Comparing the population with the extent, it thus appears that Lancashire contains more than one inhabitant to every acre,—that Warwick and Stafford have more than one to every two acres,—that Nottingham and Chester have about one to two acres,—and that the other four have about one to between two and three. These counties may, therefore, altogether be considered as exceeding the average population of England and Wales, which, compared to a superficies of 37,084,400 statute acres, gives a ratio of one inhabitant to every two acres and a half.

For some of the remaining counties, the returns are as follows:—

Counties.	Superficies in Statute Acres.	Rental, 1815.	Average Rate per Acre.	Value for Property Tax, 1815.		Parochial Assessments, 1829.	Land and Assessed Taxes, 1829.
				Schedule A.	Schedule B.		
		£	s. d.	£	£	£	£
Surrey	485,120	369,901	15 4½	1,589,702	1,664,533	321,305	272,538
Southampton .	1,041,920	894,020	11 5	1,940,547	923,714	259,123	109,368
Middlesex . . .	180,480	349,142	38 9	5,765,374	15,255,246	779,126	1,340,643
Devonshire . .	1,650,560	1,217,547	14 9	1,924,912	757,444	250,713	137,941
Norfolk	1,338,880	931,842	13 11	1,516,651	583,011	338,868	141,633
Hereford . . .	550,400	453,067	16 4	629,156	61,851	70,001	37,036
Buckingham . .	473,600	496,677	21 0½	662,672	222,961	158,484	56,667

Here we see Middlesex with a population of more than seven to a statute acre; Surrey with one to an acre; Southampton, Devonshire, and Norfolk, with about one to every three acres; Buckingham with about one to four; and Hereford with one to five acres.

In the order of the value of property, the following six of the counties of England and Wales rank foremost:—

Middlesex,	Lancaster,	Lincoln,
York,	Somerset,	Devon;

and the following six are, in that respect, of the least importance, viz.:—

Hertford,	Huntingdon,	Monmouth,
Bedford,	Westmoreland,	Rutland.

The value of the property assessed, compared with the numbers of the people, is a good test of the state of agriculture in a given district. Thus, if Bedfordshire, with a population of 95,400, is assessed at only 364,277*l.* real property, and a Scotch county (Berwickshire), with only one-third of the population of Bedfordshire, is assessed at considerably more than two-thirds of real property, the inference is, that there is some imperfection in the state of things in Bedfordshire.

If we divide England into North and South, by a line drawn from the Wash in Lincolnshire to the Severn, the total population of the eighteen counties north of the line will appear to be 6,130,581, and of the twenty-two counties south of it 6,958,755; so that the southern counties still possess the larger population, notwithstanding its rapid growth in the north. There is no coal south of the line, with the exception of comparatively inconsiderable beds in Gloucester and Somerset; and the relative condition of the labouring population in the two divisions is, in many respects, much contrasted, as will be seen on reference to the state of pauperism, of crime, and of other matters.

TABLE VI.

SUMMARY, showing the Proportion of the POPULATION of GREAT BRITAIN, engaged in and depending on each great branch of Production and Occupation. ("MARSHALL.")

	ANALYSIS.	1821—No. of Families.	1831—No. of Families.	1831—Total No. of Persons
1	Agricultural occupiers	250,000	250,000	1,500,000
2	Ditto labourers	738,956	800,000	4,800,000
3	Mining ditto	110,000	120,009	600,000
4	Millers, Bakers, and Butchers	160,000	180,000	900,000
5	Artificers, Builders	200,000	230,000	650,000
6	Manufacturers	340,000	400,000	2,400,000
7	Tailors, Shoemakers, Hatmakers	151,000	180,000	1,080,000
8	Shopkeepers	310,000	350,000	2,100,000
9	Seamen and Soldiers	319,300	277,017	830,000
10	Clerical, Legal, and Medical	80,000	90,000	450,000
11	Disabled Paupers	100,000	110,000	110,000
12	Proprietors of Annuities	190,000	316,000	1,116,398
		2,941,383	3,303,504	16,537,393

The feature deserving most attention in this Statement is the stationary number of Agricultural Employers, while the Labourers tend progressively to increase: and the comparatively inconsiderable number of Manufacturers.

TABLE VII.—An Attempt ..th Report of the Commissioners of Revenue Inquiry.

..ATES' ESTATES.

SCALE. 55 Geo. III. c. 184.	Rate of Duty.	Amount of Duty paid	..ount ..ty.	Net Amount of Property.
100	10s.	£560	00	£10,200
200	£2	1002	00	24,000
300	5	2015	00	70,000
450	8	4464	00	28,900
600	11	5467	00	45,000
800	15	7485	00	31,000
1000	22	8602	00	40,000
1500	30	19,200	00	77,000
2000	40	16,720	00	200,000
3000	50	25,800	00	70,000
4000	60	23,220	00	190,000
5000	80	19,440	00	18,000
6000	100	14,200	00	90,000
7000	120	16,680	00	138,000
8000	140	14,980	00	91,000
9000	160	11,840	00	97,000
10,000	180	15,120	00	51,000
12,000	200	25,400	00	38,000
14,000	220	15,690	00	143,000
16,000	250	13,500	00	104,000
18,000	290	18,440	00	69,000
20,000	310	15,500	00	31,000
25,000	350	26,950	00	19,000
30,000	400	21,200	00	67,000
35,000	450	14,400	00	137,000
40,000	525	19,950	00	65,000
45,000	600	13,200	00	112,000
50,000	675	12,825	00	42,500
60,000	750	29,250	00	47,500
70,000	900	15,300	00	110,000
80,000	1050	12,600	00	65,000
90,000	1200	8400	00	110,000
100,000	1350	10,800	00	190,000
120,000	1500	12,000		
140,000	1800	9000	00	£2,613,600
160,000	2100	10,500		
180,000	2400	7200	III.	
200,000	2700	5400		
250,000	3000	9000		
300,000	3750	3750		
400,000	5250	5250		
500,000	6000	6000		
		£543,250		

Amount of Duty paid by several Classes; the Number and Amount of Property in each Class.

No. of Cases under £1,000 . . 1719
Amount of Property £824,100
Amount of Duty 8,815

No. above £1,000 and under £5,000 293
Property £568,000
Duty 17,967

No. above £5,000 and under £10,000 62
Property £415,000
Duty 11,520

No. above £10,000 and under £20,000 28
Property £360,000
Duty 9,345

No. above £20,000 and under £40,000 13
Property £381,500
Duty 8,280

No. above £40,000 7
Property £510,000
Duty 11,810

. . . . £615,280
. . . . 215,910
£831,190

. . . . £32,212,700
. . . . 2,613,600
£34,826,300

* The Gross Amount of Proper..
Net is a mean proportion betwee.. paid in the Country and not classified 11,608,766

N.B. The.. passing under Probate £46,435,066

TABLES showin..the Amount of the Personalty of England.

Amount of Property passing u..
in the year ended January, 1..
Amount of Capital on which L..
year . . . .

No. VIII.

..Number of Persons to whom Half-yearly Dividends were
Excess of Proper..1822, and January, 1823, classed according to the yearly
Legacy Duty w..mentary Paper.

No. of Testators—Town . .
Do. do. Country .
No. of Intestates—Town . .
Do. do. Country .

	No. of Persons.	
. .	20,735	Capital held by these 283,958 persons . . £737,130,668
. .	41,195	Dividend thereon . £25,773,326
. .	91,542	
. .	26,949	
. .	15,459	
. .	6,141	
. .	3,243	
. .	1,782	
. .	447	
. .	215	
. .	283,958	

Amount of Property proved, &..
one year . . . .
No. of Testators and Intestat..
one year . . . .
N.B. If 33 years be consider..
the number of persons decease..
the total Population;—the sam..
Wills, &c., in one year.

No. IX.

£46,435,066 gave Probate duty £831,190

£35,806,480 gave Legacy duty . . . £1,048,692

Total Probate and Legacy duty . . . £1,879,882

on £46,435,066, viz.

£4. 1s. 8d. per Cent.

No. I. Shows the number of per..perty, the rate and the amount of probate duty levied from each class. The Stamp Act requi..ed to be under one of the grades mentioned in the schedule; upon the evidence of this affidavit ..died intestate; but it is to be observed that both tables are confined to those whose residence ..of the whole kingdom, and thus become important data in aiming at a classification of the ho..nd II. satisfactorily show the amount of personal property passing by death in one year.——N..e year possessed of personal property, distinguishing those who left wills from those who did ..cy duty, and the property paid upon, at the several rates, (which rates are regulated accordi..is a parliamentary paper, giving a classification of the fund-holders.——No. IX. Shows the am..

TABLE IX.

OFFICIAL and DECLARED VALUE of EXPORTS of British and Irish Produce and Manufactures, and Official Value of Exports of Foreign and Colonial Merchandise from Great Britain and Ireland; and Official Value of Imports into the same, for the following Years, ending 5th January.

Years ending 5th Jan.	EXPORTS. British and Irish Produce and Manufactures from Great Britain.		Irish Produce and Manufactures from Ireland.		Foreign and Colonial Merchandise from Great Britain.	Foreign, Colonial, and British Merchandise, from Ireland.	IMPORTS. Into Great Britain.	Into Ireland.
	Official Value.	Declared Value.	Official Value.	Declared Value.	Official Value.	Official Value.	Official Value.	Official Value.
1799	£18,556,891	£31,252,836	£536,544	The real Value of the Exports not recorded in these years.	£ 8,760,196	£ 68,370	£25,122,203	£ 856,087
1800	22,284,941	35,903,850	473,075		7,271,696	87,824	24,066,700	1,240,620
1801	22,831,936	36,929,007	468,531		11,549,681	62,853	28,257,781	1,381,694
1802	24,501,608	39,730,659	436,076		10,336,966	100,744	30,435,268	1,350,994
1803	25,195,893	45,102,330	436,656		12,677,431	98,749	28,308,373	1,517,837
1804	20,042,596	36,127,787	424,935		8,032,643	41,231	25,104,541	1,518,155
1805	22,132,367	37,135,746	554,942		8,938,741	40,913	26,454,281	1,365,251
1806	22,907,371	37,234,396	469,570	£ 842,748	7,643,120	44,431	27,334,020	1,227,250
1807	25,266,546	39,746,581	595,333	1,129,402	7,717,555	61,710	25,554,478	1,345,190
1808	22,963,772	36,394,443	427,442	851,434	7,624,312	49,114	25,326,845	1,407,580
1809	24,179,854	36,306,385	431,361	963,717	5,776,775	61,046	25,660,953	1,134,587
1810	32,916,858	46,049,777	625,416	1,321,616	12,750,358	84,597	30,170,292	1,580,265
1811	33,299,408	47,000,926	762,493	1,437,754	9,357,435	149,421	37,613,294	1,688,318
1812	21,723,532	30,850,618	957,868	2,040,094	6,117,720	105,049	25,240,904	1,269,289
1813	28,447,912	39,334,526	1,060,596	2,382,438	9,533,065	184,710	24,923,922	1,239,509
1814	*	*	1,139,781	2,467,824	*	157,149	*	1,050,933
1815	32,200,580	43,447,373	1,006,673	2,046,846	19,157,818	208,163	32,620,771	1,134,493
1816	41,712,002	49,653,245	1,163,994	1,949,783	15,708,435	40,119	31,822,053	1,165,348
1817	34,774,521	40,328,940	942,549	1,328,933	13,441,665	39,115	26,374,921	1,056,683
1818	39,233,467	40,349,235	877,960	1,411,817	10,269,271	23,413	29,910,502	923,797
1819	41,960,555	45,180,150	739,966	1,423,099	10,835,800	24,017	35,845,340	1,039,842
1820	32,983,689	34,252,251	650,487	956,070	9,879,236	25,677	29,681,640	1,095,170
1821	37,820,293	35,569,077	678,475	854,886	10,525,026	31,086	31,515,222	956,544
1822	40,194,681	35,823,127	637,818	832,135	10,602,090	27,605	29,769,122	1,068,590
1823	43,558,488	36,176,897	679,017	788,196	9,211,029	15,639	21,432,676	1,098,765
1824	43,166,039	34,589,410	660,568	706,918	8,588,996	14,909	34,591,264	1,307,169
1825	48,024,952	37,600,021	705,515	822,383	10,188,596	16,183	36,056,551	1,411,798
1826	46,453,022	38,077,330	697,668	793,615	9,155,305	14,187	42,660,954	1,347,849
1827	40,332,854	30,847,528	632,882	680,195	10,066,503	9,784	36,174,350	1,647,162
1828	51,279,102	36,394,817	942,832	746,518	9,806,[illegible]43	24,478	43,489,346	1,418,[illegible]97
1829	52,019,724	36,150,379	768,319	681,378	9,928,6[illegible]5	17,891	43,536,187	1,632,301
1830	55,465,723	35,212,000	747,319	617,536	10,00[illegible],400	16,948	4[illegible],311,000	1,060,009
1831	60,492,637	37,691,300			[illegible]		44,818,000	
1832	60,090,123	[illegible]			[illegible]		4[illegible],161,000	

TABLE X.

CCOUNT of the EXPORTS of COTTON GOODS, from the Year ending 5th January, 1815, to the Year ending 5th January, 1830, both inclusive, with the Duties and Drawbacks on 'Printed Goods' exported during the same period.

Years.	Official Value.	Declared Value	Duties received.	Drawbacks allowed.
	£.	£.	£.	£.
1815	17,655,378	20,033,132	1,298,057	831,040
1816	22,289,645	20,620,856	1,331,664	953,250
1817	17,564,461	15,577,392	1,127,811	719,676
1818	21,259,224	16,012,001	1,173,816	820,554
1819	22,589,130	18,767,517	1,570,636	1,079,376
1820	18,282,292	14,699,912	1,484,643	879,967
1821	22,532,079	16,516,758	1,614,049	934,955
1822	23,541,615	16,094,807	1,751,371	1,083,416
1823	26,911,043	17,218,801	1,682,701	1,182,557
1824	26,544,770	16,276,843	1,811,919	1,146,750
1825	30,155,901	18,376,515	2,040,718	1,381,941
1826	29,495,281	18,253,631	2,035,219	1,665,592
1827	25,194,270	14,013,675	1,524,664	1,020,971
1828	33,182,898	17,502,394	2,022,257	1,360,668
1829	33,467,417	17,140,114	2,098,962	1,441,206
1830	37,269,395	17,394,584	1,942,918	1,390,534
1831	. . . .	19,438,664		
1832				
1833				
1834				
1835				
1836				
1837				
1838				
1839				
1840				

TABLE XI.

ENT of the Importation of COTTON WOOL into GREAT BRITAIN for Ten Years, from 1821 to 1830; the Quantities taken ome Consumption and Exportation, Stock remaining at the close of each Year, and the Prices of different Descriptions st December in each Year.

MPORT.	1821	1822	1823	1824	1825	1826	1827	1828	1829	1830	1831	1832	1833
American	301,945	329,059	419,836	282,773	421,688	375,146	646,942	444,581	461,569	613,185			
Brasil	122,062	144,176	148,475	142,559	198,034	55,742	120,056	165,240	150,939	192,267			
West India	37,471	40,548	31,107	31,837	34,614	18,582	29,958	22,117	20,808	12,618			
East India	30,369	19,263	38,535	50,846	60,502	64,698	73,546	84,795	80,582	35,212			
Egyptian	. . .	. . .	2,000	33,745	103,419	47,362	21,998	32,855	24,712	13,596			
Total Number of Packages imported . .	491,847	533,039	670,073	541,760	821,250	581,500	892,535	749,588	747,449	871,908			
Exported	32,660	60,010	35,330	53,100	75,580	95,000	75,300	64,900	109,300	35,450			
Taken for Consumption	491,650	541,850	534,390	639,100	465,430	539,660	707,500	731,030	754,660	805,580			
Stock at the close of the Year	354,320	285,500	335,800	235,360	416,660	342,500	452,250	405,900	289,390	320,260			
PRICES on 31st Dec. Duty paid.	d. d.	d. d.	d. d.	d. d.	d. d.	d. d.	d. d.	d. d.	d. d.	d. d.			
Bowed Georgia . .	7¾ to 10½	6¼ to 8¼	7½ to 9¾	8¼ to 10½	6¼ to 9¼	6¼ to 7¼	5 to 6¾	5¼ to 7	5¼ to 7	6 to 7¼			
New Orleans . . .	8¼ .. 12½	7 .. 10⅞	8¾ .. 11	10 .. 12¾	7¼ .. 11	7 .. 8¼	5¼ .. 8½	6 .. 8	6 .. 7¼	6½ .. 7¾			
Maranham	10⅞ .. 11¼	9¼ .. 10½	10¼ .. 11¾	10¼ .. 11½	10¼ .. 11¼	9 .. 9¼	7¼ .. 8¼	7¼ .. 7¾	6⅞ .. 7	7 .. 7¾			
Pernambuco . . .	11¼ .. 12¼	10⅞ .. 11⅞	11 .. 12	10⅞ .. 12	11¼ .. 12¾	11 .. 11¼	8¼ .. 9	7¼ .. 8⅞	7⅞ .. 8	7⅞ .. 9¼			
Egyptian	. . .	. . .	— .. 11¼	10⅞ .. 12	9¼ .. 11	7¼ .. 8½	7 .. 9	7 .. 8½	6½ .. 8¼	8 .. 9½			
Surat	6¾ .. 8¼	5¾ .. 6½	5¼ .. 6¼	5¼ .. 7¼	5¾ .. 7	5 .. 6	3½ .. 5¼	3⅞ .. 5	2¾ .. 5½	4¾ .. 5¾			
Bengal	5¾ .. 6¼	5¼ .. 6	6 .. 7½	5¼ .. 6¼	5¼ .. 6½	5 .. 5¼	4 .. 5	3¼ .. 5	3½ .. 4¼	4¼ .. 5¼			

TAB. XII. COMPARATIVE COST of Manufactured Cotton between 1812 & 30.

Hanks per day per spindle. / Description of yarn.		Price of Cotton and Waste per lb.		Labour per pound.		Cost per lb.	
1812	1830	1812	1830	1812	1830	1812	1830
No.		s. d.	s. d.	s. d.	s. d.	s. d.	s. d.
40, 2	2. 7 .5	1 6	7	1 0	7¼	1 2½	1 2½
60, 1 .5	2. 5	2 0	10	1 6	1 0½	3 6	1 10½
80, 1 .5	2.	2 2	11½	2 2	1 7¾	4 4	2 6¼
100, 1 .4	1. 8	2 4	1 1¼	2 10	2 2½	5 2	3 4¼
120, 1 .2 .5	1. 6 .5	2 6	1 4	3 6	2 8	6 0	4 0
150, 1	1. 3 .3	2 10	1 8	6 6	4 11	9 4	6 7
200, .7 .5	.90	3 4	3 0	16 8	11 6	20 0	14 6
250, .5	.05	4 0	3 8	31 0	24 6	35 0	28 2

The cost has been reduced to one half.

TAB. XIII. ESTIMATE of the PRODUCE of the following MISCELLANEOUS MANUFACTURES, arising from the use of Capital combined with Human Labour and Machinery.

Beer and porter, including labour in the manufacture of malt liquor, after deducting for the raw material ....(1.)	£3,200,000
Cider, perry, sweets, and vinegar, including labour in the manufacture of each, after deducting for the raw material ....(2.)	400,000
Spirits, sweets, and vinegar, including strong waters manufactured in Ireland ....(3.)	1,500,000
Beef, pork, butter, and other provisions, labour employed in killing, preparing, and packing for exportation ....(4.)	1,400,000
Haberdashery, &c., including fringes and other small wares, sealing-wax, wafers, and ink ....(5.)	2,000,000
Straw, manufactured into hats, bonnets, &c., after deducting for the raw material ....(6.)	700,000
Dye-stuffs, labour in the manufacture of, and dying, exclusive of woollens, cottons, &c.	600,000
Furs, feathers, and skins, labour in the manufacture of into hats, muffs, &c., deducting for raw material......	60,000
Hair, hogs' bristles, &c., including labour of manufacturing into chairs, brushes, &c....................	600,000
Floor-cloths, oil-cloths, &c.; labour in manufacturing these, deducting for raw materials	40,000
Soap, including labour in manufacture, deducting for raw materials ....(7.)	700,000
Candles, including labour in manufacture, do.............	650,000
Bricks and tiles .... do.................. do. ......(8.)	900,000
Gunpowder............... do.................. do.. ......(9.)	400,000
Cooperage .... do.................. do. .... (10.)	600,000

Turnery ware, including labour in manufacture of numerous articles from ivory, horn, bone, &c.	150,000
Drugs and chemical preparations, including labour in manufacture of vitriol, varnish, glue, starch, perfumery, &c.	700,000
Tobacco and snuff, including labour in manufacture (11.)	600,000
Refined sugar, including expense of labour and machinery in refineries, deducting for raw material......	450,000
Musical instruments, cork, toys, and miscellaneous articles	350,000
Steam-engines, machinery, mills, and mathematical instruments, deducting for raw materials ....(12.)	£1,200,000
Houses, labour of persons employed in building and repairing,—masons, bricklayers, carpenters, plumbers, painters, carvers and gilders, &c. &c. ....(13.)	7,000,000
Ship and boat building and repairing, labour of shipwrights, rope-makers, &c., exclusive of raw material	2,600,000
Miscellaneous tradespeople, as milliners, tailors, umbrella-makers, fan-trimmers, shirt and twist button-makers, clear-starchers, manglers, and numerous others, many of them very profitable; for their labour in their respective branches ....(14.)	4,000,000
Salt and alum, labour in manufacturing, deducting for raw material	400,000
Total.........	£31,200,000

Explanatory Notes.

(1.)—It was estimated, in 1811, that 260,000,000 gallons of porter and beer were brewed annually in Great Britain and Ireland: considering the enormous increase in the consumption since that time, both from the cheapness of the article and the increase of population, the quantity of malt liquor of all sorts annually brewed at present, cannot be taken under 440,000,000 gallons; which, allowing only twopence a gallon for labour, machinery, &c. would give 3,200,000*l.*

(2.)—If we consider the increased consumption of cider, &c. in consequence of the reduction of duty, and the quantity of wines made from currants, gooseberries, oranges, &c., &c., this sum will appear very moderate.

(3.)—The labour, &c. in manufacturing spirits of various denominations and from various substances, is here estimated at a very moderate rate: besides British gin, immense quantities of whiskey, and cordials of all sorts, British brandy is now made from potatoes in considerable quantities: and the labour and machinery employed in rectifying rum, French brandy, &c. are to be taken into consideration.

(4.)—All articles of provisions have been already valued under the head of Agriculture: there remains the labour in salting, pickling, preserving, preparing and packing various articles for consumption and exportation.

(5.)—The individual consumption of these trifling but indispensable articles by a population of 25,000,000, amongst whom dress and neatness are so much cultivated, is very considerable, and gives employment to a great number of persons.

(6.)—The manufacture of straw into bonnets, hats, &c. is very considerable; and although the introduction of Leghorn has somewhat injured it, compensation is found in the labour required to make up this latter, and in the invention of new kinds made from grasses, &c.

(7.)—The consumption of soap may be taken at 1 lb. per week for every family: the labour employed in manufacturing the quantity required by the whole population, cannot be estimated under 700,000*l.*

(8.)—The enormous quantities of bricks and tiles annually consumed in building and repairing, may be estimated from the amazing increase of new buildings of all sorts; taking into account the considerable labour required in preparing the clay, &c., and the high wages received by the workmen employed, 900,000*l.* will be found very moderate, after deducting for the raw material.

(9.)—The gunpowder manufactured in Great Britain is of such good quality, that considerable quantities are exported.

(10.)—Under this head are included, besides casks and vats for liquors, those required for the package of glass and earthenware, tin ware, and numerous other articles, both for home consumption and exportation.

(11.)—The labour, including the interest on capital employed, in the manufacture of tobacco and snuff, the consumption of which has so prodigiously increased of late years, may safely be estimated at 600,000*l.*

(12.)—In 1803, the sum invested in steam-engines and other expensive machinery was estimated at 40,000,000*l.*; since when it has more than doubled: besides which, the manufacture may be supposed to have increased considerably since British machinery was allowed to be exported. The wages of all the people engaged in these manufactures are very high.

(13.)—The number of houses annually built in Great Britain, was estimated, in 1811, at 50,000 (or one-sixtieth part of the whole number), exclusive of those repaired; and the value of the labour, &c. of the different tradespeople employed, was estimated at 6,000,000*l.*: considering the amazing increase in this branch, and the great expense bestowed in embellishing all modern buildings, the sum stated in the Table is certainly very moderate.

(14.)—Besides the numerous trades and manufactures included under this head which are well known, there are various new ones every day starting into existence, and which, though apparently of little value or consideration, give profitable employment to a great number of people.

TABLE XIV.

PRICES of SHARES, &c., in various JOINT STOCK COMPANIES, which usually come into the London Market. Extracted from the Financial and Commercial Record, published by Wells and Son, January 1833.

Number of Shares.	CANALS.	Price per Share.	Dividend per Share per Ann.	Dividends payable.
1766¼	Ashton and Oldham.......Average 97*l* 18*s* sh.	120*l*	5*l*	Apr. & Oct.
1482	Ashby-de-la-Zouch..........Average 113*l* sh.	74	4*l*	Apr. & Oct.
720	Barnsley..........................160*l* sh	247*l*	11*l*	Feb. & Aug.
1260	Basingstoke........................100*l* sh.	5½*l*		
1003	Brecknock and Abergavenny..........150*l* sh.		4*l*	Jan. & July
4000	Birmingham................ ½ share, 17*l* 10*s*		12*l* 10*s*	April & Oct.
4000	Birm. and Liverpool Junction.........100*l* sh.	38a40*l*		
472	Bolton and Bury ....250*l* sh.	105*l*	6*l*	Jan.
600	Bridgewater and Taunton.............100*l* sh.	70*l*		
400	Chelmer and Blackwater.............100*l* sh	102	5*l*	Jan.
500	Coventry ....100*l* sh.		32*l*	May & Nov.
4545	Croydon ....Average 31*l* 2*s* 10*d* sh.	1*l*		
2060½	Dudley ....100*l* sh.	49*l*	2½*l*	Mar. & Sept.
3575½	Ellesmere and Chester.......Average 133*l* sh.	75*l*	3*l* 15*s*	Sept.
1297	Forth and Clyde.........Average 400*l* 16*s* sh.	540*l*	23*l*	Jan. & July
11,600	Grand Junction ....100*l* sh.	225a6*l* ex div	12*l*	Jan. & July
2849½	Grand Union ....100*l* sh.		1*l*	Oct.
1500	Grand Surrey.......................100*l* sh.	28*l*		
120,000*l*	Ditto Debentures 100*l*	90*l*	5*l* p. ct.	June & Dec.
3096	Grand Western ....100*l* sh. 97*l* pd.	79*l* dis		
600	Glamorganshire ......Average cost 172*l* 13*s* 4*d*	290*l*	13*l* 12*s* 8*d*	Mar. June, Sept. [& Dec.
1187	Gloucester and Berkley ....100*l* sh.	14a15*l*		
899	Ditto....(New) of 10 per Cent.	40a5*l*		
749	Grantham..........................150*l* sh.	195*l*	10*l*	May
6239	Huddersfield.........Average 57*l* 6*s* 6*d* sh.	24½a5*l*	1*l*	Sept.
23,328	Kennet and Avon .....Average 39*l* 18*s* 10*d* sh.	26½a¾*l*	1*l* 5*s*	Sept.
150	Kensington ....100*l* sh.			
11,699¼	Lancaster ....Average 47*l* 6*s* 8*d* sh.	21½a2*l*	1*l*	April
2879½	Leeds and Liverpool.................100*l* sh.	455*l*	20*l*	May & Nov.
18½	Ditto....(New).......................80*l* sh.		16*l*	May & Nov.
540	Leicester ....140*l* sh.	189*l*	15*l*	Jan. & July
5	Ditto.....ditto......................110*l* sh.		14*l*	Jan. & July
1897	Leicestershire and Northamptonsh. . Av. 83*l* 16*s*	89*l*	4*l*	Jan. & July
70	Loughborough ....Average 142*l* 17*s* sh.	1800*l*	200*l*	Jan. & July
3000	Macclesfield ....100*l* sh.	65*l*		
2409	Monmouthshire.......................100*l* sh.	195*l*	10*l*	June & Dec.
711	Montgomeryshire.....................100*l* sh.	85*l*	4*l*	August
250	Melton Mowbray ....100*l* sh.	190*l*	9*l*	July
500	Mersey and Irwell............................	700a10*l*	40*l*	June
247	Neath..............................100*l* sh.	290*l*	15*l*	Feb. & Aug.
521	Oakham ....Average about 130*l* sh.	30*l*	2*l*	June
1786	Oxford ....100*l* sh.	560*l*	32*l*	Mar. & Sept.
2400	Peak Forest............Average about 78*l* sh.	74*l*	3*l*	June
2520	Portsmouth and Arundel..............50*l* sh.			
2000	Ditto ....(New).............. 25*l* sh. 10*l* pd.			
21,418	Regent's (or London)... Average 33*l* 17*s* 2*d* sh.	16½a¾*l*	13*s* 6*d*	July
5669	Rochdale.......................Average 85*l* sh.	88*l*	4*l*	May
500	Shropshire ....100*l* sh.	136*l*	8*l*	June & Dec.
800	Somerset Coal.......................150*l* sh.	170*l*	10*l*	Jan. & July
3600	Ditto Lock Fund ....12*l* 10*s* sh	12½a¾	5½*l* p. ct.	June & Dec.
700	Stafford and Worcester..............140*l* sh.		34*l*	Jan. & July
500	Shrewsbury.........................125*l* sh.	250*l*	11*l*	May & Nov.
300	Stourbridge ....145*l* sh.	196*l*	8*l*	Jan. & July
3647	Stratford-on-Avon.........Average 79*l* 9*s* 8*d* sh.	32a3	1*l* 10*s*	August
200	Stroudwater ....150*l* sh.	500a20*l*	24*l*	May & Nov.
533	Swansea ....100*l* sh.	185*l*	11*l*	November
1300	Thames and Severn, black.............100*l* sh	25*l*	1*l* 10*s*	June
1150	Ditto.......ditto...red................100*l* sh.	29*l*	1*l* 10*s*	June
2600	Trent and Mersey................½ sh. 50*l*		37*l* 10*s*	Jan. & July
8149	Thames and Medway ....Average 19*l* 2*s* 5*d* sh	15*s*		
1000 sh. 1000½	Warwick and Birmingham..............100*l* sh	251*l*	14*l*	May & Nov.
980	Warwick and Napton ....100*l* sh.	216*l*	12*l*	May & Nov.
6000	Worcester and Birmingham, Average 78*l* 8*s* sh.	84*l*	3*l* 10*s*	Feb. & Aug.
20,000	Wilts and Berks.......Average 16*l* 17*s* 8*d* sh.	4½a¾*l*	4*s*	May
800	Wyrley and Essington ....125*l* sh.	115*l*	6*l*	
905	Wey and Arun.......................110*l* sh.	22½*l*	1*l*	May

Prices of Shares, &c., in Joint Stock Companies.—*Continued.*

Number of Shares.	INSURANCE COMPANIES.	Price per Share.	Dividend per Share per Ann.	Dividends payable.
9000	Albion Life..................500l sh. 50l pd.		3½l p. sh.	January,
50,000	Alliance (British and Foreign) 100l sh. 10l pd.	8⅝a⅞l	4l p.ct. & bs	April
50,000	Ditto (Marine)................100l sh. 5l pd.	5l	5l p.ct. & bs	January
24,000	Atlas..........................50l sh. 5l pd.	10⅛a¼l	10s p. sh.	Aug.
12,000	British Commercial Life.........50l sh. 5l pd.		5½l p. ct.	Jan. & July
20,000	British Fire..................230l sh. 50l pd.	35l	2l p. sh.	Apr. & Oct.
9000	Clerical, Medical & General Life, 100l sh. 2½l pd	3l	4l p.ct. & bs	August
4000	County Fire...................100l sh. 10l pd.	37l	2½l p. sh	December
20,000	Eagle Life.....................50l sh. 5l pd.	5½l	5s p. sh.	November
1,000,000l	Globe...............................Stock..		7l p. ct.	Jan. & July
20,000	Guardian......................100l sh. 10l pd.	25¼a½l	1l p. sh.	July
40,000	Hope Life......................50l sh. 5l pd	6l	6s 6d p. sh.	May & Nov.
2400	Imperial Fire.................500l sh. 50l pd.		5l 5s p. sh.	Jan. & July
7500	Imperial Life.................100l sh. 10l pd.	8a½l	4½l p. ct.	July
2020	Kent Fire............................50l sh.	65l	3l p. sh.	Mar. & Sept.
2000	Kent Life............................50l sh.	62l		
3900	London Fire...............25l sh. 12l 10s pd.	23l	20s p. sh.	Apr. & Oct.
31,000	London Ship...............25l sh 12l 10s pd.	23l	20s p. sh.	Apr. & Oct.
10,000	Law Life......................100l sh. 10l pd.	16a½l		
40,000	Palladium Life.................50l sh. 2l pd.	33s	5l p. ct.	Jan. & July
250,000	Protector Fire..................20l sh. 2l pd.	25s 6d a 26s	1s 1d p. sh.	July
2500	Provident Life................100l sh. 10l pd.	18¼a½l	10l p. ct.	July
190,000	Rock Life.......................20l sh. 2l pd	3⅜a⅞l	3s p.sh. & bs	October
689,219l 17s 10d	Royal Exchange......................Stock..	173½l	l p.ct. & bs	Jan. & July
	BRIDGES.			
1600	Hammersmith.........................50l sh.			
7231	Southwark...............Average 63l 2s 8d sh.			
	Ditto with new Subscription, Average 76l 2s 8d			January
3000	Ditto..(New) of 7l per Cent..........50l sh.	Shut	2½l p. ct.	January
5000	Waterloo...........................100l sh.	2½l		
5000	Ditto Ann. of 8l......................60l pd.	24l	1l 0s 8d	Mar. & Sept.
5000	Ditto do. of 7l......................40l pd	21l	18s 1d	Mar. & Sept.
50,000l	Ditto (Bonds)...............various amounts	112l p. ct.	5l p. ct.	Mar. & Sept.
5848	Vauxhall.................Average 49l sh.	18a½l	1l	June & Dec.
	IRON RAILWAYS.			
2000	Clarence (Durham)..................100l sh.	112½l		
2500	Forest of Dean.......................50l sh.	20l	18s	Apr. & Oct.
1500	Leicester and Swannington............50l sh.	55½l		
5100	Liverpool and Manchester............100l sh	18½l	8½l p. ct.	Jan. & July
5100½	Ditto...............................25l sh.	44l	8½l p. ct.	Jan. & July
6375½	Ditto...............................25l sh	44l	8½l p. ct.	Jan. & July
3762	Severn and Wye.............Average 35l sh.	17a½l	18s.	June & Dec.
1009	Stockton and Darlington, Average 106l 13s 4d	300l	8l	January
	ROADS.			
533	Archway and Kentish Town...Average 80l sh.		15s	January
300	Barking............................100l sh		1l 5s	Jan. & July
1000	Commercial.........................100l sh	100l	6l	Jan. & July
200	Ditto Joint Stock.......................100.		5l	Jan. & July
200	Ditto East India Dock Branch.......100l sh.	59l	3l p. ct.	Jan. & July
492	Great Dover Street......................70l.	47a½l	2l 13s	Jan. & July
2393	Highgate Archway.......Average 30l 7s 10½d	2½l		
11,602½l	New North Road.....................Stock..			
	GAS LIGHT AND COKE COMPANIES.			
2500	Bath................................16l sh.	33l	10l p.c.&bns	Mar. & Sept.
928	Birmingham..........................50l sh.	107l ex div	10l p.c.&bns	Feb. & Aug.
2400	Birmingham & Staffordshire...........50l sh.	39l	4l p. sh.	Mar. & Sept.
600	Brentford...........................50l sh.			April
4250	Bristol.............................20l sh	42l	10l p. ct.	Feb. & Aug.
1200	Ditto (from Oil).....................25l sh	0l		
1500	Brighton............................20l sh.	13a½l		
750	Ditto....(New)..............20l sh. 18l pd.	4a3½l dis		
5000	British (London)............40l sh. 16l pd.	½l dis	6l p. ct.	May & Nov.
5000	Ditto (Provincial)..........20l sh. 19l pd.	2a1½l dis	5l p. ct.	May & Nov.
240	Canterbury..........................50l sh	51l	5l p. ct.	Jan. & July
240	Ditto....(New)......................25l sh.	25a½l	4l p. ct.	Jan. & July
4000	Continental (consolidated)..100l sh. 51½l pd.	29½l dis	½l p. sh.	Feb. & Aug.
1000	City of London.....................100l sh.		10l p. ct.	Mar. & Sept.

Prices of Shares, &c., in Joint Stock Companies.—*Continued.*

Number of Shares.	GAS LIGHT AND COKE COMPANIES.	Price per Share.	Dividend per Share per Ann.	Dividends payable.
1000	City of London (New) ....100*l* sh. 60*l* pd.		10*l* p. ct.	Mar. & Sept.
4000	Equitable .... 50*l* sh. 20*l* pd	2¾a2½*l* dis		
10,000	Imperial.......... ....50*l* sh.		5*l* p. ct.	Apr. & Oct.
85,000*l*	Ditto Debentures, various amounts	96*l* p. ct.	4*l* p. ct.	5Jan. & 15July
2350	Independent.........................30*l* sh	41a2*l*	6*l* p. ct.	Apr. & Oct.
200	Maidstone.................... .....50*l* sh.	100*l*	9*l* p. ct.	Mar. & Sept.
9000	Phœnix . ...50*l* sh. 39*l* pd.		6*l* p. ct.	Feb. & Aug.
3.0	Poplar....................... ...50*l* sh.			
2500	Portable................... .100*l* sh. 20*l* pd.			
1000	Ratcliff ....100*l* sh. 60*l* pd.	11¾*l*	4*l* p. ct.	Mar. & Sept.
8200	United General ....50*l* sh. 44*l* pd.	7¾a¾*l* dis	4½*l* p. ct.	Apr. & Oct.
12,000	Westminster or Chartered ....50*l* sh.		6*l* p. ct	May & Nov.
6000	Ditto ....(New)..............50*l* sh. 10*l* pd.		6*l* p. ct.	May & Nov.
800	Yarmouth ....20*l* sh. 18*l* pd.	6a5½*l* dis	12*s* 6*d* p. sh.	August
	LITERARY INSTITUTIONS.			
1000	London, with Ivory Ticket ....75 gs. sh.	18a19*l*		
700	Russell ....25 gs. sh.	8*l* 8*s*		
1500	London University...................100*l* sh.	27a30*l*		
756	King's College ....100*l* pd.			
	DOCKS.			
2600&1065 ½ sh.	Commercial........................100*l* sh.		1*l* p. ct.	Jan. & July
483,750*l*	East India...........................Stock..	51*l*	4*l* p. ct.	Apr. & Oct.
1034	East Country.........................100*l* sh.			
3,114,000*l*	London..............................Stock..		3*l* p. ct.	Jan. & July
1,352,752*l*	St. Katherine.......................Stock..		3*l* p. ct.	Jan. & July
500,000*l*	Ditto Bonds................ ....100*l*		4½*l* p. ct.	5 Apr. & 5 Oct.
200,000*l*	Ditto Ditto, for 10 Years................100*l*	101*l*	4*l* p. ct.	5 Apr. & 5 Oct.
1,380,000*l*	West India ....Stock..		5*l* p. ct.	Jan. & July
2209	Bristol...............Average 147*l* 9*s* 0*d* sh.	95*l*	4*l* 8*s* 5*d* p. sh.	June & Dec.
268,324*l*	Ditto Notes, various amounts................	114*l* p. ct.	5*l* p. ct.	May & Nov.
570	Folkestone Harbour.................50*l* sh.	1*l*		
	WATER WORKS.			
4800	Birmingham..................25*l* sh. 21*l* pd.	3*l* dis		
4433	East London ....100*l* sh.	116*l*	5*l*	Apr. & Oct.
5300	Grand Junction.........Average 42*l* 19*s* 3*d* sh.		2½*l*	Jan. & July
2000	Kent ....100*l* sh.		2*l*	Jan. & July
1500	New River London Bridge Water Annuities ...	57½*l*	2*l* 10*s*	Apr. & Oct.
6486	Manchester and Salford.......Average 30*l* sh.	42*l*	1*l*	March
1500	Portsmouth and Farlington ....50*l* sh.	4*l*		
390	Ditto....(New).............. ....50*l* sh		2*l*	April
800	South London ....100*l* sh.	73*l*	4*l*	Apr. & Oct.
8290	West Middlesex...........Average 63*l* 12*s* 9*d*		3*l*	Jan. & July
1369	Yk Buildgs or Comp Lessee Proprietors 100*l* sh.	34*l*	1*l* 14*s*	Apr & Oct.
	MINES.			
10,000	Anglo Mexican ....(iss. 5*l* pm.) 100*l* sh.	9a10*l*		
4000	Ditto Subscription ......(opt. on 25*l* sh.) 10*l* pd.			
2000	Bolanos ....150*l* sh.	140a50*l*		
10,000	Bolivar ....50*l* sh. 20*l* pd	14½a14*l* dis		
10,000	Brazilian Imperial 35*l* sh. 20*l* pd. iss. 5*l* pm. ...	46a7*l*	2*l* 10*s* last div	November
6000	Ditto....National ....25*l* sh. 17½*l* pd.	2a1 dis		
5000	Ditto....St. John del Rey ......20*l* sh. 10*l* pd	6½a¾*l* dis		
20,000	British Iron Company...............50*l* sh	19*l*		
8300	Colombian ....55*l* sh. 49½*l* pd. iss. 5*l* pm.	4¾a1½*l* dis		
2850	English Mining Company ......25*l* sh. 12½*l* pd.	11½a12*l* pm		
20,000	General Mining Association .....20*l* sh. 10*l* pd.	3a2½ dis		
10,000	Hibernian....................50*l* sh. 10*l* pd			
6155	Mexican Company .... .100*l* sh. 46*l* pd.	42½*l* dis		
20,000	Mining Company of Ireland ......25*l* sh. 5*l* pd.			
1020	Penoles (Gold)...............12*l* sh. 12*l* pd.			
1000	Real del Monte ....400*l* sh.	19a20*l*		
1000	Ditto ...Subscription.. ....150*l* pd			
800	Ditto....Scrip...... . .....½ sh. 30*l* 25*l* pd			
	Ditto....Subscription Thirds..........7½*l* pd			
30,000	United Mexican.......40*l* sh. 40*l* pd. iss. 2*l* pm	3½a6½*l*		
	Ditto....Scrip.........................2*l* pd.			
	Ditto... Ditto....(New)... ....5*l* pd.	4a¾*l*		

Prices of Shares, &c., in Joint Stock Companies.—*Continued.*

Number of Shares.	JOINT STOCK BANKS.	Price per Share.	Dividend per Share per Ann.	Dividends payable.
	England.			
10,000	Birmingham........................50 sh. 5l pd.	8l pm	10l p. ct.	March
10,000	Gloucester........................50l sh. 5l pd.	3l pm	6l p. ct.	August
5000	Halifax ....100l sh. 5l pd.	12¾l pm	12½l p. ct.	February
5000	Huddersfield.......................100l sh. 20l pd.	14l pm	6l p. ct.	August
3000	Lancaster ....100l sh. 10l pd.	6l pm		
30,000	Liverpool & Manchester District 100l sh. 10l pd.	1¼a¾l pm		
20,000	Manchester.........................100l sh. 15l pd.	4a4½l pm	6l p. ct.	October
25,000	Liverpool..........................100l sh. 10l pd.	1¼a2l pm		
	Scotland.			
1,500,000l	Bank of Scotland ....83l 6s 8d sh	150a2l	6l p. ct.	Apr. & Oct.
1,500,000l	Royal of Scotland ....100l sh.	152a4l	5¾l p. ct.	Jan. & July
500,000l	British Linen Company...............100l sh.	235a7l	8l p. ct.	June & Dec.
3,000,000l	Commercial ....500l sh. 100l pd.	162a4l	6l p. ct.	Jan. & July
2,000,000l	Glasgow Union ....250l sh. 50l pd.	54a6l	5l p. ct.	Jan. & July
5,000,000l	National.....................100l sh. 10l pd.	13¼a¼l	5l p. ct.	Jan. & July
	Ireland.			
20,000	Provincial Bank of Ireland ....100l sh. 25l pd.	Shut	5l p. ct.	Jan. & July
10,000	Hibn. Joint Stock Bankg. Co. ...100l sh. 25l pd.		4l p. ct.	June & Dec.
	MISCELLANEOUS.			
1080	Auction Mart........................... 50l sh.	16a17l	1l p. sh.	Feb. & Aug.
10,000	Australian (Agricultural).....100l sh. 25½l pd.	18¼l dis		
8,600	British Rock & Patent Salt Com. 50l sh. 35l pd.	29a8½l dis	1l p. sh.	Feb. & Aug.
10,000	Canada Company...............100l sh. 17l pd.		4l p. ct.	Jan. & July
75	Covent Garden Theatre, Renter's......500l sh.	180l	25l & adm.	
300	Drury Lane Theatre, Ditto............250l sh.		12l do.	August
2122	Ditto Proprietor's....................100l sh.	5l		
4000	Devon Haytor Granite...........50l sh. 7l pd.		5¼l p. ct.	July
5000	Droitwich Patent Salt ....25l sh.	14¾l dis		
15,000	General Steam Navigation Comp. 20l sh. 13l pd.	3¼a3l dis	13s p. sh.	Feb. & Aug.
2100	Hungerford Market ....100l sh. 85l pd.	5l dis		
1800	London Corn Exchange 37½l	25l	3l p. ct	Apr. & Oct.
2000	London Commercial Sale Rooms....Av. 75l sh.	18¾l	1l	Apr. & Oct.
2754	Reversionary Interest Society ....100l sh.		4l p. sh. & bs.	Jan. & July
2754	Ditto ....New.................100l sh. 10l pd.		4l p. ct.	Jan. & July
4000	Thames Tunnel.........................50l sh.	4¾l		
10,000	Van Dieman's Land (Agricul.) 100l sh. 14l pd.	7l dis		

Foreign Income	[illegible]		[illegible]
Manufactures	Cotton	[illegible]	
	Silk	21,[illegible]	
	Woollen	[illegible]	
	Linen	14,2[illegible]	
	Leather	11,[illegible]	
	Hardware	15,000,000	
	China Glass, Pottery, &c.	17,300,000	148,050,000
	Jewellery, Plate, &c.	5,900,000	
	[illegible]	3,400,000	
	Paper, Furniture, Colours, Printing and Book Apparatus, &c. &c.	9,000,000	
	Miscellaneous (see Table XIII.)	31,200,000	
			£ 514,823,059

[illegible] of the Public and Private Property of England and Wales, Scotland, and Ireland. ([illegible])

Capital and Power.	England and Wales.	Scotland.	Ireland.	Great Britain and Ireland.
Productive Private Property.	£	£	£	£
[illegible]	[illegible]	[illegible]	[illegible]	[illegible]

Productive Private Property..............	
Unproductive....Ditto................	580,700,000
	3,575,700,000
Public Property	103.800,000
Total......	£3,679,500,000

Scotland:—

Productive Private Property	318,300,000	
Unproductive....Ditto	51,100,000	
		369,400,000

Ireland:—

Productive Private Property	622,100,000	
Unproductive ....Ditto........................	116,400,000	
Ditto............Ditto, in Great Britain and Ireland..........		738,500,000
Public Property in England and Wales	42,000,000	38,900,000
Ditto.............. in Scotland	3,900,000	
Ditto.............. in Ireland	11,900,000	
Ditto.............. in common to Great Britain and Ireland, as the Navy, Military, and Ordnance Stores, &c.	46,000,000	
		103,800,000
Grand Total.............		3,679,500,000

EXPLANATORY NOTES TO TABLE XVI.

(A.)—*Lands cultivated in Grain of all sorts, Grass, Hops, Nurseries, Gardens, &c.*

The following statement is taken from the Third Report of the Emigration Committee, 1829 :—

	Cultivated.	Uncultivated Wastes, capable of improvement.	Unprofitable.	Total.
	Acres.	Acres.	Acres.	Acres.
England............	25,632,000	3,454,000	3,256,400	32,342,400
Wales	3,117,000	530,000	1,105,000	4,752,000
Scotland	5,265,000	5,950,000	8,523,930	19,738,930
Ireland..............	12,125,280	4,900,000	2,416,664	19,441,944
British Islands	383,690	166,000	569,469	1,119,159
	46,522,970	15,000,000	15,871,463	77,394,433

In England and Wales it is calculated that the lands are distributed in the following manner :—

3,250,000	acres are employed in the cultivation of	Wheat.
1,250,000	....	Barley and Rye.
3,200,000	....	Oats, Beans, and Peas.
1,200,000	....	Clover, Grass, &c.
1,200,000	....	Roots and Cabbages, cultivated by plough.
2,100,000	....	Fallows.
47,000	....	Hop grounds.
18,000	....	Pleasure grounds.
17,300,000	....	Depastured by cattle.
1,200,000	....	Hedge rows, copses, and woods.
1,300,000	....	Ways and water courses.
5,029,000	....	Common and waste.
37,094,000 Acres.		

Colquhoun estimated the cultivated lands in England and Wales at an average of 24*l.* per acre: those cultivated in Scotland, including tithes, at one-fifth of this value: and those cultivated in Ire-

[illegible]

Total income of the Parochial Clergy	£3,4[illegible],138
Incomes of Bishops	15[illegible],[illegible]00
Deans and Chapters	275,000
Total revenue of the Established Church	£3,872,138

The patronage in England and Wales is thus distributed—

Rectories in the patronage of			
The Crown	558	1,340	1,733
The Bishops	592		
Deans and Chapters	190		
University of Oxford	202	393	
Ditto of Cambridge	152		
OtherCollegiate Establishments	39		
Private Individuals			3,444
Total Rectories			5,177

Vicarages in the patronage of			
The Crown	490	1,991	2,341
The Bishops	709		
Deans and Chapters	792		
University of Oxford	112	350	
Ditto of Cambridge	131		
OtherCollegiate Establishments	107		
Private Individuals			3,175
Total Rectories and Vicarages			10,693
Chapels in the patronage of private individuals			649
Total number of benefices in England and Wales			11,342

The following Table exhibits a summary of the value of Scotch Livings:—

172	Benefices at 150*l.* each	£25,800
200	Ditto ...... 200*l.*	40,000
200	Ditto ...... 250*l.*	50,000
200	Ditto ...... 300*l.*	60,000
100	Ditto ...... 325*l.*	32,500
76	Ditto ...... 350*l.*	26,600
948		£234,900
948	houses, with attached glebe lands, at 30*l.* each	28,440
		£263,340

The aggregate revenue of the Church of Ireland, according to Moreau, and several other writers, exceeds 1,300,000*l.* per annum;

but according to the late parliamentary returns, it is 1,232,000*l.* The population of Ireland is distributed as follows:—

Roman Catholics	5,500,000
Presbyterians	800,000
Methodists, &c.	300,000
Church of England.........................	400,000
	7,000,000

The total income of the Church in England and Wales as above stated, is	£3,872,138
———————————— in Scotland	263,340
———————————— in Ireland.................	1,232,000
Making a total income for Great Britain and Ireland of	£5,367,478

Which, estimated at the low rate of twenty five years' purchase, will give the extraordinary capital of 107,349,560*l.*!! Thus the Church of the United Kingdom is the richest in the world; and its united income is, perhaps, equal to that of the whole Catholic church in Europe. But unfortunately, this immense wealth is not justly distributed amongst all the labourers in the vineyard. "By the returns of 1827," says Lord Henley, in his Plan of Church Reform, "it appears, that of 10,533 benefices in England and Wales, there were only 4413 served by actually resident clergymen, and 6003, including those where the incumbent did duty, without the kind of residence required by law; that the duty in 4,530 parishes is performed by curates, one sometimes serving two parishes: by another return the number is only 4,254. No less than 2,989, or about three-fourths of the whole, have less than 150*l.* per annum—248 have under 40*l.*—and 69, less than 30*l.*, which is less than the wages of a common labourer." But in Ireland the state of the Church is much worse. The income of the priests not belonging to the Church of England, only amounts to 264,000*l.* The total number of clergymen, of all sorts, is 4,075; but there are parishes where there are 3000 Catholics, and only one Protestant; however, they are bound to pay the tithe of all produce to the Protestant rector, whom they detest: thus the population, at present eight millions, is in a perpetual state of agitation and disturbance. Most fortunately, a Plan for the Reform of the Church in Ireland, has been brought in by Lord Althorp; which may be expected to produce the most beneficial results. The following will be found to be a correct summary of its principal points.

1. Church cess to be immediately and altogether abolished. This will produce a pecuniary saving to the amount of 80,000*l.* annually.

2. The number of archbishops and bishops to be reduced prospectively: the first from four to two; the last from eighteen to ten: and the revenues of the suppressed sees to be appropriated to the general church fund. The archbishoprics of Cashel and Tuam to be reduced to bishoprics. Ten bishoprics to be abolished, and the duties transferred to other sees; as Clogher to Armagh, Raphoe to Derry, Kildare to Dublin, Killaloe to Tuam, &c. &c.

3. A general tax, of from five to fifteen per cent. to be imposed on all bishoprics.

4. An immediate reduction from the bishopric of Derry, and a prospective reduction from the primacy, in addition to the tax; the amount to be paid to the general fund. The plan will effect a reduction in the incomes of the archbishops and bishops of 60,000*l.*; their annual amount being at present 130,000*l.*

5. An immediate tax on all benefices, of from five to fifteen per cent., in lieu of first fruits, which are afterwards to be abolished. Benefices under 200*l.* to be exempt; and the tax to be calculated according to the value. Total income of parochial clergy, 600,000*l.*

6. Abolition of all sinecure dignitaries; and their revenues to be appropriated to the general church fund.

7. Commissioners to be appointed to administer the fund, and apply it, first, to the ordinary church cess, and the surplus to the augmentation of poor livings, to assist in building glebe-houses and churches, to the dividing of unions, &c. &c.

8. Commissioners to have the power, with the consent of the Privy Council, of dividing and altering limits of parishes.

9. Where no duty has been performed, nor minister resided, for three years before the passing of the Act, commissioners to have the power to suspend the appointment, (if in the gift of the crown or Church,) and apply the proceeds to the general fund.

10. Tenants under bishops' leases to be empowered to purchase the perpetuity of their leases at a fixed and moderate rate; subject to a corn rent equal to the amount now paid in the shape of rent and fine.

11. The proceeds of these leases to be paid to the government, *and to be applicable to purposes not connected with the Church.* The amount of all purchases, at a very moderate rate, will be from

2,500,000*l.* to 3,000,000*l.* Such are the leading features of the Plan for the Reform of the Church in Ireland.

(C.) *The Mines and Minerals* in Great Britain are as numerous as they are valuable. The richest are considered to be those of *Coal, Iron, Tin, Copper*, and *Lead:* the latter, especially those of Cumberland, are very productive: the mines of rock salt, at Norwich, and at many other places, and the mines of copper in Wales and Anglesea, are equally productive. Scotland also possesses mines of coal, lead, iron, and other metals. The chief mines in Ireland are iron and copper, and, in common with the other parts of the kingdom, there are mines of other metals, slate, &c., in abundance. The *mines of coal* are certainly worth the full amount at which they are estimated. The Newcastle coal formation alone contains 5,575,680,000 yards, extending in length twenty-three miles. In the opinion of some writers, from twenty-eight to thirty millions of tons, or thirty-three millions of cubic yards, are annually raised: about 1,700,000 chaldrons are annually consumed in London, and the average consumption is estimated by Mr. Perkins, at 1 $\frac{18}{100}$ chaldron per head per annum. The grand total of the number of persons employed in the North-country, and London departments, in the coal trade, according to a statement made by Buddle of Wallsend, (one of the best informed coal engineers,) is 45,500; the persons employed in out-ports and discharging ships not included. The grand total of the number of individuals engaged in the coal trade in all Great Britain, may be set down, says another writer, at from 160,000 to 180,000. The aggregate capital employed on the *Tyne*, as calculated by Buddle, exclusive of the craft on the river, amounts to 1,500,000*l.*: but the total capital employed in the coal trade, allowing a moderate valuation for the ships, &c., may be estimated at from 9,500,000*l.* to 10,500,000*l.*

The *Iron Mines* rank next in importance. The quantities produced in 1827, in the different districts, were ;—

Staffordshire	216,000	tons, produced by	95	furnaces.
Shropshire	78,000	....	31	...
South Wales	272,000	....	90	...
North Wales	24,000	....	12	...
Yorkshire	43,000	....	24	...
Derbyshire	20,500	....	14	...
Scotland	36,500	....	18	...
Total	690,000		284	

and the quantity annually produced at present exceeds 700,000 tons; which at 4*l*. a ton, will be equal to 2,800,000*l*., as is mentioned in the text.

The *Copper* imported into Great Britain, in the year ending 5th January, 1830, including copper ore, amounted to 38,354 cwt.; and the quantity exported, including foreign copper, amounted to 177,018 cwt., and in 1831, there were imported 52,701 cwt., and exported 179,980 cwt., besides the immense quantity consumed at home, to form an idea of which it may be stated, that the value of articles of brass and copper annually made, has been computed at 3,000,000*l*., employing 50,000 persons. Previous to 1793, England was dependent on foreigners for her supply of copper: in 1829, the quantity produced in Cornwall, exceeded 10,000 tons of pure metal; and if to this we add the produce of other parts of England, of Wales, and of Ireland, we may fairly state the quantity produced in the United Kingdom at 13,000 tons; the value of which is about 90*l*. a ton.

Of *Tin* there were imported 2,673 cwt., and exported, of British tin 32,215 cwt., and of foreign tin 2,580 cwt.: in 1832, there were imported 8,099 cwt., and exported of British tin, 21,762 cwt., independent of the very considerable consumption at home.

Of *Lead*, and *lead ore*, there were imported 1708 tons, including 163 tons of lead ore from the Isle of Man; and exported, of British manufacture and ore, 8647 tons, foreign, 1760 tons, besides the home consumption.

(D.) *Canals, Rail-Roads, Tolls, and Timber.* The length of the Turnpike-roads in 1823, was 24,531 miles: annual income 1,214,716*l*.: debt 5,200,000*l*. At present their extent is above 30,000 miles. The total length of the *Canals* in Great Britain in 1823, exclusive of those under five miles, was 2,889 miles: at present it is above 3,000 miles. In 1825, an official summary of eighty corporate canal companies, gives the following result:—

23 companies have expended		....	£3,734,910	producing no dividend yet.		
14 Ditto	......	....	4,073,678	....	£ 92,221	dividend.
22 Ditto	......	....	2,126,000	....	112,400	....
11 Ditto	......	....	2,073,300	....	216,084	....
10 Ditto	......	(div. 20 per cent.)	1,197,230	....	311,554	....
			£13,205,118		£732,259	

being an average dividend of about $5\frac{3}{4}$ per cent. The canals in Scotland are many and important; especially the magnificent canal of the Forth and Clyde, and the Caledonian[a]. In Ireland also, a canal joins Dublin with Limerick and Waterford, and there are others in the neighbourhood of the collieries, &c. Rail-roads, water-works, and docks, are not mentioned in Colquhoun's tables; but the progress in these branches since that time, has been such as would have astonished our ancestors. The rail-roads are at present sixty in number, independent of the important one between Manchester and Liverpool, which alone cost upwards of 900,000*l.* Works of such magnificence can only be compared with their prodigious public utility. The names of 'Meteor' and 'Novelty' will descend to posterity along with those of Stevenson and Ericson, their inventors: the last named engine, which obtained the prise, moved twenty-seven miles within the hour. In another trial, this engine drew eight waggons, weighing twenty-eight tons one hundred weight (precisely seven times its own weight) at the regular average rate of ten miles in one hour thirty-seven minutes and a half[b]. All this is nothing to what has since been performed; they now draw waggons conveying merchandize to the amount of two hundred and thirty tons; and a load of one hundred tons was drawn by one engine from Manchester to Liverpool (thirty miles) in one hour and a half, or at the rate of twenty miles an hour. An eight horse waggon carries eight tons a day; consequently it would

[a] The sum expended on the Caledonian Canal from 1803 to 1832, amounted to 986,924*l.*

[b] There is no exaggeration in this. The engine called the Sampson, in last May, drew fifty waggons laden with goods, making, together with its own weight, a total of 233 tons, from Manchester to Liverpool in two hours and forty minutes. The engine which conveyed Mr. Huskisson to Manchester, after the misfortune which took place on the day of the public trial, moved at the rate of thirty-five miles an hour. The Novelty moved at the rate of thirty-two miles, and at one time when its speed was noted, at the rate of forty miles an hour! The speed of migratory birds in America, according to the statements in Wilson's Ornithology, does not reach the above mentioned rate; and the speed at which the carrier pigeons travelled from London to Brussels, in July 1830, was only thirty-three miles an hour. Notwithstanding all these wonders, we may say that this branch is yet in its infancy. The improvements made since the first trials have not been considerable, on account of the difficulty of trying new experiments on the Manchester railway, and its being almost exclusively confined to one engineer. Should the Directors of the Company become more liberal on this point, improvements may be expected to take place daily. The limits to which this wonderful power can be carried are unbounded, and as the most confident hopes may be entertained that they will be practically extended to a great length—what a wonderful country will England become in half a century!

take 100 horses, working for a day on the turnpike road, to do what a single steam engine can perform in an hour and a half on a rail road. A great saving has also been effected in the consumption of fuel, which has been reduced from 1.63 lb, to one pound of coke per ton per mile. These great undertakings have been commenced, and are proceeding with spirit, at Carlisle, Leicester, and other parts of the kingdom. (See Practical Treatise on Rail-roads, by N. Wood. "Account of Competition of Locomotive Steam Carriages," in the Mechanics' Magazine, October 1829. "Observations on Steam Carriages and Turnpike-roads," by Gurney. Partington's History of Steam Engines. Cumming on Steam Carriages. Lardner on the Steam Engine.) The superiority of a rail road over a canal, is *safety, certainty, economy, and velocity.* Table XIV. affords the means of forming an accurate idea of the capital invested in canals, rail-roads, bridges, docks, water-works, &c., and their value in January 1833: from which the moderation of the estimate in the Table may be inferred.

(E.)—*Dwelling-houses not included in the value of land, including Warehouses and Manufactories, and Machinery.*

According to Colquhoun, the number of dwelling-houses not included in the rent of land, in 1811, in Great Britain, was 2,036,612; but in 1821, it was 2,429,630; and at present the number must be considerably greater. In the metropolis the number of houses has increased one-third in a few years.

In Dublin there were in 1830, of houses from the annual value of 5*l.* to 300*l.* and upwards, 17,324; of the annual value of 704,757*l.*—(Official Account.)

The increase of manufactories and warehouses since 1811 has been considerable. Buildings have been erected on a larger scale, more costly, and some of them magnificent. The progress of machinery has been still greater: in 1818, the number of power looms in Manchester, Stockport, and its vicinity, was 2000; in 1827, it was 45,000; and at present, the number is 70,000. The silk, and several other manufactories, have increased at an equally rapid rate. To give an idea of the value and extent of the machinery employed, the following statement, made by the Editor of the Quarterly Review, in 1826, of the power of machinery applied only to the single manufacture of cotton, is here inserted:—"Supposing only 350,000 men employed in the cotton manufacture: fifty years ago it would have required forty-two millions of men (or fifty-three millions according to some economists) to produce the same result: supposing the labour of these to cost 18*l.*

per annum, it would amount to 756,000,000*l.*; deducting from this sum the pay of the labourers now really employed, at the above annual rate, 280,000 × 18 would give 5,040,000; and allowing fifty millions for the wear and tear of machinery, buildings, &c.—the result is, that the machinery employed in this manufacture saves 700,000,000*l.* to the British nation." The number of men at present employed in this manufacture, is 1,200,000: but supposing it only double the number above stated, the machinery employed in this manufacture alone, would be equal to the power of eighty-four millions of men! (See Sec. XI. Part III.)

(F.)—*Manufactured Goods in progress to maturity, and in a finished state, deposited in Warehouses, Shops, &c., for sale.*

To form an adequate idea of the value of all sorts of goods and merchandise in warehouses, shops, factories, &c., to be there kept for home consumption, it would be necessary to conceive and calculate the immense annual produce of all manufactures in Great Britain.

An approximate estimate of that annual produce is given in the text, to which the reader is referred.

(G.)—*Foreign Merchandise deposited in Warehouses, Shops, &c., either paid for, or virtually paid for, in debts owing to this country by foreign merchants.*

Nothing can convey a better idea of the value of this item than Table IX., exhibiting the value of exports and imports of all kinds of goods and merchandise: it may there be seen, that the official values (which are a criterion of the quantity) have more than doubled since 1812.

(H.)—*British Shipping of every description employed in Trade, including vessels on the stocks, &c.*

An Account of the number of Vessels, with the amount of their Tonnage, built and registered in the several ports of the British Empire, in the years ending the 5th of January:

	1829.		1830.		1831.	
	Vessels.	Tonnage.	Vessels.	Tonnage.	Vessels.	Tonnage.
United Kingdom	842	88,663	718	76,635	730	75,532
Jersey, Guernsey, and Man	15	1,406	16	1,000	20	1,879
British Plantations	466	50,844	416	39,237	289	25,630
Total	1,323	140,913	1,150	116,872	1,039	103,041

J. COVEY, Registrar Gen.
23d March, 1831.

An Account of the number of Vessels, with the amount of their Tonnage and the number of Men and Boys usually employed in the navigation of the same, that belonged to the several ports of the British Empire, on the 31st of December, in the years—

	1828.			1829.		
	Vessels.	Tonnage.	Men.	Vessels.	Tonnage.	Men.
United Kingdom	19,151	2,116,373	131,306	18,618	2,168,356	130,809
Guernsey, Jersey, and Man	495	31,927	3,763	492	31,603	3,707
British Plantations	4,449	324,891	20,507	4,349	317,041	20,292
Total	24,095	2,473,191	155,576	23,459	2,517,000	154,808

	1830.			1831.		
	Vessels.	Tonnage.	Men.	Vessels.	Tonnage.	Men.
United Kingdom	18,675	2,168,916	130,000	18,942	2,190,457	
Guernsey, Jersey, and Man	499	32,676	3,646	506	33,899	
British Plantations	4,549	330,227	21,163	4,794	357,608	
Total	23,723	2,531,819	154,809	24,242	2,581,964	....

An Account of the Tonnage of Vessels in the Coasting Trade, which have entered at, and cleared out from, the Ports of Great Britain, from 1827 to 1831, both inclusive.

Years.	Tonnage entered inwards.	Tonnage cleared outwards.
1827	8,186,004	8,648,868
1828	8,811,109	8,957,286
1829	8,933,633	9,158,525
1830	9,121,619	9,439,099
1831	9,176,758	9,372,870

The following is an Official Abstract of the number of Steam Vessels:

	1829.		1830.		1831.	
	Vessels.	Tons.	Vessels.	Tons.	Vessels.	Tons.
England	241	20,611				
Scotland	75	5,953				
Ireland	26	4,791				
Total	342	31,355				

(I.)—*Agricultural Property, viz. Grain, and all the Productions of Farms, &c., &c., including Implements of Husbandry.*

Eden, in his Observations on Insurance, in 1801, estimates the total agricultural stock of Great Britain, insurable for a year, at 32,500,000*l.*, for the stock on hand of wheat, barley, rye, oats, beans, and straw: but when to these are added, rape, peas, hops, butter, agricultural utensils, &c.; and when it is considered that fifteen millions of quarters of wheat, and twenty-five millions of bushels of malt, are annually consumed in England, (the import of wheat only averaging 500,000 quarters a year,) the estimate of the value of agricultural property will be found very moderate. The agriculture in Ireland has increased so considerably in the last twenty years, according to the report of the Committee of the House of Commons in 1820, that the estimate for that country must also be considered extremely moderate. The exports of corn to England are very large: in 1806, 400,000 quarters of grain of all sorts were exported to England, and in 1830, the quantity had increased to 2,400,000 quarters; and all sorts of agricultural produce in proportion. The Committee were informed, that some of the small dealers, who were formerly turning about 400*l.* a year, can now turn, in the same article, 10,000*l.* Fifty tons weight of eggs, and ten tons of live and dead poultry, are sometimes shipped from Dublin in a single day. One of the witnesses informed the Committee, that in 1824, in eggs alone, a branch of trade entirely new, there were exported from Dublin to the value of 273,000*l.* Cattle are brought from Ballynasloe to Liverpool in little more than three days. Steam has also been applied to the navigation of the river Shannon, with the most important and beneficial consequences to agriculture. In three years the tonnage of the middle Shannon has augmented seven fold. (See Sect. I. Part III.)

(K.)—*Animals, viz. Horses, Horned Cattle, Sheep, Hogs, &c.*

It is difficult to ascertain the number of animals; however the English economists, Luccock and Stevenson, stated, as was supposed with tolerable accuracy, that the number of sheep and lambs in England amounted to 26,148,663, and of horned cattle, to about 11,000,000: a more exact idea may be formed by the fact, that 1,260,000 head of cattle are annually sold in Smithfield market only. In Ireland, the number of all sorts of cattle has increased amazingly. The number of horses cannot be estimated under 1,900,000 [a]: the number of mules is inconsiderable. A breed of crossed zebras has lately been introduced: but it is surprising that

[a] France possesses 2,400,000 horses, but imports annually from 28,000 to 30,000, and has only 6,000 riding horses.

the beautiful breed of asses of Andalusia has been neglected: these are of the same colour as the crossed zebras, but are considerably more useful, being as tall as mules, and possessing, with all the power, greater longevity than common draught horses.

(M.)—*Waste Lands at present unproductive and incapable of improvement adequate to the expense, including Ways and Waters.*

The lands not in a state of cultivation, according to the official statement, (see page 351,) are, in

	Acres.		£
England	3,454,000	which at 15*l.* per acre, as valued by Colquhoun, would be	59,760,000
Wales	530,000		
Scotland	5,950,000	1-5th the value of those of E. and W. ....do.	17,850,000
Ireland	4,900,000	2-5ths ....do. ....do. ....do.	29,400,000
British islands	166,000	1-5th ....do. ....do. ....do.	498,000
			£107,508,000

Such, following the valuation of Colquhoun, would be the value of the waste lands. The increase of thirteen millions made in the table, is therefore a very limited one. There remain nearly sixteen millions of acres called 'unprofitable,' to which no price is given, though they are certainly of no small value. Mr. Nimmo states the waste lands in Ireland to be five millions of acres: however, the number of the unemployed poor is at present as great in proportion as in the time of Sir W. Petty, who states, that in his time the inhabitants were only one million, of whom one-fifth were unemployed.

(O.)—With respect to *Wearing Apparel, Plate, Jewels, and other Ornamental Articles*, it must be observed, that the increase of these articles, particularly of plate, is very considerable; an idea of which may be formed by the following facts. The assay duty on plate during ten years, from 1800 to 1809, has been calculated at an average of 8,420*l.* a year. Now in 1828, according to the statement of Mr. Huskisson in the House of Commons, it amounted to 105,000*l.*, being equal to 88,200*l.*, at the former rate of duty *: consequently, 17,790 lbs. of gold and 1,186,973 lbs. of silver, were manufactured into plate in Great Britain *in one year only*. Huskisson says the duty has risen from less than 5,000*l.* in 1804, to upwards of 105,000*l.* in 1828, or more than twentyfold, notwithstanding the greatly diminished supply from the mines. From such facts it must be inferred, that the annual value of gold and

* The rate of duty upon silver is 1*s.* 6*d.*, and upon gold 17*s.* per ounce.—*Mr. Huskisson's Speech*, ed. 1830.

[illegible]

[illegible]

These establishments, which commenced in [illegible], have conferred considerable benefits on the poor and labouring classes. It has been generally believed and asserted, that the Government countenanced these institutions, not only on account of the beneficial effects to numerous classes of the State, but that these classes becoming interested in the National Debt, might be kept in greater subordination, and under better control. The first object, as may be seen by the progress of Savings' Banks since their establishment to the present day, has been completely realized; but the political object has entirely failed. The numerous labouring and poorer classes, far from becoming more dependent on Government, in consequence of their deposits in Savings' Banks, possess a power capable of paralysing, or even totally upsetting it. Should the ministry propose any grand measure, against the feelings or prejudices of those classes, and should the discontented, the disappointed, the *agitators*, basely act upon those sentiments and prejudices, and prevail on them to withdraw their deposits and call for gold, as is usual on such occasions, the Commissioners would then be compelled to sell stock to answer their demands: this operation would produce the most awful effects on public credit, and a great pressure upon the Bank, which, being incapable of paying one-half of the deposits in Savings' Banks in gold, must stop payment. Nothing is easier than to induce the multitude to call for their money in gold; and no Government could withstand the two-fold calamity of the shock to public credit, and the failure of the Bank. This is no idle theory. When the Reform Bill was thrown out, a specimen of this operation was given, the continuance of which was stopped by the recall of the present ministry.

The interest at present allowed by Government is 3*l.* 8*s.* 5½*d.* per annum.

The total amount of capital in 1829 was	£14,434,921
Do. in 1830	14,366,967
Do. in 1831	14,311,647

SUMMARY OF SAVINGS' BANKS IN ENGLAND, WALES AND IRELAND, 1831.

(*i* signifies increase; *d*, decrease.)

	England.		Wales.		Ireland.		Total for England, Wales, and Ireland.	
Number of Depositors under 20*l.* each	195,093	8,698 *i*	5,186	69 *i*	18,945	1,925 *i*	219,166	10,692 *i*
——— 50*l.* each	102,536	688 *i*	3,234	80 *d*	12,991	2,145 *i*	118,766	2,753 *i*
——— 100*l.* each	47,903	139 *i*	1,296	23 *i*	4,622	300 *i*	53,821	462 *i*
——— 150*l.* each	17.031	150 *d*	384	2 *i*	982	68 *i*	18,397	80 *d*
——— 200*l.* each	7,850	282 *i*	177	25 *i*	293	69 *i*	8,378	375 *i*
——— above 200*l.* each	3,756	455 *d*	97	1 *d*	65	2 *d*	3,918	448 *d*
Total Number of Depositors...............	374,169	9,212 *i*	10,374	39 *i*	37,898	4,505 *i*	422,441	13,754 *i*
——— Friendly Societies......	4,162	71 *i*	167	6 *i*	234	66 *i*	4,563	143 *i*
——— Charitable Societies ...	1,996	216 *i*	53	15 *i*	347	79 *i*	2,396	310 *i*
Total Number of Accounts	380,327	9,499 *i*	10,594	60 *i*	38,479	50 *i*	429,400	14,207 *i*
Total Amount of Investments..............	£12,916,028	3,597 *d*	349,794	4,047 *d*	1,045,825	122,642 *i*	14,311,647	114,998 *i*
Average Amount of each Depositor	£32		£31		£26		£30	

(R.)—Total Amount of the Effects of the Suitors of the Court of Chancery in the following years:—

	£	s.	d.
1819............	32,848,820	13	4
1820............	33,258,897	17	11
1821............	34,693,735	10	10
1822............	35,683,034	5	6
1823............	36,988,481	12	9
1824............	37,635,924	13	0
1826............	38,224,834	18	4
1827............	38,060,055	4	1
1828............	38,266,438	9	10
1829............	38,886,135	19	5

(S.)—*Public Buildings, Churches, Hospitals, &c.*

The Treasury, New London Bridge, Buckingham and Windsor Palaces, &c., the roads and public buildings in Ireland, and above all, the immense number of churches and chapels, have made a very considerable addition to the public property in this item. The commissioners for building and promoting the building of additional churches, stated, in their eleventh annual report, that thirty-four more churches and chapels had been completed since the last report. That on the whole, 168 churches and chapels had been now completed, and therein a total provision made for 231,367 persons, including 128,082 free seats, to be appropriated to the use of the poor: that twenty-seven churches and chapels were building; that plans had been approved for sixteen others: that they had under consideration plans for two chapels; and that they had proposed to make grants in aid of building fourteen churches and chapels. In fine, since opening the commission, that they had determined on, and made provision for, the erection of 227 churches and chapels. That the Exchequer Bills issued to this day (1830) amounted to 1,367,400*l.*

(T.)—*Public Arsenals, Castles, Forts, &c., with the Artillery and Stores thereto belonging.*

All the barracks, the magnificent arsenals, and the fortifications, at Portsmouth, Dover, Plymouth, Sheerness, Chatham, &c. &c., together with those in Scotland, Ireland, &c., are certainly worth more than the sum stated.

(U.)—*Dock-Yards, and all Materials for Ship-Building, &c.*

The sums which are laid out yearly on materials employed in building and repairing ships of war, and in keeping the immense navy of England in such splendid order, are very considerable. The magnificence and value of the Dock-yards is only to be compared with their importance, and the immense sums expended on them.

(W.)—*Ships of War, including those in Commission, in Ordinary, and Building.*

The total number of vessels composing the British navy is 574, viz.—

Vessels.		Guns.
14	carrying	120
5	——	110
3	——	108
12	——	84
9	——	78
62	——	62
7	——	52
15	——	50
62	——	46
20	——	42
365	——	from 36 to 2 guns each, in which number are included 20 Government steam-vessels.
Total 574		

(X.)—*The Military, Naval, Ordnance, and Public Stores* of all kinds in all the arsenals, magazines and store-houses of the United Kingdom, cannot be estimated under the sum stated; and as Colquhoun states, "if it were possible to suppose that these should be annihilated, it would cost three times this sum to replace them." And although ships of war, military, naval, ordnance and public stores are apparently unproductive, they are not so in reality: they are for the defence of the nation, the extension of commerce, the communication with distant colonies, the increase of their wealth, and the protection of the immense British property always floating on the seas.

Many additional particulars and further illustrations of all the above heads will be found in the text.

SECTION III.

Extent and importance of the British Possessions in Europe—in North America—in the West Indies—in Africa—in Australia—in the Indian Ocean,—and in the vast empire of India.

There does not exist the record of a nation ever ruling such a number of inhabitants, possessing such vast territories, having such immense colonies, and commanding such extensive dominions all over the world, as England does at the present time. They encircle the globe, as it were. From Heligoland to Quebec, from this stronghold to the fortified Malta[a], from the impregnable Gibraltar to the important Cape of Good Hope, from the military rock of St. Helena to the rich Ceylon,—scarcely can there be found on the surface of the globe a place, where a warehouse of British goods does not rear its head, and a squadron is not at all times ready to defend British property.

[a] Malta basin is divided into five beautiful harbours, all equally safe, and capable of containing immense fleets and shipping. Its fortifications are a most stupendous work of art. The island is a commercial depôt for all the Mediterranean. (See Brydone's excellent Tour in Sicily and Malta.) Stronger, perhaps, than Malta itself, is Gibraltar; another general deposit for colonial produce, and for British industry and manufactures. This centre of Spanish smuggling has been kept up by the ignorant fiscal system so long pursued and maintained against the Spanish revenue, and the mutual interest of both nations. The advantageous maritime and military position of the Cape of Good Hope, adapts it for another entrepôt of a similar nature; including, besides the productions of Europe and America, those of the East Indies. Sincapore has not been mentioned in the text, but its favourable position constitutes it another entrepôt of the highest importance to the Indian, Chinese, and British trade. Its prosperity has amazingly increased within the last few years, is daily augmenting, and may be expected to continue.

Thus, English capital is spread over all her dominions, and invested in forwarding the productions of her remote and extensive possessions in all parts of the world. It is true that a grand political and economical question is often agitated in respect to these colonies; namely, whether England receives a compensation for the large capital employed in these possessions; or whether she derives any commercial advantages from them, which she might not have without them; and, consequently, whether it would not be much more advantageous to the British interests, revenue, and capital, to emancipate them from her rule [*].

But leaving these vital questions to the able contending parties, and entertaining an equal regard for both, the author cannot but agree with one of them, that from the very day on which the adamantine chain above described, shall either be broken or abandoned to other powers, the mighty England will begin to cease to be the First of Nations; her influence over the commercial world will be diminished; her proud trident will undoubtedly lose the respect it now commands from all nations. But until that day happens, (and, for the happiness of the human race, may it be retarded for ages!) it must be agreed on all hands, that these possessions not only constitute an integral part of Great Britain, but that their value forms an essential portion of the aggregate capital of the British empire.

[*] Sir H. Parnell says, " there are only three ways in which the colonies can be of any advantage; 1. in furnishing a military force; 2. supplying with revenue; 3. in affording commercial advantages." " It is clear", he concludes, " that on the whole, the public derives no commercial advantages from the colonies which it might not have without them:—the Canadas cause an annual charge to the British treasury of 600,000*l*." (Financial Reform, p. 252.)

The immense amount of capital invested in these dominions, may be judged of by the sums employed in forwarding agriculture and commerce in the West Indies: they really are enormous. The annual average trade of these colonies alone, (notwithstanding the lamentable state in which the principal of them is affirmed to be,) for the last three years, exceeded twenty millions! of which the imports of British produce and manufactures were about nine millions; the remainder constituting the exports of their produce! All this results from British capital advanced and invested in them.

The capital invested in the North American colonies is even greater in proportion than in the West Indies; particularly under the head of Fortifications and Public Works and Buildings. The progressive annual increase of emigration to these colonies, furnishes them with an *animate* capital of the highest importance; which, combined with the circulating capital taken out by the emigrants, amounting to at least 200,000 sovereigns a year, constitutes a considerable aggregate of British capital annually invested in these colonies.

The commerce of the African possessions, particularly of the Cape of Good Hope, has also very considerably increased, and is carried on, as well as all the extended cultivation of the interior, with British capital; and if the Emigration Company, lately formed, continue its exertions, wealth and industry may be expected to flow to those colonies, to their great advantage and improvement.

The prosperity of the settlements in the Indian Ocean is evinced by the extraordinary augmentation in the import of colonial produce from Mauritius, which is chiefly raised by British capital.

In the immense country of Australia, which is beginning to figure as a fifth part of the world, the amount of public and private property increases most rapidly, and contributes to augment the wealth of the British empire.

In the Indian empire, a very large amount of British capital has been employed in discovering mines, digging canals, constructing roads, extending and improving agriculture, and augmenting the cultivation of indigo and other produce; increasing the inland navigation, the coasting trade, and the immense amount of shipping required to carry on the commerce of that country. (See the last East India Returns, and the Reports of the Committees on the Affairs of India and China.)

But let us begin by examining the amount of British capital in her dependencies in Europe.

SECTION IV.

BRITISH DEPENDENCIES IN EUROPE.

Capital, Population, Agriculture, Lands, cultivated and uncultivated, Trade, Shipping, Produce annually raised, &c. &c. of the British dependencies in Europe; viz. Isle of Man, Scilly Islands, Guernsey and Jersey, Alderney and Sark, Heligoland, Gibraltar, and Malta.

It is to be observed, that in these possessions, (excepting only one or two,) the increase of population has not only equalled, but even surpassed, that of England herself; consequently, the principle adopted in respect to the augmentation of property and increase of capital, must operate in a similar manner. The first six dependencies, in the ten years from 1811 to 1821, increased in population thirty-four per cent.; and from the last mentioned year to the present time, the progress has not ceased. The increase of employment, and consequent creation of produce and capital; the cultivation, circulating specie, shipping, public and private property, &c.; must all have increased at a proportionate rate: the total aggregate value of these, is estimated at 27,115,094*l.*; and the value of the produce annually raised, at 2,146,998*l.* The reader is referred to the subjoined Table and explanatory notes for the details, and for further statistical particulars.

The Seven Ionian Islands have not been numbered among the dependencies in Europe; for it must be remembered, that although they may be considered, to all intents and purposes, as English dependencies, yet this republic, entitled "The United States of the Ionian Islands", with a surface of 4,712 German miles, and 208,100 inhabitants, is an independent State, solemnly placed under the protection of the "King of Great Britain and Ireland, his heirs and successors," by the European Powers.

EXPLANATORY NOTES TO THE TABLE.

(A.)—Nearly two-thirds of the land, in the Isle of Man, is in a state of cultivation. The productions are, potatoes, grain, and flax for the manufactures consumed in the island and exported. The fisheries are considerable; immense quantities of herrings are exported.

(B.)—The Scilly Islands are only partially inhabited; but more than 2000 acres of land are in a state of cultivation. Sheep and rabbits are produced in abundance; also poultry, vegetables, &c.

(C.)—Guernsey is a beautiful spot; nearly the whole island is in a high state of cultivation. Cattle, butter, cheese, and especially vegetables, fruit, and poultry, are produced in great abundance. There is a fort adjoining the town of St. Pierre. A considerable number of ships are employed in trading to and from this island. The returns of its population were not made in 1831.

(D.)—Nearly the whole of the land in Jersey is in cultivation. The productions are the same, and equally abundant, as those of Guernsey: a considerable quantity of knit hose is made and exported; and the island carries on a good trade. The fortifications in Jersey are, Elizabeth Castle, almost impregnable, occupying nearly a mile in circuit, and Fort St. Aubyn, also well fortified.

	Houses.			Families chiefly employed in agriculture.	Families employed in manufactures or handicraft.	All other families.
	Inhabited.	Building.	Uninhabited.			
Guernsey	3,083	21	107	1,676	2,175	447
Jersey ...	4,053	28	41	2,310	2,756	747
Man	6,627	49	207	3,520	2,864	1,474
	13,763	98	355	7,506	7,795	2,668

(E.)—Alderney and Sark. The soil of these islands is similar to that of Jersey and Guernsey, of which they are dependencies. The climate of all these islands is considered remarkably salubrious.

(F.)—There is no land at Gibraltar, except what the houses and buildings stand upon, and some little laid out in gardens and pasturage. The inhabitants chiefly depend on the neighbouring States for the means of subsistence; only raising a little fruit and poultry. The extensive fortifications, upon which immense sums have been laid out, are considered impregnable.

To face page 374.]

ESTIM|ES IN EUROPE.

Comprising the Populatio|s and Imports, Circulating Specie; and an Estimate o|h Empire:—from Authentic Documents and the latest |

	'alue into ing.	Tonnage to and from the United Kingdom. Inwards. Tons.	Outwards. Tons.
Isle of Man			
Scilly Islands			
Guernsey		33,899	33,899
Jersey			
Alderney			
Sark			
Gibraltar	5	1,795	10,426
Malta including Goza	9	2,034	7,906
Heligoland		......	......
Totals	/4	37,728	52,231

	'alue ng.	Estimated Circulating Specie.	Total.
		£	£
Isle of Man	30	6,666	4,732,732
Scilly Islands	)0	666	146,332
Guernsey	56	40,000	3,503,131
Jersey	40	53,333	3,520,038
Alderney		2,666	368,199
Sark		800	246,666
Gibraltar	00	133,333	5,889,999
Malta including Goza	33	266,666	8,659,998
Heligoland	66	1,333	47,999
Totals	05	505,463	27,115,094

AGGREGATE VAL|PROPERTY.

DEPENDE|s, Arsenals, Artillery, and
.... £7,300,000

Isle of Man .... | PROPERTY.
Scilly Islands .... |
Guernsey .... |ltivated £8,154,132
Jersey .... |ultivated........ 341,332
Alderney ....
Sark 8,495,464
Gibraltar .... |ck, and Agricul-
Malta including Goza .. |.............. 424,664
Heligoland............ |s, Merchandise,
.... 9,851,198
ng 438,305
.... 505,463
19,815,094

|and Total.............. £27,115,094

(G.)—Boisgellin, in his History of Malta, states, that the land produces cotton of an excellent quality, vegetables, and fruits, particularly oranges, and some grain, but not enough for the inhabitants. Little more than half the island is cultivated, the rest being rocky and barren. The fortifications at La Valetta are a most stupendous work; the place is so strongly fortified by nature and art, as to be deemed impregnable: the great number of cannon, the arsenals, barracks, municipal buildings, as the palace of the Grand Master, the hotels of the Seven Tongues, &c., must have cost immense sums. Goza has a more fertile soil than Malta. The houses in the latter are built of stone, and the island is almost covered with houses and villages.

(H.)—The population of Heligoland principally subsist from their fisheries. There is a light-house on the island built by Hamburgh, and since repaired by the British Government: many buildings were erected during the war, for the reception of merchandize, &c.

SECTION V.

NORTH AMERICAN COLONIES.

Capital, Population, Trade, Shipping, Fisheries, Public Works, Canals, Coal Mines, Lands cultivated and uncultivated.—Property annually created.—Military and Maritime Importance, &c. &c. of the British North American Colonies, viz., Upper and Lower Canada.—New Brunswick.—Nova Scotia.—Cape Breton.—Prince Edward's Island.—Hudson's Bay; and Newfoundland.—Discovery of North America.—French administration of their North American Colonies.—Their progress and state under British dominion, &c.

THE avarice of Henry VII., combined with the enterprising spirit of an Italian, led to the discovery of Newfoundland. In 1497, only five years after the great Columbus had reached America, Cabot with his companions explored the coasts of Canada, and entered the Gulph of St. Lawrence, but without taking possession of that region. Henry was more intent on the usurious interest obtained for the money lent for these expeditions, than on the extension of his dominion in the New World. The adventurous spirit of the discoverers was communicated to the inhabitants of the French coasts: in 1506, a party from Harfleur, and in 1508, Hubert from Dieppe, made voyages to Newfoundland, and even sailed up the river St. Lawrence. The Spaniards and Portuguese, who had repeatedly visited those latitudes, struck with the foggy and dismal appearance of the coasts, thought the country not worth their attention, and good for nothing; and from their exclamation, "Que Nada!"* arose the name of Canada, which was changed to "Nouvelle France" by Veresany, when, in 1522, he took possession of it in the name of his sovereign, Francis I. Thirteen years after this event, the brave Cartier of St. Malo sailed up the St. Lawrence,

* Good for nothing.

founded several villages, formed alliances with the natives, and took their king Donnaconna to France; but as neither gold nor silver accompanied the prisoner chief, Cartier was badly received by a corrupt court, and in 1543, overcome with affliction and disappointment, died of a broken heart: a just punishment for his cruelty and infamous conduct towards the natives. He was succeeded by Lord Roberval, who quitted France for Canada, accompanied by his brothers and a crowd of adventurers; but no account has ever been heard of what became of them. In 1598, the Marquis de la Roche was appointed viceroy of Canada by Henry IV., and another new marquis was created in the person of Chauvin, who, after the death of the former, occasioned by affliction, remorse, and vexation, travelled to Tadoussac, established the fur trade, and explored the three rivers. To Chauvin succeeded De Monts, whose principal associates were Champlain and Chatte: they received, along with the territory, the power to colonize, and to kill or convert to Christianity the natives. The restless Champlain amply acquitted himself in the extermination of the natives; but, in compensation, founded Quebec, the capital of Canada (1608). However, this active and clever man was at last compelled to surrender the affairs of Canada into the hands of a company of merchants, belonging to Rouen, St. Malo, and Rochelle (1614). The Prince of Condé transferred his authority and command to the Marechal de Montmorenci, who delegated it to his imbecile nephew, the Duke of Ventadour (1623). Under his administration, the disorder, distress, and misgovernment of the colony arrived at such a pitch, that the mere appearance of an English officer before Quebec was enough: that place and its garrison surrendered to Kirk, 130 years before the famous Wolfe lost his life in achieving a similar exploit; and Champlain and the greater part of the Jesuits were embarked and packed off for France, by the conquering general of Charles I. (1629). Three years afterwards, this monarch, by the treaty of St. Germains, ceded the conquest of his brave subjects to Louis XIII.; and Champlain, the historian, traveller, mathematician, merchant, soldier, and seaman, was justly invested with the viceroyalty of the Canadas. Montmagny succeeded this talented viceroy, but was recalled on account of his misgovernment: after him came D'Aillebout, Lauzon (1650), Marquis d' Argenson, and Baron d' Avengour; but none of these governors forwarded the interests of the colony. In 1663, on the arrival of Mesy at Quebec, a new form of government was instituted, by the creation of a sovereign council composed of seven members, amongst whom were the governor, the bishop, and the intendant. They had power to take cognizance of all causes and offences, both criminal and civil, and to decide definitively on them, in conformity to the ordinances of France, and the practice of the parliament of Paris.

However, in the next year, Canada, with all its council and new institutions, was, without any ceremony, transferred by Louis XIV., like a bale of goods, to the merchants of the West India company. This mercantile corporation, convinced that population constitutes the riches of colonies as well as states, in 1668, recruited not only as many respectable women as they could, but sent out above 300 prostitutes, who were well received, and distributed amongst the Canadians: and, to encourage population, a pension was granted to every individual who had more than ten children. However, notwithstanding all these encouragements, the population of Canada in 1685, was only 10,000, of whom

3000 were capable of bearing arms: an evident proof of the mal-administration of Courcelles, Frontenac, La Barre, and the Marquis de Vaudreuil. The War of Succession in Spain, carried bloodshed and devastation to the inhabitants of Haverhill, and to the frontiers of Canada; but peace at length put an end to these butcheries; a division of territory took place, and proper limits were assigned to the districts and parishes. Beauharnois, the bastard of Louis XIV., distinguished his administration by the erection of new forts, (particularly the important one called Crown Point, 1731,) and by establishing a regular military line, rather than by promoting agriculture, industry, and commerce. The progress of these branches was very slow: the "Code Marchand" of France was never introduced into Canada. Jonquieres chiefly occupied himself in fixing the line of demarcation between the French and English territories; while the infamous intendant, Bigot, was destroying the resources of the government, and the prosperity of the people, by an unparalleled system of plunder; creating that discontent, internal weakness, and discord, which eventually occasioned the loss of Canada. This abominable robber, whose peculations reached 400,000*l.*, and whose dishonoured bills amounted to 4,000,000*l.* sterling, pursued his nefarious career of iniquity and fraud, under the influence of the profligate Marquis de Montcalm; who, aiding and commanding in person the savage Indians, showed his military talent by the capture of Fort George, and the pitiless massacre of 2000 of its inhabitants (1757). The sons and descendants of the Jesuits and the clergy (who hated Protestants even worse than Mahomedans) now united in preaching extermination against the English; and every sort of contrivance and superstition was used, to encourage them to defend their religion against the heretics. Montcalm was at the head of one of the largest armies ever seen in Canada, and military operations were prosecuted on a scale never before witnessed in that country. The English plan of campaign was, to attack the province on three points: General Amherst to attack Crown Point and Ticonderoga; Johnson to force Fort Niagara to surrender; and Wolfe to attack Quebec on the side next the sea; the armies to effect a junction at Montreal. The fate of Canada depended on the execution of this plan. Wolfe landed on the Island of Orleans with 8000 men, but Montcalm, commanding a superior force, opposed him with the greatest success. Wolfe was repulsed at the entrenchments of Montmorenci; and in England, it was thought he was ruined. But he suddenly changed his position, landing on the plains of Abraham, with great secrecy (12th Sept. 1759); where, however, he found the precipitate Montcalm opposed to him. The invading army displayed coolness, courage, and skilful evolutions; while the impetuous French attacked it with vigour and intrepidity. Montcalm and Wolfe led their respective columns to the attack, and both fell, the one in the arms of defeat, the other in those of victory. To this terrible battle succeeded the capitulation of Quebec, and the conquest of Canada: the French totally lost their North American colonies (1762).

The little progress made by them in agriculture, commerce, civilization, and population, may be gathered from the fact, that in 1714, when they had been in possession of the French for 216 years, the whole population, according to the memoirs of Chartrain, only amounted to 27,000 souls: and in 1783, twenty years after the English conquered them, and 261 years after their first possession by the French, the total population had only reached 113,000. Those French writers who are so fond of inveighing against the colonial policy of other nations, and of pointing out their slow progress in civilization and commerce, might certainly include in their invectives the policy of their own. The long catalogue of princes, dukes, marquises, counts, and barons, who ruled the Canadas during two centuries and a half, did little or nothing towards advancing their prosperity and importance.

Let us examine the state of these colonies under better government. The "Quebec Act," passed in 1774, and properly called the "Blunder Act," which placed the Canadas in a situation entirely French, and totally different from any British colony, was revoked in 1790; and by the act called "Constitutional," they were put in possession of those great advantages and enlightened institutions, which are the foundation of their prosperity. The province of Quebec was divided into two, each having its legislature or parliament, composed of a governor, legislative council, and house of assembly. The first parliament of Lower Canada, consisting of thirty-nine knights, eight citizens, and three burgesses, was opened in 1792, and Panet was chosen speaker. The progress, prosperity, and importance of these colonies have continued uninterruptedly ever since. The Berlin and Milan decrees gave a great impulse to their agriculture and commerce. In 1812, while England was deeply engaged in European wars, the United States thought it a good opportunity to attack them; but their power had become so consolidated, and their attachment to England so sincere, that in a very short time, the legislature, directed by

Panet, (who for the seventh time was speaker,) enrolled the militia, raised battalions, and mustered such a strong force as to be capable, not only of resisting the powerful armies of the United States at the first onset, but of making prisoners the rash General Hull and his whole army, who had dared to cross the frontier and violate the territory of Upper Canada.

This unfortunate and useless war, which was in reality against the true interests of both the great mercantile nations engaged in it, was carried on with various success. However, during its whole course, the most convincing proofs were afforded of the value and importance of these possessions to the British empire; whether they are considered in regard to their geographical, maritime, military, and political situation: or in respect to their immense extent of land [a], the safety and grandeur of their harbours, the wide seas by which they are surrounded, the immense lakes and great rivers by which they are intersected, and their valuable fisheries, known to be the best in the world.

The truth of the principle already insisted on, of the relative increase of population and capital, has been most fully demonstrated by these provinces. Their prosperity has increased, since the peace, beyond the most sanguine expectations. Their population, which at present exceeds a million, has doubled since 1811; while the extent of new lands brought into cultivation has *trebled*. Commerce has increased at a like rate: the annual average of shipping engaged in their trade, for the last three years, has exceeded 400,000 tons, employing 21,000 seamen: the annual consumption of

[a] The measured lands, cultivated and uncultivated, are about 145,000,000 of acres. See also, Bannister on Emigration to Upper Canada.

British manufactures has been above 2,000,000*l.*, and their exports have been not less considerable. And while private property has increased beyond all expectation, public property has kept pace with it. All public works have been carried on with the greatest spirit and expense. We learn from the Report of the Committee of Finance, "that a plan for fortifying Canada has been in progress two or three years, which is to cost 3,000,000*l.*"[a] Large sums have also been expended in roads and public establishments.

But the most important of all these works are the canals; promoting the interior navigation by forming a communication between the immense lakes or inland seas of Erie and Ontario; and opening a water communication between Montreal and Kingston by the Rideau and Ottawa rivers: the latter has cost already above 400,000*l.*, and the expense will greatly exceed half a million[b]. Never have such large sums been applied to better purpose: an amazing interior navigation of thousands of miles has been the result[c]. England, the most generous of all nations towards her colonies, in the large advances she makes, and the capital she expends in forwarding their prosperity, has exceeded, in regard to her northern colonies, all her former bounties. About 40,000,000*l.* may be stated as the sum already invested in these possessions[d].

[a] Sir H. Parnell on Financial Reform, p. 256.

[b] On the 31st of December, 1829, 349,262*l.* were already expended: the total estimated expense was 576,757*l.* (Ord. Office, 26th March, 1830. Byham.)

[c] M'Gregor, "British North America." Bouchette, "Dictionary of Lower Canada and British Dominions in North America."

[d] Sir Henry Parnell calculates it at from 50,000,000*l.* to 60,000,000*l.*:—rather too high. Lord Sheffield said, that by the war of 1739, was incurred a debt of 31,000,000*l.*; by that of

Nova Scotia, Newfoundland, and New Brunswick, have improved almost in the same ratio as the Canadas[a]; and the rich mines of coal at Cape Breton have lately given the highest importance to these possessions. The introduction of this article into the United States, its cheapness, the advantage of smaller bulk, and its immense and daily increasing consumption, will in time render that settlement one of the most profitable, important, and productive, of our North American colonies.

Calculating the increase of capital in proportion to the increase of population, according to the rule laid down, the capital of these colonies would amount to treble what it was in 1811; but taking into consideration the principle of compensation[b] (already alluded to), and following the basis adopted in the other parts of the

1755, a further debt of 71,500,000*l.*, and by the war of revolt, we have added to both these debts 100,000,000*l.* more. (On Commerce of American States, p. 240.) It has been stated, that the Canadas and West Indies cost us, in military and naval outlays, upwards of a million and a half in time of peace, exclusive of the revenue collected in them.

[a] "Account of the Provinces of New Brunswick", by Baillie.

[b] No addition whatever has been made to the estimates of the fisheries, as they are considered to have been rated too high in 1811. It is even thought that above a million might fairly be taken from that amount, and divided amongst other items, particularly public property, and canals, &c. Barrow, in his valuable article on Fisheries, in the Encyclopædia Britannica, has estimated the total value of the produce of the foreign and domestic fisheries of Great Britain at 8,300,000*l.*, which is considered by several writers as rather high. It must also be taken into consideration, that the British have no right to fish on the west coast of Newfoundland, in consequence of a treaty with France in 1816, and the convention of 1818. (Vide Chitty, Laws of Commerce, &c.) France, in 1829, employed 300 vessels, and 25,000 sea-going fishermen, according to M'Gregor's "British America."

British empire, the aggregate capital of all our North American colonies, including all public and private property, is estimated at 62,100,466*l.*; and the property annually created, at 17,620,629*l.* The details, and further information, will be found in the subjoined Table, and explanatory notes.

From this may be inferred how injudicious and ungrateful are the proceedings of that Canadian party, calling themselves "*Enfans du Sol*", who direct their impotent exertions to obstruct the course of the benefits and prosperity, which are continually flowing from England into their country. To act against the progress and tide of emigration to a country of such immense extent, and in such want of inhabitants, to impose a tax upon emigrants, to oppose the introduction of capital and industry into a country which has the greatest need of both, is certainly most unpatriotic, and even highly ridiculous. It is truly the proceeding of "enfans", and for which they deserve to be treated, by a fatherly government, like children who do not know what is good for them. The union of the legislatures will be the radical remedy for such folly. But in spite of all this, the number of settlers who had arrived at Quebec in the year 1832 up to the 15th of October, was 49,281; and the number of vessels 915, measuring 273,813 tons, or 27,932 tons more than in 1831: while in the same year, upwards of 300,000 *sovereigns!* were deposited in the Canadian banks, chiefly by emigrants, according to a letter from one of the most respectable men in Canada, a friend of the author.

EXPLANATORY NOTES TO THE TABLE.

(A.)—The territory of Canada is immense: the number of uncultivated acres capable of cultivation is almost infinite. Twenty-seven millions of acres are occupied or granted according to the last demi-official statement, besides twenty-three millions belonging to the Crown, and as many more to private proprietors. (Vide Banister and Richards.) The productions are timber, wheat, apples, &c., and they raise cattle, sheep, hogs, poultry, vegetables, &c. The consumption, on a medium of years, may be estimated at 19*l.* per head, which would give an amount of 11,628,000*l.* as the value of produce consumed; to which ought to be added the surplus exported. This shews the moderation of the estimate in the Table. The large sums expended on public property, particularly on the canal of the Ottawa river, and on fortifications, have been already noticed.

(B.)—The number of acres uncultivated and capable of cultivation, in New Brunswick, is very great. Timber is the principal production; the others are almost the same as those of Canada. The annual average consumption being estimated at 19*l.* per individual, the total would amount to 1,379,708*l.* The capital of all its fisheries was estimated in 1811 at 1,000,000*l.*; there being at that time 500 small vessels in the different harbours, ports, &c.

(C.)—There are above 160,000 acres of land in cultivation in Nova Scotia. The productions are timber, grain, cattle, poultry, &c., in great abundance. The consumption, estimated at 19*l.* a year for each person, on a medium of years, would amount to 2,708,372*l.*; besides the exports. The fisheries are very valuable: in 1764, the value of the fish taken amounted to 47,610*l.*; in 1810, no less than 328 vessels, measuring 42,222 tons, and navigated by 3,282 seamen, were employed, exclusive of small craft; and 20,000 cwt. of fish were exported to Jamaica alone.

(D.)—In Cape Breton, the cultivated lands are above 90,000 acres. The best and staple production is coal, the mines of which have become very important, and in time will constitute the riches of the country, in consequence of the increasing consumption of this article in the United States.

(E.)—The situation of Prince Edward's Island is very important to Great Britain, both in regard to its fisheries, and to the maritime power of England in America. The cultivated lands are proportionately small in extent. The capital of the fisheries was esti-

To face page 386.]

ESTIMATE and GENERAL ...ture, Cession or Settlement, how they are governed, Population, Number o... Shipping, Circulating Specie, and an Estimate of the Amount of Public ...ire. From Authentic Documents, and the latest Authorities. (1833.)

	...stimated value of Productions ...ised annually, including Fisheries.	Imports into the United Kingdom. Official Value.	Exports from the United Kingdom. Official Value.	Tonnage to and from the United Kingdom. Inwards.	Tonnage to and from the United Kingdom. Outwards.
	£.	1829 £.	1829 £.	Tons.	Tons.
Lower and Upper Canada	9,737,102	569,451	1,117,421	227,909	221,694
New Brunswick	2,551,982				
Nova Scotia	3,476,440	213,842	274,922	155,249	133,469
Cape Breton	92,402	61,701	297,966	30,146	31,738
Prince Edward's Island	288,578				
Newfoundland	1,420,792	243,628	373,817	17,820	31,246
Hudson's Bay	53,333	52,666	53,333		
	...17,620,629	1,141,288	2,118,459	431,124	418,147

...PERTY.

	...mated Value of the ...isheries.	Estimated Value of Colonial Vessels, Ships building, &c.	Estimated Circulating Specie.	TOTAL.
	£.	£.	£.	£.
Canada, Upper and Lowe...	......	191,146	400,000	32,617,811
New Brunswick	...,000,000	66,666	66,666	6,476,663
Nova Scotia	...,000,000	86,666	266,666	13,337,332
Cape Breton	50,000	6,666	13,333	641,331
St. John's or Prince Edw...	500,000	6,666	26,666	1,196,664
Newfoundland	...,000,000	333,333	66,666	7,630,665
Hudson's Bay	......	......	......	200,000
	...,550,000	691,143	839,997	62,100,466

AGGREGATE V...

Canada, Upper and Lower
New Brunswick
Nova Scotia
Cape Breton
St. John's or Prince Edward'...
Newfoundland
Hudson's Bay

PUBLIC PROPERTY.

... of Forts, Barracks, Arsenals, Artillery, and all ...ngs		£ 2,933,331

PRIVATE PROPERTY.

... of Lands, viz. cultivated	£21,960,000	
uncultivated	4,506,665	
	26,466,665	
... of Buildings, Stock, and Agricul... on Farms	8,787,999	
...e of Houses, Stores, Merchandise, ..., in the Towns	14,831,331	
...e of the Fisheries	7,550,000	
...onial Vessels, Ships building, &c.	691,143	
...lating Specie	839,997	59,167,135
	£	62,100,466

mated, in 1811, at half a million; and the value of the island at 1,022,500*l.*

(F.)—The imports into Newfoundland, average of the years 1829-30-31, were	£241,444
British manufactures	550,000
Total	£791,444

The average annual produce:—

Cod fish, 600,000 quintals, at 10*s.*	£300,000
Do. oil, 3,000 tuns at 18*l.*	54,000
Seal oil, 5,000 do. at 20*l.*	100,000
Seal skins, 400,000, at 1*s.*	20,000
Salmon, furs, &c.	20,000
	£494,000
Value of produce from Labrador exported direct, and from Newfoundland and Nova Scotia	278,400
Present annual value of Newfoundland and Labrador fisheries	£772,400

Entries and clearances of vessels, 1831:—

Great Britain	298
Foreign	193
British America	182
West Indies	72
United States	8
Total number of vessels	753

In the carrying trade to and from Newfoundland, 400 vessels are employed, measuring 50,000 tons; two-thirds of which are English, the rest colonial. ("British America", by M'Gregor.)

(G.)—The Hudson's Bay Company, in 1712, had four factories, valued at 108,514*l.* 19*s.* 8*d.*, and their capital was 100,000*l.*; it has since decreased, and in 1812 all their property was estimated at 150,000*l.* Their forts have been stated to be absolutely necessary for the protection of their business and people. The affairs of this Company do not appear to have improved; but the Directors have generously contributed both money and means towards the projected expedition for the relief of the courageous but unfortunate Captain Ross.

The

[illegible] income of all these colonies is...... £[illegible]

[illegible] expenditure .... [illegible]

		Income.	Expen[illegible]
[illegible]	1823	£24,944	£[illegible]
[illegible]	ditto	93,[illegible]	[illegible]
[illegible]	1826	39,709	6[illegible]
[illegible]	ditto	25,772	[illegible]
[illegible]	ditto	49,605	51[illegible]
[illegible]	ditto	12,514	12[illegible]
		£246,321	£[illegible]

[illegible] as follows:—

		Imports into.	Exports fro[illegible]
[illegible]	[illegible]	£250,500	£113,[illegible]
[illegible]	[illegible]	22,184	94,[illegible]
[illegible]	[illegible]	660,600	455,[illegible]
[illegible]	[illegible]	852,600	487,[illegible]
[illegible]	[illegible]	335,630	141,390
[illegible]			
		£2,121,464	£1,293,17[illegible]

[illegible]

	Exports to.	Imports from.
[illegible]	[illegible] 288	£2,118,459
[illegible]	[illegible].156	2,226,639
[illegible]	[illegible]	£4,345,098

[illegible] documents.

[illegible] as reported by his Majesty's [illegible] at Quebec:—

	[illegible]	[illegible]	[illegible]	[illegible]
England and Wales	[illegible]	[illegible]	1,048	17,481
Ireland	[illegible]	[illegible]	34,[illegible]	36,304
Scotland	[illegible]	[illegible]	5,354	5,500
Nova Scotia and New Brunswick	[illegible]	[illegible]	424	546
Other places				15
Total	[illegible]	[illegible]	[illegible]	[illegible]
Grand Total				136,[illegible]

SECTION VI.

WEST INDIA COLONIES.

Capital.—Population.—Agriculture.—Lands, cultivated and uncultivated.—Sugar and Rum Manufactories.—Produce annually raised.—Shipping.—Commerce.—Circulating Specie.—Public Works and Buildings, &c., &c. of the British West India Colonies; and importance of these Possessions.

These rich and magnificent possessions are nineteen in number; and when their importance in the balance of the world, their extension and improved cultivation, and their productiveness, embracing not only their indigenous, but even European and Asiatic productions, are considered; when the mercantile and commanding maritime positions they occupy, and the immense amount of blood and treasure expended in their preservation, are contemplated; and when the vast capital heretofore employed, and actually invested, in forwarding their prosperity, is calculated; *the fact*, that their prosperity has not increased in proportion to the other parts of the British dominions, exhibits a most extraordinary phenomenon. But when one reflects, that the evils, the distresses, and the complaints of these colonies, have now been *clamoured*, as it were, for more than half a century; and that they have been the subject of almost perpetual legislative inquiry: when one sees the ablest men in the nation, whose information is equal to their powers of reasoning, exerting and torturing themselves to discover the causes of the complaints and distresses, and of the unprogressive state of these colonies, while the causes of those evils and of that state, are so clear, so evident, so unquestionable; one must be quite convinced, that a fatality attends the great concerns of nations.

An honourable and patriotic writer, many years ago, pointed out in the most express language, the origin of the perpetual evils which are even now a subject of controversy. "The present restraining system" (says Edwards) "in forbidding men to help each other, who, by their necessities, their climate, and their productions, are standing in perpetual need of mutual assistance, and able to supply it, is the cause," &c.[a]. Pitt perceived the necessity of changing that ruinous system, and introduced a Bill on that momentous subject, but his mighty power was split, not on the rock, but on the moving waves, of the ship owners and rotten timber merchants[b]. Huskisson was not more successful. The liberal modifications introduced by him in the restrictive system, are a complete mockery; some of them are as though Parliament should compel the manufacturers and agriculturists of this country to provide themselves with raw materials from the Cape of Good Hope, while they could have the same articles cheaper and better from the Bay of Biscay. Those restrictions however have been considerably modified[c]. (Table I. at the end of this Section.)

[a] Edwards's History of the West Indies, alluding to the restrictions on the intercourse with the United States.

[b] It was stated by one of the Commissioners of the Navy before the Committee of the House of Lords, that the timber of Canada, both oak and fir, does not possess, for the purpose of ship-building, more than half the durability of wood of the same description, the produce of the north of Europe.

[c] Great praise is due to Act Will. IV., c. 4., passed in 1831, amending the previous Acts regulating the trade to the British possessions in America; by which the duties upon wheat, pork, provisions, lumber, &c., brought from the British North American colonies, are repealed; but in the same Act, temporary additional duties are charged upon the importation, from any foreign country, of staves, headings, lumber, &c.

Had not the remedy for such momentous evils been connected with the plan of this work, this digression would have been unnecessary. The discussion of the salutary remedies to be applied, tending to the general happiness of the empire, and the prosperity of these unfortunate colonies, are reserved for a fitter place. To the perpetually discontented and lamenting party, who, in a hypocritical tone, but with the most boundless confidence, incessantly affirm, "that these colonies are completely ruined", and "that their wealth and capital, far from having increased, have decreased amazingly" since 1811, it may be replied, that this assertion is in utter contradiction to the plainest facts.

The quantities of the staple articles of these colonies, sugar, rum, and coffee, have considerably augmented. The quantity of the first, imported in the years 1828, 1829, 1830, evinces an annual increase of 1,228,033 cwt., compared with the years 1810, 1811, 1812; exclusive of the immense consumption of the colonies, and of the exportation to other parts of the world; and in spite of the competition with the sugars from the Mauritius and the East Indies. (Table II. of this Section.)

In 1811, the total produce of rum in these nineteen colonies, amounted to 2,539,100 gallons; but in April, 1831, the rum imported into England from the said settlements reached 6,812,873 gallons, according to the official returns; or 4,273,777 gallons more than in 1811. The importation of coffee into Great Britain, which in 1812 was 5,679,000 lbs., amounted, in 1829, to above 19,000,000 lbs., and in 1831 to 27,429,144 lbs. The assembly of Jamaica declared, above twenty years ago, that the capital invested in coffee plantations was 20,000,000*l.* What that capital must now be, and what must be the increase of cultivation, where the produce has so considerably augmented, the reader is left to determine. The average annual income of these colonies may be stated at about 700,000*l.*, and the expenditure at about 660,000*l.* In 1826, the former amounted to 666,765*l.* and the latter to 610,537*l.* According to the account presented to the Select Committee of the House of Lords, the annual value of the produce of these colonies amounted to 22,496,672*l.* (Table III.) The population has increased, though not nearly so much as in the other parts of the empire; but the exports and imports, the shipping, commerce, amount of specie, &c., have considerably exceeded the increase of numbers. The immense sum of 140,000,000*l.*! is supposed to be at present invested in our West India possessions; this enormous capital belongs to the planters, merchants, mortgagees, and shipowners, connected with these colonies[a].

An addition might be made to the capital of these colonies, as estimated in 1811, on the most authentic and unquestionable data, according to the scale elsewhere adopted; at least it might safely be estimated at one-fifth more: but in order to ensure moderation, it is left as stated at that time. The whole aggregate value of the private and public property of all our West India colonies, was then estimated at 131,052,424*l.*, and the annual average of their produce at 22,496,672*l.*

The Tables shew the last official returns of imports and exports, trade, agriculture, population, &c. The great disproportion in the numbers of the black and white inhabitants, and their relative condition, must

[a] See the papers laid before the Finance Committee, printed by order, &c., in 1828; and the statements, calculations, and explanations, submitted to the Board of Trade, printed by order, &c., 1831. The sum has been elsewhere stated at 160,000,000*l.*

excite the most serious reflections in every thinking mind [a]. To allay the bitterness of feeling, and moderate the measures of the contending parties, on the important question of slavery, calls for the unremitting exertions of parliament. All the combined wisdom of the legislature is required to enable them to steer between the equally dangerous and difficult rocks—the zealous philanthropy and canting ignorance of one party, and the self-interest and prejudices of the other. The Table annexed, and Explanatory Notes, will furnish some useful information towards the discussion of these important and vital questions.

[a] "Practical View of the present State of Slavery in the West Indies"; also, "Effects of the late Colonial Policy of Great Britain," by Barclay. These works being of a practical kind, are entitled to more attention than those which are speculative. "A short View of the West India Question," by Franklyn,—author of the "Present State of Hayti." Ferrall's "Rambles through America." "In the agricultural states," says this writer, "slave labour is found to be quite unproductive, which causes this market (New Orleans) to be inundated: within the last two months, 5,000 negroes have been sold here. The state legislature has just passed a law regulating the introduction of slaves, and commanding all free people of colour, who were not residents previous to 1825, to quit Louisiana. Georgia has enacted a law to the same effect, with the addition of making it penal to teach people of colour to read or write! It is an occurrence of no uncommon nature to see here the Christian father sell his own daughter, and the brother his own sister by the same father: negresses, when young, are often employed as wet nurses by the white people, as also by either the planter or his friends to administer to their sensual desires;—and this frequently as a matter of speculation; for if the offspring, a mulatto, be a handsome female, from 800 to 1,000 dollars may be obtained for her in the Orleans market."

TABLE I.

Recapitulation of Restrictions on the Trade of the West India Islands.

From the Papers submitted to the Board of Trade, and ordered by the House of Commons to be printed, 1831.

Fish:—		
From Newfoundland, enhancement of cost	£75,544	
From Great Britain, ditto	68,666	
American Supplies:—		
Enhancement of cost	86,677	
——— in freight	94,803	
Restrictions and disadvantages in sale	187,576	
Total enhancement in the cost of American or Trans-atlantic Articles, caused by the restrictive system		£513,266
British Manufactures:—		
Enhancement in cost		372,575
Freights:—		
Enhancement in, to and from Europe	£438,274	
On surplus produce	75,550	
		513,824
		£1,399,665
Deduct net revenue received by the colonies, in diminution of the aggregate amount of these restrictions		7,312
		£1,392,353
To be deducted from this sum in consequence of the renewal of intercourse with America		369,054
Leaving an annual burden inflicted on these colonies in consequence of the restrictive system, of		£1,023,299

It appears from these authorities, that the amount of duties collected in 1828 on articles from America was 75,340*l.*—less 68,028*l.* *expenses of collection*, leaves 7,312*l.*

TABLE II.

STATEMENT of IMPORTS and EXPORTS of Sugar from all the British Colonies, her parts of the World, in the Years 1828, 29, and 30. Taken from the State- and Calculations printed by the Board of Trade, relative to the British West Colonies, on 7th February, 1831.

	IMPORTS into GREAT BRITAIN.						STOCK in GREAT BRITAIN.					
	1828	1829	1830	1831	1832	1833	1828	1829	1830	1831	1832	1833
	Tons.	Tons.	Tons.				Tons	Tons.	Tons.			
lantation	193,400	195,230	185,660				42,210	5,316	43,290			
s	18,510	14,580	23,740				1,400	1,350	2,340			
. . . . .	6,000	8,700	10,180				2,150	3,000	5,850			
anilla . .	1,175	1,600	5,600				1,595	690	2,600			
h . . .	1,900	5,300	6,060				1,100	2,050	3,120			
. . . . .	4,900	4,680	5,480				2,200	785	1,000			
s equal tards .	13,010	9,950	5,620				4,040	4,430	2,020			
Total . .	238,989	240,040	242,340				54,625	17,525	60,200			
	EXPORTS. Deliveries of Raw Sugar from the Ports.						HOME CONSUMPTION. Deliveries of the Raw Sugar from the Ports.					
	1828	1829	1830				1828	1829	1830			
Plantation	2,530	810	1,485				191,005	182,850	190,840			
lus	5,900	2,860	2,930				12,100	12,020	24,240			
l	2,100	2,810	1,850				4,870	6,060	8,625			
Manilla . .	1,200	1,000	2,835					150	85			
nah . . .	3,050	3,460	4,450					110	200			
. . . . .	3,770	5,000	2,995				75	150	1,150			
ses, equal astards .	. . .	60					10,360	9,850	8,030			
Total . .	18,550	16,000	16,545				218,410	211,090	233,270			
ct Exports Raw Sugar, uced into w ditto Bas-	38,830	40,290	47,650				40,530	41,420	50,090			
d	1,700	2,000	2,370									
al Consumption, including stards . . .	. . .	. . .	. . .				177,880	169,670	183,290			

CONSUMPTION IN EUROPE.

A STATEMENT Drawn by the first Mercantile Authority, January, 1831.

	1827	1828	1829	1830
	Tons.	Tons.	Tons.	Tons.
England	76,000	93,500	102,500	100,000
Germany and Baltic	46,000	57,000	70,000	80,000
Netherlands and Holland . .	35,500	35,000	44,000	33,000
Mediterranean	25,600	19,000	23,000	28,000
Tons . . .	183,100	204,500	239,500	241,000

We see by the Statement, that the Importation from the West India Colonies, in 1828, was larger than all the Consumption of Europe in 1827.

TABLE III.

From the Report of the Select Committee of the House of Lords.

VALUE OF PRODUCE.

BRITISH COLONIES.	
Jamaica	£11,169,661
Barbadoes	1,270,863
Antigua	898,220
St. Christopher's	753,528
Nevis	375,182
Montserrat	211,160
Virgin Islands	201,122
Grenada	935,782
St. Vincent	812,081
Dominica	561,858
Trinidad	735,017
Bahamas	269,806
Bermudas	175,560
Honduras	146,700
	£18,516,540

CEDED COLONIES.	
Demerara and Essequibo	£2,238,529
Berbice	629,461
St. Lucia	595,610
Tobago	516,532
	£3,980,132
British Colonies	18,516,540
Total	£22,496,672

Estimate of the value of Exports and Imports; also the number of ships, the tonnage, and number of men employed, by these Colonies:—

EXPORTS.	
Value	£8,394,484
Ships	5,448
Tons	562,751
Men	39,879

IMPORTS.	
Value	£4,530,008
Ships	4,458
Tons	531,758
Men	39,304

STATISTICAL TABLE IV.

[To face Page 397.

ESTIMATE AND GENERAL VIEW OF THE PRESENT STATE OF THE BRITISH WEST INDIA COLONIES;

shewing the Population, Date of Capture, Cession or Settlement, How they are governed, Number of Acres of Land, Cultivated and Uncultivated; Value of Productions raised, Exports and Imports, Colonial Shipping, Circulating Specie, Estimate of the Amount of Public and Private Property; exhibiting the Value of each Colony. From Authentic Documents, and the Latest Authorities (1833).

CAPITAL AND POWER.

Colonies.	Date of Capture, Cession, or Settlement.	Whether having Legislative Assemblies or governed by Orders in Council.	Population. *			Lands.		Estimated Value of Productions raised Annually, including Cattle, &c., Esculents and Fruits. C.	Imports into the United Kingdom. Official Value. D.	Exports from United Kingdom. Official Value. D.	Tonnage to and from the United Kingdom and the Colonies.	
			Whites.	Free Coloured. A.	Slaves.	Cultivated. B.	Uncultivated.				Inwards. Tons.	Outwards. Tons.

Colony	Value
Jamaica	[illegible]
Barbadoes	9,089,630
Antigua	4,264,000
St. Christopher	3,783,800
Nevis	1,750,100
Montserrat	1,087,440
Virgin Islands	1,093,400
Grenada	4,994,365
St. Vincent's	4,006,866
Dominica	3,056,000
Trinidad	4,932,705
Bahamas	2,041,500
Bermudas	1,111,000
Honduras	578,760
St. Lucia	2,529,000
Tobago	2,692,920
[illegible]	18,410,480

[illegible]
634,231 Negro Labourers.

Total 733,617

Lands.............. 2,476,095 Acres cultivated.
3,996,696 Acres uncultivated.

Estimated Value of Productions raised annually, including Cattle, &c. £22,496,672

Shipping, inwards........ 262,021
Ditto.... outwards...... 252,356
514,377 Tons.

[illegible] Value of Exports .... £5,515,[illegible]

Estimated Value of Forts, Barracks, Arsenals, Dock-yards, and all Public Buildings.. £3,853,000

PRIVATE PROPERTY.

Estimated Value of Lands: viz. Cultivated	£42,182,520
Uncultivated	3,764,198
	45,946,718
Estimated Value of Negro Labourers	42,355,280
Ditto of Buildings, Utensils, &c. on Estates	21,289,020
Ditto of all kinds of Stock on Estates	8,710,740
Ditto of Houses, Stores, Merchandise, and Furniture in the Towns	7,924,500
Ditto of Colonial Shipping	302,595
Estimated Amount of Gold and Silver in Circulation	620,500
	197,199,494
Grand Total	£171,099,494

EXPLANATORY NOTES TO TABLE IV.

(A.)—The population of the West India Islands is according to the official returns. The census of the white and free coloured population of Jamaica has not been taken.

(B.)—"In stating the lands in Jamaica, both cultivated and uncultivated, the latest survey taken by Mr. Robertson has been followed. Those in St. Vincent are also from a recent survey. An official account, during Lord Seaforth's government, is the authority for the number of acres cultivated in Barbadoes; which is supposed to have varied very little, if at all, since that period. With respect to the other Colonies we have partly consulted Edwards' History of the West Indies, and other later writers, and partly gentlemen who have for a considerable number of years resided in the Islands respectively."—(Colquhoun.)

(C.)—"It is deemed fair to estimate the consumption, as plantains, yams, fruits, cattle, poultry, &c., &c., at an average of 10*l.* per head per annum for the whole population, excepting Curaçoa and St. Thomas, which produce nothing; the former being dependent on Aruba and Bonaire, and the latter chiefly upon Porto Rico, for articles of subsistence. To this average value of the articles consumed is to be added the amount of the surplus commodities exported, including what is purchased for consumption on board the shipping during the voyage."—(Colquhoun.)

(D.)—The account of exports and imports from and to England, as well as the tonnage, is taken from the last official returns in 1829. The commerce of the West India Colonies to other parts than Great Britain, may be estimated thus: imports into, 3,100,000*l.*; exports from, 3,000,000*l.* In 1826, the imports were 2,971,627*l.*; and the exports 2,685,595*l.* In 1829, the total value of the commerce was:—

	£
Exports from, to England..................	9,087,919
Do. .... to other parts...............	3,000,000
	£12,087,919
Imports into, from England...............	5,521,169
Do. .... from other parts............	3,100,000
	£8,621,169

About 18,000 British seamen are employed in this trade.

(E.)—With respect to the value of all works of defence and public buildings in each Colony, all that can be expected is an approximation to their real worth.

(F.)—" Edwards and Sir W. Young, estimated negroes at 50*l.* each: their value has, however, since greatly increased, particularly since the abolition of the slave trade. Averaged, they cannot now be worth less than 55*l.*"—(Colquhoun.) At present they are not worth so much.

(G.)—" The lands are estimated as follows:—

	£	*s.*	
Land in a high state of cultivation, in the sugar colonies averaged at	20	0	per acre.
Idem, producing coffee and provisions	10	0	
Idem, yielding cotton and other inferior articles ...	4	0	
The best land not cleared, and not in a state of cultivation	1	0	
Land of a medium quality	0	10	
Inferior land	0	5	

(Colquhoun.)

(H.)—" In estimating the buildings, utensils, &c., on estates, we have chiefly availed ourselves of Mr. Edwards' experience and knowledge of West India concerns, assisted by information from some intelligent proprietors who have long resided on the spot. This article is taken as follows:—

Buildings of every description, utensils, &c.	on sugar estates including proprietors' dwellings	at about two-thirds the value of the lands.
Idem	on coffee settlements	at about one-third ... idem
Idem	on cotton and other settlements	at about one-fifth ... idem."

(Colquhoun.)

(I.)—According to Edwards, the stock on sugar estates may be estimated at somewhat more than one-third the value of the buildings; and the stock on cotton, coffee, and other settlements in proportion.

(K.)—" Edwards estimates the houses and other property in the towns of Jamaica at 1,500,000*l.* From the best local information we have been able to obtain as to their present value, all kinds of property having materially increased since Mr. Edwards' time, we should conceive the estimate for Jamaica may be fairly taken at 2,000,000*l.*, and the other Colonies in proportion."—(Colquhoun.)

(L.)—" The Colonial shipping, that is, vessels registered and belonging to the Colonies respectively, are estimated at the very moderate average of 12*l.* per ton."—(Colquhoun.)

(M)—"Money is become so much an article of merchandize, that it is almost impossible to ascertain the circulating medium. We learn from good authority, that a sum exceeding 200,000*l.* currency in money, is annually paid into the Colonial chest of Jamaica, for the public and parochial taxes and assessments, and that the amount of circulating gold and silver coin fluctuates, there being sometimes a considerable sum and sometimes very little in circulation. It is assumed that about 220,000*l.* sterling are generally circulated in Jamaica, exclusive of the remittances to this country. The circulating medium of the other Colonies is by no means in proportion."—(Colquhoun.)

NOTES ON THE TABLE OF THE WEST INDIA COLONIES.

(1.)—JAMAICA. This Island, discovered by the Spaniards in 1494, colonized by them in 1509, and captured by Cromwell in 1655, was the asylum of the adherents of that great man, who took refuge there after his death. Its political constitution was concluded in 1726, after the most severe struggle. In this year, the assembly agreed to grant to the crown 8000*l.* per annum as a permanent revenue, on condition:—"1st. That the quit rents, then estimated at 1460*l.* per annum, should form a part of the sum:—2d. That the body of their laws should receive the royal assent:—3d. That all such laws and statutes of England as had been at any time established, introduced, used, and accepted, or received as laws of the Island, should be and continue laws of Jamaica for ever." The legislature is composed of a captain-general, a council nominated by the crown, consisting of twelve gentlemen, and a house of assembly of forty-three members, elected by the freeholders: their sittings, as well as those of the supreme court of justice, are held at Spanish Town. The British troops stationed in this Island receive colonial pay. Jamaica is 150 miles in length, and about forty in breadth: the number of acres of land is 2,742,262, of which more than a million are cultivated. Above one hundred rivers water this beautiful Island; all sorts of fruits grow most abundantly; not only the pine-apple, the sweet-sop, cocoa-nut, avocado pear, mamea, orange, &c., but the genuine cinnamon and mango (introduced by Rodney in 1782) are produced in profusion. The population, productions, &c., may be seen in the Table.

(2.)—BARBADOES. This Island being abandoned by the Charibs, was taken possession of by the English crew of the Blossom in 1605; who erected a cross, inscribing on it, "James King of England and this Island." Its possession was contested and disputed for among the English aristocracy for a quarter of a century: when Cromwell, to punish its adhesion to Charles, enacted the famous "Navigation Act"—the promoter of British power. The dreadful hurricanes have rendered a great part of this Island almost barren but its maritime position is far more important than its productions. It is twenty miles long and fourteen broad. (Table III.)

(3.) ANTIGUA.—This little island having neither rivers nor springs, was deserted by the natives; but the enterprising Codrington constructed cisterns, and planted the sugar cane. It is about 50 miles in circumference, and contains 56,838 acres of land above one half of which are cultivated. It yields most abundantly not only sugar, but tobacco, and a variety of productions. A council composed of twelve members, and an assembly of twenty-five, direct the affairs of the island.—(Table III.)

(4.) ST. CHRISTOPHER'S.—Columbus gave his christian name to this little island containing only 43,746 acres of land, of which the greater part are perfectly cultivated. In 1626, Warner exterminated the native Charibs. D'Esnambue, a Frenchman, aided him in the work of destruction; and, by a solemn treaty, this small spot was divided between the two great but most inimical nations. The Frenchmen were at last expelled, and the descendants of Warner are at present enjoying the fruits of their ancestors' labours. (Table III.)

(5.) NEVIS—Is a mountain 24 miles round, rising from the sea in the form of a cone; probably the result of a volcanic eruption, as a hot spring of sulphuric water is found at the top. Such a spot cannot be very productive.—(Table III.)

(6.) VIRGIN ISLANDS.—These are very numerous: the principal are Tortola, Virgin Gorda, Losban Dikes, Guana, Anegada, Beef and Thatch Islands, &c.

(7.) GRENADA.—Discovered by Columbus in his third voyage (1498), had a far more numerous population than the other islands. The Frenchman, Du Parquet, deceived the natives with presents of knives, glass beads, and brandy. He then sent 300 men from Martinique with express orders "*to extirpate all the natives*"; but when the executioners arrived, Le Compte, their countryman, had already murdered them all, sparing neither men, women, nor children. The island being captured by the British was ceded to England in 1763. The duties of 4½ per cent. having been demanded, the people disputed the right to levy such contribution. The question of law was brought before the Court of King's Bench; and the Chief Justice immortalized himself by pronouncing judgment against the Crown. The islands of Curaçoa, Rondc, and a few other small ones, form its dependencies.

(8.) ST. VINCENT'S.—Columbus having discovered this island on St. Vincent's day, gave it that name. Some blacks were shipwrecked there about 1670: the negroes intermixed with the Charibs, and the race thus produced was so ferocious, that they almost exterminated the aborigines. The long and bloody contest between France and England about the possession of this island, having ended in the peace of 1783, England became possessed of this most beautiful spot, watered by 20 rivers, turning numerous mills, affording pleasure to the inhabitants, and contributing to the production of a large quantity of sugar, considered the best of all that comes from the West Indies. This is the only island, in that part of the world, which has escaped the hurricanes; but it has not been so fortunate in escaping tremendous volcanic eruptions. The one which visited it in 1812 was so terrific, that it not only covered the island with volcanic matter, but its noise was heard at the distance of more than 300 miles. Eight small islands are depending on St. Vincent.

(9.) DOMINICA—is 29 miles in length, and about 16 in breadth. The interior of its soil is light, brown-coloured mould, with all the appearance of having been washed from the mountains. Coffee answers better than sugar. The cultivation is carried to a very large extent, and is much favoured by more than 30 rivers watering it in all directions. This spot, the field of cruelty and contention between the French and English, has also been subject to the most terrible hurricanes. In 1813, two of those most tremendous visitations succeeded one another within a short interval: the losses were considerable.—(Table III.)

(10.) TRINIDAD—was discovered by the Spaniards in 1498, and possessed by them till 1801. Precisely when they had begun to spend a large capital to colonize and forward the productions of this most fertile and important colony, they ceded it to the English. It is 90 miles in length, and 50 in breadth. The soil is the most rich of America, and yields all sorts of productions—sugar, rum, coffee, tobacco, and cocoa, which is as good as that of the Caraccas:

there are forests of cocoa-nut trees extending many miles. The timber is abundant, and a lake exists in the island, the waters of which assimilate to pitch, and cause the admiration of the naturalist. The Table shews that the population, agriculture, and commerce of this most important island, have not progressed in proportion to the immense resources of which it is capable. Spanish laws, a governor, and council, regulate the affairs of the island.

(11.) Bahama Islands.—This was the first land discovered by Columbus in 1492. They are 500 in number, but are almost barren, in spite of having been fertilized with torrents of Spanish, French, and English blood: their possession was contested during more than a century. Salt is the staple production: New Providence, and particularly Turk's Island, have reaped great benefits from this article.

(12.) Bermudas.—Discovered by the Spaniard Bermudez, in 1529, were not inhabited till a century afterwards, when Sommers and Gales, having been shipwrecked, were forced to remain there nine months. These islands, like the Bahamas, are insignificant on account of their barren soil. They are of higher importance as a chief maritime station for British fleets and men-of-war; and, on that account, have been declared a free port with extensive privileges.

(13.) Honduras.—This British settlement is situated on the peninsula of Yucatan, on the "tierra firme" of South America. The territory possessed by the English is immense. Balise, the capital of the colony, situated at the entrance of the river of the same name, is one of the most healthy parts of America: the invalids of the islands resort there to recover their strength. This large and beautiful river being navigable for above 250 miles, affords facilities to the British settlers for their principal employment, the cutting of logwood and mahogany. The trade in this latter article employs at present nearly 20,000 tons of shipping; an evident proof of the amazing increase in the prosperity of the settlement. But when the extraordinary advantages which this part of America possesses are considered, in consequence, among other circumstances, of the low islands scattered all round the coast, commonly called "Keys", formerly (particularly St. George, Ambergrease, &c.) the haunts of buccaneers, it is surprising that British industry and capital, have not reaped greater advantages from this colony.

(14.) St. Lucia.—Three times taken by the English from the

French, and as often ceded to them, was, for the fourth time, captured by the British marines in 1803; and allotted to England in perpetuity at the peace of Paris, 1814. This island is as large as Martinique, and possesses one of the best and safest harbours in the West Indies.

(15.) Tobago—followed the vicissitudes of the preceding island; was captured in 1793; restored to the French in 1802; and recaptured in 1803. It could not improve under such uncertainty of dominion; but it has considerably advanced since the peace of Paris. Its length is 32 miles, and its breadth about 10. Little Tobago is only two miles long, and one broad. The soil of both is rich; the hills are beautiful, and covered with verdure; but more than one-fourth of the island is uncultivated.—(Table III.)

(16.) Demerara and Essequibo.—Every one is aware of the importance and value attached to these colonies when in possession of the Dutch. How much their importance and prosperity have increased since they came under British sway, and have been aided by British capital, may be judged of by the best of all criterions—the extraordinary amount of imports from these colonies into the United Kingdom in the last three years. The extent of Demerara and Essequibo, according to the official declaration of B. D'Urban in 1827, is 3 degrees of longitude by 5 degrees of latitude; and with the exception of 499 estates situated along the sea coast, every part of the colony is crown land. The quantity of coffee imported from Demerara, in 1830, was 6,000,000 lbs.

SECTION VII.

COLONIES IN THE INDIAN OCEAN.

Capital of the English possessions in the Indian Ocean, viz.:—Mauritius, and Ceylon: how these Colonies came into the possession of the English.—La Bourdonnau, principal founder of the prosperity of the Mauritius, his talents and reward—importance of this place—its Population, Productions, Fertility. excellence of Climate, Commerce, Agriculture, Lands cultivated and uncultivated, Produce annually raised, Shipping, Circulating Specie, Public Property, &c.—The same in regard to Ceylon, &c.

The Mauritius (so called by the Dutch in honour of their prince of that name) was discovered by the Portuguese in 1505. It was abandoned by the Dutch in 1712, one hundred and eight years after their countryman Van Neck landed there, for the Cape of Good Hope. The French immediately took possession of it, and changed its name to the Isle of France. But the British arms wrested this productive and important place from French dominion, in December 1810.

The true founder of this island was De la Bourdonnaye, who introduced the manioc, the sugar-cane, cotton, indigo, coffee, &c. He erected dock-yards, built ships, launched one of 500 tons, established iron works, made roads, constructed bridges, hospitals, barracks, fortifications, mills, canals, &c.; upholding at the same time, the dignity of the French navy. How far was that great man from thinking *then*, that he was fortifying one of the links in the chain of the British maritime power in India. Who could have imagined that all the toils and great exertions of that comprehensive mind, would be rewarded, by one of the ungrateful "Kings of the French," with the irons and horrible dungeons of the Bastile, where that extraordinary man expired?

The island falling under British sway, experienced a happier fate. Since that time, not only have its fortifications and public works been considerably improved, but its population has increased one third, and its wealth and capital may be said to have trebled. In 1811, the whole produce of sugar was 20,000,000 lbs.; in 1830, the 'import' of this article into England alone, amounted to 53,992,800 lbs.!![a] The coffee produced in the first named year, was 600,000 lbs.; in 1830, the quantity imported into Great Britain alone, was 7,066,199 lbs.: these two are staple articles of this colony. But its fertility in all sorts of produce is no less remarkable. The soil, of a reddish colour mixed with a ferruginous substance, intersected by many lakes, and watered by sixty rivers, yields, in great luxuriance, not only all the fruits of the tropical, but even those of the northern climates. "The apple, the apricot, the pear tree, &c., are, with no little astonishment as well as pleasure, seen twined with the cinnamon, pepper, clove, bamboo and nutmeg." No healthier spot is known in that part of the world. The application of steam has already begun to produce its wonderful effects in the sugar manufactories of this island; and a bank has been established to aid with its currency the planters, merchants, &c.

The demi-insurrection lately occasioned by the Orders in Council relative to the black population, and which still continues, is an ill-judged act against the kindness of the mother country. "The natives," according to the latest advices, "capable of bearing arms, are all formed into a sort of militia, and dressed in mourning; they persist in the same intent, and in rejecting the English Orders in Council as before." But

[a] The exportation of sugar from the Mauritius was, in 1822, 23,403,644 lbs., and in 1832, 79,000,000*l.*—(Revue Africane.)

fortunately for humanity, this probably is an insurrection which can be cured by itself; a sort of revolution which can be perfectly quelled, without shedding a drop of blood, and even without any military interference. England need not send her soldiers for that purpose; she need do no more than suspend the admission of Mauritius sugar and coffee into her ports, until the orders are obeyed, and the military mourners have unconditionally submitted. This simple measure would be received with the greatest rejoicings and pleasure by the West Indies, as it would afford the most satisfactory relief to that integral part of the British Empire; and would afford, at the same time, a great lesson for the future, and effectually annihilate the restless, ungrateful, and discontented French spirit of the revolutionists. Really, when the situation, power, and productions of this little island, and the difficulties surmounted in lowering the duties on the admission of its produce into England, (the only market open to it,) are considered, it appears almost inconceivable, that these colonists should be capable of acting in such a foolish and misguided manner, against their own vital interests.

Let us hope, however, that while the government mends its involuntary errors, reason and reflection will soon regain their empire; and that tranquillity and order will be restored, leading to a continuation of prosperity, and increase of capital. The whole public and private property in this island, may certainly be estimated at 13,216,450*l.*, and the annual value of produce raised, at 1,216,666*l.*

CEYLON.

This great island was once the emporium of Oriental commerce. The Arabs, in the earliest times, perceived its beautiful topographical situation for commercial intercourse. It was at Colombo and Trincomalee that these great conquerors carried on the most extensive commerce, until adventurers from the Grand Nation of that age came, from the most remote regions, to expel them.

The Portuguese became possessed of all the coast of this island, the surface of which is 27,000 square miles; its length being 270 miles from Point Pedro to Dondra, and its breadth 145 miles. The kingdom of Candy, situated in the interior, was completely surrounded by the Portuguese settlements, in 1505: they fortified the whole coast, and the wonderful works erected, and the expense and labour bestowed upon that grand object, show the knowledge and foresight of those noble and able conquerors, and the great importance which the Lusitanian heroes attached to the maritime and mercantile situation of the place.

This island, the climate of which is better than that of all the Coromandel coast, is rich in its precious productions, and singular in yielding, in different parts, the fruits of quite opposite climates. Its maritime and commanding situation, extending over all the oriental seas, gives it unquestionable advantages. Its port, Trincomalee, in particular, is the only safe shelter during the terrible season of the *monsoons*. If, in the revolution of time, in the vicissitudes of human affairs, England should lose her Indian continental possessions—should she only retain Ceylon, it may, by its topographical position, become to India, what Great Britain is to the European continent [a].

[a] Percival's Account of Ceylon. Thomson's "Account of Ceylon, and the Cape of Good Hope." Knock's "History of Ceylon." Davy's "Account of the Interior of Ceylon and its inhabitants."

The [illegible] [illegible] in possession of this im-portant [illegible] [illegible] years, and in 1656, the com-pany [illegible] [illegible] [illegible] and kept possession of it [illegible] [illegible] [illegible] 1796, when it ca-pitulated, and surrendered to the British forces. The Fort of St. [illegible] Colombo, built on a peninsula of a mile and a quarter in circumference, extremely well fortified and covered by batteries mounting 300 pieces of ar-tillery, deserves particular attention. The fortifications of Trincomalee are also of a superior class: the expense of putting them in their present state has been consi-derable: but they have rendered the place quite im-pregnable. Other public works and improvements have been effected since 18[illegible] to a great extent. Cul-tivation has amazingly increased: the gardens of Cinna-mon have been much extended and improved: the one near Colombo is twelve miles in circumference. Com-merce, &c., has augmented in proportion: the imports, which, in 1813, were valued at 6,578,939 rix dollars, and the exported goods at 2,424,940, have consider-ably increased[a]. The gross value of cinnamon export-ed, according to Colebrooke and Cameron's last reports, amounted to 133,000*l.*[b] *Trial by Jury has been in-troduced, and has produced the most beneficial results* even in that country, where the habits are so different from ours, and where despotism and barbarism have reigned from time immemorial. This furnishes a salu-tary admonition to the greatest part of European na-tions, who, boasting of their civilization, not only do not

[a] A great quantity of rice is annually imported into this island.

[b] The London charges for the sale of 223 tons of this article amounted, according to the same authority, to the large sum of 10,000*l.*!! The population is underrated by these gentlemen, who state it to be only 850,000 British subjects.

possess, but *reject* this institution—one of the best of human society. The population, consequently, has improved, and the Cingalese or natives, though the most indolent race of the East, have become more industrious through the exertions of the able governors, who have encouraged the neighbouring nations, especially the Chinese, to settle on the most productive lands, and establish themselves in the beautiful harbours.

This island, though infested by all sorts of noxious animals, is free from foxes. It produces in abundance all sorts of fruits, spices, and drugs; its pearl fisheries are renowned; they are at present carried on by a sort of company: but the chief articles of wealth are cinnamon and pepper. Its public and private property may be estimated at 14,293,331*l.*, and the produce annually raised, at 3,074,666*l.* The total capital of our possessions in the Indian Ocean may be stated at 27,509,449*l.* Further particulars will be found in the Table.

STATISTICAL TABLE.

[illegible]ATE and GENERAL VIEW of the present STATE of the BRITISH POSSESSIONS in the INDIAN OCEAN; showing the Population, [illegible] Capture, Cession or Settlement; how they are Governed; number of Acres of Land, cultivated and uncultivated; value of Productions raised; [illegible] [illegible]d Exports; Colonial Shipping; Circulating Specie; and an Estimate of the Amount of Public and Private Property, exhibiting the Value of each. From Authentic Documents, and the latest Authorities. (1811).

CAPITAL AND POWER.

	Date of Capture, Cession, or Settlement.	Whether having Legislative Assemblies, or governed by Orders in Council	POPULATION, Whites.	Free Coloured	Slaves	TOTAL	LANDS, Cultivated	Uncultivated	[illegible]	[illegible]	[illegible]	[illegible] Inwards	Outwards
							Acres	Acres	£	£	£		
[illegible] (A)	Capitulation 17th Sept. 1799	Governor and Council, and Orders of the King in Council	6,014	[illegible]	[illegible]	[illegible]	[illegible]	[illegible]	[illegible]	[illegible]	[illegible]	[illegible]	[illegible]
Isle of France, or Mauritius (B)	Ditto 3 Dec. 1810	Ditto Ditto	[illegible]	[illegible]	[illegible]	[illegible]	[illegible]	[illegible]	[illegible]	[illegible]	[illegible]	[illegible]	[illegible]
Totals			[illegible]	[illegible]	[illegible]	[illegible]	[illegible]	[illegible]	[illegible]	[illegible]	[illegible]	[illegible]	[illegible]

VALUE.

	PUBLIC PROPERTY. Estimated value of Forts, Barracks, Arsenals, Artillery, and all Public Buildings	Estimated Value of Negro Labourers	LANDS. Cultivated.	Uncultivated.	Estimated Value of Buildings, Utensils, &c., on Estates	Estimated Value of all kinds of Stock on Estates.	Estimated Value of Houses, Stores, Merchandise, and Furniture, in the Towns	Estimated Value of Colonial Shipping	Estimated Circulating Specie	TOTAL.
	£.	£.	£.	£.	£.	£.	£.	£.	£.	£.
Ceylon	[illegible]	....	[illegible]	[illegible]	[illegible]	[illegible]	[illegible]	[illegible]	[illegible]	[illegible]
Isle of France, or Mauritius	[illegible]	[illegible]	[illegible]	[illegible]	[illegible]	[illegible]	[illegible]	[illegible]	[illegible]	[illegible]
Totals	[illegible]	[illegible]	[illegible]	[illegible]	[illegible]	[illegible]	[illegible]	[illegible]	[illegible]	[illegible]

SUMMARY RECAPITULATION.

AGGREGATE VALUE OF EACH COLONY.

Ceylon .... 14,0[illegible]1
Isle of France, or Mauritius 13,216,450
£ 27,[illegible]

Population 1,084,796.
Lands 795,000 cultivated
1,802,000 uncultivated.
Estimated value of Productions raised annually, including Provisions and Fruits .... £. [illegible]
Estimated value of Exports £ 917,000
Idem Imports 654,000
Colonial Shipping, inwards 14,188
Idem outwards 9,000

VALUE PUBLIC PROPERTY.

Estimated Value of Forts, Barracks, Arsenals, Artillery, and all Public Buildings .... £ [illegible]

PRIVATE PROPERTY.

Estimated Value of Lands cultivated
uncultivated .... £ [illegible]
Idem Negro Labourers .... [illegible]
Idem Building Utensils, &c., on Estates .... [illegible]
Idem all kinds of Stock on Estates .... [illegible]
Idem all kinds of Houses, Stores, Merchandise and Furniture, in the Towns .... [illegible]
Idem Colonial Shipping .... [illegible]
Money in Circulation .... [illegible]

Notes to the Table of the Possessions in the Indian Ocean.

(A.)—Ceylon. The English are in possession of the whole sea-coast, which completely surrounds the kingdom of Candy. The inhabitants are said to be numerous, and composed of all nations and races. It is calculated that the lands are 13,000,000 of acres in extent, and that the English possess about 3,000,000, of which about 1,000,000 are cultivated. The productions are important; and though many of them are common to other parts of India, some are peculiar to this island: they are, cocoa, cinnamon, betel, pepper, tea-plant, coffee, sugar, precious stones, &c. Ceylon abounds in minerals and precious stones, of which there are not less than twenty sorts: the *sapphire, amethyst, aqua marine* and *tourmaline*, are equal to those of any other country; besides the *ruby* and *diamond:* the *tourmalines* are of various colours, the *topaz, blue* and *green sapphire, white, yellow, brown* and *black crystals*, cat's-eye, a species of opal *cornelians* and others of the same description in great plenty: the whitest pearls in abundance off the coast: *lead, tin*, and *iron* are found in the interior, but are never wrought, or applied to any purpose; there are also mines of quicksilver, but they do not appear to be much wrought. The cultivated lands, producing the most valuable articles of commerce, are taken at the low average of 10*l.* per acre, including all buildings, stock, &c.; the uncultivated are valued at 10*s*. Money is so much an article of commerce, that it is difficult to state the amount of circulating specie, as it varies considerably; the copper money, being current no where else, remains in the island.

(B.)—The surface of the Island of Mauritius, according to Abbé la Caillé, is 432,680 acres, of which above 100,000 are cultivated. The mountains are of considerable extent, and are calculated at nearly 20,000 acres. All the country is watered with a great number of rivers and rivulets (Vide Vaux Hist. Mauritius). The cultivated lands were calculated in 1811, at 20*l.* per acre, and the uncultivated at 1*l.* per acre. The productions are, cloves, cotton, sugar, and other minor articles, together with poultry, cattle, &c. Port Louis, the principal town, is defended by batteries mounting above 190 pieces, aided by the contiguous island of Tormelius, which is defended by sixty mortars of large calibre, &c.; there are several other works of defence, which line the shore for some distance. The slaves, buildings, stock, &c., and other private property are estimated at the same moderate average as similar articles in the West India Colonies. The average income of these possessions may be calculated at 580,000*l*., and the average expenditure at 600,000*l*.

	£		£
In 1826 the Income of Ceylon was	300,822,	the Expenditure	333,052
Ditto .... Mauritius	245,852,	....	228,527
Total	£546,674		£561,579

The Commerce of these Colonies to other places than Great Britain, was:—

	Imports into. £		Exports from. £
Ceylon, 1826	272,861	....	126,851
Mauritius	372,915	....	345,635
	£645,776		£472,486

Total Commerce:—

	Exports to. £		Imports from. £
Great Britain, 1829	654,666	....	327,026
Other Places, 1826	472,486	....	635,776

SECTION VIII.

BRITISH SETTLEMENTS IN AFRICA.

Capital, Agriculture, Lands, cultivated and uncultivated, Productions annually raised, Trade, Shipping, &c. of the British Settlements in Africa.—Exertions of England to extend her trade in those parts of the world: progress of the same under numerous chartered companies: large expense incurred in the two late reigns: inconsiderable returns and losses: the whole fully compensated by the important Colony of the Cape of Good Hope—its maritime position, immense extent, varied productions, trade, heterogeneous population, private and public property, &c. &c.

GREAT have been the efforts of Great Britain, during two hundred and fifty years, to introduce her colonial system into Africa. The Portuguese possessing the only trade existing there, excited the cupidity of the English, as early as 1536. Elizabeth, in 1558, granted a charter to several merchants "for the exclusive trade of the rivers Gambia and Senegal, and Goree Island." Three more chartered companies were established in the reigns of James and Charles I.; but all were equally ruined: notwithstanding which, a fifth Association was formed in Charles the Second's time. The coast lying between Capes Blume and Rouge, had been before erected into a province, and decorated with the pompous title of "Royal Senegambia," with the brilliant appendages of a military and civil government. However, the losses and disappointments of those engaged in these enterprises were greater even than their golden hopes, and persevering exertions.

Senegal was delivered to France in 1783, and conquered again in the Revolutionary War. The Island of Goree, with its Fort, was taken by the English in 1800. Sierra Leone, and latterly, Fernando del Po, have contributed to increase the waste, both of treasure and blood. The large sum of 318,806*l.* was expended on the African settlements during George the Third's reign; of which, 211,668*l.* was for Sierra Leone: and the expenses of those settlements since that monarch's death have not decreased, whilst the waste of human life has greatly increased[a].

But some compensation for the large capital expended without return in that ungrateful and barbarous land, is found in the immense maritime, political, and mercantile advantages derived from the possession of the Cape. This first link in the chain of posts, which holds our Indian Empire, is almost unbounded in the extent of its territory. The cultivated farms extend above 600 miles into the interior of the country. Several colonies have been established in the interior, and the colony, lately settled on the Bavarian River, is more than a hundred miles beyond the last English settlement. The country is described to be the most fruitful and promising ever seen; the scenery of a singular and imposing description: the valleys sheltered, without being encumbered, by groves of Mimosa trees, and full of herds of wild animals, guays, &c. pasturing in undisturbed tranquillity. The immense variety of birds, grasses, fruits, (as oranges, pomegranates, melons, grapes, &c.,) flowers, medicinal

[a] Mr. Keith Douglas is reported to have stated in the House of Commons, in July 1831, that down to the year 1824:—

The expenses of Sierra Leone amounted to	£2,269,000
And from 1824 to 1831	1,082,000
The Naval expenses from 1807 to 1824	1,630,000
The payments to Spain and Portugal	1,230,000
The expenses on account of captured Slaves	533,092
On account of mixed commission	198,000
Making a total of	£6,942,092

plants, timber, &c., is really beyond conception[a]. The population is composed of the most heterogeneous elements: French emigrants and Hottentots, English and Caffres, Dutch and Negroes, Portuguese descendants and savage Boshmen[b]. This population, which in 1811 was about 90,000, has almost doubled since that time: the increase of produce has exceeded that ratio. The principal staple articles are salt, corn, and wine. This last, from 40 tons, which was the whole imported into England in 1812, increased in 1817 to fifteen times that amount, or 4218 tons; and in 1830, no less than 10,483 pipes were imported into England, according to the official returns[c]. If we may rely upon the

[a] In one district alone, there are above a hundred more species of birds than are found in all Europe. Five hundred species have been ascertained to inhabit this possession. Great Britain and Ireland have 277 species, of which, 142 are land birds, and 135 water birds. Eighty different sorts of timber have already been recognised in this colony.

[b] See Barrow on the distribution of population.

[c] Warre, publication presented to the Board of Trade in 1823—1824:—

CAPE WINE Imported into England.

In 1812	40 tons.
1814	340
1815	1,512
1816	1,631
1817	4,218
1818	3,648
1819	1,648
1820	1,925
1830	10,483 pipes.
1831	6,108

Imports in 1831	£332,525
Exports „	176,618

SHIPPING.

calculation made by well-informed agriculturists and merchants, this colony is capable of producing 400,000 casks of wine annually; but, though the quantity producible be so enormous, the quality has disappointed the hopes of those who thought most highly of it*. The expectations of the able men, who proposed making Cape Town a free port, would have been far better realized, had that privilege been bestowed upon Saldanha Bay: the considerable and periodical maritime losses incurred in the stormy and unsheltered Bay of Cape Town, could then be avoided. However, by that measure, an emporium was created for the general sale of East Indian, African, and European productions; and a large trade was opened with the South of Africa, with the Indian Empire, and with the numerous and new British settlements in Australia. In fact, from this point, as from a centre, not only British vessels, but those of all nations, proceed to spread luxuries and riches amongst all nations of the globe.

But, great as these advantages are, they totally vanish, when compared with the importance which this colony possesses in regard to the preservation of the British East Indian Empire. Those alone who have seriously considered and calculated this great question,

Shipping.	Vessels.	Tons.
In 1830	256	118,382
1831	181	59,264

From the Committee appointed to make an appeal to the Government.

* Fisher published an interesting tract in 1813, in which he confidently asserted, "that the Stein Wine and Cape Madeira, with a little good management, proper degree of fining, and length of keeping, would surpass Sherry and Madeira;" this, however, has not been yet effected.

are able to appreciate the prodigious value of the Cape of Good Hope.

From the economical and statistical data just given, it could be proved that the aggregate value of the produce, trade, and capital of these possessions, has nearly doubled since 1811; but adhering to the general plan, the total capital, &c. of the Cape of Good Hope, Goree, Senegal, Sierra Leone, and all the other dependencies in Africa, is estimated at 6,444,398*l.*; and the annual value of the productions raised, at 1,067,065*l.* The Table subjoined, and the official accounts in the Notes, afford further details.

STATISTICAL TABLE.

ESTIMATE and GENERAL VIEW of the PRESENT STATE of the SETTLEMENTS in AFRICA; showing the date of Capture, Cession or Settlement; Population; Number of Acres of Land cultivated; Value of Productions raised annually; Exports and Imports; Shipping; Circulating Specie; and an Estimate of the Amount of Public and Private Property; exhibiting the Value of each Settlement. From Authentic Documents, and the latest Authorities. (1833).

CAPITAL AND POWER.

	Date of Capture, Cession, or Settlement.	Whether having Legislative Assemblies, or governed by Orders in Council.	POPULATION.			TOTAL.	LANDS.	Estimated Value of Productions raised annually, including Esculents and Fruits.	Imports into the United Kingdom, Official Value.	Exports from the United Kingdom, Official Value.	Tonnage to and from the United Kingdom, and the Colonies.	
			Whites.	Free coloured.	Slaves.		Cultivated				Inwards.	Outwards.
							Acres.	L.	L.	L.	Tons.	Tons.
Cape of Good Hope ....(A)	Capitulation 10th Jan. 1806	Governor and Orders of the King in Council...	35,675	37,862	35,500	129,036	400,000	779,720	238,113	393,487	8,069	7,705
Sierra Leone..........(B)	Settlement, 1787	Governor and Council	87	15,185	....	15,310	2,090	164,397	258,570	511,779	27,912	31,909
Senegal and its Dependencies ...	....	....	1,000	4,400	....	5,400	5,288	74,138				
Goree	....	....	400	4,000	....	4,400	180	48,666				
Totals........	....	....	37,182	61,275	35,500	154,046	407,578	1,067,065	496,683	895,266	35,981	39,614

VALUE.

	PUBLIC PROPERTY.	PRIVATE PROPERTY.				
	Estimated Value of Forts, Barracks, Arsenals, Artillery, and all Public Buildings.	Estimated Value of Cultivated Land.	Estimated Value of Forts, Factories, Merchandise, &c.	Estimated Value of Slaves, Colonial Shipping and Houses, Stores, Merchandise and Furniture, in the Towns.	Estimated Circulating Specie.	TOTAL.
	L.	L.	L.	L.	L.	L.
Cape of Good Hope..........(A)	1,333,333	1,333,333	....	2,300,000	70,000	5,036,666
Sierra Leone..........(B)	....	....	300,000	....	2,200	303,000
Senegal and its Dependencies	66,666	....	400,000	....	1,200	467,866
Goree	26,666	....	100,000	....	1,000	161,000
Fernando Po	....	....	....	10,000	....	10,000
Totals........	1,426,665	1,333,333	799,999	2,310,000	74,400	6,444,399

SUMMARY RECAPITULATION OF THE BRITISH SETTLEMENTS.

AGGREGATE VALUE OF EACH SETTLEMENT.

Cape of Good Hope	L 5,036,666
Sierra Leone	303,000
Senegal and its Dependencies . .	467,866
Goree	161,000
Fernando Po	10,000
	L 6,444,399

CAPITAL AND POWER.

Population 154,046

Lands 407,578 Acres cultivated.

ad infinitum uncultivated.

Estimated Value of Productions raised annually, including Esculents and Fruits . . . . L. 1,067,065

Shipping inwards . . 35,981

outwards . . 39,614

Estimated Value of Exports [illegible] Imports [illegible]

VALUE.—PUBLIC PROPERTY.

Estimated Value of Forts, Barracks, Arsenals, Artillery, and all Public Buildings . . L1,426,665

PRIVATE PROPERTY.

Estimated Value of cultivated Lands . . . . L 1,333,333

Estimated Value of Forts, Factories, Merchandise, &c. of Sierra Leone . . 799,999

Estimated Value of Slaves, Colonial Shipping and Houses, Stores, Merchandise and Furniture, in the Towns at the Cape of Good Hope . . . } 2,310,000

Circulating Specie estimated at 74,400

[illegible]

NOTES ON THE TABLE OF THE BRITISH POSSESSIONS IN AFRICA.

(A.)—The average annual income of all these colonies may be stated at 150,000*l.*; and the expenditure at 200,000*l.*:—

		Income.	Expenditure.
Sierra Leone	1828	£25,670	£25,670
Cape of Good Hope	1824	97,167	126,194
		£122,837	£151,864

The Commerce to other places than Great Britain:—

		Imports into.	Exports from.
Sierra Leone	1828	£39,911	£6,724
Cape of Good Hope	1824	98,460	67,294
		£138,371	£74,018

Total Commerce of these Colonies:—

		Exports to.	Imports from.
Great Britain and Ireland	1829	£496,703	£895,206
Other places	1826	74,018	138,371
		£570,721	£1,033,577

(B).—The population of this settlement does not exceed 26,000 souls.

SECTION IX.

SETTLEMENTS IN AUSTRALIA.

Capital, &c., of the English Settlements in Australia, viz.:—Van Dieman's Land—Swan River—and New South Wales, discovered by Cook—A Colony established for Convicts, in 1788—Soil—Natives—Animals—Population—Establishments—Trade—Shipping—Exports and Imports—Expenses, &c.

THIS new part added to the known world has a surface exceeding that of Europe by 307,000 geographical miles; and the greater part of it is under British dominion. The enterprising Cook first landed in the part now called New South Wales in 1770[a]. Banks, on seeing the land covered with numerous herbs, called it Botany Bay; and, in 1788, Philips landed the first criminals in Sidney Cove, of whom 220 were females. Such was the humble commencement of this immense colony, which is perhaps destined to perform a principal part in human affairs.

The natives of this extensive country appear to be the last link in the chain which connects the human with the brute creation: they are, in general, the most weak and degraded of the human race. The quadrupeds are neither numerous nor of great strength, and are chiefly of the opossum species: the kangaroo differs from all animals hitherto known. The birds are far more numerous than other animals. The climate, in

[a] Cook was born at the village of Manton, in Yorkshire, in 1728: he was apprenticed to a small shopkeeper, but enlisted in the navy as a common seaman. He emerged from obscurity by his talents and perseverance; studied mathematics and astronomy in his hours of leisure; and became one of the most scientific naval officers of the time; the government chose him, in 1768, to ascertain the observation of the approaching transit of Venus in the South Sea.

general, is various and excellent; the heat being never excessive in summer, nor the cold severe in winter. European productions and animals thrive and multiply amazingly. Van Diemen's Land wool has supplanted that of Estramadura and Segovia; its production is on the increase; is doubling—trebling. Five degrees south of Sidney are Port Dalrymple and Hobart Town; the public buildings in which, particularly the hospital, are magnificent, and vie with any in Europe. These places have increased in population, cultivation, shipping, and commerce, in the same, or perhaps greater proportion, than New South Wales [a]. Swan River has lately been added to the number of these establishments, though at an immense distance from them. This colony, after overcoming very considerable difficulties, is likely, eventually, to become as prosperous as the other settlements [b].

All the European productions, plants, fruits, &c., have been introduced into these colonies; but grain, hemp, and flax, answer best. The European domestic animals, as the horse, &c., are propagated, and Merino sheep are to be seen in large flocks. Manufactures of wool, potteries, breweries, &c., have attained a comparative degree of prosperity. The population, since 1811, has quadrupled; the cultivation, commerce, and industry, have increased in a greater ratio; and the navigation and shipping have been augmented thirty-fold.

[a] According to the official papers laid before parliament, the expenses of the establishment of New South Wales, in 1830, were.......£242,989 7*s*. 7½*d*.
Ditto of Van Diemen's Land....... 144,746 1 5¾

[b] See Wentworth's "New South Wales"; Cunningham's "Two Years in New South Wales"; "Friend of Australia; or, Plans for Exploring the Interior", &c.; Oxley's "Journals of Two Expeditions into the Interior of New South Wales"; Dawson's "Present State of Australia", &c.

[illegible] advantages are [illegible] by the [illegible] and [illegible] of [illegible] and [illegible] [illegible], &c.[a] All the improvements of a [illegible] [illegible] [illegible] and [illegible] [illegible] to [illegible] a part. In fact, to have a perfect idea of these colonies, we ought to imagine an entire English town transported by enchantment to a distance of 12,000 miles, with all its sorts of [illegible], [illegible], town hall, female and orphan asylums, hospitals, charitable societies, public libraries, stage coaches, markets, reviews, newspapers, &c. &c. If in this rapid manner, civilization begins at the extreme point of European refinement, what will that country become in the revolution of ages? Thus the British nation, at present so numerously spread throughout the world, will in process of time, cover its great surface with an active and intelligent race, speaking one language, and ruled by the wisdom of the most fundamentally sound and happy institutions.

However, it is but too true, that the cost of these establishments of government is considerable. The expense of the transportation of convicts is too heavy: they might certainly be sent to other colonies nearer, cheaper, and with advantageous returns.[b] But when we contemplate the grand general result to the happiness of the human

[a] A college has been in the present year, established at Sidney, on the same principles as the London University. The Church people, even in those remote parts, attending to selfish interest rather than to public virtue, opposed the plans of the indefatigable institutor, Dr. Laing; but his praiseworthy exertions have triumphed over all obstacles.

[b] Eight pounds are paid by government to each unmarried woman, between the ages of 18 and 30, who chooses to emigrate to New South Wales or Van Diemen's Land; the number not to exceed 1,200. The expenses of the passage are calculated at 16*l.* for an adult, and 9*l.* for a child.

race and the civilization of the world, we ought to feel the highest gratification in seing 300,000*l.* a year expended in such useful and magnificent objects. This would be farther increased at seeing the British nation take immediate possession of the beautiful Sandwich and Bonin Islands, which are so closely connected with the continent. The wretched state of the inhabitants of those extensive groups would then terminate; the communication with Australia would increase: the commerce with Japan would commence; the British chain round the world would be completed; and a just tribute, not yet paid, would be offered to the manes of the great Cook.

The total amount of capital of these extensive countries, yet in their infancy, is stated in the annexed Table: it has not been increased, more than that of England, although there is little doubt it has increased threefold since 1811.

TABLE.

NERAL VIEW of the PRESENT STATE of NEW SOUTH WALES and its DEPENDENCIES; showing the Population, Number of Acres of Land cultivated; Colonial Shipping; Value of Productions raised annually; Imports and Exports, Tonnage, and Circulating Specie; and an Estimate of the Amount of Public and Private Property in these Settlements. From Authentic Documents, and the best accessible Information. (1833).

CAPITAL AND POWER.

	Population, [illegible].			Lands.		Estimated value of Productions raised annually, including Esculents and Sheep.	Imports into the United Kingdom.	Exports from the United Kingdom.	Tonnage to and from the United Kingdom.	
	Whites.	Aborigines.	Convicts.	Cultivated.	Uncultivated.		Official value 1829.	Official value. 1829.	Inwards. 1829.	Outwards. 1829.
						£.	£.	£.	£.	£.
New South Wales	20,930	Not ascertained.	8,484	300,000	Ad infinitum	520,000	33,191	58,913	8,979	28,719
Van Dieman's Land	9,421									
Swan River	850	.....	.....				.....	37,210		
Total	31,201	.....	8,484	300,000	.....	520,000	33,191	96,123	8,979	28,719

VALUE.

	Public Property.	Private Property.			
	Estimated Value of Forts, Barracks, Arsenals, Artillery, and Public Buildings.	Estimated value of cultivated Lands.	Estimated Value of Houses, Stores, Merchandise, Furniture, &c., including Colonial Shipping.	Money in Circulation estimated at	TOTALS.
	£.	£.	£.	£.	£.
New South Wales	100,000	750,000	700,000	12,000	1,562,000
Van Dieman's Land	40,000	700,000	300,000	8,000	1,048,000
Swan River	.....	50,000	25,000	.....	75,000
Totals	140,000	1,500,000	1,025,000	20,000	2,685,000

RECAPITULATION.

AGGREGATE VALUE.

New South Wales	£1,562,000
Van Dieman's Land	1,048,000
Swan River	75,000
Total	[illegible]

Population	39,685
Lands, cultivated	300,000
Shipping—Tonnage Inwards	8,979
Outwards	28,719
Value of Productions annually raised	£520,000
Value of Imports	[illegible]
Exports	[illegible]

PUBLIC PROPERTY.

Estimated Value of Forts, Barracks, Artillery, &c. £140,000

PRIVATE PROPERTY.

Estimated Value of Cultivated Lands	£1,500,000	
Houses, Stores, Merchandise, &c.	1,025,000	
Money in Circulation	[illegible]	[illegible]

SECTION X.

EAST INDIAN EMPIRE.

Capital, Population, and Resources of the British East Indian Empire—Rise, Progress, and Actual State of that Empire—Political measures and great men who have contributed to its conquest—Lands—Productions—External and Internal Commerce—Exports and Imports—Shipping—Property belonging to the East India Company—Private Property—Advantages and disadvantages of the Zemindar, Ryotwar, and village systems—Revenue—Expenditure—Debt—Circulating specie—Great questions relating to the East India and China Trade, &c.

To describe the rise, progress, and present state of the East Indian empire, would require a larger space than the limits of this work afford; a short, but important sketch, comprehending all the essential and leading points required to form an idea of these immense possessions, and to enable the reader to form an opinion upon the interesting questions soon to be agitated on the occasion of the renewal of the Company's charter, is all that can be given.

The conquest of British India, effected by a company of merchants, is of such a nature and magnitude as has never before been recorded in ancient or modern history. As far back as 1549, the son of the Italian, Cabot, formed a mercantile company, aad obtained a royal charter, "to trade with the East Indies." The attempts made to reach that region by the north-east and north-west passages, in order to surpass, if possible, the Portuguese, who had discovered the circuitous route by the Cape, were persevered in till 1553[a].

[a] One hundred and forty-one years before these attempts were made, Henry II., son of Don Pedro of Portugal, (in 1412,) sent several vessels towards the coast of Africa, with the idea of disco-

Willoughby and all his crew were frozen to death in attempting that passage; but the enterprising Britons were not, on that account, deterred. The merchants of the City of London formed a company composed of 101 "adventurers", who obtained a charter from Elizabeth in 1600[a]. But the Portuguese, who, though natives of a small province, possess great knowledge

vering India. This great Portuguese, a descendant, on the side of his mother, Philipa, of the great Englishman, Edward III., directed all his talents, his energies, and his life, to that great object. His judicious plans were prosecuted with the greatest perseverance, till, in 1486, Diaz, passing the southern extremity of Africa, discovered Cabo das Tormentas, which name was very properly changed by King John of Portugal, to Cabo del Bea Esperanza, or Cape of Good Hope. With the view of keeping alive the hope of Indian discovery, the courageous Payva, and the determined Cavilha travelled to India overland. The great Vasco de Gama, commanding a fleet composed of the San Gabriel, the San Rafael, and a caravel, arrived at Calicut on the ever memorable 22d May, 1498; his brother, Paulo, was the vice-admiral of this great fleet, whose total tonnage amounted to 270 tons!— However, by such slender means this great object was accomplished by the Portuguese, while Columbus and Pinzon, under the patronage of a Spanish woman, had discovered another hemisphere of no less importance. The worlds thus discovered, and to be discovered in future, were divided and partitioned by a solemn treaty, among the Spaniards, the Portuguese, and the Pope, who, always intermeddling in the territorial affairs of this world, fulminated a tremendous bull, putting out of the pale of the Church, and excommunicating all sovereigns and kings who should dare to resort to those countries, without the express license of Queen Elizabeth of Castile; while to King Manuel of Portugal, that *modern* Roman pontiff granted the navigation, conquest, and trade of Ethiopia, Arabia, Persia, and India: much more indeed than all the pontiffs of *ancient* Rome could have imagined. Thus began the conquest of India by the Europeans.

[a] September 22d, 1599, the Lord Mayor called a meeting at Founders' Hall, and a capital of 30,113*l.* 6*s.* 8*d.* was subscribed for trading to India.

and heroism, were in full enjoyment of the extensive Indian commerce [a]: the English, commanded by Downton, joined the ferocious Mongolians, to exterminate them [b]. Such was the first step of British policy (1614) to make themselves absolute masters of the Indian trade.

In 1622, they followed the same policy and line of conduct, in assisting the Persians to massacre and expel the Portuguese from Ormus: while the calculating Dutch, who had the same object in view, retaliated upon

[a] The knowledge, courage, and excellent financial dispositions which the Portuguese displayed in the conquest of India, can only be compared with the admirable financial and economical measures which the great Cortez was adopting in another part of the world at the same epoch. At the same time that Cortez, having conquered the vast empire of Mexico, was exploring the sea and archipelago of California, and selecting proper ports and stations, Albuquerque was also choosing the best ports in the Indian archipelago, attending to the finances and doubling the revenue of Malacca, and constituting that place the key to the navigation of those seas. However, the losses sustained by the Portuguese in the Indian conquests, through the hostility of the Venetians, English, and Dutch, and from their own comparatively small skill in navigation, were very considerable. Faria gives an account stating, that from 1412 to 1640, 956 vessels sailed from Portugal, of which 150 were entirely lost; and in which he supposes that no less than 100,000 people perished. But the bad conduct of many of the Portuguese governors, and the entire neglect with which Philip II. treated the affairs and conquest of India, were the principal causes of the advantages and success of the English and Dutch against the Portuguese, and led to their almost total expulsion from a country they had conquered with so much courage and ability.

[b] One hundred and five years before the English acted in this manner against the Portuguese, the Venetians, actuated by the worst passion that can pervade a nation—mercantile avarice, sent their carpenters and shipbuilders to construct a fleet for the Sultan, with the nefarious intention of exterminating and destroying the Portuguese in the Indian ocean: but the fleet was entirely defeated by the Portuguese Almeida, in 1508.

the English, by driving them from the islands of Landoire and Puto in 1619, and by torturing, persecuting, and putting them to death at Amboyna in 1623. Notwithstanding these persecutions and cruelties, the Company's affairs were flourishing: an account was presented to the parliament in 1624, by Munn, the deputy-governor of the company, showing that their commerce amounted to 1,255,444*l.* per annum.

But a new competitor, France, stepped forward into the arena, to contest this rich trade. The French East India Company was established in 1664; and the merchants of that country were forwarding their speculations in India, while the British people were even more clamorous than at present for a "free trade", and against the monopoly of the East India Company. However, that noisy and obstinate opposition did not disturb the march of British perseverance. The small villages of Sootanutty, Girrindpore, and Calcutta, situated along the banks of "Father" Ganges, were bought in 1698: at this time, the whole territory of the Company was only three miles in extent[a]. Such was the limited foundation upon which the British Indian empire was to be raised: we shall soon see what immense extension it has received in 130 years.

Two rival English East India Companies were disputing among themselves, and contending for the trade,

[a] About this time there were four classes of merchants, all of whom were entitled to trade to India under certain circumstances: 1st. The Original Company, who possessed all the establishments: 2nd. The New Company was authorised to trade unreservedly: 3rd. The subscribers of the "General Society", who chose to trade, each on his own account: 4th. The separate traders, who were so far legalized, that all the ships sent out by them before 1698, might prosecute one voyage, which might be lengthened to any period by country voyages.

advantages, and profits. At length, Godolphin was chosen arbitrator of their differences; he gave his mighty award in 1702, and the two corporate bodies were united[a]. The great power resulting from that well-advised union was not suffered to remain idle; the combined companies soon began to act in a military as well as in a mercantile capacity.

The deposed Rajah of Tanjore implored the aid of the British merchants; which they afforded him, on a promise of the territory of Devicotah. The British, in the mean time, took possession of Tanjore; but abandoned the cause of the deposed Rajah, on condition of being confirmed in it (1749). By the treaty of Pondicherry, (26th December, 1754,) the French and English commissioners agreed, "that both nations must withdraw from all interference in the affairs of the native princes." The signatures to this treaty were scarcely dry, when this article was infringed. In June, 1757, the Subahdar of Bengal was deposed; Chandenagore was taken from the French; the British military power was consolidated by Clive, at the battle of Plassy (April, 1759); and two years afterwards, not only were all vestiges of French sway annihilated, but the Prince of Deccan, after being obliged to cede large possessions, engaged "never to suffer any Frenchman in his empire."

At this time almost all Hindostan was subject to the Mahrattas. Abdallah, Prince of Eastern Persia, directed their forces against the company; but the horrible slaughter at Paniput, and the battle of Putna, (1761,) had the effect of enlarging the territories of the Association, and increasing the amount of the tribute

[a] In July, 1702, an Act for the Union of the two Companies passed the Great Seal.

paid to them by the emperor[a]. The dividing principle and cunning system, adopted by those practised conquerors, the Romans, of aiding one sovereign against another in order to subdue both and seize their possessions, was strictly followed by the company. Warren Hastings extended and completed it, by bribery, cruelty, and tyranny. He contracted with the Nabob of Oude, "that he should pay him forty lacs of rupees, and a monthly allowance for the British troops, on condition of receiving his aid to exterminate the Rohillas." Their army was of course beaten; and, during three days, their camp plundered, villages burned, country laid waste, and the people butchered; while the English were cool spectators of this massacre and spoliation (1774). Hastings, in the mean time, continued his own system of bribery. The concubine of Japier gave him immense sums to be appointed guardian to the little Dowlah, against custom, justice, and the rights of others. Nor was she the only one who bribed that corrupt governor. The Viceroy Nundicomar, having accused Hastings of receiving many other corrupt gifts, was cruelly hanged on the pretext of forgery, amidst the tears of his subjects, and for a crime not deemed capital by the laws of India. The enormous extortions and cruelties of the English Verres, were horrible and beyond imagination: they were exposed by Burke in a trial which lasted seven years; but humanity and justice were unavenged. The Directors of the East India Company, sensible of his merits as a governor[b],

[a] "Pindary and Mahratta Wars":—a collection of treatises.

[b] There is no question of the abilities and talents of Hastings as a governor and servant of the Company; but one cannot approve, nor remember without horror, the cruelties and extortions attri-

and aware of the able and successful manner in which he had forwarded their interests, rewarded that infamous monster with an annuity of 5000*l.* for 28½ years; besides paying the expenses of the prosecution, amounting to 70,000*l.*

In 1786, Cornwallis, a better minded man, took possession of the East India government. The soil of India was considered the exclusive property of the sovereign of the country[a]: he was, in fact, the only landed proprietor. The Zemindars were the mere revenue collectors of the Great Mogul: the Zemindarship was hereditary, but they could neither sell nor alienate that privilege: the peasants were, after the sovereign, the real owners of the land. Cornwallis, with the most laudable as well as economical intentions, declared the Zemindars to be the actual landowners. Thus, in consequence of this arrangement, the East India revenues proceed from the Zemindars, as a sort of land tax. The peasants were entirely dispossessed, being declared the tenants of the Zemindars. This plan brought about a complete revolution of property and finance in India: the terrific and disastrous effects at the time, and which have not yet entirely subsided, happened against the plans, views, and feelings of the governor. However, the impulse given by this measure to the native cultivators and

buted to him by the ablest men of England, several of whom had no direct interest in the prosecution itself.

[a] Malcolm, in his excellent Work on Central India, says, that "the right of the cultivators to the property of the soil was never disputed;"—"the field that his father had tilled, was his own, and the inheritance of his children; the monarch being entitled to a tax of 10 per cent. for his support." No doubt the right might be so, but an uninterrupted series of centuries of vexation and usurpation, and conquest, had rendered that right almost extinct.

proprietors, and the inducement afforded to bring lands into cultivation, and improve those already under tillage, have fully compensated for its disadvantages. Indeed, before the permanent settlement, no native would devote either capital or labour to the improvement of the land or mode of culture, convinced as he was, that the arbitrary government would raise the assessment in proportion as the produce was greater. The good Cornwallis, aware that this principle is the main cause of the decline and downfal of empires, attempted to counteract it; and, more candid than the British legislature, entertained the most sincere, disinterested, and philanthropic ideas, about that wretched and unfortunate country.

Parliament (1782) made a solemn declaration, "that to pursue schemes of conquest, and extend dominion in India, are measures repugnant to the wish, the honour, and the power of the British nation." We shall see how this hypocritical and uncalled for declaration was fulfilled. It was scarcely known by Matthews, when he took Bidnapore (1783), Caunpore, Maujalore, &c., &c., besides immense treasures. A triple alliance was formed with the Nizam and the Mahrattas against Tippoo: the redoubts of Seringapatam were attacked: that prince ceded one half of the Mysore, paid 3,300,000*l.*, and delivered two of his sons as hostages[a].

[a] To show how awkwardly the native Princes of India, even of most renown, have conducted their military affairs and wars against the English, let us hear what General Munro says of the so much celebrated military operations of Tippoo. "Cruelty and deceit were the two great engines of his power: it would have been death for any man to be known as one who could speak or read English: intercepted correspondence gave him no insight into our intended movements. We found most of the intercepted letters of the late and former wars, lying unopened; so that we might have saved ourselves the trouble of using a cipher."—(Munro's *Life and Cor-*

The effects of the French Revolution were felt in the remote extremes of India. All the French establishments, including Pondicherry, were taken (1795); and the Dutch, who in former times abused their extensive power in India, cutting down the spice trees, and torturing their fellow creatures, were now also expelled [a]. Ceylon, Banda, Moluccas, Amboyna, &c., were captured. The brave Tippoo thought of recovering his lost possessions: he trusted to French promises, and was, of course, deceived. Seringapatam was stormed, and the prince killed. But the Nizam, to engage the protection of the Company, ceded his moiety the very next year.

The Nabob of Surat was forced to exchange his dominions for a pension of 10,000*l.* per annum. The Nabob of Furruckabad was compelled to cede all his possessions for a similar one of 108,000 rupees. The Nabob of Arcot died; and the Company's servants placed his nephew on the nominal throne, reserving for themselves all the real power. The Rajah of Berar, by a treaty (1803), ceded Cuttack and the territory of Bhurtpore; signed another convention in 1805; delivered up his sons; paid 20 lacs of rupees; and transferred to the Company all the territories before granted to him [b].

But in spite of all these advantageous conquests, the Company was several times greatly embarrassed. As far back as July 1712, a deficiency of above a million

respondence.)—If a knowledge of the designs and movements of the enemy constitutes one of the principles of the art of war; the great military Tippoo did not care much about it.

[a] Orme's "History of the Military Transactions of the British Nation in Hindostan, from the year 1745."

[b] For the amount of subsidies received from native princes and ceded countries, see Table XI.

was declared: loans upon loans were contracted; and the privileges were periodically renewed. Pitt, in 1784, passed an Act establishing a Board of Control, composed of six privy counsellors, to superintend the territorial concerns of the Company: the Court of Proprietors was not to have power against the acts of the Court of Directors, which might be approved by the Board. But the cry against monopoly was increasing with time, and the growing knowledge of mercantile affairs. In 1813, it became quite general; and the important Act of "Indian Free Trade" became necessary, both for the Company and the public[a]. By this Act the trade to India was thrown open; the commerce to China being reserved for the Company: the territorial and commercial branches were separated, as well as all accounts relating to them; and the King was empowered to create a "Bishop of India, and three Archdeacons, to be paid by the Company."

However, the Indian conquest was not yet completed; another pretext was required to accomplish it, which soon offered. War was declared, in 1814, against the Nepaul; the ultimate result of which was, that it came under British dominion. The last Paishwah of the Mahrattas was compelled to transfer Ahmednuggur and many other territories to the Company; and the capital of the Guzerat was likewise ceded, in virtue of another treaty with the Rajah of Baroda. At last, the warlike Pindaries, intimately attached to the fortunes of the Mahrattas, struggled for their independence, but in vain; they were brought under submission and subjection one after

[a] 33 Geo. III., cap. 52.—This Act renewed the declaration, disclaiming all views of conquest or dominion.—Also 53 Geo. III., cap. 155. July, 1813.

another. Bajee Row abdicated his throne, abandoned Deccan, and exchanged his empire for a pension of eight lacs of rupees.

There were no more great nations in Hindostan to be conquered: but another empire was not far off. The Burmese having encroached on the territories of the Company, an expensive war, accompanied by loss of life and treasure, was undertaken against them; for all which they paid in the end [a]. They were defeated at Prome; and the English took Ava, their capital. By the treaty of Yandaboo, the British retain Arracan, Kavay, Merguy, &c., &c.; and the Burmese are bound to pay a crore of rupees; while, at the same time, the territories of the Gwickers were seized by the Company's agents, "on account of the liquidation of a debt."

Such have been the steps, the policy, the measures, and the perseverance, by which a company of British merchants have not only expelled all other Europeans from India [b], but become conquerors of an empire of 514,000 square miles in extent, peopled by numberless distinct nations, speaking above 300 different languages [c], and constituting a population of above 89 millions and a half, besides the dependent territories under the protec-

[a] White's "Political History of the extraordinary Events which led to the Burmese War."—Marshall, "Narrative of the Naval Operations in Ava during the Burmese War."

[b] At the general peace, the English granted to the Dutch and French some of their ancient settlements. But should any misunderstanding or war arise between those nations, they will immediately fall again under British dominion.

[c] The principal languages of the Hindus are Famieul, Teloyoo, Mayalim, and Canarese. Kennedy, "Researches into the origin and affinity of the principal Languages of Asia and Europe".—Hamilton's "Geographical, Statistical, and Historical Description of Hindostan", &c.

tion of the Company, which exceeds 614,000 square miles. (Tables I. and II. at the end of this Section.)

But looking at its grand results as affecting the happiness of the human race, it must be confessed that never has a conquest turned out more advantageous and beneficial. All the immense Indian territories have been concentrated in a powerful confederation: a large river, immense deserts, and lofty mountains, constitute the strongest barriers against foreign invasion by land[a]; while an extensive sea coast, and the mighty maritime power of Britain, defend it by sea. A great power, a central government, wisely and humanely presiding over and commanding all this confederation—all this immense amalgamation of states, has put an end to all the conflicting elements, and to all the civil wars waged by numberless and cruel tyrants perpetually contending for empire: rapacity, tyranny, plunder, massacre, and savage cruelty, have entirely ceased.

It cannot be denied that the Indian Government, by a blind and misguided avarice, still promotes the most horrible and cruel superstitions, by drawing a revenue from them[b]. But the commercial intercourse of the

[a] "Excursions over the Himalaya Mountains", by Skinner.

[b] Instance Juggernaut, Tripety, Gya, &c. Some of the horrid rites are, "swinging in the air by means of an iron hook fixed in the fleshy part of the loins; swinging with the head downwards from a hook fastened to the foot: ten rupees are paid to the Company for the one, and two for the other; to say nothing of Juggernaut, the temples of Fejurry, Tripety, and Allabyad:—24 miles from Poonah there are 300 prostitutes maintained to worship the idol, and 100 men, whose characters are as bad."—(Poynder against Chaplin.) Free from any party spirit, the misguided financial views of the Company in continuing exactions of such a horrible nature must be deeply regretted. The pretext alleged, of "nea-

Company, and a knowledge of its own true interests, will gradually put an end to all these partial evils; while its capital, and maritime superiority, have communicated a great impulse to all the principal sources of Indian prosperity.

Let us see how these salutary effects have been felt since the beginning of the period of this inquiry. As soon as civil war ceased and conquest was at end, the population increased in almost every state. "In Delhi, one of the principal districts," says Fortescue, before the Lords' Committee, "when we took possession of it, there were about 600 deserted villages; and now, 400 of them are repeopled by the descendants of those who had a right of property in those villages." The same effect has been experienced generally throughout India, and in the large capitals of the different states the population is immense. Thus the population, which in 1811 was estimated by Colquhoun at 40 millions, was considered by Hamilton, in 1822, to be 83 millions, and is now, according to the latest official returns, 89,577,206. (Table I.) Agriculture and produce have augmented in a relative or greater ratio. The evidence before the Lords' Committee states, "that the land in Berar, which was before of little value, has become very high priced: the lands of Bengal have reached the price of 54 years' purchase":—one of the witnesses states, that "lands have been sold during the year, whose sale averaged 36 times the whole government revenue of those states"; and that "the rights origi-

interference in Hindu superstitions" is not a sufficient excuse. It appears, by the statement of Heber, that 5397 widows were burnt alive from 1815 to 1824: by the humane, just, and powerful interference of the government, all such barbarous cruelties and human sacrifices have been prevented.

nally attached to the Zemindarships had become worth 360 years' purchase."

Spanish America was in possession of the supply of indigo to Europe, when the trade to India was opened to British activity and capital, at the epoch above-mentioned. British adventurers and planters soon went off, to apply their capital and exert their skill on Indian soil: one individual (Davison) held no less than 100,000 acres in the cultivation of this plant! (See Evidence, &c.) No wonder the Spaniards and Americans were superseded in the European markets. This production has increased amazingly. In 1813, the total value of indigo raised was 1 crore, 46 lacs, 12,048 rupees; but in 1828, its value more than doubled that sum, amounting to 2 crores, 92 lacs, 53,615 rupees. The export of this article had increased more than 50 per cent.; and the average value of the indigo exported from Calcutta in the late years has been estimated at 2,500,000*l.* (Asiatic Journal.) This wonderful increase of produce and mercantile speculation, has been chiefly occasioned by the application of the capital and industry of from 500 to 1,000 European planters, the total of Europeans being about 2,000, (Table III.) who *have not even the right of holding land,* to the miserably defective system of Indian agriculture. (See Evidence.) If the British people were allowed to settle and hold land, capital and industry would be equally directed to the cultivation of silk, sugar, cotton, and coffee; and the same or similar effects might be expected in regard to these articles.

However, the exports and imports have greatly increased. From the papers laid before the House of Commons, it appears that previous to the renewal of the Charter (1813), the aggregate value of all sorts of merchandise exported from England to India (exclusive of China) did not amount to one million a year: in 1814, the amount of merchandise exported from India was 870,179*l.*; in 1824, it reached 3,057,741*l.*, while the private trade had increased, in the same period, tenfold:—in fine, the total value of imports and exports, in 1829, reached 10,329,548*l.*—the imports into India being 4,100,264*l.*, and the exports to Great Britain 6,218,284*l.* Table IV. shews the Exports and Imports; Table V. shews the sale amount of the goods sold at the Company's sales in each year from 1816 to 1830. The shipping employed has kept pace with the increase of agriculture and commerce. According to the abovementioned authority, it amounted, previous to 1813, to only about 42,000 tons.

The external and internal trade of Bombay amounted, according to the last official accounts, to the enormous sum of 6,931,381 sicca rupees; that of Madras to 48,684,429 sicca rupees; and that of Bengal to 89,140,258 sicca rupees, or 11,142,535*l.* in British currency, at the present rate of exchange. (Table VI.) The exports and imports of Calcutta in each year, from 1814 to 1828, are shewn in Table VII. In the last year, the former amounted to 8,730,000*l.*, and the latter to 4,150,000*l.*

But what are the revenues, the expenditure, and the debts of this extraordinary mercantile and political government? What has been their progress within the period of this inquiry, and what is their present state?

There are three governments ruling over this immense empire, under the humble name of Presidencies—Bengal, Madras, and Bombay. The revenues arising from the original possessions of the Company in these

Presidencies, in 1811, amounted to 8,720,591*l.*; and the subsidies from the ceded and conquered countries amounted to 7,958,609*l.* (Table VIII.); making a grand total of 16,679,198*l.* But the military expenses, in the same year, amounted to 7,975,995*l.*, or almost one half of that large sum; and the civil, judicial, and marine expenses, amounting to 13,909,903*l.*, absorbed nearly all the rest; leaving the sum of 2,769,215*l.* as the net revenue, after defraying all the expenses. But the effects of free trade were favourable to the revenue: British capital gave greater employment to the natives; and, in 1818, the revenue reached 19,392,002*l.*; the military expenditure was 10,451,856*l.*; and the net revenue 1,833,387*l.* In 1826, the gross revenue increased to 21,096,966*l.*, and the military expenditure to 12,881,525*l.*; in 1827, the former reached above 23 millions; and in 1829 (the last account published), it is estimated at 23,097,341*l.*; the military expenses at 9,445,707*l.*; the total expenditure, including civil, judicial, buildings, fortifications, &c., &c., at 19,536,919*l.*, and the net revenue at 3,560,422*l.* (Tables VIII. and IX.) Such has been the progress of the total gross revenue, and the relative diminution of expenditure. The Table shows the progress, not only in the different years, but in each of the Presidencies.

Table X. shows in detail the various heads and sources of this revenue. The principal of these is the income arising from land, which constitutes about two-thirds of the whole income of the Company. In the latest year for which the accounts are made up, this branch alone produced above 14,000,000*l.* sterling: and its produce would greatly increase if a more liberal and judicious economical system were adopted.

The other heads of Indian revenue appear in the

Table X.: and in Table IX. will be found an account of the receipt from native princes, or from ceded and conquered countries: which amounted in 1828-29 to the large sum of 8,066,271*l.*

But coming to general results: it appears by the official account made by the Auditor-General of the East India Company (Melville), "that the gross territorial revenue, during the fourteen years ending in 1829, amounted to 284,804,085*l.*; but the gross charges during the same period amounted to 304,188,859*l.*; exhibiting a deficit of 19,384,774*l.* The amount of the charges incurred in India was 278,911,464*l.*; whereof the proportion of military charges was 137,253,467*l.*; and of civil charges 117,606,336*l.*; the interest of the debt 24,051,666*l.*; the expenses of St Helena 13,915,134*l.*: the remainder was for charges incurred in England, amounting to 23,915,134*l.*, including 1,300,000*l.* paid on account of the loan:—the total expenses of the East India House amounting to 360,000*l.* a year." [a]

However, the debt of the Company is small in proportion to their resources and territories, the value of their possessions, and the large subsidies received from the native princes, (Table IX.) The territorial debt exceeds 39 millions; the floating debt 7 millions; both together, in 1828, to 47,506,558*l.* The commercial debt was exceedingly small, only amounting to 167,443*l.*, the grand total of both being 47,672,001*l.* The assets were 25,955,111*l.*, leaving therefore, 21,716,890*l.*, as the total amount of debt. (Table XII.) The origin and progress of these debts may be easily traced in the rise

[a] "Political and Financial Considerations on our Anglo East-Indian Empire." The Secretary's Office (56 persons) at the East India House, in 1827, cost 20,333*l*; Examiner's Office, 21,000*l.*; Military Secretary's, 5,000*l.*; Expense of the India Board, 30,000*l.*

and progress of conquest, in the measures of the Company, and in the extension of their empire.

The population, agriculture, produce, shipping, and commerce, have nearly doubled during this period; their increase, since the trade was thrown open, has been immense. The capital, public and private, might be fairly stated to have augmented in the same proportion; however, no great deviation is made from the rule laid down with respect to England. The grand total capital of all the Indian Empire was estimated, in 1811, at 1,072,427,551*l.*: in estimating its present amount at 1,611,077,354*l.*, it is certainly rather under, than overrated.

Table XIII. and the explanatory Notes furnish the details; and the means of verifying the calculations, and forming a complete idea of this stupendous empire.

It is evident that this great increase of capital is owing to two causes—the general tranquillity of the country, and the opening of the trade to British subjects in 1813. By this last measure, not only have British manufactures and commerce received a great impulse, but British capital, finding employment in India, and applied to her various and fertile soils, has improved her resources, and increased her productions and wealth. The times when Pliny lamented and bitterly complained, that the manufactures, luxuries, and dress, brought from India for the Roman ladies, absorbed an annual capital of "millies centena millia sestercium" of the empire[a], have quite passed away. On the contrary, a modern mercantile, but more powerful

[a] "Minimâque computatione milles centena milia sestercium omnibus annis India et Seres, Peninsulaque illa Arabia, Imperio nostro adimunt. Tantó nobis delitiæ et fœminæ constant."—Pliny, H. Nat. 16, 12, c. 18.

empire, sends the produce of its industry, and the luxuries of the world, to India; and British goods have entirely superseded many of her home manufactures.

Would these beneficial results continue their progress, if the trade was *quite* opened to the British nation?—Ought the British to be allowed to settle, buy lands, employ their capital, and act as the subjects of other nations do, in India[a]? Upon the decision of these questions depends the happiness or misfortune, the prosperity or distress, of millions of British European and Indian subjects. It cannot be denied, even by the party who think "that this measure would be productive of more mischief than good," that the application of British capital, activity, and industry, to Indian agriculture, deficient as it is in every respect, but especially in *means*, would produce the most wonderful results. The cultivation of sugar, coffee, tobacco, and above all, cotton, might be increased *ad infinitum*. All men conversant with the manners and feelings of the natives of India agree as to their willing disposition, and the absence of all jealousy towards the Europeans, *on these points*: all parties allow, that the soil of India, its extent, variety of climate, and fertility, are eminently adapted to the cultivation of these productions. Now, after reflecting how often the production and supply of particular articles has, in a short period, passed from one nation to another,—after remembering how the present of a few Merino sheep, injudiciously made by the King of Spain to the King of Saxony, threw Spanish wool out of the English market[b],—and considering how the

[a] The Dutch permit all Europeans to acquire property and land in Java.

[b] The import of Saxony wool into England, which, in 1812, only amounted to about 20 *lbs.*, last year reached above 26 *million lbs.*!!

cultivation of cotton passed from the Spanish colonies to the North Americans[a], and how the Spanish American indigo was superseded by its immense production in India, and this by a very limited number of industrious British individuals, and in a very short space of time,—one is really at a loss to see why the same results should not ensue with regard to sugar and coffee, and particularly, why tobacco and cotton, which are of easier cultivation, and require less skill than indigo, could not be brought to supersede the two staple exports of North America; thereby, saving five millions a year, which we now pay for the last article alone, and imposing, at the same time, a good check upon American tariffs. One cannot but think, that England would derive great advantages by opening her trade to India, and encouraging the investment of capital there; besides increasing the agriculture, industry, commerce, and above all, the shipping, of her own subjects[b]. But let these important questions be left to the wisdom of the British

[a] In 1790, not a pound of American cotton reached this country; at present, above 230 *million pounds* are annually landed here.

[b] The exports of the domestic produce of the United States for the year 1828, adopted as a fair basis, ('Encyclopedia Americana,') amounted, according to the estimates of the Custom House, to 50,669,689 dollars; those of cotton, the greatest staple of that country, were 22,487,299 dollars; and those of tobacco, 5,269,960 dollars:—these two articles amounting to more than one-half of all the produce exported! The number of bales of American cotton imported into England in 1821, was 301,945; but, in 1830, it was doubled, being 613,185. This importation was almost all effected in American ships, whose tonnage was considerable. The importation of East India cotton in 1824, (as may be seen by the Table,) was 50,846 bales; in 1826, was above 64,000 bales; in 1828, reached 84,795 bales; and in 1830, according to the official account, it amounted to 24,873,811 lbs. The common objection, that the East Indies could not supply England with cotton,

legislature: before such a mighty object, as the general and permanent welfare of all the integral parts of the empire, the private interests of individuals, and the views of corporations, sink into insignificance[a].

But having shown the combined causes which have rendered the Indian empire comparatively prosperous in its financial situation, namely, the tranquillity of the country, and the increase of capital and population,—it would be unfair to omit to mention the main causes which have prevented, and still retard, its greater advancement—causes which are actually impairing the very sources of production in that part of the empire, in the same manner as in Great Britain.

The English conquerors, in the settlement of the revenue of India, instead of following the laws of the Indian lawgiver, Menou, who most justly declared, that "the cultivated land was the property of him who cut the wood—who first cleared and tilled it," preferred

on account of its inferior quality, has no strength whatever: because this branch is at present in the hands of the natives, who have no skill, no industry, no capital, no judgment in the selection of soil. The case would be entirely different if the capital, skill, and capabilities of British planters were devoted to this article. In the immense extent of lands in India, there are, most undoubtedly, soils capable of producing as good cotton as the Sea Islands in America. One of the principal causes of the inferior prices which the East India cottons bear, is, their want of cleanness and due preparation: but these defects would soon be removed by British ingenuity. The conclusion is easily drawn, that all the immense shipping at present employed by the Americans in conveying this article, would be transferred to British subjects. This question is perhaps one of the most important that can engage the attention of the legislature.

[a] See the Report of the Committee on East India and China Affairs, which will be found very interesting.

those of the barbarous Mahomet, who, in his Koran, asserted, that "it was lawful to take the whole of the persons and property of infidels, and to distribute them amongst the Musselmen." On this principle the Mahomedan conquerors of India thought it was the greatest generosity, to take from the Indians one-half only of their incomes and property[a]. Cornwallis, actuated as he was by the best intentions in establishing the Jumma, (as above stated,) did not abandon the Mahomedan principle and doctrine, but, on the contrary, added to the already enormous taxes, the European, or Anglo-Indian, machinery of collection; not only defeating his own good intentions, but even obstructing the very sources of production to which he intended to give relief[b].

The Zemindar system was, however, established in Bengal; while that most excellent man, Munro, who deserved the name of the 'father of the country,' introduced, with equally benevolent intentions, the Royotwar system into the Presidency of Madras. He took the greatest pains in arranging the basis of that system; and spared no labour or expense in perfecting it. He estimated 45 per cent. for the produce of the land; allowed an equal share to the Ryot[c]; and the 10 per cent. remaining, was left for the village expenses. But when such an extraordinary sum is set apart for the

[a] See Buillie's "Digest of Mahomedan Law, according to the Tenets of the Twelve Imans."—And Hedaya, or Commentary on the Musselman Laws, translated by order of the Governor and Council of Bengal.—Book ix, cap. 7.

[b] Wilks, in his "Historical Sketches of India," treats with uncommon soundness the question of Indian property with regard to the conquerors, and openly denies the moiety doctrine.

[c] "Ryot" means a tenant of land paying rent.

government; when such a sum is collected by a crowd of pitiless agents, as Zemindars, Amunees, Potails, Mocuddums, Cornums, &c., and this, without any other object than the realization of a larger amount; when such a large and certain portion is absorbed by the administration, while the contingent losses of the stations and the crops, accidents, &c., fall upon the cultivator—what interest can he have to induce him to cultivate the land? Thus, the Ryotwar system[a], founded in the very prin-

[a] The following extract from a description of the Ryotwar system given by a member of the government of Madras in 1823, has been copied by Mr. Tucker into a late work of his.—" To convey to the mind of an English reader even a slight impression of the nature, operation, and results of the Ryotwar system of revenue, connected with the judicial arrangements of 1816, must be a matter of some difficulty. Let him, in the first place, imagine the whole landed interest—that is, all the landlords of Great Britain, and even the capital farmers, at once swept away from off the face of the earth; let him imagine a cess, or rent, fixed on every field, seldom under, generally above, its means of payment; let him imagine the land so assessed allotted out to the villagers, according to the number of their cattle and ploughs, to the extent of forty or fifty acres each. Let him imagine the revenue rated as above, leviable through the agency of 100,000 revenue officers, collected or remitted, at their discretion, according to their idea of the occupant's means of paying, whether from the produce of the land, or his separate property. And in order to encourage every man to act as a spy on his neighbour, and report his means of paying, that he may eventually save himself from extra demand; let him imagine all the cultivators of a village liable at all times to a separate demand, in order to make up for the failure of one or more individuals of their parish. Let him imagine collectors in every county, acting under the orders of a board, on the avowed principle of destroying all competition for labour, by a general equalization of assessment; seizing and sending back runaways to each other. And lastly, let him imagine the collector, the sole magistrate and justice of peace of the county, through the instrumentality and medium of whom alone, any criminal complaint of personal grievance suffered by the subject can reach the superior courts. Let

ciples of Mahomet's moiety system, and followed by Cornwallis, becomes subject to the same objections, and produces the same results.

The village system, which is commonly followed in Bombay, is a mere modification of Ryotwary. In India there is generally in every village or district a head man who directs and manages all the economical affairs of the town. This man, who is called Cornum, or Malik, &c., makes contracts and arrangements with the government agent, and is answerable for the revenue of the town or district where he resides, undertaking to pay it to the government, and collect it on his own account. In a great many districts this office is hereditary: but these men abuse the confidence reposed in them, and plunder the people to such an extent, that the Company's collectors are sometimes obliged to make a detailed schedule of the assessment and its distribution among the cultivators, which is posted up in the village, in order to protect them in some measure from frauds and extortions. However, the rapacity of the native servants is so great, and the control of the Company's collectors over these head men so limited, that this system is perhaps more oppressive than the Ryotwar system itself.

But nothing can convey a better idea of the dreadful effects occasioned by both systems, than the two con-

him imagine at the same time, every subordinate officer employed in the collection of the land revenue to be a police officer, vested with the power to fine, confine, put in the stocks, and flog, any inhabitant within his range, on any charge, without oath of the accuser, or sworn recorded evidence in the case. If the reader can bring his mind to contemplate such a course, he may then form some judgement of the civil administration in progress of re-introduction into the territories under the Presidency of Madras, containing 120,000 square miles, and a population of twelve millions."

clusions that are drawn from the official "Regulations" of the Marquis of Hastings; conclusions which have been completely developed, and demonstrated by a series of facts, in a most valuable publication by Rickards. The first of these conclusions is, "the utter inefficiency of our institutions, revenue, and judicial, to protect property and private rights": the second establishes the fact, that "facilities are afforded for the commission of frauds, amounting to continual confiscations of property by the public officers of the government, to an extent of atrocity which, without the authentic certificate of the highest official authority, could scarcely be credited." (See Rickards, Note, where the official regulations are published.)

Thus, as this very commendable author observes, (Vol. I. p. 312.) "the conversion of the government of India's share of the produce of lands in some districts, is as high as 60 or 70 per cent." "The assessments are in general too high and oppressive", says a witness before the Committee of Lords: "this is highly injurious to the revenue itself: such measures prevent the increase of revenue; and in those districts where they are more moderate, as in Nagpore, the population is greater, and the revenue has augmented. The tax upon carts and wheels is 40 per cent., and upon cocoa nuts, dates, &c., &c., which are all necessary articles of life, the tax is exceedingly heavy."

Thus, unfortunately, we see the same faults, the same errors, which are committed in the imposition of taxes upon the necessaries of life and sources of production in Great Britain, repeated, with equally mortiferous effects, in the most distant parts of the empire. But the Committee of the House of Commons, in its 15th Report, expresses more in a few words than could be comprehended and explained in volumes :—"the whole system (says the Report) thus resolves itself, on the part of the public officers, into habitual extortion and injustice : what is left to the Ryot is little more than what he is enabled to secure by evasion and concealment." After such a declaration by a Body so enlightened, so impartial, and possessing such means of information, to add any thing further would only be a waste of time, and would rather weaken and injure the cause, than serve to forward and advocate it.

These enormous evils must not be attributed to common motives, nor to the regular course of events: "they originate in a powerful, mischievous, and mighty cause," exclaims one of the best writers, "*the union of the commercial and political character of the Company.*" This grand, this most important question, affecting the happiness and existence of millions of human beings, and connected with the financial measures, and with the prosperity, honour, and security of the British empire, has, unfortunately, been left undecided. That high and competent body, the Select Committee of the House of Commons, expressly appointed to inquire into the affairs of the East India Company, and to form an opinion on the momentous questions connected with them, have (like the Committee on the affairs of the Bank) declined to do so : or, as they express themselves, "have abstained, as far as possible, from the expression of any opinion on the numerous and all-important subjects presented to their view ; preferring rather to submit to the House a general summary of the evidence." But if a most talented Committee, after collecting a complete body of evidence, is unable to form any opinion on it, how much more difficult must it be for a numerous and heterogeneous assembly, whose ideas are so opposite and directed to so many other objects, to come to correct conclusions, when they have only a general summary of that evidence.

It would have been more reasonable for the Committee, with such ample information and evidence, both general and detailed, to have opened the way for the House of Commons in such a difficult and interminable labyrinth. They ought not to have been so diffident of their powers of perception and judgement, lest it should be suspected that such extreme prudence originated in the fear of displeasing certain powerful and influential bodies. The interests of the whole British empire are far superior, and the happiness of millions of Indian and British subjects is of far greater moment, than the offence that might be taken at opinions expressed on questions of such importance; which are indeed worthy of the free and incorrupt parliament to whose decision they are left.

Never, indeed, have the representatives of a nation been called to a more honourable and difficult task: upon their well matured resolution rest the mercantile and manufacturing prospects of England, as well as the safety and continuation of the Indian empire under her sway. For it should be borne in mind, that England (following a different system of policy in her subjugation of India, from that pursued by Portugal and Spain in their conquests) in strictly prohibiting her subjects from establishing themselves in those regions, has taken no natural root in the Indian soil [a]. The English are *now* as unassociated in language, strangers in customs, rivals in prejudices, and contrary in religion, as they were at the commencement of the conquest:—

[a] See Orme, "Progress of British Dominion in India."

they have indeed an enormously difficult task to perform, to govern an immense people so extraordinarily situated. "Our power," say the best writers on that region, "rests upon opinion"; but an authority which rests upon so frail a tenure as the opinion of men, is exceedingly weak, and must be subject to the same changes and uncertainties as opinion itself [a]. A better financial administration, less oppressive taxation, greater commercial intercourse, greater investment of capital, and more reciprocal manufacturing and agricultural advantages, would surely be a far more solid basis to rest our authority upon, than human opinion, or than any military force whatever. For the natives having learned the European tactics and military system, having on several occasions shewn their determination and courage, and being besides endowed in general, (and particularly in some provinces,) with the highest character, capabilities, and military qualities [b]—all our mar-

[a] Sir J. Malcolm, unquestionably one of the ablest writers on the affairs of India, expresses his ideas upon this important subject most beautifully, and in a true martial style, in his "Memoir on Central India." "Our authority (he says) rests on opinion: our present condition is one of apparent repose, but full of danger: increase of territory will, in spite of our efforts, come too rapidly; but to be at all safe, the march must be gradual towards a crisis which cannot be anticipated without alarm. We have no retreat: whenever our authority is called in question—*En avant* must be the motto."

[b] James Tod, in his "Annals and Antiquities of Rajast'han, or the Central and Westerly States of India," gives the highest idea of the character, military endowments, and capabilities of the Raja'poots. The native princes have fought bravely, and have even obliged entire British corps to surrender. The many attempts to storm Bhurtpore, in 1805 and 1806, are well known in the history of the war; proving to a demonstration to what an extent the courage of the natives can be carried against the most powerful British force. No less than 25,000 men attempted that operation.

tial cries and honourable incitements would be of no avail, should the spell be broken which now binds their obedience.

The author cannot conclude this article without openly and sincerely expressing his regret that, for the sake of the general commerce and intercourse of nations and the happiness of mankind, England does not direct a part of her force, a part of her immense power in India, towards China.

For the first mercantile nation to suffer one of the best parts of the world, with a territory of 1,372,410 square miles, and a population of 155,000,000, to be almost hermetically closed against the rest; to endure daily insults from an infamous despotical government, one of whose maxims is to despise foreigners and trade[a], and which does not possess a shade of power capable of facing the mighty combined naval and military superiority of the British[b]—is certainly quite unpardonable and unwarrantable, and utterly unworthy of the British nation.

[a] One of the maxims of Confucius was to despise foreigners, and foreign merchandise and commodities. A Chinese who goes out of his country is considered a traitor, and punished with the most cruel death.

[b] When the British navy was only a shadow of what it is at present, Anson, with a 60-gun ship, set all the power of the Chinese government at defiance at Canton. What could a British squadron, accompanied by a few steam-boats, and ten thousand Indian troops commanded by British officers, perform at present? Although Klaproth, in his "History of China," gives to the Chinese empire a military force of 1,182,000 men; this force is so irregular, so ill-armed, and so deficient in tactics, as to be quite incapable of resisting the European military system.

TABLE I.

Abstract Statement of the Extent and Population of British India and of the Extent of the Allied or Protected States.

	Extent in Square Miles.		Population.
Bengal Presidency. Districts, of the Population of which Statements have been received:—			
Lower Provinces	153,802	...	37,503,2[illegible]
Upper or Western Provinces	66,510	...	32,206,8[illegible]
Fort St. George Presidency.	141,923½	...	13,508,[illegible]
Bombay Presidency. Districts, of the Population of which Statements have been received	59,438¼	...	6,251,54[illegible]
Prince of Wales' Island, Singapore, and Malacca	1,317	...	107,0[illegible]
Total ...	422,990¾	...	89,577,206
Territories, of the Population of which no account can be traced:—			
Under Bengal	85,700	...	no census.
— Bombay	5,500	...	ditto.
Total ...	514,190¾		
Add, Allied or Protected States	614,610		
Grand Total extent in Square miles of British territory in India, and territories protected	1,128,800¾		

East India House, 14th September, 1831.

Hamilton, in 1822, estimated the Population of those Districts where no census has been taken, at ...	11,000,000
And the remaining Districts, and Independent States, at	40,000,000
	51,000,000
To which, adding	89,577,206
Makes the total Population	140,577,206

TABLE II.

The following Statement exhibits the computed extent in Square Miles of those Territories on the Continent of India, which have been, by various Treaties, placed under the protection of the East India Company; so far as can be ascertained.

	Square Miles.
Dominions of the Rajahs of Travancore and Cochin	9,400
Nizam	108,800
Rajahs of Mysore	29,750
King of Oude	25,300
Dowlut Row Scindiah	42,400
Rajar of Berar, including Nagpore ...	64,270
Jeswunt Row Holkar	171,660
Guickars, including the detached Pergunnahs	36,900
Rajah of Koorg	2,230
Nabob of Kurnool.........................	3,500
Rajah of Sikhim	4,400
Nabob of Bhopal	7,360
Rajahs of Suttara, Calapore, Sewuntwarree, and the principal British Jaghiredars	21,600
Rajah of Cutch	6,100
Soubadar of Jhansi, Rajar of Dutten, &c.	19,000
Territories under British protection, West of the River Jumna, comprehending Jhopore, Bickamer, &c. ...	165,000
Seikh country, hilly districts, &c., &c., Jynteca, Cochar, Nunigiore, &c.	51,000
Total	614,610

TABLE III.

A Return of the Number of Europeans in British India, not in the Service of His Majesty or the East India Company; distinguishing those residing within the Presidencies of Bengal, Madras, and Bombay, and each of the British Settlements within the Straits of Malacca, on the 1st May, 1814, and on the 1st May, 1830; so far as can be made up.

	1815.		1830.
Bengal	1,100	......	*1,595*
Fort St. George	115	......	116
Bombay	240	......	286
Prince of Wales' Island, Singapore, and Malacca	46	......	*19*
Total	1,501	......	2,016

FISHER.

East India House, 1st November, 1831.

TABLE IV.

IMPORTS.

TOTAL VALUE of Imports into GREAT BRITAIN, from all Places Eastward of the CAPE of GOOD HOPE, (except CHINA,) according to the Prices at the EAST INDIA COMPANY'S SALES in the respective Years.

	By the East India Company.	Private Trade.	Total.
	£	£	£
1814	4,208,079	4,435,196	8,643,275
1815	3,016,556	5,119,611	8,136,167
1816	2,027,703	4,402,082	6,429,785
1817	2,323,630	4,541,956	6,865,586
1818	2,305,003	6,901,144	9,206,447
1819	1.932,401	4,683,367	6,616,768
1820	1,757,137	4,201,389	5,958,526
1821	1,743,733	3,031,413	4,775,146
1822	1,092,329	2,621,334	3,713,663
1823	1,587,078	4,344,973	5,932,051
1824	1,194,753	4,410,347	5,605,100
1825	1,462,692	4,716,083	6,178,775
1826	1,520,060	5,210,866	6,730,926
1827	1,612,480	4,068,537	5,681,017
1828	1,930,007	5,135,073	7,065,180
1829	1,593,442	4,624,842	6,218,284

EXPORTS.

VALUE of EXPORTS from GREAT BRITAIN to all Places Eastward of the CAPE of GOOD HOPE, (CHINA excepted,) according to the Declarations of the Exporters.

	By the East India Company.	Private Trade.	Total.
	£	£	£
1829	434,506	3,665,678	4,100,264

WILLIAM IRVING,
INSPECTOR GEN. of IMPORTS and EXPORTS.

Custom House, London, 12th Feb. 1832.

TABLE V.

Sale Amount of Privilege and Private Trade Goods, sold at the East India Company's Sales, 1816–17 to 1828–29, distinguishing India from China.

From the 1st March to the 1st March in each Year.	Privileged, Licensed, and Free Trade.		Private Trade Goods.		Total.	
	India.	China.	India.	China.	India.	China.
	£	£	£	£	£	£
1816–17	3,473,667		356,415	499,174	3,830,082	499,174
1817–18	3,873,523		374,918	510,582	4,248,441	510,582
1818–19	4,188,678		158,064	364,197	4,346,742	364,197
1819–20	2,349,365		219,765	434,044	2,569,130	434,044
1820–21	2,605,358		90,290	557,590	2,695,648	557,590
1821–22	2,634,435		9,088	592,048	2,643,523	592,048
1822–23	2,430,087		93,056	516,403	2,523,143	516,403
1823–24	2,586,307		130,702	445,903	2,717,009	445,903
1824–25	3,136,138		61,829	487,851	3,197,967	487,851
1825–26	3,073,998		27,079	427,923	3,101,077	427,923
1826–27	3,221,057		62,394	424,889	3,283,451	424,889
1827–28	2,502,253		3,030	473,401	2,505,283	473,401
1828–29	2,416,092		28,142	524,082	2,444,234	524,082

(Errors excepted.) THOS. G. LLOYD, Acc. General.

East India House, 21st Sept. 1829.

An Account of the Sale Amount of the Company's, the Private Trade, and the Neutral and Prize Goods, &c., sold by the East India Company in the year 1829–30.

1829–30.	Company's Goods.	Licensed, and Private Goods.
	£	£
Teas, Piece Goods, Silks, Nankeens, Pepper, Saltpetre, Indigo, Spices, Sugar, Wool, Coffee, Drugs, &c.	4,194,108	2,213,447

(Errors excepted.) WM. LEACH.

India Board, Westminster, 28th Feb. 1831.

TABLE VI.

EXTERNAL and INTERNAL COMMERCE of BENGAL, for the Year 1828–29, at Sicca Rupees 8,91,40,258; or in British currency at the Exchange it has hitherto been usual to assume £11,142,532 sterling.

IMPORTS.	Private Tra de. Rupees.	Company's Trade Rupees.	Total Rupees.
Merchandise..................	3,00,40,816	1,51,916	3,01,92,732
Treasure......................	51,68,390	17,32,900	69,02,374
Total Sicca Rupees...	3,52,09,206	18,85,900	3,70,95,106
EXPORTS.			
Merchandise..................	3,39,10,363	1,63,71,594	5,02,81,595
Treasure......................	14,63,183	3,00,000	17,63,193
Total Sicca Rupees...	3,53,73,558	1,66,71,594	5,20,45,152
Sterling............	£8,822,885	£2,319,687	£11,142,535

EXTERNAL and INTERNAL COMMERCE of MADRAS, 1827–28.

IMPORTS.	Madras Rupees.	Madras Rupees.	Madras Rupees.
Merchandise..................	93,91,228	4,18,117	98,09,345
Treasure......................	36,28,467	....	36,28,468
Total....................	1,30,19,695	4,18,117	1,34,39,813
EXPORTS.			
Merchandise..................	1,40,64,835	22,62,868	1,63,27,703
Treasure......................	10,12,726	44,64,376	54,79,102
Total	1,50,77,561	67,29,244	2,18,06,805
Grand Total.........	2,80,97,526	71,47,361	3,52,44,617

TABLE VI.—*Continued.*

EXTERNAL and INTERNAL COMMERCE of BOMBAY in 1828-29.

GENERAL IMPORTS.	Sicca Rupees.
Merchandise	2,50,55,237
Treasure	1,20,04,969
Horses	5,01,800
	3,75,62,025
EXPORTS.	
Merchandise	2,89,64,478
Treasure	20,40,178
Horses	4,47,200
Total Sicca Rupees	3.17,51,856

TABLE VII.

IMPORTS and EXPORTS of CALCUTTA, from 1814 to 1828:—from the Calcutta Custom-House Records.

	Imports.	Exports.
1813-14......	£2,120,000	£5,390,000
1814-15......	2,610,000	5,610,000
1815-16......	3,440,000	6,660,000
1816-17......	5,840,000	6,990,000
1817-18......	6,850,000	7,810,000
1818-19......	7,620,000	7,090,000
1819-20......	5,650,000	6,950,000
1820-21......	4,520,000	6,710,000
1821-22......	4,670,000	7,790,000
1822-23......	3,880,000	8,710,000
1833-24......	4,300,000	8,040,000
1824-25......	4,040,000	7,750,000
1825-26......	3,600,000	7,600,000
1826-27......	3,400,000	6,800,000
1827-28......	4,150,000	8,730,000

To face Page

An Offici[illegible]
1809
the [illegible]
or C[illegible]
Fort[illegible]
&c. [illegible]
rece[illegible]
the [illegible]

Y[illegible]
180[illegible]
181[illegible]
181[illegible]
181[illegible]
181[illegible]
181[illegible]
181[illegible]
181[illegible]
181[illegible]
181[illegible]
181[illegible]
1820
1821
1822
1823
1824
1825
1826
1827
Est[illegible]
1828

Years.
1809—10
1810—11
1811—12
1812—13
1813—14
1814—15
1815—16
1816—17
1817—18
1818—19
1819—20
1820—21
1821—22
1822—23
1823—24
1824—25
1825—26
1826—27
1827—28
Estimate. 1828—29

TABLE XII.

ABSTRACT STATEMENT of the Result of the Debts and Assets of the East India Company, in all India, on the 30th of April in each year, from 1809 to 1827, both inclusive.

	Debt.		Grand Total of Debts.	Grand Total of Assets.	Excess of Debts.
	At Interest.	Floating.			
	£	£	£	£	£
1809	27,089,831	3,722,610	30,812,441	19,930,560	10,881,876
1810	27,529,693	4,372,017	31,901,710	24,372,173	7,529,537
1811	24,202,066	4,228,066	28,430,132	23,662,893	4,767,239
1812	25,666,782	4,903,871	30,570,653	25,960,162	4,610,491
1813	26,243,219	3,917,331	30,160,550	25,124,567	5,035,983

From 1814 to 1827.

	Territorial.					Commercial.			Grand Total. Territorial and Commercial.		
	Debt.		Total Debts.	Total Assets.	Excess of Debts.	Debts.	Assets.	Excess of Assets.	Debts.	Assets.	Excess of Debts.
	At Interest.	Floating.									
	£	£	£	£	£	£	£	£	£	£	£
1814	27,002,439	3,847,950	30,850,389	22,767,230	8,083,169	286,770	3,687,238	3,400,468	31,137,159	26,454,458	4,682,701
1815	27,842,305	4,678,089	32,521,372	16,401,357	16,190,916	171,884	3,503,826	3,332,340	32,[illegible],118	19,905,243	12,787,875
1816	28,057,964	5,071,735	33,129,699	16,941,813	16,197,886	121,113	3,622,878	3,501,769	33,250,812	20,564,691	12,696,121
1817	28,821,486	4,866,530	33,687,987	17,824,755	15,863,242	79,287	3,353,579	3,274,192	33,767,384	21,188,334	12,579,050
1818	29,417,878	5,241,708	34,659,580	17,491,367	17,167,223	116,253	3,567,429	3,450,989	34,775,843	21,059,479	13,716,364
1819	31,065,846	6,296,722	37,358,570	18,482,812	18,859,958	113,534	3,318,811	3,205,277	37,475,804	21,808,123	15,667,681
1820	33,801,981	5,989,121	39,791,092	19,506,218	20,284,790	68,868	2,998,414	2,923,[illegible]	39,859,918	22,498,716	17,361,202
1821	33,104,941	6,328,137	39,456,078	22,489,312	17,028,766	75,856	3,393,971	3,318,416	39,533,[illegible]	25,723,[illegible]	13,810,380
1822	31,883,760	6,976,877	38,501,637	22,804,704	16,396,933	104,769	3,058,724	2,980,955	38,[illegible]	26,[illegible]	12,408,[illegible]
1823	29,362,860	7,457,140	36,829,990	23,726,746	13,112,915	110,094	2,848,850	2,738,916	36,[illegible]	25,574,[illegible]	10,374,700
1824	26,468,475	8,[illegible]	34,490,735	19,[illegible],340	15,[illegible]	68,944	2,780,809	2,[illegible]	35,[illegible]	22,[illegible]	12,[illegible],117
1825	27,370,050	8,440,126	35,729,175	18,301,[illegible]	17,487,780	148,[illegible]	2,672,[illegible]	2,[illegible]	34,878,979	24,[illegible]	14,977,[illegible]
1826	32,950,858	8,501,088	41,[illegible]	21,211,164	20,650,777	117,129	2,643,[illegible]	2,[illegible]	36,[illegible]	24,[illegible]	18,184,214
1827	34,706,838	8,074,040	42,[illegible]	21,[illegible]	21,367,[illegible]	113,[illegible]	2,867,770	2,714,124	41,[illegible]	[illegible]	18,[illegible]
1828	39,[illegible]	7,[illegible]	47,[illegible]	[illegible]	[illegible]	104,443	[illegible]	2,[illegible]	47,[illegible]	[illegible]	21,[illegible]

India Board, Westminster, 6th February, 1832.

ESTIMATE AN

Shewing the Population; Lands cultivated; estim

	Population. A.	Troops. B.		Area in British square Miles.
		Native.	Europ^{n}.	
Bengal................	69,710,071	96,889	15,606	220,312
Madras................	13,508,535	57,749	12,981	141,923
Bombay..............	6,251,546	32,421	7,729	59,438
Prince of Wales' Island, Sincapore, and Malacca................	107,084	....	....	1,317
Territories in the Deccan not yet attached to any Presidency...	11,000,000	....	....	91,200
China................	......	....	....	....
Allied and Independent States................	40,000,000	....	....	614,610
	140,577,206	187,057	36,604	1,128,800

Bengal..................

Madras..................

Bombay..................

Prince of Wales' Island, Si capore, and Malacca....

China..................

AGGREGATE VALUE.... £1,611,077,354

Area in

Popula

Lands,

Ditto,

Estima

Import

Export

Tonnag

Ditto.

Subsid

Revenu

Charges

Net Re

£1,611,077,354

.PLANATORY NOTES TO THE TABLE.

'he Official Table I. shows that the population of the
s territories in India, according to the last returns (1830)
to 89,577,206; exclusive of the population of a territory
' square miles in the Presidency of Bengal, and 5,500 un-
-as, altogether amounting to 91,200, for which no returns
-le; but the population of this immense territory, consti-
bove one-fifth of the Company's dominions, would undoubt-
. many millions to the numbers above noticed.
number of Christians in Calcutta, according to the Police
in 1822, was 13,138; of whom 2,254 were Europeans, and
half castes. There were 20,000 half castes in all the pro-
. the attorneys generally belong to that class. Families in
according to the evidence of Elphinstone, do not inherit by
indu, but by the Mahomedan law. If half castes marry Eu-
ı women, their offspring are not British subjects: but if Bri-
ubjects marry native women, their children inherit the right
e fathers.

5.) Abstract Numerical Strength of the Indian Army:

	Regular Troops.		Irregulars and Invalids.		Total.		
	Eur.	Nat.	Eur.	Nat.	Eur.	Nat.	Gr. Total.
Bengal	15,312	68,367	384	28,520	15,696	96,887	112,583
Madras	12,603	51,096	378	6,653	12,981	57,749	70,730
Bombay	7,667	28,613	70	3,808	7,729	32,421	40,148
	35,572	148,076	832	38,981	36,306	187,057	223,461

(C.) *Estimated value of Produce annually raised.* It is difficult to ascertain with accuracy the value of the produce annually raised in India. However, considering the enormous mass of produce required to feed, clothe, and furnish with all the necessaries and luxuries of life, such an immense population; and considering the immense quantity and value of the productions exported, which may be seen under the proper head; it will certainly be a very moderate estimate, to assume the annual value of the produce raised for consumption and exportation, at an average of 3*l.* 10*s.* per individual. This gives, for a population of 89,500,000, the sum of 313,200,000*l.*

(D.) *Imports into and Exports from Great Britain.* The commerce with India, both private and on the Company's account, has greatly increased since the trade was opened in 1813. The imports into Great Britain by private trade, are above three times more than by the Company. And of the exports, amounting in 1829 to 4,100,264*l.*, only 434,506*l.* were on account of the Company. Table IV. shows the imports and exports, and the whole internal and external trade of India is fully shown in Tables VI. and VII.

(E.)—*Tonnage*. Many of the natives are considerable ship owners; the Queen of Canore is considered one of the greatest. The number of Indian vessels, called Dhonies, trading to and from Calcutta in 1829, was 138, measuring 20,700 tons. The number for the other presidencies may be considered as at least a third of this number, which would give 27,466 tons for the whole; to which must be added the considerable tonnage of the small craft employed on rivers, &c.

Statement of the Number of Ships and Tonnage to and from Calcutta for the years—

	1827–8.		1828–9.	
	Ships.	Tons.	Ships.	Tons.
Under British Colours	251	97,888	234	101,105
French	25	8,147	34	10,560
Swedish	3	590	1	468
Portuguese	4	1,500	...	....
Spanish	1	320	...	....
Dutch	3	1,028	2	460
American	10	2,788	11	3,526
Arabs	19	7,257	13	5,118
Dhonies	370	55,500	138	20,700
	686	175,018	433	141,937

(F.)—*Subsidies from Native Princes, or from ceded and conquered Countries*. The gross amount of these was in 1828, 10,964,000*l.*, and in 1829, reached 11,580,000*l.*; and the net receipts in the same year were eight millions, as appears by Table XI. There is no doubt that the revenue derived from this source might be considerably augmented, by greater economy and better management.

(G.)—*Revenue*. The progress and amount of Indian revenue since 1810, is shewn in Table VIII. The revenue from the original possessions of the company, rose from eight and a half millions in that year to eleven and a half in 1829; and the territorial, from above five and a half in 1810 to above seven and a half in the latter year: the gross receipts of both branches from 16,464,000*l.* in 1810 to above 23,000,000*l.* in 1829: and, according to the evidence of several witnesses before the committee, they might be very greatly increased, if the taxes were lowered and rendered less oppressive.

Charges. These have increased in a much greater proportion than the revenue. In 1810, the total charges for all the presidencies were only about 13,000,000*l.*: in 1829, they were above 20,900,000*l.*

Net Revenue. This has decreased in the same period; as in 1810, it was 2,600,000*l.*, and 1829 only 1,200,000*l.* (See for these three heads, Tables VIII. and IX.)

(H.)—*Dead Stock* The company in computing their assets, value this item at only 400,000*l.*, this being the amount according to Lord Godolphin's award in 1702; whereas the whole sums of money expended by the company in fortifications, buildings, plate, furniture, plantations, vessels, stores, and other articles constituting what is called dead stock, for the maintenance and acquisition of their possessions, amount, according to the latest estimates to 15,929,243*l.*: but in order to preserve the amount of assets, as officially stated by the company, this 400,000*l.* is deducted *here;* leaving for the item of dead stock, which may be called public property, 15,529,243*l.*

It deserves to be mentioned to their credit, that in consequence of the wise dispositions of the company, India is at the present day better measured, and the latitude of her towns much better determined, than in many parts of Europe boasting the highest knowledge and civilization. Since 1814, a meridional arc has been extended by Colonel Lambton and Captain Everest, from Daumergeda to Seronj, being a length from north to south of six degrees of latitude. A tract of country has been triangled in the Nizam dominions, of 30,000 square miles in extent: and a chain of triangles has been carried on from Seronj to within fifty miles of Calcutta (a distance of about twelve degrees of longitude) for the purpose of connecting that place with the meridional arc: the position of all the principal towns in the line of route, has also been determined.

Thus this immense region has already received the fundamental bases of wealth, internal and external commerce, and prosperity: which will be fostered or retarded by the dispositions and measures that the legislature may adopt on the renewal of the company's charter: on these much of the future public welfare of India and England depend.

A consideration of all the facts and data adduced, led the author to estimate the total capital of the E. I. empire at 2,000,000,000*l.*, instead of the sum stated in the Table; but he has preferred adopting a moderate scale, leaving the intelligent and experienced reader to correct the calculations, if they should be thought to require it.

	Buildings and Fortifications, &c.		Plate, Household Furniture, Plantations, Vessels, Stores, &c.		Total.
	Political.	Commercial.	Political.	Commercial.	
	£	£	£	£	£
Bengal, 30th April, 1828.	6,177,930	377,915	4,052,675	22,067	[illegible]
Madras	2,098,115	38,229	429,964	17,393	[illegible]
Bombay	1,849,965	75,184	442,270	21,862	[illegible]
St. Helena	101,470	......	30,228	......	[illegible]
Prince of Wales' Island	165,253	......	25,658	......	[illegible]
Singapore	15,583	......	1,696	......	[illegible]
Malacca	367	......	1,752	......	[illegible]
China, 7th Feb., 1828	....	5,489	....	8,157	[illegible]
Total	10,278,983	496,818	4,984,237	69,105	15,888,743

(I.)—In the *Assets* of the Company is included the 400,000*l.* for Dead Stock, as mentioned under that head, which does not disturb the general result. The *real* value of the whole property belonging to the Company will be:—

Assets	£25,955,111
Dead Stock (less 400,000*l.*)	15,529,243
Total ...	£41,484,354

The total amount of the Company's Debts is shewn in Table XII. to be 47,600,000*l.*; but against this sum stand not only all the Assets and Capital of the Company, but their credit and sovereign right in the soil of all India under their sway. The Company, considered as a mercantile corporation, are quite right in putting the Assets against the Debts, when drawing their general account of Debtor and Creditor. But considered as sovereign rulers of an immense Empire, the total Debt of the Company must be considered on the same footing as the public debt of England or any other country. But in order to show the Capital and Stock of the Company considered as a mercantile and corporate body, the following official statement is inserted, shewing the grand total and balance.

Statement per computation of the East India Company, exclusive of their Capital Stock, drawn out in respect to England on 1st May,

1829; in respect to India, on 1st May, 1828. In continuation of the Account presented by his Majesty's command in 1830.

T. G. LLOYD.

East India House, 16th February, 1831.

Dr.		£	Cr.	£
Total Territorial and Political Debts abroad and at home		58,442,972	Territorial & Political Credits abroad and at home, afloat, &c.	28,109,481
Total Commercial Debt		2,026,081	Total Commercial Credits, abroad and at home....................	23,086,233
Company's Home Debts bearing Interest	3,780,475	3,795,892		51,195,714
Ditto Ditto	15,471		Balance deficient ..	13,068,231
Grand total ..		£64,263,945	Grand total ..	£64,263,945

This balance is subject to reduction by the amount of advances made in India from the Territorial to the Commercial branch, which may amount to 3,261,480*l.*, leaving a balance due to commerce of 4,923,021*l.*, including interest.

(K.) *Estimated Value of Lands, Stock included.*—The extraordinary increase in the value of lands under cultivation has been shewn in the evidence before the Committee for East India affairs, already quoted in the text; it is therefore unnecessary to add any thing further here. Twenty years ago, and in the absence of such important data, the cultivated lands were valued by several writers at an average of 5*l.* per acre. Estimating them at present at an average of 4*l.* 10*s.* per acre, must be considered very moderate, particularly as this includes all stock attached. Taking the number of cultivated acres in round numbers at 130,000,000, their total value will be 585,000,000*l.* The value of the uncultivated lands is left to the judgment of the reader.

(L.) *Estimated Value of Houses, Stores, Merchandise, Plate, Furniture, &c.*—It is almost impossible to ascertain with exactness the amount of property comprehended under this head. Let the immense wealth of all the natives, princes, zemindars, contractors, merchants of all classes, &c., &c., down to the lowest grades, be first duly weighed and considered, and perhaps the following classification of persons and property, may give an approximate idea of the total amount; any competent person may correct and regulate it according to his judgment and experience.

Distribution of the Property in Houses, Furniture, Merchandise, Plate, Jewels, Cattle, &c. (exclusive of specie in circulation) possessed by Europeans and Natives in India.

No. of Persons.	Average Property possessed by each Person.	Total Property.
	£	£
300,000	300	90,000,000
1,500,000	100	150,000,000
2,000,000	70	140,000,000
3,500,000	50	175,000,000
[illegible]	20	200,000,000
7,000,000	10	70,000,000
12,000,000	4	48,000,000
18,000,000	2	36,000,000
[illegible]	..	....
Total [illegible]	Total property	£909,000,000

Thus there will be property to the value of 909,000,000*l.*, possessed by Europeans and natives in India, even supposing above 40,000,000 of inhabitants to be in a state of utter poverty and destitution.

IX. *Estimated Value of Coastal Shipping.*—The number of coasting vessels, as well as the tonnage, has considerably increased since the trade was opened in 1813; however, as their value is less than at that time, the amount has been left as then estimated. There has been a decline in the coasting trade and shipping in the present year when compared with the preceding. (See Note E.)

(X.) *Estimated Amount of Circulating Specie.*—India has always been renowned for the large amount of gold and silver hoarded and in circulation. To compute the quantity of specie in circulation, even in the most civilized countries of Europe, is one of the most difficult tasks of an economist: how much more difficult must it be, to ascertain its amount in the extensive territories of India. In 1813 it was estimated by some writers, at 150,000,000*l.*, and by others at much more. Taking the same basis that was adopted in calculating the personal property, the amount of gold, silver, and copper, hoarded and in circulation, may be estimated as follows:—

No. of Persons.		Each possessing £	£
2,000,000	Many in a state of affluence, others in easy circumstances	16	32,000,000
8,000,000	Acquiring moderate incomes from agriculture, commerce, &c.	8	64,000,000
19,750,000	Lower classes employed in agriculture, trade, &c..................	4	79,000,000
59,827,206	Not supposed to possess any gold, silver, or copper whatever.........	...	....
89,577,206	Total, in circulation and hoarded		£175,000,000

SECTION XI.

General View and Recapitulation of the Capital, Resources, Population, Laws, Trade, and Shipping of the British Empire in Europe, America, Africa, Asia, and Australia.—Aggregate value of the productions annually raised in Great Britain and Ireland, by the combination of capital with animate and inanimate power; in the British dependencies in Europe; in the North American colonies; in the West Indies; in the possessions in the Indian Ocean; in the settlements in Africa; in Australia; and in the East Indian Empire.

In the preceding Sections an attempt has been made to exhibit, in the most intelligible manner, and by the aid of sound data and facts, a detailed view of the capital, resources, and productive powers of the several parts constituting the British Empire.

Let us now see what is the aggregate result of all this wealth, capital, and power, when brought under one view, and summed up in one grand total.

It appears then, that even according to the moderate calculation adopted in all these estimates, there exists, in the United Kingdom of Great Britain and Ireland, a capital, public and private, of 3,679,500,000*l.*!

The greatest part of this enormous capital is beneficially employed in creating substantial property, and in promoting industry and enterprise in the multifarious pursuits and occupations by which the necessaries, the comforts, and the luxuries of life are raised and provided. The most useful and important of these is Agriculture, which raises, in all its branches, annual produce to the value of 246,600,000*l.*; or fifty-two millions and a half more than the total produce of this branch in France, considered to be the first agricultural country in Europe[*]. The value of the produce of Mines and Minerals, in the United Kingdom, is 21,400,000*l.* The produce and profits of the numerous classes engaged in Inland Trade, amount to the large sum of 48,425,000*l.*. And of those important branches to all maritime nations, the Coasting Trade and the Fisheries, the former yields 3,550,000*l.*, and the latter 3,400,000*l.* The annual gains of all those engaged in Shipping and Foreign Trade, amount to 34,398,059*l.* The profits of Bankers may be stated at 4,500,000*l.*; and the income derived from property invested in foreign securities, including the sum annually remitted from India, is estimated at 4,500,000*l.* Lastly, the capital, labour, and machinery employed in all the numerous and extensive

[*] Dupin, "Forces Productives et Commerciales de la France".

STATEMENT of the EXPENSES and PRODUCE of FRENCH AGRICULTURE.

	North France.	South France.	Total. France.
	Francs.	*Francs.*	*Francs.*
Gross produce	2,452,842,087	2,860,321,648	5,313,163,735
Net produce	800,600,000	825,410,000	1,626,000,000
Charges of Cultivation	1,652,242,087	2.034,921,648	3,687,163.735
Working animals and materials	302,326,540	298,507,260	600,833,800
Seeds	151,979,759	169,624,482	321,604,241
Total expenditure, human expenses excepted	454,306,299	168,131,742	922,438,041
Human expenditure	1,197,935,788	1,566,789,906	2,764,725,694
Human powers	3,094,564	4,738,778	7,833,342
Annual profits of the labourer, at 260 days of work in the year	381	331	358
Price per day	1,47c.	1,27c	1,38c.
Annual earnings of a family	508	441	477

See Goldsmith's Statistics of France, who calculates the total produce of the soil of France at 4,853,628,873 francs, or about 194,145,154*l.*

branches of Manufactures, annually raise produce valued at the enormous sum of 148,050,000*l.*!

Thus the grand result of the combination of the prodigious capital above stated, with all animate and inanimate power, is the annual creation of produce and property to the amount of 514,823,059*l.*!!

Such are the astonishing effects of the wealth, talent, industry, and intelligence concentrated in this extraordinary country: such is the immense capital, and such are the amasing productive powers of this little isle—this "precious stone set in the silver sea", as the poet calls it*. But even *his* portentous imagination was far from conceiving the power which "that little world"—"that fortress built by nature"—would one day reach: he could not even have fancied that thousands of tons of goods would be conveyed with a speed greater than that of the messenger pigeons of Aleppo and Antwerp: he could not have imagined, that by the combined aid of steam and capital, the productive powers of each of "that happy breed of men" would be rendered equal to the simple exertions of several hundred individuals!

From all this may be easily concluded how imperfect have been the statements of those who have calculated the productive powers of Great Britain, and

* "This royal throne of kings, this scepter'd isle,
This earth of majesty, this seat of Mars,
This other Eden, demi-paradise;
This fortress, built by Nature for herself,
Against infection, and the hand of war;
This happy breed of men, this little world;
This precious stone set in the silver sea,
Which serves it in the office of a wall,
Or as a moat defensive to a house,
Against the envy of less happier lands."

SHAK. RICH. II. ACT 2.

compared them with those of France and other countries: this important inquiry and comparison is reserved for another opportunity; while sufficient facts and data are here stated to give the mind of the reader more just and correct ideas of the real productive powers and capital of this country; a country, however, only to be considered as the *mighty heart,* which diffuses strength and vigour throughout all the *limbs* of that gigantic body, the British Empire; while they, by a strong and reciprocal motion, return and increase its vitality, action, and power.

In the parts more immediately connected with England, and in all her dependencies in Europe, there is supposed to exist a capital of 27,115,094*l.*; and the produce annually raised, is valued at 2,146,198*l.*

The seven important North American possessions, as may be seen by the Table, have a capital of 62,100,466*l.*; and raise annually produce and property worth 17,620,629*l.*

The West India Colonies, with a capital of 131,052,424*l.* raise every year produce valued at 22,496,672*l.*

The whole British capital in Africa amounts to only 6,444,398*l.*; and these settlements, unproductive like the country itself, yield an annual produce of only 1,066,065*l.*

To compensate for this, there is in the two fertile islands in the Indian Ocean, a capital of 27,509,781*l.*; and the value of the produce annually raised is 4,291,332*l.*

While the new, but rapidly improving settlements in Australia already possess a capital of 2,685,000*l.*; and raise produce amounting to 520,000*l.*

It is almost impossible to obtain sufficient data and facts, on which to make a sound calculation of the im-

[illegible]

[illegible]

Such are the unparalleled magnitude and importance of the wealth, power, resources, and productiveness, of the British Empire. But it must not be forgotten, that against the prodigious capital and resources we have just been contemplating, stands the *National Debt*—incessantly acting upon that very capital, crippling those very resources, pressing upon that population, and producing evils of such magnitude as all these powers united can scarcely withstand.

In the next Part these evils are more fully stated and examined, and the only effectual remedy for them is pointed out.

GENERAL STATISTICAL TABLE.—General View and Estimate of the Wealth, Power, Resources, Popu[illegible] Private, Lands, Produce annually raised, Trade, Shipping, Naval and Military Force of the whole British Empire.

	Population.	Surface in Geographical Square Miles.	Capital. Public Property.	Capital. Private Property.	Capital. Total.
			£	£	£
Great Britain and Ireland	24,271,758	90,948	103,800,000	3,575,700,000	3,679,500,000
British Dependencies in Europe	247,701		7,300,000	19,815,094	27,115,094
——— North American Colonies	911,229	1,930,000	2,933,331	59,167,135	62,100,466
West Indies	733,617		3,853,000	127,199,424	131,052,424
British Possessions in Indian Ocean .	1,034,736	23,000	3,733,332	23,776,449	27,509,781
——— Africa	154,046	91,000	1,426,665	5,017,733	6,444,398
——— Australia.....	39,688	1,496,000	140,000	2,545,000	2,685,000
——— East Indies	89,577,206	826,650	15,529,243	1,595,548,111	1,611,077,354
	116,969,978	4,457,598	138,715,571	5,408,768,946	5,547,484,517

	Lands. Cultivated.	Lands. Uncultivated.	Estimated Value of Produce annually raised.	Imports into the United Kingdom.	Exports from the United Kingdom.	Tonnage. Inwards Tons.	Tonnage. Outwards Tons.	Coasting Trade. Inwards Tons.	Coasting Trade. Outwards Tons.	Force. Navy Men.	Force. Army Men.
	Acres.	Acres.		£	£						
Great Britain and Ireland...........	46,522,970	30,871,463	514,823,059	48,161,600	60,090,123	2,930,000	2,243,000	9,176,958	9,372,870	27,000	96,419
British Dependencies in Europe	208,100	39,600	2,146,998	1,622,974	55,319	37,728	52,231				
——— North American Colonies	10,309,998	135,200,000	17,620,629	1,141,288	2,118,459	431,124	418,147				
West Indies	2,476,095	3,926,698	22,496,672	9,087,914	5,521,169	263,338	252,992				
British Possessions in Indian Ocean	580,000	1,652,080	4,291,332	654,666	372,026	14,133	9,439				223,461
——— Africa	274,240	....	1,067,065	496,683	895,206	37,981	39,614				
——— Australia	300,000	....	520,000	33,191	96,123	8,979	28,719				
——— East Indies ...	134,200,000	....	313,200,000	6,218,284	4,100,264						
	194,871,403	....	876,175,755	67,416,600	73,248,689			9,176,958	9,372,870	27,000	319,880

PART IV.

EFFECTS OF THE TAXATION REQUIRED TO PAY THE INTEREST OF THE NATIONAL DEBT, AND A PRACTICAL PLAN FOR ITS LIQUIDATION.

SECTION I.

Influence of taxation on the sources of production, viz. land, labour, and capital; and its effects on society.—Similar results produced in Spain and Holland.—How the public writers of those nations maintained the same doctrines as many of the present English economists.—Evils resulting from this system, and the remedy to be applied.—Several anomalies and apparent contradictions explained.

THE taxation required to pay the annual interest of the national debt, cripples the primary sources of production; paralyzes the manufactures, commerce, and enterprise of the British empire; deprives it of the advantages resulting from a superiority of skill and machinery; prevents it from enjoying the full benefits of a state of peace, and renders it unfit for war.

In the demonstration of this proposition, the author will endeavour to abstain from going into the minute details with which it is so often encumbered. He will not, therefore, adopt the technical language and style of the financiers, who, like doctors and divines, render the plainest questions confused and unintelligible; his aim being to make himself understood by those who, though not initiated in the mysteries of the economical sciences, have no less interest in this and other momentous questions which they embrace.

All the most celebrated economists agree, that taxation takes away part of the property of individuals, and [illegible] public writers [illegible] the [illegible] ministers, [illegible] while nearly thirty [illegible] the public [illegible] from the acknowledged [illegible] any ministry [illegible] to them. The expenses must be provided for: the selecting and discriminating of taxes, therefore, must be set aside; the just limits of imposts must unavoidably be passed;

* "Les [illegible] . . ." Say, [illegible] Principes.

and consequently the sources of production must be attacked and impaired.

Let us bring these truths to the best of all tests, *facts*. The average revenue produced by taxation in Great Britain, in the five years ending in 1832, may be fairly estimated at sixty millions, (see Table XLIII. Part I.;) the greatest part of which is applied to the interest of the debt, and the remainder to the *indispensable object* of the maintenance of the state[a]. But in what mode is this income raised? The enormous sum of forty-one millions is levied upon consumption—upon the necessaries of life[b]!—upon food, coals, malt,

[a] The average expenditure to maintain the state in the last year, in the departments of civil government, justice, diplomatic services, and naval and military force, when compared with expenditure required to defray the charges of the debt, was nearly as 17 to 28.

[b] To demonstate the truth of this assertion, the following statement, extracted from the Report of the Finance Committee of 1828, is chosen in preference to one formed for a later period, on account of the respectability of the authority by which it was framed. At present, however, taxation bears in nearly the same proportion on the sources of production.

	£	
Spirits	7,921,645	
Malt	4,623,112	
Beer and hops	3,516,764	
Wine	1,700,051	
Total Liquors		£17,761,572
Sugar and molasses	5,191,280	
Tea	3,448,814	
Coffee	425,389	9,065,483
Tobacco and snuff		2,793,873
Total		29,620,928
Butter and cheese	307,794	
Currants and raisins	436,580	
Corn	193,228	
Food		937,602

 Cotton,

sugar, dress, household articles, raw produce, and the materials of manufactures. The duties on sugar, malt, and beer, in 1829, netted 13,331,155*l.*; but these articles are as much necessaries of life as bread, butter, cheese, soap, and coals, which, in the same year, were made to yield the large sum of 3,709,199*l.*; and the proportionate pressure on articles of consumption is much the same in the present day.

By such taxes the productive classes of the state are overloaded; the poorer people, with less means, contribute a greater share than the wealthy. But this is not the worst: by such measures the primary source of produce, *labour*, is injured: the elements influencing wages, as food, household expenses, &c. are raised; and consequently those elements, into which all manufactures are resolved, must be elevated in proportion. Manufac-

Cotton wool, and sheep's, imported	395,174	
Silks	345,278	
Printed goods	657,741	
Hides and skins	451,944	
Paper	723,497	
Dress, &c.		2,573,634
Soap	1,210,754	
Candles and tallow	665,758	
Coals, sea-borne	895,085	
Household articles		2,771,597
Glass	616,527	
Bricks, tiles, and slates	392,365	
Timber	1,488,498	
Building, &c.		2,497,390
Auctions	275,564	
Excise licenses	845,160	
Miscellaneous Excise and Customs	2,205,903	3,326,627
Total		£41,727,778

tures increasing in price, sales must diminish in the same ratio; and, to increase the evil, we possess no control over foreign improvements, and our home markets are extremely limited, in proportion to our daily increasing productive powers.

But it is contended, that 'this mode of taxation, being circuitous and indirect, does not produce the baneful effects on manufactures which are imagined'. This doctrine, as will be presently shewn, ruined a great manufacturing nation; but to exhibit its fallacy and absurdity at once, let us suppose a direct tax of five shillings a yard imposed upon cloth; undoubtedly cloth would not meet with buyers in the foreign market: but the result must be the same if the yard of cloth become five shillings dearer in consequence of the high rate of wages, and the high price of the materials constituting it. To expect any other result is a manifest absurdity.

But if labour is affected by these imposts acting *directly* upon it, how much more will it be crippled, when to that pressure, is added the combination of a host of *indirect* taxes? For when *labour* is thus greatly depressed, the other two sources of production being intimately connected with it, and possessing a reciprocal action amongst themselves, must be exceedingly injured. *Capital*, that agent of production, whose only country is "higher interest", will be affected first: not being able to obtain an adequate interest, it must flow to more beneficial channels, it must abandon this country for a more favourable region, or it must lie idle. Ricardo himself, struggling to maintain that the high prices of commodities occasioned by taxation are no disadvantage to this country, could not resist the evidence of truth: for he adds, that "the interest of the contributors is, to withdraw their shoulders from the burden, and to remove themselves and their capital from the country[a]. A loss of population, then, as well as of capital, will be the result; while by this twofold combination, *land*, the third source of production, will be more seriously and effectively injured. But these baneful effects will be more considerably felt in a country of limited extent like England, where, while the population is increasing, the fertility of the soil is rapidly decreasing, and for that very reason requires lower wages and an increased capital[a]. The greatest pressure, therefore, will fall upon the land. Thus, by a chain of evils so intimately connected, the three principal springs of production will be injured, and the wealth accumulated by centuries of industry will disappear in a short period. Such has actually been the awful but uninterrupted march, even in nations which possessed a more extensive and fertile soil, and were far from being in the artificial situation in which England is at present placed.

But we have not yet gone to any thing like the extent of the baneful effects produced by the taxes required to pay the interest of the debt: we have only considered the smallest part of the result of the evils. If national writers have shown the sum of 60 millions, levied in the manner described, to be hurtful, and have declaimed against the amount as enormous, before the Restriction Act ceased, they have acknowledged that,

[a] It was stated before the Committee of the House of Commons in 1822, that the best lands produced from forty to fifty-six bushels per acre; the worst, from eight to ten. Thus, four or five times the amount of capital is required for the inferior soils: the consequence is, that the land which could bear wheat first, could bear oats afterwards, then rye, and so on down to the inferior crops, until it is thrown out of tillage. See also, a "Letter to the Agriculturists of England, &c."

prices having considerably fallen since that event[a], 60 millions are at present equal to 76 millions: and even that 50 millions are equal to 70[b]! the pressure upon the sources above mentioned, must consequently have increased in proportion. But, on the other hand, the taxes necessary for the preservation of the State cannot be dispensed with. The poor rates also are unavoidable: to pay poor rates, and endure all the evils of the poor laws, is preferable to being surrounded, at every step, as in Ireland and on the Continent, by disgusting, miserable, and destitute objects: and even if it were possible to leave our fellow-creatures to perish of starvation, we may rest assured that the unemployed labourers, the disabled seamen, and the large body of artificers, who have mainly contributed to the wealth and power of the country, could not, nor would not be abandoned. The taxes raised to relieve human misfortunes, amounted, on an average of the last three years, to 8,451,572*l.*[c] (see Table I.):—not to mention the numberless other local imposts, which might be cal-

[a] See Tables I. and II., in Part III., Section II.

[b] Lowe, in 1822, affirmed that 67 millions were equal to 80: other writers estimated the difference at much more. Since that time, the prices of every thing have fallen in greater proportion.

[c] Nearly one-third of the rates being employed to pay wages, and not to support the poor, is considered here as a compensation for the difference between the prices above stated. But it must also be borne in mind, that the poor rates under the present system cannot be diminished, but, on the contrary, must go on increasing; for 53,000 poor labourers annually come from Ireland, which, combined with the growing practice of employing children in factories, instead of adults, is a two-fold and powerful cause of the decrease of wages, and of hundreds of destitute labourers being thrown upon their parishes; thus creating a permanent cause for the increase of the poor rates.

culated perhaps at an equal if not a greater sum, and which equally clog the main-springs of production.

But let us consider the net revenue received at the Exchequer at 50 millions, equal to 70 millions as above stated, to which adding 8 millions for poor rates, let us confine ourselves to the effects of these 78 millions only upon those sources. In analyzing this subject, the best writers on national economy acknowledge, that the actual pressure of a tax upon the community is not to be measured by the mere amount of such tax, but by the increased amount it has virtually acquired before it reaches its destination. Many well-informed writers, who have devoted their exertions to this subject, following a given tax through all its successive stages and chain of operations, have calculated the real burden inflicted on the public at 3*l*., and even at 6*l*. and 7*l*., for every 1*l*. levied upon the contributor, and paid to the government. Adopting, therefore, the *minimum* of these calculations, the pressure of our national income, upon the sources of production, will be equal to the enormous sum of 234 millions! a sum sufficient to cripple even the most extraordinary productive powers. In fact, it was a pressure much inferior to this, which occasioned the downfal of those once flourishing commercial and manufacturing nations, Spain and Holland. The superior quality and abundance of the manufactures of Spain rendered her fairs the general mart of all nations. But the commercial history of this nation teaches us, that all these advantages were annihilated by the operations of the causes just noticed. Holland, whose capital was so enormous that she had 62 millions sterling in the public funds of England and France, and whose commerce was so universal, fell from her eminence by a similar mode of taxation. With how much greater truth and reason might the British people apply that destructive but common saying of the Dutch, when a dish has been brought to the table, that one share of the price went to the fisherman and six shares to the government.

Were not men the same in all ages and nations, it would be strange to hear, every day, a repetition of the shallow doctrine, the artificial reasoning, the apparent patriotic principles, which, before the downfal of those nations, were triumphantly maintained by the supporters of this vicious system of taxation. They confidently affirmed, "that a tax imposed upon consumption—upon the necessaries of life, raises wages, and enhances labour, and consequently is supported and paid by those who pay the labourers." This specious argument, this fallacy, did not prevent the results predicted by the opposing though unsuccessful party. But it may be easily demonstrated that when this reasoning is applied to a country like this, it has infinitely less force: for, in such a case, wages must either be kept at their *minimum, or above it, or below it*. If at their *minimum*, then the most numerous class of society will be condemned to the borders of perpetual starvation, and will be in a much worse condition than slaves, in whose lives and comforts their masters are interested. But the increasing population, which cannot be stopped, and the progress of machinery, which no power can control, these unremittingly active powers certainly tend to keep the wages of the numerous working classes rather *under* their *minimum* [a]. But under such a

[a] See Report of Select Committee of the House of Commons (1828) on the Poor Laws, and relating to the employment of able-bodied persons paid out of the poor rate.

system, what must eventually be the condition of the country? what must be the privations and distress of those classes? The only result to be expected is, that supremest of all evils, which alone is capable of subduing, humiliating, and crushing, even the greatest and proudest nations. But supposing the most favourable state, the rise of wages *above* their level: of course their produce must become higher, the enhanced cost of manufactures must follow, and their sale and consumption must be circumscribed; as it is an infallible principle that, as commodities rise in price, they diminish in sale. The interchange of our produce with other countries must likewise be circumscribed; and, it being out of our reach to control the productive manufacturing powers of other countries, the existing range of demand for our commodities must be reduced, and gradually annihilated. By pursuing such a policy, England will cut off and deprive herself of the essential means of furnishing the supply to the foreign market; thus destroying the main foundation of her greatness. Let the reader endeavour to discover a remedy for the awful evils resulting from such a position, while we proceed to examine its disastrous effects upon the happiness of the British people.

If taxation acts as a punishment upon society [a], it is also evident that the price of every article upon which taxation falls, rises in the first instance in proportion to the amount of the tax and its concomitant additions: the object thus affected acts immediately upon another, the price of which it affects in like manner. But the

[a] Say states, "L'impôt agit comme une punition—l'impôt est une portion des proprietés particulières, l'impôt lorsqu'il est poussé tres loin, prive le contribuable de sa richesse sans enricher le gouvernement.

heavy chain of taxation extending to almost all objects produced by nature or art, in the course of its windings, communicates its influence like an electric shock to every article; commodity acting upon commodity, and price upon price, and producing a general rise throughout all branches. But to a general, a *real*, rise of prices, succeeds a *real* poverty: "a true calamity", as a clever economist calls it, takes place. Industry, that magical power, whose grand object is to produce cheap commodities to satisfy the wants and comforts of all the members of society, is frustrated in its aim. The effects of the noble conquest achieved by the productive powers of steam and machinery, so wonderful and so beneficial to the human race, are entirely lost; and in their stead arise a perpetual agitation of society, an intestine and pitiless warfare amongst all its members. Every individual struggles to throw upon his neighbour the burden of the taxed article, and its increased and oppressive price; the merchant upon the manufacturer and dealer; these two upon the consumer and labourer; the labourer upon the farmer and landowner; these upon the capitalist; and all, reciprocally, one upon another. Thus originates that wonderful and ever-renewing strife for *money*, which so eminently characterizes the people of this country; which astonishes the foreigner on first landing here, gives him the worst ideas of the British character, and compels him to form the basest opinion of the British people. From the same source springs that distressing, restless, and perpetually haunting thought, of *getting money*, which pervades and tortures all classes, from the cobbler to the king; that ever-recurring want of *money*, which prevents the enjoyment of social intercourse, and which we so often see, not only destroy the sacred ties of friendship, but even insult the laws of nature. In fact, if according to Smith's definition, "a man is rich or poor, according to the degree in which he can afford to enjoy the necessaries, conveniences, and amusements of life", highly increased prices, by diminishing the power of income, and consequently the facility of acquiring those objects, have rendered the Englishman, while swimming, as it were, in an ocean of riches, the least amused, the least contented, and perhaps the poorest being in the world.

But it must not be thought that the high and powerful class, who, while enacting the laws of taxation, took special care to diminish the burden on their own property by overcharging labour, are exempt, or can escape, from this dreadful agitation. On the contrary, their wants and necessities rising with their rank and station, the increasing difficulty of procuring the numberless objects required to satisfy those wants, undoubtedly render this important class of society quite as much tormented and agitated, and perhaps as miserable, as the others: and the haughty lawgivers themselves, by a sort of retributive justice, become involved and entangled in the strong net of high prices, which they have contributed to make. Thus the whole social body becomes violently shaken, disturbed, confused, and unhappy. But wants must be supplied; necessaries must be obtained: *means* become a secondary consideration; "virtus post nummos nunc habetur." The imperious law of necessity would compel men to that course, did not the evil passions exist to prompt and precipitate them; until at length corruption, like a general flood, will deluge all.

Those who endeavour to account for the progress and increase of crime, have here the clue to their inquiries: these facts are the best text to their calendar. (Table I.) Those who cannot conceive how thousands of Britons, proud by nature, more tenacious of their habits than any other people, and members of a community possessing the best fundamental institutions under the sun, can abandon their homes, exchange all these mighty advantages for a wandering existence in strange lands, mangling foreign tongues, and suffering themselves to be the permanent laughing-stock of their most inveterate rivals—may here discover the causes of these anomalies. Those who cannot resolve the perplexing problem, that in Great Britain, with an immense increase of maritime power, with equally increasing improvements in agriculture, with unbounded commerce and industry, and with immense wealth, individual happiness does not accompany these transcendant advantages, but on the contrary marches rapidly in the contrary road—may here find the key to its solution. Those who cannot comprehend how it is, that the improvements in agriculture, which is the spring of produce, cause distress among the classes engaged in it; how it is, that the existing superabundance of capital, which is the source of production, causes distress amongst its proprietors; how it is, that the existence of an excess of labour, which is the origin of wealth, plunges its owners into want, distress, and misery: those, in fine, who are torturing their minds to find out the causes of periodical distress, and who are unable to understand how land, labour and capital, the three main springs and agents of production, can act and react one upon another, in mutual disadvantage and destruction—may perhaps find, in these pages, the clue to explain and reconcile these apparent contradictions, and paradoxical anomalies.

But it must not be concluded from this gloomy exposition, that the actual system of taxation should be overthrown or destroyed; for, although certainly susceptible of improvement, it ought by no means to be condemned on the whole. The defects and evils of this system arise from a cause over which it has no control, and can never be effectually remedied till that cause is removed. The sum annually required for the payment of the interest of the national debt, amounts to one-half, or more correctly speaking, to nearly two-thirds of the 234 millions *virtually* raised: and as long as this interest must be annually paid, so long must the necessary taxes be levied upon the main sources of production, and in contradiction to what ought to be the real object of all taxation, the benefit of society; so long must the chief part of the produce of land, labour, and capital, be charged and set apart towards that payment, *even before any portion can be appropriated for the very subsistence of the producers*, or for the charges necessary to maintain the order and welfare of society itself. This is the true cause of all the evils and oppressions of the present system of taxation—evils which no partial or temporary expedients can obviate: as long as this cause lasts, they will go on increasing in magnitude until all superiority is lost, or until they effect the dissolution and downfal of one of the mightiest agricultural, commercial, and manufacturing nations.

The defenders and promoters of this system may, like the economists of Spain and Holland, flatter the ministry and lull the nation, by showing that "these causes are not clearly apparent"; but they are not on that account the less certain in their existence, and unremitting in their activity. They may say, "commerce, shipping, and manufactures are increasing": granted, and for that very reason those branches are approaching nearer to their last term, and the remedy of course becomes more necessary. They may add, in fine, as some of our public writers (Chalmers) assert, that "taxes are no more than a transfer of property from one individual to another"—that "indirect taxes do not hurt the sources of production". But all these agreeable maxims are in contradiction to facts and experience.

Similar palliative and fallacious doctrines, proclaimed by the Spanish and Dutch economists to console the contributors and deceive the nation, did not prevent the ruin of those countries, but precipitated them more quickly from their high mercantile and manufacturing station. Those economists, however, not having authentic precedents of the "downfal of nations", were somewhat excusable for their doctrines; but the English economists are utterly unpardonable, for they have seen the causes which crippled the resources of those nations in time of peace, and rendered them unfit to enter into war with success [a].

But those nations had only an inconsiderable debt to increase their misfortunes, and to oppress and overwhelm them: how much more powerfully, then, must the causes which brought them to ruin, act in a country where an enormous amount of debt exists to aid and cooperate with them. We have seen, in the History and Progress of the National Debt, how rapidly it has increased, and how slowly it has been extinguished by the ordinary measures, even in the most peaceful times. All the exertions of one of the best of English kings, George I., aided by perhaps the ablest ministers that have ever directed the affairs of this nation, in a time of

[a] See Note (A).

the most profound peace, could scarcely reduce the national debt ten millions. We have seen, that in a long period of eighteen years since the peace of Paris, with all the increasing prosperity of this country, with an unprecedented surplus of revenue, with unparalleled means, and with resources never before possessed by any nation, the public debt has only been diminished a few millions!! What then, it is seriously asked, will be the reduction, what will be the result, should the interest or honour of the country compel it to undertake a war! Will not the host of evils affecting the sources of production, and destroying society in its very foundations, be augmented in a tenfold ratio? Will not all this mighty fabric, the result of a combination of powerful but jarring elements, be crushed to atoms with the most astounding explosion ever heard? We must never forget, that in the present age, in a country constituted like this, multitudes of men cannot long be kept in poverty and want; they cannot look with calmness on the spectacle of the insolent and overgrown wealth of the few*; they cannot long endure this violent and unna-

* The facts here stated, and especially the bad enactments which ruined the Spanish manufactures, sufficiently show how erroneous is the doctrine of Chalmers (Political Economy in connexion with the Moral State and Moral Prospects of Society) "that all the miseries affecting the labouring classes are the result of their own errors and misconduct; that there is no possible help for men, if they will not help themselves; that it is to a rise and reformation in the habits of our peasantry, that we should look for deliverance, and not to the impotent crudities of a speculative legislation." It is of no use, in the opinion of this Doctor, to seek, in the repeal of taxes or restrictions on trade, in emigration, or in such "futile" devices, for that real and permanent improvement, which can originate "only in the diffusion of sound Christian education". The communists need not take the trouble to refute such absurdities: they refute themselves.

In 1821, according to the official returns, 33 in 100, or nearly a

tural state of things: even the numerous lower classes agitate and discuss these wide-spreading evils: woe! if they take upon themselves to cure them! But they *must* be either checked, or left to take their course. What then is the great corrective—what is the great remedy? *The liquidation of the National Debt, is the only powerful, efficient, and complete measure,* capable of remedying these misfortunes, preventing their growing increase, and arresting their rapid and overwhelming march. Such a measure alone can rescue the primary sources of production from the destructive and ever acting burden which oppresses them. It has been already shown, that the empire possesses the means to effect this liquidation: it remains to point out the plan upon which that grand operation can be safely conducted.

And first, it may be as well to examine the opinions of English writers on this momentous subject.

third of the whole population, were engaged in agriculture; 46 in 100, or nearly one-half, in manufactures and trade; and 21 in 100, or less than a fifth, were not employed either in agriculture, trade, commerce, or manufactures. At present, the proportion of population engaged in agriculture, trade, and manufactures, is considerably greater: these classes almost constitute the English nation.

SECTION II.

Opinions of English writers concerning the National Debt, and the rights of the Public Creditors.—Causes which have occasioned the payment of the Debt to be considered almost impossible, and the attempt to propose such an operation, highly ridiculous.

HAD we not superabundant proofs of the contrary elements of which the human understanding is composed, we should find ample ones in the contrariety of opinions maintained by the ablest men of this nation, on a subject as simple in its nature, as it is important in its results. In fact, the British economical world is divided on a point which appears self evident. Quoting the expressions of the authors themselves, but sparing the reader the catalogue of their names, only a few of the contending leaders will be noticed.

One set of writers maintains, that "debt and wealth are synonymous"; that "increase of debt is a true increase of riches"; that "no happiness can exist without a National Debt." "The domestic debt," says one of the highest authorities (Colquhoun), "dispenses protection and happiness, by forming mutual advantages between the rich and poor: it has produced the rapid increase of public and private buildings; of the trade, commerce, manufactures, and navigation of the country, &c." Again, "the interest of the debt, although in some respects a pressure upon the country, is a main spring by which its general industry is stimulated and promoted." Another declares, that "a part of the industry, a part of the wages, a part of the land, belongs to the stockholders"; and that "by thirty millions of expenditure being in the hands of the stockholders or dissipators, consumption is highly stimulated." (Rook.) One of the *moderates* of this party (Gray) calls Public Debt "service capital." The extinction of the Debt, in the opinion of this economical phalanx, would of course bring misfortune and evil. "It would be attended," says Colquhoun, "with greater inconveniences than at present are experienced"!!

Another class of writers, with more truth, with greater force of argument, and with more evidence of facts, contends, that "poverty, misery, and the National Debt, are also synonymous and identical terms"; that, "England can never be the seat of happiness while the Debt is in existence"; that "the Debt is an enormous evil proportioned to its magnitude"; that "taxation, incurred to pay its annual interest, oppresses the people, destroys industry, and is equal to the curse of Heaven on the agriculture, commerce, and manufactures of the nation"; that "it is absurd to imagine that any of these branches can be benefited by the expenditure either of the government, or of the stockholders." (M'Culloch, "Essay on reducing the National Debt.") "To maintain that taxation contributes to enrich the nation, because it abstracts a portion of its riches, is both a plain contradiction, and an absurdity; taxation being always an engine of destruction to all the productive classes." "To contend that should Messrs. Canard, Spence, and Colquhoun continue, for a series of years, to live above their incomes, they would become richer in proportion as their profusion and extravagance increased, is to maintain a sophistry, and a groundless absurdity." "To attribute to the Debt the increase of buildings, improvements, &c. &c. during the war, is an error of the most miserable kind. It is to be attributed, not to the increase of Debt, but to the monopoly of commerce, to the discoveries of Arkwright and Watt, and to various other causes. The nation did not improve *because* of the Debt, but *in spite* of it: for it gave birth to the nefarious practice of stock-jobbing; generating a spirit of gambling, destructive of public morals, disgraceful to the nation, and decidedly hostile to the pursuit of sober industry." "No wages, no part of the land belongs to the stockholders or dissipators; nor was any specified property pledged for the greatest part of the Debt contracted. The lenders had not at the time any property mortgaged to them, consequently they cannot have at present more specified rights than they possessed when they lent their money: to maintain the contrary is a dangerous and arbitrary assumption." "They advanced money when its value was depreciated, on an average, fifteen per cent: they never entertained the idea of receiving payment at par, when the loans were contracted at exceedingly low prices." "It would be both folly and injustice to compel the nation to pay 100 ounces of gold to the fundholders, when they had only lent less than eighty." "It is equally unjust to exempt this sort of property from the alteration in value to which every other kind of property in the kingdom is subject"; "and consequently the reduction of the Debt—that millstone, which destroys the industry and vigour of the people, multiplies taxes, and spreads pauperism, crime, and wretchedness throughout the country, can be effected without any violation of the public faith." "The nation must not suffer on account of the errors of partial or ministerial men: the happiness of twenty-four millions of British subjects ought not to be postponed for the sake of an insignificant fraction (280,000) of stockholders."

To all these doctrines and assertions may be added an observation worthy of consideration, and which perhaps has not been pressed by this party as it deserves; namely, that the lenders themselves cannot plead any sound reason to be exempted from taxes for the reduction of the debt, in case it should be required for the benefit of the nation. They possessed a full knowledge of the Act of George I., in virtue of which it was enacted, "that these annuities should be free from all taxes, charges, and impositions whatsoever"; and that of George II. to the same purpose,—"the purchasers of these annuities shall have good estates, and interest thereon for ever; and the principal money paid for the same shall be free from all taxes, charges, and impositions whatsoever". But notwithstanding these most clear and express Acts, "taxes, charges, and impositions" were laid on the public funds, under the name of income tax. This deviation from the most express and clear enactments has not been considered an injustice, nor any forfeiture of faith whatever in regard to the holders of such "annuities"; still less could a similar measure be deemed unjust, or a breach of public faith, towards those stockholders who lent their money *after those Acts had been violated and practically annulled*, and consequently with a perfect knowledge of the fact.

It is not surprising that the *ultras* of this party, amazed at the difficulty of paying the enormous debt, have exceeded the bounds of reason; contending, that "as the debt must destroy the nation, or the nation must destroy the debt, no injustice will be committed by reducing the interest or the capital; the ruin of a few individuals being of a minor and insignificant weight, when the public good, and the happiness of all the nation, are in the scale."

Having read the summary of the leading arguments and opinions of all the contending parties, the reader will observe, that if some of them have rashly exceeded the bounds of equity, others are not less guilty of maintaining the most enormous absurdities in the opposite direction. These extremes are among the chief causes which have deterred the eminent financial men with whom this country abounds, from entering into the question of the liquidation of the national debt,—a question so momentous, and pregnant with so many difficulties; and while the press teems with volumes on comparatively subordinate and speculative questions, such as high and low prices, bullion, overtrading, &c. &c. not a single work has appeared on this all-important subject, which affects not only all the sources of production of the greatest manufacturing and mercantile nation, but even the interest of all the members of society. The few able men who have had the courage to face this great question, have acted on a small scale; putting forth paltry pamphlets, and throwing out detached thoughts, without going to the main point; without sufficiently shewing the *means* of payment; without considering the subject in connexion with taxation, and with the other branches of the great financial system, upon which this agricultural, commercial, and manufacturing nation rests, and extending the inquiry to ALL the parts of the British empire. In short, the subject has never been treated in a manner commensurate with its magnitude. The result of such limited and slender attempts has been, that many high-minded men, with the best intentions, have injured this great cause instead of advancing it. Their ill-arranged schemes, combined with the large per-centage they assigned for the payment of the debt, alarmed those who were to be the payers: thus, the very people who were most interested in the liquidation became the strongest opponents of all proposals for effecting it. The men of property and the land-owners, not having their interests consulted, not finding an adequate benefit held out to them, turned all their mighty powers against the measure: the stock-holders, dreading the loss of their annual interest, called it "a flagrant injustice"; and the stupid multitude, always the same, joined in the cry. They even went further, denouncing the idea of paying the national debt as "*a dream, a madness, an impossibility*"; and throwing upon those who sought to relieve them from a host of evils, the most insufferable of all stigmas—ridicule. In this manner, a writer could not treat the most important of all national questions, without the risk of being considered almost insane.

The author is further confirmed in his opinion of the inadequate and superficial manner in which this subject has been handled, by the perusal of almost all the pamphlets and plans on the question, from the first, published by the patriotic and highly informed Archibald Hutchinson in the reign of George I., to the last, published in 1832, entitled "A Plan for the Liquidation of the National Debt." To gratify the curiosity of the reader, as well as to convince him of the correctness of this opinion, extracts from the principal of these publications are subjoined[a].

[a] The first writer who proposed a regular plan for the payment of the national debt, was Hutchinson, one of the most clever members of parliament of his time (George I.). The debt then amounted to only fifty-two millions, but unfortunately Hutchinson, in his plan, did not sufficiently consult the interests of the proprietary party; the assessments displeased the landed and other proprietors, who thought their interests neglected: they contended, that the operation would bring them no benefit, complained of its injustice.

Everybody must be perfectly aware that it is beyond the powers of an individual to form a *perfect plan*, or

and, by their power and influence, raised a host of enemies against it. The most strenuous exertions of Hutchinson were unavailing; and even Hume, in his Essay on Public Credit, disapproves and attacks one of the best and least difficult measures of this nature ever proposed.

In 1821, Wilks published a "Practical Scheme for the Reduction of the National Debt and Taxation", the leading points of which are:—

"That all lower annuities must be consolidated; namely,

The 3 per cents. at......	65
3½ ditto	73¾
4 ditto	81¼
5 ditto	100

"That an assessment of twenty per cent. shall be laid on all property and funds so consolidated.

"That an assessment of five per cent. shall be laid on private property not in the British funds.

"That the value of fixed property, except buildings, shall be estimated at twenty years' purchase.

"That this assessment be converted into a redeemable income tax, at the option of the proprietor, at five per cent. per annum.

"That a like assessment, for the term of ten years, be levied upon all net profits of trade and agriculture."

The author asserts, that the practical results of this plan would be, "that 538,814,815*l.* of three per cents. would be converted into 350,229,650*l.*; that the total nominal debt, being 794,980,000*l.*, would be lowered to 583,975,075*l.*; and that in the ten following years it would be reduced to 275,000,000*l.*", &c. &c.

It is easy to remark, in this scheme, the large amount of the assessment, its complication, and heavy pressure on one part of the community during the long period of ten years: the general interest of the whole empire is not even thought of; and, after such a lapse of time, the results are comparatively small.

In 1827, an elaborate and well written paper appeared in the Edinburgh Review, No. 92, entitled "Remarks on the Financial Situation of England", at the end of which it is proposed to pay only one half of the debt, by an assessment of twelve per cent. upon all the capital of the country; and the payment of the whole debt

a subject so difficult, embracing so many objects, connected with such important financial points, affecting

is supposed to require a similar assessment of twenty-four per cent. The objections made by Hume to the plan of Hutchinson, are triumphantly answered; the supposed difficulties of a general assessment are successfully solved; and its justice, practicability, and convenience of collection, clearly demonstrated. But being only an incidental article, it did not examine the question in all its bearings; it did not state the comparative results to the financial system of the empire, and to the interests of all the parties concerned in this great measure, in all parts of the British dominions; and as the total extent of the capital was not considered, the assessment of twenty-four per cent. was too high. Consequently, the public and the legislature took little or no notice of the sound ideas and praiseworthy intentions which it displayed.

In 1832 was published, a "Practical Plan for the immediate Annihilation of Taxes, and Equitable Liquidation of the National Debt." It proposes—"to impose a tax of 20 per cent. upon all the net real property of the country, (leaving out those persons whose property amounts to less than 100*l*.)—the amount to be paid either at once, or by instalments within five years:"—"to impose a tax of 50 per cent., for one year, upon all incomes of not less than 100*l*. a year, arising from the profits of artists and other professional men":—"that all internal taxes, excepting only the present land tax, shall immediately cease to be collected":—and "that the whole assessment shall be paid, with interest, in order that, with perfect safety to the creditors, the public may be relieved from all the present taxes, as soon as the assessments are completed".—These are the outlines of the latest publication on this subject. The observations upon the effects of the present system of taxation are very judicious. The expense of collecting the taxes, the inconveniences suffered by those on whom they are levied, the extra profits required for the additional capital employed by the various tradesmen, through whose hands the taxed articles pass before they reach the consumer, the high taxation raising the price of labour by preventing the cultivation of land, driving our manufacturers out of the market, and rendering competition with other countries more difficult, the discontent and oppressions which the taxes occasion—all these truths are clearly pointed out, and are, unfortunately, daily felt by all classes of the community. The advantageous

such a variety of clashing interests, and even touching upon the rights of property, on which social order is founded. It will be a great and bold task, to suggest the principles, to establish the basis, upon which this grand operation can be safely conducted; to demonstrate its practicability, unfold its advantages, answer objections, and concentrate, in a small compass, all the essential points which bear for or against the operation; in order that the great financial men of this country

effects of the plan to the capitalists and other proprietors are also shown. Supposing, as the author says, the owners of 5,000*l.* a year will be reduced to 4,000*l.*—they would be relieved from all internal taxes: supposing those of 500*l.* and of 50*l.* a year will be reduced, the one to 400*l.*, the other to 40*l.*; the fundholder of 500*l.* a year to 400*l.*; the great merchant or manufacturer possessing 50,000*l.*, and whose interest upon the same is 2,500*l.*, will be reduced to 2,000*l.*, &c.; notwithstanding this reduction, every kind of property will become more *really* valuable than at present: 4,000*l.* a year will be worth more than 5,000*l.* was before, &c., &c. All this is quite true, even in a plan in which 20 per cent. of property is to be given up, to secure relief from taxation: how much greater will be the advantages to the property of every individual, when the same result is obtained by less than half this sacrifice? However, it was impossible in a pamphlet of only thirty-one pages, even with the best intentions and clearest ideas, to treat this important subject as it deserves; to state the capital, and enter into the complicated ramifications of the financial system of the empire; and to consider the interests of all parties, combined with the real benefits resulting to Great Britain, in consequence of the repeal of the taxes falling on the staple articles produced by her various possessions. The preservation of the land tax, when the co-operation of the landed interest was required, and the proposal to make each individual give up one-fifth of his property, were sufficient to render this plan unpalatable to the public, and disincline them to pay due attention to this important subject.

Such are the principal authors who have written on the liquidation of the National Debt, and such is the mode in which they have treated this great question.

may fight the battle of humanity and the people, and with greater knowledge and means of information than an individual can possess, may correct his errors, and carry into effect his good intentions.

The grave and steady English reader will, perhaps, laugh most heartily at the madness of a foreigner attempting to point out the means of paying the National Debt:—a stranger belonging, moreover, to a nation, where financial men are so scarce that it is difficult, if not impossible, to find one. Indeed, the author candidly avows, that nature having denied him that easy and forbearing temper, which can endure any taunt, or any ridicule, he has been rather reserved in imparting the object of his labours, even to his own friends. But being actuated by a sincere desire to cause the happiness of a mighty nation, herself the centre of civilization; by a wish to diffuse the benefits such an operation will confer on all the commercial world; and by a hope to extend its beneficial effects towards the civilization and happiness of mankind even to the most remote and savage regions,—these noble motives have enabled him to support the sarcasms of criticism, and to brave the cutting shafts of ridicule.

But after all, it is to the British Reformed Parliament—that concentration of the collective wisdom and practical knowledge of the nation—that mighty conservative body, possessing the power as well as the means of enforcing its enactments, that exclusively belongs the noble task of directing and forming a *perfect* plan for the liquidation of the National Debt, and of overcoming all the obstacles to carrying it into execution.

However, in the next Section will be found the outline of a practical plan for effecting this important object.

SECTION III.

BASES OF A PLAN FOR THE LIQUIDATION OF THE NATIONAL DEBT.

1.

THAT 500,000,000*l.* of the national funded debt shall be paid off in full.

2.

That a general assessment of 9¼ per cent. shall be levied upon all the private property and capital whatsoever of the British Empire.

3.

That a similar assessment of 9¼ per cent. shall be levied on all incomes arising from all professions, from all civil, military, and naval appointments, from the public funds, and from all employments whatsoever, in which no capital is engaged: the wages of labourers excepted.

4.

That in making the general assessment, property to the value of 30*l.* shall be deducted and left free, in estimating the property of each family assessed. And that every individual, the total value of whose property, of whatever nature, does not exceed 30*l.*, shall be totally exempt from assessment.

5.

That all property shall be assessed, debts deducted.

6.

That all proprietors who may not be entitled to

dispose of or alienate their property, shall be legally authorized to sell a portion of such property, whether real or personal, sufficient to pay the amount of their assessment.

7.

That this authority shall convey to the purchasers of all such property sold for the above purpose, a true, perfect, and valid title.

8.

That the East India Company, the legislatures, assemblies, governors, corporations, or competent authorities in the British colonies or establishments abroad, shall be fully authorized to raise money by loans, contracts, or otherwise, sufficient to pay their respective portions of the general assessments.

9.

That the payment of the assessment shall be effected within two years, commencing in and ending . That the whole amount shall be payable by instalments in eight successive quarters, in the following proportion: in each of the first six quarters 1 per cent., in the seventh quarter $1\frac{1}{3}$ per cent., and in the eighth and last quarter $1\frac{2}{3}$ per cent.

10.

That defaulters shall be proceeded against according to the laws at present existing in regard to the payment of king's taxes; but that interest at the rate of 5 per cent. shall accrue upon the instalments from the day after that on which they become due and are not paid.

11.

That in order to adjust the assessment in an equitable manner, and render its collection easy and effectual, the regulations that were in force for the collection of the income and property taxes, shall be adopted, but free from the abuses to which they were liable: it being easy, and for the interest of the payers themselves, to correct and improve those regulations, by means of the last census, and numerous other official data and returns, which have been published since they were framed.

12.

That government shall be authorized to pay off at par, a portion of the national *funded* debt, amounting to 500,000,000*l.*, selecting such descriptions of stock as shall be judged preferable, with a due regard to existing engagements and the public benefit. And that they shall be empowered to effect the said payment in eight successive quarters, in sums corresponding to the amount of the assessment payable in each quarter, as before-mentioned.

13.

That should any deficiency arise, in consequence of the whole amount of any instalment not being paid up when due, government shall be authorized to provide for such deficiency by an issue of Exchequer Bills. And in like manner, should there be any surplus, the same to be carried to account of the next quarter, and so on to the last.

14.

That an alteration or diminution of the general rate of assessment may be taken into consideration with regard to the East India empire, and all the colonies, proportioned to the *relative benefits and advantages* that each of those integral parts of the British empire will derive, in consequence of the provisions of this measure.

15.

That the taxes on knowledge or on paper, the land tax, the house and window taxes, and the taxes on bricks, tiles and slate, shall be totally repealed.

16.

That the taxes upon malt and hops, shall entirely cease.

17.

That the taxes on soap, tallow, and coals sea-borne, shall be totally abolished.

18.

That the duties on sugar, molasses, coffee, and cocoa, shall be abolished.

19.

That supposing the amount of all the taxes repealed to be sixteeen millions, two millions shall cease to be collected after the payment of the first instalment of the General Assessment; and in like manner, two millions more in each of the succeeding quarters: and that after the payment of the eighth and last instalment, the collection of all the above taxes repealed, shall entirely cease.

20.

That the Government shall be authorized to decide whether the two millions of taxes to be reduced in each successive quarter, shall be applied to the whole of the taxes to be repealed collectively, or to some of them, or to a single one, as they may deem expedient for the public benefit and the Exchequer.

21.

That all Acts of Parliament, Laws, and Regulations, contrary to these dispositions, shall totally cease.

22.

That a Committee composed of able, resolute, and above all, practical men, shall be appointed to arrange the details of this measure, and overcome the obstacles and difficulties that may arise in carrying it into effect.

SECTION IV.

Practicability of the Plan proposed for the Liquidation of the National Debt; its advantages to all parties, even to those who might oppose it—to Capitalists, Owners of land, fixed and funded property—to the present monetary system—to the West Indies and North American Colonies—to the mercantile and shipping Interests; and its general results in regard to the whole British empire.

THE total amount of *private property* and capital in the whole empire, is shewn in Section XI., Part III., to be 5,408,768,946*l.* An assessment of 9¼ per cent. on which, as proposed in Basis 2, would yield 500,311,127*l.*, or above 311,127*l.* more than is required to discharge in full the amount of the National Funded Debt, proposed to be paid off by Basis 1. But deducting from the 500,000,000*l.* to be paid off, 46,250,000*l.* on account of the assessment of 9¼ per cent. on the income derived from Funded Property, the sum to be actually provided for will *only amount to* 453,750,000*l.* And this sum being payable in eight instalments, the sum to be paid and provided for in each quarter, will be on an average 56,718,750*l.*

Now the question is, will it be practicable to raise this 56,718,750*l.* in the first quarter? For if this can be effected, the payment of a similar sum will become easier every succeeding quarter, in consequence of the relief afforded to the payers by the progressive repeal of taxes, as proposed in Basis 19. But it has been shewn, in the First and Second Parts of this Work, that the people of *one part of the empire alone* have, on several occasions, raised much larger sums than this by taxes and other financial operations, when it was against their own interests to do so. The power, wealth, and means of all classes of the empire, which have increased one-third since the period alluded to, will certainly be enabled to raise the moderate sum required, when it is for an object in which their interests are so deeply and vitally concerned.

But supposing that, from any unforeseen circumstance, a contingency should arise; such contingency has been provided for by Basis 3, by which a surplus has been secured by the assessment laid on professions and places; by the 46,250,000*l.* arising from the assessment on Funded Property; and by Basis 13, empowering government to issue Exchequer Bills.

Considering all circumstances, therefore, there can be no reasonable doubt, that the contributors and capital of the whole empire will be enabled to pay so light an assessment in such a protracted period.

When the first instalment is paid, the grand *problem* is solved; for it can be demonstrated that the payment of the succeeding ones will be comparatively easy. It is an acknowledged truth in economical science, that the income of the contributors increases, and its purchasing power becomes greater, in direct ratio to the amount of taxes repealed [a]. Now by the time the second instalment becomes due, capital and income being relieved (by Basis 19.) from a part of the most destructive and oppressive taxes, will have acquired a relatively increased value and power of purchasing: and in like manner, the repeal of taxes always following the pay-

[a] The sentiments of one celebrated economist will suffice for the rest.—"L'augmentation de prix ou des valeurs que les produits subissent en virtu de l'impôt, équivalent à une diminution de revenu. La valeur des revenus est d'autant plus considerable, qu'ils procurent une plus grande quantité des produits; l'impôt équivaut à une diminution de revenu."—Say, Economie Politique.

ment of every instalment, this value and power will go on increasing as each payment falls due, until the eighth and last, when property and capital will have reached their full and complete power, in consequence of the abolition of the taxes which cripple and oppress them. Thus, although it might appear on a superficial calculation, that the progressive instalments would be provided for with increased difficulty, until at last the powers of the contributors would be totally exhausted; it will be found, on the contrary, that their means and resources will increase at each successive operation; and so far from being impaired, will in the end, have obtained a considerable addition to their value and amount.

Let us now see the advantages which will result to those who might be opposed to the proposed plan.

The holders of funded property have hitherto ranked first in the opposition to any measure of this description; but this time, it is to be hoped, they will be satisfied. At least they cannot come forward with their martial and threatening cry of "a breach of public faith:" they will be at once deprived of this formidable weapon, for they are to be paid in full, and at par; receiving payment in gold for money lent in depreciated paper. Thus *their* property will remain uninfluenced by alterations and diminutions in value, which every other description of property has undergone; as the inevitable rise which would take place in the price of stocks, on the mere announcement of the measure, would be a full compensation for the assessment imposed upon their property. There can be no question that they would be great gainers by the measure: the only question that could arise perhaps would be, whether the legislature could interfere, without departing from the most strict justice, to curtail the unexpected profits arising from the rise in the price of Stocks. The absentee-annuitants, instead of injuring the general prosperity as they now do, would, for the first time, be justly compelled to contribute their share towards home expenditure and taxation. The accumulators of funded property would be forced to put their capitals into quicker circulation, by investing them in agriculture, commerce, and manufactures; thus promoting the employment of all the productive classes of society.

The advantages to the *landowners* and *agriculturalists* will be great and important, it being a principle, that property is affected in value in proportion as the amount of a tax laid upon it is augmented or decreased. Of course the land owners and agriculturalists become gainers to the extent of the tax abolished; whilst the saving of the charges incurred in the collection, and the benefits resulting from the avoiding of reciprocal high prices, will be so many additional profits to these classes. But this is not all, the abolition of the land tax forms only one feature of the plan. There are 48,000 acres of land employed in the cultivation of hops. But this important branch of agriculture being relieved from the heavy duty, averaging in the last three years, 169,000*l.* per annum; in consequence of Basis 16, this sum, with the charges of collection, &c., will be another addition to the profits of the agriculturalists. Then again, there are no less than 29,000,000 bushels of malt annually consumed, the produce of many millions of acres of land. The average duty upon this necessary of life in the last three years, exclusive of the charges of collection, was 3,869,933*l.* (Table XLII. Part I.) This large sum, with the considerable charges of its collection, and the incidental benefits before mentioned, will be another large item to be added to the advantages of the landowners and agriculturalists, in which the consumers will also participate. Facts and experience, as well as reason, have proved, as may be seen by the interesting Table II., Part IV., that consumption increases in proportion as taxes are remitted: the repeal of a part only of an impost, has been followed by a double, and, in many cases, a treble consumption of the article. The total abolition of a tax, therefore, would at least operate in doubling the consumption. But supposing the total repeal of the duty upon malt caused an increase of only two thirds in the consumption, the consequence would be, that 19,200,000 bushels more of malt would be consumed; a proportionate number of acres of land would come under cultivation, and a corresponding number of labourers would be employed. Two consequences of the highest importance would follow; namely, the employment of the excess of effective labourers at present without work, and the relative diminution of poor rates, which chiefly fall upon the land. Thus two extraordinary and constantly growing evils might be radically cured by adopting Bases 15 and 16; while the health and morals of the poorer classes would be improved, and society at large would reap the greatest advantages.

But these intrinsic, economical, and moral benefits, will be followed by a political advantage, which is not to be overlooked. National writers, treating of the disadvantages under which the agriculture of this country labours, compared with that of other nations, (particularly France,) come to the conclusion, that the difference between English and French agriculture amounts to from 4 to 5,000,000*l.* sterling. (Lowe, "Present State of England; comparative burdens on

French and British agriculture.") Precisely this sum being repealed by carrying into execution the Basis 15 above-mentioned, these disadvantages, these burdens, so declaimed against, and so injurious to the country, will entirely disappear; our farmers and land-owners will be on an equal footing with those of other countries; and then, and not till then, the clamour against the corn laws will cease, and its terrible consequences will be prevented.

The land-owners and agriculturalists themselves are left to sum up the items, and calculate the *peculiar* benefits they will obtain, should the measure be adopted; for it will be easily perceived, that this large and important class will partake of its numerous advantages in common with the other classes of the community. Indeed, it may be asserted without exaggeration, that this class, instead of *paying* 9½ per cent., will have *received* a larger sum before the expiration of the last instalment. A singular mode of taxation, which, in the end, returns to the contributors double the amount taken away!

The owners of fixed property, and householders, will also be greatly benefited. The remission of the taxes upon houses and windows, the average amount of which for the last three years was 3,705,544*l.*, would operate to the advantage, and benefit the capital, of these classes, in the same manner and with the same results, as has been stated in the case of the land-owners. To this large sum must be added the considerable amount (also to be repealed by Basis 15.) of the taxes upon materials of construction, such as bricks, tiles, slates, &c., the average amount of which, for the three years above-mentioned, was 382,849*l.*, (Table XLII. Part I.,) exclusive of the charges of collection.

The repeal of these taxes would materially tend to lessen the inducement for living abroad; while the householders would share with the land-owners the benefits and great moral effects, resulting from the reduction of poor rates. The unjust assessments, the partiality, the many grievances, occasioned by the house and window taxes, and the unfairness (so justly complained of) of making the metropolis contribute more than the forty-eight counties of England [a], would be entirely removed by this measure.

But what will be the advantages to *the mere capitalists?*—a class of society who in general live to the extent of the income arising from their capital. Let us see what the effects of the liquidation would be on a middling capital of 12,000*l.*, or 500*l.* a year; and so on to the highest. By the repeal of the taxes on houses, windows, malt, soap, coals, sugar, and coffee, the domestic and household expenses would be considerably lessened; these articles being precisely those which constitute the bulk of those annual expenses. The average duty on coals in the last three years, amounted to 377,000*l.*; that on candles and tallow to 670,387*l.*; and that on soap to 130,493*l.*; together 1,177,880*l.* (Table XLII. Part I.) These duties being repealed by Basis 17, a great portion of this amount would be so much gain to the capitalists. Besides which, capital will acquire a commanding power, equal to the aggregate amount of such taxes repealed: nay, it will obtain a relatively superior purchasing power to what it had before the operation, when, in consequence of the ex-

[a] In 1830, the amount of this duty for all the kingdom was 1,585,740*l.*; of which the metropolitan districts paid 784,680*l.* The rental for Great Britain is above 11,000,000*l.*, while for Middlesex alone it is 5,000,000*l.*

penses of collection, and the profits and commissions of all the chain of dealers, the prices, not only of the articles on which taxes were nominally repealed, but of an immense number of others, were rendered higher. This increased purchasing power of capital will enable them to buy more of the necessaries and luxuries of life, during the two years in which the instalments become due; and the relative increase in the value of their capital will undoubtedly exceed the amount of the assessments. Were not this result so evident, it could be shown to demonstration, by a comparative table of household and domestic expenses; but, by so doing, the good sense and understanding of the reader would be insulted.

The opponents to the liquidation of the debt having stated, as one ground of their opposition, the many and unjust advantages it would confer on merchants, dealers, manufacturers, and labourers: and these classes not being opposed to it, it would be a waste of time to point out what every one will allow, namely, the immense advantages such an operation will bestow upon these numerous and important classes of society. The merchants, manufacturers and dealers will participate in the greater part of the benefits resulting to the other classes; to which it may be added, the particular one they will reap, from having the large capital at present employed by them in the payment of duties and charges, freed and rendered available: which considerable capital being disengaged, will become productive, and flow to other and more profitable channels, and will even feed the instalments of the general assessment.

In a great mercantile empire, where the currency influences the wealth, the interests, and the transactions of all its members, it becomes a question as important as it is complicated. Two great contending parties are endeavouring to point out the remedy for the evils and periodical distress, attributed to the present monetary system; but the sources whence their arguments are deduced are so various, the facts upon which they rely are so uncertain, and their reasoning is so confused, that it is almost impossible they can come to a right understanding; and it is to be feared the patient will expire, while the doctors are disputing about the most effectual remedy for the disease. But amidst all this diversity of opinions, one fact, one undeniable truth, is admitted on all sides; namely, that "the pressure of taxation is the principal cause of the periodical distress arising from the state of the currency; and that if this baneful cause were removed, a better and safer monetary system would follow." But as the proposed plan embraces a direct and complete removal of that very cause, by the abolition of that part of taxation which most materially affects the sources of production, it is evident that, should it be adopted, the distressing evils and misfortunes arising from the state of the currency, will be in a great measure, if not wholly, remedied.

But the financial system of Great Britain is so intimately interwoven with all her possessions, that no financial measure of any importance can be safely or advantageously undertaken without taking into consideration the interests of all the integral parts of her vast empire. Not to lose sight of this important object, the great advantages which will result to the East Indian empire, to our American possessions, and even to the most remote portions of the empire, have been weighed and calculated. The depressed and ruinous condition of the *West India Colonies* has been particularly attended [illegible] it is confidently asserted that if, by the adoption of [illegible], these evils are not quite eradicated, the relief afforded will be greater, more effectual, and more [illegible] in its consequences, than the colonists [illegible] for the prosperity and happiness of the [illegible] contemplated.

[illegible] of the principal and staple productions of the West India [illegible] is sugar. This article of universal consumption, which, after bread, is most necessary to [illegible] any article when they cannot buy [illegible] of the colonial prosperity; and the [illegible] and increase of this prosperity mainly depend upon its more extensive consumption. The actual consumption of this article may be seen in Table [illegible] in the Section on the West India Colonies; and by inspecting Table [illegible] Part IV., the reader may trace, from year [illegible], how the consumption has increased, in proportion as the duty has been repealed. In the mean time it may be briefly stated that one of the most celebrated popular writers (Sir H. Parnell on Financial Reform), though he calls the reduction of the duty on sugar three shillings a hundred weight a "great error", yet acknowledges that a similar reduction would increase consumption half a million of hundred weights. If then a reduction of three shillings a hundred weight would, in the opinion of a writer unfavourable to a reduction, increase the consumption half a million of hundred weights, a reduction of twenty-four shillings (the present amount of duty) would increase it 3,500,000 cwts.* But though the consumption would not strictly follow

* "During three years, ending in 1812, when the duty upon rum was [illegible] per gallon, there were 800,000 gallons entered for home consumption in Ireland. Mr. Vansittart raised it to 12s. 7½d., and in 1828 it sunk to [illegible] gallons." *Edinb. Rev.*

that ratio, there is no doubt, that were the whole or the greater part of the duty repealed, it would increase immensely, and would at least double in a very short time[a]. What benefits would result to the planters, to the colonists, to the mortgagees, and to all those engaged in the trade to those colonies, from such an increased consumption! What would be the advantage to the shipping interest, the deplorable state of which is so loudly complained of! Many thousand tons of shipping would be required to transport this immense additional quantity of sugar: the increase in the number of British vessels would be in proportion. The Mauritius and the East Indies would come in for a large share in these advantages; while a great benefit would be bestowed upon the millions of inhabitants of Great Britain and Ireland, by the repeal of a tax producing 4,941,234*l.* a year on an average (Table XLII., Part I.).

Cocoa plantations, which were "destroyed and withered in Jamaica", as Edwards says, "under the heavy hand of ministerial exaction", will become a new and productive source of wealth to that island, as well as to the other colonies. The Grenada and Trinidad cocoa, the quality of which is as good as the renowned Caraccas, and the consumption of which is at present reduced to the insignificant amount of 400,000 lbs., in consequence of the unjust and heavy duty of 100 per cent. upon the finer, and 230 per cent. upon the inferior sorts, will come into extensive use when this enormous duty is repealed: while the benefits to the planters, to the colonists, to the shipowners, as well as to the consumers themselves, will be very great.

Another important and staple produce of these co-

[a] The weekly consumption of a labourer's family may be estimated at two pounds and a quarter of sugar, and one pound of soap.

lonies is coffee. The consumption of this necessary article has increased at a greater ratio, when the duty has been lowered, than that of sugar itself. Its consumption, from 1,170,000 lbs. in 1807, rose, in consequence of successive repeals of duty, to 5,679,000 lbs. in 1812, to 19,000,000 lbs. in 1829, and to 27,500,000 lbs. in 1831 (Table II., Part IV.). The duty, however, is still not only very high, but unjust in its operation; as it amounts to 100 per cent. on the selling price of superior coffee, and to 150 per cent. upon inferior kinds: an evident proof of the smallness of the reduction, and of its tendency to increase in consumption, in spite of such light relief. Should this enormous duty be *totally* repealed, as proposed by Basis 18*, or only in part, it may safely be affirmed, that the consumption of coffee would be doubled or even trebled. But this article is almost always used with sugar, the consumption of which it would therefore advance in compound ratio along with its own. Supposing the increase to be 20,000,000 lbs. (in the two years assumed for the payment of the debt): what beneficial effects would such an increase in cultivation occasion to the colonists! What advantage would

* The total amount of the taxes to be repealed, on an average of the last three years, will be as follows:—

	£
Land, window, and house taxes	3,705,514
Hops	169,721
Bricks, tiles, and slates	382,849
Malt	3,869,933
Coals, sea-borne	377,142
Soap	1,304,193
Candles and tallow	670,387
Sugar	4,941,234
Coffee and cocoa	215,023
Total	15,635,996

be reaped not only by the planters and labourers, but by the mortgagees and shipowners! For this produce being more bulky than sugar, would require more British shipping to carry it: whereby the shipowners and people connected with the shipping trade, would be considerably benefited. If we consider the additional shipping that would be required for the transport of sugar and coffee, we may fairly calculate, that the tonnage would be increased in the time above fixed, two-thirds of its present amount. But supposing the increase would be only one-half, with a corresponding number of sailors, &c., what a beneficial addition this would be to a maritime power like England!

The attention of the reader is here called to the evident moderation of these calculations; and he is particularly requested to notice, that they are not the wild speculations and theories of a fertile imagination, but are founded upon a series of uncontradicted facts; upon the uniform experience of increased consumption, when a relative duty has been removed.

But in considering the beneficial results of the measure to the West India colonies; those which will result to the other parts of the empire must not be forgotten. The *North American Colonies* will be large participators in consequence of the increase of shipping. The consumption of the first staple produce of those colonies —timber, will be doubled: the timber merchants, labourers, capitalists, and all the classes employed in this branch, constituting one of the principal resources of those colonies, will be great gainers: the clearing, and consequent cultivation of new lands, will increase in the same proportion. The agriculture, shipping, and commerce of those countries will undoubtedly reap the most essential benefits, by the increased demand for corn, provisions, staves, shingles, lumber, &c., in the West India colonies, occasioned by the increased cultivation of sugar, coffee, cocoa, &c.; which, altogether, must give a double impulse to the Canadian agriculturalists, capitalists, and merchants. Thus a great general result will be attained; namely, the termination, or cessation in part, of those tremendous evils which daily distract Great Britain, and threaten the existence and even the allegiance itself of those important colonies; and all this, combined with the greatest advantages to the mother country. The application of any partial remedy, will be a transient and delusive palliative; the ultimate effect of which must be inefficacious, void, and null.

It will be unnecessary to particularize the advantages which will accrue to all the *East Indian* empire, to the *Mauritius*, the *Cape of Good Hope*, and all our possessions, by the increased consumption of all their numerous and staple productions, and by the consequent improvement of their commerce, shipping, and agriculture. The facts, reasoning, and arguments insisted upon in regard to the West Indies, North America, &c., apply with equal force to all the British possessions: while their connection with the mother country is so intimate, that they cannot fail to participate in the general prosperity.

Thus it appears, that all the great leading interests of the country will be highly benefited by the adoption of the measure proposed: the landowners and agriculturalists, by the repeal of the taxes falling upon land, whereby this main source of production will be relieved from a pressure of the most injurious and fatal tendency: the owners of fixed property, and householders, disencumbered of the high duties falling not only upon houses, but upon the materials of construction, will receive a beneficial addition to their capital. The remaining stockholders will have a real increase in the amount of their capital; while those whose stock has been paid off, no longer limited to a small annual interest, and freed from the fears which now agitate them, will find new and ample means of employment for their money, more beneficial to themselves and to the other classes of society. The evils arising from the present monetary system, and the periodical distress occasioned by the state of the currency, will be totally, or to a great extent, remedied. The capitalists, acquiring a greater commanding power of purchasing, in a direct ratio to the amount of taxes repealed, and having new and more beneficial objects of investment opened to them, will embark their capital in agriculture, manufactures, and commerce, to the great benefit of those important sources of production, and the general good of the country. The labourers and working classes, being relieved from the heavy taxes which now fall upon the necessaries of life, and obtaining full employment in consequence of the demand for labour occasioned by the increase of cultivation, shipping, trade, and manufactures, will have their comforts greatly augmented, their health and morals highly improved, their general condition greatly bettered, and its actual tendency to certain ruin, effectually prevented. In fine, a state of general comfort, happiness, content, and prosperity, will succeed to the unsettled, distressed, and agitated state, in which society, in consequence of its artificial position, is at present placed; a state which no limited or partial measures whatsoever can possibly remedy.

Such will be the general results to the whole British Empire. The advantages of the plan, even to those who might be opposed to it, have been considered: let us now examine the objections that may be urged against it.

SECTION V.

The Objections that may be made to the Plan proposed for the Liquidation of the Debt answered.

EVERY impartial person is fully aware that obstacles will arise in the execution of any financial measure of importance, much more in an operation so comprehensive and of such magnitude as the one under consideration. But are the difficulties of a measure of this nature so great and insurmountable as has been imagined?—are the objections to it unanswerable?—these are the questions which we are about to examine.

Objection.—A general assessment cannot be justly apportioned; it cannot be fairly laid upon all the classes of society; for those who possess large fixed property and capital, will be compelled to pay the greatest part of it; while the rest of the community will pay little or nothing.

Answer.—The basis proposed for the distribution of the assessment, is the very one admitted, by the most just and rigid economists, to be that upon which all contributions and taxes ought to be imposed. The landowners, proprietors, and capitalists, pay their contributions, at present, on the same principle, namely, that those who are richer and possess more, should contribute more; and that the higher consideration they enjoy in society, and the greater advantages they obtain from a civilized social community, fairly render them liable to a larger share towards its burdens. Should any inequality in the distribution of the assessment arise, it must be attributed, either to the abuses which may creep into its execution, or to the imperfections unavoidable in every operation and every scheme of human invention. And at all events, this inequality will fall far short of that which enters into many existing taxes, particularly the house and window taxes, and the stamp duties.

Objection.—But the capitalists and owners of land, and all fixed property, being unable to conceal their property, will be obliged to pay their full share; while the commercial and monied men, and perhaps a part of the manufacturers, can easily avoid the burden, and shift their proportionate share upon others.

Answer.—All contributions and taxes are subject to the same objection. Unfortunately, they sometimes press more upon one class than upon another; and no fiscal ingenuity can prevent the injustice of concealment. But should this objection stand good, all taxes whatever ought immediately to cease, and no new one could be imposed: society would be dissolved. It is beyond human power to force millions of men to be just in all respects: it is impossible to prevent them from avoiding their burdens, and throwing some portion of them upon others; this is done to a great extent under the actual system of taxation; and the inclination to do so is identified with human nature itself.

Objection.—The assessment could not be collected; or even if practicable, its collection would be exceedingly vexatious and complicated.

Answer.—The late property and income taxes were assessed and distributed, for many years, with facility and tolerable equity, even with an imperfect machinery of collection. No valid reason, therefore, can be alleged why a general tax upon all capital and property could not be assessed and collected with the same facility and equity, in a similar manner, and with the same (certainly greatly improved) machinery: for the means of making a general valuation of property, as has been already observed, are much more easily attained now than when those taxes were imposed.

Objection.—The total repeal of some of the taxes mentioned would be too considerable; and the total abolition of some of them might even prove injurious to the morals and temperance of the labouring classes.

Answer.—When any plan is proposed for execution, it is understood to be subject to alterations and modifications, according to particular circumstances; provided such modifications and alterations do not change the principle upon which it is founded. The total repeal of the duty on some of the articles mentioned might be a little modified: for instance, that on malt might be reduced to one-third or one-fourth, &c.; substituting, to make up the deficiency resulting from such an alteration, some one of the many articles under taxation, the repeal of the duty on which would perhaps produce equally beneficial results, without endangering the principle of the plan [a]. It must also be borne in mind, that in the selection of the taxes to be repealed, particular care has been taken to choose only those, the repeal of which is likely to prove most beneficial to the classes who have hitherto been, and still might be,

[a] The duties upon glass, and especially upon candles, and paper of all sorts, could also be taken into consideration. These duties not only act upon industry and labour, but their collection is vexatious and inquisitorial, while the amount they produce does not make up for these disadvantages. There are also other minor taxes, the produce of which to the revenue is insignificant, while the vexations they occasion in their collection are great and manifold.

opposed to the liquidation of the debt. The taxes selected for repeal are those which press more directly upon the three primary sources of production, demoralize the labouring classes, cripple the energies of the empire, and produce the worst of all moral effects—the disturbance of the happiness of millions.

Objection.—Merchants, professional men, manufacturers, and labourers, contribute, at present, considerably more in the shape of taxation towards the payment of the annual interest of the Debt, than the other classes: it will be unjust then to impose greater burdens on the landowners, proprietors, and capitalists, than they now bear.

Answer.—The merchants, the professional men, and the manufacturing and labouring classes, pay more taxes, and a greater amount towards the debt, because they are more numerous: the debt bears more heavily upon them for the same reason. But, being assessed according to their property or income (exceeding 30*l.*), they will be made to contribute in proportion to their means: to compel them to do more, would be neither equitable nor just. The owners of land and fixed property, besides participating, in common with the other classes, in the general advantages of the measure, will derive particular ones from it, which will undoubtedly fully compensate them for any imaginary disproportion in their burdens.

Objection.—A large quantity of property and land would be brought into the market in order to satisfy the instalments: this would occasion great loss to the sellers, and the land and property would be injured.

Answer.—The instalments are so moderate, and the periodical payments so protracted, that no such large supply of land and property can be expected to come into the market. But supposing it did, the demand would not only equal, but exceed, the supply; the number of buyers would undoubtedly surpass that of the sellers; for the fundholders being paid at par, their capital would be increased, and this augmented capital being disengaged, its proprietors must leave it idle, or they must either buy land and fixed property, or lend their money to such land and fixed-property owners, as do not wish to part with their property.

Objection.—The sum to be paid in each of the eight quarters is too large: such an amount being thrown into the market, money would become too abundant.

Answer.—When it is considered that in 1816, the sum of 130,000,000*l.* (see Parts I. and II.) was raised and expended for objects and purposes not to be compared with the results of the present operation, or with the immense benefits it will bestow upon all classes of society; when it is remembered that, in 1814, notwithstanding the opposition of the proprietors, 140 millions of five per cents. were converted into fours and partially paid, *in a few days:* when such facts as these show what *has been done*, no substantial reason whatever, no pretext of any kind, can be alleged against the practicability of the payment of 530 millions, not in a few days, but at protracted intervals of three months between each instalment; especially when that payment is one, in which the collective interests, and individual welfare, of all the members of the British empire, are deeply concerned. The operation, after all, amounts almost to a mere conversion of property, as the others were a conversion of stock.

But suppose a large sum were thrown into the market in consequence of an excess of capital; an abundance of money is not always injurious; and a multiplied demand for it would be created by the new borrowers already mentioned, and by others presently to be noticed; by the demands of the increasing cultivation; and by the investments in land, and purchases of property. Besides, that sum, however large, would be entirely and easily absorbed in a market, the magnitude of which can only be imagined by reflecting, that in one place only (London), above eight millions daily, or more than 1550 millions a-year, are balanced and paid!!!

Objection.—The market being so immense, the capital and means of the nation so large, and the benefits resulting to all parties from the liquidation of the debt so considerable, why not pay off the whole Debt?

Answer.—It is true, the whole of the Debt could be liquidated at once; but "a very small National Debt" is not injurious to a great nation; it places her in a situation to borrow, should she require it, cheaper, and with better credit. A small Debt can affect the primary sources of production but lightly. In the plan proposed, therefore, a small portion of the Debt has been purposely left unliquidated, to facilitate the operation of the liquidation itself; to afford the Government the opportunity of selecting for payment, that portion which would be most convenient and beneficial to the public interests; and to enable it to keep unbroken faith with those fundholders, who have contracted that their stock should not be redeemed until after the expiration of a certain time[a]; but above all, to consult the supreme law of "the public welfare and utility."

[a] As was the case at the last conversion in 1830, when it was stipulated, that the stock then created "should not be subject to redemption at any time before the 5th January, 1849.

In a country like Great Britain, where charitable institutions, corporations, benefit societies, schools, &c. &c., are so numerous, and the amount of property litigated is so immense, a place of deposit for their funds, legacies, &c. is absolutely necessary; more especially in the present constitution of society.

Objection.—The assessment could not be imposed upon the British subjects in the territories and establishments abroad, in consequence of their distance, and their repugnance to submit to any impost.

Answer.—Distance does not destroy the right of assessing British subjects, any more than it prevents the enjoyment of the rights and advantages which that name gives them. It does not annul the claim of those territories and establishments to be considered integral parts of the British empire: neither does it exempt them from the liability to contribute a fair share towards an object, in the benefits and advantages of which they are to be such large participators. On the contrary, it would be the height of injustice, if the burdens and inconveniences were not generally and equally distributed amongst all those who are to enjoy the general and universal benefits. If an attempt were made to impose a tax upon the colonists for purposes in which they had no concern or interest, the case would be far different: but when their own welfare and prosperity are so materially and specially consulted, they can have no reasonable ground of dislike or objection.

Objection.—Could the natives of India, and the East India Company, be justly compelled to contribute to the payment of the National Debt?

Answer.—The East India Company are in full possession of all the right and authority exercised by the conquerors and rulers to whom they have succeeded.

They possess the power of taxing their subjects to an equal or perhaps greater extent than any other government; for it has been shewn in Section X. Part III., that the soil of India belongs to them in right of conquest. But in the present instance, they need not have recourse to the whole extent of their power. The Company will be authorised to raise money by loans, or otherwise by Basis 8; it will be very easy for them to raise the sum required to pay their assessment, on more advantageous terms than they have ever yet done. The annual interest of the money borrowed can be distributed among their Indian subjects in such a manner as to fall very lightly; particularly when coupled with the advantages which the natives will derive from the repeal of the duties on their staple productions. The Company will also be stimulated to forward their agriculture, shipping, and commerce: and there is little doubt, that before the final instalment becomes due, the Indian Empire will have received substantial benefits far exceeding the amount of its contribution. In any case the result will be merely an increase of the East India Company's debt. And, if necessary, a modification of the assessment on Indian property may be made; and many other arrangements may be contrived to facilitate this grand operation, which will equally conduce to the welfare and prosperity of the natives of India, of the East India Company, and of the whole British Empire.

Objection.—The West India and American Colonies are in a particularly depressed state: besides, there is an Act of Parliament of 18th Geo. IV., by which it is declared, that "no taxes shall be laid upon the Colonies, except for their use."

Answer.—The Imperial Parliament possesses the undoubted right of legislating for the Colonies, and for all parts of the Empire. Moreover, there are numerous acts of parliament in existence imposing heavy duties upon the produce and staple articles of these Colonies, which cripple all their resources: let these acts, which are not deemed eternal, be abolished in conjunction with that of Geo. IV. above alluded to. Such a measure would confer the greatest benefits on the Colonies, and remedy many of the evils under which they labour: far from creating any new tax, it would in reality be a true discharge and repeal of the old ones; and would be the foundation of the happiness and prosperity of those countries, as has been demonstrated in another place. The value of all colonial property would be considerably raised, in consequence of the extended cultivation and consumption of its produce, which would follow a repeal of duty. The colonists, by merely subjecting themselves to the payment of a light annual interest, would have no difficulty in raising money to discharge their portion of the general assessment; and the grand result would be, that before the expiration of the two years required for its payment, a benefit to double the amount would have been obtained, as has been demonstrated in the preceding Section.

There does exist a precedent for such an arrangement, which has been already mentioned. The United States, when they were British Colonies, and scarcely possessed as great population, resources, and power as the North American and West India Colonies now do, offered to the British Government an annuity of 100,000*l.* for a hundred years, towards the payment of the National Debt, in consideration of certain advantages and concessions, utterly insignificant compared with the immense benefits which will result, both to the North American and

West India Colonies, should the duties upon their staple articles be repealed. The question for the colonists to decide is this: *whether they would rather remain in their present wretched and depressed state, or, by contributing to the payment of the National Debt, relieve themselves from this miserable state, and enter into the enjoyment of all the benefits and advantages proposed.* There can be little doubt as to which of these alternatives their own sense, and a just perception of their own true interest, will lead them to choose.

But supposing the arrangement could not be effected, either with the other possessions or the West Indies; supposing that injustice and folly should prevail against sound reason and the true interest of the parties themselves; supposing such an almost impossible case: even then, it is maintained, that the measure need not be frustrated. The deficiency could be supplied by means of a small addition to the assessment on the capital of the United Kingdom. The private capital of Great Britain and Ireland has certainly been underrated, in the Statistical Table, full 250 millions; but taking it at 3,575,700,000*l.* as there stated, an additional assessment of only two and a half per cent. upon it, would yield 89,392,500*l.*; which, joined to the surplus provided by Basis 3, would not only cover, but even exceed the amount required for the liquidation; and to facilitate its collection, the payment of this additional two and a half per cent. might be extended to two other quarters.

Objection.—Will the legislature, being entirely composed of individuals from among the classes upon which the general assessment will fall heaviest, sanction this important measure?

Answer.—This objection, which was formerly formidable on account of the great benefits and advantages that will accrue to these classes from the liquidation of the debt, having never before been clearly demonstrated, will disappear before the true and well understood interest of all parties. The members of a new and reformed parliament, called by their duty and patriotism to discuss some of the greatest questions ever agitated in a British assembly, amongst which is the difficult one of the further reduction of the burdens of the people, will be perfectly aware that all the measures they may resort to for that object, short of this operation, must be partial, inadequate, and ineffectual. Public good and private advantages are equally interested in it. This is the mighty—the *only* measure, that can effect that object; that can relieve the national sources of production, put a stop to the perpetual agitation of society, remedy the overwhelming evils of the colonies, and restore happiness to the whole British empire.

Such are the principal objections that may be brought against the plan for the liquidation of the national debt. Should there be any others of importance, of which the author is not aware, he does not hesitate to declare his readiness to give them a full and satisfactory answer. But even should his limited understanding and capacity be unequal to the task, he will remind the objectors to the measure of what one of the greatest orators and statesmen (of whom England is justly proud), said under not dissimilar circumstances:—"He," says Fox, "who talks of positive plans, should go at once to the disease: he who hopes to produce a great good without hazarding some evil, is not the person from whom, in a situation of difficulty, much advantage is to be expected; all that is left is a choice of evils." But there is no a *greater* evil, there does not exist a greater calamity than the *enormous National Debt.*

TABLE I.

of the AMOUNT of the Parochial Assessments for the Poor in England and Wales, the average Price of Wheat, Number of Commitments, Male and Female, and Number of Executions, shewing the relative increase or decrease of crime, in each year from 1821 to 1832.

	1821.	1822.	1823.	1824.	1825.	1826.	1827.	1828.	1829.	1830.	1831.	1832.
	£	£	£	£	£	£	£	£	£	£	£	£
Amount levied for the Relief of the Poor.	8,411,893	7,761,441	6,898,153	6,833,638	6,972,323	6,965,051	7,784,352	7,715,055	7,642,171	8,961,281	8,114,220	8,279,217
Average price of Wheat	62*s.* 5*d.*	53*s.*	41*s.* 11*d.*	56*s.* 8*d.*	62*s.* 9*d.*	64*s.* 8*d.*	56*s.*	54*s.* 2*d.*	63*s.* 8*d.*	64*s.*	66*s.*	59*s.*
Total number of Commitments	13,115	12,241	12,263	14,437	16,164	17,821	17,921	16,564	18,675	18,107		20,829
——— Males	11,173	10,368	10,342	11,889	13,472	15,151	15,151	13,832	15,556	15,135		17,386
——— Females	1,942	1,872	1,921	2,524	2,692	2,770	2,770	2,732	3,719	2,972		3,434
Total number of Executions	57	95	54	50	57	70	70	79	74	46		54

Number of Persons charged with Criminal Offences committed for trial and convicted, sentenced, acquitted, &c. in England and Wales in each of the last three seven years.

	Seven years ending with 1817.	Seven years ending with 1824.	Seven years ending with 1831.
Committed for trial, Males	44,150	78,364	101,638
——— Females	12,158	14,484	19,880
Total	56,308	92,848	121,518
Convicted total	35,259	62,412	85,257
Acquitted total	11,762	17,708	23,442
No Bills found	9,287	12,728	12,819
	56,308	92,848	121,518
Sentenced to death	4,053	7,9[illegible]	9,316
Executed	504	610	410

TABLE II.

EXCISE.—TOTAL QUANTITIES charged with DUTY of each of the following ARTICLES, in ENGLAND, SCOTLAND, and IRELAND, stated throughout in Imperial Measure.

ARTICLES.		1818.	1819.	1820.	1821.	1822.	1823.	1824.	1825.	1826.	1827.	1828.	1829.
Beer, including Strong, Table, Intermediate, and imported	in barrels	7,308,346	7,178,464	7,196,899	7,498,950	7,379,050	7,886,625	8,221,912	8,629,308	8,310,008	7,934,071	8,165,112	7,298,838
Do. Scotland	do.	330,488	331,969	331,894	348,915	356,160	348,067	359,344	391,873	394,176	354,746	366,738	341,090
Bricks	number	896,186,696	1,101,623,356	946,234,389	899,178,510	1,019,501,482	1,244,718,378	1,463,290,999	1,948,974,501	1,350,330,926	1,108,379,404	1,078,987,640	1,109,680,708
Do. Scotland	do.	28,102,016	25,304,278	13,899,978	14,054,590	16,399,812	20,294,487	30,194,636	42,430,777	30,683,702	20,230,368	24,069,381	25,144,291
Tiles	do.	87,489,088	95,898,834	81,984,626	71,177,785	72,090,056	79,026,720	83,716,731	94,349,445	96,054,966	88,901,157	76,731,976	74,608,717
Do. Scotland	do.	2,861,769	2,781,781	1,970,371	2,318,891	2,606,100	3,707,660	2,722,211	3,714,069	3,801,381	3,022,084	3,102,098	2,952,790
Soap	lbs.	72,618,837	76,696,380	79,312,608	86,088,810	90,880,909	94,110,480	97,941,680	99,868,757	98,308,948	101,878,400	105,446,558	100,037,182
Do. Scotland	do.	16,436,715	9,781,708	10,166,385	10,714,066	10,114,276	11,187,898	11,626,808	11,644,912	10,889,198	12,145,884	12,771,719	12,038,877
Starch	do.	4,802,127	4,825,064	4,864,493	4,694,059	5,762,212	5,175,082	4,925,628	6,074,512	5,698,087	6,736,986	6,896,245	5,554,874
Do. Scotland	do.	212,746	294,345	217,323	228,496	398,086	364,864	391,977	360,001	494,750	601,088	767,684	812,838
Hides & Skins, tanned, tawed, and dressed in oil	do.	46,140,919	46,342,555	44,957,229	45,128,080	46,185,871	51,350,841	56,445,600	55,277,951	46,332,088	46,347,128	50,896,723	46,810,214
	doz.	168,718	150,247	141,626	137,962	160,465	174,880	169,951	181,082	187,391	162,800	156,805	189,399
Do. Scotland	lbs.	4,435,625	4,501,296	4,281,786	4,282,190	4,684,219	5,042,288	6,519,998	6,888,697	5,306,427	3,778,898	6,007,141	6,012,151
	doz.	1,358	1,378	1,304	778	719	1,105	994	796	486	254	289	355
Do. Ireland	cubic feet	1,112,345	1,870,470	897,708	805,966	840,127	761,682	840,762	—	—	—	—	—
	lbs.	10,845	11,800	26,063	96,959	27,738	28,441	51,876	6,887,982	7,289,931	7,228,686	7,379,558	7,280,788
	doz.	2,456	2,525	2,784	2,880	4,094	2,680	2,825	11,294	6,418	7,269	7,208	5,829
Malt	bushels	24,630,880	22,612,290	28,364,242	28,128,438	28,688,518	24,945,156	27,615,368	30,372,742	27,335,971	25,096,287	30,517,819	23,496,074
Do. Scotland	do.	1,380,815	1,534,289	1,182,208	1,305,650	1,403,177	1,616,390	2,788,608	3,925,847	3,726,535	2,714,078	3,867,189	3,712,962
Do. Ireland	do.	1,789,686	1,742,444	1,728,671	1,949,815	1,756,391	1,706,916	2,169,989	2,797,254	2,406,369	1,806,795	2,409,548	2,012,689
Candles, Tallow, Wax, and Spermaceti	lbs.	78,695,417	88,371,789	84,337,116	89,814,469	94,358,910	98,487,110	103,304,191	108,305,817	104,751,769	109,878,980	112,289,944	110,478,728
Do. Scotland	do.	4,809,188	4,798,480	4,681,518	4,864,720	4,819,340	4,280,264	3,443,914	4,231,480	6,236,280	6,005,350	5,940,769	5,798,815
Coffee	do.	7,310,116	7,081,618	6,368,861	7,007,278	7,041,398	7,381,843	7,488,014	10,221,204	12,076,758	14,151,180	15,708,372	17,288,817
Do. Scotland	do	487,741	487,740	312,425	330,010	362,612	387,400	305,096	344,718	651,474	329,507	631,675	1,048,284
Do. Ireland	do.	340,880	361,481	297,122	283,718	285,147	245,635	306,868	318,026	473,096	385,780	302,896	359,787
Tea	do.	22,744,107	22,703,796	22,312,130	22,894,656	22,911,666	23,762,457	23,784,838	24,830,015	25,238,048	26,048,228	26,790,886	29,495,195
Do. Scotland	do.	—	—	—	28	814	13	—	—	19	—	—	19
Do. Ireland	do.	3,349,431	3,298,469	2,150,844	3,498,980	3,816,984	3,867,710	3,897,310	3,329,636	3,807,785	3,887,955	2,515,159	—
Paper	do.	41,111,281	39,465,732	41,444,341	42,458,109	45,140,689	47,181,318	50,224,732	52,294,606	42,121,966	51,197,687	54,750,018	50,168,185
Do. Scotland	do.	4,186,368	4,804,958	4,302,958	4,794,891	5,119,243	5,490,480	5,362,079	6,294,194	5,017,911	6,434,944	7,532,022	7,168,895
Do. Ireland	do.	1,342,967	1,479,680	1,289,498	1,368,842	1,611,030	1,588,821	1,934,118	2,418,111	2,085,196	2,289,706	2,342,768	2,079,129
Milboard, Pasteboard, &c.	cwt.	34,187	30,448	31,161	32,807	35,390	34,848	39,517	42,323	31,145	37,751	42,598	37,742
Do. Scotland	do.	2,189	2,079	2,943	3,155	3,294	3,207	3,808	3,480	4,168	3,201	6,202	7,585
Ditto Ireland	do.	387	312	208	186	222	192	108	202	284	193	210	221
Printed Goods, including Paper, Calicoes, Linens, and Silks	yds.	94,805,158	73,681,850	91,289,644	98,948,080	99,711,786	104,480,084	120,424,822	124,122,601	96,469,566	128,122,328	120,701,896	110,204,149
Do. Scotland	do.	17,277,310	12,800,068	14,687,794	16,362,944	18,496,975	19,362,650	24,923,962	24,718,943	15,684,127	22,895,848	25,094,976	26,114,805
Do. Ireland (Paper)	lbs.	216,725	220,666	189,417	202,007	222,264	257,621	315,472	482,108	325,368	234,600	270,880	244,156
British Spirits	gal.	4,670,036	3,888,327	3,967,406	3,880,015	4,346,248	3,521,366	4,067,293	3,442,559	7,407,292	6,671,560	7,730,687	7,700,786
Do. Scotland	do.	1,981,763	1,886,122	1,742,044	2,229,435	2,079,356	2,232,728	4,350,301	5,981,550	3,988,788	4,752,199	5,716,180	5,777,280
Do. Ireland	do.	3,427,478	2,941,213	2,620,780	2,649,179	2,328,387	3,348,305	6,690,315	9,262,744	6,837,408	8,260,918	9,937,903	9,212,224
Tobacco	lbs.	12,131,916	11,456,226	11,727,861	11,682,260	11,810,113	11,873,287	11,384,098	12,700,786	12,344,819	12,979,666	12,860,287	13,080,285
Do. Scotland	do.	1,396,485	1,388,945	1,377,908	1,466,302	1,319,109	1,621,284	1,385,069	1,900,418	1,383,522	1,894,780	1,770,097	1,828,126
Do. Ireland	do.	4,190,192	3,498,219	3,380,304	2,907,385	3,283,271	3,698,914	3,756,684	4,160,049	3,896,626	4,041,171	4,014,082	4,125,296

NOTE (A), referred to at p. [illegible]

It is generally acknowledged, that there was a time when [illegible] was the seat of all the learning, and the centre of all the [illegible] which existed in Europe; but it is not so generally known that [illegible] nation was once the first manufacturing country also. The [illegible]ing passage from one of the Spanish Economists of the [illegible] century, describing the injurious effects of taxation on the [illegible] of production and on the labouring classes, gives an idea of the magnitude of her extensive manufactures in Seville, Granada, [illegible]lencia, Medina, Avila, Caprion, Toledo, and all her principal towns. "In Toledo," says Damian de Olivares, temp. Philip III. "the annual consumption of silk has diminished 438,000 lbs; and [illegible] Mancha and Segovia, the consumption of wool has diminished [illegible] arrobas, or 16,052,500 lbs.: there were consumed in the [illegible] of these manufactures, in furnishing light, and in cooking [illegible] arrobas, or 106,715,200 lbs. of oil. All these advantages [illegible] been lost. The labourers, the farmers, the land owners, the shop-[illegible], the inn-keepers, the muleteers &c., have lost their [illegible] [illegible] business: the church has lost her tithes, the nobility their [illegible] the state its revenue: not to mention other large sums [illegible] [illegible] which in consequence of commercial intercourse, would have [illegible], because consumption is reciprocal, and one thing [illegible] upon another."—Such were the sentiments of the Spanish [illegible] of that remote time, who foresaw the ruin of their [illegible] the very system that we are now adopting. [illegible] of Turkish bonnets of 400 dozens each [illegible] were annually sent from the single town of [illegible] manufacture was so extensive, that from one of [illegible] no less than 678 masters in this [illegible] dressed like Infantas, in [illegible] but in 1624, this system [illegible] manufacturers to 72, and a few [illegible] small town of [illegible] had once a glove [illegible] years a year: but, by the [illegible] says another economist [illegible] occupation to the [illegible] went away [illegible] daughters were ruined." The Houses for the reception of the poor, and the Houses of Correction for the women, unnecessary in Spain before this epoch, are the sad testimonies of this truth. Seeing the unavoidable multiplication of institutions of this description which daily takes place in Great Britain, one cannot refrain from warning England, as those Economists warned Spain.

The same causes acting in regard to the manufactures of Avila, Seville, and Granada, the same results ensued. One hundred and forty effective looms were at work in the two latter towns, and 89,000 journeymen were employed in the manufacture of wool, in Avila and Segovia. But how did all these manufactures disappear? Osorio, and Martinez de la Mata shall tell us. The former attributes it to high wages:—"Services," says Martinez de la Mata, "for which ten reals were paid in Spain, were procured elsewhere for one real:"—"los gornales," (wages) says Compomanes (Appendice à la Educacion popular V. 4) "by enhancing the cost of manufactures, were the cause of the destruction of Spanish manufactures, and the annihilation of that numerous class employed in them." These, according to de la Mata (Epitome de sus discorsos V. 1) constituted the fifth part of the nation, and their activity and labour maintained the other four, by manufacturing all sorts of goods and merchandise forming the capital and wealth of the merchants and of the rich. Thus the numerous fairs of Spain became the mart of all nations, that of Medina keeping the lead; where, at one time, mercantile Bills were annually discounted to the amount of 1,558,823,529 reals or £15,558,235 sterling!—an amazing sum for those times. The ruins of the magnificent bazaars and splendid booths, in which the manufactures were exposed for sale in that famous town, are yet to be seen, and are the only remaining testimony of its former mercantile and manufacturing grandeur. But are they not like living and speaking monuments, warning the greatest of all manufacturing nations of the fatal consequences of the measures she is pursuing? For the decay and ruin of Spanish manufactures is not to be attributed to the discovery of America, as a crowd of superficial writers on political economy, following one another's footsteps like cattle, have long maintained: on the contrary, the discovery of America increased the demand for manufactures. Neither is it to be ascribed to the laziness of the Spaniards, as other writers, not less superficial but more unjust, pretend; for the race of men is the same. It is to her bad fiscal laws, to her bad system of imposts, to the taxes upon consumption which enhanced wages, and prevented the sale of manufactures, that the misfortunes of Spain must be attributed: these, and no other, were the true causes of that widespread devastating laziness, which still desolates and impoverishes a land deserving a better fate.

GENERAL CONCLUSION, AND APPEAL TO THE LEGISLATURE AND TO THE PEOPLE.

Thus, then, in the course of this work may be seen the origin of the taxation of the British Empire, which in this, as in all nations, is necessary for the progress and consolidation of the country; and which, from the most humble commencement, has been gradually elevated to a pitch almost inconceivable. Public income has kept pace with taxation; but, too often levied with injustice, oppression, and extortion, has generally been insufficient to supply the real or fictitious wants, occasioned by the vices, the bad policy and passions of the kings, republics, or administrations, which have directed the destinies of the empire: the ends for which the people endure taxation have been seldom or never kept in view; the sacred objects to which they consecrate its proceeds have been often and shamefully disregarded.

Injustice and bad fiscal measures being followed by increasing wants, *borrowing* was resorted to. Money was at first raised by pawning the royal insignia; loans were contracted for short periods, and the public revenue pledged before it existed. But at the revolution a new and more extensive system was introduced, and three most powerful engines were brought to aid in working that system; by means of which operations were effected on a scale almost beyond imagination. The debt, from 600,000*l.*, was increased, in periods of war, to *one thousand one hundred millions;* while the reduction has been comparatively insignificant in three successive periods of peace; in the last and longest of which, the promoters of the system and the national economists were disappointed in their reasonable expectations of a considerable reduction; the amount of the debt being almost as large *now* as at the conclusion of the war! And this, notwithstanding the surplus of revenue and the unparalleled increase of the national wealth and resources. What deep and serious matter for reflection, as to future reduction, do these facts afford to the thinking mind.

The actually distressing pressure of this enormous debt on the three main sources of production, and its baneful effects on the morals, the prosperity and the happiness of society, have been clearly pointed out; and an adequate and complete remedy has been suggested for these constantly increasing evils, by the adoption of a Plan, the practicability of which has been calculated, not upon the wealth of *one portion*, but upon the united means and resources of *all parts* of the empire. It has moreover been shewn, that the operations of the proposed plan would be perfectly just, that the national and individual capital and public credit would be unimpaired, and that it would confer the greatest benefits on all classes and all parts of the vast British empire. All this is demonstrated by the aid of incontestible facts, official documents, and authentic statements.

But it is not within the limited power and influence of an individual, to give a due impulse, and command proper attention, to a measure of such magnitude. It must be by the united efforts of all branches of the legislature, combined with the exertions of the people themselves, that this great work will be accomplished.

And first, let us invoke the aid of the King, whom fate has happily placed at the head of an immense empire, powerfully influencing all the moral, political, and commercial concerns of the world; and who, overcoming the prejudices of education, and disregarding the entreaties, the threats, and the ominous predictions of the aristocracy, resolutely sanctioned the great measure of Reform. But great as are the benefits that will be conferred upon the nation by this measure, there is no doubt that equal and superior advantages will flow from the payment of the debt; while it will not require near so great a struggle and exertion on the part of the Royal Reformer.

"It will be your duty (says the king in his speech, to the reformed parliament,) to promote, by all practicable means, habits of industry and good order amongst the labouring classes of the community." But it is impossible to carry into effect this wise and salutary recommendation while *labour* is on the decline, and continues oppressed by taxation; and it is equally impossible to lessen taxation, while the present system is continued.

Interest, duty, and danger, all tend to deeply involve the next illustrious branch of the legislature, in the results of the measure proposed. It is evidently the *interest* of the great landed proprietors, and of those who have a great stake in the country, to relieve land from the pressure of taxation, and to arrest the unavoidable ruin which threatens them. For, under the present system, the corn laws cannot be continued; while their repeal would recoil with tenfold disastrous effects, on those who neglected their own true and vital interest in time.

It is the *duty* of the aristocracy to preserve their essential power in the state, and to maintain the respect due from the people to this high branch of the legislature. But they must be aware how difficult it is to retain this homage, when the industrious classes see so large a portion of wealth concentrated in the hands of those who do not employ it productively, and find themselves oppressed with a disproportionate load of taxes. That there is danger to be apprehended is evident, when we consider that in the present age it is impossible to expect that thousands of people will remain plunged in poverty and misery, or continue tranquil spectators of the wealth and luxury of those above them.

The reformed House of Commons is solemnly pledged to abolish abuses, to invigorate the body politic, and remove the evils which oppress the people*. But this pledge cannot be redeemed while the present financial system continues; nor can this system be altered until the Debt is paid off. It is useless to deceive the nation with the empty sound of retrenchment. The affairs of an empire like this can hardly be administered under the present expenditure. Any attempt to substitute a property tax for the burdens at present pressing on productive industry, would be only a commutation of impost from one source of production to another. The nation has a right to expect that her representatives will fulfil their sacred duty. This can only be done by a real and substantial relief from taxation; which can never be effected while the debt remains.

But the People, the source of all power and all legislative measures, are above all deeply and vitally interested in this question. Never in fact has their attention been called to an investigation of greater magnitude and importance. It is a complete waste of time and labour, to meet and get up petitions for the redress of evils pro-

* "Respublicas firmandas, stabiliendas vires, sanandosque populos. . . . ."—Cic. de Leg.

ceeding from the remote *branches* of the system, while the *root* from which they spring is left in full vigour. The people meet to consider all sorts of ridiculous schemes and objects, but not a *single meeting* has ever been held to consider the fundamental and acknowledged source of all their evils and misfortunes.

But it is already high time for the leaders of the British people to direct their attention to this grand object. It is their paramount duty to call *repeated* public meetings, to propose and form a plan for the liquidation of the debt, and to contrive measures for executing it. All the materials for this discussion will be found in the preceding pages. The defects of the plan there suggested may be rectified, and a more perfect one produced, by the sound judgement and talent of the British people. The individual who has condensed such a mass of materials into this work, has executed that difficult task with the sole view of promoting the happiness of the British people, even in the remotest corners of the empire. But his wishes will be fruitless, and his labours utterly impotent, unless seconded by the people themselves. Their leaders can never devote their exertions to a higher or nobler object: British perseverance and the right of petitioning, can never be directed to a sublimer purpose, or for a more useful result. Success is certain; that greatest of all imaginable triumphs will undoubtedly be achieved, "the removal of the misery, the alleviation of the evils, and the expansion of the happiness of mankind."

G. Woodfall, Printer, Angel Court, Skinner Street, London.

Ingram Content Group UK Ltd.
Milton Keynes UK
UKHW020623240423
420680UK00007B/477